D0063229

Colombia

the Bradt Travel Guide

Sarah Woods
with Richard McColl

www.bradtguides.com

edition
3

Bradt Travel Guides Ltd, UK
The Globe Pequot Press Inc, USA

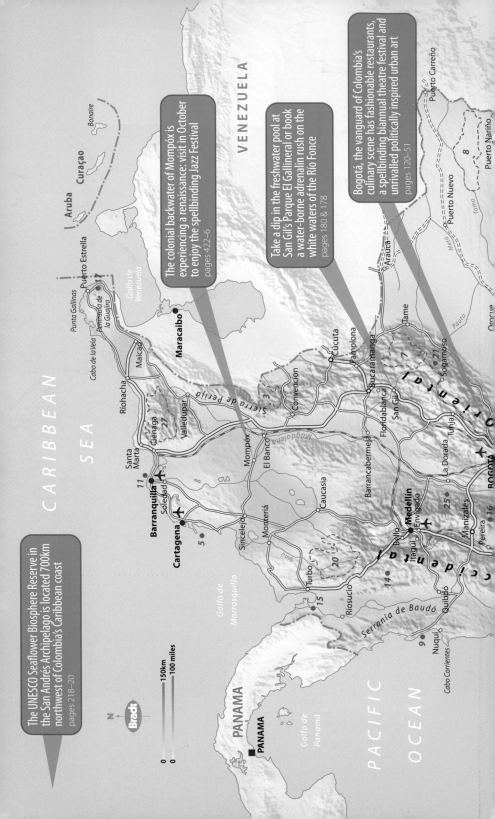

The UNESCO Seaflower Biosphere Reserve in the San Andrés Archipelago is located 700km northwest of Colombia's Caribbean coast
pages 218–20

The colonial backwater of Mompóx is experiencing a renaissance: visit in October to enjoy the spellbinding Jazz Festival
pages 422–6

Take a dip in the freshwater pool at San Gil's Parque El Gallineral or book a water-borne adrenalin rush on the white waters of the Río Fonce
pages 180 & 178

Bogotá, the vanguard of Colombia's culinary scene has fashionable restaurants, a spellbinding biannual theatre festival and unrivalled politically inspired urban art
pages 120–51

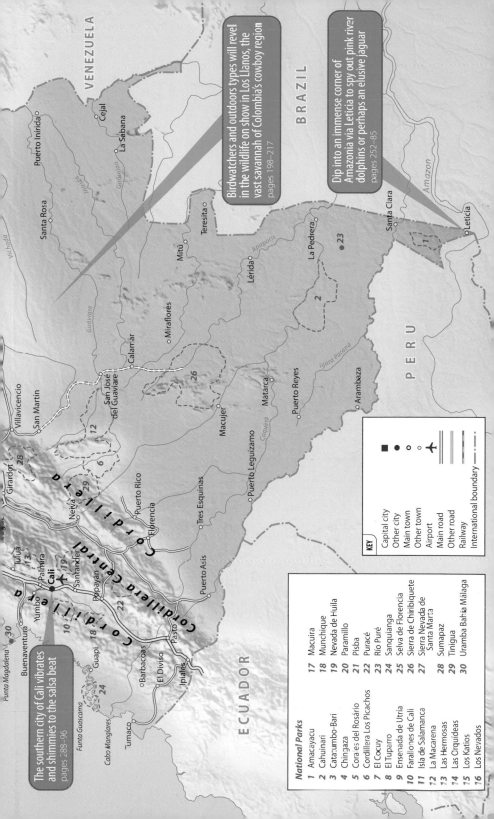

Birdwatchers and outdoors types will revel in the wildlife on show in Los Llanos, the vast savannah of Colombia's cowboy region
pages 198–217

Dip into an immense corner of Amazonia via Leticia to spy out pink river dolphins or perhaps an elusive jaguar
pages 252–85

The southern city of Cali vibrates and shimmies to the salsa beat
pages 288–96

VENEZUELA

BRAZIL

PERU

ECUADOR

National Parks

1   Amacayacu
2   Cahuinarí
3   Catatumbo-Barí
4   Chingaza
5   Corales del Rosário
6   Cordillera Los Picachos
7   El Cocuy
8   El Tuparro
9   Ensenada de Utría
10 Farallones de Cali
11 Isla de Salamanca
12 La Macarena
13 Las Hermosas
14 Las Orquídeas
15 Los Katíos
16 Los Nevados
17 Macuira
18 Munchique
19 Nevada de Huila
20 Paramillo
21 Pisba
22 Puracé
23 Río Puré
24 Sanquianga
25 Selva de Florencia
26 Sierra de Chiribiquete
27 Sierra Nevada de Santa Marta
28 Sumapaz
29 Tinigua
30 Uramba Bahía Málaga

KEY

■ Capital city
● Other city
○ Main town
○ Other town
✈ Airport
   Main road
   Other road
   Railway
—·— International boundary

Colombia
Don't miss...

Amazon Rainforest
Wearing tree-bark cloth masks and skirts, dancers representing fish spirits take part in a ritual exchange in the Vaupés Basin
(AP/A) page 256

Bogotá
La Candelaria, the old quarter of Colombia's capital, is replete with cobbled streets and brightly painted Colonial-era houses (AS/A) page 150

Los Llanos
Ride across the prairies with cattle-roping cowboys
(JH/A) pages 198–217

White-water rafting on the Río Fonce
Adrenaline junkies head to Colombia's adventure sports hub
(ProC) page 178

San Andrés Archipelago
First-class diving and home to the UNESCO Seaflower Biosphere Reserve
(SS) pages 218–51

Colombia in colour

above   Few Colonial-era towns in Colombia have been as beautifully preserved as Villa de Leyva
(PS) pages 164–71

below   Fine museums and striking architecture abound in the historic town of Guatapé (JK/S) pages 343–5

above Once a byword for danger, Bogotá has undergone a significant clean-up in recent years (SS) pages 120–51

right Colourful, Colonial-era houses line the cobblestoned streets in the lively La Candelaria neighbourhood, Bogotá (T/S) page 150

below Bogotá sits at the foot of the Andes (JK/S) pages 120–51

above Colombia's rugged and green Zona Cafetera (Coffee Zone) provides half of the country's 66-million-tonne coffee production (NE/A) pages 353–5

left Holy Week involves much pageantry and many processions in Tunja (RO/A) pages 158–62

below Dancing at a festival in Santa Fé de Antioquia: traditional folk music and dancing are a major part of Colombian culture (LR/A) pages 350–3

AUTHOR

Sarah Woods is a member of the Royal Geographical Society, the Society of Authors and British Guild of Travel Writers. She has spent extended periods in Central and South America and writes regularly for newspapers, magazines and online publications about her experience of Latin America. As the author of more than a dozen travel books, Sarah received the Guidebook Writer of the Year Award from the British Guild of Travel Writers in 2005 for *Panama* (also by Bradt). Sarah spent three years as the travel
expert on Alan Titchmarsh's sofa (on ITV) and as a holiday presenter on BBC Radio Scotland's morning show. Sarah lectures on South American themes in the UK, Spain and America and has given talks on Colombia at the Royal Geographical Society, bookshops and travel shows. Sarah won the PSA award (2013) for broadcasting and the Kenneth Westcott Prize in both 2007 and 2008. In the past few years she has worked on a documentary about Colombia's former president Álvaro Uribe (2012) and the centenary of the Panama Canal (2014). Sarah's compelling travel narrative *On a Wing and a Prayer: One Woman's Journey to the Heart of the Rainforest* was published in hardback in May 2015 (Bloomsbury) and is available in bookshops worldwide. She is currently working on a documentary about Colombia's extraordinary ancient tombs, standing stones, catacombs and funerary chambers in San Agustín.

UPDATER

Richard McColl is a British-born, Colombia-based freelance correspondent, guide and hotelier. After studying modern languages at Exeter University he pursued an MA in International Journalism in London and later became a Conflict Resolution Specialist at the Universidad Pontificia la Javeriana in Bogotá. He has been based in the Americas for 16 years and for the last nine years has made Colombia his home, travelling between the capital and his guesthouse La Casa Amarilla in Mompóx. He currently freelances for a variety of publications around the world.

PUBLISHER'S FOREWORD   *Hilary Bradt*

It was over 40 years ago that I first arrived in Barranquilla, Colombia, as a nervous lone woman traveller. I spoke no Spanish, and had only the vaguest idea of where I was going and what I would find there. Within 24 hours I was staying in the home of a delightful family in Bogotá and making great strides in learning the language. But I never did understand why the three teenage boys collapsed with laughter whenever I repeated one phrase they taught me, 'No joda' ('Stop bothering me'), and it stood me in good stead throughout my four-month trip. But I needed this book finally to learn what it actually means (page 487)!

Sarah Woods did a wonderful job in bringing this most beguiling of South American countries to life in the first two editions of this guidebook, and Richard McColl – updater of this latest edition – has continued the good work. Reading it I remembered so well the warmth of the people – surely the friendliest in the entire continent – the scenery, birdlife, beaches and numerous eccentricities that make the place so special. I only wish I'd had it with me in 1969!

Third edition published September 2015 – First published April 2008

Bradt Travel Guides Ltd
IDC House, The Vale, Chalfont St Peter, Bucks SL9 9RZ, England
www.bradtguides.com
Print edition published in the USA by The Globe Pequot Press Inc,
PO Box 480, Guilford, Connecticut 06437-0480

Text copyright © 2015 Sarah Woods
Maps copyright © 2015 Bradt Travel Guides Ltd
Photographs copyright © 2015 Individual photographers (see below)
Updated by Richard McColl
Project Manager: Claire Strange
Cover research: Pepi Bluck, Perfect Picture

ISBN: 978 1 84162 921 6 (print)
e-ISBN: 978 1 78477 131 7 (e-pub)
e-ISBN: 978 1 78477 231 4 (mobi)

British Library Cataloguing in Publication Data
A catalogue record for this book is available from the British Library

Photographers Alamy: Aurora Photos (AP/A), Natasha Ethrington (NE/A), Jeremy Horner (JH/A), Roberto Orrú (RO/A), Lionela Rob (LR/A), Emiliano Rodriguez (ER/A), WaterFrame (WF/A); Christopher Calonje; Dreamstime: Uros Ravbar (UR/DT); FLPA (www.flpa.co.uk): Frans Lanting (FL/FLPA), Thomas Marent/Minden Pictures (TM/MP/FLPA), Michael & Patricia Fogden/Minden Pictures (MPF/MP/FLPA); Marco Muscará (www.marcomuscara.com) (MM); ProColombia (ProC); Shutterstock.com: Max Blain (MB/S), Hugo Brizard (HB/S), Nicolas de Corte (NdC/S), Toniflap, (T/S), Jess Kraft (JK/S), Alberto Loyo (AL/S); Peter Stiles; SuperStock; Sarah Woods
Front cover A young boy hides behind his mother's work, a typical plate used by the Emberá people (ER/A)
Back cover The Ciudad Perdida is near Santa Marta (JK/S); colonial architecture in Guatapé (NdC/S)
Title page A colourful window in Salento (MM); waterfalls at Santa Rosa de Cabal (AL/S); Andean emerald bird (CC)
Maps David McCutcheon FBCart.S; base mapping modified by Bradt Travel Guides, provided by ITMB Publishing Ltd; colour relief map base by Nick Rowland FRGS
Illustrations Oliver Whalley
Typeset by Ian Spick
Production managed by Jellyfish Print Solutions; printed in India
Digital conversion by www.dataworks.co.in

Foreword

I was extremely pleased to learn of Sarah Woods's travel guide to Colombia as, to me, it reflects the growing interest in my country of visitors from all over the world – at last. That more and more people are prepared to come and see Colombia for themselves is great for my country and its people. I am also convinced that anyone who comes to Colombia – be it Cartagena, San Andrés, Medellín, Cali, the Amazon or my home town of Bogotá – will leave with treasured memories. Quite simply, Colombia has some of the most beautiful colonial towns, pretty beaches and unexplored jungle on earth – no contest.

I have been lucky enough to travel the world as part of my racing career and have visited some wonderful and fascinating places. However, I have always returned home to the beautiful scenery and friendly faces of Colombia – and feel constantly blessed by what I find. So, to travellers keen to explore Colombia I say keep an open mind, open eyes and an open heart. Be sure to meet the people, enjoy the many ancient cultures and, above all, discover the real Colombia – it is truly a country like no other. A warm welcome awaits you.

Juan Pablo Montoya
Former F1 racing driver, current NASCAR professional and
a UN Goodwill Ambassador.
Born in Bogotá, 20 September 1975
(*www.jpmontoya.com; see box, pages 58–9*)

Acknowledgements

I'd need a whole chapter in which to fully extend my gratitude to every Colombian who lent their support to this mammoth project. Each and every Colombian I met, without exception, had a special story about their homeland to share and I am deeply indebted to a host of people who wholeheartedly gave it their all. That this guide is so extensive owes a great deal to the impassioned know-how of these 'national tourism ambassadors' – all of whom are deserving of an official post on the basis of sheer enthusiasm for their homeland alone.

A special mention must go to two schoolgirl sisters in La Guajira, Kelly and Katiara, whose warm smiles and big hugs were a joy to behold. Arriving at the end of a long, dusty journey across arid desert sands took on an Oasis-in-the-Sahara scenario. I slept soundly in the girls' simple beachside *posada* comforted by human kindness, and lulled by rhythmic, lapping waves.

Thank you also to the indigenous menfolk who guided me deftly through the fast-rising waters of the Amazon and to the jewellery maker in Huila who gave me the chance to taste deep-fried ants. To the roadside vendor who insisted that I sell up everything in England to start a new life with him in colonial-era Cartagena; to the flower seller who helped me find the juiciest steak in Bogotá. Thanks also to my snake-hipped driver for switching me on to Colombia's hip-swinging *musica vallenata* and to the rugged Llanero cowboy who shared his life story with me on the cattle-clad rolling plains.

I also deeply appreciate the logistical help I received when criss-crossing Colombia – the list is a long one, but the following deserve a note of thanks: Nubia Stella Martinez, José Chehab, Diana Quiazua, Lina Rincón, General Salazar, Marta Lucía Palacío, Sandra Riaño, Milena Ramírez, Andrés Gonzalez, Diego Peláez, Alejandra Fajardo, Esperanza Valderrama, Mark Rausch and Jorge Rausch in Bogotá; Luisa Urueña, Jan Fernando Salazar and Emily Goodfellow in London; Ana María Charris and María Carolina Rico in Barranquilla; Juan Alejandro Duque, Norhara Landaño and Roberto Echeverry in the Zona Cafetería; Juan Carlos Castro; Magnola Beltrán and Juan Jaime in Cali; Lourdes Lopera, Miguel Ramírez; José Tique and Cecilia Acosta in La Guajira; Pedro Luis Mogollón and Nico Medez in Cartagena; Asturia Peña, Claudia Marcela, Claudia Delgado, Dairo Cuenta Casanova, Sussan Jane Stroemer de Saad and Humberto Mejia in San Andrés; Rosa in Providencia; Claudia Santos Carrillo, Rubén Darío Sosa, Álvaro Fernández, Dámaso Yepes, Lucy Páez Peñaloza and Jehimi Rodriguez in Santa Marta; Ángela Buitrago, Rodrigo Echeverry and Sandra Atalah in Los Llanos; Sergio Osorio, Diego Velásquez, Byron Arango, Lázaro López and Oscar Jhony in Capurgana; César Isaza Vásquez in Bahía Solano; Aurelio Velazco Mosquera in Popayán; Albeiro Castro in Neiva; Adriana Gonzalez and Santiago Ospina in Medellín; Iván Mustafa in Bucaramanga; Yusara Cruz, Antonio Cruz in the Amazon. Thanks also to Erik Rupert, Ron Behrens and Robert Giles at ProAves. *Muchas gracias* also to my dear friend David Short. For sending feedback and updates, thank you to Tom Woodhouse, Lou van Eycke, Ben Capell, Mark Lewis, Farah Yamin, Chris Hardyment and Matthew Parris.

John Howard Galindo in Buga has also been generous with his time and patience in double-checking Colombia's colloquialisms and linguistic quirks. Thanks to Roger Harris and Peter Hutchison for loaning their wildlife guide from *Amazon: the Bradt Travel Guide*.

Thanks also go to the sterling efforts of contributor Amanda Bower, a passionate advocate for all things Colombian and an invaluable and highly professional resource on this project. Like me, Amanda adores getting under the skin of lesser-known Colombia and this guide has benefited greatly from her enthusiasm. Thank you also to all at Bradt and to the oh so diligent Raichel Rickels without whom a greater number of inky embarrassments would lurk amongst these pages.

To Alejandro Navas, I owe a special heartfelt thank you for accompanying me on the lion's share of my journey. I learned so much about the real Colombia from a man who clearly adores his country – and who readily admits he wants nothing more than the world to love it too. To explore Colombia in Alejandro's company was a true revelation and his courteous good manners and charming smile opened many doors along the way. I defy anyone not to feel enlivened by his infectious enthusiasm and honest appreciation for his beloved home nation. That Alejandro also has an ability to remain cheerful when faced with cancelled flights, mudslides and sudden mechanical failure has also been invaluable in helping my challenging cross-country itinerary run smoothly.

Lastly, to Matthew, Joseph and darling Milly who have been so patient during my periods of absence. Thank you for supporting me when I've been hunched over a laptop over bank holidays and weekends. Much love to you all.

Sarah Woods

ACKNOWLEDGEMENTS FOR THIRD EDITION Thanks to my ever-patient wife Alba: hopefully this work will help bring a brighter future to Colombia.

Richard McColl

DEDICATION

To Matthew, Joseph and Milly with all my love

CONTRIBUTORS

Amanda Bower developed a love for cultures studying anthropology at the University of Edinburgh. She has since spent time with indigenous communities in Australia and also in the Amazonas region of Colombia during a six-month stay in the country in 2009. Here she developed a passion for the culture and diversity of Colombia, returning to visit in 2010. Amanda is also a keen photographer.

Simon Willis started his career as a sports journalist at the Press Association in Howden, Yorkshire. After two years of covering football matches on frosty Tuesday nights, he left England to sell sunglasses on the beaches in Spain and Italy. He has since worked in Indonesia, Argentina and the Czech Republic before landing in Colombia in 2012. Nowadays he's based in Medellín, though it doesn't take him long to head out on freelance assignments corralling cattle in Los Llanos, or screeching round Pacific beaches on a motorbike in search of nesting sea turtles. He updated the chapters to the northwest interior and the Pacific coast for this edition.

SEND US YOUR SNAPS!

We'd love to follow your adventures using our *Colombia* guide – why not send us your photos and stories via Twitter (@BradtGuides) and Instagram (@bradtguides) using the hashtag #Colombia. Alternatively, you can upload your photos directly to the gallery on the Colombia destination page via our website (*www.bradtguides.com*).

COLOMBIA ONLINE

For additional online content, articles, photos and more on Colombia, why not visit www.bradtguides.com/colombia.

Contents

LIST OF MAPS

HOW TO USE THIS GUIDE

MAPS
Keys and symbols Maps include alphabetical keys covering the locations of those places to stay, eat or drink that are featured in the book. Note that regional maps may not show all hotels and restaurants in the area: other establishments may be located in towns shown on the map.

Grids and grid references Several maps use gridlines to allow easy location of sites. Map grid references are listed in square brackets after the name of the place or sight of interest in the text, with page number followed by grid number, eg: [126 C3].

FEEDBACK REQUEST AND UPDATES WEBSITE

At Bradt Travel Guides we're aware that guidebooks start to go out of date on the day they're published – and that you, our readers, are out there in the field doing research of your own. You'll find out before us when a fine new family-run hotel opens or a favourite restaurant changes hands and goes downhill. So why not write and tell us about your experiences? Contact us on ✆ 01753 893444 or e info@bradtguides.com. We will forward emails to the author who may post updates on the Bradt website at www.bradtupdates.com/colombia. Alternatively you can add a review of the book to www.bradtguides.com or Amazon.

Introduction

Colombia must surely be one of the world's most bewildering paradoxes, a nation blessed with jaw-dropping natural beauty and some of the most damning headlines on the planet. Yet delve beneath the front-page drama and Colombia differs from the common perception, a country that has so much more to offer than turmoil and strife.

Spanning an area twice the size of France and about twice the size of California, Colombia is also the only South American nation with coastlines on both the Atlantic and Pacific oceans. Few countries in Latin America boast such ecological riches with an abundance of natural resources on a dramatically contrasting terrain. Rolling, dusty plains edge snow-capped mountain peaks; lunar-like craterous deserts lead to lush, vine-tangled rainforests; flower-filled meadows and coffee plantations lie dotted with pretty red-and-white fincas; palm-scattered idyllic white-sand beaches stretch out beyond fine colonial settlements in bubblegum hues. Dozens of indigenous cultures speak more than 60 languages in a land that is home to the greatest number of bird species on earth. Colombia is also the setting of Gabriel García Márquez's massively popular novel *One Hundred Years of Solitude* – a story as entrancing as the country itself. Fertile waters are rich in marine life; resplendent swathes of dense jungle teem with flora and fauna. Mighty rivers, vast canyons, magnificent waterfalls and bubbling thermal springs dot a landscape of mud-and-thatch villages, in contrast to gleaming, futuristic cities that rank amongst Latin America's most progressive. Explore creeper-clad ancient civilisations dating back to 500BC, reggae-drenched Caribbean islands and flamingo-covered mangrove thickets. Discover pre-Columbian gold and sacred sites that spawned the myth of El Dorado. Delve into forests that are home to armadillo, jaguar, tapir, ocelot, monkey and spear-hunting tribes. Journey along the inky-green might of the Amazon River amongst 3,300 butterfly species, 1,900 bird species, 80,000 insect species, 2,000 species of reptile and amphibian, 3,200 species of fish, 51,220 plant species – in a region that is home to a staggering 10% of all species found on the planet.

Yet this enigmatic nation isn't all about good news, as more than 60 years of horror stories will bear out. A legacy of civil war has left Colombia with something of an image problem, even though the country has left the mess of 15 years ago behind. Once inextricably linked with drug lords, gang violence and guerrilla warfare, Colombia has achieved notable success in dismantling cartels and demobilising more than 30,000 left-wing and paramilitary fighters. The widespread common delinquency of the 1990s has given way to fierce national pride. Today a thriving forward-thinking society has a rising middle class with modern cities that boast some of the finest healthcare facilities and universities in the region. Peace talks have brought tranquillity to large areas of the country and today Colombia is a safer place to visit than much of the US and Mexico. Poised on the cusp of a promising future, Colombia is entering a brand-new era, bolstered by a wave of national confidence that has the country in a buoyant mood. Colombian citizens and foreign and national companies alike have ploughed significant amounts of investment into the country, while much-improved infrastructure has encouraged millions of vehicles to drive across a once-deserted road system. In 2007, American magazine *BusinessWeek* named Colombia 'the most extreme emerging market on earth', with tour operators reporting a roaring trade in ecotourism where people once feared to tread. Today, travellers in Colombia are unlikely to encounter anything more dangerous than a hungry mosquito – not bad for a country that once had the tourist appeal of a camping trip in central Baghdad.

Over 1.4 million visitors explored Colombia in 2010 with annual tourism growing at around 10.7%. In the same year, readers of *Wanderlust* magazine voted it their favourite emerging destination worldwide. Cruise ships sail into Cartagena, one of the most important colonial cities in the Americas, and the country attracts the third-largest market share of tourism in South America – a clear sign of things to come. In 2014, the number of tourists to Colombia exceeded four million. What a turnabout! Soccer-mad Colombia even made a serious bid to host the 2014 World Cup – prompting a state of near-delirium and parties nationwide, but most important was the Cafeteros' emotional and exhilarating play in Brazil – winning over neutral supporters and seeing them lose to the hosts in unfortunate circumstances.

So, it just leaves me to say 'enjoy Colombia', have a great trip, *buen viaje*. I'm certain that a few myths regarding this rather fine country will be dispelled along the way. I'm also sure you'll meet some of the friendliest, most genuine people in Latin America and will be dazzled by the trademark Colombian smile. One word of advice: try not to make the all-too-common mistake of spelling Colombia with a 'u' (as in Columbia). Few things are as likely to turn a smile into a scowl!

AUTHOR'S STORY

Colombia first came to my attention as a nine-year-old at junior school when, in a geography lesson, I learned about the Spanish settlement of fortified Cartagena. I studied pastel drawings of colonial streetscapes and marvelled at sketches depicting Colombia's ancient indigenous tribes. Almost 30 years later, after completing *Panama: the Bradt Travel Guide*, I journeyed to Colombia and was able to make those illustrations from my childhood come to life. For even in modern Colombia, I could pass through vast, open expanses of countryside gloriously free of traffic, noise and people. I savoured jaw-dropping scenery dotted with pretty, rustic towns and grazing cattle and witnessed indigenous people practising ancient rituals as they'd done for many centuries past. I realised quickly that Colombia is a very special country, a nation poles apart from the one so often primitively depicted in the news headlines.

Like many travellers, I was frustrated by the scant coverage offered in the back-end of regional 'South American' travel guides, so I am glad that in my own small way I am able to help redress the balance. In all honesty, I could fill an entire bookshelf describing what Colombia has to offer visitors. Thank goodness that the Bradt team were there to remind me that travel guides need to be portable and should weigh in at under a ton.

Re-reading this guide brings back memories of the many life-enriching experiences I owe to Colombia and its people. One simple, but memorable example of the Colombian hospitality I encountered was a handwritten note handed to me by a young girl in Huila welcoming me warmly to her country. I still have the note, stained purple by the freshly picked berries we shared in the sunshine, while swapping stories and etching pictures in the blood-red dust of the road.

Part One

GENERAL INFORMATION

COLOMBIA AT A GLANCE

Name República de Colombia
Location Northern South America, bordering the Caribbean Sea, between Panama and Venezuela, and bordering the North Pacific Ocean, between Ecuador and Panama
Border countries Brazil 1,644km, Ecuador 590km, Panama 225km, Peru 1,800km, Venezuela 2,050km (border total 6,309km)
Type of government Democratic Republic
Head of state President Juan Manuel Santos (since 2010): Independent Liberal
Independence 20 July 1810 (from Spain)
Capital Bogotá
Population 48 million
Climate Steamy tropical conditions along coast and eastern plains; cool with less humidity in highlands
Topography Flat coastal lowlands, central highlands, high Andes Mountains, eastern lowland plains
Coastline 3,208km (Caribbean Sea 1,760km, North Pacific Ocean 1,448km)
Lowest point Pacific Ocean (0m)
Highest point Pico Cristóbal Colón (5,775m)
Major rivers Magdalena, Cauca, Meta, Guaviare, Caquetá, Putumayo, Atrato, Vaupés, Vichada
Currency Colombian peso (COP/$)
Rate of exchange £1 = 4,100COP, US$1 = 2,600COP, €1 = 2,900COP (July 2015)
Economy GDP: US$171.6 billion comprising agriculture (12.1%), industry (35.2%), services (52.7%), with key products and industries coffee, cut flowers, bananas, rice, tobacco, corn, sugarcane, cocoa beans, oilseed, vegetables, forest products, shrimp, textiles, food processing, oil, clothing and footwear, beverages, chemicals, cement, gold, coal, petroleum and emeralds
Language Spanish; also 65 indigenous languages
Religion Catholic (90%); also Episcopal and Jewish faiths
Time GMT/UTC –5
International dialling code +57
Electricity 110V, 60Hz
Electric plug American-style plug with two parallel flat blades
Flag Three horizontal bands of yellow (top, double-width), blue and red. The yellow represents the richness of Colombian gold; the blue the Pacific Ocean and Caribbean Sea; the red the lives lost during the fight for independence and also the blood of Jesus, reflecting Colombia's Christian roots.
Public holidays (based on 2016 calendar) 1 Jan (New Year's Day), 11 Jan* (Epiphany), 21 Mar* (St Joseph's Day), 24 Mar (Maundy Thursday), 25 Mar (Good Friday), 1 May (Labour Day), 9 May* (Ascension), 30 May * (Corpus Christi), 6 Jun* (Sagrado Corazón; Sacred Heart), 4 Jul * (St Peter & St Paul), 20 Jul (Independence Day), 7 Aug (Battle of Boyacá), 15 Aug* (Assumption), 12 Oct* (Columbus Day), 7 Nov* (All Saints' Day), 14 Nov* (Independence of Cartagena City), 8 Dec (Immaculate Conception), 25 Dec (Christmas Day). *Observed the following Monday if falls on any other day.

1

Background Information

GEOGRAPHY

Few countries boast such striking physical variety as Colombia, a land where rugged topography combines with a location near the Equator to create an extraordinary diversity of climates, vegetation, soils and crops. Spanning 1,141,748km² (an area double the size of France or California), Colombia also boasts the distinction of being the only South American nation with coastlines on both the Pacific Ocean and Caribbean Sea. Shaped like an oversized fraying bedsheet, Colombia is South America's fourth-largest country (after Brazil, Argentina and Peru), overwhelming its many diminutive neighbours with a landmass that is as geographically complex as it is physically vast. At the Pasto Massif, near the Ecuadorian border, the mountains divide into the Cordillera Occidental (Western Range), which runs parallel to the Pacific coast, and the Cordillera Central (Central Range), which, with its numerous volcanoes, forms a dominant spine across most of the country north to south, rising to well over 5,000m. The Eastern Cordillera extends southeast from the Colombia Massif to the peaks of the Perijá Mountains in La Guajira. The valleys of two great rivers – the mighty Magdalena and fast-flowing Cauca – act as dividing channels from the Atlantic coastal lowlands into the very heart of the country.

Crystalline rocks are exposed on the brooding flanks of the Cordillera Central and are home to sandstone, shale and gold and silver deposits dating back several million years. Ash and lava from more than two-dozen ancient volcanoes form soaring peaks that are permanently covered in snow at over 4,600m. In contrast, the Cordillera Occidental is non-volcanic and the lowest and most sparsely populated, forming a barrier between the Cauca Valley and the Pacific coast. Elevations less than 1,500m mark the lowest point between the cities of Cali and Buenaventura with higher crests reaching 3,960m at Mount Paramillo in Antioquia at the point where the mountains fan into three distinct forested mountain ranges – Abibe, San Jerónimo and Ayapel. Antioquia is also the site of a magnificent weather-ravaged granite intrusion, an exposed plateau averaging 2,500m above sea level, divided in two by the depths of the Porce River. This vast, irregular, deep-seated mass of intrusive igneous rock is riddled with gold-bearing quartz veins: a rich strata of lesions that once saw colonial mining prosper. The Baudó Mountains are a far less dramatic topographic attribute than their batholithic counterpart but boast one of the fastest-flowing rivers on the planet. A staggering 4,900m³ of water per second is emptied into the Caribbean Gulf by the currents of the Río Atrato. The Baudó Mountains represent a southward extension of the Isthmus of Panama where the range becomes known as Serranía del Sapo and stretches into the Darién.

Estranging the Magdalena Valley from the Llanos are the statuesque slopes of the Cordillera Oriental, a range composed of foliated metamorphic rock and marine sediments and ancient deposits of igneous matter. Rising to 5,493m with high plateaus formed by residues from nearby lakes in the Quaternary Period, the

3

Cordillera Oriental culminates in the towering Mount Cocuy before branching off into two skinny mountain ranges, one extending into Venezuela and the other creating a northern boundary.

The isolated, mystical mountains of Santa Marta boast the highest point in the country along its fault-bounded granite massif at 5,775m atop the twin peaks of Cristóbal Colón and Simón Bolívar. Rising sharply from the Caribbean littoral it sprouts up to ice-covered summits with the Atlantic lowlands behind it, forming an imposing if compact group surrounded by lands with elevations below 200m: an isolated array of ecosystems and the world's fifth most prominent summit.

Extending north to south almost the entire length of Colombia, the Andes Mountains dominate the central and western parts of the country, with two-fifths of the west of Colombia lying in their highlands. Lofty tablelands and fertile valleys form a dramatic contrast with steep, rugged rocks that descend into the rolling coastal plains of the Pacific and Caribbean regions across the eastern interior towards the Orinoco and Amazon rivers.

Colombia's two coastlines have very distinct characteristics: from the boggy horseshoe bays, inlets and jutting marshland peninsulas that epitomise the Pacific shoreline to the Caribbean's sandy beaches, palm-fringed islands and saline lagoons.

Between the Andes and the frontiers of Venezuela, Brazil, Peru and Ecuador are some 600,000km² of very sparsely populated steamy lowlands and swamps that form catchments for the tributaries that empty into the Orinoco and Amazon rivers. To the north lies the gaping savannah of Los Llanos at roughly 250,000km², a huge open stretch in the basin of the Orinoco River. This vast semi-arid terrain of grass plains contains thick forests along the riverbanks. At more than 400,000km² the Amazon engulfs southeast Colombia, a land dominated by dense rainforest and riddled with magnificent vine-tangled rivers.

Another of Colombia's important geographic facets is its numerous outlying islands, including the photogenic cluster of white-sand palm-fringed isles located 750km northwest of the mainland in the Caribbean Sea. The islands of San Andrés and Providencia boast seven groups of coral reefs and cays just a few hundred miles from the Mosquito Coast of Nicaragua. Also near the Caribbean coast are San Bernardo and the Islas del Rosario, while Malpelo and Gorgona are located in the Pacific Ocean in Colombia's southwest. In the Pacific, Colombian territory encompasses Isla de Malpelo at about 430km west of Buenaventura. Nearer the coast, a former prison colony is located on Isla Gorgona. However, the combined area of all these offshore and outlying islands does not exceed 65km².

NATURAL DISASTERS Colombia is susceptible to volcanic eruptions, earthquakes, periodic droughts and flooding and is located in an active seismic zone. In 1979, an earthquake and tsunami destroyed six fishing villages along the Pacific coast. Hundreds of people died in the state of Nariño with tremors felt in Bogotá, Cali, Popayán, Buenaventura and other major cities and villages in Colombia as well as Guayaquil, Esmeraldas, Quito and other parts of Ecuador. In 1985, four towns in the Andes region were buried under ash spewed from the Nevado del Ruiz volcano, causing a horrific mudslide that claimed 23,000 lives. Worst affected was Armero, the province of Tolima's second-largest city, about 50 miles from Bogotá. Fatalities were particularly high because the eruption occurred at night when most of the town's 27,000 residents were asleep. Nevado del Ruiz, known locally as 'the Sleeping Lion', had not erupted for nearly 150 years. In 1999, at least 1,000 people were killed and more than 4,000 injured when an earthquake measuring six on the Richter scale struck the heart of the country's coffee-growing region. The most powerful quake to hit Colombia for 16 years destroyed large sections of the cities of Armenia and Pereira, trapping people in the rubble and in landslides and leaving 200,000 homeless. In November 2004, a state of emergency was declared across eight states, as torrential downpours caused dangerous floodwaters and landslides. Hundreds died and many were injured in the districts of Atlántico, Bolívar (particularly in the cities of Cartagena, Achí and San Jacinto del Cauca), Guajira, César, Córdoba, Magdalena, Sucre and Santander, affecting 49,660 families and 251,717 people. In 2005, the Galeras Volcano erupted in the Nariño department, sparking a mass evacuation of more than 9,000 people living on its slopes near the border with Ecuador. The threat to life was complicated by hundreds of people who refused to leave their smallholdings, despite a pledge by the Colombian government to pay evacuees US$40 a month to help with temporary accommodation. In January 2006, heavy rains deluged much of Colombia causing severe flooding across the country, particularly in the northeast. In the same year, eight boy scouts and their guide were killed by a mudslide at the foot of Nevado del Ruiz volcano. Bad weather took the group by surprise as a huge flow of water carried them into rocks. The expedition was swept away while bathing in a canyon known as La Gruta when heavy rains upstream caused the Chinchiná River to swell. In 2010, Colombia suffered its worst ever natural disaster as widespread heavy rains swept away roads, villages, schools and vehicles and triggered deadly landslides. In the suburbs of Medellín, severe weather devastated houses and killed hundreds of people as torrential rains eroded huge swathes of the landscape. Colombian officials and the Colombian Red Cross battled to recover bodies as water swept illegal rubbish dumps through slum neighbourhoods to render over 1.5 million people homeless. According to meteorologists the 2010–2011 rainy season was the worst the country had seen in 60 years: a unpredictable weather front caused by 'La Niña' that effected US$5.2 billion of damage and which has led to a decrease in production in various agro-industrial sectors that has taken several years to recover. Major cities continue to be jolted into action by frequent tremors, the largest and most recent being in March 2015 which reached 6.6 on the Richter scale, with its epicentre located in the town of Los Santos, Santander. While the nearby town of Betulia was left in ruins, there were no deaths and the shocks were felt strongly as far away as on the Caribbean coast and in Bogotá.

CLIMATE

Colombia lies almost entirely in the so-called Torrid Zone: a part of the earth's surface between the tropics of Cancer and Capricorn characterised by hot weather. However, Colombia's climate varies as a result of the differences in altitude with seasons defined by periods of lesser or greater rainfall, with little or no temperature change. Weather-wise, the country can be divided vertically into four regions with the hot country (*tierra caliente*) stretching from sea level to roughly 1,100m. In the temperate zone (*tierra templada*) elevations reach 3,000m while the remaining land is dubbed 'the cold country' (*tierra fría*) as it exceeds 3,000m. The cold zone's upper area marks the treeline and roughly denotes the limit of human habitation. Adjacent to the *tierra fría* are Colombia's treeless regions. These can reach 4,500m and are bleak areas referred to as the *páramos*, usually with permanent snow (*nevado*). Expect an average of 24–27°C in the hot low-lying regions along the Caribbean coastline and outlying islands, but don't be surprised if they rarely exceed 22°C in lofty Bogotá. Medellín is known as 'La Ciudad de la Eterna Primavera' (or 'City of the Eternal Spring') throughout Colombia for its pleasant year-round climate with minimal temperature variations.

Precipitation is heavy along the Pacific coast and in the Andean regions while on the leeward side of the Guajira Peninsula light rainfall is the lowest in Colombia. Northern Colombia has one long rainy season while other regions have a 'dry' season followed by a 'wet' season in three-month cycles. In Bogotá annual rainfall averages about 1,060mm per annum while in Barranquilla around 800mm is the norm. In recent years, Colombia's seasonal cycles have been unpredictable – a symptom, experts say, of climate change. If your trip is centred on exploring the country's great outdoors then it is important to avoid the worst of the rains, when many hiking trails are rendered impassable owing to mudslides and flooding. Water levels in the Amazon can also be unpredictable during the rainy season. Jungle expanses, islands and entire villages can be engulfed during this period, when a continuous deluge can cause the river to rise by up to 13m.

For further information contact the Colombian Meteorological Institute (Instituto de Meteorología) (*Calle 25D, No 96 B–70, Bogotá;* \ *352 7160; www.ideam.gov.co*).

NATURAL HISTORY

Colombia is one of the most biologically diverse countries in the world. Within its borders you'll find hot and sticky humidity, chilly high-altitude temperatures, both Caribbean and Pacific coastlines, palm-laden islands, mountains reaching 5,000m, dry scrub, volcanic hills and a chunk of thick subtropical Amazon Basin that hosts extraordinary, untamed ecosystems. This eco excess is remarkable considering Colombia's size, and makes the country an extremely attractive destination for wildlife enthusiasts. Colombia supports more species of bird than any other country and the second-largest number of amphibians in the world. To date, over 1,880 species of bird and 700 amphibians have been recorded there. This includes the rather bizarre-looking beached toad discovered in the heart of the Colombian jungle on the Pacific coast in 2010 – a species that is smaller than a human thumbnail. With deep purple skin and small blue blotches, the toad was discovered by a British-led scientific team. They also catalogued a red-legged tree frog with distinctive black streaks from nose to body and a brown toad with red eyes – both also new additions to the zoological record. Other exciting discoveries include a trio of new bird species, with two tapaculos (scytalopus) recorded in the central Cordillera and the Yaringuies brush finch (*Atlapetes latinuchus yariguierum*) discovered in the Serranía de los Yariguíes. The latter, a vibrantly coloured finch with a scarlet head, gold chest and dark wings and tail, has impressed wildlife enthusiasts globally. In 2010, researchers also discovered a new species of antpitta in the montane cloudforests of western Colombia. The thrush-like bird with brown and grey plumage was captured, banded, measured, photographed and sampled for DNA before being released alive back into the Colibri del Sol Bird Reserve, managed by Fundación ProAves and founded in 2006.

Mammals number over 400 species and range from jaguars and pumas to spectacled bears. Not surprisingly, plant life is abundant; around 130,000 species have been recorded, of which a third are endemic. Colombia is renowned for its orchids, but there are endless exotic plants, from the wax palm (*Ceroxylon quindiuense*; the country's national tree) to giant water lilies so vast they can hold a child.

Sadly, rapid deforestation in Colombia is threatening a growing number of species; a staggering 10,000 plant species are believed to be facing extinction as well as around 10% of the country's mammal species. Deforestation is depleting forests annually, due to logging, illegal mining, industrial corporations, commercial crops and locally produced charcoal (page 255). In addition, strong pesticides deployed in aerial coca crop spraying further threaten the country's flora with extinction. Numerous zones in the country are pinpointed by the Alliance for Zero Extinction (AZE) (*www.zeroextinction.org*) and a number of environmental groups are now actively involved in conservation such as Proyecto Tití (Project Tamarin) (*http://proyectotiti.com*) and the Wildlife Conservation Society (*http://www.wcs.org/saving-wild-places/latin-america-and-the-caribbean/valle-de-cauca-colombia.aspx*).

SPOTTING WILDLIFE Most wildlife is concentrated on the spine of the Andean chain, the Western Cordillera, the Central Cordillera and the Eastern Cordillera, three mountain ranges that cross the country. However, due to deforestation, the region is fragmented and now many areas are stripped of their previous habitat. In new urban expanses a lot of wildlife has been shot or simply frightened out of town. Monkeys, mammals and birds are easiest to find in national parks that can provide maps and guides to what you can expect to see. At the time of writing, the best place to spot migrating humpback whales is in the deep waters of Bahía Málaga on the Pacific coast, just north of Buenaventura.

ORCHIDS Parts of Colombia are festooned with orchids, and in some areas the flowers literally blanket the trees. The flowers are spectacular and attract people on a global scale. Some 15% of the world's orchid species are found here and it is claimed that up to 21,500 plants have been recorded per hectare in the Nariño region. So valuable are these ornate flowers that horticulturist Tom Hart Dyke was kidnapped on the Panamanian side of the border with Colombia while searching for plants in 2000 (he was released after nine months). Indeed, the country is so enamoured with orchids it has made the *Cattleya trianae* (Flor de mayo; May flower) its national flower. It is indigenous to Colombia and named after Colombian botanist José J Triana and English botanist William Cattley (1788–1835). The flower grows without soil in 15 different colours in the central departments of Tolima, Huila and Cundinamarca, and is sadly now threatened due to loss of its natural habitat.

There are now around 3,500 orchid varieties found in Colombia and orchid fever has spread throughout the country. Regional orchid societies in Bogotá, Pereira, Cali, Manizales and Medellín are respected by enthusiasts all over the world and hold regular local shows. There is also huge national pride in the annual Exposición Internacional de Orquídeas de Colombia (Colombian International Orchid Show), which is hosted by a different city each year. Colombia even has its own award system designated by the Comité Colombiana de Orquideología; it awards only Colombian species.

The Sociedad Colombiana de Orquideología, the oldest society in the country, hosted the seventh World Orchid Conference in 1972, in Medellín. The society was founded 50 years ago and promotes cultivation and conservation. Another group, the Orchid Foundation of Tolima, an NGO in central Colombia, maintains an 'orchidary' where visitors can enjoy 150 species that are under threat.

Where to spot an orchid Orchids grow best between 1,800m and 2,500m above sea level. However, Colombia's countless species vary in requirements and can be found almost anywhere, from jungle to mountain; even by the beach. The Zona Cafetera is probably the best area to find orchids, but those looking for a more organised display should head to Bogotá Botanical Gardens. Tour operators are generally accustomed to visitors wanting to find orchids and should have well-informed guides available. De Una Colombia (page 66) is in contact with orchid organisations and can arrange trips with professional guides.

1

FUNDACIÓN PROAVES

Founded in 2001, the ProAves charity (*www.proaves.org*) is Colombia's largest conservation NGO. It aims to protect around 50 of the country's 88 threatened bird species, as well as endangered amphibians and some mammals. The organisation owns and maintains forest reserves, which serve as effective protection areas for birds. In addition, ProAves is involved in ongoing, extensive research programmes and runs environmental education programmes for children. These local programmes are taken to local communities around the country in the 'Loro Bus' (Parrot Bus) and the project is highly respected in Colombia. There are currently 21 ProAves reservations including:

PAUJIL The reserve covers 1,200ha at an altitude of just 300m so the climate is tropical and very humid. It's located close to Puerto Pinzón, Boyacá, an 8-hour drive from Bogotá, the last 40km of which is unpaved so it is not easy to reach. However, there is accommodation with both private and shared rooms, air conditioning and internet. More importantly you'll get the chance to see a blue-billed curassow, saffron-headed parrot and variegated spider monkey. Rubber boots are advised.

ARRIERITO ANTIOQUEÑO Situated close to Anori, Antioquia, the 610ha reserve is a 4-hour drive from Medellín. Accommodation is basic, but has electricity. Set at an altitude of 1,500m the temperature is subtropical and humidity is high. The main bird species to look for is the chestnut-capped piha.

LORO OREJIAMARILLO This subtropical 120ha specialist reserve, set at 2,200m, consists of dry forest and is named after the yellow-eared parrot that inhabits it. Accommodation is basic, with electricity, but there is a selection of good hotels in the local area to choose from. It is situated close to Jardín Antioquia, a 3-hour drive from Medellín.

EL DORADO One of the most accessible of ProAves reserves, this subtropical park covers 245ha, at an altitude of 2,000m, and is located close to Minca Magdalena, outside Santa Marta. Popular with students, teachers and biologists the accommodation is superb and the park offers a chance to see 17 endemic bird species, such as the Santa Marta parakeet and the Santa Marta sabrewing hummingbird, and three endangered frogs, two of which (*Atelopus laetissimus* and *Atelopus nahumae*) were once presumed extinct until they were rediscovered in 2006. The reserve is a 2½-hour drive from Santa Marta, 1½ of which is unpaved. However, EcoTurs (*www.ecoturs.org*) will organise a jeep to collect you from Santa Marta.

EL MIRADOR Mirador reserve covers 1,950ha of mountain habitat high up in the páramo at an altitude of 3,500m. Perfect for adventurers, the ascent is tough and

Using a guide will ensure you get the most from a trip in the more remote national parks. Most offer all-inclusive packages that allow plenty of time to watch for birds and other wildlife.

NATIONAL PARKS Over the last few decades the government has promoted Colombia's eco-diversity and, impressively, there are 55 designated national parks and protected areas in Colombia that cover around 8.5% of the country.

you'll need to travel 2½ hours by horse. EcoTurs (*www.ecoturs.org*) will organise horses and a guide to stay with you throughout your trip. Accommodation, however, is basic with hydro-electricity, but there is cell phone reception. The environment of lichenous forests and valleys feels fresh but the temperature drops sharply at night so warm clothing is essential. You can observe endangered parrots here such as the fuertes parrot, as well as the brown-banded, bicoloured and crescent-faced antpitta, rufous-fronted parakeet and mirador parrot. Situated close to Génova, Quindío, it's a 2-hour drive from Armenia, 20km of which is unpaved.

EL PANGAN At an altitude of just 800m, the wet subtropical reserve of El Pangan covers 810ha and is located a 2-hour walk from Junín, Nariño, 2½ hours from Tumaco. The accommodation is basic, with hydro-electricity. Look for the long-wattled umbrella bird, chocó vireo, banded ground-cuckoo and Pangan poison-arrow frog. Rubber boots are advised.

COLIBRI DE SOL In a similar location to El Dorado, Colibri de Sol covers 2,800ha at an altitude of 3,500m and is accessible only by a 2-hour horseride from Urrao, Antioquia (4 hours' drive from Medellín). Accommodation is basic but does have hydro-electricity. Spectacled bears inhabit the park, and although it is highly unlikely you will catch a glimpse of one, the chance is exciting. You should get to see dusky starfrontlets, rusty-faced parrots and the chestnut-bellied flower-piercer.

REINITA CERÚLEA (CERULEAN WARBLING RESERVE) This 205ha reserve is popular with many Americans who are concerned about the endangered cerulean warbler's future. This tiny, blue-grey bird migrates from the US to Colombia during winter and now faces extinction due to deforestation in Colombia. At the reserve, ProAves has established a hillside coffee plantation, where coffee beans grow in the shade, providing an ideal environment for the warblers who love such a habitat in forest environs. The coffee itself is harvested and sold within the local co-operative. The park, set at 2,000m altitude, is humid and subtropical; look out for gorgeted wood-quail, black inca and the white-mantled barbet as well as the warblers. Accommodation is good and provides internet access. It is located close to San Vicente in Santander, a 2-hour taxi drive from Bucaramanga.

HORMIGUERO DE TORCORMAMA A smaller tropical reserve, with 120ha set at just 600m altitude and situated close to Ocaña (15 minutes by taxi), Norte de Santander. There's no on-site accommodation, but there are several good local hotels. The climate here is dry, and not as humid as some parks; look for recurve-billed bushbird and Todd's parakeet.

These include ten Santuarios de Fauna y Flora (Sanctuaries of Fauna and Flora), two natural reserves, Nukak and Puinawai, the Vía Parque Isla de Salamanca and Los Estoraques, Área Natural Única (Unique Natural Area). Colombians are extremely proud of their environment; even FARC (Revolutionary Armed Forces of Colombia) claim to protect the jungle and forest in areas it inhabits. However, national park status hasn't meant that these areas are fully protected; aerial coca spraying, which is carried out in some parks, is reputed to be a particular threat. There has also been some cultural dispute over the recent development of luxury five-star accommodation within some national parks, which has created a backlash among locals who feel they are priced out of enjoying the areas themselves.

Many national parks are off-limits due to paramilitary and guerrilla activity. Furthermore, some of the most spectacular are those that remain almost untouched by human life, making them almost impossible to reach. Visitors attempting to reach remote parks must check their safety before their trip and must get permission and advice from the relevant park warden. It is vital to check that a park is safe to visit when planning a trip as some occasionally attract guerrillas. Contact the park authorities and discuss the full itinerary, including all routes and trails. Up-to-date advice should also be sought on on-site facilities to establish exactly what gear to take. The Natural National Parks of Colombia office in Bogotá can also be contacted for information (⟨ 353 2400; e ecoturismo@parquesnacionales.gov.co; www.parquesnacionales.gov.co).

A full spectrum of climate zones ranges from coral-fringed islands, glacial mountain ranges and dry scrub to steaming jungle and sticky Amazonian bogs in the parks that are accessible and much safer to visit. It is possible to witness, and occasionally interact with, indigenous communities living in some parks, but it is vital to respect any regulations that require visitors to stay away from particular tribes. Several national parks are currently open to tourists and offer good basic facilities, such as restaurants, information centres (some with language translations) and advice on footpaths and trails. Accommodation ranges from basic camping and hammocks to luxurious 'eco-habs'. Travellers planning to camp in a park should bring equipment, including ropes and tent pegs, and be prepared for all eventualities. It is also important to check with the relevant authorities (see national park contact details below) regarding the rules for each park as some prohibit campfires or cooking outside designated zones. All specify that non-biodegradable rubbish should be removed from the park and it is illegal to take home any flora or fauna. Admission to Colombia's national parks is relatively inexpensive with concessions available for children. In 2007, the Colombian government announced the creation of a new national park to protect one of the greatest areas of biodiversity in the country, inhabited by such rare and endangered animals as the Andean bear, jaguar, puma and tapir. The new park – **Serranía de los Churumbelos Auka-Wasi** – stretches from the lowlands of the Amazon Basin to the slopes of the Andean Mountains over 97,180ha. Some 461 species of birds have been registered in the region, equivalent to 26% of the birds in all of Colombia. The mountainous Churumbelos area is recognised for its incredible biodiversity and contains 30 species of amphibians, 16 species of reptiles, more than 140 species of butterflies and 825 species of plants.

The following are Colombia's most accessible and therefore most popular natural parks. In the absence of local telephone numbers, each can be contacted via the main national parks office (www.parquesnacionales.gov.co).

Amacayacu (Hammock River, Quechua) (est 1975) (e dtao@parquesnacionales. gov.co) Covering 293,500ha, Amacayacu is perhaps one of the country's most interesting parks, located deep in the jungle basin, a half-hour boat ride from Leticia, Colombia's southernmost point. Few tourists venture so far south, but the park is very popular with Colombians and is by far the best way to experience the Colombian Amazon. You may see pink river dolphins (*botos*) in the rivers and black-mantle tamarins in the forests.

The park is also home to around 500 bird species and 150 mammal species; look for the golden lion tamarin, the jabuti tortoise (the world's largest freshwater tortoise) and macaws. The observatory platforms provide a fantastic vista of untouched forest for creature spotting. The terrain offers both dry vegetation and the thick humid jungles typical of the Amazon. There is also a visitors' centre with renovated accommodation facilities that sleep 40 people, as well as a museum, auditorium and research centre.

Cahuinarí (est 1987) Some 575,000ha of dense tropical rainforest, lagoons and piranha-filled rivers are situated in the regions of Caquetá and Putumayo in Colombia's south-central Amazon. During the 19th century many trees here were felled for rubber, much of the park was destroyed and indigenous people exploited. The area, and the indigenous Cahuinarí, hunter-gatherers that live within the park, is now protected. Endangered species here include the jaguar, giant river otter, puma, black caiman and the now extremely rare charapa (giant river turtle). Parks in Peril (PIP) (*www.parksinperil.org*) are currently supporting the park and have carried out training of the Cahuinarí people to work as park wardens as well as launching the Charapa Conservation Plan. In 2001, a co-operative agreement enabled joint management between the local community and Unidad de Parques, Colombia.

Catatumbo-Bari (est 1989) (✆ *566 2139*) This park covers 158,125ha of humid tropical forests and mountain terrain, located in the Oriental mountain range in Norte de Santander, close to the Venezuelan border. There are an estimated 114 species of mammal here and 616 species of birds. Several indigenous communities live here, including the Yuko-Yukpas, Dobokubis and Barí, whose numbers have been decimated since the area was ravaged for oil during the early 20th century.

Chingaza (est 1977–78) (✉ *atencionusuario@parquesnacionales.gov.co*) Chingaza spans 76,600ha and rises to over 4,000m above sea level. The park is situated close to Bogotá in the Cordillera Oriental in the regions of Cundinamarca and Meta. The tropical mountain forests contain spectacled bears and pumas, deer, coati and monkey as well as the Andean condor and toucans among many others.

Corales del Rosario y San Bernardo (Rosario and San Bernardo corals) (est 1977) (✉ *ecoturismo@parquesnacionales.gov.co*) A total of 120,000ha of water and islands. A spectacular archipelago located 45km from the Bay of Cartagena, the park is host to 52 species of coral, 45 species of sponge, hundreds of species of molluscs and crustaceans and numerous multi-coloured fish that bask in the clear tropical waters of the Caribbean Sea. There are also important mangrove networks on Barú Island. The park is geared towards tourism and there's a popular aquarium at the Oceanario Islas del Rosario as well as the Museum of Marine Life.

Cordillera Los Picachos (Picachos mountain range) (est 1977) Some 447,740ha of humid subtropical jungle mountain situated between the Orinoco and Amazon rivers, to the west of the Meta region. The park is closed to tourists.

Cueva de los Guácharos (Cave of the oilbirds) (est 1960) South of Picachos, in the Oriental mountain range in the region of Caquetá, Guácharos occupies 700ha. Guácharo birds (small, thin relatives of the nightjar) are protected here and nest in fascinatingly formed caves carved out along the Suazas River. The park has been sited as a UNESCO Biosphere Reserve along with the Puracé National Park and the

Nevado del Huila National Park. There are basic tourist facilities here including a restaurant and camping area with an outdoor kitchen set-up.

El Cocuy (est 1977) Around 306,000ha of subtropical forest, mountain lakes and glacial peaks in the Cordillera Oriental in the regions of Boyacá, Arauca and Casanare, northeast from Bogotá. The park offers breathtaking climbing and trekking opportunities and visitors can camp with guides on the mountain. There are reputedly plans for cable cars in the future here.

El Tuparro (est 1970) (e *amazonia@parquesnacionales.gov.co*) Around 548,000ha of dry savannah, woodland and swamp along the Orinoco River in the region of Vichada, inhabited by jaguar, tapir and otter. Indigenous communities live within the park but they remain isolated from outside contact.

Farallones de Cali (Cali Headlands) (est 1968) Located on the Occidental mountain range, in the region of Valle del Cauca, the Cali Headlands cover 205,266ha of subtropical forest overlooking the Pacific Ocean. As you ascend the temperature drops from around 25°C (77°F) to 5°C (41°F). The spectacled bear roams here, as do pumas and five species of monkey. Emberá Amerindians inhabit some of the lower regions on the park.

Parque Nacional Natural Alto Fragua Indi-Wasi (Fragua Indi-Wasi Natural National Park) (est 2002) (e *amazonia@ parquesnacionales.gov.co*) An interesting part of Colombia's cultural heritage as well as precious Amazonian flora and fauna, Indi-Wasi spans 68,000ha and is inhabited by a wide ethnic mix of South American indigenous peoples. Some have migrated from Ecuador and Peru, but others, who live in the south of Putumayo, are reputed to descend from groups who refused to bow down to the conquistadors. Sadly, the park has no facilities and is currently closed to tourists.

Isla Gorgona (Gorgona Island) (est 1984) Named by conquistador Francisco Pizarro after the Greek gorgon, due to the island's many snakes, and located in the Pacific, off Cauca on Colombia's west coast, Gorgona and neighbouring Gorgonilla islets cover around 62,000ha of rich, vibrant jungle on volcanic islands. Surrounded by coral reef, the islands are home to white-faced monkeys and the three-toed sloth as well as numerous bird species such as the blue honeycreeper. The wet season here is September/October; however, it is worth noting that humpback and finback whales mate offshore from September to December. You may need proof that you have had a vaccination against yellow fever.

La Paya (est 1984) (e *amazonia@parquesnacionales.gov.co*) This remote park covers 422,000ha of thick, humid tropical jungle along the Putumayo River close to the Peruvian border in Colombia's western Amazon region. Spectacular and remote, and now protected by PIP, the park is home to the giant anteater, woolly monkey, red howler monkey, pygmy marmoset, red brocket deer, jaguar and manatee, not to mention macaws, toucans and hawks. It is currently closed to tourists.

Las Hermosas (Beautiful) (est 1977) Some 125,000ha of fog-smothered, rugged mountain range in Colombia's central cordillera, in the regions of Cauca and Tolima, are inhabited by tapir, spectacled bear, puma and deer. There are reportedly 500 lagoons here that have developed from the mountain glaciers and run down to supply the surrounding towns and villages. There are currently no tourist facilities here.

Las Orquídeas (The Orchids) (est 1973/77) Around 32,000ha located in the Occidental mountain range in the region of Antioquia, northwest of Bogotá. Around 300 species of orchid have been recorded here. The park is currently closed to tourists.

Parque Nacional de Los Katíos (Los Katíos National Park) (est 1973) Located in the Chocó, in northwest Colombia, the lush swampy jungle of Los Katíos forms part of the Darién National Park in Panama. Rich in eco-diversity, endemic flora and wildlife, the park was designated a UNESCO World Heritage Site in 1994. It covers 72,000ha of tropical forest and hillside and the thick swamps of Tumaradó and is home to jaguars, tapirs, crocodiles and rare orchids. Because of the park's location, anyone wishing to visit *must* check with authorities *before* they plan a trip. The area can be frequently used by paramilitaries and guerrillas. The area steams with heat and humidity and accommodation is basic.

Parque Nacional de Los Nevados (Los Nevados National Park) (est 1973) This 58,300ha park in the central Andean mountain range crosses Caldas, Risaralda and Quindío, and is popular with hikers for its snow-capped volcanic peaks, palm forests, Ruiz and Rancho hot springs and Lake Otún and Guali Falls. In addition there's a chance you'll glimpse bear, tapir and deer. At 2,500–5,000m above sea level it is cold and the temperatures average 3–14°C. Accommodation is currently being renovated here.

Macuira (est 1977) (e *ecoturismo@parquesnacionales.gov.co*) The tropical forest here is warm and dry; Macuira covers 25,000ha on a mountainous peninsula that juts into the Atlantic. Various indigenous groups as well as cloudforests and an abundance of wildlife inhabit the area. There's no entrance fee and although there are no government-constructed tourist facilities, the indigenous Wayúu rent hammocks in their *ranchos* to visitors. Check the area's safety before visiting.

Munchique (est 1977) Spanning 44,000ha, Munchique is located in the Cordillera Occidental, northwest of Popayán. The park is formed by several peaks and tropical rainforest and has been noted for the recent discovery of the Munchique wood-wren (*Henicorhina negreti*, named after the Colombian ornithologist, Álvaro José Negret). Visitors are currently restricted.

Nevado del Huila (est 1977) Around 158,000ha of rocky terrain, snow-covered peaks and active volcano, set in Colombia's central mountain range that reaches to 5,775m above sea level. The park straddles the departments of Cauca, Huila and Tolima and is currently not open to visitors.

Parque Nacional Old Providence McBean Lagoon (Old Providence McBean Lagoon Nature Park) (est 1995) Some 890ha of the 9.95km² park are underwater; the land part covers the 150m Iron Wood Hill on the northeastern end of the volcanic island of Providencia. The area is notable for the intricate ecosystems of the McBean mangrove, which includes red mangrove (*Rhizophora mangle*), yellow mangrove (*Avicennia germinans*) and white mangrove (*Laguncularia racemosa*). Along the shore are the palm-laden lagoons Crab Key and Three Brothers Key that are protected by substantial reef. Look out for the large black, dramatic man-of-war or frigate bird. You can stay in huts provided by the local community. Park tickets cost US$10, concessions US$3.

Paramillo (est 1977) (e *ecoturismo@parquesnacionales.gov.co*) Mountainous terrain and humid subtropical forest across 460,000ha, including the Paramillo Massif, situated to the north of the central Andes to the south of Córdoba.

Pisba (est 1977) Some 45,000ha rising 2,000m above sea level in the Oriental mountain range in Bocayá, northeast of Bogotá. The forests attract spectacled bears and deer, but are currently closed to tourists.

Puracé (est 1961) Located in the central mountain range, close to Popayán, the park spans 83,000ha and includes the Andean Almaguer Massif and Volcán Puracé, an active volcano that's a 4-hour hike from the visitors' centre. Laguna de San Rafael is situated 8km from Pilimbalá, and the waterfall, Cascada del Bedón, is a further 5km from the lagoon. There are a number of other rivers and waterfalls, as well as an orchid area, and walks here can be beautiful. There are currently three *cabañas* that sleep up to six people in each and four camping spaces.

Río Puré (Puré River) (est 2002) (e *amazonia@parquesnacionales.gov.co*) Dense Amazonian forest covers 1,000,000ha of lush jungle and river networks (including the Río Puré) between the Caquetá River and Putumayo River basins. A previously unknown fish, the Batman (*Otocinclus batmani*, named after the fictional character), was recently discovered in the Río Puré. The Carabayo-Aroje, an 'uncontacted people', inhabit the park.

Sanquianga (est 1977) This cluster of islands and a chunk of mainland covers 80,000ha on the southwest pacific coast, north of the Nariño region. Mangroves and sandy beaches attract an abundance of tropical flora and fauna, in particular protected nesting sea turtles. The park is currently closed to tourists.

Serranía de Chiribiquete (est 1989) (e *amazonia@parquesnacionales.gov.co*) Humid Amazonian mountain range, covering 1,280,000ha located in the regions of Caquetá and Guaviare. Currently closed to tourists.

Serranía de los Yaraguies (Yaraguies mountain range) (est 2005) Warm, dry terrain on the Oriental mountain range in Santander, spanning 78,837ha and set 1,700–2,300m above sea level. Both dry and humid forests cover the páramo attracting the spectacled bear among other mountain creatures.

Sierra de la Macarena (est 1971) (e *amazonia@parquesnacionales.gov.co*) Dense tropical jungle across 629,280ha in the department of Meta. Tourism is new to the area but largely seasonal given the flowering algae in the Cano Cristales, for which the region is now famous.

Sierra Nevada de Santa Marta (est 1964) (e *ecoturismo@parquesnacionales. gov.co*) Colombia's highest peaks and the world's highest coastal mountain peaks, the Sierra Nevada's highest point reaches 5,775m. The mountain sits just 26 miles from the Caribbean Sea and is not connected with the country's central Andean chain. It now supplies the water to 1.5 million Colombians and the country's largest indigenous groups live in the region. Located to the north of Colombia, the park itself covers 383,000ha of tropical lowlands, cloudforest, snowy ledges and glaciers. All of the reptiles and amphibians above 1,000m are reported endemic as well as numerous species of mammals and birds below that level, including the white-tipped quetzal.

Tourism is growing here, accommodation is available and a cable-car system is planned that will carry people to Ciudad Perdida and Pueblito.

Sumapaz (est 1977) Around 178,634ha of mountain terrain that rises to an altitude of 4,000m above sea level. The park includes rivers and cloudforests and is situated in the Oriental range just south of Bogotá, in the Meta region. There are some trails in the park, but visitors must first apply to the warden.

Tamá (est 1977) The park spans 48,000ha and is located to the north of the Cordillera Oriental, in Norte de Santander. It meets the Parque Nacional El Tamá de Venezuela, over the border. The climate zones range from tropical jungle to rough terrain and snowy peaks. Some 172 bird species have been recorded here, as well as the spectacled bear, puma, armadillo and otter.

Tatamá (est 1987) Located south of the Chocó in the Pacific region, the park covers 51,900ha and rises to 4,000m above sea level. A visitors' centre (Centro de Visitantes 'Planes de San Rafael'), can accommodate 40 people in shared dorms and offers a restaurant and park information.

Tayrona (est 1964) It is not difficult to see why Tayrona is Colombia's most popular national park. Occupying a strip of land and sea on the north coast's Magdalena region, the jagged shore is lined with golden beaches, caves and lagoons whilst inland the tropical jungle is humid and verdant, reaching an altitude of 1,000m above sea level. Around 49,000ha of the park is mainland jungle and forest and 1,200ha is ocean, reef and Caribbean marine life. Accommodation comprises eco-habs which have recently been updated from basic to luxury cabins offering cable television, air conditioning and a high-season price tag of almost US$200 per night. The renovations have been successful and are very attractive to tourists, but some local people are now unable to afford the park themselves. Close to cruise-ship ports and the holiday areas of Cartagena, Santa Marta and Barranquilla, the park offers opportunities to spot toucans and monkeys.

Tinigua (est 1989) Some 208,000ha of humid jungle and forest in the Amazonian region, in the department of Meta. The park has no facilities for tourists.

Utría (est 1987) Around 54,300ha of tropical jungle, mangrove swamps, estuaries and coral reefs in the Departamento del Chocó in the Pacific region of northern Colombia. Emberá communities utilise the jungle lakes for fishing and trading by boat. There are numerous reptiles and poison arrow frogs and it is possible to see migratory whales and dolphins. There is some lodging in the park.

SANCTUARIES OF FAUNA AND FLORA Together with numerous private initiatives, the Colombian government has set up several important conservation zones in which rare and endangered plant and tree species are protected.

Ciénaga Grande de Santa Marta and the Isla Salamanca (est 1977)
(e *ecoturismo@parquesnacionales.gov.co*) Around 23,000ha of land and ocean

situated in the Caribbean Magdalena region and easily reachable from Santa Marta or Barranquilla. The park hosts fishing eagles, coloured corals, reptiles, iguanas, caimans, turtles and manatee.

El Corchal 'El Mono Hernandez' (cork forest sanctuary) (est 2002)

(e *ecoturismo@parquesnacionales.gov.co*) Named in memory of scientist Jorge Ignacio Hernandez Camacho (1935–2001), who was known by his peers as 'the Monkey' or 'Hernandez the wise man'. An important reserve, covering 3,850ha, located on the Caribbean coast, flooded plains support five species of mangrove, marsh and swamp ecosystems and fine, organic clay sediment. Inland there are hectares of cork forests that are home to howler monkeys among other tropical creatures. There are currently no facilities for tourists here.

Galeras (named after the Galeras Volcano) (est 1985) This volcanic park

spans 18,800ha and reaches an altitude of 4,800m. Water from the park supplies the surrounding towns and the mountainous region feels invigorating, vibrant and overflowing with life. There's an abundance of canyons, lakes and crystal-clear waters pouring from rocky fissures. Overlooking the city of Pasto, the high

HIKING IN COLOMBIA

Colombia offers some of the best trails in Latin America and trekking is often at the top of the to-do list for tourists visiting the country. The mountain peaks of the **Sierra Nevada del Cocuy** are perhaps the most popular choice as they offer several routes that vary from enjoyable one-day climbs to a challenging seven-day mission. The views from the Nevada's 20 snow-topped peaks are breathtaking and visitors will find the glass-like lakes and rocky plateaus a euphoric reward to the climb. **Los Nevados National Park** offers dry scrub plains, remote cactus-clad hills, waterfalls and hot springs (El Rancho). However, it is hard to believe you're still in Colombia when you hit the glaciers at the summit of the volcano **Nevado del Tolima**, which stands at 5,215m above sea level.

For those on a stopover, or just wishing to stay closer to Bogotá, there are several superb hiking possibilities. Colombia's multi-faceted environment oozes diversity; on a day trek, the plants alone offer a firework display of vibrant colours and shapes ranging from alien-like lumpinas plants to tiny, ghostly white orchids. As an alternative to the high-altitude hikes of Cocuy and Los Nevados national parks, a gruelling six-day hike to **Ciudad Perdida** (Lost City) in the Sierra Nevada offers a very different experience. The vegetation is tropical and the climb highly rewarding – the highest point on Ciudad Perdida is 1,200m. Instead of tucking up in a tent in thermals, you can sleep in outdoor hammocks or cabins, and your food is carried by porters.

Remember, long treks can be incredibly tough so it is imperative you seek professional advice before embarking, and for these types of hikes a guide is essential. The Dutch company De Una Colombia (page 66), are hiking aficionados and provide a wealth of information on trekking in Colombia. Specialist guides at De Una say the possibilities for custom-made tours are endless – and they themselves want to explore more of hidden Colombia. The company's most popular trek is a five-day hike to **Púlpito de Diablo** (Devil's Pulpit) at the top of Pan de Azúcar in Cocuy National Park. The campsite is located next to Laguna de la Plaza, one of Colombia's most stunning lakes. The hike starts at 3,800m above sea level and ascends 200m on the first day and 1,100m on the second, with 200m páramo is a popular climb and the views are spectacular. Temperatures range from 3°C–15°C and the cloud-reaching heights of the Andean forests are often swirling in mist. The Consacá hot springs are an attraction as well as the lakes Laguna Negra, Laguna Mejía, Laguna Telpis and Laguna Verde and the Galeras Volcano crater. There are also 16 species of hummingbird to spot here.

You need to fill in an application before you can embark on this climb, which can be done in Pasto.

Guanentá Alto Río Fonce (est 1993) A 10,429ha stretch of cold Andean forests and deserts along the Oriental mountain range in southern Santander that is home to threatened species of deer, bear and wildcat. There's no lodging here but Virolín Ecological School, in Encino, and Hacienda Cachalú can provide shelter.

Iguaque (est 1977) The sanctuary covers 6,750ha along the páramo of the Oriental mountain range in Boyacá, which rises over 3,000m above sea level. The area is important to the locals who inhabit the surrounding area, not least because their water supply comes from the forest springs, but also, according to Muisca legend, because Lake Iguaque is believed to be the source of human

climbed with crampons. The trek provides a chance to climb the glaciers of Cerro's de la Plaza and experience a De Una custom of diving into a freezing cold lake.

PARQUE NACIONAL EL COCUY This 306,000ha national park was founded in 1997, stretching from temperate forests to snow-capped peaks and arid, desert land. Wooden lower plains rise to glacial terrain with alpine lakes. Lush valleys are home to waterfalls and rocky crags. Dominated by the Cordillera Oriental's highest peak, Ritacumba Blanco's 5,330m tip, Parque Nacional El Cocuy is regarded as one of Colombia's most resplendent reserves. Indigenous Indian tribes occupy the western flank of the park environs and mountain trails are relatively easy to navigate with an experienced guide. Access points are the towns of Guicán and El Cocoy located approximately 230km of Bogotá where it's possible to stock up on basic essentials ahead of an overnight stay in the park. Pack warm weather clothing and a thermal sleeping bag for camping as temperatures can drop to 0°C. An absence of on-site facilities means that you'll need to bring all food and equipment. Hikers also need to stick to official trails and engage the services of an authorised guide – solo treks are not allowed. Age restrictions also apply, so unless you are under 60 and over ten it is unlikely you'll be allowed in. Insurance is madatory.

Several tour companies offer trips into Parque Nacional El Cocuy, including many with a strong ecological focus – an important consideration given the park's fragile status. According to the Colombian Institute of Hydrology, five major glaciers in the park that in 1983 were expected to last at least 300 years are now under serious threat. Measurements taken in 2006 suggest that they may all disappear within 25 years. Dwindling numbers of several species of the park's rich abundance of wildlife are also a cause for concern, including eagles, spectacled bears and mountain tapirs. Items that pose a threat to the frailty of the ecosystem are also prohibited, so leave non-biodegradable plastic bags and aerosols behind. For further information contact Parques Nacionales de Colombia (*www.parquesnacionales.gov.co*) and follow the links to the Cocuy park pages.

POPULAR TREKS

By Erik Rupert at DE UNA Colombia Tours (www.deunacolombia.com). Erik is a seasoned adventurer and specialist tour operator who offers several hiking itineraries for visitors keen to explore Colombia's most enjoyable climbs.

For me, there are some unbeatable trekking and climbing opportunities within the **Los Nevados National Park**, although only a few are well marked. Another concern for hikers is poor visibility. Incoming clouds can suddenly restrict visibility to just a few metres to leave hikers prone to disorientation, so that they are likely to become lost – a very good reason why a guide is important. Popular treks include the following:

* Three-day climb to the summit of Nevado del Tolima from Ibagué. Lowest point: 2,400m (El Silencio); highest point: 5,215m (summit of Tolima) – 275,000COP
* Four-day trek from Pereira to Manizales passing by the lakes of Laguna del Otún and Laguna Verde Encantada. Lowest point: 2,100m (El Cedral); highest point: 4,600m (pass between Ruiz and Olleta) – 425,000COP
* Five-day trek from Valle de Cocora to Manizales passing by the lakes of Laguna El Encanto, Laguna La Leona, Laguna del Otún and Laguna Verde Encantada. Lowest point: 2,400m (Valle de Cocora); highest point: 4,600m (pass between Ruiz and Olleta) – 500,000COP
* Five-day trek from Valle de Cocora to Ibagué, climbing Nevado del Tolima. Lowest point: 2,400m (Valle de Cocora); highest point: 5,215m (summit of Tolima) – 450,000COP

As the home of 20 snow-capped mountains, the **National Park El Cocuy** is a real favourite with the challenging six-day itinerary of my preferred trail (at a cost of 800,000COP).

Prices are per person (minimum of four persons; ask for prices for smaller groups). Price includes necessary transport from and to Cocuy/Güican, park fees, camping fees, cooking equipment and bilingual guide from De Una Colombia. Good physical condition is required for all the above treks and climbs.

life. These sacred waters are a 3-hour walk into the park, but there are also some interesting rock paintings to see. There is a restaurant, some accommodation and a camping area. Locals recently blocked a proposed development for more upmarket tourist facilities.

La Corota (est 1977) Located in the Andean region of Nariño in the south of Colombia, La Corota is an island of wild grasses, paloerosa, myrtle and ferns on the ancient high plateau lake of La Laguna de La Cocha. The forests, which can be cloaked in clouds, were once the place of worship by the now extinct Quillacinga, an ancient indigenous culture. The island, of volcanic origin, spans just 8ha, rises 2,830m above sea level and can be extremely cold.

Los Colorados (est 1977) (e *ecoturismo@parquesnacionales.gov.co*) A thousand hectares of both dry and tropical forest situated near the Caribbean coast in the department of Bolívar. Some 288 bird species have been recorded here and the mammals present include Colorado monkeys, tamarin, coral snakes and boa constrictors. There are no tourist facilities on site, but in the nearby town of San Juan de Nepomuceno there are hotels, restaurants and camping areas.

Los Flamencos Sanctuary (Flamingos Sanctuary) (est 1977) Located in La Guajira on the Caribbean, Los Flamencos offers a breathtaking view of striking pink flamingos. The birds strut about in shallow lagoons formed in the coastal marshes of Manzanilla, Laguna Grande, Navío Quebrado and Tocoromanes. There are other birds here such as pelicans and herons, as well as many migratory birds, but the flamingos are the most spectacular. Flamingos come to shore March–June and September–November, but this is also rainy season so come prepared. The park spans 17,000ha and the climate is hot and humid.

Malpelo (est 1985) The tiny island of Malpelo – 350ha – lies in the Pacific Ocean 506km from the southwest Colombian mainland. However, the park also covers a staggering 860,000ha of surrounding ocean and has now become known as one of the best diving locations on the globe. The marine park's inhabitants are varied and include hammerheads, giant manta rays and many endangered and rare species such as the short-nosed ragged-toothed shark. The park is a designated no-fishing zone – the largest in the Eastern Tropical Pacific – and was added to UNESCO's World Heritage List in 2006.

Otún Quimbaya (est 1986) Joining the Los Nevados National Park, Otún Quimbaya is a 485ha forested region in the central Andes. As the park ascends from 1,800m to 2,500m above sea level, the climate is a mix of tropical warmth during the day and cold mountain air at night, with temperatures averaging 16°C (60.8°F). Spectacled bears are present in the park, although it is extremely rare to spot them. A research and information centre is available for public use.

RESERVAS NACIONALES (NATIONAL RESERVES TO PROTECT INDIGENOUS COMMUNITIES) (e amazonia@parquesnacionales.gov.co) The park spans 855,000ha and is located in the department of Guaviare in the Amazon region. The Makús (from the Piaroa linguistic family) inhabit the mountain range of Tunahí, and the area between Papanauá and Inírida. Their communities live on subsistence farming within the Amazon forest. There are no facilities for tourists.

Área Natural Única Los Estoraques (Los Estoraques Unique Natural Area) (est 1988) A haunting rise of ancient geological rock formations that has been shaped over millennia due to weather erosion. Located in the Oriental mountain range in the region of Norte del Santander, the park spans 640ha and is open to tourists. A public footpath winds through the rocks. Various formations have been named such as El Rey (the King), El Barco (the Boat) and Ciudad Perdida (the Lost City). There is no lodging on site, but you can find hotels in nearby Ocaña and make day trips to the park.

Puinawai (est 1989) (e amazonia@parquesnacionales.gov.co) Puinaves, Kurripacos and Cubeos peoples inhabit the 1.1 million hectare park in the department of Guainía, in the Amazon region to the east of Colombia on the Brazilian border. There are no facilities for tourists.

1

Vía Parque Isla de Salamanca (est 1964) (e *ecoturismo@parquesnacionales. gov.co* or *dtca@parquesnacionales.gov.co*) The park covers 56,200ha and is located in the department of Magdalena, on the northern Caribbean shores. It incorporates the shoreline, estuaries, lagoons and dunes as well as the Río Magdalena's overflows, swamps, bogs and marshes and mangroves. There's an abundance of flora and fauna here, including 98 species of invertebrate; 35 reptile species, such as caiman, both marine and freshwater turtles; more than 140 species of fish; 199 species of birds; and 33 species of mammal, including the manatee. There are public footpaths between some mangrove sites and it is also possible to tour the 'bogs' in a local boat; however, you must go with a guide. There's no lodging on site, but in nearby Barranquilla you can find good hotels that offer excursions to the park.

CONSERVATION

We are in danger of losing our natural heritage if we don't dedicate ourselves to protecting it. This is critical, given all that is at stake.

Fabio Arjona, Conservation International, Colombia, 2007

Modern Colombia has struggled to manage its environmental issues during its most turbulent chapters in history, and today deforestation, soil erosion and poor water quality are serious concerns. Excessive pesticide usage has caused damage to agricultural land while air pollution is sparking widespread unease, especially in Bogotá where vehicle emissions are high. Other urban environmental issues include health disorders linked to inadequate refuse disposal and contaminated food.

Colombia's diminishing forests are another key concern. More than 700,000ha of forests are cut down each year for wood and paper and to create farmland for crops and cattle. This is in part the consequence of continued poverty in the countryside and a legacy of the prejudiced land distribution policies that date back to colonial times.

At this rate, Colombia's forests will be almost completely wiped out by 2050, creating a major environmental catastrophe and destroying many of its wildlife species, plants and marine life. Such large-scale deforestation has already caused widespread soil destabilisation in Colombia's rural heartlands, annihilating the natural habitat of dozens of species of birdlife, while increasing the propensity of flooding and causing rivers to fill with silt.

Another large ecological conundrum for Colombia relates to its drive to bolster a global, market-based economy and the pressure that brings on the environment when it comes to developing land. Sizeable swathes of countryside in Boyacá and along the Caribbean coastline have already been eaten up by large-scale construction projects such is the demand for swish designer condominiums, new hotels and gated golf resort complexes. Mineral extraction on the Pacific side continues to forge ahead as part of an ambitious plan to strengthen the fragile economy of this often marginalised community. Poverty is rife in many of the Afro-Caribbean coastal towns along the Pacific stretch and few local inhabitants have the heart for ecological conscience when it comes to trying to feed their families. Environmentalists continue to attempt to spark serious debate about the dilemmas caused by Colombia's wealth imbalance.

Another pressing conservation concern is the loss of forest to Colombia's drugs trade. More than 50,000ha are chopped down each year in order to plant coca, opium and marijuana, primarily deep in virgin rainforests of the Amazon region and the Andes. As you'd expect, Colombia's cocaine producers care little for ecology, dumping the noxious by-products of cultivation and production into streams and poisoning water supplies with toxic waste. In 2011, conservationists called on the government to do more to protect the natural habitat of the 30+ species of monkey found in the country – five of which are unique to Colombia. According to experts, Colombia's rich primate diversity will only survive if new protected areas are established, as a number of endangered primate species are currently found only in unprotected regions.

Many of Colombia's biggest urban concentrations have benefited from city-funded environmental initiatives such as Bogotá's 300km of cycle paths that have encouraged millions of Bogotanos to trade their cars for two wheels. In 2000, Bogotá was honoured with the Stockholm Challenge Award for making the city car-free once a month on a Sunday. More than 120km of Bogotá's main arteries are closed to vehicles for 7 hours, allowing the city's eight million population to walk the streets, ride bicycles, jog and appropriate their city without traffic fumes or tooting horns. Traffic-free Sunday remains the largest and most successful car-free initiative of its kind in the world today.

Bogotá is also home to a UN-sponsored tree-planting project in partnership with the city's schoolchildren. Some 50 pupils planted 275 native trees provided by the city's botanical garden (Colombian laws do not allow the planting of non-native species). In Cali, a similar replanting programme funded by the botanical garden is part of a large-scale ecological restoration process, designed to promote the growth of native vegetation in the degraded hillsides at the edge of the city.

Rubbish, waste disposal and recycling are hot topics with Colombian environmentalists, despite a concerted effort by government ministers to promote recycling since the early 1980s. However, to date, no legally imposed recycling restrictions or programmes have been developed or implemented. Waste laws remain extremely complex and full of loopholes. There are also numerous ongoing disputes between the Ministry of Economic Development (Mindesa), the Ministry of Health (Minsalud) and the Environment Ministry (MinAmbiente) regarding the exact scope of their jurisdiction and control. In 2006, the Colombian Senate announced a bill that would repeal the existing hazardous waste framework law (Law 430/1998), banning all imports of hazardous wastes into the country – it had little impact. 'Scavengers' Houses' have been more beneficial, opening in Colombia's main cities to provide schooling for children, training for adults (particularly women) and meeting centres for families of the *recicladores* (around 25,000 families/125,000 people have been helped this way).

Today, the government estimates that there are over 20 non-government household rubbish recycling programmes in its major cities. Five recycling plants countrywide also supply schools and libraries with refurbished computers as part of the 'Computadores para Educar' programme. Other items that are recycled successfully to lower income communities via Colombia's rubbish-tip recicladores (see box below) include batteries, electrical parts, telecommunication products and televisions. One of Colombia's finest citizen-run recycling schemes can be found in the tiny village of Puerto Nariño in the Colombian Amazon, where waste is managed by a network of community volunteers. Its pristine neighbourhoods and 6,000 ecologically aware house-proud residents have been hailed as an environmental beacon by green campaigners in Colombia. Ironically, Puerto Nariño is also fast becoming a centre for conservationists studying the impact of untreated sewage, illegal pesticides and industrial waste on the Amazon's eco system.

Colombia is party to the following international agreements: Antarctic Treaty, Biodiversity, Climate Change, Climate Change-Kyoto Protocol, Desertification, Endangered Species, Hazardous Wastes, Marine Life Conservation, Ozone Layer Protection, Ship Pollution, Tropical Timber 83, Tropical Timber 94 and Wetlands. It has signed but not yet ratified the Law of the Sea.

WHAT A WASTE!

Colombia's major cities are home to an estimated 50,000 scavenger families (*recicladores*) who earn a living collecting rubbish from local tips. Conditions are grim and the work is hard for these professional scavengers who spend many hours trawling Colombia's piles of waste. Many recicladores work within family groups to run a non-stop dawn-to-dusk shift. Ages range from pre-school children to the elderly. Many of them suffer from serious health conditions because of ongoing exposure to contaminated waste and hazardous materials.

A programme launched in 1986 has helped to better organise Colombia's unofficial recyclers. First, the Asociación Nacional de Recicladores (ANR) was formed, using local NGO assistance. Improving working conditions was high on the list of priorities. The ANR also realised that the recicladores would better understand the value of the rubbish collected via education relating to markets, products and quality control. NGO advisers helped implement facilities for storing collected waste properly and also developed simple waste management systems and trained communities of scavengers in stock control. Educational programmes equipped the recicladores with supply-and-demand market information and helped train them in selective rubbish harvesting and identified items to avoid.

So far, more than 125,000 individuals from Colombia's garbage-picking families have benefited from such projects, many as a result of help from Fundación Social. The upshot has been a 30% increase in revenue stream for the recicladores with a greater level of productivity and improved medical care and social security support. The ANR has also opened so-called scavengers' houses in Colombia's main cities, including Bogotá, Medellín, Cali, Barranquilla, Cartagena, Neiva, Pasto, Popayán, Buga, Armenia, Manizales, Pereira, Soledad and Sincelejo. Some ANR branches have successfully negotiated contracts and joint ventures with many of the nation's largest private companies. On the north coast, 14 co-operatives of recicladores are represented by ARCON (Association of Recyclers and Collectors).

Colombia's history is nothing short of compelling – just when you think it can't get any more dramatic, another chapter unfolds. Few countries can claim a historical account so complex and utterly haunting, with Colombia's past a colourful, if emotional, fusion of intrigue, turmoil, pain, violence and hope. Getting to grips with Colombian history isn't easy and those who seek a rounded account will need to do some serious study. Numerous sources exist – many of them conflicting (see pages 490–1). Others home in on specific themes or eras, such as the modern-day guerrilla conflict. However, Colombia's pre-Columbian history is rich in indigenous culture while the colonial period spawned some of the finest architecture in the Americas. The following account offers a starting point for those keen to learn more.

KEY DATES IN COLOMBIAN HISTORY

1525	Rodrigo de Bastidas founds first permanent Spanish settlement in Santa Marta.
1810	Colombia declares independence from Spanish rule.
1819	After a successful campaign waged by Simón Bolívar the Republic of Gran Colombia (the present republics of Panama, Venezuela, Colombia and Ecuador) is founded.
1829	Venezuela breaks away from the republic.
1830	Ecuador also breaks away and the republic dissolves. Remaining member states form a new republic, Nueva (New) Granada.
1849	Conservative and Liberal parties founded.
1861	Nueva Granada restores its name to Colombia.
1861–85	The country becomes divided by Liberal Party rule segmenting Colombia into nine largely autonomous entities. The Church also separates from the state.
1885	Power is recentralised ahead of 45 years of Conservative Party rule with Church influence restored.
1899–1903	Around 120,000 people are killed in the 'The War of the Thousand Days' – a violent civil war between Liberal and Conservative activists during a long period of political instability (1899–1902).
1903	Panama breaks away from Colombia with help from the US.
1903– **mid 1940s**	Colombia enjoys a period of relative calm with President Alfonso. Lopez Pumarejo (1934–38) able to implement political reform.
1946	Conservatives return to power.
1948	Popular left-wing mayor Jorge Eliécer Gaitán is assassinated. Rioting ensues in Bogotá with thousands killed and injured.
1948–58	Political conflict between Liberal and Conservative party supporters spreads out to Colombia's rural communities, resulting in 300,000 deaths during a bloody era known as 'La Violencia'.
1957	General Rojas Pinilla, Colombia's only 20th-century military dictator, is ousted after four years at the helm.
1958	Liberal and Conservative parties agree a power-sharing deal (National Front) to run until 1974.
mid 1960s	Colombia's guerrilla groups, the Revolutionary Armed Forces of Colombia (FARC), Maoist People's Liberation Army (EPL) and National Liberation Army (ELN), are established.
1971	The M-19 guerrilla group is formed.

1978	Liberal leader Julio César Turbay elected president. He conducts a tough counter-insurgency campaign and launches an intensive fight against drug traffickers.
1982	Conservative president Belisario Betancur grants guerrillas amnesty and frees political prisoners.
1982	Drug cartels in Medellín and Cali consolidate their respective drugs trades. Paramilitary groups, hired initially for self-defence purposes, emerge as a significant force within the drug-trafficking industry.
1982	Conservative Belisario Betancur becomes president and takes the first serious steps towards a negotiated settlement of Colombia's guerrilla conflict.
1985	FARC establishes a political party, Patriotic Union (UP). M-19 takes over Palace of Justice in Bogotá but although the military seizes back control of the building more than 100 people are killed, including 11 senior judges.
1989	M-19 guerrillas demobilise and establish a democratic political movement legally after reaching a peace agreement via protracted negotiations with the government.
1989–90	Gunmen from the Medellín drug cartel assassinate Luis Carlos Galán – a favourite to win the 1990 Liberal Party presidential nomination. Some 200 policemen are also killed in what is a marked escalation of drug-related violence. President Barco (1986–90) appeals to the international community for support in the struggle against the narco-traffic trade.
1991	A new constitution is drafted by the Constituent Assembly with former guerrillas well represented.
1991–92	Various rounds of peace talks between government of President Gaviria (1990–94) and FARC and ELN guerrillas fail to make headway.
1993	Medellín's infamous drug cartel leader Pablo Escobar is killed by police in the city.
1994–98	The Liberal administration under President Samper Pizano is dogged by drug-related corruption scandals. He is subsequently charged and cleared of receiving drug money for his election campaign and goes on to achieve some success in dismantling the Cali cartel.
1998	Conservative Andrés Pastrana wins the presidential seat as an Independent candidate.
2000	Pastrana's 'Plan Colombia' receives almost US$1 billion in mainly military aid from America to fight drug trafficking and rebels who profit from and protect the trade.
2002	After three years of peace talks, President Pastrana breaks off negotiations with FARC and terminates their demilitarised zone. Peace talks with ELN also fail.
2002	Dissident Liberal Álvaro Uribe wins presidential elections, standing for the independent Primero Colombia Movement. The inauguration ceremony on 7 August is attacked by FARC mortar grenades. Twenty people are killed and within days a state of emergency is declared. Uribe vows to crack down hard on rebel groups.
2003	United Paramilitary Groups (AUC) announces a unilateral ceasefire, allowing formal peace talks to take place with the government. The AUC commits to demobilisation by the end of 2005, although observance of the ceasefire is very patchy.

2004	The AUC signs a further agreement to provide a 'location zone' of 360km² in Santa Fé de Ralito. The zone grants paramilitary leaders amnesty from arrest or extradition for the duration of the demobilisation process as verified by the Organisation of American States (OAS). More than 5,000 AUC members collectively demobilise by the end of the year.
2005	The government establishes the Justice and Peace law as a legal framework for the demobilisation process. Detractors claim it is a 'law of impunity' that makes too many concessions to rebels. Defenders of the law point to the need to eliminate armed guerrillas from the conflict, and claim it as a positive step.
2006	AUC demobilisation is complete with a reported 30,150 paramilitaries handing over some 17,000 weapons, 117 vehicles, three helicopters, 59 urban properties and 24,000ha of land under the terms of the Law of Justice and Peace. Álvaro Uribe secures a second, four-year tenure as president.
2008	FARC release Ingrid Betancourt, arguably Colombia's most famous kidnap victim. The French-Colombian politician was freed with 14 other hostages after rebels holding them were tricked into handing them over by a crack team of Colombian soldiers. Ms Betancourt was held by the FARC for more than six years and ranked as their highest-profile captive. Her two children had worked hard to keep her captivity in the spotlight since her abduction in February 2002 (see page 488)
2010	On 7 August Juan Manuel Santos inaugurated as the next Colombian president. Santos, whose great-uncle was Colombian president 1938–42, was a Minister for Foreign Trade, Finance and National Defence as part of President Uribe's administration. Prior to this, he was chief executive of the Colombian Coffee Delegation to the International Coffee Organization in London and also held a number of senior posts at his family-owned newspaper *El Tiempo* (see page 110)
2011	Chinese government officials announce a proposal to construct a rail link between Cartagena on Colombia's Caribbean coast to an unspecified site on the country's Pacific coast to better facilitate Chinese imports. The announcement creates a frenzy of worldwide media interest and is billed as a project that bewitched Spain, ruined Scotland, stumped France and empowered the US: a 'dry' inter-oceanic cut-through that will rival the Panama Canal (see page 36).
2011	Death of FARC leader Alfonso Cano on 4 November.
2012	Peace negotiations begin in Havana, Cuba between a government negotiating team and members of FARC regarding a six-point agenda of how to bring the long-running armed conflict to an end.
2014	President Santos wins second term as president, defeating his conservative Uribista rival Oscar Ivan Zuluaga in the second round. Santos pledges to achieve peace with both guerrilla groups. FARC declare indefinite unilateral ceasefire in December and call on the government to scale back the military campaign.
2015	Paulina Vega is the latest Colombian to become Miss Universe.

Elected to the presidency in 2010, President Juan Manuel Santos quickly set out his stall to distance himself from his former mentor, the warrior-like Álvaro Uribe Velez, and push Colombia down a road towards international investment and peace. Peace dialogues with the FARC guerrillas were started in November 2012 in Havana, Cuba with the guarantor nations of Chile and Norway in attendance as well. The six-point agenda for the dialogues included the topics of agrarian reform, political participation, illicit drugs, victims of the conflict, disarmament and finally, how to implement this peace process. At the time of writing three of the six points on the agenda had been concluded and the FARC had declared an indefinite unilateral ceasefire in December 2014. Exploratory talks have also been taking place between the government and the country's second-largest guerrilla group, the ELN (National Liberation Army) but as of January 2015, no dates had been set for formal discussions. Whatever the case, peace in Colombia seems achievable with political commentators suggesting that now the dialogues with the FARC have 'passed the point of no return' and that good progress is being made. As to be expected in a conflict which has, according to Human Rights Watch, caused the deaths of 220,000 people and displaced upwards of five million others since 1964, there remains a great deal of suspicion regarding the motives of the guerrilla groups as the long-suffering Colombian people have been let down before.

PRE-COLUMBUS Before Spanish rule, Colombia was populated by indigenous peoples. Most were hunters or nomadic agriculturists, but one part of the country, the high basins of the Eastern Cordillera, was densely occupied by the Chibcha people who had become sedentary farmers. Numerous indigenous groups travelled through Colombia from North and Central America, using it as South America's overland gateway. Many tribes disappeared after unsuccessful migration. Others, such as the Inca, built major settlements further south. Of the enduring monuments today, Colombia's finest include San Agustín (pages 304–7), Cuidad Perdida (pages 448–9) and Tierradentro (pages 307–8), although large collections of artefacts, gold and fossils can be found in museums countrywide. Colombia's first human inhabitants occupied small settlements all over the country with the main groups choosing to live along the fertile waters of the Pacific and Atlantic coasts and the Andean region. Although some inter-tribe trading existed, most of Colombia's tribes evolved independently, with vastly different cultures, languages and belief systems. Each of these hunter-gatherer communities developed its own political system along with that of the Muisca people, one of the most developed in South America. Other Amerindian groups included the Calima, Nariño, Sinú, Tolima, Tumaco, San Agustín and Quimbaya.

THE SPANISH ARRIVE From the moment the Spanish conquistadors arrived, El Dorado became an obsession – and this mythical land of untold riches was a motivating force behind many expeditions into Colombia's harsh interior regions. Although named after Christopher Columbus, the explorer never actually visited Colombia. It was his comrade, Alonso de Ojeda, who set foot on Colombian soil in 1499 – the first European to do so. In many ways, El Dorado was born out of Ojeda's awe at the Amerindian treasures and wealth he encountered with tales spreading (and growing in stature) over time. Although the Spanish never did discover the land of gold and emeralds, the searches they undertook with great determination were the dynamo behind Colombia's colonisation. After establishing several short-lived settlements along the coast, the Spanish founded the town of Santa Marta in 1525 with conquistador Rodrigo de Bastidas at the helm. Pedro de Heredia then went on to establish Cartagena in 1533 and this coastal trading hub soon became a principal port for shipments of supplies and slaves. In 1536, three independent advances forged towards the interior from different directions, led by Sebastián de Benalcázar, Jiménez de Quesada and Niklás Federman. Each had the goal of plundering Amerindian treasures after hearing tales of carpets of glittering jewels and vast piles of dazzling gold. After deserting from Francisco Pizarro's army during an assault on the Inca Empire, Benalcázar launched an expedition from Ecuador reaching the newly founded Santa Fé de Bogotá in 1539 after establishing Popayán and Cali *en route*. Bogotá had been founded just a year prior to Benalcázar's arrival by Jiménez de Quesada who had conquered two clans of Muiscas after climbing the Cordillera Oriental from Santa Marta via the Valle del Magdalena. Federman began his expedition from the Venezuelan coast and arrived in Bogotá shortly after Benalcázar, having crossed Los Llanos and the Andes. All three advances claimed supremacy and many battles ensued. In 1550, King Carlos V of Spain eventually brought the colony under single rule, establishing a court of justice in Bogotá under the leadership of the Viceroyalty of Peru.

THE COLONISATION ERA The New Kingdom of Granada (Nuevo Reino de Granada) comprised a collection of Spanish colonial provinces in northern South America that today correspond primarily to modern Colombia. It was established in 1564 as a new governing system by the Spanish crown and had military and civil power and self-ruled to a greater degree. Civil government had already been installed in the former New Granada but it was when a *presidencia* or governor was established with executive power that Nuevo Reino de Granada was born as a Captaincy General – a colony under the control of the Viceroyalty of Peru. All of Colombia (except what is known today as the Valle de Cauca, Cauca and Nariño) fell under its jurisdiction along with Panama with a mixed population of indigenous tribes, Spanish invaders and African slaves. Colombia's slave trade was concentrated on the port of Cartagena from where shipments were distributed throughout the many coastal mines and plantations along the Pacific and Caribbean coasts. Colombia's racial mix soon became more diverse once the three ethnicities began inter-breeding. So many slaves were shipped to the colony during the 16th and 17th centuries that people of African origin or descent soon outnumbered the indigenous tribesfolk. However, it was the Spaniards who held all the power – a stronghold that would last until 1819.

Fight for independence Although Spanish domination continued across the continent it stirred up strong feelings of dissent and protests became more prevalent in the early 18th century. People were angry at the throttlehold the Spanish had on land, wealth and commerce and became incensed by rising taxes – resulting in an uprising in Socorro in 1781. The Revolución Comunera was sparked by new crown-imposed levies and was the first open protest in Colombia's colonial period. In 1808, Napoleon appointed his own brother king – to the outrage of the Spanish colonies. Each refused to recognise the monarchy and a four-year wave of political infighting and chest-beating ensued. By 1812, a soon-to-be hero of the independence cause was causing ructions across the region, and eventually winning independence for Colombia in 1819 – Simón Bolívar (see box, page 28).

1

INDEPENDENCE In 1819, the new state of Gran Colombia was formed in a euphoric post-independence congress in Angostura (the modern-day Ciudad Bolívar in Venezuela). The union joined Colombia, Venezuela, Panama and Ecuador, although sizeable parts of Venezuela and Ecuador remained technically ruled by the Spanish. A second assembly took place in Villa del Rosario near Cúcuta in 1821 when the strong opposing political views of each country came to the fore. These

Despite our just resentment toward the ubiquitous Spaniards, our magnanimous heart still commands us to open to them for the last time a path to reconciliation and friendship; they are invited to live peacefully among us, if they will abjure their crimes, honestly change their ways, and cooperate with us …

15 June 1813, Simón Bolívar (1783–1830)

Without a doubt, Simón Bolívar was one of South America's greatest generals, a leader of men who triumphed over the Spanish to win independence for Colombia, Bolivia, Panama, Ecuador, Peru and Venezuela. A wealthy orphan of rich parentage, Bolívar was born in Caracas, Venezuela. He travelled across Europe as a young man and returned home with strong ideals. Bolívar joined the group of patriots that temporarily seized Caracas in 1810 and attempted to proclaim independence from Spain. After travelling to Great Britain in an unsuccessful bid for funding, Bolívar returned to Venezuela to take command of a rebel army. In 1813, he recaptured Caracas from the Spaniards earning the name El Libertador – The Liberator. However, the Spaniards forced Bolívar to retreat to New Granada (now Colombia) where in 1814 he raised a Colombian force to capture Bogotá. A defeat saw Bolívar return to Venezuela after rallying an army of skilled horsemen from the Colombian plains of Los Llanos. Strengthened by the British Legion, Bolívar marched over the Andes into New Granada in 1819. After a succession of winning battles he defeated the Spaniards in Boyacá in 1819, liberating Colombia and assuring independence. He then returned to Angostura (now Bolívar) and led the congress that organised the original republic of Colombia (now Ecuador, Colombia, Panama and Venezuela). Bolívar became its first president on 17 December 1819.

However, not everything that the so-called 'George Washington of South America' did for Latin America had a positive impact and many of Simón Bolívar's actions were the cause of numerous lasting negative effects. Giving up his presidential position allowed a class structure to return to Latin American society, allowing those of Spanish and Portuguese descent to assume power and wealth. Next in the social chain came the Creole people with European ancestry, with the *mestizo*, African American and indigenous citizens at the bottom of the class system. The rich were also politically strong and were able to ascend to rule. Bolívar himself said, 'We have ploughed the sea' in reference to his disappointment at the poor results achieved by revolution. Despite liberating Latin America from the Spanish, he didn't achieve quite the republic he had dreamed of – a place where no class distinctions prevailed, with an equality of wealth and power. He died rejected and penniless having admitted, 'There have been three great fools in history: Jesus, Don Quixote and I.'

divided into two factions: federalists and centralists. Bolívar pushed for a centralist republic and got his way, gaining a presidential election. However, the state of Gran Colombia was doomed to failure such was its size and political diversity. Second-in-command, Francisco de Paula Santander was a federalist at heart and struggled to govern such a large territory on a centralised basis. By 1830, Gran Colombia had disintegrated into three separate nations – the end of Bolívar's dream of unifying the countries he had liberated.

As an independent nation, Colombia got off to a troubled start. Two political parties born out of the centralist v federalist conflict were formalised in 1849 and galvanised fierce support. Bitter rivalries between the Conservatives (centralists) and Liberals (federalists) soon spawned a succession of civil wars and factions – between 1863 and 1885 alone there were more than 50 anti-government uprisings with eight 19th-century civil wars. In 1899, a federalist rebellion sparked a full-blown civil war resulting in over 120,000 deaths. It was ultimately a centralist victory but the carnage rocked the social foundations of the nation. This instability provided the US with the perfect opportunity to support Panama in its efforts to become an independent republic. Colombia, distracted by its own affairs, reacted with considerable fury, withdrawing diplomatic ties with both nations. It eventually agreed to recognise the sovereignty of Panama in 1921 and patched things up with the US, but the issue remains a sore point in the hearts and minds of Colombians nationwide.

LA VIOLENCIA In order to understand the sheer bloody brutality of La Violencia it is important to get to the heart of Colombian culture. In Colombia, religion and politics are crucial hereditary traits, defining characteristics that are upheld with considerable pride. Generations of Colombians are raised from birth with political affiliations. Politics is in their blood, in their hearts and in their minds – it's almost innate. So, when these political principles are challenged, things get incredibly heated – some of Colombia's bloodiest conflicts are testament to this. La Violencia ranks amongst the most deadly clashes in the western hemisphere, a violent struggle that broke out in Colombia in 1948 and eclipsed all other battles. On 9 April, the first of many urban revolts (known as El Bogotázo) took hold of the capital after Jorge Eliécer Gaitán was assassinated. As one of the Liberal movement's most popular leaders, Gaitán's loyal following were incensed. They took up arms and launched a vicious onslaught on the nation's Conservatives. The retaliation was brutal and during the 1940s and 1950s Colombia was engulfed by a wave of hereditary hate-crimes with thousands of atrocities that included murder, mutilation and rape. Much of the violence of this intense bipartisan conflict centred on the rural provinces with organised self-defence groups and guerrilla units fuelling the fire. A coup led by General Gustavo Rojas Pinilla in 1953 remains the only military intervention in Colombia's 20th-century history – but failed to last. In 1957, the Conservatives and Liberals signed a 16-year power-sharing agreement known as the National Front (Frente Nacional). The pact banned other parties from power, thus encouraging other groups to operate outside of the official political arena. Both parties served alternating four-year terms in a system that many blame for helping to nurture Colombia's guerrilla revolutionaries.

ARMED AND DANGEROUS Colombia's political underbelly was ripe for more ideological tensions in the mid 1960s. Disillusioned components operating within the conventional political structure turned to the outer extremes. Militias were raised and security forces recruited as the political divides in Colombian society turned their back on dialogue and protest. Today, Colombia's Marxist guerrillas

1

and right-wing paramilitaries have been at the forefront of a civil conflict spanning more than four decades. Government troops continue to wage war on these militant factions in bloody rural offensives. Over the years, many Colombians have had no option but to flee their homes to escape the violence – now Colombia has around three million internally displaced people, second only to Sudan.

More than a dozen rebel groups operate according to individual philosophies and political aims. Each has well-planned, well-organised and well-armed military strategies. Many have abandoned ideological causes for the commercial rewards of drug money to finance horrendous acts of terror. Extortion, robbery and kidnapping are other key sources of income. Military analysts suggest that FARC (Revolutionary Armed Forces of Colombia) alone earns US$250–300 million through criminal acts, of which 65% is derived from the drugs trade. This shift in political focus has clouded the popular perception that guerrillas are 'freedom fighters' with a cause. Civilian massacres, enforced enlistment at gunpoint and the banning of any form of religious/spiritual expression have transformed the image of a rebel from a Che Guevara-style role model to terrorist. Nebulous political goals and involvement in drug trafficking have seen local support for guerrilla groups plummet. At their peak, Colombian guerrillas controlled up to 40% of the countryside – a region the size of Switzerland. Today membership is much diminished with guerrilla activity largely concentrated in Colombia's deep south. Many guerrillas and paramilitaries have laid down their arms to take advantage of a government amnesty that has offered programmes of retraining, rehabilitation and reintegration to former members of FARC, AUC, M-19 and the ELN. However, conflict continues to blight Colombia's domestic headlines, with the following the main guerrilla and paramilitary groups.

Fuerzas Armadas Revolucionarias de Colombia (FARC) (*www.farc-ep.co*)

FARC is the oldest and largest left-wing rebel group and is also one of the wealthiest and most powerful guerrilla armies on the planet. It was founded in 1964 in order to overthrow the government and establish a communist-agrarian state. Its beliefs stem from highly nationalist and anti-capitalist rhetoric rooted in early progressive ideology. However, its political focus shifted in the 1990s and it has since become increasingly involved in the drug trade. Kidnapping and extortion are both now often ends in themselves. FARC is governed by a seven-member secretariat in an HQ in Colombia, chaired by its octogenarian original founder, Manuel Marulanda Vélez. Marulanda was born Pedro Antonio Marín but is renowned throughout Colombia by his *nom de guerre*. He is also nicknamed Tirofijo by his comrades – meaning 'Sureshot' – on account of his aim. Some 30% of FARC are female and most are younger than 19. FARC targets anyone suspected of conspiring with the military and paramilitaries, using explosives, landmines and bombs camouflaged as necklaces, footballs and soup cans. It also forcibly enlists people aged between 13 and 60 to work coca or poppy plantations and serve in its military battalions. After a period of relatively peaceful co-existence, FARC and the National Liberation Army (ELN) started fighting each other again in 2006 in a marked escalation of violence in southern Colombia. Today, FARC remains the most active and well organised of the country's guerrilla groups, although large numbers of operatives have voluntarily given up arms as part of a government amnesty. Morale is said to be at an all-time low throughout the FARC ranks following the capture and trial of several long-serving commanders and the shooting of other high-ranking officials by the Colombian army. Peace dialogues between FARC and the government began in November 2012 in Havana, Cuba.

Ejército de Liberación Nacional (ELN) (*www.eln-voces.com*) The National Liberation Army was inspired by the Cuban revolution and established by a group of Colombians trained in insurgent warfare in Havana in 1964. Under the leadership of Fabio Vásquez Castaño, the ELN reached the height of its power in the late 1990s with some 5,000 fighters. Today it remains Colombia's second-largest leftist guerrilla group but is much depleted after taking a hammering from right-wing paramilitary forces and the Colombian military. Today its numbers have dropped to around 3,500. The ELN pledged a ceasefire in 2007 on the basis that the government dropped a free-trade pact signed in 2006 with the United States. The ELN has so far rejected a government demand that would confine the guerrillas to a demilitarised area. When he was in power, former Colombian president Álvaro Uribe insisted the rebels hand over their weapons, declare a ceasefire and free some 500 hostages. President Santos has been courting possible peace dialogues with the ELN but as yet (March 2015) nothing concrete has been defined.

Autodefensas Unidas de Colombia (AUC) (*www.colombialibre.org*) This umbrella group for a collective of small right-wing paramilitary factions was formed in 1997 and the United Self-Defence Forces of Colombia has strong links with the drugs trade. Wealthy landowners and drugs cartels form the backbone of the organisation with its roots in the paramilitary armies. AUC claims it took up arms in self-defence, in the place of a powerless state. More than 70% of its funding comes from drug lords. It is known to have carried out massacres and assassinations, targeting left-wing groups. The AUC has demobilised almost 30,000 fighters since 2004 in a process beset by endless ceasefire violations and amnesty demands. Many of those that demobilised and agreed to prison sentences have now been released after serving their eight-year sentences. While the AUC no longer formerly exists, the group with their remaining members splintered off into new paramilitary gangs known as the Aguilas Negras and the Rastrojos. Currently a new wave of organised crime by smaller outfits is strafing the country. These are now known as the BACRIMs (newly emerged criminal gangs); amongst these are the Urabenos and the Clan Usaga.

M-19 The 19th of April Movement (Movimiento 19 de Abril) or M-19, demilitarised in 1990 to become a legal political party called the M-19 Democratic Alliance (Alianza Democrática M-19), or AD/M-19. M-19's ideology is a mixture of populism and nationalistic revolutionary socialism, with a membership that peaked during the mid 1980s to make it once the second-largest rebel group in Colombia. On giving up its weapons, the members of M-19 received pardons and publicly renounced the armed struggle. One of their own, Gustavo Petro Urrego became the Mayor of Bogotá in 2012 for a thus-far scandal-filled four-year term.

THE COCAINE TRADE

According to reports produced by Human Rights Watch and other NGOs, since 1958 an estimated 220,000 people have been killed in violence stemming from Colombia's internal conflict. How many of these deaths can be directly attributed to the cocaine trade within Colombia remains up for debate, but rest assured that the money raised from the illegal coca crop and production of cocaine has played more than a central role in funding and continuing the conflict between the warring factions found here.

Large tracts of land are still given over to producing coca given that the profits are so high; regions such as the border areas of Arauca near to Venezuela, rural Cauca,

Putumayo bordering Ecuador and the Amazonian region of Caquetá should be avoided. However, it's not all doom and gloom as Colombia has now, according to reports, fallen behind both Peru and Bolivia in terms of cocaine production due to eradication efforts, the lack of policy against institutional corruption in the other two countries and emerging criminal groups taking advantage of these weaknesses.

The cocaine trade is one that not only profits guerrilla activity but also spreads like disease through entire communities. The UN puts total cocaine production at 640 tonnes a year, but UK law enforcement sources claim it is as high as 1,000 tonnes – that's £6 billion based on average market prices. Demand is so high that coca growers in Colombia are using genetically modified plants to dramatically boost cocaine yields. Dozens of routes are used by thousands of smugglers to transport the cocaine to the US and Europe – reports suggest it can be snorted in a London party within 24 hours of export. Yet Colombians are baffled that Europeans and North Americans fail to make any connection between their own Saturday night snort and the conflict that has blighted the nation for over 40 years. 'Don't people realise that each time they buy a bag of coke they are financing a war that is killing our country?' is a common heartfelt question.

A 434-page document entitled 'Basta Ya! Colombia: Memorias de Guerra y Dignidad' ('Enough Already: Memories of War and Dignity', available to download in Spanish for free from www.centrodememoriahistorica.gov.co), published in 2013, has detailed in some profundity the massacres, kidnappings and atrocities to have taken place in Colombia. The report documents 1,982 massacres between 1980 and 2012, attributing 1,166 to paramilitaries, 343 to rebels, 295 to government security forces and the remainder to unknown armed groups. It estimates the number of Colombians forcibly displaced by the conflict at 5.7 million. Cocaine production and trade routes are at the heart of the problem.

The cocaine trade has left Colombia in tatters with warring gangs continually evolving to find new ways to transport the drugs and new people to manipulate. There have been reports of left-wing guerrilla groups working with right-wing paramilitaries – despite their obvious political differences – to facilitate the transhipment of cocaine through disputed territories in Colombia. And the cities in many cases have been carved up and are controlled by different cartels.

The most infamous drug cartels include that of Medellín, run by former petty criminal and ruthless Colombian drug lord El Patrón, Pablo Escobar (1949–93) who once controlled over 80% of the cocaine trade with the United States. He continually evaded capture, despite a lengthy manhunt by a special 1,500-strong team. He was killed in 1993 after being on the run for 499 days and amassing a small fortune, luxurious homes, expensive cars, aeroplanes and hotels. Escobar had an effective, inescapable strategy to silence anyone who got in his way. It was referred to as *plata o plomo*, Colombian slang for 'money or bullets', intended to mean 'accept a bribe or face assassination'. In 1989 *Forbes* magazine listed him as the seventh-richest man in the world.

Yet, Colombia isn't just a cocaine supplier – Colombian police backed by US forces are now fighting the exportation of tonnes of pure heroin per year. In 2006, eight suspected traffickers were captured in Cali, a city with a lengthy association with the drugs trade. A half-tonne haul had an estimated street value of up to US$90 million. In 2007, two Mexicans were arrested after US$4 million was found in their carry-on bags as they arrived at a Colombian airport. Customs officials have long suspected links between Colombia and a Mexican drug cartel. Mexico receives US$40 million a year for anti-drug efforts from the United States and is thought to be a major transhipment point for narcotics bound for American shores.

In 2008, President Uribe issued invitations to celebrities in the public eye across the world with a known history of cocaine use to visit Colombia's major areas of drug production – the response was one of eerie silence. However, Alex James – an English musician, songwriter, journalist and cheese maker best known as the bass player with Brit-pop band Blur – accepted. The result was a documentary television series called *Cocaine Diaries: Alex James in Colombia* which premiered on BBC America, in partnership with the BBC *America Reveals* programme. As the documentary progresses, James – who admits to having used cocaine extensively during Blur's hedonistic heyday – learns about Colombia's violent drug export trade. The guitarist estimates spending up to £1 million on cocaine and champagne, and is clearly shocked when he meets local drugs farmers, sellers and enforcers and faces the 'reality' of the narcotics industry and what it means to those involved in it at source. In 2010, the International Narcotics Control Board (INCB) – a monitoring body for the implementation of the United Nations' international drug control conventions – dropped Colombia from its list of countries requiring 'special observation'. It said Colombia remained the world's biggest producer of cocaine but had made progress in its war on drugs, seizing more drugs than any other state in the world in the past ten years. Colombian authorities continue to seize stealth submarines in operations along the Pacific coast in the mangrove swamps close to the port cities of Buenaventura and Tumaco. These wood-and-fibreglass submersibles, apparently belonging to FARC rebels and other criminal gangs, are used to transport tonnes of cocaine to destinations in Central America.

At the time of writing, an agreement had been reached between the FARC guerrillas (involved in peace dialogues with the Colombian government since November 2012) on the issue of illicit drugs. While details of the agreement are not completely clear, popular belief is that the guerrillas will stop producing coca in return for increased government spending in the countryside and subsidies to enable alternative crop production such as cacao.

GOVERNMENT AND POLITICS

> When God started creating the world, he put gold into South Africa. Finding he had some left over, he gave it to Colombia. Brazil received emeralds and tropical fruits. Again, God had some left over and gave them to Colombia. He put coal into Appalachia, with Colombia getting the leftovers. The Middle East got a pot full of oil with the remainder poured into Colombia. Flowers went to the South Pacific islands but there were some of these left over too, so God gave them to Colombia, along with some surplus minerals, including iron and nickel.
>
> 'Wait a minute,' exclaimed a watching angel. 'Do you realise that you're making Colombia one of the most powerful nations on the planet?'
>
> 'Yes,' replied God, 'but don't worry. I haven't given them their politics yet.'
>
> 19th-century Colombian satire

Colombia is officially Latin America's oldest and most stable democracy although its chequered history and colourful politics boast the drama and intrigue of a Graham Greene thriller. Although fair and regular elections are the norm, Colombia's political make-up has still been contentious. Yet an ingrained respect for political and civil rights still prevails countrywide.

Traditionally, two parties – the Liberals and the Conservatives – have battled for power since the mid 19th century. Fiercely fought elections have seen the two share the role of governing party in rotation, with Colombia's armed forces seizing

1

power on three occasions in 1830, 1854 and 1953. Since declaring its independence from Spain in 1810, Colombia has had 11 constitutions. The last was adopted on 4 July 1991 and serves to strengthen the unitary republic of today. In 1821 and 1830 the statute removed significant might from Colombia's departmental governments. However, three additional federal constitutions later awarded considerable powers to the nation's administrative subdivisions (*departamentos*) and paved the way for elected departmental assemblies. The 1886 constitution sought to resolve the great federal–unitary debate head-on, tackling the role of the Roman Catholic Church and the thorny issue of a robust central government versus a decentralised federal structure in straightforward terms. It states that sovereignty resides in the nation to ensure guaranteed civil liberties, including freedom of religion, speech, assembly, press and education along with the right to strike (unless in public service), petition the government as well as own property. Citizens over 18 years old were also granted greater legal rights (subject to owning a citizenship card and registering on the electoral roll). Exceptions include active military personnel and members of the police, both of whom are prohibited from voting and participating in political activities. Those working in an administrative capacity for the Colombian government are also barred from political involvement, although they are permitted to vote.

Colombia's constitution has undergone large-scale, frequent changes over the years, including significant amendments in 1910, 1936, 1945, 1957, 1959, 1968, 1979 and 1991. Colombia has always been a nation hungry for change and in the past student demonstrations, strikes and riots have helped effect this when government reactions have been slow. Colombia's present constitution was enacted to bolster the administration of justice. Key reforms included civil divorce, dual nationality, the election of a vice president and departmental governors – as well as extending the basic rights of Colombian citizens to seek immediate court action (known as *tutela*) in the event of any violation of their constitutional rights.

The politics of Colombia takes place in a framework of a presidential representative democratic republic led by the President of Colombia, who is both head of state and head of government. The national government has separate executive, legislative and judicial branches. Colombia's president is elected after a four-year tenure by direct popular vote and, until 2006, was constitutionally prohibited from seeking consecutive terms. Former president Álvaro Uribe, who was first elected in 2002, changed the constitution so he could run for a second term in office. The amendment permitted a single re-election and was ratified by Congress in December 2004 before approval by the Constitutional Court in October 2005. Mr Uribe was re-elected for a second presidential term in May 2006, becoming the first president to be consecutively re-elected in Colombia in more than 100 years. Uribe received about 62% of the vote, consisting of about 7.3 million ballots in his favour. However, under the standard terms of the constitution, a former president may run again for the presidency only after sitting out one term. Other stipulations are that the president must be a native-born Colombian aged 55 years or over. He or she must also be in full possession of his or her political rights and should have served as a congressional or cabinet member, governor, government official or university professor (for a minimum of five years) or as a practising member of a liberal profession requiring a university degree. In 2010, Uribe stepped aside to champion a successor. Juan Manuel Santos pledged to continue in the progressive, hard-line style of his predecessor. He was inaugurated on 7 August after winning a landslide victory. Santos ran on the Social Party of National Unity or 'La U' ticket promising to campaign in continuation of Uribe's policies. In 2014, President Santos was elected to a second term and continued with his campaign for peace in

Colombia and to distance himself from Álvaro Uribe, now an acting senator for the conservative Centro Democratico Party.

Colombia's president oversees the executive branch of government as chief of state, consisting of a 13-member cabinet, a host of administrative agencies and a couple of hundred or so semi-autonomous bodies. The president has the power to elect the cabinet and is also responsible for appointing leaders to head the many administrative agencies under his control without the approval of congress. The governors of Colombia's 23 territorial departments are also under his charge, as are the heads of nine national territories. In addition to administrative powers, the chief executive has considerable legislative authority. The president is also obligated to maintain law and order, defend the nation and resolve domestic unrest as commander-in-chief of the armed forces and the national police.

Yet, for a nation with a long democratic tradition, Colombia's high level of political violence is a contradictory feature and today the list of people who have lost their lives to politically motivated violence is long. Former president Uribe personally made left-wing insurgency, right-wing paramilitary terrorism and the threat of narco-violence his focus while around him rural poverty was left unresolved with per-capita income barely reaching half the national average. Santos has continued in much the same vein. A continued application of traditional trade and tax policies has also been criticised by social commentators for only benefiting private and foreign investors rather than offering help to small farm owners and workers.

ECONOMY

According to the World Bank, Colombia has achieved stable Gross Domestic Product (GDP) growth in recent years – up 46% since 2004. Although Colombia's GDP per capita is still below some Latin American countries, initiatives in the nation's public and private sectors have helped the GDP almost double. At the time of writing, Colombia's economic foundation remains firm. The World Bank continues to table Colombia's economic growth in a positive light with GDP growth at 4.0% in 2012, 4.7% in 2013 and 2014 and a predicted 4.0% for 2015.

The Colombian economy, which experienced its first recession in nearly 70 years in 1999, has achieved a strong rebound. Unemployment dropped slightly during 2010 (0.2%) with over 700,000 jobs created in that year, according to government statistics. All these indicators, added to reduced insecurity, have fostered greater confidence among domestic and foreign investors. Despite the worldwide financial crisis, the Colombian economy grew by 4.5% in 2010. Since then, while tumbling oil prices and the slowdown of the Chinese economy and need for raw materials will affect Colombia in 2015, the country looks set to positively outperform her regional neighbours.

Colombia has always relied on geography for its economic fortunes. As a nation bordered by two oceans located where the American continents meet, Colombia's two major river valleys – the Magdalena and the Cauca – ensured vital links with Central America, South America and the Caribbean. In the 1990s, economic liberalisation (a process known as *Apertura*) opened Colombia's economy up to international trade and inward capital investment by slashing tariff duties, ditching non-tariff barriers and negotiating freetrade agreements. It also reformed foreign exchange and tax rules, labour regulations and foreign investment legislation. State enterprises, ports, railroads and banks were privatised and the sectors of telecommunications, energy and tourism reborn in a new spirit of commercial advancement. At the time of writing, America is finally about to ratify a controversial

COLOMBIA'S SHORT CUT

Though it has long dreamed of creating an alternative to the Panama Canal, Colombia has only been able to marvel at its neighbour's role as a strategic transit hub. So when China first mooted the idea of building an ocean-to-ocean 'dry canal' in 2010, Colombia put all its efforts into making this pipe dream a reality. President Juan Manuel Santos courted Chinese officials and enthused about the plans to connect the Pacific Ocean and Caribbean Sea by railway. At the time of writing Colombians are already planning for the day when their country can rival Panama's legendary crossing. Plans are advanced in the building of the Colombian inter-oceanic railway, which will involve the construction of a purpose-built city for half a million people on the Caribbean coast. According to Santos, China's railway engineers intend to connect an unspecified Pacific port to the new city where Chinese factories would assemble products for transportation to the United States – and beyond.

The multi-billion-dollar project would need to be highly efficient to pose a real threat to the Panama Canal. A single ship can transport huge quantities of goods that would require about 80 train journeys to compete. However, Colombia is determined to prove that the project is feasible, economically, commercially and environmentally to achieve what intrigued Spain, bankrupted Scotland, stumped France and empowered the US: a short cut from the Atlantic to the Pacific Ocean.

Free Trade Agreement (FTA) with Colombia under President Obama several years after it was agreed in principle and came into effect in May 2012. Widely criticised by international aid agencies, the FTA was condemned by Oxfam because of its negative impact on farming communities throughout Colombia. The deal is America's biggest in the western hemisphere for over 15 years and has ensured that more than 80% of US consumer and industrial exports to Colombia are duty-free. Ratification of the FTA has further increased tension between the US and China, following China's strengthening of Colombian ties (see box, above). Colombia is also developing robust commercial links with Iran, Turkey and India.

Colombia's sturdy economy was projected to continue growing bullishly but, with public debts increasing and a deceleration of the economy in the final trimester of 2014, the forecast is less positive. While Colombia is not as dependent on the price of oil as neighbouring Venezuela, the country has been knocked by spiralling international prices.

A grim determination by the government to reduce public debt coupled with a strong export strategy and a formidable effort to improve security has seen businesses thrive Colombia-wide. However, four decades of armed conflict and violence have taken their toll on personal wealth – studies show that if peace had been achieved in the 1980s the income of an average Colombian today would be 50% higher. Today, the government is faced with several economic challenges, including reforming the country's pension system and bringing down unemployment, to managing a passage of fiscal reform. Petroleum ranks as the principal export, although declining oil production requires significant investment in new exploration. Apart from oil, Colombia's leading exports include coffee, vegetables, chemicals, coal, textiles, fresh-cut flowers, bananas, sugar, gold, emeralds and cattle. Illegal drugs also rank high among the country's exports with the country being an illicit producer of coca, opium poppy and cannabis – Colombia supplies most of the drugs on the

US market. Colombia's annual exports earn US$13.1 billion with mechanical and electrical equipment, chemicals, food and metals the country's prime imports. The US remains Colombia's main trading partner with Venezuela, Germany, Japan, the Netherlands and Peru all significant markets. In the last year, China, the Dominican Republic and Brazil have increased their share dramatically to rank as some of the main trading destinations. The United Kingdom is Colombia's eighth-largest trade partner. In early 2014, the Colombian government estimated that exports for that year would total a record-breaking US$54 billion to surpass all previous years.

Colombia's Bank of the Republic issues all of the nation's money and shares responsibility for monetary policy with the government. More than 25 commercial banks, development banks and other financial institutions operate in Colombia with stock exchanges that serve the cities of Bogotá, Medellín and Cali. Colombia is an original member of the Andean Community (1969) and has been a signatory of the GATT since 1981 and a member of the World Trade Organization (WTO) since that institution's creation in 1994. Colombia entered into two other trade associations in 1995: the Group of Three (Mexico, Venezuela and Colombia) and the Association of Caribbean States (ACS).

In 2010, **tourism** was up 10.7% on 2009 figures (when 1.35 million people visited Colombia) and this figure has grown year on year since. Apart from visitors from the US, Spain and immediate neighbouring nations (Venezuela, Ecuador and Peru), travellers from the UK are the biggest single group of tourists – a market that is growing significantly year on year. Under the banner 'Colombia is Passion', a government campaign to boost tourism has attracted global press interest. Travel and tourism employs around 30% of total employment and is forecast to grow by 3.6% per annum to 2017. The Colombian tourism sector is ranked 53rd in terms of absolute size worldwide, 147th in relative contribution to national economies and 138th in long-term (ten-year) growth out of the World Travel & Tourism Council's 176 countries. By the end of 2014 Colombia broke records in having received more than four million international visitors showing a huge growth in interest in Colombia as a new destination, effective government campaigns and the result of the justifiable perception of a significant improvement in security.

In addition to domestic goals of keeping inflation and interest rates low and maintaining a stable currency, the Colombian government has placed a heavy emphasis on developing international trade. Colombia climbed 42 positions between 2007 and 2010 in the World Bank Economic Freedom in the World and Index of Economic Freedom 'Doing Business' Report. In 2014, now ranked at 34th, Colombia has also been named as Top 10 reformer for the last four years' indices, which attempt to measure the degree of economic freedom in a nation using a scoring system for ten broad factors of economic freedom. Statistics from organisations like the World Bank, the IMF and the Economist Intelligence Unit are just a few that are used as sources. Key points measured are business freedom, trade freedom, fiscal freedom, freedom from government, monetary freedom, investment freedom, financial freedom, property rights, freedom from corruption and labour freedom. At number one was Hong Kong, while North Korea ranked at number 178.

The Colombian government has actively sought to expand trade beyond its traditional partners of the US (Colombia's largest trading partner at 41% of its world total). Today, Colombia remains the United States' fourth-largest trading partner in Latin America, behind Mexico, Brazil and Venezuela, with more than 200 American companies operating in nearly every sector of its national economy. However, Colombia is keen to secure wider diversification in global trade terms and is looking to broaden foreign direct investment flows into the country significantly.

Forget coffee and coconuts – one of Colombia's greatest exports is its people, with 10% of Colombians currently living abroad, according to figures from the National Administrative Department for Statistics (DANE). That's over four million Colombian migrants working overseas, with most of them sending regular money back home. In fact, Colombians abroad wire more than US$3.17 billion to their families per annum – a whopping 4% of Colombia's GDP. More than 50% of this significant source of international currency is sent from Colombians living in the United States, according to the World Bank – particularly New York and Florida. International Organisation of Migration (IOM) research suggests that approximately 90% of these remittances are used to cover basic needs, education and health with 6% repaying family loans and 2% for saving. Most Colombians living abroad are originally from the Valle del Cauca department (24.1%) and Bogotá (18.7%) with the main destination other than the US being Spain (23.4%). However, unlike two decades ago, the trend is to return to Colombia, according to statistics from the Administrative Security Department (DAS). A 2007 study of Colombian migration commissioned by national newspaper *El Tiempo* entitled 'Colombia: migrations, transnationalism and displacement' directed by National University anthropologist Gerardo Ardila from the Centro de Estudios Sociales shows that the number of Colombian citizens abroad has stabilised in recent years.

More than 700 multi-national companies have invested in Colombia, including Nestlé, Marks & Spencer, Du Pont and Unilever.

Foreign Direct Investment (FDI) flows into Colombia totalled US$16 billion in 2013, according to the Central Bank (Banco de la República). The UK is the second-largest investor in Colombia, accounting for an estimated invested stock of up to US$18 billion. According to the Economic Commission for Latin America and the Caribbean (ECLAC), Colombia ranks amongst the top destinations for foreign investment in Latin America – and hopes are high that government plans to further fine-tune foreign investment policy will establish the country as a financial dynamo within the region. In 2013, Colombia was formally invited to join the OECD signifying a strong belief in the country's economic prowess and future, despite the obvious challenges, but will remain on the sidelines until the country's Inland Revenue service is overhauled.

A key attraction for investors is Colombia's 22 million labour force. Some 22% is engaged in agriculture, forestry and fishing with 19% in industry and mining, and most of the remainder in service industries. Foreign investment is governed by Law 9 of 1991 Resolutions 51, 52, and 53 of the Council on Economic and Social Policy (CONPES) and Resolution 21 of the Board of Directors of the Central Bank. Investment is permitted in all sectors of the Colombian economy, except those related to national security and hazardous waste. Foreign and national investments are viewed as the same legally and administratively with no restrictions on the amount of foreign capital invested. Red tape has been simplified with the electronic submission of required documents to Colombian authorities now permitted. Foreign businesses in Colombia are, however, governed by labour laws that stipulate firms with more than ten employees should not allow more than 10% of the general workforce (and 20% of specialist skills) to be non-nationals. According to Proexport, Colombia's trade agency, key reasons to invest in Colombia include:

- One of the most qualified labour markets in Latin America
- One of the highest adult literacy rates in Latin America
- Competitive labour costs and flexible working hours
- Colombia's ten Duty Free Zones and five Special Economy Export Zones
- Colombia is strategically located as a middle point between North and South America
- Both Pacific and Atlantic coasts have modern port infrastructure
- Easy access to North American, European, Asian and Latin American markets
- Significant investment in high-tech telecommunications infrastructure
- Increasing investment in transportation infrastructure
- Seven international airports

All foreign investments must be registered with the Central Bank's foreign exchange office within three months of the transaction date to assure the right to repatriate profits and remittances and to access official foreign exchange. All foreign investors, like domestic investors, must obtain a licence from the Superintendent of Companies and register with the local Chamber of Commerce, who can also provide practical help and guidance to a wide range of industries. Key considerations include corruption, according to CONFECAMARAS (Confederation of Colombian Chamber of Commerce) which estimates up to US$3 million of income is lost in Colombia each year. Not true, says the World Bank, which estimates that corruption in Colombia tops US$480 million annually. Joint initiatives by the Colombian government, World Bank and other non-governmental institutions have actively sought to tackle corruption since 2001, with assistance from a wide variety of trade bodies. Another point to ponder is Colombia's appetite for industrial action, although this waned considerably during Uribe's term as president. The right to strike constitutionally is guaranteed to all employees not working for public utilities with the Central Unitaria de Trabajadores (CUT, Unitary Federation of Workers) and the Confederación de Trabajadores Colombianos (CTC, Confederation of Colombian Workers), Colombia's most dominant trade unions. Each year, the Colombian government, following negotiations with the main employee unions, trade groups and business associations, establishes a minimum wage for a 48-hour workweek. Colombia has no wage categories or a minimum wage for specific jobs. Employer and employee are free to agree on a different wage, provided it is no less than the minimum wage, or the wage established in collective bargaining agreements, or than the wage resulting from arbitration rulings. In 2010, the Colombian government increased the national minimum wage by 3.64% to 514,987COP (US$252) and this has increased year on year at an average rate of between 3.5% and 4.6%, making it round off in 2015 at 644,350COP – although this applies to just over four million of the country's workers. A 48-hour working week covers Monday to Friday or Saturday from 06.00 to 22.00. Workers on shifts between 22.00 and 06.00 earn 35% above the hourly wage. Hours worked in addition to the normal workweek are compensated as overtime at 25% per hour.

The *World Competitiveness Yearbook* (WCY) ranks Colombia tenth out of 60 countries for the quality of its management staff. It also placed Colombia 24th in terms of availability of IT skills, ahead of countries such as Brazil, Spain and Mexico.

PEOPLE

We are black, white, Indian and mixed blood. We are Colombia. We are a family. We care about our country. We believe in our homeland.

Pedro Medina, *Yo Creo en Colombia* (*I Believe in Colombia*), 1962

Colombia is the most populous nation of Spanish-speaking South America, with 48 million people and a population density of almost 45 persons per square kilometre. Colombia now boasts the distinction of being the third most populous country in Latin America, after Brazil and Mexico. Its people are a diverse mix of ethnicity derived from Colombia's three main groups, namely its indigenous Amerindians and those of Spanish and African descent. This multi-culturalism mirrors Colombia's colourful history and today more than 58% of its population claim *mestizo* heritage (mixed white and indigenous). Whites represent 20% of the population, 14% are mixed white and black, 4% black and 3% mixed black and indigenous. Scholars estimate that the population at the time of the Spanish conquest numbered 1.5–two million yet today indigenous peoples account for just 1% of Colombia's modern population. Recent studies also indicate an increased number of immigrants in Colombia, especially from the Caribbean, other Latin American countries (especially Peru) and Turkey. In 2011, one of Colombia's most remote and endangered indigenous tribes faced an increased risk of extinction after FARC activists hijacked a boat carrying medical aid for them following an outbreak of serious sickness.

Colombia is divided into four distinct regions, each with a major city at its core. More than three-quarters of Colombians live in urban congregations. Principal centres are located in the Magdalena and Cauca river valleys and along the Caribbean coastal region. With a population of eight million, the capital Bogotá forms the heart of the centre of the country. The nation's 'second city' is Medellín, the hub of the northwest of Colombia with a population of 2.5 million. In the southwest, the city of Cali is only a smidgen smaller than Medellín at 2.4 million. On the Caribbean coast the capital Barranquilla (population 1.3 million) is the nucleus of this region, the popular tourist town of Cartagena being the second largest here.

Colombians are generous, gregarious and friendly people whose acts of kindness and compassion form a sharp contrast to the mean, vicious and violent stereotypes their homeland's troubled history has popularised across the world. Expect high levels of courtesy, good manners and a considerable pride for all things Colombian – characteristics that are truly refreshing for travellers worn down by the indifferent welcome favoured by so many supposedly more civilised nations. And despite the bleak depiction of Colombian life in international news headlines, 2014 brought the news that according to the New Economic Foundation's Happy Planet Index (HPI), which documented ecological footprint, life satisfaction and life expectancy, Colombians are the second-happiest people on the planet. What's more, travellers will find that the average Colombian is keen to interact with international tourists and is openly thrilled when asked for tips on what to see and do. They are also extremely proficient at networking and this natural skill for putting people together will almost certainly mean introductions to family, friends and contacts throughout the country, from the address of a kindly uncle who owns a flower-filled *pensionado* in Cali to the telephone number of a former colleague in Mompóx with fabulous tales to tell.

FAMILY LIFE Regardless of class, Colombia's family structures tend to be authoritarian, patriarchal and patrilineal with strong ties to relatives and considerable importance applied to respect. Even modern families view the Roman Catholic Church as a dynamo behind marriage and the family unit and for the vast majority of Colombians Catholic marriage remains the ideal and preferred legal, social and sexual family foundation. In recent decades, the patriarchal extended family structure has declined in urban societies largely because of increased geographic and social mobility and the greater independence this affords younger members. However, these weakened kinship ties haven't diminished the importance of the family in Colombian society and it is still commonplace for teenage children, parents, grandparents, uncles and cousins to socialise several times a week. However, surveys suggest that today 58% of Colombian families are nuclear, 30% extended, 5.5% compound and 6.5% one-person households. The family also takes centre stage in other ways and is often a prime source of support and advice. Great loyalty is shown to other family members, especially the elder members, who are revered. In 2015, it remains common for children to live at home until they marry. Since the 1990s, contraceptive use had risen dramatically throughout Latin America, and in Colombia this is reflected in households of three to four children instead of the six to eight common four decades ago. However, almost 20% of Colombian children have no birth certificate, which makes it difficult for the state to care for them. The under-five mortality rate is 21 per 1,000, while more than 20,000 babies die under the age of one from preventable causes according to UNICEF figures. For further information contact Profamilia (*Calle 34, No 14–52, Bogotá;* ❧*(1) 339 0900;* e *info@profamila.org.co; www.profamilia.org.co*).

MEN IN SOCIETY Colombia's male citizens aged 18 and over must complete one to two years of military service. Some 207,000 people serve in the Colombian armed forces, although the popular (if illegal) option of 'buying out' of the obligation remains commonplace in the middle and upper classes. Like many Latin American societies, Colombia is accepting of the traditional machismo attitudes of its men. Masculinity in Colombia is generally viewed as a positive characteristic and few men, even those in the lower socioeconomic bracket, help with housework or child rearing. Colombian males also typically subscribe to the sexual attitudes characterised by double standards, where men are permitted sexual freedom while 'decent' women are limited to sexual activities largely within the confines of marriage for reproductive purposes, even though this view of sexual conduct is at odds with the teachings of the Catholic Church. Although many of these societal values have changed and the status of women has improved considerably, 80% of men surveyed in 2006 admitted that

ALL JOKING APART

Colombians have an irrepressible love of humour and joking – a sense of fun that bubbles up in all aspects of everyday life. Although Colombian television doesn't boast a comedy tradition like Mexico or Spain, joking around is very part of the national psyche. Expect strangers to share their witticisms, jokes to be scrawled on walls and serious amounts of silliness. Dubbed American comedies known locally as *enlatados* (meaning 'canned' as in canned food) satisfy the Colombian need for a giggle. During the late 1990s, Colombian comedian José Ordoñez became a national celebrity by setting a world record for spending the longest time telling jokes on the radio. Other popular comedic talents include Andrés López Forero, Martín de Francisco and Santiago Moure along with Jaime Garzón, who died in 1999. The following joke cropped up on a menu in a rainforest watering hole:

Man: My love, why don't you learn to cook like the maid? It will save on the cost of a housekeeper.
Woman: My dear, why don't you learn to make love better – it will save on the cost of a chauffeur.

they viewed a man's infidelity as less serious than a woman's because he is biologically driven, whereas women's infidelity is not. According to UN figures, a Colombian man can expect to live on average for 70 years.

WOMEN IN SOCIETY Until a change in the constitution in the 1950s, Colombian women, at least in theory, stayed at home. Without political rights and governed by her spouse under law, a woman in Colombian society had little power, status or authority. In this subordinate role women often had limited access to education or money and lived the life of second-class citizens. Since being awarded suffrage, however, some marked changes have ensued. Today, women are evident throughout corporate entities, government bodies and grassroots movements. Colombia has one of the highest numbers of female politicians in South America with almost a quarter of all cabinet, congress and mayoral posts filled by women. Powerful role models also exist in Colombia such as pop star Shakira, who at 26 became the youngest official Goodwill Ambassador to UNICEF, the world's leading organisation for children. During his presidency Álvaro Uribe also appointed an unprecedented number of women to his cabinet during his tenures, including positions with defence and foreign affairs portfolios. In fact, a law passed in 2000 set quotas for the executive branch of the Colombian government, stating that 30% of appointment positions be filled by women. Indeed, a hotly tipped contender in the 2010 presidential election was Naomi Sanin, a highly polished Colombian lawyer and politician who was ambassador to the United Kingdom, as well as ambassador to Spain and Venezuela. Sanin also served as Colombia's minister of foreign affairs from 1991 to 1994, and was the Conservative Party presidential nominee in 1998 and 2002 before standing with Uribe's endorsement in 2010. Women remain powerful voices in Colombia and are active in campaigning. In 2001, female residents in the small town of Barbacoas in the Nariño province of Colombia embarked on a sex ban to highlight the town's lack of basic infrastructure, after years of protest and hunger strikes failed to grab the headlines. To date, around 40 million COP has been earmarked for a major road, although this leaves 30km unpaved, so the women have vowed to keep their legs crossed until this is addressed. In 2011, there was a national outcry by female rights groups after Colombia's national football team coach made the headlines for punching a woman in a Bogotá bar but kept his job.

Women do, however, continue to take prime responsibility for the lives and care of their children. These family obligations certainly challenge the pursuit of a career, especially in Colombia's infamous world of late-night, back-room dealings. However, many Colombian women see no conflict in using their attractiveness to further their status – a strategy often encouraged by the mother from an early age via modelling and beauty pageants. Indeed a number of Colombian catwalk queens have made it in the hard-nosed world of public office, including a minister of culture and a minister of defence. In Cali and Medellín, women are particularly keen on plastic surgery to enhance their God-given assets, while Colombia-wide there's an overriding sense of sexual confidence from females of every age.

However, despite considerable progress, few would argue that machismo and its discrimination against women have been eradicated from Colombian life. Year on year, the number of single mothers continues to increase within the poorer classes (in 2006, 200,000 girls and adolescents between 15 and 19 became mothers), while divorce has only been possible since 1992. Abortion is still ostensibly illegal in Colombia although an estimated 300,000 backstreet terminations are performed each year. However, in 2006 Colombia's highest court ruled that abortion is permissible in certain circumstances, such as when a pregnancy threatens a woman's life or health, in cases of rape, and in cases where the foetus has abnormalities incompatible with life outside the womb. Bungled abortions account for a significant number of maternal mortalities, especially in the lower classes. Wealthier women have the option of leaving the country to seek a termination in the US.

The average life expectancy for a woman is 78 years, according to UN figures, although UNICEF studies reveal 900 die from childbirth-related causes each year.

CHILDREN IN SOCIETY Colombia's children enjoy vastly contrasting fortunes, depending on the economic situation of their family. Those in the lower classes often experience extreme poverty in family structures that have broken down. Some suffer at the hands of their parents or other family members due to alcoholism, drug taking and mental illness. The National Institute for Child Welfare (ICBF) has a steady job on its hands and reports show that between January 2012 and 2013, 16,457 children were treated because of some form of abuse or another, physical or psychological.

In middle- and upper-class families, children are generally cared for considerably better, with low reported levels of child abuse. Many children from middle- and upper-class homes enjoy private, co-educational air-conditioned classrooms complete with IT facilities, laboratories, libraries, gym, swimming pool and auditorium. They are also encouraged to study to university level to achieve the status and profession of their class. In rural areas, it is not uncommon for middle- and upper-class families to 'adopt' a child of a local farmer. This is usually a girl, who may serve as a maid in their home. In return, the child will be given a salary, full schooling, room and board, and will become, in essence, a member of the family. This arrangement usually ends at the age of 17, but can sometimes last into middle age and beyond.

Conservative estimates suggest Colombia has almost one million orphans aged under 17, many of them in the care of organisations such as SOS Children's Villages in Bogotá. The Colombian government recognises the rights of the nation's 18 million children under a 1989 convention. However its controversial 2006 Child and Adolescent Code has been denounced by aid agencies worldwide that see it as a step backwards in children's rights and an act that offers no practical help. The legislation, which criminalises and penalises children coerced into working in armed groups or the drug trade, affects those aged 14–18. Jail terms of five to eight years apply in accordance with Colombia's penal code. In 2001, Movimiento de los Niños por la Paz (Children's Peace Movement) received the World's Children's Honorary Award for success in promoting children's rights. Members total more than 100,000 children from 400 different youth organisations Colombia-wide.

In 2007, Bogotá authorities launched a poster campaign in a bid to tackle child abuse, erecting 40 6m x 2m billboards citywide. Each displays the photos and personal details of convicted paedophiles along with their crime and sentence. The age and sex of their victims is also displayed. Lawyers for the prisoners had argued that the campaign violated the men's constitutional rights. When it was first announced, the campaign was the subject of more than 30 unsuccessful legal challenges.

RACISM Although most Colombians will deny that there is such a thing as racial segregation in their county, the reality is that in many circumstances people are still judged by the colour of their skin. In Colombia most people are born, marry and die within their caste and – like it or not – racial, economic and social discrimination are all problems in modern Colombian society. Creed and colour have a direct link to Colombia's all-important social strata (page 40). The lower the strata the fewer your chances are to advance in society. Aspirations to live a better life than the previous generation may not be solely governed by race in Colombia, but they are truncated because of a person's social status, in which race often plays a part.

Very few 'people at the top' – in political, civic, industrial and intellectual circles – are Afro-Caribbean in Colombia. This may not be palatable but it is, unfortunately, the truth. In 2001, on the International Day for the Elimination of Racial Discrimination in March, the UN chose to call on Colombia to criminalise discrimination against Afro-Colombian people. It urged the Colombian government to 'send a strong message to Colombian society that the rights and dignity of Afro-Colombians, Raizales and Palenqueros must be respected'. Los Raizales (Roots People, see box, page 221) are people of African origin living in the San Andrés Archipelago whose ancestors were transported from English-speaking Caribbean islands, while Palenqueros are the inhabitants of communities founded by self-liberated former slaves. Over 4.5 million Afro-Colombian people are Colombian citizens (10% of the population). More than 100 municipalities, according to UN figures, have an Afro-Caribbean population of 30% or more. In these communities, life expectancy and infant mortality are higher than in other parts of the country. Afro-Caribbeans also have extreme rates of poverty in many rural and urban ghettos. Areas with the worst quality of life are those with the highest concentrations of Afro-Colombians.

LANGUAGE

Spanish is the official language of Colombia and is spoken by everyone apart from some isolated Amerindian communities. English is the second language but is a rarity away from Colombia's main cities. Mastering a few Spanish basics is essential for those heading to the interior provinces where anything else will be as alien as an intergalactic tongue. However, English is being increasingly taught in schools and colleges as a mandatory subject across the country and is the primary language on the island of Providencia and commonly found in San Andrés. The average Colombian is receptive to anyone willing to have a decent stab at Spanish, offering much encouragement and attempts at Spanglish – and politely ignoring all grammatical faux pas. Colombian Spanish is relaxed, informal and generally easy to understand although even accomplished linguists will find numerous inventive *Colombianismos*, words and phrases that are wholly unique. Latin American Spanish is also littered with American influences, rather than Spain's formal European style. The most obvious difference is the absence of the 'th' lisping used in European Spanish for a 'z' and a 'c'. This is pronounced as a soft 's' in Colombian, as in much of Latin America. Greetings also tend to be much more elaborate in Colombian style, comprising a long exchange of incalculable pleasantries rather than the perfunctory '*Hola*'. Slang has also infiltrated the Colombian language to a large extent and *Streetwise Spanish*, a guide to Latin American Spanish, is especially useful countrywide (page 491). Some tribes in remote areas still speak their own languages. The current constitution, adopted in 1991, recognises the languages of ethnic groups and provides for bilingual education. *Cundiboyacences* (those from Cundinamarca and Boyacá) are distinctive in linguistic terms as they use the second-person pronoun *sumercé*. See also pages 486–7.

RELIGION

Colombia is often referred to as 'the most Roman Catholic of all South American countries' – and in terms of its out-and-out religious devotion it remains very much a colony of Spain. Although modern Colombia's immigrant Lebanese, Turkish and Jewish populations each have their own places of worship, more than 90% of Colombia's population is Roman Catholic. A ratio of priests to inhabitants of 1:4,000 is one of Latin America's highest with such primary rites of the Church as baptism, first communion and marriage viewed as key turning points in life. Small Protestant communities can be found on the former English colonies of San Andrés and Providencia where gospel-singing congregations rub shoulders with those practising ancient slave rituals and African beliefs.

EDUCATION

In the past 30 years the Colombian government has made great inroads in improving accessibility to primary and secondary education, but the gaps in the country's schooling are still immense. In 2001, the ratio of pupils to teachers in primary school was 26:1 and in secondary school 19:2 but as recently as 1994 just five of every ten children aged 12 to 17 years of age were in regular attendance. Colombia's poorest people have always received the least education. In urban areas children are schooled for an average of seven years, double that of the rural communities. The quality of education in public primary and secondary schools is also substandard in rural areas due to a lack of the materials prescribed in the curriculum. In three decades, public expenditure on education as a percentage of gross domestic product (GDP) hasn't changed a great deal: 2.85% in the 1970s, 2.99% in the 1980s and 3.03% in the 1990s. After President Uribe came to power in 2002 he cut the education budget in order to pump more capital into his military campaigns. Access to higher education by Colombia's youth population is also lagging behind by international and regional standards. The country's 22% enrolment rate does not meet the country's needs in terms of technological and economic development.

In Colombia, 70% of education is private, and there are 900 private higher education institutions compared with 32 public ones. Instruction in Roman Catholicism is standard in all public schools, most of which are controlled by the Roman Catholic Church. In 2000, some 5.2 million pupils annually attended primary schools with 3.6 million students at secondary school.

Among the largest universities are the National University of Colombia in Bogotá, the University of Cartagena, the University of Antioquia in Medellín and the University of Nariño in Pasto. Since 2003, Colombia's national programme for literacy and basic education for young people and adults has benefited 275,000 people with several specialised adult education methods winning UNESCO literacy prizes. International Literacy Day is celebrated on an annual basis. Considerable effort has been devoted to eliminating illiteracy in Colombia since the 1970s, and today 93% of all citizens over the age of 15 can read and write. In recent years Bill Gates has been instrumental in helping raise IT skills in Colombia through the Bill & Melinda Gates Foundation. Gates has set up computer learning centres in areas where demobilised paramilitary fighters are in dire need of job training, at a cost of US$1 million. Another deal has helped put 15,000 more computers in Colombian schools. The nation has one computer per 40 students and Gates wants that to drop to 25. With the government-led campaign ViveDigital, designed to bring the internet to even the most isolated parts of the country, in 2014 it was reported that 80% of Colombians have access to the internet.

SOCIAL STRUCTURE

Colombian society exhibits strong class divisions and regional distinctions with people often referred to in terms of the administrative departments in which they live, such as Antioqueños, Nariñenses, Bogotanos, Santandereanos, Tolimenses and Boyacanses. There is also a tradition of identifying Colombians by their colour, dress, diet and speech, and class structure remains based on a combination of occupation, wealth and ethnicity. Colombian society is split into six numerical socioeconomic strata (*estrata*): poor; lower working class; working class; upper working class; more affluent working class; and upper class. These groupings are of great importance to Colombians, so much so that even the most modest person will allude to their stratum – should it be sufficiently high. However, above all else, strata are about location.

According to the World Bank, Colombia's rate of inequality is one of the highest in Latin America. Colombians from the top quintile retain 60% of the national income, in strong contrast to Sweden, for example, where the top quintile retains 34% of the national income.

However, the majority of Colombia's 43.6 million people belong to the so-called 'marginal' classes, a sector of society without regular employment that tends to eke out a living by any possible means. This lower class relies on manual labour for a sporadic income and largely comprises those of African, Amerindian or mixed race who are politically powerless, poorly educated and living below the poverty line. Few of the benefits of economic growth have reached Colombia's poorest members of society, who put up with a standard of sanitation, housing and healthcare that is inadequate at best. In 2010, Colombia initiated a law to criminalise racism after being criticised by the UN for its failure to outlaw discriminatory practices.

Colombia's middle classes tend to be skilled professionals who lack the wealth, connections and pure European heritage of their upper-class compatriots. In order to infiltrate the upper echelons of society, middle-class people must transform aspiration into *real* connections. As a relatively small and politically passive group, Colombia's middle classes have traditionally settled in their comfort zone, although during President Uribe's tenure a greater number of small business owners and merchants felt the confidence to rise through the ranks.

In the upper echelons of Colombian society, professional occupations aren't that dissimilar to the middle classes. However, this social segment is dominated by a relatively small group of wealthy families of mainly pure Spanish background who control most of the country's land and property. Many of Colombia's rich elite can trace their lineage to the aristocracy of the colonial era, although this privileged group also includes those who have made their money in more recent times through entrepreneurial wheeler-dealing. Colombia's exclusive wealthy cliques are preoccupied with the protection of family pride, name and assets (*abolengo*) and these family links are key to the business and political life of every member of the upper classes.

Colombia's chasm between rich and poor was described by the United Nations in 2004 as 'the worst humanitarian crisis in the Western hemisphere' – and little has changed since. Despite pockets of considerable wealth Colombia's average daily income remains at about £4, less than a tenth of the UK's, with an annual per-capita gross income of US$2,500, according to the UN. However, a US$4 billion wealth tax imposed on Colombia's 6,000 richest citizens and biggest companies in 2007 by the Uribe administration was seen as a positive step in attempting to redress the imbalance. In 2011, President Santos also promised to take a wider look at ending Colombia's decades-long armed conflict by tackling the country's vast disparity between rich and poor. Government announcements are positive, with President Santos declaring that during his first tenure 3.6 million Colombians were no longer living in extreme poverty and that if investment and policies remained on track, this scourge could be eradicated in the country by 2025.

CULTURE

Colombia has a lengthy arts tradition born out of the nation's innate compulsion to seek out new creative outlets. Colombian artists have been renowned for their energy and spirit throughout history, from great literary and musical movements to the modern mediums of photography, cinema and television. Today, a genuine desire to retain Colombia's artistic heritage prevails throughout the country along with a considerable commitment to furthering a wide range of contemporary arts across numerous ethnic and mixed-race groups.

In 2011, the Colombian Ministry of Culture and International Council of Museums (ICOM) produced a 'red list' of the country's cultural heritage that is at risk of looting and illegal art trafficking. Containing archaeological artefacts and furniture dating back to colonial times until the early 20th century, the list was circulated to 10,000 police and customs officials, museums, auctioneers, private collectors and art dealers around the world in five languages to help identify and rescue the country's national heritage. The Colombian government has called on all buyers of Colombian art objects in or outside the country to inform themselves about the origin of the artefacts to avoid being involved in illegal trade. Part-funded by a US$99,000 donation from US State Department's Bureau of Educational and Cultural Affairs the list was compiled using 'red lists' of endangered cultural assets issued by China, Cambodia, Iraq, Peru, Mexico and African countries, which have successfully retrieved large numbers of stolen or illegally traded art objects.

Colombians remain hugely proud of their Nobel Prize winners and make much of the fact that more celebrated home-grown poets (men of the pen) than military men (men of the sword) have made it to the presidency role.

MUSIC AND DANCE

Voy a beber del veneno malevo de tu amor
(I drank from the malevolent poison that was your love)
yo quedé moribundo y lleno de dolor
(I remain a dying man and full of pain)
respiré de ese humo amargo de tu adios
(I breathe in that bitter second of your goodbye)

Juanes, *La Camisa Negra* (*The Black Shirt*), 2005

Colombia's most deeply rooted musical tradition, the folkloric tunes and melodies of the indigenous peoples, is found in distinct geographic pockets in both its pure and modern forms. Spanish elements blend with native rhythms and a hybrid of American, Trinidadian, Cuban and Jamaican styles.

Broadly speaking, Colombian music falls into four musical geographic zones: the Andean region, the Atlantic coast, the Pacific coast and Los Llanos (the plains). Andean melodies boast strong Spanish influences. Instruments used include the *tiple guitarra* and piano in genres such as the *bambuco, pasillo guabina* and *torbellino*. Music in the Caribbean (Atlantic) is a pulsating mix of hot, steamy rhythms, such as the *cumbia, porros* and *mapalé*. On the Pacific coast the *currulao* uses heavy pounding drumbeats tinged with some telltale Spanish inflections while the music of Los Llanos (*música llanera*) is usually accompanied by a harp, *cuatro* (a sort of four-string guitar) and maracas.

These older musical styles have been joined by two important newer additions that now dominate Colombia's music scene countrywide. Because of its popularity, 'la salsa' seems endemic to Colombia, yet it didn't arrive until the late 1960s when it spread like wildfire and is now a music-and-dance mainstay. Sexy, sassy and fluid, new-style salsa has become a symbol of pride and cultural identity for Latinos and is found on every street corner in the salsa epicentres of Cali and Barranquilla. The other omnipresent musical form is the infectious *vallenato*, a celebrated genre from the northern tip of Colombia that fuses European-style accordion riffs with traditional folkloric themes.

Reggae, calypso and *socca* are the most popular music styles on the islands of San Andrés and Providencia, where dozens of waterfront bars and restaurants sway to hypnotic rhythms 24 hours a day. *Reggaetón* has also been prevalent throughout San Andrés since gaining popularity in the mid 1990s. This oh-so-cool fusion of hip hop and Jamaican dancehall with Latino beat has its own unique rhythm, a hybrid of various musical genres from the Caribbean, Latin America and the United States. *Reggaetón* has attracted criticism for its sexually explicit lyrics that allegedly exploit women, although fans insist the message is non-violent, albeit a little risqué. Further controversy surrounds *perreo*, a bump-and-grind dance with explicit sexual overtones associated with Colombia's *reggaetón* scene. Some **ancient musical forms** from the colonial period have survived in Colombia, according to the Academy of American Franciscan History. Numerous folkloric festivals celebrate these ancient traditions nationwide.

Vallenato According to historian Tomás D Gutiérrez Hinojosa, *vallenato* music is traditionally played with an *acordeón vallenato* (accordion), a *caja vallenata* (large bongo) and a *guacharaca* (bamboo *guiro*), with commercial groups adding a singer (*cantante*), two harmony singers (*coros*), a conga player (*conguero*), a bass player (*bajista*), a guitarist (*guitarrista*) as well as a timbales player (*timbalero*). Traditionally, *vallenato* has been inextricably linked with the songwriter Rafael Escalona, a pioneering recording artist in the 1950s and 1960s. Other well-known songwriters of the same era are Leandro Díaz, Emiliano Zuleta, and Tobías e Pumarejo, to name just a few. Today, a modern form of so-called *techno vallenato* is popular throughout Colombia, with big-selling artists who include Carlos Vives.

Colombia stages a number of *vallenato* folkloric festivals and competitions with highly coveted awards for categories such as 'professional accordion player', 'amateur accordion player', 'young accordion player', 'best new *vallenato* song' and '*piquerías*' (verse singers).

Vallenato festivals include the 41st Annual Festival de la Leyenda Vallenato (*Valledupar, César; www.festivalvallenato.com*), Festival Cuna de Acordeones (*Villanueva, Guajira; www.elvallenato.com*), Festival National de Compositores de Música Vallenata (*San Juan del César, Guajira; www.fundacionbat.com.co*), Festival Tierra de Compositores (*Patillal, César*), Festival Folclórico del Fique (*La Junta, Guajira; www.miriohacha.com*), Festival de Acordeoneros y Compositores de Chinú (*Chinú, Córdoba; www.parrandavallenata.com*) and Festival Sabanero (*Sincelejo, Sucre*).

Cumbia This complex mix of African rhythms was popularised on Colombia's Caribbean coast with primal percussive drums, simple vocals and a tit-for-tat-style dance. Courtship rituals are depicted through a flirtatious performance with shuffling footwork said to portray slavery in ankle chains. In the 1940s, many of Colombia's urban communities discovered *cumbia*, which soon evolved from its rural form to a more refined style. The so-called golden age of cumbia was the 1950s when Colombians nationwide embraced the rhythmic performances with gusto, often in large groups of male and female couples. Cumbia is characterised by women playfully swirling long skirts while holding a candle, whilst each man, wearing a red handkerchief around the neck, dances behind with one hand on his back. The remaining hand pulls his hat on and off and waves it flamboyantly. Until the mid 20th century, *cumbia* suffered from a poor reputation and was considered a vulgar dance, practised only by peasants. Today it remains a stalwart of Colombia's working classes with drums and claves giving an instantly recognisable backbeat. Modern *cumbia* is fused with other genres, such as *vallenato*, pop and rock music, and has been popularised by Grammy Award-winning artists (see *www.grammy. com/latin*) such as Colombia's dreadlocked heart-throb, Carlos Vives. A former soap-opera star, Vives has become a national hero for championing *vallenato*, *cumbia* and *porro* for a new, young audience. He has worked with English producer Richard Blair as well as a range of veteran Latino musicians on the albums *Los Clásicos De La Provincia*, *La Tierro del Olvido* and *Tengo Fe*.

Música llanera This harp-led music originates from the Colombian plains but has become part of a national tradition renowned for its verbal contests, *contrapunteo*, a form of sung poetry performed head to head. *Joropo* musical style resembles the waltz with an accompanying dance that mixes African and European influences with its roots in Venezuelan and Colombian folklore. *Música llanera* (*www.musicallanera.net*) also features a *cuatro* (a type of four-string guitar) and maracas with lyrics redolent of the rural cattle-farming life of the *llanos* region.

Colombian salsa Although originally born among Puerto Ricans and Cubans, salsa soon spread to a receptive audience in Colombia and during the late 1960s it truly captured the hearts and souls of music lovers nationwide. By 1970, salsa was fast becoming an epidemic as Colombia took the reins of Latin America salsa music, with its irrepressible, sexy, sultry rhythms popularised by Fruko y sus Tesos. This Cali-based crowd-pleasing band of musicians led by Ernesto Fruko Estrada enjoyed huge popularity throughout Latin America with big-selling albums that include *Pura candela*, *El preso*, *Cali de rumba*, *Son de la loma*, *El patillero* and *Charanga campesina*. Today Fruko and his boys still rank among the best Colombian salsa bands, famed for their hardcore, swing-inspired music of the highest quality. Joe Arroyo began singing in Fruko y sus Tesos in 1971, wooing the salsa world with his vibrant vocal style and mischievous dance moves. He finally started his own band, La Verdad (The Truth), in 1981, with a talented orchestra of musicians. He was born in Cartagena, and his father had 40 sons with many different women, a story that he famously tells during his set. A versatile singer of many Caribbean rhythms, Joe Arroyo is a vivacious performer of sones and boleros as well as the *cumbias* and fandangos of his native region. Today he remains highly popular and much revered within Colombia, and regularly invents new rhythms and styles with roots in his local salsa traditions.

Santiago de Cali (better known as simply Cali) is Colombia's undisputed 'Capital de la Salsa' with hundreds of clubs, festivals, dance schools and concerts that pay homage to the city's infatuation. An annual week-long summer salsa festival takes place in Cali in early July, attracting many of the world's greatest salsa bands and devotees to a host of dance shows and competitions. The rivalry is fierce between salsa connoisseurs and aficionados, who try to out-do each other with fancy moves to vintage long-lost salsa tunes. January 2008 also heralded the 50th anniversary of the Feria de Cali, the largest salsa festival in the world. More than three million *salseras* and *salseros* descend on the city for the mother of all Cali's famous parties. The event includes the World Salsa Championship and the World Salsa Congress and accounts for a massive hike in the sales of rum and *aguardiente*.

1

COLOMBIAN MUSIC GLOSSARY

baile	meaning dance
balada	Spanish romantic popular music, as in ballad
bambuco	an Andean style of dance music or Andean lyric
bandola	used in *música llanera*, stringed musical instrument similar to a mandolin
bandolin	larger style of bandola
bombo	drum used in folklore music on the Caribbean coast, traditionally used in cumbia
bullerengue	traditional flute-and-drum music
caja vallenata	a goatskin drum used in *música vallenata*
campana	traditional cowbell
capachos	traditional maracas
champeta	gutsy Atlantic coastal music, Afro-Colombian in origin
contrapunteo	an improvised, verbal duel to music
cuatro	small guitar used in *llanera* music
guache	seed-filled rattles used in *música vallenata*
joropo	courtship dance endemic to cattle-ranching culture
llamador	traditional drum used in *cumbia*
melómano	a true music lover
parrandero	a person who loves to party – a lot
pasillo	Andean lyrical song
porro	brass band flute-and-drum music
salsoteca	a salsa venue
tiple	small stringed instrument used in *música llanera*
zarzuela	traditional Colombian operetta

Pop music

No puedo pedir que el invierno perdone a un rosal
(I can't ask winter to spare a rose bush)
No puedo pedir a los olmos que entreguen peras
(I can't ask an elm tree to bear pears)
No puedo pedirle lo eterno a un simple mortal
(I can't ask the eternal of a mere mortal)

Shakira, 'La Tortura' 'The Torture', 2007

Think Colombian pop music and Shakira is bound to spring to mind, yet on domestic soil artists like Fonseca (*www.fonseca.net*), Juanes (*www.juanes.net*), Carlos Vives (*www.carlosvives.com*) and Mauricio y Palo de Agua (*mauricioypalodeagua.co*) are headline-grabbing musical icons. Bogotá-born heart-throb Fonseca's acclaimed double-platinum album *Corazón* blends *vallenato*, *bullerengue*, *tambora* and African drums with a hint of classic salsa and features the heart-warming 'Te Mando Flores', a big-selling single in 2006. Triple Grammy Award-winner Medellín-born Juanes launched his solo career in 1998. His sophomore album, *Un Día Normal*, was certified platinum throughout much of the Spanish-speaking world, and its lead single 'A Dios le Pido' topped singles charts in 12 countries. Juanes is also renowned for his extensive humanitarian work, especially with aid for Colombian victims of anti-personnel mines. Hailing from the Pacific coast and the city of Quibdo, the three-person hip-hop outfit ChocQuibTown, including Tostao, Goyo and Slow, should not be overlooked. With Latin Grammy-winning song 'De Donde Vengo Yo' and the catchy 'Somos Pacifico', they should be on everyone's playlist. Yet it is undoubtedly two-time Latin Grammy Award-winner Shakira (*www.shakira. com*) who remains Colombia's biggest musical celebrity, selling 50 million albums and establishing herself in history as the only Colombian artist to reach number one on the Billboard Hot 100 and UK Singles Chart. In July 2006, she earned the distinction of performing the last-ever song on British music programme *Top of the Pops*, with 'Hips Don't Lie', after seven weeks in the charts. A number of free concerts play host to some of Latin America's most popular rock, R&B and pop acts each year in Bogotá's Simón Bolívar Park.

Classical music

It's as if he is conjoined to the music, he is one with its energy.

Música Clásica article, 2006

Colombia is justifiably proud of its shining classical star Andrés Orozco-Estrada, a handsome 30-something with incredible musical pedigree and flair. Born in 1977 in Medellín, he started playing the violin at the age of five and by 15 was conducting an orchestra. Today this darling of the orchestral circuit is fast emerging as one of the most creative conductors. 'He is dazzling, a master. A genius,' said one critic in 2007. Orozco-Estrada has conducted the Colombian National Orchestra and the Philharmonic Orchestra of Bogotá. Today he frequently works with the most prestigious orchestras in Colombia, including the Orquesta Filarmónica de Medellín, Orquesta Filarmonica del Valle, Orquesta Sinfónica Universidad Eafit, Coral Tomás Luis de Victoria in Medellín and Coro Polifónico de Medellín.

THEATRE Each of Colombia's main cities boast a wide range of theatres and venues that stage an array of performances spanning the conventional and classical to the bizarre. Colombia's theatre tradition was born in the mid 19th century, but it wasn't until the emergence of its National Theatre almost a century later that the arts benefited from a firmer footing and significantly higher profile nationwide. Today, Bogotá, Cali and Medellín remain the main centres for theatre groups with more than 150 amateur, semi-professional and professional troupes countrywide. A growing number of theatrical academies are feeding the future development of Colombia's national theatre, from social projects in deprived communities via the amateur dramatic association and programmes at the Escuela Nacional de Arte Dramático in Bogotá. A ballet school in Bogotá has a growing international reputation, while a male voice choir in Medellín has put the city's choral societies on the map. Every two years Bogotá plays host to the Iberoamerican Theater Festival, when the best of scenic arts from five continents, 33 countries, 45 international companies and 140 guest Colombian groups fill 12 theatre halls, six coliseums, 20 parks, the bullfighting arena and Bogotá Fair venue to deliver 556 shows and over 1,200 performers. Concerts range from classical music, dance, avant-garde performances, circus troupes and plays to street theatre in every auditorium, public park, coliseum and street space throughout the capital, attracting upwards of 30,000 visitors from all corners of the globe.

For further information contact the Colombian Amateur Dramatic Association (Corporation Cultural Nuestra Gente) (*Calle 99, No 50 c38, Barrio Santa Cruz, Medellín, Colombia;* ✎ *4 258 0348;* e *nuestragente@une.net.co; www.nuestragente. com.co*), Iberoamerican Theater Festival (*www.festivaldeteatro.com.co*) and Fundación Teatro Nacional (✎ *4 211 1741;* e *teatronacional@teatronacional.com.co; www.teatronacional.com.co*).

1

LITERATURE Since independence from Spain, Colombia has enjoyed a long and glorious literary tradition. Numerous authors of note have achieved international acclaim, including one Nobel Prize in Literature winner.

Gabriel García Márquez (1928–2014)

In my ninetieth year, I decided to give myself the gift of a night of love with a young virgin.

Gabriel García Márquez, *Memoria de Mis Putas Tristes*
(*Memories of My Melancholy Whores*) 2004

Because of his strong political views, Colombia's most famous novelist, journalist, publisher, political activist and celebrity García Márquez lived much of his life in exile in Mexico City. He began his career at a local newspaper working on regional giants such as *El Heraldo* (Barranquilla) and *El Universal* (Cartagena) when he joined forces with other writers and journalists to form what became known as the Barranquilla Group. These creative, influential compatriots became a strong source of inspiration for García Márquez who went on to work in Paris, Barcelona, Caracas and New York as a foreign correspondent. He openly criticised Colombia's political situation, which provoked accusations from the government regarding his support of guerrilla groups, such as the FARC and ELN, although there has never been any evidence to back up these claims. García Márquez is noted for his friendship with Cuban president Fidel Castro and in 2006 he joined other international figures to demand sovereignty for Puerto Rico. He also joined the Latin American and Caribbean Congress for the independence of Puerto Rico to push for the island-nation's right to independence, at the behest of the Puerto Rican Independence Party. His first novel, *La Hojarasca*, was published in 1955 (translated in 1972 as *Leaf Storm and Other Stories*) but it was *Cien Años de Soledad* in 1967 that thrust García Márquez into the international limelight, gaining him acclaim worldwide (published in English in 1970 as *One Hundred Years of Solitude*). Affectionately known as Gabo, García Márquez is a master of the literary style known as magic realism. In 1982, he became the first Colombian to win the Nobel Prize in Literature, just one of 104 winners worldwide since 1901.

Today, García Márquez still ranks as one of South America's greatest 20th-century authors. Born in the town of Aracataca in the department of Magdalena on 6 March 1928, García Márquez is the father of television and film director Rodrigo Garciá. After being diagnosed with cancer in 1999, García Márquez started work on his memoirs, an event that in 2000, prompted premature reports of his death in Peruvian newspaper *La República*. The first volume, *Living to Tell the Tale*, was published in 2007. The same year also saw the release of the film version of Márquez's seminal novel *Love in the Time of Cholera*, set in Cartagena and directed by Mike Newell (*Four Weddings and a Funeral*). The screenplay was written by García Márquez himself. García Márquez' passing in early 2014 was a cause for national mourning with simultaneous memorial events taking place in Mexico and Colombia. Such is Gabo's importance in Colombia that there are discussions about having his portrait on a new Colombian peso note.

Jorge Isaacs (1837–95)

Isaacs studied for a medical career before becoming a journalist, poet and writer, drawing on his childhood, growing up in a small Jewish community in Cali. In 1987, his only novel *María* (published in English in 1890 as *María: A South American Romance*) became one of the most notable works of the romantic movement in Spanish literature. Many of his poems portray the Valley of the Cauca. Isaacs also lived in Popayán before moving to Bogotá in 1848.

Porfirio Barba-Jacob (1883–1942) Miguel Ángel Osorio Benítez was better known by his pseudonym Porfirio Barba-Jacob and was also dubbed 'The Poet of Death' for his avant-garde writing style. Born in Santa Rosa de Osos in Antioquia, Jacob founded the literary magazine *El cancionero antioqueño (The Antioquian Songbook)* in Bogotá under the pseudonym Marín Jiménez. He also wrote a novel *Virginia* that remains unpublished because the original manuscript was seized by authorities due to its alleged immoral themes. In 1906, he moved to Barranquilla under the name Ricardo Arenales, a name he would use until 1922. For the rest of his life, he lived as Porfirio Barba-Jacob, enjoying the success of poems *Árbol viejo*, *Campiña florida* and his most famous work *Parábola de la vida profunda (Parable of the profound life)*. Jacob died in 1942 of tuberculosis in Mexico City where he had become famous for his poetic style, known as *nueva sensibilidad*.

José Asunción Silva (1865–96) The poems of Bogotá-born José Asunción Silva are renowned as some of the most beautiful in the Spanish language, marked by haunting angst and a brooding spirit of pessimism. The best known is *Nocturno III*, an elegy for his sister, Crepúsculo, and *Día de difuntos (Day of the Dead)*. Silva also wrote a novel, *De Sobremesa*, notable for its rejection of realist conventions and its intense emotional themes.

Unfortunately José Asunción Silva's life was overshadowed by periods of deep depression, caused by the loss of a crucial manuscript, family debt and the death of a beloved sister. In 1896, he committed suicide, leaving a debt of US$210,000. The lasting legacy of this most gifted writer is a collection of poetry called *Los Nocturnos* in which Silva displays extraordinary genius. Baldomero Sanín Cano subsequently published many of his works in Paris in 1913.

John Jairo Junieles (1970–present day) This young Colombian poet has won considerable acclaim since winning the prestigious 2006 II 'Ciudad Alajuela' International Poetry Award in Costa Rica with his book *Passenger with a Ticket to a Strange Land*. Junieles, who received US$5,000 and the publication of his book, was born in Sincelejo, Sucre, Colombia in 1970. He currently resides in Bogotá.

Juan Gabriel Vasquez (1973–present day) One of the new wave of young Colombian writers making inroads internationally, Juan Gabriel Vasquez has been awarded prizes in France and Spain and has seen his works translated into 17 languages. Pushing the style away from that of magic realism Vasquez's notable offerings include *The Informers*, *The Secret History of Costaguana* and most recently taking on the difficult issue of the Escobar years in Colombia, *The Sound of Things Falling*.

CINEMA, TELEVISION AND RADIO

> I'm going to get Daniel a new horse to ride … That didn't sound as dirty in my head.
> Betty Suárez, *Ugly Betty (Yo Soy Betty la Fea)*, ABC, 2006

Colombian television programmes appear to move seamlessly from light and fluffy escapist trash to the harsh reality of the nation's social discourse. Cinema tends to be harder hitting, exploiting these themes to much acclaim as in films such as *Rosaria Tijeras* in 2005 and 2004's *Sumas y Restas*. Although widely ignored outside Colombia, these gritty celluloid triumphs achieved sizeable success on home soil with their dark tales of narco-traffickers and contract killing.

Colombians, like most Latin Americans, adore *telenovelas* (soap operas) and no self-respecting household isn't a slave to at least one each night. These kitsch mishmashes of drama, comedy and topical themes regularly fight it out for national ratings via increasingly bizarre and outrageous storylines. A favourite at the time of writing is RCN's *Los Reyes*, a mix of controversy, woes and hardship with just the right hint of drama and glamour. Another RCN show, *Yo Soy Betty la Fea*, inspired ABC's hugely popular American prime-time hit *Ugly Betty*, the tale of a bespectacled, bushy-browed, braces-wearing heroine played by América Ferrera (*Real Women Have Curves* and *The Sisterhood of the Traveling Pants*). Most recently and perhaps spurred on by dwindling viewer ratings, Colombian television stations have resorted to detailing the bloody contemporary history of their country with soap operas such as *El Patron del Mal* (Escobar), *Las Munecas de la Mafia* (the mafia dolls) and even one about the controversial *vallenato* star Diomedes Diaz. American imports are also popular in Colombia, especially reality television shows.

At the Film Festival, Colombian president Juan Manuel Santos pledged his support to Colombia's aim to become a 'mecca' for cinema and announced a strategy to attract directors, producers and investors, especially from the United States and India, to make movies in the country. He also outlined plans to stimulate investment in the wider audio-visual sector. So far Fox International and Sony Pictures Television have already based their Latin American operations in Colombia.

Colombia has hundreds of great radio stations that broadcast everything from religious classics and political talk shows to pumping rock and salsa. Stations come and go but the following are currently worth a listen:

• El Vallenato (97.4)	*vallenato*
• Tropicana FM (102.9)	salsa
• La Z – Bogotá (92.9)	salsa
• Los 40 Principales (89.9)	*reggaetón*
• La Mega (90.9)	*reggaetón*
• SuperEstación (88.9)	rock
• RadioActiva (97.9)	rock
• Vibra Bogotá (104.9)	rock and pop, retro 80s music, news
• CaracolRadio (94.9)	news and pop
• WRadio (99.9)	news and retro pop
• UNRADIO (Universidad Nacional de Colombia) (98.5)	all genres
• Javeriana Esteréo (Pontificia Universidad Javeriana) (91.5)	jazz, rock, pop
• Javeriana Esteréo Cali (107.5)	salsa
• Amor Estéreo (93.9)	retro 70s, 80s and 90s pop
• RCN (104.4)	news
• LaX (103.9)	retro pop and news

ARCHITECTURE Those who dismiss Colombia as an architectural wasteland are guilty of overlooking some of South America's most handsome buildings. For Colombia has a wealth of incredible good-looking structures, from the gleaming Miami-esque skyline of Cartagena's shoreline and the ramshackle faded colonial façades of Bogotá's La Candelaria district to some of the finest preserved 16th- and 17th-century architecture in Latin America at Villa de Leyva and the walled city of Getsemaní. Cali, Medellín and Bogotá each boast plenty of futuristic, needle-thin spires, while Barranquilla's white stucco and red-tiled buildings in the historic El Prado district and Popayán's resplendent aged streets and churches are truly deserving of acclaim. Styles that dominated the 16th and 17th centuries were the elaborate Plateresque (as seen at the Tunja Cathedral), Mannerism (exemplified by Bogotá's San Ignacio Church) and the extravagant, ornate Baroque (epitomised by the Palace of the Inquisition, Cartagena). In 2006, the prestigious Golden Lion Award for Architecture recognised Colombia in its tenth International Architectural Awards, rewarding Bogotá for its positive stance in applying Mies van der Rohe's dictum 'less is more' to its civic space. Judges were impressed by the city's widespread redesign that saw its streets improve aesthetically as well as in economic and social terms.

In 2007, the Biblioteca Pública Piloto de Medellín para América Latina (Medellín Pilot Public Library for Latin America) staged an exhibition entitled '100 years of Architecture in Colombia', a photographic journey through Colombia's architectural heritage in conjunction with UNESCO and the Memory of the World Programme. Numerous books have been published on the subject, including *Casa Republicana: Colombia's Belle Epoque*, in which author Benjemín Villegas takes a look at Republican architecture and examines the era of ornate design. *Country Houses in Colombia* sees authors Alberto Saldarriaga and Antonio Castenda Buragua explore how indigenous plants (such as *guadua*, a local bamboo) have influenced the Colombian architectural form. Similarly, *Casa De Hacienda: Architecture in the Colombian Countryside* by German Tellez showcases some of the finest old rural properties in Colombia's rural provinces. In 2010, Bogotá received the Latin American award in Urban Planning and Information Platforms from New York's Environmental Systems Research Institute, which acknowledged the strides that the Ministry of Planning has made to integrate communities, build better neighbourhoods and manage sustainable projects. And the plaudits have not ended there – Medellín was voted in as the World's Most Innovative City in 2013 in an online *Wall Street Journal* poll. Bogotá was also garlanded by the prestigious C40 Siemens award for the work done to mitigate climate change gases through improving urban transportation.

PAINTING AND SCULPTURE Religious themes dominated much of Colombia's artistic scene prior to independence, with Bogotá-based Gregorio Vásquez de Arce y Ceballos (1638–1711) one of the colonial era's finest. On his death he bequeathed more than 500 pieces of his work to the nation. These are now found in an array of museums and churches across the country, including some particularly fine paintings in the cathedrals of Bogotá. Colombia's artists became considerably more experimental after independence when European influences began to permeate traditional outlets, leading to more creative, rave and expressive original art. Distinct styles and themes began to emerge during the 1930s and 1940s, heralding a defining moment in Colombia's artistic history. At the forefront of this exciting creative explosion were a host of masters, including painter and sculptor Luis Alberto Acuña; watercolour, oil and mural artist Pedro Nel Gómez; Alejandro Obregón, a fine abstract painter; Eduardo Ramírez Villamizar, an artist renowned for his geometric style in three-dimensional space; Guillermo Wiedemann, a German-born painter who made Colombia his artistic home; and Rodrigo Arenas Betancur, Colombia's most celebrated monument creator. In the footsteps of these artistic forefathers came Colombia's most international renowned artist, Fernando Botero (see box, page 56), as well as a painter famed for his erotic, nude work, Leonel Góngora. Today, Colombia is at the heart of Latin America's fine arts scene and boasts numerous exhibitions of international repute in galleries nationwide. Genres range from pre-Columbian to modern contemporary and include art,

... by the time you come to create art yourself you're spoilt – you're tired of beauty as such and want to do something else. With me it was quite different. I wasn't tired of beauty; I was hungering for it.

2008

When Medellín-born Fernando Botero came into the world on 19 April 1932 he immediately began to look at it through unique eyes, according to his parents. This creative early bloomer had his own exhibition at the Leo Matiz Gallery in Bogotá while still in his teens, developing an instantly recognisable style of painting and sculpture characterised by the use of distorted proportions. The following year he was awarded a second prize at the National Salon, using the money he earned to travel to Spain, France and Italy to study the work of the old masters. Botero's neo-figurative works are often described as fat – but this is a gross oversimplification of the subject matter. Situational portraiture is his trademark, using exaggerated elements and shifts of scale. Botero also plays with the corpulence of the figures in his art with proportion manipulated to distort colour, shape and size.

Many paintings depict influences from a traditional Colombian upbringing. Botero describes himself as 'the most Colombian of Colombian artists' and some astute social commentary is also woven throughout his work. Paintings of small-town Colombian life centre on themes that range from political figures and military men to criminals, prostitutes and nudes. Many possess comic qualities that satirise power and excess, while family portraits depict greater affection and restraint. Those that dwell on the death of his son are particularly touching.

Botero moved to New York in 1960 but left in 1973 for Paris. Today he divides his time between Paris, New York, Tuscany and his homeland. In 2004, he donated a series of 23 oil paintings and 27 drawings to the National Museum of Colombia, depicting the country's long-lasting violence. In early 2005, Botero also unveiled a series of 50 controversial paintings graphically representing his anger at prisoner abuse at the Abu Ghraib jail. After exhibiting at the Palazzo Venezia in Rome, and later in Germany and Greece, Botero took this headline-grabbing collection to New York in October 2006, where they were shown at the Marlborough Gallery to great critical acclaim. In 2009, the man dubbed the 'Picasso of Latin America' returned to London for the first time in 25 years. His collection, entitled The Circus, was displayed at Thomas Gibson Fine Art for 30 days only. It contained nearly 20 watercolours and oil paintings.

design, photography and cutting-edge high-tech visual mediums. Many of the nation's finest galleries are free to the public, including the magnificent El Museo Botero de Bogotá.

For further information contact the Colombian Fine Arts portal (*www.colarte.com*).

HANDICRAFTS Colombian handicrafts are easily found in markets, street stalls and shops throughout the country, from the woven shoulder bags of the Arhuaco indigenous people of the Sierra Nevada de Santa Marta to the exquisite *sombrero vueltiao* made by the people of Córdoba. Other beautifully crafted items include hammocks of San Jacinto in Bolívar, decorated figures of Pasto, Nariño, and cheerful pottery of Ráquira in Boyacá – not to mention the Paez people's wonderfully thick, homespun triangular shawls (*ruanas*). In Bogotá, in the cloister of Las Aquas, a neighbourhood just off La Candelaria, Artesanías de Colombia (*Las Aguas Cra 2, 18A–58, Bogotá;* \ *286 1766; www.artesaniasdecolombia.com.co*) stocks everything from straw umbrellas to hand-woven ponchos. Atop Cerro Nutibara in Medellín in the recreated typical Paisa village plaza an impressive range of *artesanías* sell bags and jewellery, while on the basis of choice alone, the colourful array of handicraft stores in the old dungeons in the walls of Cartagena is difficult to beat.

SPORT
Football

Every defeat is a victory in itself.

Francisco 'Pacho' Maturana,
defender in 1982 Colombian World Cup squad, 1983

Colombians are passionate about football (soccer) with fierce regional competitiveness that leads to highly emotional matches between rivals. The Colombia Football Federation (Federación Colombiana de Fútbol) is the national game's governing body, dating back to 1924. It has been affiliated to FIFA since 1936 and is a member of CONMEBOL (Confederación Sudamericana de Fútbol). Professional football in Colombia was established in 1948 by DIMAYOR, now the Asociación de Clubes del Fútbol Profesional Colombiano. Today football is a national pastime with high levels of support from fans on a local and national level. Known as Los Cafeteros, Colombia's home-grown football talent includes the skilful past heroes Willington Ortiz and René Higuita, who shone in the 1970s and 80s. Other great idols include Jorge Bermúdez, Iván Valenciano, Freddy Rincón and the wild-haired Carlos Alberto Valderrama Palacío. More contemporary figures include Radamel 'El Tigre' Falcao in 2015 plying his trade at Manchester United, Juan Cuadrado at Chelsea and James (pronounced Hamez) Rodriguez at Real Madrid. Futbolred.com, Colombia's dedicated soccer website, attracts over 17 million visits per month – 75% from home-based fans and the balance from the rest of Latin America and the wider world. It is even possible for Colombian soccer fans who live for their team to wear club colours in the afterlife too. Medellín funeral director San Vicente makes caskets for soccer-crazed fans in green for Atletico Nacional and red for Independiente Medellín. Club emblems are also embroidered on the inside lining of the casket lid – all for around 150,000COP.

Colombia's greatest international achievements include winning the America Cup of 2001 (which it hosted) and the Central America Cup (1946 and 1970), second place in the America championship in 1975, winning the South American Youth Championship in 1987 and the South American Under-17 in 1993 – as well as qualifying for the World Cup in 1962, 1990, 1994 and 1998. However, Colombia's cavalier approach cost them dearly in their early qualifying games for Germany 2006. In the same year, Colombia joined (but lost) the race to host the World Cup in 2014, challenging CONMEBOL's nomination of Brazil as the sole applicant from South America. Colombia was awarded the 1986 event but withdrew for financial and safety reasons. Mexico stepped in as a replacement host.

Colombia's national squad has also been involved in some of the greatest personal tragedies to hit football in recent years. In 1994, defender Andrés Escobar was murdered on his return to Colombia after scoring an own goal in a World Cup against the US. In 2003, spectators watched in horror as Cameroon midfielder

Marc-Vivien Foé died on the pitch from a heart condition playing against Colombia in a Confederations Cup semi-final in France. In 2004, striker Albeiro Usuriaga (nicknamed 'Palomo') was gunned down in a nightclub in Cali. In 2006, Elson Becerra was also shot and killed in his home town of Cartagena. Becerra was hailed a hero for his attempts to revive Marc-Vivien Foé after his collapse, and played in four games in qualifiers for the 2006 World Cup.

In 2011, Colombian football made worldwide headlines when Deportivo Pereira's Panamanian defender Luis Moreno kicked an owl off the pitch, prompting the crowd chant 'murderer' at the player. Moreno later apologised, saying: 'I apologise to the fans, it wasn't my intention.' He claimed to have mistaken the massive bird with feathers, eyes and a beak for a football – an excuse that the Colombian league

COLOMBIA'S FASTEST GUY

He was so little when he started racing that he learned to drive by looking through the hole in the steering wheel.

Juan Pablo Montoya's father, Pablo, 2004

When Juan Pablo Montoya Roldán was born in Bogotá in September 1975, his father had a feeling he'd be a star. After mortgaging the family home, Pablo helped his five-year-old son begin karting and to win both local and national titles in the Children's Kart Championship and Kart Komet Division. But money was often a struggle and Montoya couldn't even afford to travel by public transport, so he used roller blades to go from one place to another. He secured a scholarship at the famous Skip Barber School in the US before moving to Britain to race in the Formula Vauxhall series with Paul Stewart Racing. He then made a move to the Copa Formula Renault Series in Colombia, capturing five poles and four wins in eight races. He spent a year in F3, notching two wins, one pole position and five fastest laps, before moving on to the International F3000 series – a long-awaited break that came in 1997.

Landing a drive with the crack Super Nova outfit for 1998, he duly took the title with four wins and seven pole positions. He tested for Williams's F1 squad and was then summoned to participate in his first Formula One test before getting signed to a multi-year testing contract in 1998. In addition to his testing duties, Montoya competed again in the Formula 3000 series and grabbed the FIA International Formula 3000 Championship. The young Colombian would soon find himself heading to the United States in 1999 as part of a driver swap between Williams and Ganassi. The exchange resulted in Montoya taking over for two-time CART Champion Alex Zanardi at Ganassi's Indianapolis-based open-wheel shop, while Zanardi returned to Formula One.

Immediately, Montoya made his presence known in the CART Series, and all across the United States. At the age of 24, the rookie driver proceeded to set several series records en route to claiming his first and Ganassi's fourth consecutive CART Championship. Altogether, he collected more wins, pole positions, laps led and earnings than any other driver during the 1999 CART season. In 2000, as the defending series champion, Montoya added three additional wins to his CART CV. In addition to the regular CART season, Ganassi decided to enter his teams in the Indy Racing League's Indianapolis 500 for the first time since 1995. After just missing the pole and starting second on the grid, Montoya set a rookie record by leading 167 out of 200 laps on his way to an Indy 500 victory. That same weekend, Williams announced Montoya had signed a two-year deal to drive for them in the Formula One Series.

weren't buying. Describing it as a 'painful, horrible act of intolerance' football officials instructed judicial authorities to press charges after the owl – the Atletico Juniors' mascot – died later of respiratory failure. Moreno was suspended for two matches and fined US$560 and punished by his club. He has since been the target of insults and newspaper editorials condemning his behaviour and was forced to go into hiding following death threats.

The Colombian national team appears to have turned the corner and have become a side with enough quality and heart to beat any team on their day. The Cafeteros' showing in the 2014 World Cup in Brazil won over many impartial supporters, not only for their joyful interpretation of the beautiful game but also for the *joie de vivre* shown in their 'Ras Tas Tas' celebratory dance. Other teams attempted to imitate

Montoya made his debut with BMW Williams in the premiere open-wheel series at the Australian Grand Prix in 2001, and then captured his first F1 victory at the Italian Grand Prix at Monza. The rookie racer also tallied three pole positions and four podium finishes during his freshman season to finish sixth in the Drivers' Championship standings. In 2002, Montoya fared even better, even though Ferrari dominated the season. He finished third, turning the fastest qualifying laps in seven out of the 17 races and earning four runner-up finishes. During this season he lit up the track at Monza by posting a record-fast qualifying lap with an average speed of 259.84km/h. In 2003, Montoya finished third in the Drivers' Championship with 82 points, and captured two victories. He also had six additional podium finishes – four second and two third places. He announced his departure from BMW Williams at the end of the 2004 season to move over to the McLaren Mercedes team – but not before finishing fifth in the 2004 F1 Drivers' Championship, taking the chequered flag in Brazil.

Juan Pablo Montoya wasted no time making his presence known in the NASCAR world after transitioning from open-wheel cars to the 2007 NASCAR Sprint Cup Series. Not only did he become the first Latino to win in NASCAR's premier Series and capture the 2007 Sprint Cup Rookie of the Year title, but he earned the respect of his team, his competitors and fans as well, adding his name to an elite list of drivers who have achieved top-level racing success across the Sprint Cup Series, IndyCar Series, Grand-Am Prototype cars, stock cars and Formula One. The only other driver to accomplish such a feat is Mario Andretti. Montoya is also the only driver to have competed in all three major events at Indianapolis: the Indianapolis 500, the US Grand Prix, and the Brickyard 400.

Today, Juan Pablo Montoya continues to chalk up racing success in the Sprint Cup Series. With his wife Connie he also runs the charitable foundation, 'Formula Smiles' for underprivileged children with ambition. The self-confessed Twitter fiend was honoured for his charitable works in 2010 by MTV Latin America in conjunction with the Inter-American Development Bank when he was presented with a 'Chiuku' award as an MTV Agent of Change. 'Chiuku' is a fictional creature, originally from the Amazon, with a special power conjured by the mystical Chiukotek tribe that enables the ability to speak the universal language of music and communicate with humans. Chiuku seeks to reach the most important and influential people, who in turn will spread his message all over the world. Montoya received his award 'on behalf of all Colombian ambassadors'. For more information visit www.formulasmiles.com.

Background Information CULTURE

1

this but not one came close to the Colombian style. High points included James Rodriguez's wonder strike against Uruguay, winning him the FIFA Puskas prize for the best goal of 2014. Unfortunately Colombia fell to Brazil in an ill-tempered match that saw Brazilian star Neymar injured.

Cycling Colombia has a strong cycling tradition with up-and-coming cyclists benefiting from some of the world's most inhospitable mountain ranges as their personal training ground. Fierce peaks in the area surrounding Armenia and the Andean cordilleras have both helped create some of the greatest climbing cyclists in the world. Many have competed internationally in events such as the Tour de France.

Colombia has several hundred thousand ardent cyclists and the areas that surround cities like Bogotá, Cali and Medellín are deluged with two-wheelers each Sunday when enthusiasts take to the hills. In 2006, three Colombians left Bogotá to cycle to Ushuaia in Argentina, in a bid to support the Colombian Campaign to Ban Landmines and to draw international attention to their country's extensive landmine problem. Colombia's capital also boasts 300km of cycle paths, known as the Ciclovia. This cycle-friendly initiative costs US$1.5 million a year to run, but is part-funded by Colombia's many cycle-mad corporate sponsors. The annual Tour of Colombia takes place in March and April; El Vuelta de Colombia covers 2,000km in 12 days.

Yet Colombia's professional cycling scene is not without controversy. In 2006, the Colombian Cycling Federation (Federación Colombiana de Ciclismo) (⊠ *(1) 211 6659;* e *contacto@ciclismodecolombia.com; www.ciclismodecolombia.com*) cleared Santiago Botero of doping charges, following investigations that forced him to withdraw from the Tour de France. Among those arrested included Dr Eufamiano Fuentes, who was Botero's team doctor when the Colombian rode with the Kelme team during 1996–2002. In the 2004 Athens Olympics, Colombian cyclist María Luisa Calle was stripped of her bronze medal after testing positive for the banned substance Heptaminol. She was third in the women's points race in the velodrome, giving Colombia its first medal of any colour in the short history of women's Olympic track cycling.

In 2007, the 39-year-old Colombian cyclist Hernán Buenahora defied his critics to win an overall victory in the 42nd Vuelta al Táchira in Venezuela. The evergreen Colombian (nicknamed *escarabajo* or cockroach) triumphed after 14 stages over a 15-day period. He joins a long list of illustrious winners of the race inaugurated in 1966. It was the first Colombian victory in the race since Hernán Muñoz in 2003 with Buenahora the 17th Colombian to claim the crown. Like many Colombians, he is a natural climber whose hard graft in the mountains of his homeland paid dividends when he turned professional in 1990. In 1995, he put on a scintillating display in the Tour de France, gaining a very respectable tenth place. Yet for most Colombians, the 1985 Tour de France is an emblematic moment, for this is when working-class hero Luis 'Lucho' Herrera won a mountain stage after crashing and opening a deep gash on his temple. In a true display of grit, Herrera got back into the saddle and pounded on up the mountain, even as a medic tried to stem the bleeding from a car speeding alongside. Television images of a blood-soaked Herrera crossing the finish line provoked considerable displays of patriotism within Colombia. *El Tiempo* newspaper declared: 'We came, we suffered, we won.'

For further information, Matt Rendel's excellent book *Kings of the Mountains: How Colombia's Cycling Heroes Changed Their Nation's History* is recommended. (See also page 493.)

In 2010, Colombian female cycling pro Angela Parra won La Ruta de los Conquistadores in Costa Rica – one of the region's toughest cycling challenges. In

December of the same year, the city of Cali staged the UCI World Cup Track Cycling championship for the tenth time at the showpiece Alcides Nieto Patino velodrome.

Colombian cycling seems set for a great future if only looking at Nairo Quintana's second place in the 2014 Tour de France and Rigoberto Uran's silver medal in the 2012 London Olympics. And it doesn't end there as Colombia also possesses the current No 1 Women's BMX competitor in Mariana Pajon who won gold at the London Olympics.

Rugby An international sevens tournament is held every November in Bogotá, following the introduction of rugby to Colombia in 1986. Initially played solely by groups of European expats, the game started to generate wider interest in the early 1990s, attracting local participation in 1992. Today, there are over 25 clubs in six Colombian cities, the two main ones being Bogotá and Medellín. Colombia's home-grown players are showing lots of raw potential. However, as a minority sport rugby suffers from a lack of funds and proper organisation, despite being enjoyed by a growing number of people keen to reach the top of their top game. For further information contact the National Union of Colombian Rugby (*www.fecorugby.co*).

Golf Colombia is home to a growing number of golf courses, especially in and around the major cities and Caribbean coast. The popularity of golf has been helped by the success of golfers such as Camilo Villegas, who finished second in the FBR Open behind John Holmes from the United States in 2006. Villegas hails from Antioquia and achieved the best performance ever by a native Colombian golfer in the PGA Tour. The Colombian Golf Federation (Federación Colombiana de Golf) (*Carrera 7a, No 72–64 int 26, Santa Fé de Bogotá;* \ *(1) 310 7664;* e *fedegolf@ federacioncolombianadegolf.com; www.federacioncolombianadegolf.com*) stages a packed year-round calendar of events across the country, including those in the Coffee Zone. Cristóbal von Rothkirch's first-class book *Campos de golf en Colombia* (Villegas Editores, 2005) takes a look at more than 50 of the nation's finest golfing establishments and includes blueprints, maps of the greens and signature holes. In 2010, Bogotá played host to the PGA Open, attracting a field of 135 top golfing pros from the US, Europe and Latin America.

2

Practical Information

WHEN TO VISIT

Like many countries, Colombia is experiencing a blurring of the seasons and unpredictable and atypical weather patterns have flummoxed meteorologists in recent years. However, generally speaking, Colombia's *verano* (summer) is from December to March. These months and those from mid-June to mid-August tend to be the best times to visit, with the exception of the northern plains where the wet season continues. Some 90% of Colombia's territory is below 915m, tropical and warm with temperatures averaging around 25°C. The Caribbean coast and the Amazon are extremely humid and rain is sporadic and unpredictable even in the dry season. As you ascend Colombia's Andes the temperature will drop around 6% per 1,000m. And, at an altitude of 1,980m, you'll find yourself amongst glaciers, where temperatures can be as low as –17°C.

This range of climate and scenery is one of Colombia's best assets and the country offers visitors the full spectrum of travel opportunities. Adventurous travellers can hop between the snow-capped peaks of the Colombian Andes and the Caribbean's tropical turquoise waters and golden sands. Those looking for a more relaxed break can simply pick their preferred holiday – mountain hike, Caribbean beach, city jaunt or jungle trek are just some of the many, many choices available.

High season in Colombia can be busy with hordes of domestic vacationers. Visit during the celebratory months of Carnaval (in Barranquilla, February/March), Semana Santa (Holy Week, March/April) or Navidad (Christmas) and plans should be made well in advance with hotels and transport booked. In addition, check for regional celebrations, when towns, villages and even roads close entirely to enable locals to enjoy the fiesta. Unless you dislike big or lively crowds, these regional and national festivals are a great way to become immersed in Colombia's different cultures. Witness colourful rituals, dancing and the relaxed side of local life, as businesses close for the holiday and people revel in a party atmosphere that can last several days – at least.

HIGHLIGHTS

RAFT THE FAST-FLOWING RAPIDS ON THE RÍO FONCE Colombia's adventure sports Mecca, San Gil, is home to kayaking, climbing, rappelling, paragliding and pot-holing on a dramatic mountainous terrain dotted with rocky, gushing streams. Less radical pursuits include horseriding and fishing with craggy ravines, canyons and gorges crossed by a riddle of fine hiking trails. (See also pages 178–80.)

HEAD TO THE UNESCO SEAFLOWER BIOSPHERE RESERVE Located in the reggae-drenched San Andrés Archipelago; dive amidst sunken galleons home to 57 species of coral, 24 species of sponge and over 270 fish species. Octopus, dolphin, nurse shark and spotted eagle ray are commonly sighted in warm, tropical waters frequented by migrating whales. (See also pages 225–30.)

CYCLE, ROLLERBLADE OR STROLL Bogotá has 121km car-free roads and 300km *ciclovías* (cycle paths) open on Sundays and public holidays, or you can stroll through over 4,500 leafy public parks in South America's third-highest capital city, a dizzying 2,630m above sea level and edged by rivers and mountain peaks. (See also page 128.)

JOURNEY ALONG THE VINE-TANGLED INKY-GREEN DEPTHS OF THE AMAZON RIVER It's home to at least 7,500 species of butterfly, 1,900 birds, 80,000 insect species, almost 2,000 species of reptile and amphibian, and 3,200 species of fish – a staggering 10% of all species found on the planet. The watershed is also home to several hundred indigenous tribes who speak more than 100 languages and dialects, with thick swathes of impenetrable jungle covering almost one-third of the Colombian territory.

EXPLORE THE ROLLING SAVANNAHS OF LOS LLANOS (THE PLAINS) ON HORSEBACK Ride with cattle-roping cowboys across undulating prairies dotted with ranches and corrals. Learn lassoing skills from the gaucho-like Llaneros (plainspeople) in a hard-working region rich in provincial culture that is home to folklore, legends and heartfelt *música llanera* – lilting cowboy music played with a *cuatro* guitar or harp.

CLIMB THE SNOW-CAPPED NEVADO DEL RUIZ The 5,400m peak is one of five permanently white-tipped volcanoes in Los Nevados National Park (*www.parquesnacionales.gov.co*). Guided treks are available from Manizales.

TRY OUT SOME NEW MOVES IN CALI Colombia's sultry salsa capital (*www.cali.gov.co*) is a haven of dirty dancing.

STAY ON A COFFEE FARM Over 300 *haciendas* offer lodging to tourists and can arrange walks through the coffee fields as well as horseriding, fishing, mountain biking and trips to local villages.

STEP BACK IN TIME IN COLONIAL COLOMBIA While the jewel in the crown is undeniably Cartagena you could spend weeks exploring the ornate smaller offerings available here including, but not exclusive to, Villa de Leyva, San Gil, Barichara, Playa de Belen, Mompóx, Santa Fé de Antioquia and Popayán to name just a few.

TOUR OPERATORS

UK

Black Tomato ☎0207 426 9888, +1 877 815 149 (US); www.blacktomato.co.uk. Upmarket company with a top-notch reputation for super-smooth, fascinating itineraries in Bogotá, Caribbean Coast & major cities. Offers tailored schedules.

GAP Adventures Matrix Studios, 91 Peterborough Rd, Fulham, London SW6 3BU; ☎0870 999 0144; www.gadventures.com.

Boundary-pushing adventure travel firm with a far-reaching world itinerary.

Journey Latin America 401 King St, London, W6 9NJ; ☎ 020 3432 1525; www.journeylatinamerica.co.uk. Slick, smooth outfit with an impressive portfolio of Latin American itineraries.

Last Frontiers The Mill, Quainton Rd, Waddesdon, Bucks HP18 0LP; ☎01296 653000;

www.lastfrontiers.com. Specialists in tailor-made travel to South & Central America. For sample itineraries check out the website.

Rainbow Tours Layden House, 76–78 Turnmill St, London EC1M 5QU; 020 7666 1272; e info@rainbowtours.co.uk; www.rainbowtours.co.uk. Pioneers of responsible travel, Rainbow Tours specialise in tailor-made & small-group tours to Africa, Madagascar & Latin America. Their well-travelled team can arrange custom-made trips for couples, families & groups. See ad, 2nd colour section.

Tucan Travel 316 Uxbridge Rd, Acton, London W3 9QP; 020 8896 1600; www.tucantravel.com. Specialist adventure tour operator with hundreds of affordable worldwide destinations, including South & Central America (Winner of the Small Tour Operator of the Year 2009).

Worldgate Travel 13 Hogarth Pl, Earls Court, London SW5 0QT; 020 7927 7566; e enquiries@worldgatetravelservices.co.uk; www.worldgatetravelservices.co.uk. Try this firm for flights as it has good deals from 150 airlines together with hotels, car hire & tours all over the world, including Latin America.

EUROPE

Aternum Viaggi Vía Mazzini, 162/164 65122 Pescara, Italy; +39 085 4210557; e info@aternum.com; www.aternum.com

Tagus Madrid C/Buen Suceso, 14 28008 Madrid, Spain; +34 91 547 1044; e tagus-madrid@tagusviajes.com; www.tagusviajes.com

Voyages Wasteels 5 Rue de la Banque, 75002 Paris, France; +33 1 42 61 69 87; www.wasteels.fr

US

GAP Adventures 225 Franklin St, 26th Floor, Boston, MA 02110; +1 800 676 4941; www.gadventures.com

Latour 233 Park Av South, New York, NY 10003; +1 800 243 7460; www.isram.com

Miller South America 3003 Van Ness St NW Ste S-823, Washington, DC 20008; +1 202 250 6004; www.miller.travel

CANADA

GAP Adventures 19 Charlotte St, Toronto, Ontario M5V 2H5; +1 800 708 7761 (North America), +1 416 260 0999 (outside North America); www.gadventures.com

AUSTRALIA

Adventure Associates Level 7, 12–14 O'Connell St, Sydney, NSW 2000; +61 2 8916 3000; www.adventureassociates.com

BFirst Travel Suite 203, 74 Pitt St, Sydney, NSW 2000; +61 2 9232 0048; www.bfirsttravel.com

GAP Adventures +61 1300 85 33 25; www.gadventures.com

South America Tourism Level 1, 178 Collins St, Melbourne, 3000, Victoria; +61 3 9654 7977; www.southamericatourism.com

Tucan Travel 217 Alison Rd, Randwick, NSW 2031; +61 2 9326 6633; www.tucantravel.com

NEW ZEALAND

GAP Adventures +1 416 260 0999; www.gadventures.com

COLOMBIA

Agroecotur Los Abedules 21, Circasia, Quindío; (1) 315 585 7937/310 421 5250; e info@agroecotur.org; www.agroecotur.org. This Bogotá-based network of ecotourism specialists offers made-to-measure tours in the Amazon, Eastern Plains (Orinoco region), the Andes & the Caribbean coast, includes homestay accommodation with local farming families, lodging on nature reserves & programmes relating to biodiversity conservation.

Aventure Colombia Av Jiménez No 4–49, Bogotá; 510 4856; e info@aventurecolombia.com; www.aventurecolombia.com. This French-run outfit has an exemplary record in service & made-to-measure tours for groups & couples. They excel in trips to the Guajira & the Coffee Zone and have offices in Bogotá, Cartagena & Santa Marta. See ad, page 155.

Awake.travel m 322 365 5135; e info@awake.travel; http://awake.travel. Offering a wide variety of outward-bound-style excursions from 1 day to multi day, Awake Travel is run by a young & enthusiastic group of Colombians keen on making a difference in their country. Trips to Cano Cristales, Casanare & Tuparro are amongst the favourites but they also do multi-day hikes to El Cocuy & a 5-day kayaking trip along the Magdalena River. See ad, 2nd colour section.

Beyond Bogotá m 321 272 3528; e bogotaandbeyond@gmail.com; www.bogotaandbeyond.com. Aiming to change the common perception of Colombia by organising unique tours & events that encourage interaction between travellers & locals, founder Thomas

Dutton believes in a community-based approach to tourism, & has created a network of locally run tours all around the country. Currently they offer day trips to Chicaque, La Chorrera, Chingaza Park & even a scavenger hunt during the Sun Ciclovia.

Birding Tours Colombia m 315 585 7937/310 421 5250; e daniel@birdingtourscolombia.com; www.birdingtourscolombia.com. This Colombia-based company organises birding tours that concentrate on the endemics & speciality birds found in the Central & western Andes, around Bogotá, the Madgalena & Cauca valleys, the Santa Marta Mountains & the dry forests of La Guajira.

Bluefields Carrera 13, No 98–61, Bogotá; (1) 635 1521; www.blue-fields.org. One of Colombia's most impressive tour operators, offering new dimensions to standard options as well as tailored alternatives off the beaten track. Established in 1997, the company has 1st-class service supported by state-of-the-art equipment. All tour guides have a certificate in first aid, as well as advanced courses in management of emergencies in wild areas. They cover all areas of Colombia & is one of the only outfits to include Los Llanos & the Pacific coast as well as the Amazon, the Guajira & the Caribbean.

5Bogota m 313 278 5898; www.5Bogota.com. A new & dynamic group of young Bogotanos keen on promoting their city through the 5 senses: highlights include learning how to barter in a traditional market, an *empanada*-cooking course & a bike tour of the city's vibrant graffiti scene with a graffiti artist. Professional & fun, these tours are aimed at those people seeking out something more authentic than regular offerings.

Colombia 57 6 886 8050; m 311 372 6594; info@colombia57.com; www.colombia57.com. Manizales-based operator founded in 2003 by Brits Simon Locke, Russell Coleman & Brendan Rayment, who have both travelled extensively throughout Latin America & come highly recommended. They offer tailor-made holidays to Colombia.

Colombia Birdwatch www.colombiabirdwatch. com. Custom & fixed-date tours in friendly, exciting & small groups. Based in Cali.

Colombia Eco Travel m 311 319 3195; e tours@ colombiaecotravel.com; www.colombiaecotravel.

com. Based in the coffee region this small family-run outfit created by Daniel Buitron sets high standards & require that all of their providers make efforts to be environmentally aware. Excellent day trips & multi-day expeditions all around Colombia are offered.

Colombia Paragliding m 312 432 6266/301 352 8839; e richifly@colombiaparagliding.com; www. colombiaparagliding.com. Runs 10-day tours for paragliding enthusiasts all over Colombia as well as a range of shorter itineraries & tailored tours.

De Una Colombia Tours Carrera 24, No 39b–25, La Soledad 501, Bogotá; (1) 368 1915/805 3733; e info@deunacolombia. com; www.deunacolombia.com. Run by Erik & Thomas, 2 Dutchmen who emigrated to Colombia several years ago after falling in love with the country, De Una combines adventure with respect for both the local environment & culture. De Una promotes local tourism & ecotourism. See ad, page 62.

Ecoguías Carrera 7, No 57–39, Oficina 501, Bogotá; (1) 347 5736/212 1423; e info@ecoguias. com; www.ecoguias.com (English/Spanish/ German). This Anglo-Colombian tour company has been running overland transport services in Colombia for almost 10 years with the combined experience of a biologist & a travel expert.

Educamos Viajando Carrera 23, No 124–87, Bogotá; (1) 620 5359; e tiquetes@eduvi.com; www.eduvi.com. Educational travel with lots of fun for family groups Colombia-wide with over 30 years of experience.

New Frontiers Adventures Calle 27, No 1C–74, Santa Marta; (1) 318 736 1565; e info@newfrontiersadventures.com; www. newfrontiersadventures.com. Company offering tours throughout Colombia, led by experienced bilingual guides.

Sal Si Puedes Carrera 7, No 17–01, Oficina 639, Bogotá; www.salsipuedes.org (Spanish). Over 30 years of experience in offering nature-based travel, treks & tours makes this a popular choice with wildlife-lovers, walkers & conservationists.

Viajes Celtour Av 15, No 106–50, Mz 01, Bogotá; (1) 612 7020; www.celtour.net. Local & international tour options.

RED TAPE

Citizens from most western European countries (including the UK), Australia, New Zealand, the USA and Canada only need a valid passport to enter Colombia.

A 30-, 60- or 90-day tourist visa will be issued on entry without the need to apply for any other visa in advance. Those planning to stay for up to 90 days should notify immigration officials as they tend to issue 30 or 60 days as standard. Once in the country, extended stays of over 90 days should be arranged by visiting the Office of Immigration Affairs (*Calle 100, No 11–27*) in Bogotá to submit an application. Those planning to work or study in Colombia will need to apply for the relevant visa from the Colombian consulate in their home country before they leave. Citizens from restricted countries need to apply for a tourist visa in the Colombian consulate in their country of origin.

Whether arriving by plane or land, visitors must hold a return or onward ticket to prove an intention to leave the country. Furthermore, the ticket out of the country should be dated within 90 days to avoid difficulties at immigration. It is also entirely possible that proof may be required to show sufficient funds exist to cover your stay. Passport and visa requirements can change without much notice, so check with the Colombian embassy in advance of your trip.

Don't forget to allow for the airport tax on departure, which is currently 71,000COP for a 90-day stay but less for a 60-day stay. Make sure your passport is stamped on both arrival and exit, whether you enter by air, land or sea, or you may be liable to a fine. Individuals entering or leaving Colombia are only entitled to carry up to US$10,000 in cash. Anything in excess of this may be confiscated. Recently, a British national carrying US$14,000 had US$4,000 confiscated by the authorities at the airport, despite his argument that the money belonged to both him and his wife, who was travelling with him.

Those entering by sea must report to the port's local immigration office for a passport entry stamp within one day of arrival.

EMBASSIES
Embassies in Colombia

🄴 **Australia** Oficina del Hotel Radisson, Calle 113, No 7–65, suite 908 , Bogotá; ☎ (1) 657 8700

🄴 **Canada** Carrera 7, No 115–33, Piso 14, Bogotá; ☎(1) 657 9800

🄴 **France** Carrera 11, No 93–12, Bogotá; ☎(1) 638 1400

🄴 **Germany** Edificio Torre Empresarial Pacífic, PH Calle 110, No 9–25, Piso 11, Bogotá; ☎ (1) 423 2600; e info@bogota.diplo.de; www.bogota.diplo.de

🄴 **Israel** Calle 35, No 7–25, Piso 14, Bogotá; ☎(1) 327 7500

🄴 **Italy** Calle 93B, 9–92, Bogotá; ☎(1) 218 6680; e ambbogo.mail@esteri.it; www.ambbogota.esteri.it

🄴 **Netherlands** Carrera 13, No 93–40, Piso 5, Bogotá; ☎(1) 638 4200

🄴 **Panama** Bogotá: Calle 92, No 7–70; Bogotá; ☎(1) 257 4452; Cali: Av 4a Oeste No 5–97, Oficina 316 Cali; ☎(2) 486 1116; Medellín: Carrera 43A, No 7–50, Oficina 1607, Medellín; ☎(4) 268 1358

🄴 **Spain** Calle 94A, No 11a–70, Bogotá; ☎(1) 593 037; www.exteriores.gob.es

🄴 **Sweden** Calle 72, Bis No 5–83, Piso 9, Edificio Av Chile, Bogotá; ☎(1) 325 6100; e marie.andersson.de.frutos@foreign.ministry.se; www.swedenabroad.com

🄴 **Switzerland** Carrera 9, No 74–08, Oficina 1101, Bogotá; ☎(1) 349 7230

🄴 **UK** Bogotá: Carrera 9, No 76–49, Pisos 8 & 9; PBX; ☎ (1) 326 8300; e EmbajadaBritanica.Bogota@fco.gov.uk; www.ukincolombia.fco.gov.uk; Cali: Calle 22, Norte No 6–42; ☎(2) 661 7745/1031;

🄴 **US** Calle 22D, Bis No 47–51, Bogotá; ☎(1) 275 2000; Consular section; ☎(1) 315 1566; USAID ☎(1) 423 6880; http://spanish.bogota.usembassy.gov/; Consular agency in Barranquilla: Calle 77B, No 57–141, Piso 5, Centro Empresarial Las Américas, Barranquilla, Atlántico; ☎(5) 353 2001

🄴 **Venezuela** Carrera 11, No 87–51, Piso 5, Bogotá; ☎(1) 644 5555 ; Calle 32B, No 69–59, Medellín; ☎(4) 351 1614

BY AIR Colombia's major international airports are El Dorado (*www.eldorado. aero*) in Bogotá (BOG), Alfonso Bonilla Aragón, Cali (CLO), José María Codova, Medellín (MDE), and Rafael Nuñez, Cartagena (CTG). Other popular international airports include Barranquilla (BAQ) and Bucaramanga (BGA). National airline **Avianca** (*www.avianca.com*) serves all international airports from most Latin American destinations as well as some cities in North America, London and Spain. The Avianca VIP lounge at El Dorado International Airport won the 'Priority Pass Airport Lounge of the Year' award in 2006.

Air France (*www.airfrance.com*) operates from most western European destinations with stopovers on some routes. **Iberia** (*www.iberia.com*) flies from Madrid to all the above airports, via Bogotá. **American Airlines** (*www.aa.com*), **Northwest** (*www.nwa.com*), **Continental** (*www.continentalairlines.com*) and **Delta** (*www.delta.com*) are the major airlines between the US and most of Colombia's international airports. **Copa** (*www.copaair.com*) also provides services to New York, Miami and Orlando from Barranquilla, Bogotá and Cali. **Lufthansa** (*www. lufthansa.com*) has direct flights from Frankfurt, **KLM** (*www.klm.com*) from Amsterdam. **TAP** (*www.tap.com*) are in discussions about a flight from Lisbon. **Jet Blue** (*www.jetblue.com*) has affordable flights to Bogotá from Orlando and Fort Lauderdale and **Spirit Airlines** (*www.spirit.com*) reaches Armenia, Bogotá, Cartagena and Medellín from Fort Lauderdale. From Bogotá, **LAN Airlines** (*www.lan.com*) connects to Miami, Quito, Ecuador and other South American destinations via stopovers. **LACSA** (*www.avianca.com*) and **TACA** (*www.taca.com*) both connect between Bogotá and Latin America and some US destinations. Flying time is around 10½ hours from Madrid, 12 from Paris and 13 from London (exc stopover). Flying from New York takes 4½ hours and from Los Angeles 8 hours.

In December 2007, American Airlines increased its flights to Colombia with daily flights from Miami to Barranquilla – an excellent option for travellers heading to Cartagena. In addition AA will increase its flights to Medellín, Bogotá and Cali on a daily schedule. At present the following international connections apply: Aruba (from Bogotá, Medellín and Barranquilla), Alicante (from Bogotá), Barcelona (from Bogotá), Buenos Aires (from Bogotá), Caracas (from Bogotá), Curaçao (from Bogotá), Fort Lauderdale (from Bogotá), Guayaquil (from Bogotá), Lima (from Bogotá), Los Angeles (from Bogotá), Madrid (from Bogotá and Cali), Mexico City (from Bogotá), Miami (from Bogotá, Medellín, Cali, Barranquilla, Cartagena and Pereira), New York (JFK) (from Bogotá, Medellín, Cali, Barranquilla and Pereira), Panama City (from Bogotá), Punta Caña (from Bogotá), Quito (from Bogotá), Rio de Janeiro (from Bogotá via São Paulo), Santiago (from Bogotá), São Paulo (from Bogotá), Valencia (Venezuela) (from Bogotá).

OVERLAND Arrival overland from Panama can be hazardous and anyone thinking of attempting it should first contact the Foreign and Commonwealth Office (*www. fco.gov.uk*) for advice. There is no road between the countries; instead you'll have to skirt around the edges of the vast Darién rainforest – known as the Darién Gap – by boat (between Puerto Obaldía in Panama and Sapzurro in Colombia) and bus along the Caribbean coast. Although at the time of writing this area is safer than it was, a risk remains from guerrilla activity. In January 2006, two Spanish nationals were kidnapped in the Darién region, close to the Colombian–Panamanian border.

Immigration officers staff the borders of Ecuador and Venezuela. At Ipiales, the Colombian border town that crosses to Tulcán in **Ecuador**, the office is open between

06.00 and 17.00 daily. There is no charge for leaving (or entering) the country. In February 2010, Ipiales and Tulcán signed an agreement that strengthened their cross-border working partnership with a pledge to 'iron out' a lot of the frustrating delays and unexplained hold-ups. Both countries had accused the other of failing to properly control the border region in the past. Today, an increase in problems relating to illegal armed groups, drug smugglers and well-organised contraband operators makes it essential for all cross-border travellers to be vigilant, alert and patient. The Colombian and Ecuadorian immigration offices sit either side of the border, which is a road bridge over the Río Carchi. First, present your passport to the immigration office of the country you're leaving (being sure to collect your exit stamp). Then, walk across the bridge to the immigration office of the country you're entering (to collect your entry stamp). You *must* stop at both booths – in and out. Failure to do so may result in a fine. Should the immigration office on the border be closed, seek assistance at the next nearest office of the Migración Colombia. Buses run from Ipiales on the border from the corner of Calle 14 and Carrera 10.

Travellers entering from or departing to **Venezuela** should cross at Cúcuta and not Arauca or Riohacha/Maicao, according to British Foreign Office advice. However, the Venezuelan crossing at Cúcuta has been 'unpredictable' in the past due to tension between the Colombian government and Nicolas Maduro, the President of Venezuela. Since the swearing in of new Colombian president Juan Manuel Santos, the situation has eased greatly thanks to some diplomatic schmoozing. However, anyone considering a border crossing between Colombia and Venezuela should keep an eye on the headlines just in case there is a random political spat. In the past, the border has been closed instantly without warning. Travellers should also be warned that the Venezuelan crossing is much used by guerrillas, paramilitary groups and coca cultivators and can be volatile and unsafe as a result.

The British Foreign and Commonwealth Office advice is not to travel in this area – but many travellers do. A tourist visa (US$30) can be purchased from the Venezuelan consulate in Cúcuta (*Av 0 & Calle 8, 713 983/781 034; 08.00–noon & 13.00–16.00 Mon–Fri*). Travellers will need a valid passport, recent photograph, sufficient funds to cover the trip, and a return or onward ticket. National buses leave regularly to and from the border.

BY SEA Most tourists entering by sea do so on cruise lines (pages 86–8), where all necessary entrance formalities are taken care of by cruise staff. Several shipping companies dock on the Caribbean coast and it is possible to take a boat tour from both Colón and Kuna Yala (San Blas) in Panama to Colombia's Cartagena. Those that do arrive in Cartagena by boat must visit the immigration office on the day of arrival for a Colombian entry stamp in their passport – fail to do so and you will be illegal in the country after 24 hours.

Before travelling to Colombia it is worth checking all pre-existing travel insurances to ensure they adequately cover your trip. White-water rafting in the Coffee Zone, jet skiing in San Andrés and trekking through the wilds of the Amazon may all be activities that are exempt from a standard policy. There may also be some stipulations in regards to the length of stay. **IAMAT** is a good source of advice on insurance topics and should also be able to provide a list of recommended doctors in Colombia (page 80). Those planning to scuba dive should consider the specialist insurance plan offered by the **Divers Alert Network** (DAN) (*Peter B Bennett Center, 6 West Colony Pl, Durham, NC 27705, USA;* \ *+1 800 443 2671;* e *dan@diversnetwork. org; www.diversalertnetwork.org*). This non-profit organisation was founded in 1990 and now has 200,000 members, providing medical R&D services and health and safety support to recreational scuba divers in association with Duke University Medical Center. The organisation offers two plans that cover eventualities from emergency air evacuation to hyperbaric chamber treatment, plus a wide range of equipment and medical safety aspects.

HEALTH *with Dr Felicity Nicholson*

Healthcare in Colombia is reasonably good, especially in cities where getting modern medical treatment fairly fast poses little problem. In rural areas, however, don't rely on finding any medical care. Arrive prepared with any medicines that might be needed and a first-aid kit, and plan for unforeseen emergencies.

Health centres in most towns should be able to treat minor ailments and costs are usually very low. However, treatment is paid for at the time it is administered so it is important to have access to cash. Ask for a receipt if you intend to claim on your health insurance and be prepared to pay upfront if an ambulance is required. Medical staff in towns or rural areas may not speak English, so it may pay to look up some useful Spanish phrases beforehand, such as the names of allergies to medicines or words about pregnancy, etc. Take out health insurance before your visit to Colombia, and if you intend to trek or hike – a policy should cover every eventuality, including being evacuated for more advanced hospital care.

IMMUNISATION Preparations to ensure a healthy trip to Colombia require checks on your immunisation status: it is wise to be up to date on tetanus, diphtheria and polio (now given as an all-in-one vaccine, Revaxis, that lasts for ten years), and hepatitis A. Immunisations against yellow fever, typhoid, hepatitis B, and rabies may also be recommended. Other vaccines that may be mentioned include BCG for TB, and MMR for measles, mumps and rubella.

Colombia is considered to be a yellow fever endemic country, at least in parts. There are two reasons for immunising against yellow fever, firstly to protect against the disease, and secondly as a certificate requirement to gain entry into a particular country. The World Health Organization (WHO) recommends that this vaccine should be used in those nine months of age and over. The yellow fever vaccine and its certificate were until recently said to last for ten years. It is now accepted that the vaccine offers protection for many decades and from the middle of 2016, it will no longer be necessary to have proof of yellow fever vaccine within the preceding ten years. This means that as long as you have had the yellow fever vaccine and can prove it then you won't need to repeat the vaccine every ten years. If you have not been vaccinated before then you need to seek specialist advice from a registered yellow fever centre. Whether or not you need the vaccine for health has to be determined on an individual basis, based on the risk of the disease versus the risk to the traveller. There are certain medical conditions that mean the vaccine would be contra-indicated. If you are unable to take the vaccine then you may be advised to avoid the risk areas within certain countries, for example the Amazon Basin. Whilst the risk of yellow fever is not as high as in West Africa, the disease has a significant mortality in people who catch it who have never met the disease before and have never been vaccinated, ie: are non-immune.

Hepatitis A vaccine (Havrix Monodose or Avaxim) comprises two injections given about a year apart. The course costs about £100, but may be available on the NHS; it protects for 25 years and can be administered even close to the time of departure.

Hepatitis B vaccination should be considered for longer trips (two months or more) or for those working with children or in situations where contact with blood is likely. Three injections are needed for the best protection and can be given over a three-week period if time is short for those aged 16 or over. Longer schedules give more sustained protection and are therefore preferred if time allows. Hepatitis A vaccine can also be given as a combination with hepatitis B as 'Twinrix', though two doses are needed at least seven days apart to be effective for the hepatitis A component, and three doses are needed for the hepatitis B. Again this rapid schedule is only suitable for those aged 16 or over. Children aged one–15 can be vaccinated with Ambirix which consists of two doses given six–12 months apart.

The newer injectable **typhoid** vaccines (eg: Typhim Vi) last for three years and are about 75% effective. Oral capsules (Vivotif) are also available for those aged six and over. Three capsules over five days lasts for approximately three years but may be less effective than the injectable forms as they rely on good patient compliance. Vivotif is also a live vaccine, which is not suitable for everyone. Typhoid vaccine should be encouraged unless the traveller is leaving within a few days for a trip of a week or less, when the vaccine would not be effective in time.

Vaccinations for **rabies** are ideally advised for everyone as Colombia is a high-risk country, but are especially important for travellers visiting more remote areas, especially if you are more than 24 hours from medical help and definitely if you will be working with animals (page 78).

Experts differ over whether a BCG vaccination against **tuberculosis** (TB) is useful in adults: discuss this with your travel clinic.

In addition to the various vaccinations recommended above, it is important that travellers should be properly protected against **malaria** in those countries that have it. For detailed advice, see pages 73–5.

Ideally you should visit your own doctor or a specialist travel clinic to discuss your requirements if possible at least eight weeks before you plan to travel.

HEALTH INFORMATION AND TRAVEL CLINICS
A full list of current **travel clinic websites** worldwide is available on www.istm.org. For other journey preparation information, consult www.nathnac.org/ds/map_world.aspx (UK) or http://wwwnc.cdc.gov/travel/ (US). Information about various medications may be found on www.netdoctor.co.uk/travel. All advice found online should be used in conjunction with expert advice received prior to or during travel.

FIRST-AID KIT
No visitor to Colombia planning to spend time out of the main cities should arrive without a decent first-aid kit, especially those travelling to the islands or the Amazon region. While Cali, Bogotá, Medellín and Barranquilla boast

top-notch medical facilities, many with English-speaking doctors; elsewhere the standard of healthcare is unlikely to be so reliable, or easy to access. Large stretches of rainforest remain accessible only by boat or on foot, so all it takes is a spell of poor weather or engine trouble to put medical help out of reach. On the islands, health facilities tend to be rudimentary and clinic-based. Mainland hospitals in some rural communities are often also woefully under funded, relying on NGO assistance to provide the most basic service, without any frills.

A good first-aid kit for Colombia will vary depending on where you plan to travel. Contents should reflect the weather conditions and availability of replacement items, eg: pack as much mosquito repellent as you can for the Amazon but swap this for blister treatments if you're hiking across the Coffee Zone. If you suffer from altitude sickness then ask your doctor about a course of acetazolamide (Diamox).

Other suggestions as follows:

- Antiseptic wash
- Blister patches
- Bandages and plasters
- Sachets of rehydration mix
- Painkillers
- Antifungal cream
- Travel sickness tablets
- Lots of mosquito repellent
- Antibiotics
- Cold cure sachets
- Throat lozenges
- Eye and ear drops
- Indigestion tablets
- Iodine or alcohol wipes
- Your own prescription medicine
- Female hygiene products including tampons/towels, as well as anti-thrush creams

DRINKING WATER Colombia's bottled Agua Manantial comes from a natural spring 3,330m above sea level near Bogotá. Not only is it cheap, it's delicious – and widely available. As a result many travellers opt for the bottled stuff rather than risk the tap. However, Colombia is one of the few Latin American nations where tap water is good enough to drink without worry – with just a few exceptions. In the Guajira region travellers are advised to avoid the local water and to refrain from ordering drinks with ice. In contrast, the water in Manizales is of optimum quality as it comes straight from a pristine natural source near a *nevado* (snow-covered spring). Order bottled water here and the locals will think you're loco – or are sure to be mightily offended. Travellers venturing out to the wilds of the Amazon region should pack water purification tablets just in case or, better still, take a water filter bottle such as Aquapure which relies on a mechanical filter. Some of the rivers in the Andes are showing signs of pollution from the coca crop-spraying programme – an initiative that has made water unsafe for drinking or bathing and which has destroyed local fishing stocks.

MEDICAL PROBLEMS
Deep vein thrombosis (DVT) Although relatively rare, there is an increased risk of deep vein thrombosis if you fly for longer than 8 hours. If you have a long-haul flight ahead, consider taking medical advice from your GP before you leave to

check you are not in a high-risk category. DVT occurs when blood clots that form naturally in an immobilised body get stuck in the lungs. Travellers should not be alarmed as clots form regularly in the body without causing a problem. However, some people, such as cancer and heart disease sufferers and the elderly, are considered to be at a higher risk of DVT than others. If you think you are high-risk make sure you get your doctor's approval to fly. In general anyone on a long-haul flight should move about the plane regularly throughout the flight, stretch their legs at regular intervals and rotate their ankles frequently, avoid heavy sedation, such as alcohol or sleeping pills and drink plenty of water and/or fruit juice. You can also try socks that have been designed to reduce the risk of DVT (*www.legshealth.com* or *www.donttravelwithoutit.com*).

Malaria The most dangerous form of malaria, Plasmodium falciparum, occurs in low-lying (below 800m) tropical areas of Colombia, in particular Chocó and northwest Antioquia. Malaria is contracted by a bite from an infected female Anopheles mosquito and it multiplies in the oxygen-carrying red blood corpuscles (cells). The incubation period varies from seven days to three months and sometimes up to a year. Signs of malaria include fever, shaking and shivering, a temperature of more than 38°C rising and falling, flu-like symptoms, headaches, nausea and vomiting and diarrhoea. Falciparum is an extremely dangerous form of malaria and if you think you may have it, it is vital to seek medical attention immediately. In the unlikely chance you get malaria whilst taking antimalarials, make sure you tell any doctor treating you exactly what antimalarials you are taking. Remember symptoms of malaria may not appear until after your return.

Malaria prevention There is not yet a vaccine against malaria that gives enough protection to be useful for travellers, but there are other ways to avoid it. Seek current advice on the best antimalarials to take: usually atovaquone/proguanil (eg: Malarone), doxycycline or mefloquine (particularly for small children or for adults who have used it before).

Atovaquone/proguanil (eg: Malarone) is highly effective in preventing falciparum malaria which is the most serious type of the disease. It has the advantage of having relatively few side effects and need only be continued for one week after returning. However, it is expensive and because of this tends to be reserved for shorter trips. Atovaquone/proguanil may not be suitable for everybody, so advice should be taken from a doctor. The Advisory Committee for Malaria Prevention have advised that it is safe to take atovaquone/proguanil for as long as it is tolerated, ie: far longer than the product licence suggests. There is a paediatric form of the tablet for children under 40kg and the dose is calculated by body weight.

The antibiotic doxycycline (100mg daily) is a credible and cheaper alternative. Like atovaquone/proguanil it can be started two days before arrival. In about 1–3% of people there is the possibility of allergic skin reactions developing in sunlight; the drug should be stopped if this happens. It is unsuitable for children under 12 years, in breastfeeding mothers and in pregnant women over 11 weeks' gestation. It can be used in people with epilepsy but can sometimes make antiepileptic medication less effective.

Mefloquine (Lariam) is a very effective drug but needs to be started ideally 2½ weeks (three doses) before departure to check that it suits you and to ensure that it has reached an effective level; stop it immediately if it seems to cause depression or anxiety, visual or hearing disturbances, severe headaches, fits or changes in heart rhythm. Side effects such as nightmares or dizziness are not medical reasons for stopping unless they are sufficiently debilitating or annoying. Anyone who has been treated for depression or psychiatric problems, has diabetes controlled by oral therapy or who is epileptic (or who has suffered fits in the past) or has a close blood relative who is epileptic, should probably avoid mefloquine. Small children tend to tolerate this drug very well, and as it is a weekly dosing tends to be more convenient for them.

In the past doctors were nervous about prescribing mefloquine to pregnant women, but experience has shown that it is relatively safe and certainly safer than the risk of malaria. That said, there are other issues, so if you are travelling to malarial areas whilst pregnant, seek expert advice before departure.

All tablets should be taken with or after the evening meal, washed down with plenty of fluid and, with the exception of atovaquone/proguanil (page 73), continued for four weeks after leaving.

Despite all these precautions, it is important to be aware that no antimalarial drug is 100% protective, although those on prophylactics who are unlucky enough to catch malaria are less likely to get rapidly into serious trouble. In addition to taking antimalarials, it is therefore important to avoid mosquito bites between dusk and dawn (page 73).

There is unfortunately the occasional traveller who prefers to 'acquire resistance' to malaria rather than take preventive tablets, or who takes homeopathic prophylactics thinking these are effective against killer disease. Homeopathy theory dictates treating like with like so there is no place for prophylaxis or immunisation in a well person; bona fide homoeopathists do not advocate it. It takes at least 18 months residing in a holoendemic area for someone to get some immunity to malaria so travellers will not acquire any effective resistance to malaria. The best way is to prevent mosquito bites in the first place and to take a suitable prophylactic agent.

- Cover up your arms and legs, especially at dusk, by lakes and in rural areas. Tuck your trousers into your boots, and use elastic or hair bands around your wrists to keep mosquitoes out of your sleeves
- Choose a good insect repellent, with about 50% DEET (as the optimum strength) and remember to keep reapplying as per the manufacturer's instructions. Repellents should be applied in the daytime as well as in the evening to all exposed skin.
- Sleep under a mosquito net impregnated with permethrin (an insecticide) in high-risk areas – ask in rural hotels if you are unsure though to be sure it is best to bring your own
- Avoid areas with stagnant water

Malaria: diagnosis and treatment Even those who take their malaria tablets meticulously and do everything possible to avoid mosquito bites may contract a strain of malaria that is resistant to prophylactic drugs. Untreated malaria is likely to be fatal, but even strains resistant to prophylaxis respond well to prompt treatment. Because of this, your immediate priority upon displaying possible malaria symptoms – including a rapid rise in temperature (over 38°C), and any combination of a headache, flu-like aches and pains, a general sense of disorientation, and possibly even nausea and diarrhoea – is to establish whether you have malaria, ideally by visiting a clinic. From seven days or more into your trip, assume that any high fever over 38°C lasting more than a few hours is malaria regardless of whether you have any other symptoms or not. Also remember that it is still possible to develop malaria several months (technically up to a year) after leaving a malarial area so make sure that you tell the treating doctor where you have been.

Diagnosing malaria is not easy, which is why consulting a doctor is sensible: there are other dangerous causes of fever in South America, which require different treatments. Even if you test negative, it would be wise to stay within reach of a laboratory until the symptoms clear up, and to test again after a day or two if they don't. It's worth noting that if you have a fever and the malaria test is negative, you may have typhoid or paratyphoid, which should also receive immediate treatment.

Carrying a course of malaria treatment may be recommended for travellers on long overland trips, or those working or volunteering in more remote Amazon regions in Colombia where access to good medical care may be very limited. Some people advocate taking a rapid diagnostic test kit with them, though these have been shown to be difficult to use by people who are sick or who haven't had a lot of practice using them. Ideally you should get to medical help as soon as possible and let those with experience make the diagnosis. With malaria, it is normal enough to go from feeling healthy to having a high fever in the space of a few hours (and it is possible to die from falciparum malaria within 24 hours of the first symptoms). In such circumstances, assume that you have malaria and act accordingly – whatever risks are attached to taking an unnecessary cure are outweighed by the dangers of untreated malaria. Experts differ on the costs and benefits of self-treatment, but it is hard not to agree that treatment may save your life. There is also some division about the best treatment for malaria, but either atovaquone/proguanil (eg: Malarone) or Coarthemeter are the current treatments of choice. Discuss your trip with a specialist ideally before you travel.

Other insect-borne diseases Malaria is by no means the only insect-borne disease to which the traveller may succumb. Others include dengue fever, sleeping sickness and river blindness (page 76).

Dengue fever Dengue fever is more common than malaria in many parts of South America and there are many other similar arboviruses, such as Chikungunya. These mosquito-borne diseases may mimic malaria but there is no prophylactic medication against them.

The dengue fever virus belongs to the family Flaviviridae, genus *flavivirus* (which includes yellow fever and Japanese encephalitis).

The mosquitoes that carry the dengue fever virus typically bite during the daytime, so it is worth applying repellent if you see any mosquitoes around. Symptoms include strong headaches, rashes and excruciating joint and muscle pains and high fever. Viral fevers usually last about a week or so and are not usually fatal. Complete rest and paracetamol are the usual treatment; plenty of fluids also help. Some patients are given an intravenous drip to keep them from dehydrating. It is especially important to protect yourself if you have had dengue fever before, since a second infection with a different strain can result in the potentially fatal dengue haemorrhagic fever.

Chagas disease Also known as American trypanosomiasis, this is a potentially life-threatening illness caused by the protozoan parasite *Trypanosoma cruzi* (*T. cruzi*). In Latin America the disease is mostly vector-borne, where it is transmitted to humans by contact with the faeces or urine of the triatomine bugs, which are also known as kissing bugs in some countries. The bugs live in the cracked walls of poorly constructed houses in both rural and suburban areas. They are active at night when they feed on human blood. The bugs typically bite on the face and then defecate next to the wound. The parasite enters the body when the infected faeces are smeared into the open wound or into mucous membranes such as the eyes or mouth. Travellers can also contract this disease by eating infected food.

Chagas disease has two phases. The acute phase lasts for about two months after the initial infection. Most cases during this phase have few or no symptoms. Less than half have skin lesions or present with fever, headache, enlarged lymph nodes, abdominal or chest pain. During the chronic phase, the parasites hide in the heart or digestive muscles. About a third of patients suffer from cardiac disorders, some fatal, and up to 10% have digestive problems.

Benznidazole and nifurtimox can effectively treat Chagas disease if given early in the acute phase. They are less effective the longer a person has been infected.

It can be reduced or avoided by doing the following:

- **Avoid sleeping in a mud, thatch or adobe house;** these types of residences are more likely to harbour triatomine bugs
- **Use permethrin-impregnated bed nets** when sleeping in thatch, mud or adobe houses
- **Use insecticides** to remove insects from your residence
- **Use DEET-based insect repellent** on all exposed skin

Onchocerciasis This disease, which is also known as river blindness, is hypoendemic in Brazil, Venezuela and Colombia. The risk of infection is greatest in the dry season.

It is caused by a nematode worm (*Oncocerca volvulus*) and is spread by the bite of a black fly (*Simulium species*) which breeds in fast-flowing water. The black fly bites mostly at dawn and dusk. The microfilaria released by the black fly cause skin irritation with intense itching which usually occurs months or years later. The cornea can be affected, leading to blindness (hence the name), but this is rare in travellers.

Usually infection follows multiple bites, so those staying in the endemic countries listed such as aid workers, missionaries, and military personnel are potentially at higher risk. Travellers who are living near rivers, particularly camping, are again at higher risk. The risk for most travellers is low. The recommended treatment is ivermectin, which needs to be given every six months for the lifespan of the adult worms or for as long as the infected person has evidence of skin or eye infection.

Prevention Cover up and use DEET-containing insect repellents on all exposed skin. Sleep under permethrin-impregnated mosquito nets.

Leishmaniasis In South America this disease is caused by a protozoan parasite (*Leishmania braziliensis*). It is spread by the bite of an infected sand fly (*Phlebotomus* spp) which is mainly night biting and is most prevalent in forest or jungle areas.

There are two forms of the disease: cutaneous (affecting the skin) and visceral (affecting the organs). Brazil has the highest prevalence of both these forms in South America. The visceral form is usually fatal without treatment but thankfully the disease is rare in travellers. Those at highest risk are those trekking or living in the jungle. Treatment with liposomal amphotericin B is used for the visceral form and in most cases treatment is not needed for the cutaneous form but amphotericin B can be used.

Prevention As sand flies bite close to the ground the risk is reduced if beds are raised off the ground and you sleep under a permethrin-impregnated bed net. Sand flies are small enough to be able to get through the mesh of the net.

Schistosomiasis (bilharzia) Schistosomiasis affects only a handful of countries in South America, namely Brazil, Venezuela, Suriname, Guyana and French Guiana. It is caused by a microscopic flatworm (fluke) of the genus *Schistosoma*. The form that exists in South America is *Schistosoma mansoni*.

It is an unpleasant problem that is worth avoiding, though can be treated if you do get it.

The risk is greatest for travellers who swim and bathe in fresh water (not sea or chlorinated water) particularly slow-moving or sluggish water, or who are exposed to water provided for washing from local lakes or rivers.

By understanding a bit about the life cycle then it is easier to prevent the disease, or recognise that you have it and therefore get treatment.

Eggs of the flatworm are excreted in faeces, which are then washed into the lake. The eggs hatch and the larvae that emerge infection certain species of snail. The snails then produce about 10,000 cercariae (larvae) a day for the rest of their lives.

Winds will disperse the snails and cercariae. The snails in particular can drift a long way, especially on windblown weed, so nowhere is really safe. However, deep water and running water are safer, while shallow water presents the greatest risk. The larvae penetrate intact skin, and find their way to the liver where they continue to multiply.

Although the adults do not cause any harm in themselves, after about four–six weeks they start to lay eggs, which cause an intense but usually ineffective immune reaction, including fever, cough, abdominal pain, and a fleeting, itching rash called 'safari itch'. The absence of early symptoms does not necessarily mean there is no infection. Later symptoms can be more localised and more severe, but the general symptoms settle down fairly quickly and eventually you are just tired.

Schistosoma mansoni end up in the gut wall and can lead to abdominal pain, diarrhoea and symptoms of anaemia due to blood loss – either frank or occult. Often though there are no symptoms at all.

With long-standing untreated infection complications such as fibrosis/stenosis of the bowel can occur. Liver involvement can lead to hepatosplenomegaly, cirrhosis and portal hypertension.

Although bilharzia is difficult to diagnose, it can be tested at specialist travel clinics. Ideally tests need to be done at least six weeks after likely exposure and will determine whether you need treatment. Fortunately it is easy to treat at present.

Avoiding bilharzia If you are bathing, swimming, paddling or wading in fresh water, which you think may carry a bilharzia risk, try to get out of the water within 10 minutes.

- Avoid bathing or paddling on shores within 200m of villages or places where people use the water a great deal, especially reedy shores or where there is lots of water weed
- Dry off thoroughly with a towel; rub vigorously
- If your bathing water comes from a risky source try to ensure that the water is taken from the lake in the early morning and stored snail-free, otherwise it should be filtered or Dettol or Cresol added
- Bathing early in the morning is safer than bathing in the last half of the day
- Cover yourself with DEET insect repellent before swimming: it may offer some protection

HIV/AIDS The prevalence of HIV is higher in nearly all South American countries than the UK and the risk of sexually transmitted infections is greater whether you sleep with fellow travellers or locals. About 80% of HIV infections in British heterosexuals are acquired abroad. If you must indulge, use condoms or femidoms, which help reduce the risk of transmission. If you notice any genital ulcers or discharge, get treatment promptly since these increase the risk of acquiring HIV. If you do have unprotected sex, visit a clinic as soon as possible; this should be within 24 hours, or no later than 72 hours, for post-exposure prophylaxis.

Rabies Rabies is carried by all warm-blooded mammals (beware the village dogs and small monkeys that are used to being fed in the parks) and is passed on to man through a bite, scratch or a lick of an open wound. You must always assume any animal is rabid as they can often look well but can still be infectious. Have a low threshold for seeking medical help as soon as possible after any potential exposure. Meanwhile scrub the wound with soap under a running tap or while pouring water from a jug for a good 10–15 minutes. The source of the water is not important at this stage but if you do have antiseptic to hand then put this on afterwards. The soap helps stop the rabies virus entering the body and along with an antiseptic will guard against wound infections, including tetanus.

Pre-exposure vaccination for rabies is ideally advised for everyone, but is particularly important if you intend to have contact with animals and/or are likely to be more than 24 hours away from medical help. Ideally three doses should be taken over a minimum of 21 days. All three doses are needed in order to change the treatment needed following an exposure.

If you are bitten, scratched or licked over an open wound by any mammal, then post-exposure prophylaxis should be given as soon as possible, though it is never too late to seek help, as the incubation period for rabies can be very long. Those who have not been immunised before will need four–five doses of rabies vaccine given over 28–30 days and should also receive a product called Rabies Immunoglobulin (RIG), either human or horse. The RIG is injected round the wound to try and neutralise any rabies virus present and is a pivotal part of the treatment if you have not had pre-exposure vaccine. RIG is expensive and may not be readily available as there is a global shortage so it is important to insist on getting to a place that has it. This is another reason for having good insurance.

Tell the doctor if you have had pre-exposure vaccine, as this will change the treatment you receive. You will no longer need to have RIG and will only need a couple of doses of vaccine ideally given three days apart. And remember that, if you do contract rabies, mortality is almost 100% and death from rabies is probably one of the worst ways to go.

Tick-borne diseases
Rocky mountain spotted fever This is caused by the obligate intracellular gram-negative spirochete bacteria *Rickettsia rickettsii*. It is spread by the bite of the ticks that live on rodents and dogs and is more risky for travellers if they are camping and hiking in rural areas.

The incubation period is two–14 days. The patient presents with an acute onset of fever, headache, abdominal pain, hypotension, rash, myalgia and arthralgia to name a few. There is a case fatality of 1.4%. It is treatable with tetracyclines, such as doxycycline 100mg twice daily for seven–14 days.

Prevention is always better than cure, so if you are going to be walking in rural areas ensure that you are dressed appropriately with long sleeves, long trousers tucked into boots and a hat. At the end of the day check each other for ticks.

Ticks should ideally be removed as soon as possible as leaving them on the body increases the chance of infection. They should be removed with special tick tweezers that can be bought in good travel shops. Failing that you can use your finger nails: grasp the tick as close to your body as possible and pull steadily and firmly away at right angles to your skin. The tick will then come away complete, as long as you do not jerk or twist. If possible douse the wound with alcohol (any spirit will do) or iodine. Irritants (eg: Olbas oil) or lit cigarettes are to be discouraged since they can cause the ticks to regurgitate and therefore increase the risk of disease. It is best to get a travelling companion to check you for ticks; if you are travelling with small children, remember to check their heads, and particularly behind the ears.

Spreading redness around the bite and/or fever and/or aching joints after a tick bite imply that you have an infection that requires antibiotic treatment, so seek advice.

Travellers' diarrhoea (TD) Around 60% of travellers get TD at some point on their journey, so do not be shocked if it happens to you. Opinion is divided about TD: some argue it comes from contaminated food and water, others believe it is caused by a change in diet. It's wise to stick to bottled (or boiled) water, avoid eating from dirty-looking street stalls, and avoid cooked food that has been sitting around for a while and salads that might not have been washed. TD is unpleasant, with symptoms that vary in severity from person to person. In general, symptoms settle within 48 hours but it is imperative you replace lost fluids, salts and sugars, as dehydration can be quick, and very serious. Take rehydration sachets mixed with bottled or cool boiled water and avoid food for 24–48 hours. Don't drink alcohol or caffeine for several days as these can dehydrate you and cause cramping. If you experience diarrhoea for longer than 48 hours seek medical attention, just in case you have something more serious. Some travel clinics – eg: the Hospital for Tropical Diseases (*www.thehtd.org*) – sell very effective antibiotic treatments for TD.

Sun and heat It is tempting to lie in the sun, especially in the tropics where you might picture yourself lying under a palm tree sipping something exotic. However, the incidence of skin cancer due to sun exposure is rising. UV rays from sunlight trigger DNA cell change which can initiate melanoma, a malignant skin tumour now responsible for around three-quarters of all skin cancer deaths. Fair-skinned people are more susceptible than dark-skinned, but everyone should take precautions and avoid excessive sun exposure. It is advisable to avoid the midday sun, apply a sunscreen with sun protection factor (SPF) of 25 or higher with both ultraviolet A of four stars or more (UVA; wavelength 315–400nm) and ultraviolet B (UVB; wavelength 280–315nm) protection, as well as wearing a wide-brimmed hat and sunglasses. Reapply cream regularly, and especially after swimming. Babies and children are at great risk from the sun and should be covered with long-sleeved swimsuits, high-factor sun cream (SPF 50) and wide-brimmed hats, whenever they are outside.

Heatstroke is caused by excessive sun exposure; drinking alcohol or taking strenuous exercise in the sun are also factors. Symptoms include dizziness, nausea, headache, unclear vision, confusion and unreasonable behaviour. If you suffer heatstroke get out of the sun immediately. Drinking plenty of fluids, keeping cool with wet towels and resting for at least 24 hours can treat mild cases. You may also find after-sun creams or aloe vera gel a soothing comfort to burned skin. For severe sunstroke seek medical attention immediately as you will need rehydration.

Remember, it is just as crucial to wear sunscreen at high altitude (mountain) or on rivers and at sea, where snow and water reflect ultraviolet light despite the air temperature.

Fungal infections Fungal infections are common in hot, humid climates where they thrive on moisture. They usually flare up in crevices of the body that sweat in the heat, in particular the groin area and between the toes. However, fungal infections are not serious and respond well to antifungal creams. Wear loose-fitting clothing in natural fabrics and if possible expose the area as much as possible.

WOMEN'S HEALTH Cystitis and other urinary tract and bladder infections are extremely common in female travellers, especially those on long-haul trips and/or on a budget. Spending hours on old buses, sleeping in less than sanitary conditions and not getting the chance to wash properly for long periods all help to raise the risk. Such infections can be extremely uncomfortable and cause a painful burning sensation while urinating. To make things worse, it will make you feel as though you constantly need the toilet, even when you do not. It is vital to drink plenty of water, which will help wash out the infection. Over-the-counter medicines can help. If symptoms persist, seek medical attention, as the infection can be dangerous if it spreads to the kidneys.

Like fungal infections, vaginal yeast infections such as thrush are also common, but react well to over-the-counter treatment. Buy creams or pessaries before you leave and have them in your first-aid kit just in case. Some people recommend applying fresh yoghurt to the area; it could help with the itchiness. In rural areas it may be difficult to buy tampons, so if these are your preferred method of period care, bring some from home.

USEFUL CONTACTS
Bogotá
Ambulance
Ambulancias Médicas (1) 214 8304/620 5107–5
Ambulancias Transmedica (1) 625 6910/258 6669, tell them to take you to Servicio de Urgencias Fundación Santa Fé, Calle 119, No 9–10; (1) 629 0477
Colombian Air Ambulance Aeromedicos – Ambulancia Aérea, El Dorado International Airport, Entrance 2, Int 1, Oficina 105; (1) 413 9160/8915
Suma Emergencias (1) 621 0630; m 310 229 9696

Hospitals
Fundación Santa Fé de Bogotá Calle 116, No 9–02; (1) 603 0303; www. fsfb.org.co (English/Spanish)
Clinica del Country Bogotá Carrera 16, No 82–57; (1) 530 0470; www.clinicadelcountry.com
Hospital El Tunal Santa Fé de Bogotá, Carrera 20, No 47B–35, Sur; www.hospitaleltunal.gov.co (Spanish)
Hospital Universitario Cliníca San Rafael Carrera 8a, No 17–45, Sur Bogotá; (1) 328 2300; www.clinicasanrafael.com.co
Red Cross La Cruz Roja Colombiana y el Departamento de Sanidad Portuaria del Aeropuerto El Dorado, Muelle Internacional,

Bogotá; www.cruzrojacolombiana.org. Can give vaccinations such as for yellow fever.

Pharmacies
Cafam (1) 646 8000 ext 1240
Colsubsidio (1) 343 0080
Olímpica Carrera 40, No 22C–10; (1) 368 9246
Sideral Calle 22, D Bis, No 42B–11; (1) 244 8757

Cali
Fundación Clínica Valle del Lili Carrera 98, No 18–49; (2) 331 7474; www.cardiolili.org (Spanish)

Medellín
Clínica Las Américas Diagonal 75B, No 2A, 120 Oficina 309, Centro Comerical Plazoleta Las Américas; (4) 341 6060; www.pmamericas.com
Hospital Universitário San Vicente de Paul HSVP Calle 67 (Barranquilla); www.elhospital. org.co (English/Spanish)

Cartagena
Cruz Roja de Bolívar Barrio España Cl, 30 No 44D–71; (5) 662 5267/5311/5514

Although conflicting stories abound about safety in Colombia, the issue of travelling without incident here remains an important consideration. Those planning to criss-cross the country should do plenty of thorough research – whilst remaining mindful that Colombia thrives on urban myth and is prone to circulating safety information that is out of date. This country remains a place where there is danger, although the present security situation is much improved. Today, it offers the safest travel conditions for many decades and visitors who apply common sense should expect an incident-free stay. Take safety warnings extremely seriously and stay away from regions that are totally out of bounds. Red Zones under the control of warring factions are found in the south of the country, while some city slum areas are highly dangerous no-go areas where violence is rife.

On a positive note, Colombia is no longer the 'Most Dangerous Place on the Planet' according to international specialist iJet Intelligent Risk Systems. In its 'Dangerous Destinations 2014' list Colombia was ranked as number 13 due to major segregations in the country. Another misconception is that Colombia is the 'World's Murder Capital' but in fact rates have reduced. The UN Office on Drugs and Crime (UNODC) said the murder rate in Colombia was 30.8 homicides per 100,000 people in 2012. This is a dramatic fall from a decade ago when the homicide rate in Colombia was 61 per 100,000 people. However, with guns widely available – Bogotá's firearms black market alone made profits of over US$4.9 million between 2009 and 2010, according to city officials – petty crime in Colombia can easily escalate into violence.

KIDNAPPING Although Colombia was once the so-called 'Kidnap Capital of the World', this dubious honour is now thankfully out of date, although continued struggles amongst FARC, the right-wing paramilitary group (AUC), left-wing

MY KIDNAPPER

In 2003, Mark Henderson was one of eight backpackers taken hostage while trekking in the Colombian jungle. He was released unharmed after 101 days of captivity. Out of the blue, almost a year after his release, Mark received an email from Antonio, one of his kidnappers. One of his fellow hostages also received a Facebook friend request from Antonio's girlfriend, another of their captors. This bizarre communication was the beginning of a series of friendly exchanges between hostage and kidnapper that eventually tempted Mark back to Colombia to face the man who had once denied him his freedom.

In 2010, Henderson made a film of his emotional journey back into the heart of the jungle – the result is a deeply personal, authored documentary told from all sides that was released in 2011. Together with some stunning coverage of the beautiful Sierra Nevada mountains the film contains some poignant, disturbing and bewildering moments. The hostages themselves seem to struggle with the answers to the questions they've wanted to ask for so long. However, the film does serve to highlight how perfectly innocent and friendly Colombians have been caught up in the guerrilla conflict. So many have been forced to play a part in something they later regret – and in *My Kidnapper*, two are offered the chance to say sorry. See www.mykidnapper.com for more information.

paramilitary (ELN) and the cocaine trade ensure that Colombia still has a kidnapping problem – despite President Uribe's hardline stance achieving a 78% drop during his eight-year tenure. Official kidnap figures indicate that a total of 282 people were abducted in Colombia in 2010 – compared with over 3,000 in 2002. Around 60% of these are criminal attempts at extortion rather than the traditional kidnaps of leftist guerrillas, according to the National Foundation for the Defense of Personal Liberty (Fondelibertdad). Military and police intelligence indicates that around 30 professional kidnapping gangs operate in Colombia, with FARC believed to be responsible for 23.5% of cases, the ELN for 10% and common criminals for 27%. In a third of cases it was not possible to establish who the kidnappers were. At the beginning of 2012, the FARC banned kidnapping and, according to the official statistics, kidnapping subsequently dropped 23%. However, even before the guerrilla group vowed not to kidnap again, common criminals were already suspected of having taken over the horrid crime. Some 590 reported kidnapping victims are still missing.

In 2011, President Juan Manuel Santos issued a strong statement to all international companies operating in Colombia insisting that no organisation should pay kidnappers 'a single peso'. Warning that anyone found doing so would be automatically kicked out of the country, Santos's message resonated throughout Colombia's rebel groups to whom abduction is traditionally paid. The warning came two days after 22 of 23 employees of South American Exploration, a subcontractor of Canadian oil company Talisman Energy and Colombia's Ecopetrol, were freed by their kidnappers. Some of those taken hostage said their company had paid a ransom – a criminal offence under Colombian law.

The British Foreign and Commonwealth Office (FCO) (*www.fco.gov.uk*) offers up-to-date information on which areas are dangerous and currently advises against all travel to certain areas. To lower the risk of abduction, avoid all Red Zones and don't travel after dark in the countryside. Flying is the safest form of travel as it keeps travellers well away from remote rural guerrilla or paramilitary roadblocks. Take daytime buses whenever possible and only travel with a reputable company on safe routes. Avoid unofficial tours and be wary of anyone who approaches you without good reason. Take heed of the popular Colombian saying '*no se puede dar papaya*' ('don't give papaya'), meaning 'don't let your guard down'.

ROBBERY Robberies are probably no worse in Colombia than in any other Latin American country; however, there are basic precautions that every traveller should take – wherever they are.

For evenings out, shopping or day tours, allocate some money for the outing. Leave your passport behind with credit cards and travellers' cheques – preferably locked securely in the hotel safe. Don't take out anything other than what you'll need; just carry a photocopy of your passport as ID – a Colombian requirement.

Use a money belt and try not to carry bags and purses that are easy to grab hanging off your shoulder. Don't flaunt wealth, jewellery or music players, camcorders or cameras. Put an extra note in your shoes, or somewhere discreet, so if the worst happens you can still get back to your hotel. Never walk around after dark on your own, whether you are male or female. Avoid difficult neighbourhoods (ask your hotel for the best routes before you leave) and use only licensed taxis. Be extremely careful in downtown areas at night, such as La Candelaria in Bogotá. Remember that, unlike many cities in Europe, firearms and weapons are often carried as a matter of course so even the pettiest crime can turn nasty.

The US press has reported that drugging travellers has become a disturbing trend, although there have been few confirmed reports. A derivative of the drug scopolamine known as *burundanga* is thought to be administered via drinks or even cigarettes – it is colourless, odourless and tasteless and can easily be sprinkled on to food. Victims become so docile that they have been known to hand over belongings without batting an eyelid. Others awake in a state of grogginess having been robbed of all possessions. To avoid becoming an unsuspecting victim, don't accept anything from strangers – even a cookie or a cigarette. Travellers thinking of using prostitutes (male or female) should also remember that the drug can be put on parts of the body and be licked. Incidents of being 'scopolamined' in Colombia have increased on the Bogotá to San Agustín night bus in 2011. Travellers should be particularly vigilant on this route and only eat food they know with real certainty is safe.

EMERGENCY/USEFUL NUMBERS

24-hour Healthcare line ☏125	**Police (emergency)** ☏156
Citizens' Information Line ☏195	**Police** ☏112/428 0677
Civil Defence ☏144/640 0090	**Red Cross ER** ☏132/428 0111
Department of Immigration ☏153	**Tourist police** ☏337/4413/243 1175
Fire ☏119/217 5300	**Traffic police** ☏127/360 0111
GAULA (anti-kidnapping) ☏165	

DRUGS Whatever you hear about Colombian cocaine it is unwise to seek it out – most pushers are part of a dangerous underworld criminal element and you will be placed in immediate danger of robbery, contaminants, violence or worse. Drug-taking in Colombia is illegal and travellers caught in possession are likely to receive a prison sentence. To date, the only two foreigner arrests since 1997 in the tourist resort of Cartagena have been drug-related. Please don't forget the consumption of cocaine significantly damages Colombian society. Money spent on cocaine goes directly to support armed groups, fighting in Colombia's internal conflict, leading to assassinations, kidnappings, massacres and one of the world's largest refugee problems. Consuming cocaine means not less than to have somebody's blood on your hands.

LANDMINES Despite widespread efforts to address the problem, landmines remain a threat to civilians and travellers in rural Colombia. According to the Colombian army and independent landmine monitors, Colombia is second only to Afghanistan for its number of landmines, with the Colombian countryside littered with unexploded devices. A total of 10,900 people were killed or wounded by landmines in Colombia between 1990 and March 2014, accounting for 10% of the world's landmine casualties during that period, the presidential programme against landmines, or Paicma, concluded in a 2011 report. The FCO offers the following advice, 'In 2005, more people were killed or injured in Colombia by landmines than in any other country in the world. When travelling in rural areas you should always follow local warnings about the presence of landmines.' Colombia signed the Mine Ban Treaty on 3 December 1997, which was ratified on 6 September 2000. Of Colombia's departments, only one – the Caribbean Archipelago Department of San Andrés, Providencia and Santa Catalina – is not affected. The worst area, as of June 2006, was Antioquia, accounting for 22.6% of incidents registered since 1990, followed by Meta and Santander. Between 1990 and 1 June 2006, the Observatory recorded 8,439 landmine and (Explosive Remnants of War) ERW-related incidents in Colombia, including 1,236 people killed and 3,916 injured. In 2010, the Colombian army began training rodents to specifically sniff out landmines in an unconventional initiative that has achieved excellent early success. In 2011, police seized 1,053 landmines in Antioquia, believed to be the property of FARC operatives as part of a planned attack by the guerrilla group's 9th Front. The mines were buried in an area near El Carmen de Viboral, a small rural settlement. Since then work has been progressing and both the military and foreign NGOs have been working to rid Colombia of the landmine scourge yet one of the major problems has been the topography, tremors, floods, landslides and so on which have shifted the original positions of said mines making them even harder to locate.

WOMEN TRAVELLERS Colombian women are highly politically active and appear extremely confident in social situations. However, machismo still plays a large role in Colombia and female travellers may feel less vulnerable in a group. Those travelling alone should be prepared for the occasional come-on, flirty comment and wolf-whistle from Colombian men – it is part of the culture and something that is best accepted with good grace. Expect it to happen wherever you are, be it a city or rural village – react without hostility but firmly ignore the attention. Avoid acting coy, shy or giggly as this may be misinterpreted as interest. Dressing in short skirts or revealing tops will only exacerbate the situation so stick to conservative clothing – even if the local girls are flaunting their bodies. Some travellers resort to wearing a wedding ring in order to put off male advances – it may work but will rarely stop a persistent suitor. Women who plan to party or drink in bars should remember that dancing with men or accepting drinks may also be construed as interest. Avoid drinking to excess as this will make you vulnerable and when leaving a bar or party make sure you are in a group. Never accept a lift, or walk home, with someone you don't know, or have just met. Attacks on female tourists are rare with robbery a more common motivation than sex crimes. However, if anyone you don't know approaches you on the street or on the beach, offering tours (or anything else), don't wait to hear his patter – walk away.

SOLO TRAVELLERS Travelling alone in Colombia is more than possible, although fair-haired solo females (ie: those obviously non-national) may find this hard going (see *Women travellers*, above). Women do get hassled in Colombia, ranging from some fairly harmless sexual innuendo to being doggedly pursued and intimidated. This tends to be worst along the Caribbean coast. Other travellers have found that the service they receive in hotels, bars and restaurants significantly improves when they have a friend in tow. A companion will certainly help save on single-room supplements. It can also help spread the cost of charter travel arrangements, such as hiring a boat to island-hop in Cartagena. Long car journeys can also be more fun as a shared experience, unless you're a traveller who really enjoys their own space. Outside of the cities, a Spanish-speaking travel buddy can be very useful. Other incentives to pair-up include improved security on the basis that there is often safety in numbers, wherever you are in the world.

Keen to hook up with like-minded travellers? Then check out the following websites:

www.companions2travel.co.uk Since establishing in Jul 2004 to bring like-minded travellers together, Companions2Travel has attracted over 14,000 members looking for new friends to travel with worldwide.

www.gumtree.com This UK-based, classified ads & community site has expanded significantly since its launch in 2000 & it now includes a travel-buddy bulletin board.

www.solotravel.org Has a section written by someone who criss-crossed Colombia alone that contains some useful & reassuring information for people keen to do the same.

www.travbuddy.com TravBuddy contains several thousand travel blogs about Colombia posted by travellers & Colombian nationals. It also has an excellent travel-buddy search facility using country or region.

www.wayn.com Log details of your upcoming trip to find others in the same place at the same time. A user search helps find people by location.

There's also WAYN instant messenger to contact millions of members across the world.

TRAVELLERS WITH A DISABILITY Colombia isn't the easiest place for travellers with a disability, especially those keen to leave the major cities behind. Provincial roads tend to be unpaved, pot-holed and are often little more than dirt tracks. Although wheelchairs and mobility aids are available in large malls and shopping centres, they are rare in rural areas. Adaptations and amenities also vary from place to place. This inconsistency makes planning ahead difficult. However, Colombia's National Institute for the Blind (Instituto Nacional para Ciegos, INCI) (*Grupo de Desarrollo Tecnológico, Carrera 13, No 34–91, Bogotá;* e *inci@presidencia.gov.co; www.inci. gov.co*) has made considerable inroads in campaigning for public information to be available in Braille. There are just over two million deaf people in Colombia, according to Federación Nacional de Sordos de Colombia (Colombia's National Deaf Association, Fenascol) (*Av 13 (Autopista Norte), No 80–60, off 202, Bogotá;* ✆ *256 1467/68;* e *contacto@fenascol.org.co; www.fenascol.org.co*), an organisation established to promote sign language (known as LSC) in 1984. Two constitutional laws for deaf people passed in 1996 recognise Colombian sign language and requires captioning or sign language on television.

Wheelchair ramps are also mandatory in new public buildings, although compliance is poor in this respect outside of urban centres. The Murillo Toro post office building in Bogotá has an entrance ramp, as does the Ministry of Education, but older buildings are rarely modified for disabled access and usually contain steep flights of steps. Much of Colombia's public transportation system is also inaccessible, impairing the free movement of people with disabilities countrywide. The exception to this is the TransMilenio in Bogotá and Medellín's metro system, both of which have special facilities for disabled passengers and wheelchair users.

However, Colombia is playing an increasingly active role in the preparation of a Convention on the Human Rights of Persons with Disabilities as promoted by the United Nations. As a nation it defines disability on World Health Organization (WHO) guidelines and has been responsive to change. Although there are no firm figures, the WHO estimate that up to 12% of the Colombian population are likely to have some kind of disability – that's roughly 5.5 million people. Lightweight travel wheelchairs are in their infancy but have already revolutionised travel for some disabled people. Weighing no more than 10kg and small enough to store in tight spaces, travel wheelchairs are designed to be assembled quickly but can carry the same weight as a standard chair (90kg). None of Colombia's airlines makes additional charges for wheelchairs.

If you need assistance from airport or airline staff at any stage of your journey, contact the airline at least 48 hours before you fly. Travellers who require a companion may be offered a reduced fare for a second ticket. Passengers with a sensory, physical or learning disability can also take advantage of the following services free of charge:

- Assistance to reach check-in
- Help with registration at check-in
- Orientation of the layout of the cabin and briefing in emergency procedures
- Assistance with embarking/disembarking
- Help with luggage
- On-board wheelchair when available
- Transport around the airport

Practical Information   SAFETY

2

Airline staff may ask you to complete an Incapacitated Passengers Handling Advice (INCAD) form and/or a Medical Information Form (MEDIF). You can fill in the INCAD yourself, but your doctor needs to complete the MEDIF. Each airline has a different policy in place regarding disabled passengers and people with medical conditions; yours should be able to supply you with a copy of its provisions in this respect or may have its disabled persons policy online. A Department of Transport code of practice 'Access to air travel for disabled people' aims to make air travel more accessible to disabled people, but only relates to the UK air travel industry including travel agents, tour operators, airlines and airports. The code sets out the good practice needed to make sure disabled and less mobile passengers enjoy trouble-free journeys by air. It includes information for airport operators who are legally bound by the Disability Discrimination Act 1995 (DDA). It also advises airlines on how to provide better services to disabled people on a voluntary basis. At present, it is a voluntary code for UK companies only, but much of its content is reflected in similar European and international best practice codes.

For more information on the services available for disabled travellers (and to download a copy of the Access to Air Travel for Disabled People code in PDF format), visit www.direct.gov.uk/en/DisabledPeople. The website also includes details of the facilities for disabled people at UK airports, such as transfer arrangements, parking and wheelchair-accessible toilets.

OLDER TRAVELLERS Colombians are extremely respectful of older people, bestowing reverence on those aged 50 and over. Subsequently, older travellers will find themselves well treated in Colombia's bars and restaurants where they are often seated as priority. Hotels also tend to look after their older guests with staff more prepared to go that 'extra mile'. Many theatres, cinemas, attractions and museums offer generous senior discounts, so older travellers should be sure to always have their ID close at hand. Cheap travel is also offered to senior citizens in Colombia with a 10% discount on some domestic airlines and reduced fares on public transport nationwide. A significant number of foreign volunteer workers in Colombia are aged 50–65. However, some of the country's high-altitude regions present older people with some medical challenges. The sheer physical demands of the Amazon can also make this a tough region to explore. Retired Backpackers (*www.retiredbackpackers.com*), started by Jonathan Peace after his father said he wanted to visit South America, has a number of members keen to travel to Colombia. It comprises a mix of solo travellers and married couples who are independent in spirit. (See also pages 84–5.)

CRUISE PASSENGERS

The number of cruise ships docking in Colombia is growing and cruise-ship activity in Colombia has grown by nearly 13% since 2012, bringing over 275,000 tourists to port on 193 voyages, according to statistics circulated at the Florida Caribbean Cruise Association (FCCA) Conference and Trade Show.

The main operators to include Colombia on their itineraries are the Royal Caribbean, Princess and Celebrity. The Colombian cruise-ship destinations are Santa Marta, Cartagena, and Isla de San Andrés and Isla de Providencia, two small islands nestled in the turquoise waters off the east coast of Nicaragua. Cartagena remains the most popular stop-off, but Santa Marta, San Andrés and Providencia are now being added to more cruise itineraries.

WHAT TO EXPECT ON A CRUISE VISIT Cruise ships usually dock for a full day (excluding evenings) in each location, so you should have several hours to explore. Santa Marta is great for those seeking sunshine and Caribbean waters, whilst the islands of San Andrés and Providencia offer tiny, deserted beaches and spectacular reef snorkelling.

CARTAGENA EXCURSIONS The excursions offered in Cartagena are professionally guided and may vary slightly. There is a variety of choices. For a mix of contemporary city life and historic culture, the **City Drive and La Popa Monastery** tour is a good option. Set on a 150m-high hill, Convento de la Popa has spectacular views overlooking the city plus an ornate 22-carat gold-foil altar and a relaxing flower-festooned courtyard. The tour continues down to the 18th-century Spanish dungeons, Las Bóvedas, which were constructed in the thick city walls and are now used for handcrafted souvenir shops. You'll also be driven through the residential area of Bocagrande with the chance to browse the emeralds and handicrafts in the shops. The trip takes around 3½ hours.

Those interested in architecture should try the **Deluxe Cartagena and Fortress** tour, which starts with a browse around the Manga residential area, noted for its Republican architecture and beautifully restored houses. Afterwards, you'll visit Convento de la Popa and the 17th-century fort, San Félipe de Barajas, which was one of the strongest forts ever built by the Spanish in colonial Latin America. Next, you'll be taken to Las Bóvedas for shopping, and then will pass through Simón Bolívar Square to the spectacular Inquisition Palace that now houses an interesting museum. Finally, you'll visit the Church of San Pedro Claver – the patron saint of slaves – and finish with a shopping expedition at Bocagrande. The trip lasts 4½ hours. For a more strenuous tour outside the city, try the **Mangroves and Swamp Ecological Tour**. This is a 3¾-hour guided canoe ride through the Swamp of the Virgin, an important sanctuary in Cartagena for tropical birds, fish and crustaceans as well as the ornate and intricate mangrove system that oxygenates the water.

For a colonial reminder and an overview of the history of Cartagena, take the **Panoramic Tour around the Bay**. You'll sail on a replica of a Spanish galleon, past the private port of Muelles El Bosque and the statue of the Virgin and the site of the Fort of Manzanillo that guards the eastern entrance to the Inner Bay. The boat makes a loop between the island of Tierra Bomba and the peninsula of Castillo Grande. To enhance the experience, a traditional show based on local folklore takes place on board. The trip lasts 2 hours.

You can visit the national park area of Rosario Islands on the **Rosario Island Tour**, some 35km to the south of Cartagena. The tour stops first at Isla del Sol, for a drink and exotic fruit, after which you can take the boat around 27 islands and visit the local aquarium at Isla de San Martín. Lunch is on Isla del Sol, where you can snorkel (equipment not included in the price), swim or lounge by the swimming pool. The **Best of Cartagena** is a fairly flighty overview of the city's sites. You'll visit the Manga residential area, Convento de la Popa, the Fort of San Félipe de Barajas, Las Bóvedas (The Dungeons) for handicraft shopping, the Church of San Pedro Claver, the Navy Museum for refreshments followed by a short shopping spree at Pierino Gallo Mall and return to the ship via Bocagrande and Castillogrande residential areas.

COLOMBIAN CRUISE PACKAGES All cruises that dock in Colombia offer the country in combination with other destinations in the region.

Celebrity Cruises ☏0845 456 1520; www.celebritycruises.co.uk. Offer a 12-night cruise on the *Celebrity Quest*, leaving from Miami, Florida, calling at Port Antonio (Jamaica), Santa Marta & Cartagena (Colombia), Colón (Panama), Puerto Limón (Costa Rica), San Andrés Island (Colombia) & Playa Del Carmen (Mexico). A 14-night cruise on the same ship, also leaving from Miami, stops at Port Antonio, Santa Marta, Cartagena, Puerto Limón, Panama Canal (cruising), Fuerte Amador (Panama), Puerto Caldera (Costa Rica), San Juan Del Sur (Nicaragua), Huatulco & Acapulco (Mexico). Prices start at £932 pp, based on double occupancy (£1,620 single occupancy); prices can rise during the high-season months of Dec & Jan.

Princess Cruises ☏+1 800 PRINCESS (US); www.princess.com. Includes Colombia in their Panama Canal trips with a 10-night itinerary including Aruba, Cartagena, Panama Canal partial transit, Cristóbal, Limón (Costa Rica) & Ocho Ríos. They offer 2 full Grand Canal 15- & 17-day transits between Fort Lauderdale & San Francisco or Vancouver with calls at Cabo San Lucas, Acapulco, Huatulco, Puntarenas (Costa Rica), Panama Canal, Cartagena & Aruba. Prices start from US$1,199 pp, based on double occupancy.

Royal Caribbean Cruises ☏0844 493 4005; www.royalcaribbean.co.uk. Offers a range of Latin American itineraries that incorporate the rainforests of Brazil to the snow-capped Andes Mountains of Chile & Colombia's finest colonial-era city, Cartagena. For the ultimate thrill, take to the skies & go parasailing over the breathtaking beaches of Uruguay or take to the saddle & ride through the surf. When in stylish Buenos Aires, you can learn how to tango like a local or take a less energetic turn around the elegant shops. Check online for latest prices, special offers & hot deals.

GAY/LESBIAN RIGHTS

Laws are not enough; an important cultural shift is needed… for discrimination to end.
Marcela Sanchez, Colombia Diversa, 2007

Colombia has a relatively small gay scene confined to its major cities but has witnessed significant improvements in gay and lesbian rights in recent years. However, discrimination remains rife, despite Colombia's increasingly liberal social attitudes. Today, it may be easier to be openly homosexual in major cities but in rural areas the attitude towards gays and lesbians shows little sign of softening. Dozens of groups in Colombia have conducted anti-gay campaigns under such names as 'Death to Homosexuals'. Even a human rights ombudsman once described homosexuals in a television interview as 'abnormal faggots' that should be subject to 'social control'.

However, Colombia does have openly gay politicians, an active gay and lesbian information network and an active gay rights group – Bogotá-based Colombia Diversa, founded in 2004. Consensual homosexual activity was decriminalised in 1980 with amendments to the Criminal Code so there is a single age of consent of 14. In 2003, following strong opposition from the Catholic Church, an extremely progressive bill to give legal recognition to lesbian and gay partnerships was shelved. However, in February 2007, the Colombian Constitutional Court ruled that same-sex couples are entitled to the same inheritance rights as heterosexuals in common-law marriages. Even Colombia's powerful Catholic hierarchy backed the bill on the basis that it didn't include same-sex marriage or adoption. According to Colombia Diversa at least 100,000 couples will benefit from the new legislation, which is one of the most progressive gay rights reforms in Latin America. In 2010, gay rights advocates gathered in protest in Bogotá after Colombia's Constitutional Court voted five to four to dismiss a lawsuit arguing for a change in the country's civil code that would allow same-sex marriage. In 2014, a gay rights activist was murdered in his home in what appeared to be a hate crime, so do be vigilant. While Colombia has come along significantly, there are still challenges ahead.

Centro Comunitario LGTB www.colombialgbt.com. This gay support group has an excellent online guide to the Colombian gay & lesbian scene. A city-by-city search facility covers most of the country & lists everything from cafés & bars to nightclubs & porn shops.

Colombia Diversa \(1) 483 1237; e info@colombiadiversa.org; www.colombiadiversa.org. This non-profit organisation promotes the rights of lesbians, gays, bisexuals & transgendered (LGBT) persons in Colombia. It was founded in Bogotá in 2004.

WHAT TO TAKE

All visitors arriving in Colombia by plane are blessed with the opportunity to make the most of Bogotá's plentiful shopping. Malls, retail zones and department stores can be found in abundance in a city where almost anything is available for cash. Need a pair of designer shoes for a night in the hottest club downtown? No problem – nor is finding tent pegs, pharmacy supplies and a Gore-Tex jacket for that jungle trek. That supplies are so widely available is a real boon for travellers as it dispenses with the need for squeezing everything (plus the kitchen sink) into a backpack ahead of a trip. However, it is worth remembering that some essential items are likely to be more expensive in Colombia. Others may have limited availability year-round.

The old travel adage 'pack half the clothes you think you need and at least twice the money' is pretty apt for Colombia. It is rarely cold, so unless you plan to ski in the Andes or camp in the Cerro Monserrate, it is worth keeping clothing pretty light. Choose items that can cope with the climate, the terrain and activities such as watersports, trekking and hopping in and out of a boat around the islands. There are many advantages in taking only a single rucksack in Colombia, including avoiding charges for excess baggage on many of its domestic flights. Buses and taxis can also be pretty tight on space. A smaller pack also makes it more practical to keep your luggage with you at all times, rather than be forced to stash it out of sight in a boot.

CLOTHING Colombia's altitude plays a crucial part in planning what clothes to pack. Some of the country's coolest parts are found in the Nevado del Ruiz Natural Park where the air is crisp, cool and can chill at times. On the upper slopes it is common to find snow year-round, while even on the Pacific coast the Baudó Mountains are often shrouded in cloud cover and damp mists. Visitors who plan to climb or camp in the peaks of Iguaque National Park should be sure to pack a fleece jacket, waterproofs and warm clothing. In the Cordillera Oriental the peaks are renowned for unpredictable, cold temperatures and hypothermia is a real risk to climbers who tackle them unprepared. Even in Bogotá some silk micro-knit underwear can prove invaluable on a chilly day. However, broadly speaking most travellers should get by on a pair of jeans, a couple of pairs of shorts, two or three T-shirts, a hat, swimming gear, a long-sleeved shirt and trousers, and a lightweight waterproof jacket. Rubber-soled shoes are great for hopping on and off boats. Some hiking boots are essential for Colombia's tougher treks, with a pair of trainers for walking ideal in bigger cities.

CAMPING EQUIPMENT Pack a sleeping bag designed for tropical conditions, a sheet or sarong and a lightweight hammock. High-altitude camping will necessitate blankets and a heavy-duty sleeping bag. A lightweight tent with plenty of ventilation and a separate rain fly is ideal for Colombia. A length of strong nylon cord makes an invaluable clothesline with other essential items a nest of aluminium cooking pots, a lighter and a box of waterproof matches, a small multi-fuel stove, compass, a first-aid kit, torch, sunscreen, insect repellent, spare batteries, three-in-one camping utensils, bottled water, toilet paper, a small container of soap and a scouring pad.

JUNGLE CLOTHING/EQUIPMENT Spending a significant amount of time in Colombia's jungle or remote rural areas will make the following items a worthy consideration:

- Strong boots with drainage holes
- Lightweight hiking boots
- Two pairs of cotton-polypropylene/nylon socks
- Two pairs of wool-blend socks
- A pair of washable pumps
- Waterproof air-inflated sleeping mattress
- Plenty of mosquito repellent (pump-spray and lotion, 50% DEET minimum)
- Waterproof poncho/jacket
- Lightweight trousers (specialist quick-dry ventilated make, eg: Rohan)
- Lightweight shorts (specialist quick-dry ventilated make, eg: Rohan)
- Quick-dry blanket (specialist make, eg: Rohan), thick for highland/light for lowland

MISCELLANEOUS It is essential to have photo ID at hand wherever you travel in Colombia and for a wide variety of practical reasons it may not be wise to rely solely on your passport for this. Pack a driving licence (if it has a photograph) or anything else that clearly identifies you. This will not only help your passport stay in good nick for longer, it will also make it less likely to go astray at yet another of Colombia's many checkpoints. Outside of the major cities, a torch is essential as most streets are unlit and electricity can cease as early as 21.00. Pack a spare stock of batteries, sunglasses, a candle and a box of good-quality waterproof matches as well as a tiny MW/FM radio to make the most of Colombia's several hundred great local music channels. Spare camera film and memory cards, a handful of safety pins, a travel sewing kit, spare plastic carrier bag and cotton buds (great for all manner of things) are also useful. Bring a spare pair of contact lenses or glasses (and a spare prescription), a travel plug (Colombia uses the US-style two-pin 110V, 60Hz), and a healthy supply of plasters. A Spanish phrase book is essential outside the major cities and English-language reading material is also thin on the ground countrywide. Women will also discover that tampons are harder to find than press-on towels in Colombia so squeezing a decent supply in your backpack is more than worthwhile.

ELECTRICITY Colombia's main cities are served by reliable electricity that comes from a mains source and is therefore assured in most hotels, offices, shops, bars and restaurants. However, away from the major metropolitan centres, the electrical supply is much more shaky, with many villages and areas off the beaten track powered by elderly generators. What this means for the visitors in remote rural areas is unreliable access to electricity – a key consideration for anyone in need of recharging camera batteries and mobile phones or using electronic equipment. In most instances, even the most basic of posada will offer its guests an hour or so of electricity per day; usually at around 18.00–19.00. However, be warned: this is vulnerable to power surges and can be adversely affected by storms and poor weather. Also, the supply can often stop abruptly without warning. Around three million people in Colombia have no power at all and continue to rely on open fires, candles and paraffin lamps.

Colombia's voltage is 110V – very similar to those in the US, Canada and Japan. The electrical frequency in Colombia is 60Hz. The plugs used in Colombia are A and B types. You'll need an adapter for 'Type A' JIS C 8303 / NEMA 1-15 (non-grounded, non-polarised) and an adapter for 'Type B' NEMA 5-15 (grounded, non-polarised) even if you have a North American plug, as although the electrical sockets are similar to those in North America they may not be compatible. There are some exceptions to the rule, so to be on the safe side, invest in an adapter as a fallback. Rather than risk damage to valuable electrical items it may be advisable to seek advice prior to travel. For example, with some voltages the adapter itself is insufficient as it doesn't address the incompatibility, but would just 'fry' it. Only a voltage transformer can change one voltage to another, for 220–240 to 110–120 volts.

Other electronic goods Colombia uses DVD Region 4, the same as Australia, Mexico, Argentina and Central America. A Region 4 DVD cannot play on a DVD player supporting another region. There are, however, some region-free DVD players available that can be used to overcome this.

Colombia uses Blu-ray Region A, the same as the rest of the Americas as well as Japan, Taiwan, North Korea, South Korea, Hong Kong and southeast Asia. Compatibility is rarely an issue as Blu-ray products are increasingly region-free.

MONEY

Carrying anything other than small amounts of cash is not recommended in Colombia, so most travellers rely on an ATM for daily needs and settle everything else on a credit or debit card. Colombia's national currency is the peso, which is expressed as COP or $ but shouldn't be confused with the US dollar. It comprises 50, 100, 200, 500 and 1,000 peso coins with paper notes in denominations of 1,000, 2,000, 5,000, 10,000, 20,000 and 50,000 pesos.

CASH Although US dollars aren't widely accepted they can come in useful as they offer the best rate of exchange with the peso, unlike the British pound or the euro. However, a large number of homemade counterfeit US dollars circulate in Colombia. In fact, more than 25% of the fake notes on the planet are thought to have originated from counterfeiters in Cali. These are often US$20 bills and are so good they are indistinguishable from the genuine article, so it is advisable not to purchase these from a money changer on the street. Fake 1,000 peso coins also exist, so these are best to avoid and they are often difficult to offload. Fast, safe money-changing services are offered by Colombia's *casas de cambio* – authorised bureaux located in most big towns and major cities. Business hours vary, but expect to find them open from early until 18.00 Monday to Friday. Most close at noon on a Saturday. Rates may be lower than the banks but changing cash is quick and easy, taking less than 10 minutes for a US dollar-to-peso transaction. Numerous companies operate as *casas de cambio* and rates and services vary – so for the very best deal to stretch a budget further it really does pay to shop around.

CREDIT CARDS AND ATMS Credit cards (especially Visa and MasterCard) are welcomed pretty much everywhere in Colombia, from the side-street stationery stores in Bogotá to almost every hotel across the country. Most visitors make their first withdrawal on arrival at Bogotá Airport, to cover transfer costs, bellboy tips and that all-important first-night *cerveza*. ATMs are found in plentiful supply in major towns and cities, although care should be taken when withdrawing cash from machines right on the street. Opt for an ATM in a mall, hotel lobby or city supermarket to be on the safe side – and much like any other place on earth be sure not to wave the cash around. Both banks and ATMs can be used for credit-card cash transfers. However, to prevent any hiccups it pays to notify the bank in writing well ahead of boarding the plane – sorting out a frozen account from Colombian soil can be highly problematic. At the time of writing, a number of foreign travellers have reported having their credit cards 'cloned' in Cartagena. Although their cards were eventually 'frozen' by the banks who detected abnormal spending patterns, this action was a little too late as thieves had already spent large amounts on clothing, electronics and CDs in shops all over town. Travellers who fall foul of this type of crime can call a hotline dedicated to credit-card fraud – there is one for each city (*Bogotá: 3355509; Barranquilla: 3691887; Medellín: 3110932; Cali: 6674974*), plus a Línea Nacional (National Line) of 01 8000 1).

Using a credit card in Colombia requires a passport or photo ID. Don't be surprised if the teller asks you how many months you'd like the payment spread over – 'cuantas cuotas?' – this is a standard option in most retail outlets.

CHANGING MONEY Some banks change currency and travellers' cheques, but many don't – and this can vary from branch to branch of the same institution. Travellers' cheques are now rarely used and ATMs are more common. If you do find a bank willing to take them, they are changed at up to 5% lower than the official rate, with cash exchanged at up to 3% less. Be sure to take along your passport and muster up as much patience as possible, as even the simplest transaction involves dozens of forms in triplicate and can easily take up to an hour. Banking times also differ but are generally 08.00–11.30 and 14.00–16.00 Monday–Thursday, and 08.00–11.30 and 14.00–16.30 Friday. The exception is the banks in Bogotá, which close an hour earlier. Many of Colombia's banks only provide currency exchange services for a limited period each morning, so it pays to get there early – especially as every branch in the country closes at 12 noon on the last working day of the month.

BUDGETING

KEEPING COSTS DOWN Those with a meagre purse will discover that Colombia isn't a dirt-cheap option for travellers. However, food costs are minimal – unless you simply can't survive without dining on top-notch à la carte each day. This is especially true in the major cities, where an excellent array of low-priced tasty food represents great value for those on a shoestring. Expect to pay 8,000COP for an excellent bowl of *ceviche*, 3,500COP for a beer and 1,400COP for a *café con leche*.

TIPPING

Gratuities are now becoming the norm in most restaurants and bars. In restaurants, a service charge can sometimes be automatically added to your bill; your wait staff will now ask you if you would like to include the recommended 15% service charge to your bill before totalling it up for you. Taxi drivers will be perfectly happy if you round up the fare. In hotels, the bellboy will expect 500–1,000COP per bag and room-service waiters will be pleased with the same. Tour guides should be tipped around 10% of their fee. Hairdressers, beauticians and chambermaids are generally awarded discretionary amounts of 1,000–3,000COP. In a bar, it is customary to leave a token amount for the bartender based on a rounding up of the bill. However, if you decide to run a tab into the wee small hours always be sure to scrutinise the final tally.

Finding somewhere low-cost to stay isn't difficult, but many of the budget joints throw up the issue of safety so are often best avoided. Although backpacker hostels have rooms for less than 20,000COP per night many international backpackers opt for a more comfy mid-range hotel. Allow 150,000COP for a double room in Bogotá and 100,000COP in Cali, while an all-inclusive stay at a beach resort in Cartagena will set you back 800,000COP for three nights.

TRAVEL Colombia relies on a mix of ground transportation, internal flights and boats out to the islands. Overland travel is often impacted by Colombia's latest security concerns, so visitors should check this out thoroughly before booking anything from Bogotá to the country. Another factor to consider when planning how to get from A to B is Colombia's sheer size, especially if spending 20 hours on a crowded bus with poor suspension is your idea of hell. On the plus side, the nation's bus companies are famously aggressive when it comes to price wars, so fares are often negotiable for those with the patience (and Spanish) to haggle. Expect to pay 1,500COP for a cross-city *buseta* trip in Bogotá and around 75,000COP for a 10-hour overland slog to Medellín. A more comfortable option is to hire a driver and car at about 250,000COP a day – an appealing transfer option for groups of four when faced with any measure of personal safety risk. Domestic airfare tickets also needn't bust the budget if purchased well in advance. In Bogotá, navigating the city's 300km of pristine cycle paths makes an excellent alternative to doing battle with the traffic. Another way to stretch the budget further is to visit museums on the 'free day' – usually the last Sunday in the month. Students should also wave their student ID at every opportunity as this often produces a discount when booking air, cinema and gallery tickets.

NO NEED TO BUDGET? Colombia boasts many of the finest gastronomic haunts in Latin America with five-star French bistros, stylish chichi cafés and award-winning pan-Asian fusion cuisine. Foodies keen to join Colombia's elite nouveau riche will find plenty of high-class dining hangouts complete with menus where the prices aren't listed and where fine wines start at 15,000COP a glass.

The best hotels in Colombia tend to be concentrated around the major cities, although some of the all-inclusive resorts on the Caribbean coastline pander to a luxury clientele. Expect to pay 500,000COP for a five-star suite in Bogotá and 400,000COP in Medellín, while a night in one of Cartagena's chicest boutique hotels costs from 800,000COP per person.

Exploring Colombia with little regard for budgetary constraints allows for cross-country journeys by private plane. Book direct with the airline or even better engage a reputable tour operator, who will almost certainly organise a ground transfer in an air-conditioned car as part of the charter package. Private jets, helicopters, chartered yachts and chauffeured limousines are some of Colombia's more upmarket modes of travel – expect to pay US$5,000 for executive cross-country flights and US$350–500 per hour for helicopter charter.

GETTING AROUND

BY AIR Flying is by far the safest, easiest and most convenient way of getting around the country, with around 984 airports (although only around 100 have paved runways). Most domestic flights take less than 60 minutes' flying time. Some offer business class and economy tickets and serve a snack and a drink.

Avianca, Latin America's first airline (est 1919; \ *+1 404 7862; www.avianca. com*), **CopaAirlines** \ *+1 320 9090; www.copaair.com*), **LAN** (\ *+1 800 094 9490;*

www.lan.com) and **Satena** (☎ +1 281 7071; *www.satena.com*) are some of the large domestic carriers, although there are others (for a comprehensive list of Colombian airlines visit www.comunidadandina.org).

The following towns are served at the time of writing, although routes are prone to change: Armenia (from Bogotá), Barrancabermeja (from Bogotá), Barranquilla (from Bogotá and Medellín), Bucaramanga (from Bogotá), Cali (from Bogotá, Medellín, Cartagena, San Andrés, Pasto and Tumaco), Cartagena (from Bogotá, Medellín, Pereira and Cali), Corozal (from Bogotá and Medellín), Cúcuta (from Bogotá), Ibagué (from Bogotá), Manizales (from Bogotá), Medellín (from Bogotá, Cali, Cartagena, Barranquilla and Santa Marta), Montería (from Bogotá), Neiva (from Bogotá), Pasto (from Bogotá and Cali), Pereira (from Bogotá, Cartagena and Barranquilla), Quibdo (from Medellín), Riohacha (from Bogotá), San Andrés Island (from Bogotá, Medellín, Pereira and Cali), Santa Marta (from Bogotá and Medellín), Tumaco (from Cali), Valledupar (from Bogotá).

Flights can be reserved and tickets paid for with some carriers online or by telephone. Another option is to book with a tour operator (pages 64–6). Always book in advance where possible as seats are usually in demand. Return journeys should be reconfirmed, especially when departing San Andrés. Some areas of Colombia are served by small turbo planes that seat 35–56 passengers – a bumpier ride than on a regular aircraft but often with better views.

BY RAIL/METRO

Colombia has over 3,000km of working railway. However, as yet there are no real services for passengers available.

The city of Medellín operates the country's only metro system. It's connected to an aerial cable car that transports passengers from Acevedo station to the hilltop district of Santo Domingo Savio. Over 90 cars offer a service every 12 seconds between four stations.

BY BOAT

There is an estimated 18,000km of waterways in the country. Both the Río Magdalena (Magdalena River) that intersects the country to the north of Bogotá and the Río Cauca (Cauca River) are navigable in parts (some 1,500km). However, you should thoroughly research any such project first. Wide rivers and jungle canals sound intriguing, but they can lead you to some extremely remote destinations, which could be dangerous in the light of the current guerrilla and paramilitary situation. Jungle canals around Leticia provide a safer option, and tour operators can supply advice.

There are a number of ports on both the Caribbean and Pacific. The main ones are Buenaventura, Tumaco, Santa Marta, Barranquilla, Cartagena, Muelles El Bosque, Puerto Bolívar, Santa Marta and Turbo.

BY BUS

Flying is the safest form of travel in Colombia. However, if you want to bus it, there's a good service that will take you around the country (excluding the Amazon) and on to other parts of Latin America. Each city has a central bus station – *terminal de pasajeros* – although some are located out of town a short taxi or local bus journey away. Unless you are travelling during a public holiday bookings aren't essential and it is easy to purchase tickets on arrival at the terminal. It is advisable to take daytime buses wherever possible with travelling by night bus on unpaved roads best avoided.

For those travelling relatively short distances, *corriente* or *sencillo* are cheap buses that cover a vast network of villages and towns. These basic rust-buckets, like local town buses, tend to pick up passengers who flag them down on the roadside. They

ON THE RIGHT TRACK

Colombia's railway system got off to a promising start in the early 1900s, guided by Europe's most skilful engineers. Projects were lavished with generous amounts of funding, components being shipped in from the developed world. John Charles Gibney, an Englishman, was awarded the government contract to connect Bogotá with the coast. Building a railway wasn't easy on Colombia's challenging mix of terrains and the work was hard and slow-going. Progress was hindered by disease and heavy downpours, often in stifling heat.

However, once completed, the long-awaited railway received rough treatment. Poor investment sent it into disrepair while warring guerrilla and paramilitary factions took turns to blow stretches to smithereens. As a result, Colombia's railways were already in steady decline by the late 1960s. Today, the ageing, decrepit tracks that still remain are few and far between – testament to transportation from a bygone age. Apart from Medellín's state-of-the-art new metro system, Colombia has no passenger-carrying railway system. Of 3,380km of track just 1,746km are in use, most of which is narrow gauge. Shuttle trains connect Colombia's main coal mines to the country's maritime port, Puerto Bolívar. A rolling stock of 30 battered engines form part of a fleet of around 1,500 obsolete passenger and freight wagons.

In 2008, Colombia's National Development Plan included plans to centralise the country's railway system with the construction of railroads for both touristic and cargo-carrying use. Priority has been awarded to the departments of Magdalena, on the north coast of Colombia, and Cauca in the central Pacific region, where goods and mined minerals require shipment.

Today, a sightseeing steam train connects Bogotá with savannah districts north of the capital on Saturday, Sunday and public holidays, at a cost of 27,000COP per person (children 17,000COP). Contact Turistren Ltda (*Estación de la Sabana, Calle 13, No 18–24, Bogotá;* \+57 (1) 375 0557–9; *www.turistren. com.co*).

Similarly, the Tren Turistico Café y Azúcar offers steam train journeys to day-trippers from Cali to Buga, La Tebaida and Cumbre, while a rum-fuelled 'rumbero' option offers a party trip from 20.00 to 03.00 at weekends. Pick up a timetable from the central station in Cali or contact the reservations office (*Av Vásquez Cobo, No 23N–47, Piso 2;* \666 6899/620 2324; e *trenturistico@ert. com.co; www.facebook.com/trenturisticocafeyazucar*).

can be cramped and crowded so be prepared for a tight squeeze. Pullmans travel in roughly the same area but are much more respectable and offer a smoother ride.

Buses that serve long-distance routes tend to be much more comfortable and usually have air conditioning, toilets and movies (most of which are in Spanish). These *ejecutivos* are professionally run by private firms from major bus terminals. They may travel longer distances at night and often stop a couple of times *en route* at roadside cafés. Travellers planning long-distance bus journeys should pack plenty of books, music and snacks. Air-conditioned buses can also get chilly so some warm clothes are advisable. Although reported incidents are rare, travellers have been 'scopolamined' in Colombia on buses: a tactic used by thieves who operate on long-distance public transport that involves spraying biscuits or other snacks with burundanga (a strong sedative). (See also pages 82–3.)

Bogotá to Cali takes 20 hours (US$45); Bogotá to Bucaramanga 10 hours (US$25); Bogotá to Medellín 9 hours (US$30); Medellín to Cali 9 hours (US$16); Medellín to Cartagena 14 hours (US$40); Cali to Bogotá 12 hours (US$24); and Cartagena to Santa Marta 3 hours (US$5). Be certain to pre-book bus travel during public holidays, such as Christmas, Easter or regional holidays, like Carnaval Barranquilla, when crowded bus terminals and vehicles make reservations essential to guarantee a seat.

Urban buses All Colombia's main cities have a good bus and transit network so getting around cheaply (no journey should cost more than 1,500COP) isn't hard. A variety of buses suit all tastes, from the rowdy *busetas* to the very respectable TransMilenio in Bogotá. One set price applies to each journey, no matter how far you are going, although it can vary depending on the style of bus. Official bus stops – or *paradas* – are not abundant outside of the major cities so those who want to board simply stick their arms out and wave their hands – a system that works well and should be seen as a bonus, as there is rarely the need to run for a bus.

Busetas are the cheapest and liveliest mode of public transport but are not for the faint-hearted, especially if you don't like scary cruising speeds or deafening salsa music. Many areas use ex-American school buses, sometimes deemed unroadworthy in the US. They honk and growl as they career around the city spewing out fumes and rattling alarmingly. Lots have been lovingly decorated by their drivers in a rainbow of spray-can colours, motifs and slogans. Pay the driver on entry and try to find a seat to avoid being swung about on corners. Getting off is as haphazard as getting on; you'll need to let the driver, or conductor, know where you want to stop, or call out '*por aqui, por favor*' (please stop here) above the din.

Colectivos are small buses, or large people-carriers, that operate in both small towns and major cities. They provide a comfier ride than regular buses, although they are slightly more expensive. The better, newer ones can be quite plush with soft padded seats and air conditioning, especially on the most popular routes and longer trips from town to town. Although *colectivos* may have roughly scheduled times (hourly or every half-hour for example), most will only depart once full.

Colombia's three main cities each has its own state-of-the-art integrated transport network, known as a Bus Rapid Transit (BRT) system. Bogotá has TransMilenio, Medellín the Metro and Cali the MIO (Masivo Integrado de Occidente); Bogotá's system was the first to be built and has served as the model that the others have followed. Introduced to the capital in 2001, it has become a worldwide blueprint for sustainable urban design. The system was put in place after plans for a metro system were abandoned and now works like an overland metro system. The TransMilenio buses that operate on the system run on exclusive bus lanes. Buses will take up to 160 passengers, although only 42 can be seated, and they can also get very crowded during rush-hour periods. However, they are clean and comfortable and there's just one price for all routes of 1,700COP. Included in the price is a transfer on to *alimentadores* – buses that go further out of the city than the TransMilenio currently can. Main TransMilenio stations (*cabeceras*) are called *portales* and located at the beginning and end of each route. In between, *intermedias* stops serve major intersections and simple stops (*sencillas*) around each 500m. At the time of writing a number of other cities are planning their own Bogotá-style mass-transportation systems, including Cartagena and Barranquilla.

BY CAR Driving a car in Colombia is rarely recommended for tourists as it can be risky in certain areas, especially if the vehicle carries foreign licence plates. For years it has been considered unwise for tourists to obviously display that they are non-Colombian as this may attract attention from guerrillas or paramilitaries. However, it is perfectly safe to drive on about 70% of Colombian roads during daylight although road quality varies dramatically across the country. Routes remain unsafe in the south of the country and anyone planning to self-drive should always seek local advice 'on the ground'. Travelling by air is considered far safer but those who decide to drive should be sure to avoid the so-called Red Zones of conflict.

Colombians drive on the right and all passengers are required to wear a seat belt. Police or military roadblocks are common and stopping is mandatory. Other than this, don't stop for anyone on the road, no matter how innocent the situation looks, especially in isolated areas.

Aside from the large chunk of land that forms the southeast of the country, the road network is relatively good. However, the landscape is rough and uneven and in Colombia's most humid areas paving doesn't last long. Pot-holes can develop over relatively short periods of time and there are still many unpaved roads to contend with – a real challenge, even in a 4x4. The main driving roads in the country are the Pan-American Highway that runs from Cartagena to Bogotá and the Simón Bolívar Highway that connects Bogotá with Caracas in Venezuela and Quito in Ecuador.

Driving can be extremely stressful in Colombia's main cities where roads are highly congested. More than one million cars use Bogotá's city centre alone and drivers can be reckless and quick to cut you up. Travellers who do decide to take to the wheel should find the right balance between assertion (not hesitating) and alert and quick-thinking. If possible, drive a car with a local plate and always plan your route in advance. Have a map or sat nav system to hand. Keep doors locked at all times, especially at traffic lights and intersections, and avoid driving after dark.

Drivers heading from Central to South America are faced with a decision – to import their car by sea or air around the impenetrable Darién Gap (between Panama and Colombia) or to simply buy another vehicle in Colombia. Paperwork and transport to bring in a car can be extremely costly, although there are companies that are prepared to entertain haggling. Colón to Cartagena is the main Panama to Colombia route; check www.shipmyvehicle.com for professional advice.

Rental cars Having charge of a car can be an unwanted burden of responsibility in congested cities with few safe places to park. However, if rental is the only option, the good news is that is it relatively easy; there is a variety of reputable companies to choose from. Rates can be high so it pays to shop around. It is also important to check the fine print regarding insurance clauses as it may be necessary to pay the extra for complete insurance security. Although car hire provides drivers with a Colombian licence plate (considered a safer option than crossing the border by land in a foreign vehicle), a rental plate is still a potential source of attention - so travellers may decide it is safer to stick to public transport in Colombia's remote regions. In the main cities or visiting popular destinations, it probably works out cheaper to fly or take the bus. Taxis can also often be booked by the hour, or per day – a good alternative option (see below).

You'll find a list of car-rental offices in Bogotá at www.bogotaturismo.gov.co/directorios/alquiler_vehiculos and www.bogota-dc.com/dir/cars.html. It is best to go for a well-known company such as **Hertz** (*main office: Carrera 14, No 27–21, Bogotá; www.hertz.com*) or **Budget**, which has an office at Bogotá Airport (*www.budget.com*). You'll need a valid driving licence and a credit card with suitable funds to cover an insurance deposit (can be up to US$1,000).

Driving rules In Bogotá there are rigorous laws regarding when and where you can drive a car. Driving is forbidden on Sunday in the city centre and parking in public places is restricted. In addition, the Pico y Placa law, introduced to reduce traffic congestion, means you can drive your vehicle only on certain days of the week. Days are arranged according to the letters on your vehicle licence plate, but the schedule changes periodically. To be certain, check with your car-rental company for details or visit www.bogota-dc.com/trans/bog-tra.htm.

BY TAXI Most travellers arrive at Bogotá airport and take a taxi into the city centre. Look for the signs pointing to the taxi rank outside of the airport building – a small official taxi booth will point you in the right direction. A taxi official will issue a slip of paper confirming the price, which you then take to one of the taxis waiting. This constitutes an order and sets the price. Should the driver ask for more, don't buy it – a common ruse is to claim that it is just a base price and that some sort of premium or surcharge applies. This is nonsense, as any surcharge would be clearly stated on the price slip.

Elsewhere, taxis are easy to find, day and night, in every main city. They are also cheap even though there is a tendency by some drivers to hike up prices for tourists. Agree on a price before entering the car or insist the driver uses the meter – in Bogotá, a taxi's meter fare is priced in units per 100m at 0.55COP. An average rate per kilometre is 750COP, although charges to and from airports tend to be higher. In rural areas taxis with meters are non-existent so ask around town for the usual rate – and be prepared to negotiate with the driver.

Don't get into a taxi if there is anyone else in the car. Also, don't be tempted to hail a taxi off the street – get your hotel or restaurant to call one to order. Avoid taxis that appear to be unlicensed – check the front window or dashboard for an official badge. Download helpful APPs for your smartphone such as Easy Taxi, Tappsi or Uber. You can lodge complaints about bad service at www.denunciealtaxista.com.

BY BIKE Cycling the length of Latin America is becoming more popular and cyclists are no longer giving Colombia a wide berth. Crossing the country on two wheels is fast becoming a real phenomenon fuelled in part by the Colombian passion for cycling as a national pastime. Bogotá now boasts a 300km network of *ciclo rutas* (bicycle routes), the largest in Latin America, constructed under the instruction of the ex-mayor of Bogotá, Enrique Peñalosa. The mayor also restricted car parking in public spaces and introduced the Ciclovia policy – an initiative that banned cars from the inner 120km of the city centre's roads on Sundays and holidays. This has allowed Bogotá's 8 million population to cycle, jog, walk or rollerblade as they please. Bogotá now has one of the world's longest pedestrian-only streets at 17km and over 5% of the city's population cycle on a regular basis.

Peñalosa was awarded the Stockholm Challenge Prize for his efforts – quite an achievement given Latin America's reputation for over-polluted cities. But even outside the city cycling is a highly popular pastime and visiting cyclists will find that they are well respected on the roads. The trip along the Pan-American Highway from Cartagena to the Ecuadorian border offers spectacular views and it is also possible to ride along the Caribbean coast to Venezuela. Cycling is also popular in the Llanos Orientales region and Boyacá – although not all roads in the country are safe for cyclists and safety precautions (combined with thorough research) should be undertaken before a trip. Seek professional advice on the roads from a specialist tour operator (pages 64–6) – it may pay you to hire a cycling guide to help plan the journey. Vehemently stick to your route, stay on the road and don't be tempted to stray into unknown areas that may be dangerous. Never cycle after dark and allow plenty of time to hit a town before daylight dwindles.

Bogotá has some excellent cycle shops that sell repair kits and helmets – items that may be impossible to find in provincial areas. It is also possible to tour Bogotá by bike as part of fun and free-spirited – but well-organised – cycle sightseeing tour (see *Bogotá Bike Tours*, page 130). This award-winning company also hires bikes at highly competitive half- and full-day rates. For one man's experiences across Colombia in the saddle, check out www.roundtheworldbybike.com.

ACCOMMODATION

Colombia's hotels range from simple, sparse, cut-price rooms to grand, city, no-expense-spared hotels. Backpackers will find plenty of cheap options in the most touristy areas of the country with plenty of hotels in the major towns, resorts and cities to suit most budgets and tastes. However, most visitors to Colombia balance their personal preference with a need for good security, and this is generally the key deciding factor when it comes to finding a decent place to stay. Costs vary, but expect to pay up to around 60,000COP for a double room in a budget hotel, less in many backpacker hostels.

HIGH END Those looking for a range of facilities that often include restaurants, bars, internet, room service, cable television, concierge services and 24-hour security will find plenty of upmarket hotels in Colombia that fit the bill. Unlike many mid-range options, rooms tend to be fitted with a safe, a phone and industrial-standard door locks. There is also a good likelihood that the hotel will offer luggage storage, a round-the-clock reception desk and safety deposit boxes. However, prices aren't always a good indication of quality – and before forking out upwards of 90,000COP it is advisable to ask to see a room. Check the area out too, as not all five-star options are blessed with the nicest of locations, especially in Bogotá where traffic noise can be an issue.

MID RANGE Typically, Colombia's mid-range hotels are centred on or around the Plaza de Bolívar, making it ideal for visitors keen to explore on foot. Though these functional buildings tend to be soulless affairs without any real creature comforts, they benefit from the buzz of

ACCOMMODATION CODES

Approximate price of a standard double room per night

$$$$	500,000–800,000COP
$$$	150,000–500,000COP
$$	40,000–150,000COP
$	<40,000COP

LOVE HOTELS

Forget any notion of romance and candles in Colombia's so-called love hotels, for these soulless, functional rooms exist solely for the purpose of sex. Expect tacky décor, plastic undersheets and low-watt lighting. Condoms and lubricant are also often sold in the style of a minibar. Yet for all its sordidness this is less the domain of the prostitute than the illicit affair or pre-marital romp. Payment is by the hour for a room with a double bed and private bathroom. Couples that lack privacy because they live in an extended family unit also frequent love hotels. Garish, neon-lit exteriors and names like '99 Degrees' and 'Red Flamingo' distinguish them from regular hotels. Find them on the edge of town, set back from the road.

being in the thick of it, with bars, restaurants and attractions within easy reach. Facilities include private bathrooms and rooms are generally equipped with a fan or air conditioning. However, standards in this mid-range bracket vary enormously. Some entrepreneurial owners charge astronomical prices for a room that's one step up from a cupboard. Others offer extraordinary value with prices at just 90,000COP for plenty of space and striking city views.

BUDGET Colombians use a variety of terms for accommodation, including *pensión*, *hosteria*, hotel and *residencia*, although in many areas of the country there are very few obvious distinctions in standards or price. Location is a giveaway when it comes to finding something dirt-cheap, as most budget options are found in the noisiest part of town. Expect a basic room without a private bathroom, although it will probably be fitted with a ceiling fan but almost certainly without air conditioning. This type of shoestring accommodation often comes without hot water in the hottest parts of Colombia, but it's a necessity in the hostels in cooler Bogotá. A sheet, blanket and towel often come as part of the deal. Some also provide door locks for added security and may offer a deposit system for guarding belongings against theft. Prices vary, but range from 20,000COP to 50,000COP for a single and 50,000COP to 80,000COP for a double.

CAMPING A growing number of campsites are springing up across the country, although most Colombians fail to appreciate why anyone sane would want to sleep under canvas outdoors. The sites that do exist usually offer basic washroom facilities but little else, although some are based within the gardens of small hotels or private homes where meals can be purchased. It is more than possible to camp almost anywhere other than Colombia's designated campsites, but on the basis of safety very few people do. Those who decide to try it should seek permission from neighbouring *campesinos* to benefit from a few basic facilities and a watchful eye. Expect to pay 5,000–8,000COP per night.

EATING AND DRINKING

In the last decade Colombia has experienced a gastronomic explosion, attracting world-class chefs to its thousands of restaurants to create a culinary scene that is one of Latin America's best-kept secrets. Much of this modern gastronomic ID is found in Bogotá's über-cosmopolitan restaurant districts, where Colombian Creole classics and champagne and oyster bars rub shoulders with pan-Asian fusion

100

What am I without aguardiente? I'm a nation without people, a tree without roots.

The lament of a Colombian émigré

This patriotic tipple is much like whisky is to the Scots. It's fiery, harsh and extremely potent, yet Colombians swear that *aguardiente* is hangover-free. It has also led to many late-night tearful ramblings by misty-eyed bards. What does it taste like? Well, the name is a bit of a giveaway, meaning 'burning water'; this is an aniseed-flavoured drink. In the mid 1600s, the King of Spain tried to ban aguardiente, but to no avail. Colombia fought tooth and nail for their beloved tipple right up until independence in 1810. Today it is at least 50% alcohol and remains the national drink to be enjoyed countrywide.

Served cold in shot-sized glasses, this sugarcane liquor is usually downed in one by Colombians. Tastes vary, so the amount of aniseed differs from region to region. Key brands include Antioqueño (in Antioquia), Líder (Boyacá), Cristal (Caldas), Nectar (Cundinamarca), Doble Anís (Huila), Llanero (Meta), Quindiano (Quindío), Superior (Santander), Tapa Roja (Tolima) and Blanco (Valle del Cauca). Aguardiente knows no class barriers and is a communal experience. With dramatic aplomb, bottles are slammed on to the centre of the table. Glasses are then filled, toasts are made and proclamations declared. Then in one, single synchronised movement, glasses are emptied in unison in a single gulp. Businessmen enjoy aguardiente in swanky wood-panelled lounges as much as the farmers who drink it from plastic cups in the fields. More than 6.6 million cases of aguardiente are sold in Colombia each year. The Caldas distillery, at the base of a thickly forested mountain outside Manizales, now makes sugar-free Cristal – at just one calorie per glass. Billboards across the region proclaim 'Aguardiente Cristal. No sugar. No regrets.' But after a bottle or so it is still inadvisable to make any significant plans for the morning.

diners and stylish French brasseries. Yet Colombia's sophisticated international culinary triumphs aren't just confined to the swish bistros of the capital city. Mini gastronomic circles are springing up in cities such as Cali and Medellín and the resort areas in Cartagena, creating an exciting alternative to Colombia's traditional culinary staples. Yet, fear not – typical Colombian fare (*comida criolla*) remains very much in evidence on every street corner, from the pavement vendors selling paper-wrapped *tamales* to the hearty plates of chicken, rice, fried plantains and red beans served as *comida corriente* (set meal) in *cantinas* nationwide.

Expect to find plenty of variations on *comida criolla* during a journey across Colombia, each with its own distinct twist. On the Caribbean coastline the focus is seafood, especially lobster, while in the Andes a guinea pig dish is a regional delicacy. In Bogotá, *ajiaco* (a stew of chicken and potatoes) promises to keep city-dwellers warm during seasonal frosts, while generous helpings of *sancocho* soup are served using at least 100 different recipes in every town from Leticia to El Cabo. See pages 104–5 for more regional specialities.

RESTAURANT PRICE CODES

Average price of a main course:

$$$$$	100,000–200,000COP
$$$$	65,000–100,000COP
$$$	35,000–65,000COP
$$	10,000–35,000COP
$	<10,000COP

Practical Information EATING AND DRINKING

2

At the heart of every Latin American nation is a beer of the people. In Colombia, they have five. Much of Colombia's beer tradition revolves around the **Cervecería Bavaria** (Bavaria Brewery) (*Calle 94, No 7–47, Bogotá;* ✆ *(1) 638 9000;* e *servicioalcliente@grupobavaria.com; www.bavaria.com.co*), a Colombian brewing institution founded in 1889 by German immigrant Leo S Kopp. Today 'Bavaria' is a byword for thirst-quenching nectar, thanks to its best-selling cerveza that Colombians hold so dear. To many people **Aguila** ('A-gee-la') (*www.cervezaaguila.com*), the country's top-selling beer, is Colombia, such is its distinctive oh-so Colombian taste. Drive along any highway and you're sure to see the perfect, rounded butt-cheeks of Aguila's bikini-clad *chicas* on the billboards. It's also the beer of choice at thousands of events, festivals and parties countrywide. Aguila is perfect in Colombia's tropical regions as it's a crisp, clear Pilsner with a sweet, mild taste. Served with lemon it's a refreshing way to ingest an alcohol content of 4% – as is its brother beer, Aguila Light. Brava is much more of a macho sup, made for those who enjoy a beefy beer with an intense taste and high alcohol content. This deep-coloured lager beer is 6.5% alcohol. It's another Pilsner variety but is characterised by a hoppy flavour and a slightly bitter residual content. Few would deny that **Club Colombia** (*www.cervezaclubcolombia. com*) is the country's premier lager, Colombia's so-called perfect beer, which is extra dry and carefully crafted as a classy brand with an alcohol content of 4.7%. **Costeña** (*www.bavaria.com.co*) is geared towards Colombia's youth market and has been skilfully targeted at university students aged 18–25. This medium-bodied, golden Pilsner is Bavaria's third-largest seller nationally. It contains 4% alcohol, so is perfect for those big nights out before a thesis beckons. In rural Colombia, **Leona** is the second-largest-selling lager. People describe it as the drink that's ideal for people who don't need an excuse to enjoy a beer. Antioquians favour **Pilsen**, a brewing tradition since 1909. The locals defy anyone not to want to sink a second bottle of this clear, gold festive beer. OK, **Póker** may sound like a dumb name for a drink, but this smooth beer is a big hit with Paisas in Colombia's southwest. Beer is viewed as the right of every Colombiano/a – and is priced accordingly. Even in a hotel minibar it'll rarely cost more than 48p for a 330ml bottle, to ensure no sector of Colombian society is excluded from a decent swig. Do keep an eye out for the growing micro-brew industry in Colombia.

VEGETARIAN FOOD Colombia has a growing number of good vegetarian restaurants, although these are confined to the larger cities. Most are in Bogotá, Cali and Medellín, but there are a few surprises in Buenaventura, Meta and Barranquilla to name just a few. Juice bars, organic food shops, health stores and delicatessens are also found throughout the capital. Some of Colombia's vegetarian diners feature on the international listing www.happycow.net. Entries also state if the menu is vegan, lacto, organic, eat-in or take-away.

PUBLIC HOLIDAYS

| 1 January | Año Nuevo (New Year's Day) |
| 11 January | Día de los Reyes Magos (Epiphany)* |

21 March	Día de San José (St Joseph's Day)*
March/April	Jueves Santo (Maundy Thursday) and Viernes Santo (Holy Friday)
1 May	Primero de Mayo (Día del Trabajo/Labour Day)
9 May	La Ascensión del Señor (Ascension)*
20 May	Corpus Christi*
6 June	Sagrado Corazón (Sacred Heart)*
4 July	San Pedro y San Pablo (St Peter and St Paul)*
20 July	Día de la Independencia (Independence Day)
7 August	Batalla de Boyacá (Battle of Boyacá)
15 August	La Asunción de Nuestra Señora (Assumption)*
12 October	Día de la Raza (Columbus Day)*
7 November	Todos los Santos (All Saints' Day)*
14 November	Independencia de Cartagena (Independence of Cartagena)*
8 December	La Immaculada Concepción (Immaculate Conception)
25 December	Navidad (Christmas Day)

Based on 2016 calendar. * These holidays are moved to the following Monday to ensure a long weekend, if the date does not fall on a Monday.

FESTIVALS

FERIA DE CALI (25 December–1 January) The Cali 'town' fair, which some think an odd label for a city of two million, is a long-established event presenting the region's cultural identity. Great processions feature horseriders and impressive masked and costumed dancers. Music and revelry are passionate and continue until the early hours throughout the event. True to Latin tradition, there's a spectacular beauty pageant, but the bullfighting, which takes place in the Plaza de Cañaveralejo, is almost as popular. A highlight is watching the dancers in the salsa marathon on the banks of the Cali River; the buzz is infectious and you'll find it hard not to join in. The event has been criticised in the past, mainly for the gold-clad horseriders in the 'Cabalgata' parade; some have suggested these are in fact prosperous drug dealers flaunting their wealth. However the fair is renowned across the country and witnessing it is a great way to experience Cali-style fiestas, which range here from classical performances to late-night salsa.

CARNAVAL DE BARRANQUILLA (February/March) Travellers in the country during the four days preceding Lent who like a party shouldn't miss the chance to do the Mardi Gras Colombian-style. Colombia is extremely proud of this highly traditional event, proclaimed one of the 'Masterpieces of the Oral and Intangible Heritage of Humanity' by UNESCO in November 2003.

The Carnaval's heritage reaches back to the late 19th century and combines a diverse mix of ethnicity, from the indigenous to European to Caribbean, apparent in the elaborate costumes and dances. Colombians spend months planning the Carnaval. Throughout the four-day event, celebrations take over Barranquilla; everything closes down while residents enjoy the party. Decorated floats, rows of traditionally dressed street dancers and orchestral festivals fill the streets; cumbia music floats in the air and crowds are fuelled with aguardiente over ice. Those who can see past the liquor-infused merriment of the hour can observe a wide range of cultural dances such as traditional Spanish *paloteo* and African *congo*. A must-see is the Gran Parada, a display of Afro-Amerindian Colombian dancers following the opening battle of flowers procession. The crowning of the

REGIONAL SPECIALITIES

Colombia's rich regional culinary diversity may not be immediately obvious from a menu, as many dishes are found nationwide. However, ingredients and seasoning differ greatly from village to village and city to city. The result is a national gastronomic tradition that offers a vast array of recipes and flavours. Order a bowl of *sancocho* in Cali and it will taste wholly different from that in Cabo de la Vela, while the Caribbean-style *la fritanga* bears little resemblance to that on the Pacific coast.

CUNDINAMARCA
El ajiaco Chicken soup with three varieties of potatoes (*sabanera, criolla, pastusa*) and *hojas de guascas* (wild leaves) served with corn, cream and avocado.
El piquete de la Sabana A variety of meats with fried or broiled giblets served with yellow potatoes, fried green slices of bananas and corn.
El puchero Soup of manioc, green bananas, *arracacha* (a mountain root vegetable) and pork, beef and chicken meat served with *el aji* (hot sauce), boiled egg and avocado pulp.
La mazamorra Cooked corn mixed with milk and water.
El cuchuco con espinazo Wheat soup thickened with vegetables and pork loin.

ANTIOQUIA
Los frijoles con garra Red beans thickened with fried pigs' trotters.
La bandeja paisa A hearty plate of red beans, chopped meat, spicy sausages, rice, fried egg, avocado and slices of fried sweet bananas.
Los chicharrones Fried, crispy pork rind.
La mazamorra White corn cooked plain and natural.
Los buñuelos A corn puff with cheese and egg.
La natilla A thick pudding of sweet maize.
Las arepas Colombia's omnipresent corn pancake.

CARIBBEAN COAST
Las arepas con huevo A corn pancake topped with a fried egg.
El sancocho A soup of boiled meat with manioc, yam and sweet banana.
El bollo limpio Mashed young corn in a corn leaf wrap.
El bollo de yucca Mashed manioc in a corn leaf wrap.
Los patacones Fried mashed green plantain.
La cazuela de mariscos A delicious seafood soup.
La fritanga Fried meat and giblets.

PACIFIC COAST
El sancocho A soup of boiled chicken and other meats with manioc, green banana and potatoes.
Los envueltos Steamed corn pastry in a corn leaf wrap.

Carnaval Queen is of course highly popular, but Colombians here also crown a children's King and Queen as well as a Popular Queen, reflecting the festival's family focus.

The event ends with a somewhat tongue-in-cheek re-enactment of the funeral of Joselito, an age-old Carnaval character, and an impressive firework display.

La fritanga Fried beef, pork and giblets served with manioc and fried bananas.
El cuy Roasted guinea pig.
Las empanadas de pipian Yellow potato fritter with meat.

SANTANDER
Los tamales Cornflour pastry with pieces of pork and sausages steamed in a corn leaf.
El cabrito Spicy meat with fried manioc and *arepa* (corn pancake).
Las hormigas culonas Fried ants.
El moute Whole corn soup with tripe in sauce.
La pipitoria Blood sausage (similar to black pudding).

TOLIMA
El viudo de pescado Freshwater fish served with green bananas and manioc.
El tamal Rice, corn pastry, chicken, pork and bacon steamed in a corn leaf wrap.
La lechona Suckling pig stuffed with rice and peas, cooked in a clay oven.

AMAZONIA
La charapa Stewed tortoise meat.
La gamitana An Amazonian fish.

LLANOS ORIENTALES
La ternera a la llanera Venison cooked over a wood fire.

COLOMBIAN DESSERTS
Los turrones Sweet, white nougat.
La cuajada con melao Thickened milk dish served with sugarcane syrup.
El postre de natas Milk skin cooked with sugar, cinnamon and raisins.
Melcochas Sugarcane worked until tender with butter, like a soft caramel.
El manjar blanco A thick, sweet milky pudding.
Las cicadas Grated coconut with golden syrup.

DRINKS
El tinto Popular light, sweet coffee.
El guarapo Old Colombian Amerindian drink of pineapple skin fermented in water.
Aguardiente Fiery aniseed liquor made from distilled sugarcane (see page 101).
La chuchuguaza 'Firewater' of the indigenous people of the Llanos region.
El masato Fermented rice and corn with cinnamon, served cold.
El jugo Fresh tropical fruit juices.
La colombiana The nation's favourite soda of tamarindo.
Cerveza (see box, page 102)

CARNAVAL DE NEGROS Y BLACOS, PASTO (4–6 January) One of the oldest festivals in Latin America, this event takes place in the southern town of Pasto in the Atriz Valley. Its history stems from the early Spanish colonial practice of giving black slaves a day off during which they were, ironically, supposed to revel in happiness. It is reflected today in the Pasto carnival where on 5 January everyone paints themselves black and on 6 January everyone paints themselves white. The festivities are now seen as a reflection of both integration and racial diversity and the event was declared part of the National Cultural Heritage by Colombian congress in April 2002.

A pre-carnival water-fest takes place on 28 December, which is Colombia's national All Fools' Day – known as the Day of Innocent Saints. On 4 January, elaborate floats parade the streets heralding the arrival of the Castañeda family and the start of the Carnaval. The Castañeda characters are a sight to behold, based on a large family, believed to have migrated into the Pasto Valley in 1928. They arrive on a festival float surrounded by mountains of luggage, old mattresses, pots and pans, naughty children, a pregnant daughter and eccentric granny. However, as with most Carnavals it is the fun that takes precedence rather than the real story behind the festivities. The following two days see lots of black paint and white talc, processions, shows and street celebrations.

CARNIVAL OF THE DEVIL, RIOSUCIO (January, every other year – odd numbers, ie: 2007, 2009, 2011) This lively bohemian festival attracts poets, songwriters, artists and musicians. Known as the Devil's Carnival, it originates from the mid 19th-century festival of the King's Magicians which celebrated the union of two feuding neighbouring towns, one native, one Spanish, to create the Riosucio district in northwest Colombia. A fascinating array of colourful masks and 'diablada' costumes – some more than a little scary – adorn locals parading the streets.

COLOMBIAN FESTIVAL OF FOLKLORE, IBAGUÉ (last week in June) Known as the Music Capital of Colombia, Ibagué throws a great fiesta of traditional Colombian folk music such as the *bunde*, *bambuco* and *pasillo*. The **National Bambuco Folklore Festival and Beauty Pageant** in **Neiva** is also an important musical event, and takes place around the same time.

FERIA DE MANIZALES (Second week in January) Colombia's second-biggest celebration, after Barranquilla Carnaval, Manizales Fair is extremely popular. The fair oozes history and costumed and masked locals parade in 'manola' processions. The city attracts Colombian musicians and artists from other parts of Latin America and there's an interesting variety of local crafts and coffees, as well as an impressive firework display during the opening event. The show has become renowned for bullfights, a custom here since the founding fair in 1951 marked the city's first centenary. However, it's most famous for its International Coffee Beauty Pageant that elects a Reinado Internacional del Café (Miss Coffee Queen). Manizales also hosts the **Manizales Jazz Festival** and the **International Theater Festival** each September.

INTERNATIONAL THEATER FESTIVAL OF BOGOTÁ (Easter every other year, even numbers, ie: 2008, 2010, etc) This fantastic event has run since 1988 and now attracts international interest. It offers a great chance to experience Colombian theatre, as well as work from many other Latin American nations. In addition there are lots of events for children and families. See www.festivaldeteatro.com.co.

FESTIVAL DE LA LEYENDA VALLENATA, VALLEDUPAR, CÉSAR (April) In 1968 former Colombian president, Alfonso López Michelsen, *vallenato* composer and Governor of César, Rafael Escalona, and journalist then Minister of Culture, Consuelo Araújo Noguera created the Leyenda Vallenata Festival. It combines the Rosario Virgen festival with a regional love of Colombian *vallenato* music. The

Valledupar – understood to be the birthplace of the iconic accordion-based *vallenato* music heard all down Colombia's Caribbean coast and across the country – is a well-kept secret. Even less well known amongst travellers than the place itself, the Festival de Leyenda Vallenato (Festival of the Vallenato Legend) in Valledupar is arguably one of Colombia's greatest and most important celebrations, bursting at the seams with life and soul and local tradition. For travellers who find themselves in the department of Cesar (or indeed in Colombia) in April, this is the event which should be top of the list. Still a relatively undiscovered party, you'll find yourself thrown in amongst crowds of Colombians and South American tourists who have travelled from far and wide to spend five days in this pretty town, listening to classic Colombian *vallenato* folk tunes, drinking Ron Medellín and sporting every variety of Colombian sombrero. You can't help but get into the vibe as you weave in among the seemingly endless performers, stages, shows and food stalls, watching contesters move up through the ranks, each hoping they'll be the next Vallenato King.

For more information on the Festival of the Vallenato Legend each April visit www.festivalvallenato.com.

colonial legend – which could only have come from the Spanish camp – tells of the Tupes and Chimilas, two tribes from Tayrona. They fought against the Spanish colonies after an indigenous woman was publicly whipped. During the attack the Lady of the Rosary rose from the temple, her cloak blocking the arrows and thereby saving the building. Later the natives tried to poison the drinking water in the 'Sicarare lake', but were foiled again by the Virgén del Rosario who revived the poisoned Spaniards. The indigenous people were finally defeated.

The event has become a historic icon and the Fundación Festival de la Leyenda Vallenata (Vallenato Legend Festival Foundation), a non-profit foundation, was set up to promote and run it. The main attraction is the contest for greatest accordion player; the players are passionate and it's all taken very seriously. Musicians are also judged on *paseo*, *son*, *puya* and *merengue* rhythms – a great chance to sample some excellent Colombian riffs. If you do attend, don't miss the chance to watch the musicians battling with each other with spontaneous lyrics, much like the recent Western hip-hop trend.

SAN MARTÍN CUADRILLAS, META (7–11 November) Actors perform the historic clash between Moors, Christians, Amerindians and 'Negroes', showing how the contemporary blend of ethnicities was formed. The event is also popular for the *coleo*, a local-style rodeo, where Colombians ride horses to round up cattle.

SHOPPING

Many Colombians love to shop and the centre of every city, town and rural community has some retail opportunity at its heart. In Bogotá, you'll find several so-called shopping zones as well as numerous designer stores, malls and department stores. It's much the same in Cali and Medellín. In Cartagena and Santa Marta there are dozens of handicraft stalls selling baskets and ceramics. Visitors to the Guajira region will find it almost impossible not to leave without buying a

Practical Information   SHOPPING

2

mochila (handbag), while in the Andes it is Colombia's handmade woollen poncho (*ruana*) that is *de rigueur*. Bucaramanga's fragrant flower markets are a true delight and matched only in colour by the brilliant array of handmade jewellery stalls on Isla San Andrés. Pasto abounds in carvings and varnished tableware with gold jewellery sold in every city nationwide. Although Colombia is famous for its first-grade emeralds there are few true great deals. However, the same can't be said about its wonderful, rich home-grown coffee, so be sure to pick up a decent-sized bag if you pass through the Coffee Zone. Smart shoppers compare the government-sponsored Artesanas de Colombia prices with those of private vendors. Shopping hours tend to be 09.00–20.00 Monday–Saturday, but in Bogotá many stores don't open until 11.00.

A growing number of international retailers are entering Colombia's sector. In 2006, the Chilean department stores Casa & Ideas and Falabella opened for the first time here as did Zara, the Spanish clothing store. In Bogotá, Starbucks promises to create strong competition for a range of well-positioned domestic companies, including the Juan Valdez and Oma coffee shops. Locatel, the Venezuelan chain of drugstores, and Chilean supermarket Yumbo both plan to increase their presence nationwide.

Further information can be obtained from the Federación Nacional de Comerciantes (National Retail Federation, FENALCO) (*Carrera 4, No 19–85, Piso 7, Bogotá;* ❧ *(1) 336 7800;* e *sabas@fundecomercio.com.co; www.fenalco.com.co*).

PHOTOGRAPHY

Unlike the Kuna people of neighbouring Panama, none of Colombia's indigenous groups places a charge on photography within their communities, although some do place restrictions. The Ministerio de Cultura (Colombian Ministry of Culture) (*Carrera 8, No 8–09, Palachio Echeverry, Bogotá;* ❧ *(1) 342 4100; www.mincultura. gov.co*) recommends that all visitors seek permission before snapping away at indigenous peoples. In Minca, for example, the Amerindians believe photography robs them of their soul. In the Amazon, photographing tribal rituals and ceremonies without consent is wholly unacceptable. Be mindful that openly carrying a camera may provoke considerable suspicion in some of Colombia's more remote regions because of a continued culture of distrust. Any unauthorised filming is also likely to be viewed by most indigenous groups as a serious lack of respect. Some may even fear that a camera is a weapon, accordingly reacting with aggression.

MEDIA AND COMMUNICATIONS

INTERNET In 2013, the number of Spanish-speaking internet users in the world topped 222 million, according to Internet World Stats. Located in 20 countries in the Americas and Spain, this group represents the fourth-largest language group of internet users, after English, Chinese and Japanese. In recent years, the number of internet users in Latin America has increased at a rate of 100% per month. More than 6.7 million people have internet subscriptions in Colombia, according to the Colombian Telecommunications Regulating Commission (CRT), with over 21,529,415 internet users (December 2009) – almost 50% of the total population, ranking Colombia in joint fifth place in the region, at the same level as Peru but behind Chile, Argentina, Uruguay and Brazil. This is a massive jump since 2000 when the figure was 878,000 and is a staggering two million up since 2005. Much of this increase is due to a surge in broadband subscribers, up 97% in 2007 alone. Dial-up usage in Colombia is declining year on year and currently represents fewer than 300,000 subscribers. Broadband has been available in Colombia since 1997 and boasts the fastest growth rate in Latin America. Over 4.2 million of Colombia's 6.7 million internet subscribers use mobile internet technology. And now 80% of Colombians are regularly accessing the internet either via their phones or computers.

There are numerous internet cafés in all Colombian cities, and more and more are springing up in many of its smaller, rural towns. Most open early, usually at 07.00. Closing time can be as late as midnight but is generally around 22.00. Many are now open seven days a week, but Sundays can't be taken as read. Almost all of Colombia's internet joints offer printing, scanning and faxing. Some also sell computer peripherals, such as ink, disks and paper. Costs vary from place to place around the country but expect to pay 1,500–2,500COP per hour on average. Larger hotels almost always have an internet facility for guests that is more pricey, but convenient. An hour in a five-star in Bogotá will cost around US$6 per hour while it could reach US$10 in one of Cartagena's top-notch hotels. Wi-Fi is also becoming increasingly more accessible in Colombia's urban centres, including some of the main shopping malls. Every *Yellow Pages* region-wide contains a list of local cybercafés with many public libraries also housing internet services. NB: for the @ symbol use Alt + 64.

TELEPHONE The international dialling code for Colombia is +57. The outgoing code depends on which network is used to dial out on (eg: 005 for Orbitel) followed by the relevant country code (eg: 00544 for the United Kingdom). For calls to other Colombian cities, use the blue-and-yellow or red long-distance booths marked '*larga distancia*'. They only accept 500 peso coins. To make credit-card and collect/reverse-charge calls through an AT&T operator, dial 980 11 0011. For MCI, dial 980 16 0001. For Sprint, dial 980 13 0010.

Making a regional call is on a par with using the American phone system, but is more complicated than the UK. The access code to make a call within the country from another area depends on what network is used. For example, the area code for Bogotá is 1, but using Orbitel it would be dialled as (05)1 and for Telecom (09)1. Within Colombia, the three-digit city code prefix is dropped when making local calls. Regular coin-operated street payphones accept 200 and 500 peso denominations. For directory assistance within Colombia, dial 113.

Colombia's healthy mobile-phone market has numerous roaming agreements with international network operators. CLARO, the Brazilian-owned company, is Colombia's primary network provider with 17.8 million lines (64% of the market). Spain's Telefónica is second (with 7.75 million) and Colombia Movil SA third with 2.15 million lines. Colombia is blessed with large numbers of international payphones with well-staffed CLARO telephone offices in most towns and cities countrywide. Colombia uses the GSM frequencies GSM 850/GSM 1900. Travellers will need to check compatibility of their mobile-phone technology with Colombian frequencies. The following countries are matched either wholly or in part: Anguilla (100% match), Antigua (67% match), Belize (67% match), Brazil (83% match), Cayman Islands (83% match), Cuba (83% match), Dominican Republic (83% match), Ecuador (83% match), Haiti (83% match), Honduras (100% match), Jamaica (67% match), Mexico (67% match), Nicaragua (83% match), Panama (100% match), Puerto Rico (67% match).

Hiring a cell phone is a wise investment in Colombia as it is almost impossible to co-ordinate travel plans without one. On a safety basis, carrying a mobile is also a worthwhile precaution. Network coverage is generally pretty good although rural and mountainous areas can be patchy. In the Amazon, the roaming function goes into overdrive given the proximity to Brazil and Peru. Thousands of enterprising Colombians actively sell airtime on their cell phones to the general public at 200,000–300,000COP a minute. All manner of roadside signs, sandwich boards and posters in windows advertise this service all over the country, from streetside fruit stalls in Boyacá to the plazas of Medellín. Buying a cheap 'pay as you go' mobile phone is another option. Expect to pay around US$50 for a decent model; phonecards are sold everywhere in Colombia in 2,000COP, 5,000COP and 10,000COP values.

POST Today, ADPOSTAL's workload has been taken over by 4/72 (National Postal Services, SPN) with the Colombian postal system a complicated jigsaw of domestic and international services delivered by a number of suppliers. All international airmail is handled by Avianca, Colombia's largest airline. Airmail post offices are normally next to the airline's offices and are open 07.30–18.00 weekdays, 08.00–noon Saturday. Colombia's regular post offices are generally open 09.00–15.00 weekdays but offer a domestic service only. Sending a letter by airmail to Europe costs 16,000COP (7,500COP to the US) via a reliable service that takes between seven and 14 days. Postcards are cheaper at 10,000COP to anywhere outside of Colombia.

Avianca also operates the poste restante system and will hold letters for up to 30 days. Be sure to take a passport along when collecting letters from Avianca's offices. Some understand the concept of poste restante far better than others, so also prepare to be patient. The main office in Bogotá is by far the most organised of the bunch. Post should be addressed as follows:

YOUR NAME
C/o Lista de Correos Avianca
Edificio Avianca
Carrera 7, No 16–36
Bogotá
Colombia

NEWSPAPERS, MAGAZINES AND NEWS AGENCIES News is an important part of Colombian culture as historically communication between the regions has been sparse. This is partly due to the country being so divided geographically and also because the roads were once so difficult to travel that people rarely journeyed far from home. Therefore, Colombians have always regarded news and information as highly important and have respected reliability and accuracy. Journalism in Colombia is a skilled profession with newspapers written and edited well. They are still depended on and trusted and widely available nationwide.

Colombia's news sources include seven broadcast outlets with 15 internet news media, nine news magazines (including the English-language *Economist*) and five press agencies in English, Spanish and German. Colombia's three daily newspapers (all Spanish-language) wield considerable power but are just a small part of the nation's many regional titles – at the last count 37 and rising. Bogotá's leading newspaper is *El Tiempo* (*www.eltiempo.com*) with *El Mundo* (*www.elmundo.com*) and *El Colombiano* (*www.elcolombiano.com*) in Medellín, and *El Occidente* (*www. occidente.co*) and *El Pais* (*www.elpais.com*) in Cali. *El Espectador* (*www.elespectador. com*) is another popular Bogotá-based newspaper. There are two English-language newspapers in Bogotá: *The City Paper* (*www.thecitypaperbogota.com*) and *The Bogotá Post* (*www.thebogotapost.com*).

Colombia's press and regional radio in zones of conflict are the most exposed. This phenomenon of impunity is the major threat to press freedom in Colombia and in Latin America.

Journalist Enrique Santos Calderón, *El Tiempo*, 2005

Despite both national and international press-freedom organisations in Colombia reporting a significant decrease in the number of journalists murdered in relation to their work, journalism remained one of the most dangerous professions in the country in 2010 according to the Committee to Protect Journalists (CPJ). Twenty-eight journalists were murdered, while five others disappeared, in eight Latin American countries in 2009 alone, according to the Commission to Investigate Attacks Against Journalists (Comisión Investigadora de Atentados a Periodistas, CIAP), affiliated with the Latin American Federation of Journalists (Federación Latinoamericana de Periodistas, FELAP). Since 1976, some 800 journalists have been slain in Latin America, with 83 killed in Colombia between 1996 and 2006, according to the Organization of American States' Office of the Special Rapporteur for Freedom of Expression. In 2005, the World Press Freedom Index (*www.ifex.org*) ranked Colombia 128th out of 168 countries, placing it second to last among American continent countries but above Mexico at 135th.

Media for Peace, an NGO of journalists, has members in Bogotá, Medellín, Cali, Monteria, Sincelejo, Pasto, Florencia, Valledupar and Barrancabermeja. In 2006, three Colombian journalists were murdered (Gustavo Rojas Gabalo, Mariano Pérez Murga and Francisco Bonilla Romero) while seven others were forced to flee their homes after receiving death threats. Prayers are said for the 100-plus journalists killed in Colombia since 1980 on World Press Freedom Day each year (*http://portal.unesco.org*). This United Nations' initiative is designed to raise awareness of the importance of worldwide press freedom. It was established in 1993 and is held on 3 May.

Since 1997, the UNESCO/Guillermo Cano World Press Freedom Prize has been awarded on this day to a deserving individual, organisation or institution that has made an outstanding contribution to the defence and promotion of press freedom. The prize is named in honour of Colombian journalist Guillermo Cano Isaza who was assassinated in front of the offices of his newspaper, *El Espectador*, in Bogotá in 1986.

For further information, contact Reporters Without Borders (*www.rsf.org*), the International Federation of Journalists (*www.ifj.org*) or the Committee to Protect Journalists (*www.cpj.org*).

BUSINESS

Colombian business executives tend to like certainty, conservatism and conformity, much like many of their Latin American counterparts. Although there is a certain regard for those prepared to bend the rules, Colombia's business world also retains a respect for regulations. It also likes controls and is slow to accept change so decisions are made slowly. Most business people would readily admit to being risk-averse, with little desire to put everything on black without good reason. Red tape makes effecting change a sluggish process.

Relationships are everything in Colombian business circles, with a high emphasis placed on close ties with individuals. Most people are tolerant of Colombia's vast inequalities of wealth and power. They are also accepting of the country's masculine business clans, despite recognising the growing number of high-powered female business leaders.

Colombia's Catholic faith plays a large part in many people's belief that there is an absolute 'truth' – and this conviction is a strong and powerful force in the nation's commercial world. Colombians tend to be astute, wise and detail-orientated. However, despite good intellect, many often remain ultimately ruled by emotions and their heart.

How you dress when doing business in Colombia depends on location, as formality increases the more inland you are. On the Caribbean, a short-sleeved shirt and shorts can be OK for a meeting but elsewhere more conservative attire is a sensible option, with suits in dark colours preferred. Don't be surprised by the proximity of Colombian face-to-face discussions. Personal space is not being invaded; it is just the Colombian way to stand closer together than Europeans or North Americans. Business appointments should be scheduled in advance, but once made punctuality is an altogether more relaxed affair. Foreign business people should have their business cards printed in English on one side and in Spanish on the other. At a business lunch, let the host make the first toast and expect a fight over the bill. Handshaking is the customary greeting in business, while amongst friends an *abrazo* (embrace) is the norm.

In Colombia, titles are important, so address a person correctly by profession, such as *arquitecto* (architect), *profesor* (teacher), *ingeniero* (engineer) or *abogado* (lawyer). Persons without a professional title should be addressed as *señor* (Mr), *señora* (Mrs) or *señorita* (Miss), plus their surnames. To be polite, stick to conversations about history, football and the weather and be sure to avoid topics that relate to politics, drugs and religion. Colombians will also be keen to ask you, as a foreigner, about your favourite experiences of their homeland, so it pays to have a few chosen anecdotes up your sleeve.

Most Colombian cities have a chamber of commerce office, as do some smaller rural towns.

Barranquilla Chamber of Commerce Antiguo Edificio de la Aduana, Vía 40, No 36–135, Barranquilla; ☎ (5) 330 3700; e comunica@camarabaq.org.co

Buenaventura Chamber of Commerce Calle 1, No 1A–88, Buenaventura; ☎ (2) 242 4508/3623; e ccbuvpresidencia@correopeopleonline.com.co; www.ccbun.org

Buga Chamber of Commerce Carrera 14, No 5–53, Buga; ☎ (2) 228 0088; e camara@ccbuga.org; www.ccbuga.com.co

Cartagena Chamber of Commerce Calle Santa Teresa, No 32–41 AA 16, Cartagena; ☎ (5) 660 0793/95/63; e camaradecomercio@cccartagena.org.co

Cauca Chamber of Commerce Carrera 7, No 4–36, Cauca; ☎ (2) 824 3625; e cccauca@cccauca.org.co; www.cccauca.org.co

Ipiales Chamber of Commerce Carrera 11, No 15–28, Ipiales; ☎ (2) 773 2465/3926; e ccipia@telecom.com.co

Manizales Chamber of Commerce Carrera 23, No 26–60, Manizales; ☎ (6) 884 1840/0919; e infoccm@ccm.org.co; www.ccmpc.org.co

Neiva Chamber of Commerce Carrera 5, No 10–36 Piso 3, Neiva; ☎ (8) 871 3740/3666; e info@ccneiva.org; www.ccneiva.org

Pereira Chamber of Commerce Carrera 8, No 23–09, Local 10, Pereira; ☎ (6) 338 7800; e información@camarapereira.org.co; www.camarapereira.org.co

Tunja Chamber of Commerce Calle 21, No 10–52, Tunja; ☎ (08) 740 2000; www.ccomerciotunja.org.co

Valledupar Chamber of Commerce Calle 15, No 4–33, Valledupar; ☎ (5) 574 9021/4448; e camaravalledupar@telecom.com.co; www.ccvalledupar.org.co

Villavivencio Chamber of Commerce Calle 39, No 31–47, Villavivencio; ☎ (8) 671 3737; e informacion@ccv.org.co; www.ccv.org.co

BUYING PROPERTY

In Colombia, under law a foreigner has the right to buy, own, register, sell and rent real estate. They can also repatriate all proceeds from the sale of property to their country of origin on equal terms to Colombia citizens. Although most analysts agree that a real estate boom is unlikely to happen until Colombia achieves countrywide peace, this hasn't stopped prime cities and coastal resorts experiencing significant rises in the value of property. Individual foreign investors from the US, Europe and other Latin American countries are injecting some serious money into the Colombian economy. In 2007, the world witnessed a whole new era of confidence in Colombia's real estate market, with an unprecedented number of non-nationals snapping up property 'ahead of the crowd' to take advantage of low prices. Prime hot spots include all of Colombia's major cities, including Bogotá, Medellín, Cali and Barranquilla. Yet it is Cartagena and Santa Marta on the Caribbean coast that boast the largest density of foreign property owners. Most have invested in colonial-era homes in the centre of town or swish, new high-rise apartments along the coast. Expect to pay an average cost per square metre of approximately 12,000,000COP for a property in a nice location in good condition. Variables that impact on price include bathrooms, kitchens, swimming pools, dedicated parking spaces, gardens, etc. Additional fees to consider include monthly administration fees for an apartment. Construction quality is high in Colombia as there is often a tendency to 'over-design' and 'over-spec' a property because they are obligated under law to guarantee their work personally for five years. To reduce or eliminate potential structural problems, most building companies add more steel and concrete than commonly used. Labour costs are also much lower in Colombia, having a direct effect on price.

Annual property taxes vary, depending on the municipality, but are levied at between 1% and 6%. Market values are usually higher than assessed values, eg: for an apartment that cost 180,000,000COP but which is assessed at 120,000,000COP the amount due in tax is 780,000COP (0.65%) per year. Medellín, like other major cities in Colombia, is undergoing a housing boom. New apartment projects are springing up all over the city, with resale properties enjoying a brisk demand. El Poblado is considered the most desirable area in the city. Other prime areas are Laureles, Estadio, Conquistadores, Velodromo, Floresta, Belén La Palma and Santa Mónica. An apartment will start at 682,500,000COP – at least. In Barranquilla, some neighbourhoods have seen housing increase in value by 20% since 2005 with average price tags of 400,000,000COP for a luxury two-bedroom flat. Another boomtown is Cali where numerous luxurious apartment blocks are under construction. Expect to pay upwards of 500,000,000COP for a swish apartment that could benefit from 40% capital appreciation within a couple of years.

Further information can be obtained from Cartagena Real Estate (*www.cartagenacolombiarealestate.com*), Colliers International (*www.colliersmn.com*) and Medellín Real Estate (*www.medellininfo.com/realestate*). Bogotá-based Colombia International has a strong presence in the capital (*www.colombiainternational.co*).

CULTURAL ETIQUETTE

Like many Latin nations, Colombians are extremely hard-working, but timing is not their strong point. Meetings can be relaxed and it is not uncommon for Colombians to be a little late on arrival, but this is not always the case. Timings for events, buses, trains and tours can range from punctual to seriously random – but it pays to arrive on time with the attitude that waiting a little isn't a problem.

Colombians are glad to receive foreign visitors and will often go out of their way to help them. Close friends will usually share an *abrazo* (embrace) and a kiss on the right cheek – and physical exchanges, such as a touch on the arm or a pat on the shoulder, are common even between acquaintances. Colombians are often happy to offer directions and recommendations and will happily add their own opinion on the best places to eat or stay. They have a tendency to exaggerate: you may, for example, receive ambiguous directions, but this is purely because they would rather please you than let you down. The term 'Locombia' was coined by a columnist of the Bogotá daily newspaper *El Espectador* to reflect Colombia's blessed (or cursed) touch of madness-cum-gusto – and the enthusiastic language they use mirrors this zest for life.

I feel fantastic!	*Me siento fenomenal!*
That was delicious!	*Estaba buenisimo!*
I think I've had one too many!	*Creo que he tomado una de más!*
This is insane!	*Esto es una locura!*
Is this a local custom?	*Esto es una costumbre local o nacional?*
That was amazing!	*Eso fue incredíble!*
That's great!	*Eso, eso!*
Come on!	*Venga vamos!*
This place is great!	*Es un lugar bárbaro!*
It's been great meeting you!	*Me ha encantado conocerte!*
That's beautiful, isn't it!	*Qué precuiso, no?*
I love it here!	*Me encanta esto!*
How cool!	*Qué bárbaro!*

Although different customs apply throughout Colombia some important generalisations can be made. Colombians tend to have expectations regarding the manners of visitors to their country. This will vary from person to person so it is

LEARNING THE LINGO

No hablas español? Well, it's not an insurmountable problem. However, things are considerably easier if you pick up more than just a smattering of tourist Spanish. Fluency in the language is essential for those keen to stay more than a few weeks. Both the Universidad Santiago de Cali Institute of Languages and the Pontifica Universidad Javeriana in Cali offer affordable Spanish-language tuition for foreigners with Berlitz classes in Bogotá – plus an endless list of Spanish-language schools. Hiring a private tutor is an easy and inexpensive option. The British Council also has an extensive database of English–Spanish tutors nationwide.

International House www.ihes.com. Spanish-language courses in Bogotá, includes intensive studies, 1-to-1 courses & group tuition. From US$350.

Nueva Lengua www.nuevalengua.com. Courses in Bogotá, Cartagena & Medellín in numerous shapes & sizes with prices from 20hrs a week at US$200 per week plus a range of accommodation options. University affiliated.

PEPE Colombia www.nativeenglishcenter.com/PEPE/. Offers Spanish lessons to foreign students with private lessons & group tuition (max 12 people). From US$347 for 4 weeks, includes accommodation & all meals.

impossible to avoid every faux pas. However, ignoring some ingrained beliefs and behaviours is a sure way to upset someone somehow. The following may help you avoid looking rude, foolish or worse.

- Colombians tend to use exaggerated gestures. They also engage in physical contact and will be openly 'touchy feely' even with strangers.
- Many Colombians use smaller dimensions of personal space than people from English-speaking cultures. Avoid the temptation to step away as it sends out negative signals.
- Using a gesture of an upwards palm with the fingers curled back is considered a romantic solicitation in Colombia.
- Gifts are never opened in public unless the giver insists.
- Older people are treated with considerable respect. Men are often referred to as Don and women as Doña, followed by their first names.
- Small talk is an essential preamble to every discussion in Colombia. Don't rush it, for this seemingly trivial exchange is considered important. 'Getting to the point' straight away is viewed as pushy and impolite.
- Unless it is raised by a Colombian, shy away from talking about politics.
- It is also important to avoid criticising the Catholic Church or discussing Colombia's drug trade, as these are both delicate topics.

LIVING IN COLOMBIA

Many English-language expatriates in Colombia work as English teachers, as native English tutors are in considerable demand. Teaching jobs usually require a university degree and applicants with a teaching certificate are highly sought after. Other expat job options include those at major hotels or with multi-national corporations. Several major global companies have a presence in Colombia, including Michelin, Mobil, DHL, Fuller, Xerox, Microsoft, Coca-Cola, Siemens, Sony and Mazda. Medical care, nursery schooling, child care and domestic help are all widely available and reasonably priced.

Key lifestyle benefits for expatriates include Colombia's low cost of living, excellent infrastructure and high standard of restaurants, spas, hotels and leisure facilities. Most cities are close to either the mountains or the coastline in a country that embraces fresh air, exercise and enjoying quality family time. British and American schools offer a high educational standard. Colombia is also just a 3-hour jaunt to Florida or the Caribbean with daily flights into the UK. Of course, all this needs to be weighed against the continued safety concerns within a country still struggling towards peacetime. Yet, Colombia's growing number of foreign residents is testament to the nation's potential as a haven for expatriates.

Further information is available from the British Council in Colombia (*www. britishcouncil.org/colombia*).

TRAVELLING POSITIVELY

FRIENDS OF COLOMBIA FOR SOCIAL AID (FOSCA) (*72 Humber Rd, Blackheath, London SE3 7LU;* e *friendsofcol@aol.com; www.friendsofcolombia.co.uk*) This UK-based charity is devoted to improving the lives of some of Colombia's most disadvantaged children by supplying much-needed medical and educational equipment. Each year, it is inundated with requests for help from children's hospitals and charities and is looking for funding and sponsors in a bid to fulfil the demand. FOSCA is currently working with the Hospital de la Misericordia in Bogotá, the Guardería Hogar Infantil La Esmeralda in Popayán, Liga contra la Epilepsia Capítulo Valle in Cali, the Asociación Benéfica Cristiana ABC Prodein in Bogotá, the Liga Colombiana de Hemofílicos y otras Deficiencies Sanguineas in Bogotá, Guarderia Infantil Niña María in Cazucá, the Hospital San José in Samaná, the Fundación CRAN in Bogotá and the Hospital Club Noel in Cali.

FUNDACIÓN CAMINOS DE IDENTIDAD (FUCAI) (*Calle 54, No 10–81, Oficina 301, Bogotá; www.bernardvanleer.org*) In support of the indigenous people of Colombia, the Fundación Caminos de Identidad has a strong family focus, working with a number of tribal groups, including the Uitoto of La Chorrera in the midst of the Colombian Amazon region. Mothers with young children in some of Colombia's most remote riverside village communities are given help with childrearing. FUCAI also supports those encountering domestic violence. Local people are given training in promoting education in close collaboration with teachers and volunteers. The foundation is a charity established in 1949 in the Netherlands by Bernard van Leer, a Dutch industrialist and philanthropist who died in 1958. Today it supports more than 140 major projects in 21 countries worldwide and has been working in Colombia since 1998 with a large international volunteer force. FUCAI desperately needs volunteer workers, funding and specialist social workers (Spanish-speaking).

FUNDACIÓN CARVAJAL (*Carrera 25, No 2–01, Cali;* ✎ *(2) 554 2949; e comunica@ fundacioncarvajal.org.co; www.fundacioncarvajal.org.co*) Since 1981, the Carvajal Foundation's primary area of activity has been the district of Aguablanca, a very poor area of Cali with 350,000 inhabitants in an area of less than six square miles. Most of the Aguablanca community earns a living from scavenging the local rubbish dumps. Fundación Carvajal has helped to organise these efforts in more commercial terms. Waste materials of industrial use are now sold by the community to finance basic services, such as water supplies, sewer systems, electricity and street paving. The charity provides three centres in each of Aguablanca's three neighbourhoods. It also runs a 'materials bank' depot for housing construction companies in the area. Volunteer workers are in short supply but are very welcome, as are funds and donations. Spanish-speaking travellers with specialist skills are particularly welcome.

HEALING COLOMBIA: FAMILY CARE (*www.healingcolombia.org*) This small, Bogotá charity is totally youth-focused, working in inner-city areas where Colombia's problems with poverty, drug-taking and gang crime are most prevalent. In partnership with government institutions, the therapeutic community and other NGOs in Bogotá, it runs programmes for the underprivileged. It also delivers humanitarian aid to Colombia's poorest communities. Projects include a drug prevention programme in Bogotá's slums, a drug rehab programme in the Colombian prison system, health and lifestyle counselling, music therapy sessions, sports programmes and other recreational activities, English-language courses and a year-long mentoring programme. Healing Colombia is actively seeking a wide range of volunteer workers and is fundraising for donations via the Family Care Foundation in the US (✎ +1 800 992 2383). Managers Mario Torres and Sophia Dow are also in desperate need of teaching materials, Spanish-speaking counsellors and rehab specialists, plus musicians to help implement their highly successful music therapy programme.

MOI POUR TOIT FOUNDATION (*Rue de la Délèze 27, 1920 Martigny, Switzerland;* \ *+41 27 722 6246;* m *+41 79 221 0246; www.fundacioncolombia.com*) This non-governmental Swiss–Colombian organisation supports mistreated and abandoned children in the Pereira region, providing a refuge for *'gamines'* (homeless kids) to ensure they have warmth, shelter, legal protection, education and hope for the future. Launched in 1991 from a head office in Martigny, Switzerland, by journalist Christian Michellod, Moi Pour Toit is managed by director Juan Pablo Bedoya Florez in Colombia. Comprising three major sectors – an emergency centre for boys, a farm in the country, and a house for girls – the foundation can house 70 children aged five–18. The foundation functions on the principle of direct aid, with every donated Swiss franc reaching its intended destination intact. All administrative expenses are covered by the sale of clothes, handicrafts and Colombian coffee but the Moi Pour Toit Foundation relies on donations to provide for its 70 children and 30 employees. Volunteers, donations and equipment (especially white goods) are particularly welcome.

PEOPLES OF THE WORLD FOUNDATION (*www.peoplesoftheworld.org*) The US-based Peoples of the World Foundation is looking for additional people to join its board of directors as well as forum moderators to manage its indigenous peoples discussion board. Translators are also in demand to work on multi-language materials, especially those who can translate into any of the many native tongues. Peoples of the World champions the rights of indigenous peoples to gain access to education and as well as its work in Colombia it also campaigns against marginalisation throughout the world. Online application forms offer a wide range of volunteer opportunities.

SOS CHILDREN'S VILLAGES (*www.sos-childrensvillages.org*) SOS has had a presence in Colombia since 1968, and 1971 saw the first arrivals in its Children's Village in Bogotá. The capital attracts large numbers of displaced persons from the country's rural areas and has a sizeable poor community. As a consequence, the number of orphans in Bogotá is particularly large. Today SOS Children's Villages has five centres across the country, including those in Bogotá, Ibagué, Rionegro and Bucaramanga. However in a country where over one million children aged five–17 are working and more than one million have been displaced in the last 15 years, the challenges are tough. As well as providing long-term care for orphaned and abandoned children in Colombia, SOS Children's Villages is involved in caring for street children in Bogotá. In the San Vitorino district many children find that stealing and drug dealing are their only means of survival. SOS provides food, shelter and education for these abandoned children, many of whom have never had an education or the support of a family unit. The oldest Bogotá Village is run by the inspirational Fabio Curtidor Argüello and contains 12–18 homes for 'families' of ten children in close-knit settings. They are desperate for musical instruments, sports equipment and art materials. They also need funding and sponsors and are keen to attract volunteers for project work, preferably Spanish-speakers. Contact Fabio Curtidor Argüello directly (*Aldeas Infantiles SOS Colombia; Carrera 28, No 94 A–49, Barrio La Castellana;* \ *+57 (1) 256 4208/634 8049; www.aldeasinfantiles.org.co*).

COLOMBIA ONLINE

For additional online content, articles, photos and more on Colombia, why not visit www.bradtguides.com/colombia.

Part Two

THE GUIDE

3

Bogotá

Telephone code 1

En la patria no hay otra ni habrá
(There isn't another in the nation, neither will there be)
Nuestra voz la repiten los siglos: Bogotá... Bogotá... Bogotá!
(Our voice is repeated over the centuries: Bogotá... Bogotá... Bogotá!)
Bogotá anthem, Pedro Medina Avendaño

Once a byword for danger, the city of Bogotá (also on occasion officially referred to as Bogotá DC as in Bogotá, Distrito Capital) has undergone a significant clean-up act in recent years, following a passionate campaign aimed at nurturing societal change. Visionary leadership has ignited fresh fire into the belly of Bogotá's eight million inhabitants and 11 million in its catchment area, via a host of pioneering strategies that have helped change the mindset and behaviour of a once unruly urban sprawl. Today, Bogotá is a cosmopolitan city on the up, a metropolis that bears the signs of modern self-improvement. Sleek skyscrapers and a futuristic transit system are symbols of an (almost) transformed city that boasts 4,594 public parks. Thousands of cyclists of all ages criss-cross Bogotá's wide, green expanses on Latin America's largest bike-path network. Car use is restricted to lessen congestion. Vehicles no longer park on pavements and basic traffic laws such as stopping at a red light, giving priority to pedestrians, and buses stopping only at bus stops are largely obeyed (except perhaps by *busetas*). Citizenship is no longer a laughable concept in the city and today the mood is one of highly charged optimism. Designer stores, swanky cafés, lounge bars and fine restaurants are testament to Bogotá's ambition to become one of the most desirable cities on the radar. Sunday in the city is a family day when the streets take on a party atmosphere of clowns, music and picnics in the parks. Food vendors, churchgoers and mothers with pushchairs converge on the plazas and compete for space with armies of pigeons. Jugglers take centre stage on empty roundabouts while old women on flower stalls sit amongst a fragrant kaleidoscope of varicoloured blooms. Paths are freshly swept and roads free of rubbish in a place where choking smog once dominated the cityscape. Today the people of Bogotá love and respect their city – it is now oh-so *chévere* (cool) to be Bogotano, a far cry from the sentiment of a decade ago when it was a place that was truly loathed.

Yet modern-day Bogotá still has its many problems, some of which are born out of a rapidly expanding refugee population displaced from Colombia's rural provinces. Constant streams of migrants arrive in the capital full of high hopes, only to find the city's streets aren't paved with gold. Most of these poor peasants end up in the makeshift shanty towns that sprawl along Bogotá's fast-decaying southern nub. Conditions are nothing short of horrendous with sanitation and fresh water scarce. Piles of rotting rubbish are scavenged for a glimmer of hope in sewage-swamped streets that are as lawless as they are vile. Pickpockets plague the shopping malls and all sorts of evils roam the streets after dark, yet, despite this,

Colombia's 'first city' refuses to be in the doldrums. Bogotanos are largely a morally responsive, socially conscious and fashionably introspective bunch – so the mood within vast swathes of the city is upbeat. Big hotels are also expressing confidence in Bogotá's promising future – Hilton returned to open a swanky US$27 million hotel in 2009 and the Marriott chain is now here, with two enormous hotels representing a clear show of faith. However, the vast disparities that exist between the affluent north and poverty-stricken south are nothing short of shocking – two very different faces of Bogotá, wrapped around the bubblegum-coloured colonial core of the old quarter of the city.

HISTORY

Called Bacatá by the Muiscas long before the Spanish colonised the area, the fertile highland plateau on which Bogotá sprawls was once an advanced pre-Columbian ancient civilisation composed of numerous small villages. Although no historical documents exist, it is widely accepted that the Spanish settlement was founded on 6 August 1538 by Gonzalo Jiménez de Quesada. He named it 'Santa Fé de Bacatá' after his birthplace Santa Fé in Spain, affixing it to the local 'Bacatá'. At the time of its foundation, Bogotá (known as Santa Fé) consisted of a dozen wooden huts and a small chapel. The Muisca built up large collections of gold, manufacturing a diverse range of pieces, including small anthropomorphic or zoomorphic figures (*tunjos*) that were offered to the gods as funerary and sacred gifts. They also made necklaces, bracelets, earrings, pectorals, nose rings and other pieces used for self-adornment – and were also excellent at weaving and outstanding potters. The Spanish razed all of the Muisca's sacred sites to the ground to make way for churches. Communities were plundered and an indigenous population of more than half a million ultimately destroyed.

In 1810, the citizens revolted against Spanish rule but the resulting fragile government was plagued with internal discord. Spanish military loyalists reassumed control of the city temporarily from 1816 to 1819. After Colombia gained independence from the Spanish, Bogotá was affirmed as the capital of Gran Colombia, a federation combining the territories of modern Panama, Colombia, Venezuela and Ecuador. When that republic was dissolved, Bogotá remained the capital of New Granada, later to become the Republic of Colombia, and by the middle of the 19th century the city had grown considerably in stature and size. A 1789 census recorded 18,161 inhabitants and by 1819 the city population amounted to 30,000, distributed in 195 blocks. More than 30 churches and at least a dozen schools served the city with a mule-powered tramway built in 1884. Railway access to the trading ports on the mighty Río Magdalena signified boom time ahead of a period of industrialisation that prompted Bogotá's further growth. In 1832, a census recorded 36,465 inhabitants. In 1881, the city's population was 84,723, reaching nearly 100,000 by the end of the century. Yet Bogotá still had very little industry with an economy that relied on artisan work grouped in the city's struggling commercial sectors. Slowly, retail outlets began to open around the Plaza de Bolívar, a popular centre of hat stores and women's fashion. Several shops selling imported goods began to spring up around Calle Ocho with four main banks opening offices in the city between 1870 and 1883. When the Bavaria Brewery established a base in Bogotá in 1889 it became one of the city's major industries. In 1923, a US compensatory pay-off in relation to Panama brought increased prosperity to the capital, attracting foreign investment and improving infrastructure and expanding the urban economy. However, violence began to erupt countrywide in the mid 1940s, drawing a steady stream of migrants to the city – yet with assassinations, kidnappings, hostage-takings and murders, Bogotá wasn't quite the safe haven many hoped it would be. Social disorder wreaked havoc in the makeshift shanty towns that began to spring up around the city – expanding it to over 33,000ha. This influx of peasants fleeing the violence of rural Colombia tripled the population, from 700,000 in 1951 to 1.6 million in 1964 and 2.5 million in 1973. By 1985, the number of inhabitants in the capital had increased to 4.1 million, and by 1993 almost six million people called Bogotá home.

By the mid 1990s, Bogotá was one of the world's most dangerous cities with a homicide rate of 80 per 100,000. In the last decade, however, Bogotá has gone to great lengths to change both its crime rate and its image. By 2005, Bogotá had a murder rate of 23 persons per 100,000 inhabitants – a 71% drop in ten years. Today, in terms of homicides, it ranks well below Washington DC, Caracas, São Paulo, Mexico City and Rio de Janeiro, with a rate of 16.7 per 100,000, largely resulting from a handgun prohibition introduced by the city's controversial mayor Gustavo Petro.

Bogotá is now known as the 'Athens of Latin America' on account of the city residents' education (16% of its 8 million population are students) and cultural appreciation. Every two years it plays host to the Iberoamerican Theater Festival – the biggest theatre festival on the planet. In 2007, Bogotá was named 'Book Capital of the World' due to the Luis Angél Arango Library receiving a staggering 7,000 daily visits (2.2 million in total in 2006). Since 1999, it has been the most attended library on earth, with more annual visitors than New York Public Library, the British Library and the Pompidou Centre in Paris.

GEOGRAPHY

Bogotá is a difficult city to explore on account of its sprawl, with an urban perimeter that continues to expand. Seven urban zones attempt to make sense of the structure of the metropolis with the city then split into 20 sectors, each governed by a local mayor and administrative board under the control of the main mayoral office. Located on tableland in the eastern mountain chain of the Andes 2,630m above sea level, Bogotá is bounded by the Río Bogotá to the west, the Sumapaz páramo to the south and the agricultural plains of the Sabana to the north. It is also surrounded by the Arzobispo, San Cristóbal, San Francisco and Tunjuelito rivers and zoned as follows:

ZONA 1 NORTE (NORTHERN ZONE 1) Home to the city's key financial centres, main museums, shopping, nightlife (Zona Rosa/Pink Zone), churches and cultural attractions as well as the city's most affluent and modern suburbs

ZONA 2 NOROCCIDENTE (NORTHWEST ZONE 2) Includes many large-scale industrial parks and retail outlets

ZONA 3 OCCIDENTE (WEST ZONE 3) Contains industrial areas, parks, the National University, athletic stadiums and El Dorado International Airport

ZONA 4 SUR (SOUTH ZONE 4) Primarily an industrial and working-class sector with large shanty towns on its outer edges

ZONA 5 CENTRO (CENTRAL ZONE 5) Includes the historic quarter La Candelaria and the neighbourhoods around the International Center where most of the city's political and most important commercial, cultural, governmental and financial offices are located

ZONA 6 (ZONE 6) Surrounding areas

ZONA 7 (ZONE 7) Other cities

Carrera 14 (Avenida 14) is the city's major artery, connecting the centre with the north and south. Bogotá's urban plan is based around *calles* (roads) running east to west with *carreras* (streets) that run north–south in direction. In simple terms, the city is divided into two, with around 200 blocks north and 100 blocks south.

CLIMATE

As South America's third-highest capital city after La Paz and Quito, Bogotá is often crisp and cooler than many visitors expect. The city's average temperature is 14°C year-round, plummeting to around 9°C at night – although as Bogotá is climatically variant, highs of 25°C can suddenly catch you out. Generally, expect it to hit around 19°C each day and pack a light sweater as a just-in-case measure. Be prepared for showers and plan for clear skies and dizzying altitude. The main dry season runs from December to March with a second from July to August. Bogotá's annual rainfall averages about 1,020mm, with April and October the wettest months.

ARCHITECTURE

Bogotá won the prestigious Golden Lion Award in 2006 at the 10th International Architecture Exhibition. In 2010, it received the Latin American award in Urban Planning and Information Platforms for its green spaces and community focus. In 2013, the city won the coveted C40 and Siemens Urban Transportation category for its TransMilenio + E-Taxis project and was identified as a world leader in introducing electric taxis and expanding the TransMilenio bendy-bus system to reduce gases that contribute to climate change. These international accolades forced the city's detractors to see it in a different light. Bogotá isn't a stunning, flawless urban centre – far from it; there is still plenty to do and the ongoing debate surrounding a proposed metro system continues to rumble on despite promises to the contrary by President Juan Manuel Santos. However, there is undoubtedly something rather pleasing about the Colombian capital's eclectic mishmash of architectural styles. Perfect pavements meet crumbling concrete slabs on wonky pavements edged by multi-coloured, pebble-dashed apartment blocks and fairy-tale gabled buildings. Faded colonial façades stand dominated by futuristic high-rise towers amidst an urban jigsaw of red brick, chrome, graffiti and mirrored glass. Painted shutters and ornate balconies look out on patches of manicured lawns. Ritzy bars and centuries-old monuments sit behind rubbish-strewn alleyways alongside topiary and blooms. Golden Lion judges decided that Bogotá is a beacon of hope for other cities, whether rich or poor – and its ultra-smart commercial and financial districts seem to signify a city poised for further growth.

GETTING THERE AND AROUND

BY AIR All international flights to Bogotá land at El Dorado International Airport, one of the largest cargo airports in Latin America. El Dorado is the fifth busiest in the region in terms of passenger traffic, handling upwards of 13 million passengers in 2014. It lies about 15km/20 minutes' drive west of the city centre, connected to Calle 26. The shiny new El Dorado, recently restored and updated, is a much-needed boost for air travel in Colombia and is now connected to the rest of the city by the TransMilenio bus system. Authorities in Bogotá are keen that El Dorado becomes a South American hub and this appears to be the case, with connections now easily facilitated to the rest of the continent from here.

Two passenger terminals – El Dorado (✆ 413 9053) and Puente Aéreo (✆ 413 9511) – are distinctly separate. The first handles a mix of international flights and the second purely serves Avianca. In **El Dorado**, check-in counters, ticket booths, immigration officials and customs are located on the lower level. Flight information screens, seating, emigration, duty-free stores, food outlets, newsstands, three bureaux de change and an ATM are located on the upper level. There is also a Telecom office offering international and national calls, as well as fax and internet services, between 07.00 and 19.00.

The **Puente Aéreo** terminal handles more than 120 daily flights – both international and domestic – but solely those of Avianca and its subsidiary SAM. It has a good range of shopping facilities, national and international telephone services, taxi booths, ATMs, restaurants and fast-food outlets, bookshops and newsstands. As Avianca also operates out of El Dorado terminal it is important to check the departure point for each flight. The turn-off for Puente Aéreo is 1km before the bigger terminal on a different approach road.

Schedules for both and details of services and opening times can be found online at http://eldorado.aero/. At the time of writing an increase of 76,800COP (or US$36) in the departure tax has been announced.

The following airlines have offices in Bogotá:

✈ Aerolíneas Argentinas	✆592 1737	✈ LAN Chile/LAN Peru	✆294 0330
✈ Aeromexico	✆742 4746	✈ Satena	✆423 8530
✈ Air Canada	✆296 6353	✈ Spirit	✆547 8306
✈ Air France	✆650 6002	✈ TACA	✆629 5507
✈ American Airlines	✆745 7646	✈ Tame	✆317 9099
✈ Avianca	✆587 7700	✈ TAP Portugal	✆745 8894
✈ COPA	✆638 3323	✈ United	✆800 944 0219
✈ Delta	✆549 4482	✈ Viva Colombia	✆489 7989
✈ EasyFly	✆414 8111		
✈ Iberia	✆508 7515		

Getting to/from the airport [map 135] All buses marked 'Aeropuerto' serve both airport terminals, including the *busetas* and *colectivos* that depart from Calle 19 and Carrera 10. You can find the very convenient and well-advertised TransMilenio bus service that goes to the airport along the Carrera Septima and down the Calle 26. Do remember that you will need to have purchased a prepaid ticket for this service available wherever you see the 'TuLlave' sign. A taxi to the airport is subject to a surcharge of 2,500COP – bringing the total cost to around 21,000COP from the centre of town. There used to be a set fare depending on your destination but this has been done away with. You are advised to go with official yellow taxis found outside of the terminal; avoid the pirate operators who will approach you in the taxi ranks and pay careful attention to the prices listed on the scale found in each vehicle.

BY BUS AND *BUSETA* Bogotá's large bus terminal (✆ 423 3600) is a major hub for national and international routes across Colombia and to Ecuador and Venezuela. Located out of town to the west of the city [map 135], the terminal has three well-organised departure halls, each handling a different part of the country. Rather

MAJOR BUS ROUTES FROM BOGOTÁ

Destination	Distance (km)	Fare (approx)	Time (hr)
Barranquilla	1,000	150,000COP	18
Bucaramanga	430	100,000COP	10
Cali	480	150,000COP	12
Cartagena	1,130	150,000COP	20
Cúcuta	630	100,000COP	16
Manizales	290	80,000COP	8
Medellín	440	80,000COP	10
Neiva	310	50,000COP	6
Pereira	340	50,000COP	9
Popayán	615	150,000COP	15
San Agustín	530	85,000COP	12
Santa Marta	970	150,000COP	16
Tunja	150	25,000COP	3

conveniently, these are simply called Norte (North), Oriente y Occidente (East and West) and Sur (South) – all very orderly and straightforward. Reaching the terminal requires taking a taxi (around 15,000COP) or grabbing a seat on the shuttle marked 'Terminal' from Carrera 10.

Long-distance buses to Colombia's main cities run with slick efficiency throughout the day, often departing every 20 minutes or half-hour. Most have air conditioning and some have a video player – fares vary with the operators, so it pays to ask a few. Bartering for a decent ticket price is also normal behaviour, as competition is fierce on the longer routes; don't be afraid to chance your luck.

Smaller buses (*busetas*) are the lifeblood of Bogotá's public transport, hurling passengers around the city at breakneck speed. Simply hail one down as it passes (wherever you happen to be) and pay the driver on boarding. When you're ready to get off, ding the bell – or shout loud instructions. Each vehicle displays a sign stating its destination with fares that range from 1,700COP to 1,800COP, depending on the route.

Getting to/from the bus terminal Frequent buses and *colectivos* nip back and forth between the terminal and the city centre, but the service doesn't run much later than 21.00. Traffic congestion out of the city can make the journey rather torturous with the route taking anything up to an hour at peak times. Look out for a vehicle displaying a sign for 'Terminal' from Carrera 10, Calle 13 and the streets between Calle 19 and Calle 26 heading north – but if you're stuck for time choose a taxi (15,000COP).

BY TAXI In Bogotá, the phone numbers of the city's dirt-cheap official taxi companies trip off the tongue with ease – choose from **Taxi Libres** (✆ *311 1111*), **Taxi Express** (✆ *411 1111*), **Radio Taxi** (✆ *288 8888*) and **Taxi Real** (✆ *333 3333*). Vast numbers of Korean-made custard-coloured taxis whizz around the city at speed; each is metered with rates that are clearly on display.

Unfortunately, despite a government crackdown, around 25,000 of Bogotá's 55,000 taxis remain unregistered – and however tempting the offer, these illegal cabs should be avoided at all costs. Look out for drivers with a companion and a vehicle that displays irregular markings and view them with suspicion. Never

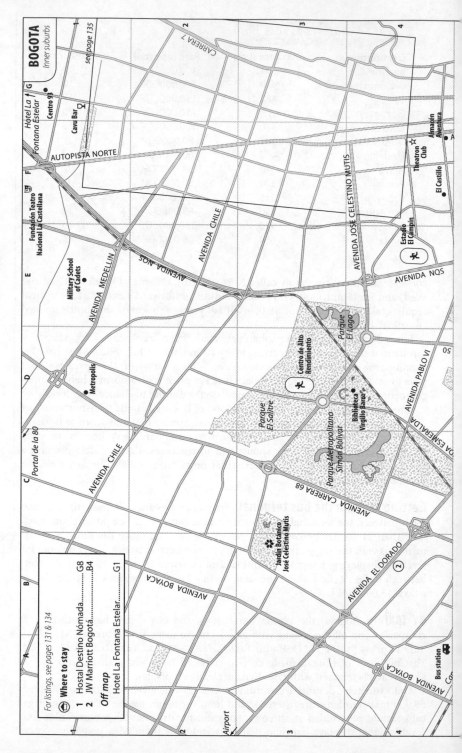

BOGOTA
Inner suburbs

see page 135

CARRERA 7

Hotel La
Fontana Estelar

Centro 93

Cavú Bar

AUTOPISTA NORTE

Fundación Teatro
Nacional La Castellana

AVENIDA CHILE

AVENIDA MEDELLIN

AVENIDA NQS

AVENIDA JOSÉ CELESTINO MUTIS

Military School
of Cadets

AVENIDA NQS

Estadio
El Campín

Theatron
Club

El Castillo

Almacén
Aventura

A

Metropolis

Portal de la 80

Parque
El Salitre

Centro de Alto
Rendimiento

Parque
El Lago

AVENIDA PABLO VI

50

AVENIDA CHILE

Parque Metropolitano
Simón Bolívar

Biblioteca
Virgilio Barco

AVENIDA ESMERALDA

AVENIDA CARRERA 68

Jardín Botánico
José Celestino Mutis

AVENIDA BOYACA

AVENIDA EL DORADO

2

AVENIDA BOYACA

Bus station

Airport

For listings, see pages 131 & 134

① Where to stay
1 Hostal Destino Nómada..........G8
2 JW Marriott Bogotá..............B4

Off map
Hotel La Fontana Estelar............G1

126

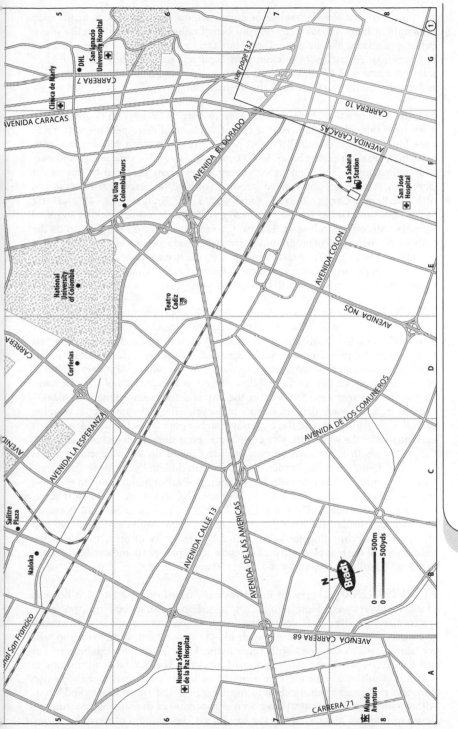

see page 132

Bogotá GETTING THERE AND AROUND

3

127

get into a taxi that already has one or more passengers – and to be sure, get your restaurant or hotel to book a cab on your behalf rather than hail one on the street. Passengers should also be aware that many taxi drivers are armed (for good and bad reasons). Alternatively you can download one of the handy APPs to your smartphone such as TAPPSI and Taxi Express which can triangulate your position and ensure you take an accredited and licensed car.

BY CAR Although there have been huge improvements in safety on Bogotá's roads, it has been difficult to totally rid the city of a culture of disrespect towards traffic laws. More than 50,000 road accidents per year result in about 900 deaths – with more than 18,000 speeding buses, 55,000 madcap taxis and one million private cars making driving in Bogotá only for the very brave. Those prepared to chance the city's congested streets and choked freeways will find numerous **car-hire** options with **Abc Rent-a-Car** (☎ 691 8113), **Avis** (☎ 629 1722), **Budget** (☎ 745 4811), **Hertz** (☎ 756 0600) and **Dollar Rent-a-Car** (☎ 691 4700), just a few of the 30 or so rental agencies with offices in Bogotá. However, a key consideration should also be the city's traffic-management programmes that restrict vehicular movement from 06.30 to 09.00 and from 17.00 to 19.00, depending on the licence-plate number. Another source of confusion is that roads such as Carrera 7 also change the direction of traffic flow, with cars in the south lane only running east–west from 17.00 to 20.00.

BY BICYCLE On Sundays and on public holidays Bogotá becomes a cycling paradise between 07.00 and 14.00, when the city's 121km of streets become traffic-free. Over three million cycling Bogotanos make the most of the peace and quiet in what has become a model programme in South America, if not the world. Bogotá also has one of the most extensive cycleways (*ciclorutas*) on the planet, with over 300km of paths exclusively for people riding bikes. Since the construction of the *ciclorutas*, bicycle use has increased five-fold in the city and today an estimated 300,000–400,000 trips are made daily in Bogotá by bicycle. The *ciclorutas* are an ongoing project with plans to extend the cycleways, highly popular as the network doesn't currently serve the whole city. Key cycle routes built since 1998 include Calle 170, Calle 127, North-Downtown South, Avenida Ciudad de Villavicencio, Avenida Ciudad de Quito, Avenida Boyacá, Fontibón-Dorado UniAndes, Bosa-Américas-Centro, Avenida Ciudad de Cali, Park Simón Bolívar, Avenida Carrera 68-Calle 100, Avenida Centenario, North-Usme Highway, Calle 80, Avenida Mariscal Sucre, Calle 63, South Railroad Corridor, Calle 53, Calle 134, Franja Seca, El Porvenir, La Toscana, Florida-Juan Amarillo and Avenida Suba, Avenida 1º de Mayo and Homecenter. Cycling Bogotanos are incredibly respectful of other people in the saddle. One of the best places to pick up cycle gear, spare parts and cycling tips is at Bicicletas Castillo on the corner of Carrera 30 and Calle 68.

BY TRANSMILENIO Few transit initiatives have transformed a city like Bogotá's TransMilenio (*www.transmilenio.gov.co*), a massive public bus transportation system that took over three decades to design. Sleek, fast and efficient, a network of buses provides a system very much like an above-ground metro using self-contained stations equipped with route maps, libraries and art exhibitions. For just 1,800COP, passengers can hop aboard a bus that is clean, safe and running to schedule. Vehicles operate on their own line well away from vehicular congestion on routes that range from standard to super-express. The TransMilenio and 'Rutas Alimentadoras' (feeder routes) have been at the centre of the Bogotá government's desire to improve mobility about the capital, yet the addition of new blue buses, faster systems and more TransMilenio vehicles has yet to overcome the challenges presented in the city. You can get to just about anywhere in Bogotá on the TransMilenio and there are helpful APPs with which to plan your journey. At the time of writing the most frequently used and reliable were Easy Taxi and Tappsi. Main links for the TransMilenio run north–south along the Avenida Caracas, and east–west along the Avenida de las Americas. Try to avoid rush hours and crowds of people and plan your journeys on the TransMilenio for after 10.00 and before 15.00 or prepare to share your transport with crowds of people. Pickpockets are rife, so be vigilant with your belongings. Additionally, there is the so-called TransMilenio 'Light' which consists of a new service of red buses along the Carrera Septima from downtown on the Carrera 10 and the Museo Nacional to the Calle 125 in the north. These buses are fast and convenient and run in their own bus lanes, thus avoiding many of Bogotá's traffic jams.

ON FOOT Part of Bogotá's 'Mobility Master Plan' has been to encourage pedestrian use of the city, after an era when fear restricted walking – even during daylight. Pedestrian pathways were built to connect key parts of Bogotá's urban landscape, such as the University Network linking the Nacional, Javeriana, Piloto, Gran Colombia and other universities located between Calle 45 and Calle 39. Others include the Athletic Network, a route that links the Botanical Garden with the Salitre Park and Simón Bolívar Park. The Cultural Network runs from the historical centre of La Candelaria out to residential neighbourhoods. Getting more people to travel around Bogotá on foot has played a large part in improving safety, although it is still unwise to walk through the city after dark. Pedestrians should always stick to popular routes, even during daylight. A highly visible police presence makes street mugging and theft less likely in modern-day Bogotá, unless you stroll around the backstreets wearing obvious jewellery, with a bulging wallet stuffed in your pocket and a mobile phone plugged to your ear.

TOURIST INFORMATION

Seven tourist information points (Puntos de Informacion Turisticos or PITs) can be found throughout the city, including a tourist police booth at the El Dorado Airport (✆ 295 4460/428 2424 ext 698). Specialist tourist advisers are located on the Plaza de Bolívar in La Candelaria and the Terminal De Transportes (✆ 423 3600) as well as the domestic (✆ 425 1000 ext 2155) and international (✆ 425 1000 ext 2156) terminals of the airport. At the Teatro Jorge Eliécer Gaitán on Carrera 7 and the Recinto Ferial De Corferias on Carrera 40, tourist offices operate during key events. Most are open 08.00–18.00 except the airport offices, which close at 20.00.

The main tourist office, Instituto Distrital de Cultura y Turismo [132 A3] (*Carrera 8, No 10–83;* ✆ 327 4916; *www.bogotaturismo.gov.co*), is located right on the Plaza de Bolívar and is open 08.00–18.00 daily.

Other useful sources of information include the Bogotá local government website (*www.bogota.gov.co*) and the website of the city of Bogotá (*www.bogota-dc.com*).

LOCAL TOUR OPERATORS

5Bogota m 313 278 5898; e info@5Bogota. com; www.5Bogota.com. 5Bogota is a new & dynamic group of young Bogotanos keen on promoting their city through the 5 senses. Highlights include learning how to barter in a traditional market, an empanada cooking course & a bike tour of the city's vibrant graffiti scene with a graffiti artist. Professional & fun, these tours are aimed at people seeking out something more authentic.

Bogotá Bike Tours [132 B4] Carrera 3, No 12–72, La Candelaria; 281 9924/312 502 0554; e bogotabiketours@gmail.com; www. bogotabiketours.com. This award-winning addition to the capital's tour scene offers a bike rental/guided tour service that centres on La Candelaria. Hire from 15,000COP for a half-day/30,000COP for a full-day. The office also doubles as a bookshop with used books in English, French, Dutch & German.

Bogota Foodie e feedme@bogotafoodie.com; www.bogotafoodie.com. Run by Loon Lio, an ex accountant from Australia, Bogota Foodie offers a Bogotá 'food safari' so that visitors to the city can enjoy trips to local markets to experience the culture up close & try different & exotic foods perhaps not offered in most restaurants. Describing himself as offering a trip that is a bit like 'Bourdain with a dash of James Bond', Loon infuses energy & culture into his tours.

Coches y Carruajes [132 B3] Plaza de Bolívar; 233 0440/289 1519. Specialist tour company offering sightseeing trips in horse-drawn carriages around the historic streets of La Candelaria.

De Una Colombia Tours [127 F6] Calle 39, No 28–49, Le Soledad; 368 1915; e info@ deunacolombia.com; www.deunacolombia. com. European-run & established in 1999, this highly recommended outfit is perfect for anyone keen on hiking, climbing or walking, as its tours of Colombia's national parks & mountains are second to none. Visit their De Una Travel Café in the Candelaria at Calle 11, No 2–98 (see also ad, page 62).

Empresa Turística y Cultural Candelaria [132 B2] Carrera 8, No 11–39; 281 5569/283 2319. A specialist in romantic evening walking & sightseeing tours around Bogotá's historic quarter.

Viajes Chapinero L' Alianxa [135 B6] Carrera 10, No 26–33; 596 0160. As well as the standard sightseeing tours, this company offers shopping & gastronomic trips around the city – during the day & after dark.

Voyage Colombia [off map 135 D1] Carrera 13A, No 96–18; 600 0098; www.voyagecolombia. com. Offering trips to all over the country, this agency can offer you day trips out to the Salt Cathedral in Zipaquirá & to Guatavita as well. Tours can be given in English, French & German.

🏠 **WHERE TO STAY** *See maps, pages 126–7, 132 and 135.*

Bogotá has an excellent array of accommodation options, including some budget hostels. However, on the basis of safety most foreign visitors choose to stay at something mid- to upper range. Most consider the extra cost worth it for 24-hour security, access-controlled lifts and in-room safety deposit boxes. They also tend to be in the nicer areas of the city close to bars, restaurants and nightlife. Budget hostel accommodation is aimed at shoestring travellers, and these tend to come and go. For an up-to-date list in Colombia visit www.colombianhostels.co, which has details of fully authorised and licensed accommodation in this category. Travellers simply looking for a couch on which to kip for the night should check out www.globalfreeloaders.com and www.couchsurfers.com, where you can find a plethora of Bogotá-based people offering free accommodation, many in the city's central neighbourhoods.

Visitors planning to stay a few weeks or months in Bogotá will find that it's relatively easy to find an apartment to share or rent – just ask the guys at Alegría's or post a message at some of the other traveller hangouts around La Candelaria. Some, but not all, of the hostels offer long-stay discounts. Almost every hotel in town is open to negotiation for longer stays, so don't be afraid to barter. Another good option is an apart-hotel. For further information try one of the following websites:

* http://www.apartaestudioslacandelaria.com/
* www.bedandbreakfastbogota.com
* www.colombiahotels.com

HIGH END

🏠 **Casa Medina** (60 rooms/suites) Carrera 7, No 69A–22; 217 0288/312 0299; http://www. hotelcharlestoncasamedina.com. Casa Medina was declared a National Historical Conservation Monument in 1985 & the building, which was built in 1945, combines Spanish & French design to very good effect. Wrought-iron railings & banisters, stone walls & pillars, hand-carved wood ceilings & veneers; decorated with classic & antique furniture with rooms of classical style. There's also an on-site restaurant, bar & business centre. **$$$$**

🏠 **Hotel de la Ópera** (30 rooms) Calle 10, No 5–72; 📞 336 2066/5285; e sales@hotelopera. com.co; www.hotelopera.com.co. Suites are the standard accommodation at this truly gorgeous historic property. A bright, light, leafy courtyard bar & restaurant attract Bogotá's wealthy elite with a fresh juice bar & coffee bar, sumptuous spa & beautifully restored colonial exterior. Expect to see TV crews patiently waiting outside for some celebrity or visiting politician – this is one of Bogotá's places to be. **$$$$**

🏠 **Hotel La Bohème Royal** (66 rooms) Calle 82, No 12–35; 📞 644 7132; www.hotelesroyal.com. A favourite resting place with a jet-setting business clientele, this swish 5-star option is located in the Zona Rosa close to theatres, coffee shops, boutiques, shopping malls & restaurants. The recently refurbished rooms are equipped with high-speed internet access. Comfy queen or large twin beds are standard. On-site amenities include a business centre, dining room & cocktail bar. **$$$$**

🏠 **Hotel La Fontana Estelar** (215 rooms) Av 127, No 21–10; 📞 615 4400; e ventas@ hotelesestelar.com; www.hotelesestelar.com. This rather fine 5-star, 6-storey city hotel employs a high percentage of English- & German-speakers & has a cosmopolitan feel. The pleasant rooms all include minibar, fridge, cable TV, internet, safety deposit boxes & twin phone lines. There's also an excellent coffee bar, pub & restaurant on site with a large shopping mall just across the road. Expect friendly, co-operative staff who are prepared to do their utmost to make your day. **$$$$**

🏠 **Hotel Tequendama Crowne Plaza** (578 rooms, also has suites) Carrera 10, No 26–21; 📞 382 0300; e bogota@ihg.com; www. crowneplaza.com. This 5-star hotel in the downtown district boasts a sterling reputation as one of Bogotá's oldest establishments. The 239 double, 339 single & 103 suites are well appointed with 24hr room service, cable TV, minibar, safety deposit boxes & voicemail. Guests can use a business centre with high-speed

internet access & there is also a laundry & valet service as well as an on-site casa de cambio, gym & ATM. A café, restaurant, lobby bar, tour operator & English-style pub are all located around the foyer where there are also jewellery stores, boutiques & handicraft stalls. Ask for a room at the back of the building to avoid the worst of the traffic noise. **$$$$**

🏠 **JW Marriott Bogotá** (264 rooms) Calle 73, No 8–60; 📞 481 6000; www.marriott.com; Everything that you would expect from this international chain aimed at the high-end business traveller. This hotel is sumptious, well located in the heart of the financial district & only walking distance from the bars & restaurants of the Zona G. Rooms are spacious & contain every comfort required as well as a filling buffet b/fast, possibly the best in the city. **$$$$**

🏠 **Park Inn by Radisson** (64 rooms) Carrera 18, No 93–97; 📞 403 4000; www.parkinn.com/ hotel-bogota. You will find this über-stylish, small boutique hotel tucked away on a quiet backstreet just 2km from Bogotá's city centre. Slick & contemporary, with a business edge to it, this unique hotel boasts quiet luxury. Large suites with kitchenettes, plasma screens & hot tubs have a truly indulgent feel to them, with handy high-speed Wi-Fi, & all-round excellent service. **$$$$**

🏠 **Abadia Colonial** (12 rooms) Calle 11, No 2–32; 📞 341 1884; e abadiacolonial@gmail.com; www.abadiacolonial.com. This charming boutique hotel is set in a beautiful colonial house with clean rooms, private bathrooms & a heater in each room – a real boon if you feel the cold in chilly Bogotá. There's also a tearoom & a nice communal area. **$$$**

🏠 **Bogotá Marriott** (224 rooms) Av El Dorado, No 69b–5; 📞 485 1111; www.marriott.com. This property is a favourite with business travellers as it is located just 10 easy mins by cab from El Dorado International Airport. Soundproofed rooms are equipped with a host of techy amenities such as high-speed internet, work desks with plug panels & 37" LCD TVs. On site there's a lap pool, an Italian restaurant & a sushi & tapas bar. Just outside are 2 shopping malls & the chamber of commerce. **$$$**

🏠 **Casa Deco** (20 rooms) Calle 14, No 2–30, La Candelaria; 📞 283 7262/7032; e reservas@ hotelcasadeco.com; www.hotelcasadeco.com. This homely accommodation in a beautifully restored historic building is one of the area's

3

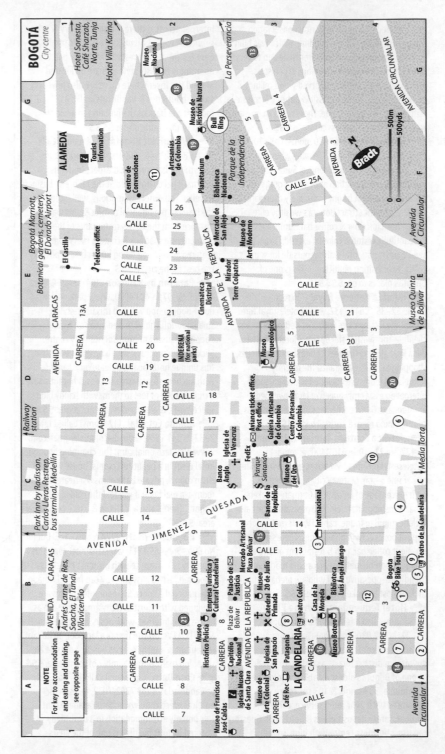

newest additions. Since opening in Sep 2009, it has become a firm favourite with travellers looking for a stylish option. Guests rave about the cleanliness, friendly staff & ambience of this place & its 20 colour-coded Art-Deco rooms. **$$$**

⌂ **Hotel Sonesta** (126 rooms) Carrera 15, No 127–03; www.sonesta.com. The brochure describes this hotel as 'fun, modern & sophisticated' – & the Sonesta certainly aims to deliver on all 3 counts. Bright, bold & daring décor characterises the lobby, lounge & rooms. Amenities include big, soundproofed windows that let in lots of natural light together with giant LCD TVs, complimentary high-speed internet, iPhone/iPad charger, a range of 'mood' lighting, blackout shades & bathroom with tub. **$$$**

MID-RANGE

⌂ **Hotel Ambala** (24 rooms) Carrera 5, No 13–46; ☎342 6384/341 2376; www.hotelambala. net. Another perfectly acceptable option for those looking for mid-range accommodation. Rooms have a private, hot-water bathroom & TV. **$$**

⌂ **Hotel Casa Galeria** (7 rooms) Carrera 2, No 12B–92, Callejón del Embudo; ☎342 5225; e info@hotelcasagaleria.com; www. hotelcasagaleria.com. Welcoming, eclectic & mildly bohemian, this establishment is perfect for those wishing to explore the environs of the Candelaria on foot. All rooms have private bathrooms although not necessarily inside the room, so be sure to ask. B/fast inc. **$$**

⌂ **Hotel Casa Platypus** (17 rooms) Carrera 3, No 12F–28; ☎281 1801; www. casaplatypusbogota.com. Owned by the one and only German Escobar, responsible for bringing tourism to the Candelaria, this offshoot of the original Hostel Platypus (now under new management) is an upmarket but well-priced boutique option in the downtown area. Delicately restored with all the relevant comforts, including a rooftop terrace offering great city views, the Casa Platypus is an excellent option for those wanting the adventure of the Candelaria but the comfort of uptown. B/fast inc. **$$**

⌂ **Hotel San Sebastián** (36 rooms) Av Jiménez, No 3–97; ☎334 6041. This place won't win any awards for décor or style, but is a decent enough mid-range option – another hotel favoured by bland businessmen on a budget. Large, clean rooms are perfectly adequate with a private bathroom & TV. **$$**

⌂ **Hotel Villa Karina** (27 rooms) Calle 30, No 17–47; ☎287 1445/5309/1298 & 285 6547. Visitors keen to hang out in the ultra-avant-garde Macarena area will find this middle-sized option appealing. It's close-ish to the bohemian arts district & attracts Colombian business executives eager to economise on their expenses. Friendly service, a decent cheap restaurant & reasonable room rates are all good reasons to book here – & there's a dirt-cheap laundry across the road. **$$**

BUDGET

⌂ **La Casona del Patío Amarillo** (sleeps 20) Carrera 8, No 69–24; ☎212 8805/1991; e casona@ telecom.com.co; www.lacasonadelpatio.net. This lovely ochre-coloured L-shaped building has been recently renovated & offers gardens, patios & a tiled terrace & some very nice rooms. It's a great budget option, in the northern suburbs of the city just 2 blocks west of Carrera 7 & served by 24hr public transport with a straight connection to La Candelaria, a 15min bus ride away. Brightly painted dorm rooms are adorned with modern art & sleep up to 5 people. **$$**

🏠 **Masaya Hostel** (12 rooms) Carrera 2, No 12–48; m 310 609 2782; e bogota@masaya-experience.com; www.masaya-experience.com. Located in the historical centre, Masaya Hostel is a stylish hostel in a colonial house, with free Wi-Fi, computers, pool table, Ping-Pong, guitars, traditional Colombian games & a fully equipped kitchen. Dormitories & private rooms available. **$$**

🏠 **Hostal Destino Nómada** (7 rooms) Calle 11, No 00–38; ✆ 352 0932; m 312 300 6895; e contactus@destinonomada.com; www.dnhostels.com. Ideal for anyone planning to visit the museums or Monserrate. Nicely restored colonial building with clean rooms; choose from a mix of private or shared rooms, some with en suite. Internet available, tours offered, storage lockers & good buffet b/fast included in rate. Popular with a young international crowd. **$–$$**

🏠 **Alegria's Hostel** (8 rooms) Carrera 2, No 9–46; ✆ 286 8047; e reservations@alegriashostel.com; www.alegriashostel.com. Set over 2 delightfully restored colonial buildings in the Candelaria, Alegria Meza, the owner, has put her heart & soul into her hostels which ooze character & charm. Dormitories & private rooms with & without bathrooms available. **$**

🏠 **Hostel Anandamayi** (sleeps 40) Calle 9, No 2–81; ✆ 341 7208; e anandamayihostel@yahoo.com. This comfortable, inexpensive backpacker hostel is housed in a lovely colonial house in La Candelaria & is blessed with a pretty garden with patios, hammocks, geranium bushes, waterfalls, fish ponds & hummingbirds plus plenty of charm. Guests can use the internet & enjoy sunrise views over the Monserrate in a relaxed place popular with writers, painters & poets – the owners allow long stays. Rates include linen, towels, safe box, luggage storage, & pizza on Fri. Rooms are clean & comfortable with a range of mixed dorms, twin & double options. **$**

🏠 **The Cranky Croc** (18 rooms) Calle 12D, No 3–46; ✆ 342 2438; e info@crankycroc.com; www.crankycroc.com. Owned & operated by a long-time Australian guide in South America, the Cranky Croc has been thought out & designed with the needs of the backpacker in mind. Trips to points of interest can be organised at the reception, & the good communal area with an open fireplace is a fine place to strike up conversation with other travellers. Do not miss the legendary barbecues. **$**

✗ WHERE TO EAT AND DRINK See maps, pages 126–7, 132 and 135.

Bogotá is filled with almost 20,000 truly exciting places to wine and dine, from the rustic Colombian eateries serving hearty bowls of *Santafereño sancocho* (a typical Bogotá soup) to numerous bistros, cafés, restaurants and diners specialising in Italian, Middle Eastern, Greek, Mexican and Asian cuisines. *Condé Nast Traveller* ranked the city as one of the finest culinary centres in the world and as a gastronomic capital Bogotá rarely disappoints. The city has over 300 quality carbon-grill joints, 200 seafood restaurants, 250 oriental eateries, dozens of fast-food outlets and umpteen elegant French à la carte options. Plenty of budget places offer price tags that cater for shoestring diners with numerous mid-range restaurants and others that offer the ultimate in culinary excess. Opening hours vary; many small food outlets open early for breakfast and close whenever the last plate is cleared. For an updated list of restaurants and dining reviews check out www.bogota.gov.co – click on to 'leisure' and follow the gastronomy link.

HIGH END

✗ **Astrid y Gastón** Carrera 7A, No 67– 64; ✆ 211 1400/1143; www.astridygaston.com; ⊕ noon–16.00 & 19.00–midnight Tue–Sat. This ultra-fancy Peruvian restaurant housed in a converted mansion also has branches in Peru, Chile & Venezuela & serves upmarket dishes at lunch & dinner, Tue–Sat. Expect lots of seafood in rich Peruvian spices, such as blue crab *angolotti*, octopus with mango & peanut sauce, & grouper with pink peppercorns. **$$$**

✗ **Bandido** Calle 79B, No 7–12; ✆ 212 5709; ⊕ noon–01.00 Mon–Sat. Slick, bustling & very popular with the beautiful people. Arrive early for dinner if you don't want to be disappointed. Excellent & huge portions in this French bistro-

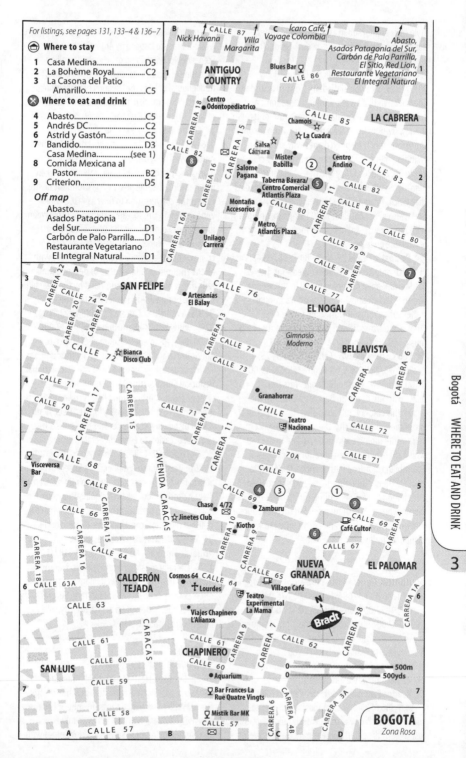

For listings, see pages 131, 133–4 & 136–7

Where to stay
1 Casa Medina.........................D5
2 La Bohème Royal..................C2
3 La Casona del Patio
   Amarillo............................C5

Where to eat and drink
4 Abasto................................C5
5 Andrés DC...........................C2
6 Astrid y Gastón....................C5
7 Bandido.............................. D3
   Casa Medina..................(see 1)
8 Comida Mexicana al
   Pastor............................... B2
9 Criterion.............................D5

Off map
Abasto.................................D1
Asados Patagonia
   del Sur..............................D1
Carbón de Palo Parrilla.....D1
Restaurante Vegetariano
   El Integral Natural..........D1

CALLE 87
Nick Havana   Villa
               Margarita
Ícaro Café,
Voyage Colombia
Abasto,
Asados Patagonia del Sur,
Carbón de Palo Parrilla,
El Sitio, Red Lion,
Restaurante Vegetariano
El Integral Natural

ANTIGUO
COUNTRY

Blues Bar
CALLE 86

LA CABRERA

Centro
Odontopediatrico

CALLE 85

Chamois
La Cuadra

CARRERA 18

CALLE 15

CALLE 82
Salsa
Cámara
Mister
Babilla
Centro
Andino
CALLE 83

CARRERA 16
Salome
Pagana
Taberna Bávara/
Centro Comercial
Atlantis Plaza
CARRERA 11
CALLE 82

CARRERA 16A
Montaña
Accesorios
CALLE 80
CALLE 81

Metro,
Atlantis Plaza
CARRERA 9
CALLE 79

Unilago
Carrera
CALLE 78
CALLE 80

CARRERA 22
A
CALLE 77

SAN FELIPE
CALLE 76

Artesanías
El Balay
EL NOGAL

CALLE 20
CALLE 19
CALLE 74
CARRERA 13
CALLE 74

CARRERA 17
Bianca
Disco Club
CALLE 72
CALLE 73

Gimnasio
Moderno
BELLAVISTA

CARRERA 7
CARRERA 6

CALLE 71
CARRERA 15
Granahorror
CHILE

CALLE 70
CARRERA 12
Teatro
Nacional
CALLE 72

CARRERA 11
CALLE 70A
CALLE 71

Visceversa
Bar
CALLE 68
CALLE 70

AVENIDA CARACAS
CALLE 69

CALLE 67
Chase 4/72
Zamburu

CARRERA 16
CARRERA 15
Jinetes Club
Kiotho
CARRERA 9
Café Cultor

CARRERA 18
CALLE 66
CALLE 69
CARRERA 4

CALLE 63A
CALDERÓN
TEJADA
Cosmos 64 CALLE 64
Lourdes
Village Café
NUEVA
GRANADA
EL PALOMAR

CALLE 63
Teatro
Experimental
La Mama
CARRERA 38
CARRERA 1A

Viajes Chapinero
L'Alianxa
CALLE 65
CARRERA 9
CARRERA 7
CALLE 62
Bradt

CALLE 61
CARRERA 6

CALLE 60
CHAPINERO
CALLE 60

SAN LUIS
Aquarium
0   500m
0   500yds

CALLE 59
Bar Frances La
Rue Quatre Vingts
CARRERA 6
CARRERA 3A

CALLE 58
Mistik Bar MK
CARRERA 4B

A CALLE 57   B   CALLE 57   C   D

BOGOTÁ
Zona Rosa

style restaurant, hidden away on a side street, are accompanied with live jazz on w/ends. The cocktails are killer. $$$

✕ Criterion Calle 69, No 5–75; ✆310 1377/1538; ☺ noon–late daily. Keen to splurge? Then head to this award-winning restaurant as it could give any fine Parisian kitchen a run for its money. Owners Jorge & Mark Rausch whip up only the finest French-inspired dishes with an ever-changing menu that includes lamb *gigot* & crab *en croûte*. Expect a fancy clientele that comprises high-flying wheeler-dealer executives, CEOs, ladies that lunch, TV moguls & starlets who enjoy a rather fine wine cellar containing 300 European vintages with no-expense-spared taster menus at a very reasonable price pp. $$$

✕ Donostia Calle 29, No 5–84; ✆287 3943; ☺ lunch only Mon–Fri, dinner Wed–Sat. The Mediterranean–Colombian menu at this trendy hangout has an army of fans, with traditional dishes subtly infused with some rather nice European touches. Diners can expect plenty of hip music with live bands on a Wed night. $$$

✕ Leo Cocina y Cava Calle 27B, No 6–75; ✆286 7095/281 6267; ☺ noon–16.00 & 19.00–01.00 Mon–Fri. Ranked by *Condé Nast Traveller* in 2006 as one of the 80 best restaurants in the world, this chic Colombian–Asian fusion specialist is still the talk of the city. Day or night, expect its stark white dining room to be packed to the rafters whilst chef-owner Thorny Leonor mixes coastal Colombian traditions with French–Asian haute cuisine. Menu highlights include snail carpaccio with lemon & olive oil, stuffed *carimañolas* of rabbit, white fish sashimi served in coconut sauce, mango purée & mint granite & green salad with giant Santander ants. $$$

MID RANGE

✕ Abasto Carrera 6, No 119b–52, Usaquén; ✆215 1286 & Calle 69A, No 9–09 ✆675 0492; ☺ 07.00–22.00 Mon–Thu, 09.30–22.00 Sat, 09.30–17.00 Sun. With 2 branches, 1 in Usaquén in the north of the city & the other in the centrally located Quinta Camacho district, you have no excuse not to go & try one of Bogota's most popular & innovative gastro pubs. $$

✕ Asados Patagonia del Sur Calle 117, No 7–54; ✆215 6525; www.patagoniaasadosdelsur. com; ☺ lunch & dinner daily. Weekly tango shows are just some of the entertainment staged at this lively

Argentine grill restaurant where tables, chairs, posters & bric-a-brac are inspired by Argentinian traditions. Scenes depict horseriding gauchos in the rolling Argentine plains with much use of wood & brick throughout. Find it in the Usaquén neighbourhood. There is also a branch in the Candelaria on the corner of Calle 10 & Carrera 6 (☺ *lunch only*). $$

✕ Carbón de Palo Parrilla Av 19, No 106–112; ✆214 5452; ☺ early–late daily. This much-loved grilled-meat joint serves legendary man-sized plates of beef, pork, rabbit & chicken in a traditional atmosphere of gastronomic gusto. Expect the conversation to flow as fast as the wine – even in the so-called quiet hours between lunchtime & dinner – with tables of families, couples & co-workers squeezed into every nook & cranny. Choose a *grande punta anca* (steak) with all the trimmings, add a bottle of decent Spanish red wine & be pleasantly surprised by the final bill. Dress up or down – it doesn't matter 1 iota. $$

✕ Casa Medina Carrera 7, No 69A–22; ✆312 0299; www.hotels-charleston.com; ☺ 17.00–23.00 daily. Renowned Bogotá chef Francisco Rodriguez matches the finesse of his surroundings with his creative French menu in this fine National Historical Conservation Monument. Amidst wrought iron, marble, stone & carved wood diners are treated to game, scallops, lobster, beef, lamb & veal dishes in a stately setting that adds a true sense of occasion to every delectable dish. $$

✕ Gostinos 69 Calle 28, No 6–77; ✆313 0612/0601; ☺ lunch & dinner daily. Expect to be able to feast on fine seafood, choosing from dozens of delicious recipes for *ceviche*, including Thai-style, red hot chilli, lemon garlic & zingy lime. Swish service & chill-out music in a contemporary-modern décor. $$

✕ Sopas de Mama y Postres de la Abuela Carrera 9, No 10–59; ✆243 4432/342 3973. Literally meaning 'mum's soups & granny's puddings' this restaurant, as its name suggests, offers simple, homely Colombian fare. Several branches have cropped up across the city, all boasting reasonable prices. $$

BUDGET

✕ Al Wadi Calle 27, No 4A–14; ✆334 1434; ☺ all day daily. Nestled in the bohemian district of La Macarana amidst artists' studios & bookshops, the Al Wadi is every inch the atmospheric Lebanese hideaway. Choose from a handful of tables surrounded by Arabian scenes & *shisha* pipes with a small menu of shish kebabs, breads, hummus & falafel. $

✕ Alina Calle 9, No 2–81; ✆ 341 7208; ⊕ all day daily. Colombian-American patron Mario serves up some of the best pizza in the city. Choose from a dozen toppings & a menu of pasta dishes. $

✕ Autoservicio Luna Nueva Carrera 7, No 13–55; ✆ 342 6806; ⊕ 08.00–20.00 daily. This simple little Colombian café opens for b/fast each day & serves good-value dishes until evening. Set lunches are particularly good for shoestring diners. $

✕ Café Sharzab Carrera 16, No 48–79; ✆ 285 5716; ⊕ noon–22.00 daily. Choose from a mouthwatering menu of Persian meals, snacks & desserts at this delightful little find – it's open for lunch (*nahar*) & dinner (*shahm*). Expect super-soft breads, rice, yoghurt drinks & meats cooked with nuts, dried fruit & pulses. $

✕ Candela Café Calle 9, No 4–93; ✆ 283 1780; ⊕ b/fast, lunch & dinner daily. This popular lunch venue serves a super menu & is also open for dinner when the lights are dimmed. Expect salmon gratins, creamy pasta dishes, grilled chicken salads & spicy meatballs. $

✕ Comida Mexicana al Pastor Carrera 16A, No 83–47; m 300 561 2021; ⊕ noon–late daily. You can't miss this canary-coloured Mexican cantina where budget-priced quesadillas, tacos, enchiladas & nachos come served in generous portions. $

✕ Restaurante Vegetariano El Integral Natural Carrera 11, No 95–10; ✆ 256 0899; ⊕ 09.00–18.00 Mon–Fri, noon–18.00 Sat. Set veggie lunches are the main draw at this dirt-cheap

café with simple rice dishes, soups & sandwiches. $

✕ Restaurante La Pola Calle 19, No 1–85; ✆ 566 5654; ⊕ 11.00–17.00 daily. This great little local food joint serves up big portions of Bogotá specialities, from grilled plates of meat, bowls of *ajiaco* (chicken soup with cream & potatoes) & *puchero sabanero* (a hearty mixed soup). $

AROUND BOGOTÁ

✕ Andrés Carne de Res Calle 3, No 11A–56; ✆ 863 7880; e acr@andrescarnederes.com; www. andrescarnederes.com; ⊕ lunchtime & for dinner until late. Ask every Bogotano about Andrés Carne de Res & the response will be a glowing reference, as this fast-paced party restaurant is a firm favourite with city-dwellers of all ages. Located in Chía in Bogotá's city limits (a 50,000COP taxi ride from the centre), this legendary fun-fest is always packed, be it lunchtime or after dark. Steak is the order of the day, served big & tasty. Expect loud music, dancing waiters, raucous sing-songs & wooden menus that retract into the rafters on bungee cords. Dress up or down. Budget for a splurge & be prepared to queue for a table – or better still, pre-book. $$$

✕ Andrés DC Calle 82 interior centro comercial el retiro, No 12–21, ✆ 863 7880 http://www. andrescarnederes.com/es/andres_dc; ⊕ noon–01.00 Sun–Wed, noon–03.00 Thu–Sat. Building on the immense popularity of the original restaurant in Chia, Andrés DC brings their unique brand of decadence to the Zona Rosa. Expect much of the same raucous celebrations but, mercifully without the long taxi ride home! $$$

ENTERTAINMENT AND NIGHTLIFE

Bogotá offers all manner of fun and frolics for every conceivable taste, from cinema, theatre and salsa dancing to numerous restaurants, bars, cafés and clubs. In a city that is keen to talk in terms of zones, Bogotá's nightlife sectors are 'unofficially' referred to as the M Zone (Macarena), G Zone (the Gourmet sector), T Zone (where the main roads meet in a 'T'), Zona Rosa (around and including Carrera 13), the V Zone (referring to Usaquén, the area above the T Zone) and Parque de la 93 (around and including Calle 93). Bars, in particular, tend to be clustered around the pedestrianised district of T Zone in the heart of the Zona Rosa (Pink Zone), where tourists and Bogotanos alike party in their droves. Other key nightspot venues can be found in the city's Chapinero neighbourhood, the gay hub of Bogotá. For the definitive guide to Bogotá's nightlife and entertainment, check out http:// rumbabogota.com for nightlife, and for cultural events listed in English, look no further than the city's monthly anglo newspaper *The City Paper Bogotá* (*http:// thecitypaperbogota.com*).

NIGHTCLUBS Partying night-owls are spoilt for choice in Bogotá, where hundreds of nightclubs offer every musical style from techno and trance to reggae, tango, rumba, rap and salsa. La Candelaría's bars and clubs are clustered along Calle 15 and Carrera 4, with most of the inexpensive student hangouts around Carrera 7 and Calle 51. Things are a little bit more upmarket in the über-cool Zona Rosa where the mood ranges from pretentious designer beats to ultra-chic downright moody – head to the streets between Carrera 11 and Carrera 15 and Calle 81, Calle 84 and Calle 82 to be in the thick of it. Highlights include the mega-spacious **El Sitio** [off map 135 D1] (*Carrera 11a, No 93–52;* ☎ *530 5050*) and the eclectic **Mister Babilla** [135 C2] (*Calle 82, No 12–15;* ☎ *617 1110*). Travellers keen to find a British-style pub should check out the **Red Lion** [off map 135 D1] (*Carrera 12, No 93–64;* ☎ *691 7938*), **Lloyd's** [off map 135 D1] (*Carrera 14, No 94–26;* ☎ *616 0499*) and the **Eight Bells Inn** [map, page 152] (*Calle 120A, No 6–23;* ☎ *213 7669*). The Bogotá Beer Company is the city's very own microbrewery with a branch seemingly on every corner. Some of the best are the lively Parque de Usaquén, El Parque de la 93, Zona T, and where Calle 122 meets Avenida 19 – be sure to try the signature 'Jirafa' (giraffe), a yard-long glass full of the beer of your choice.

Sounds and rhythms of Latin America
Bogotanos love to sing along to music from the region and dance to classics from Mexico, Argentina and Cuba – as well as melodies from their homeland. Although Cali is Colombia's true salsa city (see pages 288 and 293), the capital has some decent up-tempo *salsatecas* where the pace is fast and furious. Check out the latest threads at http://salsabogota.blogspot.com for details of where's hot and not.

Salsa
☆ **Lázaro** [map, page 152] Calle 108, No 15–80; ☎ 213 8811

☆ **Salome Pagana** [135 C2] Carrera 14, No 82–16; ☎ 218 4076

☆ **Salsa Cámara** [135 C2] Carrera 14, No 82–45, Piso 2; ☎ 256 4869

☆ **Taberna Bávara** [135 C2] Centro Comercial Atlantis Plaza; ☎ 530 7519

Mexican music
☆ **Chamois** [135 C2] Calle 85, No 11–69; ☎ 218 3285

☆ **Ícaro Café** [off map, 135 D1] Carrera 13, No 93–60; ☎ 623 3223

☆ **La Cuadra** [135 C2] Carrera 12A, No 83–29; ☎ 616 3674

☆ **Plaza México** [map, page 152] Transversal 26, No 117–26; ☎ 214 2846

☆ **Villa Margarita** [off map 135 C1] Carrera 15, No 93B; ☎ 610 2982

Cuban music
☆ **Habana Club** Calle 68, No 73–68; ☎ 252 8231

☆ **Nick Havana** [off map, 135 B1] Calle 122, No 25–59; ☎ 214 2083

CINEMA Bogotá has almost 50 cinemas, ranging from tiny little art houses showing retro movies in French to sprawling multi-screen complexes where blockbuster films are all the rage. Some of the most interesting screenings are found at the various university *cinematecas* and art cinemas where cutting-edge documentaries and foreign films tend to be the order of the day:

▆ **Cinemateca Distrital** [132 E2] Carrera 7, No 22–79; ☎ 283 5598; www.cinematecadistrital.gov.co. This rather nice art theatre shows foreign & national films in the Jorge Eliécer Gaitán Theater.

▆ **Museo de Arte Moderno** [132 F3] Calle 24, No 6–00; ☎ 286 0466; e cine@mamBogotá.com; www.mambogota.com. Check out the regular schedule of screenings at this exciting in-house art house, as it favours the unusual.

As homosexuality becomes slowly more accepted in Colombia, the city of Bogotá is at the forefront of pushing the boundaries of convention. In 1996, Colombia's first Gay Pride parade attracted just 32 participants, but just 15 years later more than 175,000 people joined in the parade in a colourful, flamboyant parade that did much to prove that Bogotá is no longer sexually repressed.

Expulsions of gay high school students have become a rarity, and reports of 'gay bashing' are much reduced. Newspapers no longer use lurid headlines to report gay issues. The downfall of Catholic morals is no longer singularly blamed on homosexuals. Even the Bogotá mayor has championed gay rights and denounced Colombia's culture of machismo – joining Gay Pride revellers on the city's parade route. A decade ago, Bogotá's gay community lived life in fearful anonymity. Today, the city's Chapinero neighbourhood resembles Greenwich Village with a centre specialising in health, legal and psychological services for gays and lesbians. Bogotá also has a number of openly gay hotels (*http://www.guiagaycolombia.com/hoteles*) – although reports about this place are best described as mixed. Same-sex couples can now register civil unions and enjoy most of the rights of marriage – except for the right to adopt children. While there was a vote in the courts and congress regarding the issue of same-sex marriage in 2012, no final agreement was reached either in favour or against, leaving this topic in limbo. However, many Notaria offices have started to legally marry same-sex couples despite the polemic situation.

There is a mood of considerable optimism throughout the gay community following a series of progressive rulings in recent years. Today Bogotá is home to more than 100 bars, nightclubs, saunas, clothes shops and video stores aimed at a gay clientele. All the best places are listed on www.guiagaycolombia.com/bogota – with the following some of the city's finest gay haunts:

☆ **Bar Frances La Rue Quatre Vingts** [135 B7] Calle 79, No 11–42; ☏ 317 6539
☆ **Bianca Disco Club** [135 A4] Calle 72, No 16–48; ☏ 314 5187/217 1983
☆ **Blues Bar** [135 C1] Calle 86A, No 13A–30; ☏ 616 7126
☆ **Cavu Bar** [126 G1] Carrera 15, No 88–71; ☏ 530 2356
☆ **Chase** [135 B5] Calle 67, No 4A–91; ☏ 249 3090
☆ **Ego Disco Bar** Calle 45, No 16–25; ☏ 245 2531
☆ **El Café** Calle 59, No 13–32; ☏ 249 6512
☆ **El Clóset Lounge & Club** [off map, page 152] Vía La Calera; ☏ 254 5230; www.elclosetbogota.com
☆ **Jinetes Club** [135 B5] Vía La Calera; ☏ 648 6009/292 7456/520 1091
☆ **Kiotho** [135 C5] Calle 66, No 10–75; ☏ 211 4068
☆ **Lottus Bar** Calle 58, No 10–42; ☏ 249 2092/235 6879
☆ **Metro** [135 C2] Calle 61, No 13–81; ☏ 248 0388
☆ **Mistik Bar MK** [135 B7] Carrera 9, No 57–76; ☏ 217 9409; m 310 563 9686
☆ **Ra Bar & Lounge** Calle 64, No 13–52; ☏ 235 6308
☆ **Theatron Club** [126 F4] Calle 58, No 10–32; ☏ 249 2092/235 6879; www.theatrondepelicula.com
☆ **Village Café** [135 C6] Carrera 8, No 64–29; ☏ 346 6592
☆ **Visceversa Bar** [135 A5] Calle 68, No 21–07; ☏ 235 7767
☆ **Zamburu** [135 C5] Calle 67, No 9-41; ☏ 610 2262

THEATRE AND CONCERTS Bogotá's highly developed theatre scene offers plenty to choose from year-round, from small independent avant-garde productions and amateur dramatics to large-scale Broadway adaptations.

🎭 **Fundación Teatro Nacional La Castellana** [126 F1] Calle 95, No 30–13; ✆257 0893. Expect a range of shows, from light entertainment to serious, weighty theatre from this group of actors, who stage regular shows of varying styles.

🎭 **Teatro de la Candelaria** [132 B4] Calle 12, No 2–59; ✆281 4814. This small repertory company stages a wide range of performances, some of them on controversial themes, & is a leading force in progressive theatre in Bogotá.

🎭 **Teatro Experimental La Mama** [135 C6] Calle 63, No 9–60; ✆211 2709. Edgy, experimental theatre is the speciality of this venue where local amateur groups perform year-round alternative shows.

🎭 **Teatro Colón** [132 B3] Calle 10, No 5–32; ✆341 0475. This beautiful, aged auditorium lends considerable grandeur to the backdrop & attracts numerous visiting international touring groups staging large-scale musicals & drama.

🎭 **William Shakespeare Theater** [map, page 152] Av 19, No 152–48; ✆614 9747. This small independent theatre within the Anglo-Colombiano High School stages British classics & Shakespeare festivals.

🎭 **Auditorio León de Greiff** [127 E5] Cnr Carrera 30 & Calle 45; ✆316 5562. Sat concerts feature orchestras from all over Colombia & Latin America at this university auditorium with tickets for less than 4,000COP.

🎭 **Biblioteca Luis Ángel Arango** [132 B4] Calle 11, No 4–14; ✆343 1212. Midweek concerts by international artists attract a wealthy highbrow crowd with local acts performing each Mon appealing to a more grassroots audience.

🎭 **Media Torta** [off map, 132 C4] Cnr Calle 18 & Carretera Circunvalación; ✆281 7704. Free Sun concerts are popular with a student crowd who flock to this stage behind La Candelaria, from noon to 16.00 each week.

SHOPPING

Bogotá has more than 70 large shopping centres with a great variety of boutiques, craft shops, chain stores and malls all over the city. Prime shopping areas are located in the north and northwestern areas, as shown below:

🏬 **Alhambra Plaza** [map, page 152] Calle 114A, No 33–54

🏬 **Aquarium** [135 B7] Calle 60, No 9–83

🏬 **Atlantis Plaza** [135 C2] Calle 81, Carrera 14

🏬 **BIMA** [map, page 152] Autopista Norte, No 232–35

🏬 **Bulevar Niza** [map, page 152] Carrera 52, No 125A–59

🏬 **Cedritos 151** [map, page 152] Diagonal 151, No 32–19

🏬 **Centro 93** [126 G1] Calle 93, No 14–20

🏬 **Centro Andino** [135 D2] Carrera 11, No 82–71

🏬 **Cosmos 64** [135 B6] Calle 64, No 11–37

🏬 **El Castillo** [126 F4] Carrera 7, No 72–64; ✆211 4321

🏬 **Galerías** Calle 54, No 26–41

🏬 **Granahorrar** [135 C4] Calle 72, No 10–34; ✆312 7077

🏬 **Hacienda Santa Bárbara** [map, page 152] Carrera 7, No 115–60

🏬 **Iserra 100** [map, page 152] Calle 100, Av Suba

🏬 **Los Héroes** Transversal 18, No 78–99; ✆257 0459

🏬 **Mazurén** [map, page 152] Autopista Norte, No 150–46

🏬 **Metropolis** Carrera 68, No 75A–50

🏬 **Palatino** [map, page 152] Calle 139, Carrera 7

🏬 **Portal de la 80** [off map, 126 C1] Transversal 100A, No 80A–20

🏬 **Portoalegre** [map, page 152] Carrera 52, No 137–27

🏬 **Salitre Plaza** [127 B5] Carrera 68B, No 40–39; ✆416 9737

🏬 **Santafé Shopping Center** [map, page 152] Calle 185, No 45–03; Autopista Norte

🏬 **Subazar** [map, page 152] Calle 140, No 91–34

🏬 **Titan Plaza** [map, page 152] Carrera 72, No 80–94, Calle 80, No 80–94; ☎ 466 0828
🏬 **Unicentro** [map, page 152] Av 15, No 123–30

🏬 **Unicentro de Occidente** [map, page 152] Carrera 111C, No 86–05; ☎ 434 8797
🏬 **Unilago Carrera** [135 B3] Carrera 15, No 78–33

HANDICRAFTS AND SOUVENIRS Bogotá has way too many craft shops, flea markets and souvenir stores to mention all of them, but some of the best are clustered around Carrera 7 near to the Plaza Bolívar and in the Parque Santander, ideal for combining with a trip to the Museo del Oro. Check out the **Mercado Artesanal Plaza Bolívar** [132 B3] on Carrera 9, No 12–52; the **Centro Artesanías de Colombia** [132 C3] on Carrera 3, No 18-60; the **Galería Artesenal de Colombia** [132 C3] on Calle 16, No 5–70; and the **Artesanías El Balay** [135 B3] on Carrera 15, No 75–63. The **Mercado de San Alejo** [132 E2] on Carrera 7 between Calles 24 and 26 is probably the best flea market – it's held 09.00–17.00 every Sunday.

EMERALDS AND JEWELLERY Every parade of shops in Bogotá contains at least a couple of *joyerías* (jewellery stores), although the main centre for emerald shopping is in and around Carrera 6 between Calle 12 and Calle 13 and in the Centro Internacional, where at least 90 outlets cater specifically for this market. There's also an emerald traders' street market on the corner of Avenida Jiménez and Carrera 7, and most hotel boutiques stock a small range of Colombian gold.

SPORT

Bogotá's fanatical football (soccer) scene is highly charged, with matches at the **Estadio El Campín** [126 E4] (☎ 315 8726) on a Wednesday and Saturday night often played to maximum crowds. The 46,018-seater stadium opened in 1946 and is the home ground of the Independiente Sante Fé and Millonarios club teams as well as the Colombian national squad. For tickets for local games call the Millonarios (☎ 347 7080) and Santa Fé (☎ 544 6670) box offices. Tickets for international games are available from the Federación Colombia de Fútbol (☎ 288 9838; *www.colfutbol.org*).

OTHER PRACTICALITIES

ALTITUDE SICKNESS A former motto of Bogotá was that it was '2,600 metres closer to the stars' – a direct reference to its altitude above sea level. Some travellers may find that the rapid ascent into Bogotá can lead to altitude sickness, with dizziness, sweating and breathlessness the most common effects. Should these symptoms persist, seek medical attention or contact Bogotá's 24-hour health line by dialling 125. Alternatively, a range of over-the-counter medicines available at pharmacies can help to alleviate symptoms.

BOOKSTORES, NEWSPAPERS AND LIBRARIES Bogotá was appointed the 'World Capital of the Book' for 2007 by UNESCO in recognition of its role in promoting reading initiatives. Unlike many Latin American cities, Bogotá has a large number of bookstores, although very few stock English-language publications. Non-Spanish-language newspapers, such as *The Sunday Times, Herald Tribune, Le Monde, New York Times, Süddeutsche Zeitung, Jerusalem Post, Financial Times* and *Mainichi Shimbun*, are stocked by a newsagents on the retail level at El Dorado Airport, although these can be up to two weeks out of date. Of Colombia's 400 public libraries, Bogotá has 33, of which the city's **Biblioteca Nacional** [132 F3]

(*Calle 24;* ☎ *243 5969*) is the backbone. A collection of more than 800,000 books and manuscripts can be enjoyed in numerous reading rooms – tourists need to apply for a library card in order to visit, but it's worth the red tape. Another recommendation is the **Biblioteca Luis Ángel Arango** [132 B4] (*Calle 11;* ☎ *343 1212*) in the heart of the historic district of La Candelaria – without a doubt one of the best-equipped libraries in Latin America. Large reading rooms lead to magnificent art galleries and auditoriums that are home to a dazzling array of year-round temporary exhibitions. Other libraries include the **Biblioteca Virgilio Barco** (adjacent to Simón Bolívar Park) where a collection of 25,000 books and 64 reading areas are open to the public free of charge. **Biblioteca El Tunal**, in south Bogotá, has over 110,000 titles – find it on Carrera 48. Bogota's English newspapers can be found in the Zona Rosa and Zona G in most restaurants and cafés and both *The City Paper Bogotá* (*http://thecitypaperbogota.com*) and *The Bogotá Post* (*http://thebogotapost.com*) are free of charge and provide excellent listings for events in and around the capital.

LAUNDRIES AND DRY CLEANERS   Hotel laundry services in Bogotá are generally fast and cheap – some charge by the weight of a bundle of garments, others on an item-by-item basis.

MEDIA AND COMMUNICATIONS   Most of Bogotá's major hotels offer internet access to guests, some for a nominal charge. **Wi-Fi** is found almost everywhere in the city including in TransMilenio stations in a drive to make the city more socially inclusive, in all Juan Valdez and Oma cafés and most shops. If you do not have your own phone or laptop, most hotels, hostels and *pensiones* will have one available for guests' use. Otherwise, you won't have to walk far before finding an internet café – there's one on almost every block!

Most of Bogotá's internet cafés also offer **international phone calls** at rates of around 1,000COP per minute. **Telecom** (☎ *561 1111;* ⊕ *07.00–19.00 daily*) has offices throughout the city, including a large base on Calle 23, No 13–49. Services include domestic and international phone calls and faxes.

Colombia's **postal service**, 4/72 [132 B3] has offices in La Candelaria (*Cnr Carrera 7 & Calle 13;* ☎ *353 5666*) and the Centro Internacional (*Carrera 7, No 27–54*) with **DHL** [127 G5] (☎ *212 9727*) on Calle 72, No 10–70, and **FedEx** [132 C3] (☎ *291 0100*) on Carrera 7, No 16–50. **Avianca's** city-centre branch [132 C3] (☎ *342 7513*) has a poste restante on Carrera 7, No 16–36, with a branch at the Centro Internacional (☎ *342 6077*).

MEDICAL SERVICES   A high level of medical care comparable to that in industrialised countries is available in Bogotá, and the city has many hundreds of clinics, medical centres and hospitals, both private and state-funded. Having medical insurance will allow you to visit a private doctor where facilities tend to be better and English more widely spoken. Bogotá's ophthalmology clinics already enjoy a good reputation for their pioneering use of new technology, and the city also has world-class facilities in areas such as fertility treatment, prosthetics, cancer treatment, transplants, cardiovascular medicine and plastic surgery. Latin America's first baby born after in vitro fertilisation was born in Bogotá. The city also has the region's most advanced blood bank and transfusion centre. In 2002, city authorities in Bogotá launched a medical tourism initiative, promoting the capital as a place that is 'good for your health'. Particularly good facilities can be found at **Clínica de Marly** [127 G5] (☎ *343 6600*) on Calle 50, where a number of doctors cover most specialities, with a wide range of travel-related medical services offered at the Centro de Atención al Viajero – including vaccinations and laboratory tests. For a list of hospitals and private clinics, visit http://www.bogota-dc.com/dir/clinicas.html. Bogotá is also blessed with some excellent dentists, including **Antonio José Hurtado Soto** [map, page 152] (*Calle 134;* ⟍ *627 2684/258 1281*), and **Centro Odontopediatrico** [135 B1] (*Calle 12;* ⟍ *312 3739/211 3484*). For a list of more than 50 orthodontists, visit www.bogota-dc.com/profesiones/odontologos.html.

MONEY AND CURRENCY Hundreds of money-exchange specialists operate in Bogotá with 24-hour booths at the airport, outlets in most major hotels and offices on almost every street corner citywide. A large concentration of *casas de cambio* can be found downtown at Jiménez Avenue, around El Rosario Square, the Centro Comercial Avenida Chile on Calle 72, the International Center and between Calle 90 and Calle 95. Most buy and sell foreign currency, travellers' cheques and handle international drafts. One of the largest chains is **Money Gram** (*www.moneygram.com*) but shop around as rates can vary enormously. Credit cards are widely accepted in Bogotá's larger hotels and restaurants but expect to pay cash (often in advance) in the cheaper hostels and *pensionados*.

Unlike the rest of Colombia, **banks** in Bogotá close at 15.00 Monday to Thursday, 15.30 on Friday, but stay open over the lunch period – a quirk that catches many first-time visitors out. Not all handle foreign currency or offer cash advances on credit cards, but most have an ATM, including the Banco Popular on Calle 24 and the Bancocolombia and Banco Unión Colombiano on Carrera 8. For a list of ATM locations visit www.bogota-dc.com – there are dozens citywide.

SHOWERS, EQUIPMENT AND LUGGAGE El Dorado Airport has showers with towels, disposable slippers, soap and shampoo – find them at Module 4. There are also luggage lockers at modules 1, 2 and 3 – great for those keen to explore Colombia without lugging the entire contents of their backpack around, and a way to beat luggage-weight restrictions on smaller planes. Bogotá has several very good camping supply stores that stock a decent array of tents, trekking equipment, gas canisters, sleeping bags and backpacks. Two of the best are **Almacén Aventura** [126 F4] (*Carrera 13, No 67–26;* ⟍ *248 1679*) and **Montaña Accesorios** [135 C2] (*Carrera 13A, No 79–46;* ⟍ *530 6103*).

SOLO TRAVELLERS AND MEETING FRIENDS Lone travellers in Bogotá who fancy meeting up with like-minded people have plenty of options. Scour the noticeboards in backpacker hostels in the city and you'll spot plenty of 'solo traveller seeks similar' postings, usually from Europeans and Americans seeking company on the next leg of their trip. Another option is to post details of your travel plans on WAYN.com (Where Are You Now), a website aimed at helping travellers keep in touch that has members in Bogotá. Sal Si Puedes (⟍ *283 3765*) is a group of outdoor-minded people who enjoy walks in the countryside on the outskirts of the city. Ecoguías also arrange weekly group walks for each Sunday (⟍ *347 5736*).

WHAT TO SEE AND DO

MUSEUMS Bogotá has over 80 public and private museums – all of which are well managed and funded. Collections range from archaeological and colonial exhibits to modern art, sculpture and religious artefacts – and are well worth a visit. Sundays can be busy, as some museums offer free admission then. Avoid the last Sunday of the month, when every collection can be visited free of charge – the crowds are vast. The following are just some of the highlights.

Museo del Oro (Gold Museum) [132 C3] (*Calle 16, No 5–41;* ⟍ *284 7450; www. banrep.gov.co/museo;* ⊕ *09.30–16.30 Tue–Sat, 10.00–16.30 Sun & public holidays; admission 2,000COP*) More than 34,000 gold pieces from most of Colombia's major pre-Hispanic cultures (Calima, Quimbaya, Muisca, Tairona, Sinú and Tolima amongst others) are contained in this innocuous modern building – making it one of the most important collections of its type worldwide. A sign states that 'birds are fundamental symbols of the shaman. Like them, he can fly, see a long way, link the earth to the sky, and take part in reproducing nature' – and throughout the exhibition the natural world is represented at every turn. Parrots, macaws, fish and iguanas feature in resplendent magnificence on this vast collection of '*ofrendas alos dioses*' ('offerings to the gods') comprising masks, necklaces, bracelets and hundreds of figurines. At the heart of this collection is a circular exhibition pod with automated illumination in sections – don't miss the atmospheric display that starts off dark and culminates in a dazzling array of gold. Although most of the exhibits are signed in Spanish there are English-language tours each day (at 11.00 and 15.00 at the time of writing). The collection spans two floors and is just a small, handpicked selection of a vast collection held in the museum's guarded vault. Part of this National Monument is a display of 20,000 bone and ceramic objects.

Museo Botero (Botero Museum) [132 B4] (*Calle 11, No 4–41;* ⟍ *343 1331;* ⊕ *09.00–19.00 Mon–Sat, closed Tue, 10.00–17.00 Sun; free admission*) This magnificent 208-piece collection was donated by Colombia's most famous artist Fernando Botero (see box, page 56) and contains 123 of his own works along with 85 by an impressive range of European masters – including pieces by Picasso, Chagall, Dalí, Renoir, Matisse and Monet. Housed in a beautifully restored colonial mansion (Casa Luis López de Mesa), the Botero collection is catalogued as the most important art exhibition in the country and comprises drawings, paintings, sculpture using some fine watercolour, oil and pastel techniques.

Casa de la Moneda (Coin House) [132 B3] (*Calle 11, No 4–93;* ⟍ *281 3146;* ⊕ *09.00–19.00 Mon, Wed & Sat, 10.00–17.00 Sun; free admission*) As the immediate neighbour of Museo Botero, this fine historic building is often visited as part of a walking tour around the area. The city's former mint boasts a succession of rooms containing several permanent exhibitions and collections, including coins, bills, printing presses and artefacts relating to the strongroom.

Museo Nacional (National Museum) [132 G2] (*Carrera 7, No 28–66;* ⟍ *381 6470; www.museonacional.gov.co;* ⊕ *10.00–17.30 Tue–Sun; free admission for all permanent exhibitions & a nominal fee for temporary exhibits*) Colombia's oldest museum is housed in a British-designed old stone-and-brick building that dates back to 1823. Thomas Reed created this panopticon as the city's prison, using fortress-style architecture that includes arches, domes and columns in the shape of a Greek cross. More than 100 prison cells were constructed behind a solid façade housing both male and female prisoners up until 1946. In 1948, the building was adapted significantly to house the National Museum. It underwent further restoration in 1975 to add extra rooms and modern services and today contains a collection of over 20,000 pieces, including archaeological artefacts, indigenous and Afro-Colombian art, paintings, documents and cultural objects. There are also 57 paintings by Fernando Botero, Alejandro Obregón and Guillermo Wiedemann in this three-storey collection that spans Colombia's history from the pre-Hispanic era.

God made us walking animals – pedestrians. As a fish needs to swim, a bird to fly, a deer to run, we need to walk, not in order to survive, but to be happy.

Enrique Penalosa, former mayor of Bogotá

Vast, sprawling Bogotá continues to grow at an alarming pace and offers far too much ground to cover in a single visit. However, getting to grips with the neighbourhoods of La Candelaria and Plaza de Bolívar is more than achievable in a day or two – you won't have time to see everything but it'll be a decent introduction to the city's heart and soul. The distance between the pigeon-scattered Plaza de Bolívar (Bolívar Plaza) and the Parque Santander (Santander Park) is less than 2km but as the route is jam-packed with museums, churches, craft shops, cafés, bars and markets, allow at least a day if you plan to break for lunch.

Set off from the steps of the vast **Catedral Primada** (page 148), one of Bogotá's finest colonial structures, and head to the commemorative collection in honour of the 1810 Creole Rebellion at the **Museo del 20 de Julio** (Museum of Independence, page 146). Next it's on to the beautiful **Casa de la Moneda** (Coin House, page 144) and the fascinating artworks at **Museo de Botero** (Botero Museum, also known as **Donación Botero**, page 144) – an exhibition that is practically a review of late 19th-century art history and includes original pieces by Corot, Monet, Matisse, Picasso, Dalí, Chagall, Bacon and de Kooning. Take Calle 10 downhill from the corner of Calle 4 past the quirky roof-mounted sculptures that adorn some of the bubblegum-coloured houses to the **Palacio de San Carlos** (Sain Carlos Palace), the former government HQ before it was moved to the Palacio de Nariño. It was from this fine old palace that Bolívar fled through a window to escape a murder attempt, leaping half-naked from a bathtub, covered in soap. At Carrera 6, turn left to view the rather magnificent religious art collection at **Museo de Arte Colonial** (Museum of Colonial Art, page 146) before heading on to the ancient Iglesia de San Ignacio (San Ignacio Church) and the Iglesia Museo de Santa Clara (Santa Clara Church Museum). Push on up Carrera 7 from the grand **Plaza de Bolívar** (page 150) to discover shops, boutiques and outlets galore before crossing Avenida Jiménez to the handicraft stalls, buskers and food vendors at **Parque Santander** (Santander Park). A visit to the resplendent **Museo del Oro** (Gold Museum, page 144) provides a fitting finale to touring Bogotá on foot. Despite the extensive pillaging of pre-Columbian art by the *conquistadores* and the mass exportation of South American gold, the museum boasts the finest collection of pre-Columbian gold on the continent. It contains 33,000 individual pieces, from simple bangles to some of the most beautifully crafted masks and figures in the world.

Museo Histórico Policía (Museum of Police History) [132 B2] (*Calle 9, No 9–27;* \ *233 5911/281 3284;* ⊕ *08.00–17.30 Mon–Fri, closed noon–13.00, 10.00–16.00 Sat; free admission*) Most people visit this exhibition to see the blood-stained jacket of Colombia's most notorious drug baron, Pablo Escobar. The jacket was worn by Escobar on the day he was shot dead by police gunmen after a high-profile (and controversial) 499-day manhunt. Museum rooms are organised chronologically to allow a running

history of the Colombian police force from its inception in a building that became the national police HQ in 1923. The museum has lots of exhibits that focus on laws, penalties and punishments, containing guns, radios, uniforms and insignia.

Museo Arqueológico (Archaeological Museum) [132 D3] (Carrera 6, No 7–43; ✆ 243 1048; ⊕ 08.30–17.00 Mon–Fri, 09.30–17.00 Sat, 09.00–16.00 Sun; admission 3,000COP) This extensive collection of archaeological relics is housed in the beautifully restored Casa del Marqués de San Jorge, a fine 17th-century colonial building that is a museum piece in itself. Expect lots of fine ceramic pieces from Colombia's main pre-Columbian Amerindian groups, many of which are some of the most magnificent artistically ever found in the region.

Museo de Arte Colonial (Museum of Colonial Art) [132 A3] (Carrera 6a, No 9–77; ✆ 341 6017; ⊕ 09.00–17.00 Mon–Fri, 10.00–16.00 Sat/Sun; admission 2,000COP) Originally a Jesuit college, this grand 17th-century building was inaugurated as a museum in 1942 and contains an impressive array of paintings, silverware, books, furniture and carvings from the colonial era. A collection of works by painter Gregorio Vásquez de Arce y Ceballos is the largest in the world and comprises 76 oils and 106 drawings – all of them truly memorable.

Museo 20 de Julio (Museum of Independence) [132 B3] (Calle 11, No 6–94; ✆ 334 4150; ⊕ 09.00–17.00 Tue–Fri, 10.00–16.00 Sat/Sun; admission 4,000COP) Located on the site of the Creole revolution against Spanish rule on 20 July 1810, the Museum of Independence looks over the Plaza de Bolívar and is housed in the Casa del Florero. A rather sterile collection of papers and paintings relates to the Colombian fight for independence – it's nothing mind-blowing but it does a decent job of telling the tale.

Museo de Arte Moderno (Modern Art Museum) [132 F3] (Carrera 24, No 6–00; ✆ 286 0466; www.mambogota.com; ⊕ 10.00–18.00 Tue–Sat, 12.00–16.30 Sun; admission 4,000COP) This large collection of temporary displays of 20th-century visual arts changes frequently. It opened in the mid 1980s and contains painting, photography and sculpture by national and international artists – although home-grown talent is the focus.

Museo Quinta de Bolívar (Bolívar Homestead Museum) [off map, 132 E4] (Calle 20, No 2–91; ✆ 336 6410/6419; e quintadebolivar@excite.com; www. quintadebolivar.gov.co; ⊕ 09.00–16.30 Tue–Fri, 10.00–15.30 Sat/Sun; admission 3,000COP) Built in 1880 and given to Simón Bolívar in 1820, this grand mansion was restored in 1998 and declared a National Monument as a testament to Bolívar's era. A fine example of rural colonial architecture, the museum contains furniture, garments, armoury, documents and objects belonging to The Liberator and is set in splendid gardens in the foothills of the Cerro de Monserrate.

Iglesia Museo de Santa Clara (Santa Clara Church Museum) [132 A3] (Carrera 8, No 8–91; ✆ 337 6762; ⊕ 09.00–17.00 Tue–Fri, 10.00–16.00 Sat/Sun; admission 2,000COP) This fine colonial church no longer opens for worship but as a museum it is still well worth a visit. Built between 1629 and 1674 as part of the Poor Clare convent, it typifies Bogotá's single-nave church structures and has a stunning interior with over 100 wall paintings, ornate altarpieces and statues dating from the 17th and 18th centuries.

In 1995, mathematician, philosopher and political novice Antanas Mockus traded in a senior position at the Colombian National University to run as Mayor of Bogotá. He won, and using his skills as an educator set about turning Bogotá into one of the most ambitious social experiments on the planet.

At the time, Bogotá was on the cusp of chaos, choked with violence, lawlessness and corruption. People were desperate for a change and for moral leadership, and Mockus fitted the bill. He focused on changing hearts and minds by empowering Bogotá's citizens as individuals and getting people to think about good and bad behaviour. He had already gained notoriety for the use of some rather unconventional teaching techniques, once dropping his pants and mooning a class of rowdy art students to gain their attention.

As a leader, Mockus was equally avant-garde, hiring 420 mime artists to control the traffic in Bogotá's rush-hour chaos. They shadowed pedestrians who didn't follow crossing rules and poked fun at reckless drivers, as Mockus believed that Bogotanos were more afraid of being ridiculed than of being fined. He also launched a 'Night for Women', decreeing that the city's men should stay home. On the first night alone of this three-day event, more than 700,000 women enjoyed free concerts and bars, clubs and restaurants, marching through Bogotá in celebration and applauding men who stayed at home or were seen taking care of children. The police commander on duty that night was a woman, as were all 1,500 police officers in charge of Bogotá's security.

Mockus also appeared naked on television during a water shortage, taking a shower but soaping without water and asking his fellow citizens to do the same. Within weeks, the city's water consumption dropped by 40%. He also asked for volunteers to pay 10% in extra taxes – an initiative that 63,000 people agreed to. In 2002, Mockus collected more than three times the taxes that had been gathered in 1990. His leadership also saw 7,000 community security groups formed; a 70% fall in the homicide rate; drinking water provided to all homes (up from 79% in 1993); and sewerage provided to 95% of homes (up from 71%). He had stars painted on the streets where 1,500 pedestrians had been killed in traffic accidents – prompting a 50% drop in fatalities. 'Saving a single life justifies the effort,' he said.

In 2010, Mockus was hotly tipped to be the next president of Colombia but polled second for the Green Party to Juan Manuel Santos, leading to a run-off election which Santos won. Mockus had resigned from his mayoral role to campaign for the presidency after serving two non-consecutive terms. While on the campaign trail, Mockus revealed he was suffering from Parkinson's disease. He is currently the president of Corpovisionarios, an organisation that consults cities about addressing their problems through the same policy methodology that was so successful during his terms as Mayor of Bogotá.

Bogotá WHAT TO SEE AND DO

3

Museo de Francisco José Caldas (Francisco Jose Caldas Museum) [132 A3] (*Carrera 8, No 6–87*; \ *289 6275* ⊕ *10.00–17.30 Tue Fri, 10.00 15.00 Sat/ Sun; admission 3,000COP*) Located in the premises of Presidential Guard Infantry Battalion, this fascinating museum contains a range of exhibits of scientific instruments, writings and books belonging to Sabio Caldas, Colombia's most famous naturalist. Browse through documents of scientific-historical interest,

It may come as a surprise to visitors to the capital that the coffee culture here is only really in its infancy due to the fact that most locals prefer to drink inexpensive shots of '*tinto*' from vendors armed with *panela*-sweetened offerings sold from thermos flasks on street corners. Of course, this is a result of years of only the best crop being exported and whatever was left used for domestic consumption. We are happy to report that this practice is now confined to the past. Once, gourmet coffee was the sole business of national chains such as Oma and Juan Valdez, and now the ubiquitous Starbucks (the first store opened in 2014), but now you can find pop-ups, indie locations, containers and specialist coffee destinations so you can placate those caffeine urges! For some fabulous insights into the national crop check out any or all of the following options: **Café Cultor** – [135 D5] Calle 69, No 6–20, Chapinero; **Azahar** – Carrera 14, No 93A–48, Parque 93; **Café Rec** – [132 A3] Carrera 6, No 7–08, La Candelaria. Café Rec is worth a special mention as you can actually enjoy a coffee-tasting session with a resident expert.

including expedition plans, cartographic maps and surveys of Colombia's geographic areas. Displays also feature all manner of engineering instruments consisting of telescopes, hypsometry, metal detectors and microscopes.

CHURCHES Although only a handful of Bogotá's many churches look anything much from the outside, don't let this fool you – a great number offer plenty of surprises. Many have ornate interior decoration and elaborate furnishings despite a dull exterior. Most date back to the 17th and 18th centuries and some contain paintings by Gregorio Vásquez de Arce y Ceballos, one of Colombia's most famous colonial painters and a Bogotá legend. There are too many fine and interesting churches to list them all individually. Some of the highlights include the following.

Catedral Primada [132 B3] (*Plaza de Bolívar;* \ *341 1954;* ⊕ *09.00–10.00 Mon–Sat, 09.00–14.00 Sun*) This hulking great Neo-classical building stands on the site where the first Mass was celebrated on the founding of Bogotá in 1538. At that time, there was just a simple thatched chapel, although several larger replacement structures have been built over the years. The first, in 1556–65, collapsed in a pile of rubble due to poor workmanship and the second, built in 1572, was reduced to ruins by an earthquake in 1785. The present building dates back to 1807 but wasn't fully completed until 1823 and is by far Bogotá's largest church. The body of the city's founder Jiménez de Quesada is entombed in a chapel off the right-hand aisle away from a vast array of pews in echoing spaciousness.

Iglesia de San Francisco (San Francisco Church) [132 C3] (*Cnr Av Jiménez & Carrera 7;* \ *341 2357;* ⊕ *07.00–19.00 Mon–Fri, 07.00–13.00 & 18.00–19.00 Sat/Sun*) Bogotá's oldest surviving church has a beautifully elaborate interior that includes some fine Mudéjar ceiling ornamentation and a magnificent 17th-century gilded altarpiece – so don't let the rather austere exterior put you off. The building dates back to 1556 and has a loyal and flourishing congregation, so expect packed pews. .

Iglesia de San Ignacio (San Ignacio Church) [132 A3] (*Calle 10, No 6–35;* \ *342 1639;* ⊕ *09.00–18.00 Mon–Fri, closed noon–15.00, 09.00–noon Sat/Sun*)

Originally founded in 1610 by the Jesuits, the building remained unfinished until their expulsion in 1767 but has been a place of worship since 1635. Today it remains one of Bogotá's most lavishly decorated churches and as befitting a large colonial relic it contains a wealth of magnificent art.

Iglesia de la Veracruz (Veracruz Church) [132 C3] (*Calle 16, No 7–19;* 342 1343; ✆ *for Mass only at 08.00, noon & 18.00*) An important burial place for the heroes of independence, the tomb of the martyrs of the Veracruz church is known as the National Pantheon throughout Bogotá. Between 1810 and 1819, some 80 patriots who were killed by the Spanish came to rest in the church's catacombs. Although it has a simplistic interior, the Iglesia de la Veracruz has some fine altarpieces and an impressive panelled vault.

OTHER SIGHTS
Cerro de Monserrate (Monserrate Hill) [map, page 152] (*Quinta de Bolívar;* 284 5700; ✆ *10.00–midnight Mon–Sat, 10.00–16.00 Sun; admission 16,400COP*) This dominant mountain peak shapes Bogotá's cityscape and has a handsome white church built on its summit at 3,200m. Devotees of the Señor Caído (a statue of the fallen Christ) inside the church make Sunday pilgrimages to the mountaintop, where some of the best panoramic views of Bogotá can be enjoyed unless a build-up of smog gets in the way. Looking down on the chaos of the city from Monserrate Hill on a clear day is nothing short of breathtaking, with incredible views that extend from the banks of the Río Bogotá to La Candelaria's red-tiled roofs. There's a handicrafts market, cafés and a couple of excellent restaurants – all of which stay open until midnight. A half-hourly *teleférico* (cable car) or tram departs from Monserrate station near Quinta de Bolívar for the 15-minute journey to the peak.

Mirador Torre Colpatria (Colpatria Tower Look-out) [132 E2] (*Carrera 7, No 24–89, Piso 50;* 609 2448; ✆ *14.00–20.00 Sat/Sun & public holidays*) More stunning 360° views abound from the top of Torre Colpatria, home to the highest building in Colombia at 180m. Look out across the city's western hills, Parque de la Independencia (Independence Park) and Torres del Parque (Park Towers) over criss-crossing streets, rooftops and bridges. Take a lift to the top at a cost of 4,200COP, where there are numerous telescopes and a coffee shop on the 50th floor.

Bogotá WHAT TO SEE AND DO

3

Jardín Botánico José Celestino Mutis (Jose Celestino Mutis Botanical Garden) [126 B3] (*Calle 57, No 61–13;* ✆ *437 7060; www.jbb.gov.co;* ☉ *08.00–17.00 Tue–Sun, closed noon–14.00; admission 2,700COP*) This botanical park and centre of scientific investigation is named in honour of botanist José Celestino Mutis (see box, page 388). Climate-controlled exhibits of flora boast staggering temperature differences and reflect the varied regions of Colombia. There is also an exhibit of 5,000 indigenous orchids – one of the most exquisite collections in the nation. Beautiful grounds offer a comprehensive selection of plants and shrubs with gardens stocked with a huge diversity of flora. A good-quality restaurant serves pan-Colombian fare.

Maloka [127 B5] (*Carrera 68D, No 24A–51;* ✆ *427 2707; www.maloka.org;* ☉ *08.00–17.00 Mon–Thu, 10.00–19.00 Fri–Sun; admission 10,500COP*) One of the most impressive science and technology centres in South America, Maloka has become a byword for high-tech fun. An interactive museum with a thematic structure, it allows visitors to play science-related games and view documentaries in a giant domed-roof cinema on physics, chemistry, maths, biology and geography. The name of the museum derives from the Amerindian word *maloca* – a meeting house that indigenous communities believe is the centre of the universe and life, a symbol of family integration and a place to share ideas and solve problems.

La Candelaria [132 A3] Bogotá's old historic quarter has some magical, captivating qualities – with gorgeous blue, pink, gold, turquoise, magenta, ochre and canary-yellow colonial buildings adorned with balconies painted crimson, white and deep blue. Pretty cobbled streets cluttered with bohemian shops, craft stalls and galleries climb up towards a hazy mountain peak. Eccentric rooftop sculptures draw the gaze skywards while a cacophony of street musicians, chattering students and food vendors rises from parks and plazas. Handsome boulevards open up on to Plaza de Bolívar, a handsome and crowded meeting point with the people and pigeons of La Candelaria. Visit swish hotel courtyard cafés or trendy student juice bars in a fine aged city centre that is wonderful to explore by bike or on foot.

FESTIVALS AND EVENTS
Festival Iberoamericano de Teatro (March/April; *www.festivaldeteatro.com.co*) This vast theatrical extravaganza takes place every even-numbered year. Over 200 theatre groups comprising 2,400 artists from five continents and 42 countries stage performances across dozens of Bogotá's most iconic venues, attracting an audience of over 2.5 million people to a host of plays, dramas, musicals and comedy in one of Latin America's most elaborate theatrical events.

Feria de Libro de Bogotá (April/May; *www.feriadellibro.com*) Since the first book fair was launched in 1988 the event has gone from strength to strength with more than 95% of Colombia's editorial industries participants in 2007. Expect 300,000 visitors from across the globe during the 13-day event where over 100,000 titles and 500 exhibitors occupy 15,000m² of space.

Carnaval de Bogotá (August) This citywide celebration of TransMilenio's Hispanic foundation includes masquerades, dances, processions and parades culminating in an array of activities, concerts and sports events centred on the Parque Simón Bolívar. A host of warm-up pre-carnival festivities begin each year in July with beauty pageants, folkloric shows and live music.

Jazz al Parque (September) This two-day open-air jazz concert in the Parque de los Novios attracts a high-calibre international line-up with class acts taking to the stage from 21.00 to midnight each night. It's free and a highlight in Bogotá's crowded festival calendar, and was established in the city in 1996.

Hip Hop al Parque (October) Hip Hop in the Park brings beats and rhymes to the city's Parque Simón Bolívar with two days of the finest hip-hop music. An 8-hour set starts at 13.00 each day. Since launching in 1998, this mega rap event has attracted a strong international line-up and an enviable crowd of international DJs.

Rock al Parque (October) Rock in the Park is the biggest annual rock festival in Latin America, attracting 300,000 rock fans to Parque Simón Bolívar with a wide variety of international, national and local bands – all of which perform for free. In the weeks leading up to the event, local up-and-coming groups take part in a battle of the bands for the privilege of performing.

Festival de Cine de Bogotá (October; www.bogocine.com) Since it was established 25 years ago, Bogotá's annual film festival has become one of the most respected in Latin America, attracting films from all around the world and providing a showcase for Colombian film-making and cinema well beyond the mainstream. The festival bestows its 'Pre-Columbia Circle Awards' for Best Film, Best New Director and Best Colombia Film with numerous star-studded events across the city.

AROUND BOGOTÁ

Once you've left the city behind, the topography determines the climate, and such is the variety of landscape surrounding Bogotá that this can offer significant temperature changes. Expect steamy lowlands in the west and chilly open highlands in the east – all within a couple of hours or so from the swish boutiques of urban Bogotá. Beautiful forests, lakes, streams and mountains hide hundreds of small towns and settlements on a landscape that was an important sacred site for the Muisca people.

PARQUE NATURAL CHICAQUE (CHICAQUE NATURAL PARK) (✆ 368 3118; e info@ chicaque.com; www.chicaque.com; admission 14,000COP) You'll find this private nature reserve just half an hour outside the centre of Bogotá, 20km to the west. It contains more than 15km of maintained paths that weave through 300ha of spectacular cloudforest packed with flora and fauna, at a height exceeding 2,700m. Muggy and damp, the forest averages 74% humidity, with October and November the most humid at around 80%. The reserve has gorges, creeks and rocky crags with gradual slopes and inclines, hundreds of species of plants and 200 species of birds. Temperatures fluctuate between 11°C and 17°C in the reserve, where it is possible to stay overnight in a cabin for 93,000COP (including all meals) or camp at 50,000COP per person.

Getting there and away Hop aboard a **buseta** or **colectivo** in Bogotá's centre to the town of Soacha and haggle with a local **taxi** driver to get a good deal to the reserve. The administration is about 4km off the Soacha–La Mesa road, so budget for about 15,000COP for the trip.

ZIPAQUIRÁ (*Telephone code 1*) More than 70,000 people live in this mountain town 49km north of Bogotá where salt mines (*salinas*) are the main employers.

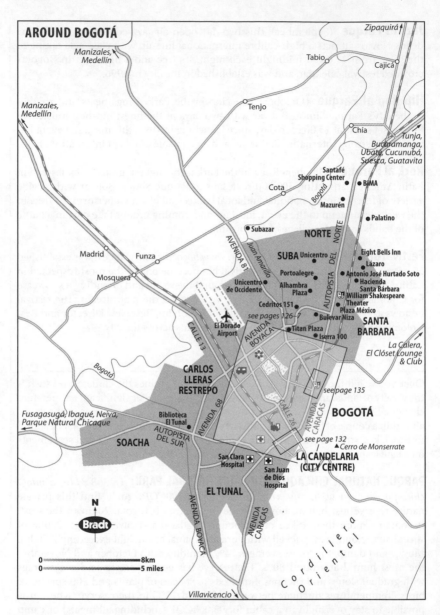

AROUND BOGOTÁ

Zipaquirá
Manizales, Medellín
Tabio
Cajicá
Manizales, Medellín
Tenjo
Chía
Tunja, Bucaramanga, Ubaté, Cucunubá, Suesca, Guatavita
Santafé Shopping Center
BIMA
Cota
Mazurén
Palatino
Subazar
NORTE
SUBA Unicentro
Eight Bells Inn
Lázaro
Portoalegre
Antonio José Hurtado Soto
Unicentro de Occidente
Alhambra Plaza
Hacienda Santa Bárbara
William Shakespeare Theater
Cedritos 151
Plaza México
see pages 126–7
Bulevar Niza
SANTA BARBARA
El Dorado Airport
Titan Plaza
Iserra 100
La Calera, El Clóset Lounge & Club
Madrid
Funza
Mosquera
CARLOS LLERAS RESTREPO
see page 135
BOGOTÁ
Fusagasugá, Ibagué, Neiva, Parque Natural Chicaque
Biblioteca El Tunal
SOACHA
see page 132
Cerro de Monserrate
San Clara Hospital
LA CANDELARIA (CITY CENTRE)
San Juan de Dios Hospital
EL TUNAL
N
Bradt
0   8km
0   5 miles
Villavicencio
Cordillera Oriental

Huge reserves of salt make Zipaquirá famous throughout Colombia and the town's **Catedral de Sal** (Salt Cathedral) has been a popular tourist attraction since 1954 (✆ *852 9890;* ⊕ *09.00–17.30 daily; admission 23,000COP*). Carved out of natural salt rock by the miners who worked in Zipaquirá, the Salt Cathedral is a vast and impressive feat of human endeavour that can accommodate a staggering 8,400 people and is 18m high at its loftiest point. Visitors walk through a network of hand-hewn tunnels buried deep beneath the surface of the mine. You'll see altars, statues and a fully operational cathedral carved from the salt rock where Sunday services are still conducted and weddings and christenings are often held.

Dimly lit corridors are unsuitable for anyone with claustrophobia, although the route itself is well maintained and easily walked in around 90 minutes at a slow pace. There's also a **Salt Museum** (⊕ *10.00–16.00 Tue–Sun; admission 3,000COP*) and a **Museum of Archaeology** (◣ *852 3499;* ⊕ *09.30–16.30 daily; admission 3,000COP*), where a number of collections feature Muisca art and ceramics – phone before making a special journey as this place is often closed without explanation. Zipaquirá was founded in 1606 and named after the Chibcha word meaning the 'Land of the Zipa' – Zipa being the territorial king. A large plaza still boasts some fine colonial architecture, including the imposing green-and-white town hall building.

Getting there and away Every 10 minutes a **bus** departs from Bogotá's TransMilenio northern terminus for Zipaquirá. It's a 1½-hour journey (1,800COP) with an added 20-minute walk from central Zipaquirá to the mines on the edge of town. Another option is to hop aboard the **Turistren** (◣ *375 0556; www.turistren. com.co*) from Bogotá on Sundays and public holidays – a ticket for this quaint *Puffing Billy*-style steam train costs 20,000COP. It departs at 08.30 and reaches Zipaquirá after a brief stop at Usaquén station. It returns at 14.00, making it a perfect trip for lunch – but be sure to pre-book.

SUESCA (*Telephone code 1*) Rock climbers across the world are fast becoming aware of this town of 14,000 people as it sits amidst some fantastic mountaineering terrain. A small climbing school, **Campo Base** (e *deaventuraporcolombia@yahoo. com*) runs guided climbs and offers basic accommodation for around 10,000COP per person. Expert guide **Hernán Wilke** (m *310 216 8119; www.monodedo.com*) also offers popular classes for all levels, from novice to expert. He rents out equipment and offers guided half- and full-day trips. Another recommended rock-climbing guide is **Hugo Rocha** (m *315 826 2051*) who can be hired at around 80,000COP per day. Many of Suesca's 200 or so climbs are less than 20 minutes from town, some within a 5-minute walk along some railway tracks. Expect sandstone crags with beautiful flowering plants. A good source of information is the small climbing shop run by Fernando and Tatiana Gonzolas – Fernando is a veteran of some of the most impressive climbs on the planet, including K2 and Everest. Although Suesca can be quiet during the week it springs to life at weekends, when the mountaineering fraternity descends on the town, 65km north of Bogotá. By public transport, head to Suesca on the TransMilenio to its northern terminus and catch a bus – they depart with some frequency (40 minutes, 4,000COP).

GUATAVITA (*Telephone code 1*) Although the original town of Guatavita was demolished to make way for a reservoir in 1967, the so-called 'New Guatavita' has been built to replicate its colonial style. It's been beautifully done with white façades, rustic masonry, red-clay roof tiles and heavy wooden doors and shutters. The central square is framed by a necklace of handicraft and food stalls and is popular with milling local children. Sunday is a good time to visit as the church bells ring melodically and best-dressed locals take to the streets.

However, most people think of the Laguna Guatavita (Guatavita Lagoon) when they hear the name Guatavita – as this small circular lake 50km northeast of Bogotá is a famous Muisca sacred site. At the heart of the mythical El Dorado, the Laguna Guatavita is supposedly full of gold. Certainly, 500 years ago the gold-dusted Zipa (the Muisca king) would throw gold items into the lake as offerings to the gods. Many have been retrieved and now form the basis of the magnificent collection at

Bogotá's world-famous Museo del Oro (Gold Museum), where 30,000 pieces form a dazzling display.

Visitors to the Laguna Guatavita can enjoy a number of pleasant walks around the lake and into the forests along well-maintained trails that were extensively restored in 2006. Paths reach an elevation of 3,000m and offer spectacular views across the lake and surrounding countryside. English-speaking guides are sometimes available. Facilities include a visitor centre and a café. Permits are required to visit the park with numbers strictly monitored. To apply, contact the Corporación Autónoma Regional de Cundinamarca in Bogotá (✆ *320 900; www.car.gov.co*).

CUCUNUBÁ (*Telephone code 1*) This agricultural outpost is home to 1,699 people, almost all of whom work on the land or rely on farming or mining for a living. Located 88km north of Bogotá, the settlement was founded by Luis Enriquez on 2 August 1600. Today almost 15% of the economy is based on cattle, with an average of four animals per smallholding. Modern Cucunubá owes a lasting debt of gratitude to architect Pedro Gómez Potter, who was born in the town. A famous Colombian exponent of progressive urban architecture across the country, he built the first commercial centre of Bogotá and won awards across the whole of Latin America. However, his success didn't distract him from improving his shabby, humble home town. Gómez Potter set about redesigning and investing in Cucunubá, building a well-planned town to better serve its residents whilst being incredibly pleasing on the eye. Part of his urban layout featured workshops for local wool-knitters whom he organised into a co-operative. He then set about selling their wares to many of Bogotá's swankiest clothing boutiques. Today Cucunubá has hotels, shopping malls and neighbourhoods of residential housing – a triumphant testament to a home-grown talent prepared to give something back.

UBATÉ (*Telephone code 1*) This rural town of around 7,000 people has dairy products coursing through its veins, with streets of shops and food stalls selling cheap eats on a milk or cheese theme. Named after the Muisca word meaning 'Bloodied Land' the town was founded in 1592 and has been the site of many ancient battles. Renowned as the 'Milk Capital of Colombia', Ubaté has a rather fine Gothic-style cathedral and is also famed for its San Luis Convent. Construction of the church began in 1927

HIKING BOGOTÁ

Should your visit to the Colombian capital fall on a weekend and you are not suffering from the ill effects of a Friday night on the tiles or from altitude sickness, there is an option for the more outdoorsy traveller. Located on the Avenida Circunvalar and Calle 72 and accessed through an old water board entrance is one of Bogotá's best-kept hiking secrets, the Quebrada la Vieja. Open to the public from 05.00 until 10.00 every Saturday and well-policed and very popular with the locals, this is a wonderful way of reconnecting with nature and enjoying the pine-covered hills if the bustle of the city is too much. The hike up should take no more than an hour; it is well marked and you'll be in good company as ex presidents and former mayors have been spotted exercising here, and once you arrive at the large crucifix the views out west over Bogotá on a clear day are unrivalled. Do plan ahead, wear the appropriate clothing and factor in a couple of hours for the whole excursion.

with modifications by the Dutch architect Antonio Staufe. It was inaugurated on 27 October 1939, and finally blessed by Monsignor Carlos Serna in 1941.

At an altitude of 2,556m, Ubaté boasts average temperatures of 14°C. It tends to be overlooked by tourists, but if you're passing through be sure to stop at one of the roadside cheese stalls – don't miss a chance to try one of the finest-tasting cheeses in all Colombia, the oh-so-creamy San Carlos Queso Tipo Holandes. It's sold in slabs and has a golden rind and is gooey and delicious. There's also a permanent seven-days-a-week market where you can feast on a whole roast chicken and all the trimmings for 25,000COP. All in all, Ubaté is a great place to chow down just 97km outside central Bogotá.

4

North of Bogotá

Commonly referred to collectively as 'north of Bogotá,' the departments of Boyacá (*www.boyaca.gov.co*), Santander and Norte de Santander form a teardrop-shaped land bridge between the capital and the Caribbean coast. This breadbasket of Colombia is a picturesque farmland region, boasting magnificent countryside that is so resplendent in colour the locals call it *el tapiz* (the tapestry). Rolling pasture lies dotted with pretty red-roofed *fincas* and *campesino* shacks. Well-maintained roads weave through a lush landscape of flower fields edged by stalls weighted with slabs of cheese and churns of cream. Sombrero-wearing herdsmen usher goats through pocket-sized villages. Scrub-clad peaks overlook gushing rivers and deep rocky gorges. Machete-holding farmers tend to vast maize crops littered with broken-down farm machinery. Chickens peck at scraps of corn under apple, pear and peach trees home to tethered horses. Chubby sheep scramble up steep grassy banks navigating large piles of pumpkins and potatoes. Children run through bloom-filled meadows. Grain stores are guarded by weathered old women in ponchos woven from cheap grey wool. Proud rural traditions thrive in Colombia's crop-growing communities in a heartland region renowned for its revolutionary spirit.

As one of the Colombian mainland's safest areas, the region north of Bogotá is easily navigable with good, paved main routes and well-lit roads. Military checkpoints are less frequent than in many provinces of Colombia, although it is wise to avoid travelling off the beaten track after dark.

Changing altitudes affect the climate in the undulating region with Tunja at 2,820m averaging a cool 13°C. Low-lying areas such as Cúcuta average a hot and sticky 28°C. Pack a fleece and a cold-weather sleeping bag if you plan to camp or spend time in the mountainous areas. In muggy Bucaramanga it pays to keep clothing light.

HISTORY

Colombian patriots nationwide hold this region in high regard as it is a hotbed of nationalistic passion. It stoked the flames of independence and stood up to Spanish rule and it was here that Simón Bolívar rallied a makeshift army of proud separatists to do battle with the Spanish infantry. Fierce, conclusive wars were fought at Puente de Boyacá and Pantano de Vargas. Colombia's first constitution was also drawn up here in the Villa del Rosario. However, this historic region is also an important site of Amerindian occupation. Large numbers of Muisca and Guane tribes once had their homes here trading with Spanish conquistadors and spawning the mythical legend of El Dorado (see box, page 167).

GETTING THERE AND AROUND

From the south, roads out of Bogotá offer spectacular scenery atop leafy mountains but can get congested with hordes of fanatical **cyclists** – especially on Sunday

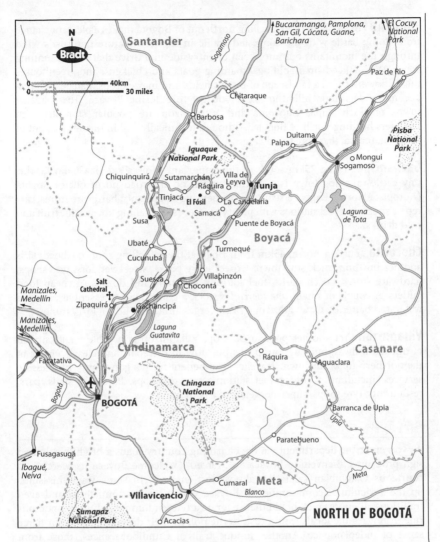

Map labels (reading within the image):

N
Bradt

Santander

Bucaramanga, Pamplona, San Gil, Cúcata, Guane, Barichara

El Cocuy National Park

Sogamoso

Paz de Rio

0 ——— 40km
0 ——— 30 miles

Chitaraque

Barbosa

Duitama
Paipa

Pisba National Park

Iguaque National Park

Mongui
Sogamoso

Chiquinquirá   Sutamarchán   Villa de Leyva   Tunja
Ráquira
Tinjacá   El Fósil   La Candelaria
Samacá
Susa   Puente de Boyacá

Laguna de Tota

Boyacá

Ubaté
Cucunubá   Turmequé

Villapinzón
Suesca   Chocontá
Salt Cathedral †
Zipaquirá   Gachancipá

Laguna Guatavita

Manizales, Medellín

Cundinamarca   Casanare

Ráquira   Aguaclara

Facatativá

Bogotá

Chingaza National Park

Manizales, Medellín

Barranca de Upia
Upía

Paratebueno

Fusagasugá
Ibagué, Neiva

Cumaral   Meta
Blanco

Meta

Villavicencio

Sumapaz National Park   Acacías

NORTH OF BOGOTÁ

morning and holiday *ciclovías*. If you enjoy two-wheeled challenges then there are few better places in Colombia to hill-climb on a bicycle. A number of companies offer bike hire. Another option is to pick up a cheap Colombian- or Chinese-made bike in stores such as Jumbo or Exito. Nicer bikes of questionable provenance can be found in the pawn shops along Avenida Caracas.

Although the region's transportation network suffers from poor development, a major **railway and highway** pass through the Boyacá department's capital Tunja, and other major centres.

A number of different **bus** companies run services across the region; Tunja is a 2½-hour journey from the capital (15,000COP) with good connections with Bucaramanga and Medellín. **Minivans** also connect cities to small towns with a frequent timetable every 30 minutes. **Taxis** are in good supply in larger conurbations with bike and horse hire available in the more touristy towns of Villa de Leyva and Bucaramanga.

THE ROAD FROM BOGOTÁ Travelling north out of Bogotá makes a pleasant change from doing battle with the congested traffic in the city. Picturesque roads wind through the mountains out into green countryside in a drive that offers stunning views. Wire-fenced smallholdings, roaming goats and chickens, and greenhouses full of flowers sit on a landscape of potato fields and maize crops. Patches of grass become wide rolling hills the closer you get to entering Boyacá. The roadside towns of Gachancipá, Chocontá and Villapinzón are popular stop-offs with travellers heading north of Bogotá. Although technically still in the department of Cundimamarca, these are listed here.

Gachancipá Lying 25km south of the important Muisca site of Guatavita, this tiny cattle-ranching town is a useful stop-off on the road north out of Bogotá (Autopista Norte). Expect a string of inexpensive restaurants, hardware stores, car-repair shops and fuel stations with plenty of street stalls selling hot snacks, fruit and cold drinks.

Chocontá Further north, 45km from Bogotá, the refuelling spot of Chocontá is another bustling truck-stop town. Expect lorry parks, street vendors, tyre shops, hardware stores, coach parks, fuel stations, oil stalls and dozens of cheap food outlets. A couple of small *supermercados* stock a good range of essentials, such as water and batteries. Cows graze on grassy verges amidst clouds of lorry fumes.

Villapinzón Yet another popular pit stop, Villapinzón is notable for its stretch of unused railway, built by Europeans but now in disrepair and clearly visible at the northern tip of the town. Travellers can benefit from a good range of roadside services, including a Texaco fuel station, car workshops, hardware stalls, bars, restaurants, tyre shops, supermarkets and a laundry.

BOYACÁ

As you enter the department via the charming country roads a brightly coloured sign proclaims 'Bienvenido Boyacá Su Merced' (Welcome Boyacá Its Mercy) – a courteous Colombian salutation almost lost in time. In some ways this sums up the agricultural communities of Boyacá where time is immaterial and aged traditions all important. Should there ever be a referendum regarding autonomous rule in Boyacá the locals would rush to the poll in their droves such is their fierce sense of independence. Another unique trait of Cundiboyacences (those from Cundinamarca and Boyacá) is to use a second-person pronoun *sumercé*, a rather quaint and old-fashioned act of respect – but a potential source of some confusion for visitors already struggling with Colombian Spanish.

Boyacá lies in east-central Colombia, spanning over 23,000km^2 of fertile terrain, from the cool Andean uplands in the west and forested basins to the undulating *llanos* (plains) in the east. The department's agrarian economy largely relies on coffee, tobacco, cereal crops and fruits. Emeralds, iron ore and coal are also mined in the region and Boyacá produces most of Colombia's steel. The Chivor Dam, one of the highest rock-filled dams in the world, on the Batá River, is a source of hydro-electric power. People from Boyacá are known as Boyacense – and it is not uncommon to spot red-haired blue-eyed locals who are a legacy of interbreeding with European settlers.

TUNJA (*Telephone code 8*) One in five residents in Tunja (*www.tunja-boyaca.gov.co*) is a student and Boyacá's historical capital is very much the funky university town.

THE FOOD OF BOYACÁ

Boyacá's regional cuisine is the hearty diet of farming folk, using the cattle and chickens of the Spanish and different potato varieties, herbs and root vegetables of the indigenous tribes. A thick soup called *ajiaco santafereño* mixes three varieties of potato with sweet corn, chicken, an indigenous herb called *guasca*, cream and capers, while *cocido boyacense* (a robust stew usually consisting of beef, pork and chicken in the mix!) contains a wide variety of herbs and root vegetables such as *chuguas*, *hibios* and *cubios*. Boyacá is also characterised by its baking, including *almojábanas* (rice-flour fritters) and *pandeyucas* (sweet pasty made from yucca) amongst others.

The founding of the Pedagogical and Technological University of Colombia in Tunja in 1953 redefined the city. Today, along with its fine colonial churches, handsome mansions and imposing central plaza there are internet cafés, bookshops and CD stalls. Burger restaurants and coffee bars rub shoulders with statues and monuments. On street corners, undergraduates gather to swap notes and gossip. Posters advertise the arrival of a hot new DJ in town amidst magnificent examples of Hispano-American Baroque art.

Tunja was founded on 6 August 1539 by the Spanish captain Gonzalo Suárez Rendón on the site of Hunza in the domain of 'El Zaque', one of the chiefs of the Muisca tribe. Sadly very little evidence of this pre-Hispanic Muisca settlement remains in the city. The legacy of Colombia's indigenous people was effectively erased once the town was built. Tunja was historically known as 'The Loyal and Noble City of Santiago of Tunja' and served as an operating base for Simón Bolívar in 1819 ahead of his victory over the Spanish at the Battle of Boyacá, 8km to the south. Today it is famous for its architectural riches and is also home to some of the most unique artwork in South America – Mudejar works that are Islamic in style dating back to the 12th century.

Tunja lies in the high valley of the Río Teatinos (or Boyacá River) and as well as its academic centre the city is a communications, commercial and agricultural hub. Cattle from the rolling plains of Llanos region to the east are traded in Tunja and the area is also rich in gold and emerald mines. At an elevation of 2,820m above sea level, Tunja is Colombia's highest and coldest departmental capital. An alpine climate prevails year-round with an average temperature of 13°C. Tunja is a celebrated cultural centre and stages three notable festivals with great gusto: the Cold Festival in October, the International Festival of Culture and Expressions and Aguinaldo Boyacense in December – one of the most important celebrations held in the region.

Getting there and around Tunja is situated on the Pan-American Highway linking Cúcuta with Bogotá – it's a straightforward drive or there's a frequent **bus** service linking the two. The 147km journey takes about 3 hours and costs around 15,000COP with buses departing every 15 minutes or so. Tunja's bus terminal is located on Avenida Oriental to the southeast of Plaza de Bolívar. An hourly bus to Bucaramanga costs 45,000COP and takes 7 hours, while Villa de Leyva takes 45 minutes by **minibus** at a cost of 10,000COP.

🏠 **Where to stay** *See map, page 160.*

🏠 **Hotel Boyacá Plaza** (38 rooms) ☎ 740 1116; e reservas@hotelboyacaplaza.co; www. hotelboyacaplaza.co. Service is brisk at this mega-efficient hotel to satisfy the demands of

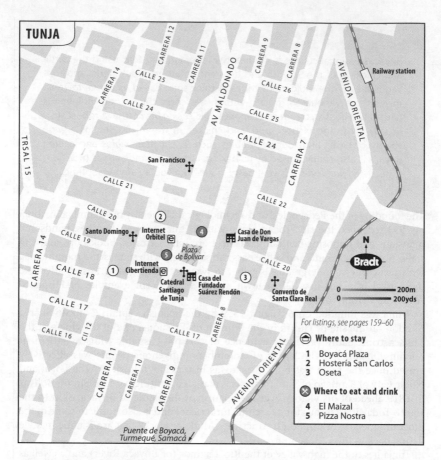

TUNJA

San Francisco

Santo Domingo
Internet Orbitel
Plaza de Bolívar
Internet Cibertienda
Casa de Don Juan de Vargas
Catedral Santiago de Tunja
Casa del Fundador Suárez Rendón
Convento de Santa Clara Real
Railway station

Puente de Boyacá,
Turmequé, Samacá

N

Bradt

0   200m
0   200yds

For listings, see pages 159–60

⊖ **Where to stay**

1   Boyacá Plaza
2   Hostería San Carlos
3   Oseta

✕ **Where to eat and drink**

4   El Maizal
5   Pizza Nostra

the business executives it attracts. Private parking makes this an easy option for travellers with a vehicle. The room rate includes a generous b/fast. **$$**

⌂ **Hotel Oseta** (27 rooms) Carrera 19, No 7–64; ☎742 2886. www.hotelocetatunja.com. Choose from single, double & triple rooms at this popular shoestring option. About a dozen bright,

clean rooms come with a private bathroom & TV. Sleeps 40. **$**

⌂ **Hostería San Carlos** (5 rooms) Carrera 11, No 20–12; ☎742 3716. This is another of Tunja's most pleasant budget hotels where simple rooms offer single, double & family (5 persons) accommodation in a cosy old home. Ask to see a couple of rooms, as they vary in size. **$**

✕ **Where to eat and drink** *See map, above.*

For big plates of cheap local grub head to **El Maizal** (*Carrera 9;* ⊕ *24hrs daily;* **$**) where packed tables are testament to the popularity of this shabby-looking place. What it lacks in glamour El Maizal makes up for in good value with simple chicken-and-rice dishes. Around the plaza and beyond you'll find a cluster of fried-food joints and fast-food outlets, including the **Pizza Nostra** (☎740 2040), where a man-sized margarita will set you back just 8,000COP. Numerous **cafés** by the plaza offer pastries, doughnuts and coffee with dozens of street vendors selling *arepas*, *tinto* and juice from early until late.

Other practicalities Tunja has a large number of **internet cafés** due to the demands of its student population. Most are clustered around Calle 10 and Calle 20,

Colombia has over 50,000 known species of flower – an estimated 10% of the world's total – although many species remain uncatalogued and many thousands unidentified. As a major exporter of blooms, Colombia's flower trade blossomed out of the Andean Trade Preference Act (ATPA) of 1991, renewed and expanded by the United States' Trade Act of 2002. The second-largest exporter of flowers in the world, behind the Netherlands, Colombia's flower exporters boast annual sales of around US$900 million. At least 65% of those flowers end up in the US; an estimated 75% of all roses sold in America on Mother's Day have originated from Colombia. More than two billion stems of Colombian flowers are sold for Valentine's Day alone with 98% of the chrysanthemums and 90% of the carnations bought in the US and Canada coming from Colombian soil. As many as 35 flower-packed planes a day do the 3-hour flight to Miami. In the UK, many of the flowers sold in Asda have been grown in Colombia. The flower industry creates 83,300 direct jobs and 75,000 indirect jobs, making its concentration of employees per hectare the highest in Colombia's agricultural sector. Some 65% of flower workers are women.

Floral yields were dealt a blow by the torrential rains of 2010, but have bounced back in recent years.

Further information is available from Asociación Colombiana de Exportadores de Flores (*www.asocolflores.org*) and ProFlora Fundación (*www. proflora.org.co*).

including the **Internet Cibertienda** (m *310 563 5665*) and **Internet Orbitel** (℅ *743 0955*). Most offer CD burning and international telephone services. Opening hours generally correlate with university hours with prices around 2,000COP per hour.

What to see and do The city of Tunja has a significant number of 16th-century churches, some of which are considerably finer than others. One of the most notable is the **Iglesia y Convento de Santa Clara Real** (Royal Santa Clara Church & Convent) (*Carrera 7, No 19–17;* ℅*742 5659;* ⊕ *08.00–18.00 daily, closed noon–14.00; admission 2,000COP*), founded in 1571 and thought to be the first convent in Nueva Granada. It was the home of Colombia's Mother Teresa figure, Madre Francisca Josefa del Castillo, from 1689 to 1742. In 1863, the nuns were evicted and the convent was used as a hospital although the church itself remained a place of worship. Today it contains a magnificent collection of religious art from the 16th, 17th and 18th centuries, some of which depicts themes relating to the Muisca belief system – a ploy to encourage the local people to convert to Catholicism.

Other churches worth a look include the **Catedral Santiago de Tunja** (Saint James of Tunja Cathedral) on Carrera 9, No 19, Plaza de Bolívar – the city's most elaborate and largest, built between 1569 and 1600. Although it doesn't look much from the outside, the **Iglesia de Santo Domingo** (Church of Holy Sunday) on Carrera 11 between Calles 19 and 20 built in 1658 has colourful and ornate décor with a sumptuous interior of gilded carved wood and Baroque art. An altar statue of the Virgén del Rosario is layered in mother-of-pearl and reflecting glass. A fine Capilla del Rosario (Rosario Chapel) here has been dubbed the Sistine Chapel of New Granada's Art (La Capilla Sixtina del Arte Neogranadino) and is the showpiece of this stunning interior decoration design by Quito's Fray Pedro Bedón. The **Iglesia**

de San Francisco (Saint Francis Church) on Calle 10, between Carrera 21A and 22, was built between 1550 and 1572 and contains gilded archways, a handsome presbytery and a sculpture of Christ, Cristo de los Mártires.

Some of Tunja's historic buildings are open to the public and the **Casa del Fundador Suárez Rendón** (Founder Suárez Rendón's House) (*Carrera 9, No 19–56;* \ *742 3272;* ⊕ *08.00–18.00 daily, closed noon–14.00; admission 2,000 COP*) is definitely one not to be missed. Originally the home of the founder of the city, this grand mansion is every bit the resplendent residence of nobility. It was built in the mid 16th century and has numerous swanky aristocratic touches. Another fine example of Tunja's architectural splendour can be found at the **Casa de Don Juan de Vargas** (House of Don Juan de Vargas) (*Calle 20, No 8–52;* \ *742 6611*), where beautifully painted ceilings and colonial artwork, dating back to the 16th, 17th and 18th centuries, are stunningly displayed. To delve further into Tunja's history and its importance to the Muisca people, check out the Cojines del Zaque found at the western edge of the city. These large haphazardly placed carved rocks were of great significance to the local people for sun worship prior to the arrival of the Spanish.

Festivals
Semana Santa (Holy Week) Religious celebrations revolve around a large procession through the city streets on Maundy Thursday and Good Friday.

Festival Internacional de la Cultura (September) This multi-site festival programme includes all manner of artistic shows and musical performances, from concerts in the Iglesia de San Ignacio to exhibitions in the main plaza.

Aguinaldo Boyacense (December) This week-long event runs up to Christmas when Tunja stages a wide range of religious concerts, fancy dress parades and a carnival-style procession through the city.

AROUND TUNJA
Turmequé This tiny, unassuming town is little more than a couple of rustic eateries and a string of *fincas* but it enjoys a countrywide reputation as being the birthplace of the game of *tejo* (see box, page 163). Turmequé's dedicated Camp de Tejo is a social focal point. Passers-by will also find some rather nice ceramic stalls along the roadside with plenty of kiosks and vendors selling fresh peaches and pumpkins.

Puente de Boyacá Set on the Río Teatinos, the Puente de Boyacá was the scene of Simón Bolívar's last battle on 7 August 1819. Despite having no soldiers or weapons, Bolívar was determined to defeat the Spanish on the bridge, so he mustered an upstart army from the surrounding fields and villages. Against all the odds Bolívar and his 3,000 peasant troops were victorious – a crucial battle in the wars for Latin American independence. Spanish forces were cut off at the bridge, resulting in 1,800 prisoners being captured. Bolívar proceeded to take control of Bogotá on 10 August where he was hailed the liberator of New Granada. After establishing a provisional government Bolívar journeyed to Angostura in Venezuela where he announced his plan to establish the Republic of Gran Colombia.

Today Simón Bolívar is honoured in fitting style at the Puente de Boyacá. Pristine, manicured lawns sweep down to the river's edge. A succession of magnificent paved plazas encircle a grassy hillock on which a bronze monument to Bolívar towers. The bridge itself is small and white and almost unnoticeable on such a dramatic canvas. A perpetual flame burns in tribute to Latin America's revered hero and his makeshift army.

Samacá This typical Boyacense town is reputedly Colombia's biggest beer-swilling community, quite a feat for such a small place. It is also dedicated to the pursuit of *tejo* and regularly attracts crowds of players from all over the country. A 15km unmade pot-holed dusty road leads directly into town and although this is prone to flooding it is easily passable (albeit in bone-rattling style) in the dry season. To the left an abandoned stretch of railway track disappears into the distance. Beyond, the fields are dotted with tiny white *fincas* as the rocky shrub-lined road rolls slowly into town.

Samacá is a charming place blessed with friendly people and all the basic essentials – including plenty of places to buy beer. Since 2002, the town has more than quadrupled in size to 23,000 people from what was once a pinprick-sized hamlet. Today, an attractive plaza is edged by a bank (with ATM), church, photo shop, pharmacy and a handful of decent chicken-and-rice joints. On the edge of town there's an Esso garage, car wash and mechanic. Travellers looking for plenty of small-town character will find it in Samacá. Expect poncho-wearing *campesinos* selling fruit, onions, peas, red beans and potatoes and butchers stringing up loops of homemade sausages. Samacá is also famous for its cheese bread, a traditional delicacy that is baked at 16.00 each day. Arrive at 15.45 to join the growing queues before stocks run out – some of the finest is produced by Alberto Whittingham whose English name is testament to his European heritage. His forefathers moved from England five generations ago to supply iron to the nation's railway industry (see box, page 95). Today, Alberto runs a charming bakery just off Calle 5. Everyone knows him – especially Samacá's womenfolk who swear his bread and flaky pastries are Colombia's finest.

Driving out of Samacá towards Tunja is another journey jam-packed with stunning views. A stretch of craterous, dusty road crosses small bridges and sheep fields. Cows feed on the roadside against a backdrop of mountains and honey-

BEER AND BANGS: *TEJO*

Colombians, especially those from Boyacá, are passionate about the game of *tejo* – so much so that in June 2000 it was declared a national sport. Originating in Turmequé over 500 years ago, today this humble farming community has a Campo de Tejo at its heart. Once known simply as Turmequé by the Chibcha people, this spirited throwing sport has evolved over time. In the past it was played using stones and pieces of wood. Today, things are different. A small 2kg metal disk is chucked at a gunpowder detonator on a clay-filled target – all in the name of good fun.

Tejo takes place in a small circular area usually behind a local bar. The goal is to make the disk strike triangle-shaped *mechas* (gunpowder) in the middle of the target. Many professional *tejo* teams compete nationwide. Most are sponsored by beer companies because drinking is a vital part of the game. Even the Amerindians used to consume vast quantities of *chicha* (a potent drink made from corn) on match days. Today Boyacá's many *tejo* players drink *cerveza* – and lots of it. Beer-swigging contests take place before, during and after the game. *Tejo* is played to nine or 21 points – or until players pass out. The person who makes the most explosions is the winner – at which time the losers must buy the next round.

coloured rocks. Fieldworkers hack at cactus scrubland and hedgerows by religious icons set in stone. Eventually, at a T-junction opposite a Texaco garage, a sign points left to Villa de Leyva and right to Tunja. At this point the landscape alters dramatically to palms and parched, hardy shrubs. Dramatic, time-sculpted orange rock forms magnificent contoured towers. Vast peaks change colour from grey to black to pink to gold marred only by the occasional carefully painted political slogan. On a spiralling road the sheer enormity of the terrain can be overwhelming – prepare to feel like an ant crawling over an intergalactic land.

VILLA DE LEYVA (*Telephone code 8*) Lying about 60km from Tunja and about 207km from Bogotá, few entire towns in Colombia have been as beautifully preserved as Villa de Leyva (*www.villadeleyva-boyaca.gov.co*). Bordered by Arcabuco and Gachantivá to the north, Sáchica to the south, Chíquiza to the east and Sutamarchán to the west, Villa de Leyva was declared a National Monument in 1954.

Gloriously free from any ugly modern buildings, it is a triumph of architectural conservation, a stunning whitewashed colonial town with cobbled streets. Octogenarians snooze on benches in an expansive plaza edged by bottle-green shuttered buildings adorned with flower-filled window boxes. Tiny little mews-style shops sell handicrafts and fresh vegetables in a town once renowned for its abundant olive crops. Pretty backstreets hide some charming boutique hotels and cafés. Although the olive groves have long gone, many of Villa de Leyva's businesses and buildings still bear the names of the industry. At 2,144m in altitude, the town is also notable for its numerous fossils from the Mesozoic and Cretaceous periods.

Stroll through the Plaza Mayor at dusk to join tourists, locals and famous faces alike as they congregate at the steps of the cathedral. Grab a table under flower-filled balconies to enjoy a glass of freshly squeezed *feijoa* (pineapple guava) juice to the sound of strolling musicians and *cuenteros* (storytellers). Choose from an array of fine restaurants or nibble on *besos de novia* (bride's kisses), a local meringue-cake sold in every *panaderia* (bakery) in town. In 2007, Colombian production company RTI shot a Spanish-language *telenovela* (soap opera) of the Zorro story in Villa de Leyva. Part of the Werner Herzog film *Cobra Verde* was also filmed here.

History

> ...that he marked... all the land between a bright red gorge and some oak trees found
> in the water of the ravine at the foot of the mountain range of the new Villa, to the edge
> of the mountain, passing through a small hill made of stones, and below Juan Barrera's
> mill; continuing down the hill from the ravine...
>
> Don Juan de Otálora (19 December 1572)

Villa de Leyva was founded in 1572 by Captain Hernán Suárez de Villalobos after being charged by President Andrés Díaz Venero de Leyva with finding suitable land in the region to house the region's military upper echelons. His sidekick, Don Juan de Otálora, travelled far and wide before reporting back to Villalobos – he had discovered the perfect spot. On Thursday 12 June 1572, a group of Tunja's most prominent top brass headed to the fertile, forested valley known as Saquencipá by the Chibcha people. Recording the legal foundation (*acta*) of the 'Villa de Nuestra Señora de Santa María de Leyva', they appointed St Anthony of Padua as patron of the new settlement.

In 1573, the *caciques* (Amerindian chiefs) of neighbouring villages began work on the construction of the first church in Villa de Leyva. In 1642, the King of Spain, Don Félipe IV, signed a *real cédula* (royal decree) creating a Carmelite convent in Villa de Leyva. It took three years to build but in April 1645, the convent welcomed its six founding nuns. Today Villa de Leyva, with its 14,000m² plaza and fine colonial streets, is one of Boyacá's most popular tourist centres. That it has survived intact throughout Colombia's most turbulent years is nothing short of a miracle – and is testament to how Villa de Leyva is held dear in the hearts and minds of Colombians nationwide.

Getting there and around Only two direct daily **buses** link Villa de Leyva with Bogotá (4 hours, 35,000COP); another option is to take one of the frequent departures to Tunja and change. Note that you can also travel to the Portal del Norte on the TransMilenio bus system and then cross the road – south to north side – where you will find buses waiting for Tunja and Chiquinquira. This way you can avoid an unnecessary trip to the bus terminal. **Minibuses** run back and forth between Tunja and Villa de Leyva every half-hour until late afternoon. Expect the journey to take around 45 minutes and to cost about 10,000COP.

Tourist information

i **Oficina de Turismo** Carrera 9, No 13–11 ; ☎ 732 0232; ⊕ 08.00–18.00 daily, closed noon–15.00. Free maps, tour bookings & an abundance of local leaflets & brochures.
i **www.villadeleyva.net** Local tourism website.

Tour operators Taxi drivers offer standard local tours that usually include a trip out to El Fósil, the Convento del Santo Ecce Homo and El Infiernito (at around 50,000COP). Trips further afield tend to take in Ráquira and La Candelaria (at around 85,000COP). Specialist tour operators offer a much more sophisticated set of services and numerous off-the-beaten-track options, such as night hikes, rappelling, horseback tours, bike trips/hire, camping and walking tours. Two of the best are **Guías & Travesías** (☎ 732 0742) on Calle 12 and **Colombian Highlands** (☎ 732 1862) at the Renacer Guesthouse. Guías & Travesías offer bike rental by the hour, half-day or day at 10,000COP and upwards. Umpteen hiking trails around the town offer a variety of different degrees of difficulty. Horseriding is easy to arrange with a number of local rental agencies. Expect to pay about 10,000COP per hour.

Where to stay *See map, page 166.*

There's no need to worry about finding a decent place to stay in Villa de Leyva – the town has more than its fair share of good hotels. Choose from budget *hospederías*, campsites and modest *hostales* to stylish boutique hotels. However, pre-booking is highly recommended, especially at weekends when the number of tourists can triple overnight and room rates reach a premium.

🏠 **Hostería del Molino La Mesopotamia** (10 rooms) Carrera 8, No 15A–265; ☎ 732 0235; e hosteriamesopotamia@hotmail.com; www.lamesopotamia.com. This swish restored former flour mill dates back to 1568 & many of its old original features are still on show. It's a stunning building with pretty gardens & a large freshwater swimming pool reputed to have therapeutic qualities. About 10 rooms are split between the old part of the house & the newer section – so if you want max 440-year agedness be sure to put in a request. **$$$**

🏠 **Hotel Plaza Mayor** (32 rooms) Carrera 10, No 12–31; ☎ 732 0425; e info@hotelplazamayor.com.co; www.hotelplazamayor.com.co. This pricey option right on the main plaza is worth every penny for the wonderful attention to detail it offers to ensure guests are truly rested. Expect friendly service & plenty of added-value extras at this prime location hotel. Room sizes available including king-size & a large family-sized suite. **$$$**
🏠 **Hotel Plazuela de San Agustín** (20 rooms) Opposite Parque Ricaurte; ☎ 732 1275; m 310 299 6221; e reservas@hotelplazuela.

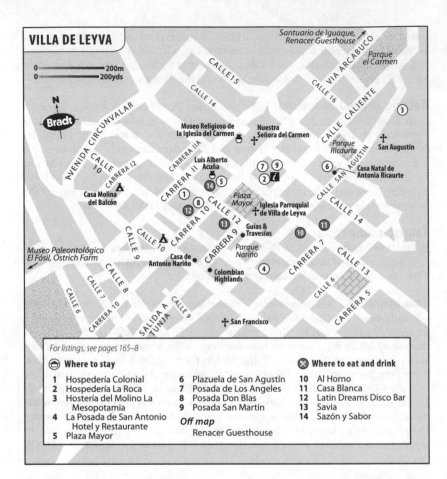

VILLA DE LEYVA

```
0 ————— 200m
0 ————— 200yds
```

Santuario de Iguaque,
Renacer Guesthouse

Parque
el Carmen

VIA ARCABUCO

CALLE 15

CALLE 14

CALLE 16

CALLE CALIENTE

N

Bradt

AVENIDA CIRCUNVALAR

CALLE 10

CARRERA 12

CARRERA 11A

CARRERA 11

Museo Religioso de
la Iglesia del Carmen

Nuestra
Señora del Carmen

Parque
Ricaurte

San Augustin

CALLE SAN AGUSTIN

Luis Alberto
Acuña

⑥   Casa Natal de
            Antonia Ricaurte

⑦ ⑨
②ⓘ

⑭ ⑤

Casa Molina
del Balcón

⑦

⑧

⑫

Plaza
Mayor

Iglesia Parroquial
de Villa de Leyva

CALLE 14

CARRERA 10

CALLE 12

⑬   Guías &
        Travesías

CARRERA 9

⑩   ⑪

CALLE 9

Museo Paleontológico
El Fósil, Ostrich Farm

Casa de
Antonio Nariño

Parque
Nariño

④

CARRERA 7

CALLE 13

CARRERA 5

CALLE 8

CALLE 7

CARRERA 10

CALLE 6

Colombian
Highlands

CALLE 6

SALIDA A
TUNJA

CALLE 9

✝ San Francisco

For listings, see pages 165–8

🍴 **Where to stay**

1 Hospedería Colonial
2 Hospedería La Roca
3 Hostería del Molino La
   Mesopotamia
4 La Posada de San Antonio
   Hotel y Restaurante
5 Plaza Mayor

6 Plazuela de San Agustín
7 Posada de Los Angeles
8 Posada Don Blas
9 Posada San Martín

Off map
   Renacer Guesthouse

❌ **Where to eat and drink**

10 Al Horno
11 Casa Blanca
12 Latin Dreams Disco Bar
13 Savia
14 Sazón y Sabor

---

com; www.hotelplazuela.com. Step over floors inlaid with thousands of fossils to enter this stylish hotel opposite the park. The very pleasant rooms overlook a courtyard & really nice tiled-floor restaurant & range from singles to larger suites. Each is decorated to a high standard & some have exposed beams. **$$$**

🏠 **La Posada de San Antonio Hotel y Restaurante** (30 rooms) Carrera 8, No 11–80; 📞732 0538; e reservas@ hotellaposadadesanantonio.com; www. hotellaposadadesanantonio.com. This handsome colonial-era building has been decorated to an exceptional standard with exquisite antiques, rich fabrics & delightful exposed stone & woodwork. A tiled-floor library leads to a private chapel & on to a charming restaurant where wooden tables look out on to a courtyard centred on a stone fountain. The lovely rooms range from singles to king size &

vary in price depending on the season. **$$$**

🏠 **Hospedería La Roca** (22 rooms) Calle 13, No 9–54; 📞732 0331; www.hospederialaroca. com. This former cheap budget option has significantly raised its game – with prices to match – & b/fast is not included. However, it is difficult to knock its great location & its plentiful supply of pleasant rooms with TV & private bathrooms. **$$**

🏠 **Posada de Los Angeles** (11 rooms) Carrera 10, No 13–94; 📞732 0406. This step up from low-budget option has a range of charming rooms of various sizes with private bathrooms, with rates including b/fast – but has been known to hike its rates up at busier times of the year. However, it remains a very nice mid-range choice on the basis of location overlooking the Iglesia del Carmen. Friendly staff & generous b/fasts. **$$**

🏠 **Posada San Martín** (6 rooms) Calle 14, No 9–43; 📞732 0428; e posadasanmartinleyva@

At this time they stripped the heir to his skin, and anointed him with a sticky earth on which they placed gold dust so that he was completely covered with this metal. They placed him on the raft... and at his feet they placed a great heap of gold and emeralds for him to offer to his god.

Eyewitness report from Juan Rodriguez Freyle, 1636

The story of El Dorado was one of the most influential myths born out of the New World. Stemming from reports from conquistador Gonzalo Jiménez de Quesada in the 1530s, tales of a gilded man of untold riches began to ignite the curiosity of every traveller. Quesada had discovered the Muisca people in the Andes of present-day Colombia in what are now the highlands of Boyacá, in 1537. Rituals were observed that involved offering gold to the gods and soon rumours became mixed with exaggeration.

The myth was spawned by a Muisca ritual that sees an Amerindian chief plaster his naked body with gold dust before plunging into the depths of Lake Guatavita. After this ceremony, his subjects threw jewels and gold into the water as gifts to the gods. As the story was retold, the legend of 'El Dorado' was soon imaged as a place – an empire, a kingdom and a city with a golden king. A succession of conquistadors sought to locate this realm of riches over two centuries, during which time the myth continued to feed on itself. The resulting El Dorado enticed explorers but was always just beyond reach.

One of the most famous doomed searches was undertaken by Francisco de Orellana in 1541 (pages 254–5). It was a disaster but afforded Orellana the distinction of being the first explorer to journey the Amazon River all the way to its delta. Other expeditions to El Dorado include that of Phillip von Hutten in 1541 and Sir Walter Raleigh in 1595. In 1531, a man claimed to have been rescued from a shipwreck by El Dorado himself.

Today the landscape around Lake Guatavita bears a curious scar carved by Antonio de Sepulveda, a Bogotán merchant who attempted to drain the lake in the 1580s to uncover its wealth. Gold was discovered but the project abandoned when the hillsides collapsed, killing many of the workers. Later excavation has uncovered numerous treasures that are now in Bogotá's magnificent Gold Museum (page 144). Today, El Dorado has become a byword for a place where wealth can be made quickly. It is also used as a metaphor to represent an ultimate prize or holy grail. Towns across Latin America bear the name El Dorado, as do many in the United States. The El Dorado story is also immortalised in an array of films and literature, including Milton's *Paradise Lost* and Voltaire's *Candide* and two Walt Disney comic books, *The Gilded Man* and *The Last Lord of Eldorado*.

hotmail.com. This charming historic home set behind the main plaza is run by a friendly couple who have earned a deserved good reputation for their b/fasts as they run beyond the standard menu of eggs & eggs. Room price includes a private bathroom & b/fast. Expect high standards of cleanliness, cable TV & unlimited supplies of hot water. **$$**

🏠 **Hospedería Colonial** (20 rooms) Calle 12, No 10–81; ☎ 732 1364. Not all of the rooms at this perfectly acceptable cheapie have private bathrooms. Expect to pay 15,000COP pp or 30,000COP per room, just a block from the main square. **$**

🏠 **Posada Don Blas** (8 rooms) Calle 12, No 10–61; m 987 320 406. Don't expect any frills or fuss at this basic budget joint where 2nd-floor rooms are clean & comfy. **$**

🏠 **Renacer Guesthouse** (5 rooms/3 dorms); ✎732 1862. This pleasant colonial-era out-of-town option is run by the owner of tour company Colombian Highlands (page 165) & rooms can be booked directly with the knowledgeable Oscar Gilede by heading to the office in town. It has no official street address & is located a pretty 15min walk uphill from the centre of town. Catch a taxi

here from the bus terminal & the Renacer will cover the cost. Rooms look out over the mountains & a network of hiking trails. It's one of the only true backpacker-type places in Villa de Leyva & is aimed at this market, so there is an unlimited supply of hot water & the décor is comfortable. B/fast is an extra 5,000COP. It's also possible to camp here at 7,000COP per night & there are spaces for campervans & caravans. **$**

Camping There's an unmarked 'camping zone' on the corner of Calle 10 and Carrera 10 – it's basically just a large patch of half-decent grass with a wall around it. Stick up a tent and the patron will pop over for the money. Rates vary but expect to pay 5,000–7,000COP per person per night for a spot with an OK shower and some basic bathrooms. It's a similar set-up at the **Casa Molina del Balcón** on Carrera 12, although this time there is a sign. Parkland-style gardens offer trees for shade and privacy. Head to the house and pull the bell-cord to signify your arrival – rates are 5,000COP per person and there's a shower block and bathrooms. Although **El Solar** (*Calle 10a, No 10–60*) is fairly new it's already become a firm favourite with shoestring travellers. Friendly owner Martha offers camping at 10,000COP per tent and also has dorm-room beds at 20,000COP per night with an outside shower in the garden just beyond the plaza. It's also possible to camp in the grounds of the Renacer Guesthouse (✎ *732 1862*) at 7,000COP – it's run by a local tour guide and located 1km out of town but makes a good option if you want a cheap 'all-in' package.

✕ Where to eat and drink See map, page 166.

A number of Villa de Leyva's fun eateries can be found in immense and sprawling old mansions now lovingly converted into galleries, shops and bars, many of which share the same address. Just pop your head inside and take a pick; there are often lunchtime specials on offer during the week when tourism noticeably drops.

✕ **Al Horno** Calle 13, No 7–95; ✎732 1640; ⊕ lunch & dinner. There's something really pleasant about simply hanging out in this popular bistro where bright artwork & a cheerful décor combine to give it a funky feel. An international menu contains a dozen different pizzas along with salads, pasta dishes, sandwiches & crêpes. **$$**

✕ **Restaurante Casa Blanca** Calle 13, No 7–16; ✎732 0821; ⊕ lunch & dinner. Simple set meals offer some of the best-value food in town with à la carte options not likely to break the budget. **$$**

✕ **Savia** Plaza Mayor; ⊕ lunch & dinner. Bohemian ambience & an enigmatic menu of healthy, organic food – dishes range from pan-Indian lentil wraps to Morocco-inspired dips. There's also a really unusual bar popular with

backpackers where the barman 'El Pote' lives up to his reputation as Villa de Leyva's real character. Script-clad walls, oddball artefacts & walls sprinkled with eucalyptus leaves make this place a real must. **$$**

✕ **Sazón y Sabor** Plaza Mayor; ⊕ lunch & dinner. This place serves a changing menu of delicious cut-price dishes. Travellers on a budget will find it difficult to find a reason not to eat here each day. **$**

♀ **The Latin Dreams Disco Bar** ✎732 1042. This may be a decorative homage to the Beatles but it is every inch the Colombian *salsoteca*. It opens early evening but doesn't hit full throttle until midnight when the speakers are cranked up to maximum and the atmosphere is highly charged.

Shopping There are dozens of handicraft shops in Villa de Leyva as well as a number of artisan vendors. Most sell some rather fine basketry, jewellery, bags and ponchos (*ruanas*) as well as fossils, woven blankets and rugs. Villa de Leyva's popular **Saturday market** is famous throughout Colombia and often attracts visitors from miles around. It starts up bright and early and is busiest in the morning – find it southeast of the Plaza Mayor. On the plaza itself three beautifully restored colonial buildings contain various artisan shops and crafts. Casa Quintero, Casona La Guaca and Casa de Juan de Castellanos each have a gorgeous patio area with seating and cafés that serve snacks and cold drinks.

Other practicalities Head to the Plaza Mayor for a bank with an ATM, a money changer, photocopy shop and telecom office for international and regional calls. Of the internet cafés in town, the **Movistar** on Calle 14 is probably the best – the machines are new and reasonably speedy but a tad pricey at 3,000COP per hour. For maps head to **Guías y Travesías** (✆ *732 0742*; e *guiadevilladeleyva@yahoo.com*), where owner Enrique Maldonado has a decent stock at 6,000COP.

What to see and do To escape the dust and heat of the summer streets head to the **Hostería del Molino La Mesopotamia** (The Mill of Mesopotamia Hostel) (*Carrera 8;* ⊕ *during daylight hours*), where it's possible to swim in a beautiful spring-fed swimming pool for 4,000COP – there's an old wooden pool house for changing but no towels.

Only two of the town's handsome churches are open to the public, although the **Iglesia de San Francisco** and the **Iglesia de San Agustín** are worth a look from the outside.

Iglesia Parroquial de Villa de Leyva (Parochial Church of Villa de Leyva)
(*Plaza Mayor*) Built in 1608, the Iglesia de Nuestra Señora del Rosario (Church of Our Lady of the Rosary), is known as simply 'la catedral' by the locals although nobody is quite sure why. The most likely explanation is that its location on the plaza is reminiscent of the cathedral in Bogotá, which also has an atrium over the square.

Iglesia de Nuestra Señora del Carmen (Our Lady of Mount Carmel Church)
(*Calle 14;* ⊕ *subject to volunteer staff*) With its adjacent cloister, this striking building belongs to a Carmelite monastic order and contains some beautiful paintings, including an image of the Virgin of Carmel.

Casa de Antonio Nariño (Home of Antonio Nariño)
(*Carrera 9, No 10–25;* ✆ *732 0342;* ⊕ *09.00–17.00 Mon, Tue, Thu–Sat, 08.30–17.00 Sun*) General Antonio Nariño, the precursor of Colombian independence, lived out his last days in this house until his death in 1823. He suffered from illness following long periods of imprisonment by the Spanish and diseases caught in the battlefields and so moved to Villa de Leyva in a bid to restore his health. Nariño was a staunch defender of human rights and the building has numerous artefacts relating to his work. The day before his death, he asked that an epitaph be placed on his tombstone. It reads: 'I loved my Country. How deep was that love, one day history will tell. I have nothing to leave to my children but my memories; to my Country I leave my ashes.' Nariño won acclaim for translating Thomas Paine's *Rights of Man* into Spanish and is revered throughout Colombia for his commitment to fostering socioeconomic justice.

Casa-Museo de Luis Alberto Acuña (Homestead Museum of Luis Alberto Acuña) *(Carrera 10, No 12-85; ☏ 732 0422; ☉ 10.00–17.00 Tue–Sun, closed 13.00–15.00; admission 4,000COP)* This fascinating museum honours the life and works of Luis Alberto Acuña (1904–93), one of Colombia's great painters, writers and sculptors. One of the founders of the radical Bachué art movement (1930–40) so named after the mother of the human race according to Chibcha mythology, Acuña is renowned for creating beautiful oil murals on wood. One of his most famous works is *Teogonía de los dioses chibchas (Theogony of the Chibcha Gods)* – on display in the Hotel Tequendama in Bogotá. Located on the northwest side of the plaza, this beautiful old colonial house was painstakingly restored by Acuña himself during the last 15 years of his life. A *galería de pinturas* contains numerous original works while the *sala de antigüedades* exhibits artefacts from the colonial era. Sculptures are displayed along with three large murals including one that depicts the region of the Valle de Saquencipá (Valley of Saquencipá), where Villa de Leyva was located during the Cretaceous period. Others include a beautiful interpretation of the Chibcha deities. A *colección de tapices* includes indigenous artefacts from different regions of the country with the ceiling of the old dining room decorated with stunning Baroque motifs.

Casa Museo de Antonio Ricaurte (Homestead of Antonio Ricaurte) *(South corner of the Parque Ricaurte, Calle 15, No 8–17; ☉ 09.00–17.00*

DRUMMER TO THE KING

After his father's untimely death in Bogotá at the young age of 33, Bill Lynn's mother moved with her six-year-old son to start a new life in Miami. Even as a boy, he would drum on pots and pans along to Chuck Berry, Duane Eddy, Buddy Holly and Little Richard records. By the time he was a teen, Lynn had raised enough money by delivering newspapers and shining shoes for a secondhand drum set at a cost of US$20. To practise he'd play along to the radio in the garage that adjoined his home, forming a country & western band. At 16 he added two years to his age to work in bars around America and began to earn a reputation as 'The Drummatic Bill Lynn' on account of his frenzied style. In 1960, he signed a contract with ABC Paramount Records in Nashville as a session player and Lynn was playing with Ray Charles and Bobby Vee. He was introduced to Elvis Presley during a recording session in a neighbouring studio. The King's drummer had popped out for coffee so Bill Lynn stepped in – playing drums on 'It's Now or Never'. A year later, Elvis sent Lynn a golden record to thank him for his collaboration – and a lasting partnership began. Lynn worked for Elvis Presley on his films and recordings until 1970 – the year that Priscilla demanded that Presley's hand-picked team be dismissed. Lynn went on to launch an Elvis bar in Bogotá called Legends and Superstars. He also ran an Elvis-inspired bar Don D'Bill in Villa de Leyva and specialised in music vacations and tours to Graceland. Lynn died at his home in Villa de Leyva after developing breathing difficulties following a serious bout of flu. Even in his latter years, he always wore his staff TCB pin on a chain around his neck. The letters are an acronym of 'Taking Care of Business' – a nickname for the Elvis crew and a prized memento of their 17-year friendship. In 2007, Lynn's road-worn nine-piece Power Remo drum set was auctioned on eBay for US$2,499.95.

Wed–Fri, 09.00–18.00 Sat/Sun, closed noon–14.00; admission 1,500COP) This great hero of Colombian independence was born in this magnificent colonial building in June 1786 and it has since been beautifully restored. Located in front of a park bearing his name and a statue in honour of his heroic death in San Mateo, Venezuela, the museum contains a large collection of artefacts relating to his act of self-sacrifice to defeat Spanish aggressors. Ricaurte fought under Simón Bolívar and while encircled by the Spaniards he defended an armoury under attack. After letting them approach he ignited gunpowder kegs to cause a mighty explosion that killed everyone – including himself.

Casa Sede del Primer Congreso de las Provincias Unidas de la Nueva Granada

(Plaza Mayor; free admission) This colonial building was where the First Congress of the United Provinces of New Granada was installed on 4 October 1812. Today there are a few documents displayed to denote the significance of this house, including details of the various representatives from each region of Colombia and how the charter was ratified.

Museo Religioso de la Iglesia del Carmen (Religious Museum of the Carmel Church)

(Plazuela del Carmen; free admission) This well-stocked museum of religious artefacts is adjacent to the Iglesia de Nuestra Señora del Carmen. A sizeable collection of religious objects includes altarpieces, carvings, paintings and communion vessels from the 16th century onwards.

Festivals

Fiesta de las Cometas (August) Crowds of kite-fliers descend on Villa de Leyva in Boyacá's windiest month, including many from other nations. It's a really colourful display with a variety of different competitions as well as numerous stalls, music and food to boot.

Fiesta de Luces (December) This impressive firework spectacular is an exciting prelude to Christmas festivities. It takes place in the first or second week of the month and illuminates the whole of town.

Outskirts of Villa de Leyva

The area around the town is rich in natural splendour with petroglyphs, caverns, ruins, waterfalls, lakes and creeks to explore. Some of the sights are within walking distance with gorgeous leafy trails that wind out of town. Others can be reached on horseback or by bike and taxi – all of which are in plentiful supply.

Museo Paleontológico (Palaeontology Museum)

(http://ciencias.bogota. unal.edu.co/paleontologico; ☉ 09.00–17.00 Tue–Sat, closed noon–14.00, 09.00–15.00 Sun; admission 3,000COP) This out-of-town fossil-fest is about 1km from the centre of Villa de Leyva but is worth the trip for those not planning to visit El Fósil (see below). Find it on the road to Arcabuco to the northwest of town – it contains a large collection of locally found fossils that date back to the Cretaceous era.

El Fósil *(6km west of Villa de Leyva on the road to Chiquinquiá. The bus to Ráquira doesn't pass right by but can drop-off about 1km away. Otherwise it's a 15,000COP taxi ride or an hour-long walk; m 310 570 0243; ☉ 09.00–18.00 daily; admission 6,000COP)* This 120-million-year-old prehistoric marine reptile is a 7m baby kronosaurus that has been left in the exact spot where it was found in 1977. Although it has lost its tail (the fully complete fossil would have been around 12m in size), this carnivorous plesiosaur reptile is pretty impressive nonetheless. The kronosaurus lived in open oceans and breathed air. They caught prey with massive jaws and rows of sharp teeth up to 25cm long. A huge head had a large mouth and big eyes with an offset pair of nostrils gave it directional 'water-sniffing' ability. Although other kronosaurus fossils have been discovered in Australia, the specimen in Villa de Leyva remains the world's most complete.

Ostrich farm (*5km southwest of Villa de Leyva in the direction of El Fósil;* m *315 854 9456;* ⊕ *09.00–16.30 daily; admission 4,000COP*) Although it's known as the 'ostrich farm' this place also has llamas, horses and sheep but it is a field of 120 massive, strutting birds that pulls in the crowds. A small kiosk sells a variety of ostrich-related paraphernalia, including ostrich leather shoes, smoked ostrich meat, ostrich feathers and giant ostrich eggs. An on-site restaurant also has plenty of ostrich-inspired dishes from about 18,000COP, but this is usually open just at the weekend. Guided tours involve demonstrations of how strong ostrich eggs are – usually by a member of staff standing on one.

El Infiernito (*2km north of El Fósil, about a 30min walk;* ⊕ *09.00–17.00 Tue–Sun, closed noon–14.00; admission 5,000COP*) This ancient Muisca Indian observatory dates back to the early centuries AD and contains ancient phallic stones. La Estacíon Astronómica Muisca was used to identify the seasons by determining the distances of shadows cast by the stones at different times of the year. These three-dozen stone monoliths have been sunk into the ground in a meticulous pattern exactly 1m apart in two parallel formations separated by a 9m gap. By measuring the shadows the Muisca were able to gauge when to plant and harvest. The site also became a sacred place of rituals – much to the annoyance of the Catholic colonialists. In a bid to prevent the God-fearing Spanish from stepping on their land, the locals named the spot El Infiernito, meaning 'little hell' in Spanish, to imply association with the devil.

Convento del Santo Ecce Homo (Convent of the Holy Ecce Homo) (*Catch a bus to Santa Sofia & ask to be dropped off at the turn & you'll only need to walk for 15mins to the convent. Otherwise it's a taxi at around 15,000COP for a car that'll take 4 people;* ☏ *732 0839;* ⊕ *09.00–17.00 daily; admission 3,500COP*) This large stone convent is about 13km from Villa de Leyva and is notable for its magnificent chapel, founded by the Dominican fathers in 1620. A small image of Ecce Homo can be found on a stunning gilded retable reached via a beautiful courtyard of whitewashed archways and old tiled paths. Cobble-flanked gardens are full of brightly coloured flowers with wooden benches and wrought ironwork. Walls are inlaid with fossilised seeds and flowers with clusters of fossils around the base of a statue and in the garden. A picture of Christ in the west cloister offers an optical illusion with eyes opening and closing depending on the angle from which it is viewed.

AROUND VILLA DE LEYVA
Santuario de Iguaque (Iguaque Sanctuary) This beautiful expanse of wilderness offers some fine hikes up to a group of eight alpine lakes. Spanning more than 67km² of mountainous terrain the cool, leafy trails reach an altitude of 3,700m along the highest point of the mountain spine that stretches up to Arcabuco. Located to the northeast of Villa de Leyva, the reserve played an important role in

ancient Muisca beliefs, with the Laguna de Iguaque considered the sacred cradle of humankind in ancient culture. According to Muisca legend, a beautiful woman named Bachué rose from the waters of the lake with a baby in her arms. Once the boy became an adult, they married and had children together and populated the planet. In old age, the couple transformed themselves into serpents before diving back into the hallowed waters of the lake. Such is the importance of the lagoon that it gave the whole reserve its name. More than 400 species of trees, large swathes of highland shrubs and craggy peaks make this a pleasant place to hike and camp. A walk from the entrance of the reserve uphill to the lagoon takes about 3 hours at full pelt. Add in some additional sightseeing and it could easily be a 6-hour trek.

Temperatures drop dramatically in the Santuario de Iguaque so it is important to pack plenty of warm clothing and cold-weather camping gear. It's also pretty wet, so waterproofs and boots are recommended. Some trails can become impassable in the rainiest months so stick to January and February or July and August. Entrance to the park is 18,000COP per person.

Getting there and around Four **buses** a day leave Villa de Leyva for Arcabuco – at 07.00, 10.00, 13.30 and 16.00. Ask the driver to drop you at a place called Los Naranjos – it's about 11km from Villa de Leyva. From here it's a 3km walk uphill along an unmade track to the entrance of the reserve.

Where to stay and eat The **visitor centre** at the entrance of the reserve has a number of beds in shabby-looking dorm rooms for 18,000COP per person and also offers meals at a very reasonable 16,000COP for breakfast, lunch and dinner. Pre-booking is required via the national park office in Bogotá (*www.parquesnacionales.gov.co*).

Sutamarchán This busy little pit stop 25km west of Villa de Leyva is famous for its long, skinny chorizo sausage *longaniza*. Bogotanos make a special journey to dine on Sutamarchán's spicy delicacy, especially men who eat it on large plates with piles of *papas Criollas* (Creole potatoes) and fried plantain with a chuck of greasy black pudding on the side. Numerous small bars and a handful of restaurants sit right on the crossroads. To locate a *longaniza* vendor simply follow your nose.

Where to stay Sutamarchán's only decent accommodation option is the **Hotel Cabañas** (✆ 725 1447; **$$**), a roadside lodge run by a guy called Pedro.

Tinjacá There are some useful shops in this little town between Chinquinquira and Sutamarchán, including a couple of small supermarkets, a drinks stall, kiosk, bakery and an arts and crafts centre. A fuel station opens early until late on the road to Chinquinquira with a small Campo de Tejo nearby.

Ráquira Bubblegum-coloured colonial buildings and a pretty central square make Ráquira a popular place for tourists to spend an hour or two. Cross over a narrow yellow bridge past a terracotta pot factory and a couple of roadside ceramic vendors to enter the town on a winding road. With a population of a little over 1,600 Ráquira is no metropolis, but it does have an impressive number of art shops, craft stalls and souvenir outlets. Specialities include jewellery, pottery, woven bags, baskets, beads and carvings – much of which adorns the façades of the many colourful buildings in Ráquira's beautiful centre. There are also a handful of mediocre restaurants that deserve overlooking – so unless you're really hungry head to Sutamarchán instead.

Getting there and away Just a handful of **buses** each day travel through Ráquira along the Tunja–Chiquinquiá road to and from Bogotá. To get back and forth from Villa de Leyva hop aboard a minibus for 3,000COP – there are four departures and the trip takes about 45 minutes.

🏠 **Where to stay and eat** At the time of writing, none of the hotels in Ráquira would win any awards for opulence. Some are best described as unkempt – a real shame for such a pretty town. The following two options are by far the nicest.

🏠 **Hostería Nemqueteba** (11 rooms) Carrera 3, No 3–08; 🔌 735 7016. Ráquira's most cheerful option offers bright double & triple rooms. Each has a private bathroom & a TV & the hotel has a restaurant, a pleasant patio & a pool. **$**

🏠 **Hotel Suaya** (10 rooms) Calle del Comercio; 🔌 735 7029. This charming wooden boarding house just off the plaza has nice bedrooms of varying sizes – some sleep up to 6. There's also a restaurant on site. **$**

La Candelaria

Almost everyone heading to this tiny community 6km beyond Ráquira is in La Candelaria to visit its monastery, founded by Augustinian monks in 1597. The **Monasterio de la Candelaria** (Candelaria Monastery) (⊕ *09.00–17.00 Mon–Sat*) is an impressive place, set against a backdrop of dry, dusty hills at the end of a slippery mud road. Arrive on foot from Ráquira's main plaza along an uphill path that drops down into La Candelaria, taking about an hour. Only part of the building is open to the general public, but this includes the chapel, a library and a small museum. Monks guide visitors around the cloisters and are very knowledgeable about the many fine 16th- and 17th-century artworks on display. A leafy courtyard and magnificent gardens are a wonderful place to relax, contemplate and soak up the spiritual ambience.

Chiquinquirá

Frayed palms line the streets of this busy town, renowned across Colombia as a religious centre for devout Catholics. Faith-based tourism is big business here with dozens of shops, stalls and vendors selling a vast array of holy icons in every conceivable form. Located 115km north of Bogotá, Chiquinquirá is known as the 'religious capital of Colombia' because of a mid 16th-century miracle involving a painting called the *Virgin of the Rosary*.

In 1562, the Spanish painter Alonso de Narváez created a portrait of the Virgin Mary using pigments and dye from soil and flowers on woven cloth. The 1m image of Mary is holding baby Jesus and smiling sweetly wearing a white toque, a rose-coloured robe and a light-blue headdress. A rosary hangs from the little finger of her left hand and in her other hand she is holding a sceptre. Mary is looking towards the baby cradled in her left arm. He has a small rosary hanging from his left hand with a little bird tied to his thumb. Mary is flanked by St Anthony of Padua and St Andrew the Apostle. Narváez left the painting in a hut with a leaky roof where it was ruined by humidity. In 1577, the portrait was discarded in Chiquinquirá and propped up in an unused room of the chapel. Nine years later it was rediscovered by a woman called María Ramos who, despite the painting's dreadful state, felt drawn to it. Ramos would often sit in contemplation in front of the canvas and long for its repair.

A further nine years later, a miracle occurred. Chiquinquirá was stunned to discover that the painting had been inexplicably restored to its former glory overnight. Today, Friday 26 December 1586 is honoured for this extraordinary event. The miracle had transformed the portrait from a shabby, faded wreck to a bright, vivid canvas. Tears and holes had also self-healed.

Pope Pius VII declared Our Lady of Chiquinquirá patroness of Colombia in 1829, granting a special liturgy. In 1915, 'La Chinita', as her people call her, was canonically crowned. The chapel was declared a basilica in 1927 and renamed Basilico de Nuestra Señora del Rosario de Chiquinquirá. The city was visited by Pope John Paul II in 1986.

Aside from religious tourism, Chiquinquirá has some nice architecture and a rather lovely plaza. It also has a photocopy shop, drugstore, pharmacy, banks (with ATM), hardware stores, barber shops, shoe-repair stalls, supermarkets, a post office and laundry. A market has numerous vendors plying training shoes, T-shirts and fast food. Around the town there are plenty of food joints serving *tinto* (coffee) and *comida Criolla*. Several street stalls also sell Chiquinquirá's famous sweet, pink candy (*cañitas*).

Susa This small cattle- and horse-trading town on the road from Chiquinquirá to Ubaté is a hive of activity, hosting cattle shows and horse fairs year-round. A number of local vendors sell all sorts of associated paraphernalia, from saddles and stirrups to ropes and sombreros. Hungry travellers will also find a couple of hot-food stalls selling *tamales* and *arepas*. There are also a couple of *aguardiente* and *tinto* joints and a kiosk selling water, soda and beer.

Parque Nacional el Cocuy (Cocuy National Park) (*Parques Nacionales de Colombia;* ✆ *353 2400;* e *ecoturismo@parquesnacionales.gov.co; www. parquesnacionales.gov.co)* This 306,000ha national park was founded in 1997, stretching from temperate forests to snow-capped peaks and arid, desert land. Wooden lower plains rise to glacial terrain with alpine lakes. Lush valleys are home to waterfalls and rocky crags. Dominated by the Cordillera Oriental's highest peak, Ritacumba Blanco's 5,330m tip, Parque Nacional El Cocuy is regarded as one of Colombia's most resplendent reserves. Indigenous tribes such as the U'wa occupy the western flank of the park environs and mountain trails are relatively easy to navigate with an experienced guide. Access points are the towns of Guicán and El Cocuy located approximately 230km from Bogotá where it's possible to stock up on basic essentials ahead of an overnight stay in the park. Pack warm-weather clothing and a thermal sleeping bag for camping as temperatures can drop to 0°C. An absence of on-site facilities means that you'll need to bring all food and equipment. Hikers also need to stick to official trails and engage the services of an authorised guide – solo treks are not allowed. Age restrictions also apply, so anyone over 60 or under ten is unlikely to be allowed in. Insurance is mandatory for visitors to the park.

Getting there There are two **buses** overnight from Bogotá (altitude 2,600m) which take 10–11 hours to El Cocuy (altitude 2,700m). You are advised to take that first day easy preparing your kit and procuring a guide in El Cocuy, acclimatising to the high altitude especially if you have come from lower areas such as Bucaramanga (1,000m and 10 hours away).

Several tour companies offer trips into Parque Nacional El Cocuy, including many with a strong ecological focus – an important consideration given the park's fragile status. According to the Colombian Institute of Hydrology, five major glaciers in the park that were expected to last at least 300 years in 1983 are now under serious threat. Measurements taken in 2006 suggest that they may all disappear within 25 years. Dwindling numbers of several species of the park's rich abundance of wildlife are also a cause for concern, including eagles, spectacled bears and mountain tapirs. Items that pose a threat to the frailty of the ecosystem are also prohibited, so don't bring non-biodegradable plastic bags and aerosols.

Advice for hiking December is the best month as it is almost always sunny. Failing that, January and Feburary are also good months to visit. You can bank on heavy precipitation here though. Night-time temperatures are around 0°C and freezing gales that blow in the mornings require the appropriate warm gear. The midday sun will have you in shorts and T-shirt. Don't forget the sun is remarkably strong at 4,500m so use sunscreen.

The El Cocuy to Guican circuit (or reverse) is traditionally done in six days based on 8 hours of hiking per day. Seasoned hikers have done it in less. Some of the passes and high points you'll encounter along the way include Cusiri (4,460m), Patio Bolas (4,380m), Balcones (4,450m), El Castillo (4,600m), De la Sierra (4,700m), Frailes (4,260m), Cardenillo (4,420m), La Cueva (3,850m), Laguna el Avellanal (4,430m), Laguna del Pañuelo (4,350m), Laguna de la Plaza (4,350m), Laguna Pintada (3,950m), Laguna Grande de Los Verdes (4,070m) and Laguna el Rincon (4,400m).

You have to register upon entering the park either in **Guican** (*Municipio El Cocuy, Calle 5, No 4-22;* \ *789 0359;* ⊕ *07.00-11.45 & 13.00-16.45 Mon-Fri*) or **Cocuy** (*Municipio Güicán de la Sierra, Transversal 4a; No 6-60;* \ *789 7280;* ⊕ *07.00-11.45 & 13.00-16.45 Mon-Fri*). In 2014-15 the cost for entry for foreigners was 50,000COP per person.

ADDITIONAL TOWNS IN BOCAYÁ DEPARTMENT
The department of Antioquia is not alone when it comes to small, perfectly formed towns in which to while away the days: Boyacá also plays host to an embarrassment of riches. You could spend weeks just exploring the glorious rolling hillsides of Boyacá, tracing the striking mountains before descending along the Ruta del Libertador (Bolívar's Route) into the lowland savannahs of Casanare and beyond. Should you find yourself with time and a desire to explore, head northeast from the tourists' favourite Villa de Leyva and strike it out to any of the following small towns.

Playa Blanca and Laguna de Tota
The expansive and beautiful Laguna de Tota is reached by passing through the unremarkable towns of Duitama and Sogamoso and climbing to an altitude of 3,200m above sea level. At 55km² Laguna de Tota is Colombia's largest freshwater lake. At the lake's southwestern corner is Playa Blanca and if you visit at the right time you could be fooled into believing that this could be the Caribbean given the white sand and clear-blue skies ... only the chill factor says otherwise. There are dozens of hotels to choose from and camping is possible near to the Playa Blanca. Don't forget to try the region's speciality of rainbow trout.

⌂ *Where to stay and eat*
⌂ **Hotel Refugio Rancho de Tota** (12 rooms & 7 *cabañas*) m 311 273 7863; e info@hotelranchotota.com; http://hotelranchotota.com. With several multi-person *cabañas* & nicely appointed rooms overlooking the northeast corner of the lake, the Refugio is one of the better places to rest your head here. There is also a Turkish bath, sauna, restaurant & on-site spa available. **$$**

Mongui
Turn off the road at Sogamoso and heading west for 14km you'll come to Mongui (population 5,000), one of Colombia's most beautiful towns. Located at 2,900m above sea level the scenery is that of the highland plains and the weather can be biting at times but don't let this deter you as Mongui is perfectly cared for, wonderfully colonial as it was founded in 1555 with the majority of its architecture dating back to the 16th century. The beige-coloured bricks and tidy cobblestone streets immediately remind you that you are here in the sacred region of the mystical

Sagamuxi. There are decent hikes to enjoy nearby into the Páramo de Ocetá and if this isn't enough, Mongui is famous for producing footballs!

Where to stay

Mongui Plaza Hotel (10 rooms) Carrera 4, No 4–13; m 321 429 4772, 312 584 2309; e monguiplaza@gmail.com. Clean & basic but in an excellent location on the corner of the main plaza of the town, you'll be well looked after here. Hot water is provided & essential but be sure to insist in case of a lukewarm stream! $

Paipa Known for having an abundance of curative hot springs in the town itself, Paipa has a population of 28,000 and is a Colombian destination *par excellence* owing to its proximity to Bogotá (170km). Visit during the week and you'll have Paipa and the hot springs to yourself though. Aside from bathing in hot natural waters, history enthusiasts will be more than contented with a side trip from here to the nearby attraction of the battleground of **El Pantano de Vargos** (Vargas' Swamp) where Simón Bolívar saw off an attack by Spanish forces with the help of the British Legion on 25 July 1819.

Where to stay

Hotel Cabañas el Porton (30 rooms) Av de las Piscinas; ⟋ 785 0168; e info@elportonpaipa. com; www.elportonpaipa.com. With their own hot springs on site, the Hotel Cabañas el Porton is one of the better options in town & guests will find their rooms to be basic, yet clean & comfortable. $$

SANTANDER

This central-northern department lies east of the mighty Río Magdalena bordered to the south and east by Boyacá and to the north by Norte de Santander. Magnificent gushing rivers, craggy ravines, canyons, gorges and mountain peaks make Santander a popular region for adventure-sport enthusiasts. Thrill-seekers can enjoy kayaking, climbing, rappelling, rafting and pot-holing on a dramatic rugged terrain. Spiralling mountainous trails rise and fall amidst rocks and trickling streams. Santander has carved out quite a name for itself as an ecotour centre around the fast-flowing Río Fonce. Inheriting its name from one of the nine original states of the United States of Colombia, Santander also has some delights for those seeking a more genteel pace. Several fine museums can be found in the capital city of Bucaramanga with the architecture of San Gil, Barichara and Girón a genuine treat.

HISTORY Prior to the arrival of the Spanish conquistadors, the mountainous territory now known as Santander was inhabited by numerous indigenous tribes, including the Muiscas, Guanes, Chitareros, Laches, Opón, Yariguí and Carare. They honed farming skills to exploit the rugged terrain and developed terrace-style agricultural plots and irrigation systems, planting yucca, maize, beans, *arracacha*, cotton, tomatoes, guava, tobacco and pineapple crops. The first Spanish arrived in 1529 led by Antonio de Lebrija, but it was the aggressive stance of German explorer Ambrosius Ehinger that wiped out most of the ethnic groups via a bloody campaign. Colonisation began in earnest in 1539 when the village of Vélez was founded by Martín Galeano. The remaining Amerindian tribes were enslaved and forced to labour on the land and work in the mines. Today the Guane are the only Amerindian group in Santander not to have been fully subjugated by Colombia's colonial past.

SAN GIL (*Telephone code 7*) Modern-day San Gil (*www.sangil.com.co*) has firmly established itself as Colombia's 'White-water Rafting Capital' and is without a doubt the nation's premier adventure-sport hub. Alongside a host of extreme-sport options and madcap thrills, San Gil has numerous less radical pursuits, including horseback riding, fishing and mountain hikes. Most visitors arrive in San Gil clad in outdoor garb in preparation for some serious interaction with the surrounding countryside. Much of this centres on the rapids and tributaries of the Río Fonce, the 1,867 trees of Parque El Gallineral and the trails that riddle the surrounding mountain peaks.

However, San Gil is more than just a place for adventure nuts to gather – the town's streetscape of unspoilt colonial buildings is divine. Stroll through the town's 18th-century plaza – the Parque La Libertad – amidst balconied buildings seemingly untroubled by time. Giant *ceiba* trees and flower-filled planters lead to a fine cathedral while the foliage in Parque El Gallineral is truly spectacular year-round.

Getting there and around San Gil is on the road between Bucaramanga and Bogotá and is therefore blessed with an efficient and frequent **bus** service to both cities. Bucaramanga takes about 2½ hours and Bogotá a little over 6 hours. The bus terminal is 2km west of the city centre – it's a 5,000COP trip by taxi, or flag down a *buseta* on the corner of Carrera 10 and Calle 15. Buses that pass also frequently serve the nearby village of Barichara – a very rewarding day trip just 20 minutes or so away.

Tour operators A number of specialist eco-adventure tour agencies offer full-day and multi-day packages, the most popular of which is an 11km white-water rafting expedition down the class 3 rapids of the Río Fonce. After some basic instruction in the art of rafting survival etiquette, small groups of rafters are guided to the rapids for a water-borne adrenalin rush. The river is also used by experienced kayakers and is renowned for its whirlpool undertow and tumultuous cascades. The 11km trip takes about 1½ hours and costs around 35,000COP. Most of San Gil's tour companies are clustered around the entrance of park El Gallineral. Almost all offer short and long rafting trips (grades 1–3), caving, hiking, kayaking, climbing, paragliding and rappelling. Other excursions include the Río Chicamocha (grades 1–4) and all tour prices in San Gil are regulated so costs rarely vary by much. The main adventure tour operators include:

Aventura Total ☏723 8888; www.
aventuratotal.com.co
Brujula Promotora San Gil ☏723 7000
Colombian Rafting Expeditions m 311

283 8647; e info@colombiarafting.com www.
colombiarafting.com
Ríos y Canoas ☏724 7220; e riosycanoas@
hotmail.com, www.riosycanoas.com.co

Where to stay The number of hotels in San Gil is growing rapidly and a host of budget options are springing up all over town. Most are clustered around the centre of town and are simple, no-fuss affairs.

Hotel Abril (20 rooms) Calle 8, No 9–63; ☏724 8795. There's nothing special about this mid-range option but it is perfectly comfortable. Fan-cooled rooms are simply furnished with private hot-water bathrooms, TV & free Wi-Fi. Amenities include a tour desk, room service & on-site parking. **$$**

Hotel Agualuna (approx 6 rooms) Calle 13, No 10–33; ☏724 7220; www.sangilhotelagualuna. com. A range of differently sized rooms offer various bed configurations in this simple family-run small hotel – & some are better than others. Each has hot-water showers, TV & a terrace. A convenient location close to an ATM, coffee shops, bakeries & the main plaza a short walk from the bus terminal. **$$**

🏠 **Hotel Capri** (29 rooms) Calle 10, No 9–31; ☎ 724 4218; e hotelcaprisangil@yahoo.es. This is one of San Gil's better mid-range options with clean, sparsely furnished rooms that are bright & comfortable – each seems to have a different price so ask to see a couple. **$$**

🏠 **Sam's VIP Hostel** (sleeps 20+) Carrera 10, No 12–33, Top Floor, BBVA Bldg; ☎ 724 2746/ m 310 249 7400; e samshostel@gmail.com; www.samshostel.com. When you stay at Sam's you become part of a traveller community – a family of sorts with Sam as the great sage at its heart. With an active online network of Facebook users swapping tales, tips & messages & a growing number of regular guests that keep coming back, this place is continuing to evolve. Conveniently located in the centre of San Gil near to Gringo Mikes & the Maconda it has a range of rooms (so ask to see a couple) from dorm beds (sleeps 6) to a variety of configurations, including singles & doubles. Other amenities include a free luggage store, communal kitchen, bar, internet, swimming pool, sauna, 24hr reception, adventure tours & parties. **$–$$**

🏠 **Centro Real** (20 rooms) Calle 10, No 10–41; ☎ 724 0387. Each of the rooms at this bright & modern hotel is different with a range of singles,

doubles & triples. As one of San Gil's nicer options it tends to get booked solid so it pays to pre-book. **$**

🏠 **Hostel Santander Aleman** (2 buildings with dorms & private rooms) Calle 12, No 7–63; ☎ 724 2535; e hostelsantanderaleman@gmail. com; www.hostelsangil.com. Clean & organised, these well-located options spread over 2 houses are a fine option for those on a budget & looking to be at the heart of the action. **$**

🏠 **Macondo Guesthouse** (8 rooms) Carrera 8, No 10–35; ☎ 724 8001; e info@macondohostel. com; www.macondohostel.com. If you've ever stayed in an Antipodean backpacker hostel you'll feel right at home here – the Aussie owner runs it just like one of Darwin's finest. As one of the area's most savvy accommodation options the Macondo offers guests a choice of dorm beds & a number of newer private rooms with & without en-suite bathrooms, as well as cooking facilities, hammocks, a laundry, book exchange, fast internet & free Wi-Fi. Expect lots of laid-back home comforts & plenty of adventurous spirit with tours that range from hiking, rafting & caving to paragliding. **$**

🏠 **Posada del Conde** (13 rooms) Carrera 10, No 13–17; ☎ 724 2170. This simple budget option is right on the main square & offers clean, homely rooms with a bed, TV & fan with a comfy, cosy feel. **$**

✖ Where to eat and drink

✖ **El Turista** Calle 10, No 10–27; ☎ 724 7029; ☺ 07.00–21.00. All-day food joint; generous b/ fasts. Typical lunch & dinner menus include grilled goat dishes. **$–$$**

✖ **Gringo Mike's Sandwiches** Calle 12, No 8–35; ☎ 724 1695; e info@gringomikes.net; www. gringomikes.net; ☺ 17.00–22.00 Thu–Tue. This American-owned food joint is part snack bar & part tour company, a schizophrenic enterprise that serves tourists just fine. While you study a menu of fresh sandwiches, burritos, panini, wraps & salads made to order & look longingly at the array of

cookies & brownies, you can also mull over a range of downhill mountain-biking tours & swap tales with other travellers doing much the same. **$–$$**

✖ **Cafetería Donde Betty** Cnr Carrera 9 & Calle 12; ☺ daybreak–midnight. This simple little local eatery serves a hearty b/fast, fruit juices, lunches, snacks & dinner throughout the day. **$**

✖ **El Mana** Calle 10, No 9–10; ☺ early until late. Locals in the know rave about the food at this charming restaurant where the quality is reliable, the portions generous & the ambience truly convivial. **$**

Shopping There's a handful of handicraft vendors strung along the road that leads to the Parque El Gallineral. Expect to find ceramics, scarves, bags, jewellery and basketry.

Other practicalities A **Bancolombia** on Calle 12 has a 24-hour ATM. On Calle 10, **Foxnet internet café** (☎ 724 6659) offers connections at 1,800COP per hour 07.00–20.00 daily, closing for lunch 12.30–14.00.

What to see and do

Parque El Gallineral (Gallineral Park) (*Cnr Malecón & Calle 6;* ⊕ *08.00–18.00 daily; admission 6,000COP*) Without a doubt, this is San Gil's premier attraction. Edged by the waters of the Quebrada Curití (Curití Creek) and the Río Fonce (Fonce River), this wedge-shaped 4ha island contains over 1,800 trees covered with strands of silver-grey bromeliads that give it a mystical, fairy-tale feel. An inviting freshwater pool is edged by creeper-clad bushes, making it a very pleasant place for a stroll and a dip just 10 minutes from the town centre. A 1km trail (Sendero Guane) weaves through the trees and down to the river. Here, the Playa del Río Fonce is really just a muddy strip, but its grassy banks are a nice spot for a picnic.

Las Cascadas de Juan Curi (Juan Curi Waterfalls) Bike the 22km from San Gil on the road to Charalá or catch the bus from the main bridge in central San Gil to these magnificent 180m-high waterfalls. They can be reached by a little path by a small house – ask to leave your bike with the woman who owns it and she may well make you some fresh lemonade for the 15-minute hike. Some kind soul has fixed some wooden ladders at the base of the waterfalls so access to a large pool underneath and the rock face higher up the hills is easy. It's a superb place to take a dip in the heat of the day, so pack a picnic – during the week you're likely to have the place to yourself. The abseiling here is some of the best in the area down the sheer 50m face.

AROUND SAN GIL

Barichara (*Telephone code 7*) Resplendent colonial architecture abounds in this truly gorgeous little town 22km northwest of San Gil, and most people agree that Barichara is one of the most beautiful settlements in Colombia. Movie-set good looks give it an almost dreamlike ambience with immaculate streets of stunning whitewashed buildings and brightly painted shutters. Sympathetic restoration has painstakingly conserved the characteristics of Old Spain with pretty stone roads and fine churches dominated by a magnificent cathedral. In 1702, a field worker discovered a rock with what was considered to be an image of the Virgin Mary on it. Three years later, in recognition of this implied religious significance, Don Francisco Pradilla y Ayerbe erected a church at the scene of the miracle. It was named Villa de San Lorenzo de Barichara after the Guane word meaning 'place to relax' on account of its lofty views, year-round 22°C temperature and cooling afternoon breezes. Barichara was declared a National Monument in 1975 to protect its unique architecture and historical significance. Modern construction is outlawed, as are neon signs and billboards. Even posters and shop window displays have to conform to strict municipal codes. Located high above the Río Suárez, Barichara offers superb views across some striking mountainous terrain. As a centre for stonemasons, painters and artisans, it has become a favourite for international tourists in recent years.

Getting there and around Buses go to and fro every 45 minutes between San Gil and Barichara but only until 19.00 each evening – catch one from the main plaza. The trip costs about 3,000COP and takes about 35 minutes. A **taxi** will set you back around 15,000COP.

Tour operators Most of the tour operators that serve San Gil will run trips to and around Barichara if requested.

Santa Bárbara

CARRERA 11

CARRERA 10

CARRERA 9

CARRERA 8

CARRERA 7

CARRERA 6

CARRERA 5

CARRERA 4

CALLE 2 · CALLE 3 · CALLE 4 · CALLE 5 · CALLE 6 · CALLE 7 · CALLE 8

N

Bradt

0 ____ 100m
0 ____ 100yds

BARICHARA

For listings, see pages 181–2

🏠 **Where to stay**

1 Coratá
2 Hospedería Aposentas
3 Hostal Misión Santa Bárbara
4 La Casa de Hercilia
5 Posada La Nube
6 Tinto Hostel

🍴 **Where to eat and drink**

7 Arequipes Barichara
8 Arequipes Glorida
9 Color de Hormiga
10 La Braza
11 La Casona
12 Plenilunio Café
13 Shambalá

Catedral de la Immaculada

Capilla de Jesús Resucitado

Parque Principal

Capilla de San Antonio

🏠 Where to stay *See map, above.*

Barichara has around a dozen hotels, plus some homestay options – all of which tend to get booked to capacity during public holidays. If the hotels are full, many enterprising locals often rent out rooms to visitors at very reasonable rates – simply ask around town.

🏠 **Posada La Nube** (sleeps 16) Calle 7, No 7–39; ☎334 8677; e info@lanubeposada. com, www.lanubeposada.com. Possibly the only lodging in Barichara that could justifiably call itself boutique, this beautiful & comfortable house has been restored & renovated with minimalist design. Swimming pool & on-site restaurant, too. **$$$$**

🏠 **Hostal Misión Santa Bárbara** (sleeps 80) Calle 5, No 9–08 ; ☎635 1432; www. hostalmisionsantabarbara.com. A range of large, comfortable single, double & triple rooms in this grand colonial *hospedaje* have been carefully restored to ensure that plenty of character remains. All have large wooden beds, rugs, tiled floors & private hot-water bathrooms. Some also have patios & terraces. A fine restaurant serves good

local food & there is also a laundry service on site. Rooms aren't cheap but the rate does include a buffet b/fast. **$$$**

🏠 **Hospedería Aposentas** (5 rooms) Carrera 6, No 6–40; ☎726 7294. This quaint little family-run hotel sits right on the central plaza & comes highly recommended by travellers on a budget. Patron Miguel Bermúdez Ruiz enjoys chatting to foreign visitors & can also organise tours & guides. The rooms each have private bathrooms & TV & are set around a pleasant courtyard. **$$**

🏠 **Hotel Coratá** (10 rooms) Carrera 7, No 4–08; ☎726 7110. Barichara's finest hotel is a magnificent architectural gem with a fine exterior & interior décor deserving of *Homes & Gardens* magazine. This prized historical building dates back more than 280 years. Expect wooden balconies, vaulted ceilings, carved furnishings & numerous antiques. A charming garden centres on a large bottlebrush with plenty of surrounding leafy blooms. Rooms are in demand so pre-booking is highly recommended, especially at w/ends. Each has a TV & a private bathroom & a beautiful décor. **$$**

🏠 **La Casa de Hercilia** (sleeps 13) Calle 3, No 5–33; m 300 223 9349; e info@lacasadehercilia. com; www.lacasadehercilia.com. Unpretentious & welcoming, the Casa de Hercilia is both charming &

accommodating. With a capacity of only 13 guests you feel part of the family here as you swing idly, disconnecting from the world in one of the hammocks strung around the courtyard. **$$**

🏠 **Tinto Hostel** (12 rooms) Carrera 4, No 5–39; ✆726 7725; e tinto-hostel@hotmail.com; www.tintohostel.com. Just 3 blocks from the main plaza, the Tinto is the backpacker's digs of choice for location, price & quality. Spacious dorms & *privates* are offered in this rustic yet inviting home. Pool on site & excellent information on activities in & around Barichara. **$**

✗ *Where to eat and drink* See map, page 181.

In addition to restaurants in the town's hotels, there are now a number of excellent options in Barichara. Head to the **Plenilunio Café** (*Calle 6*; ✆ *726 7485*) for some Italian comfort food at around 10,000COP or the **Restaurante La Casona** for cheap grilled meats. Both are on Calle 6. The **Restaurante La Braza** on Carrera 6 serves many of Santander's traditional local delicacies at lunchtime, such as grilled goat. Barichara's finest *arequipe* (see above) can be sampled at **Arequipes Glorida** on Calle 6 and **Arequipes Barichara** on Carrera 8. For vegetarian and vegan platters look no further than **Shambalá** (*Carrera 7, No 6–20*); for something more upmarket head to **Color de Hormiga** (*Calle 6, No 5–35*), where the chef incorporates local delicacies such as the *hormigas culonas* to complement a succulent *filet mignon*.

Entertainment and nightlife If Barichara has any nightlife it is carefully hidden from view. The place appears totally deserted after 20.00 when even the restaurants shut up shop. A couple of kiosks sell cold beers and *aguardiente*. For a cracking hangover try the *chicha de maíz* – a potent cornmeal homebrew (see box, page 186).

Other practicalities A small **post office** opens at 08.00 on Carrera 6 and doesn't close until 20.00 (shut for lunch noon–14.00). Barichara has a small **hospital** on Carrera 2 (✆ *726 7133*) and a **police station** on Calle 5 (✆ *726 7173*).

What to see and do Barichara's main attraction is the Parque Principal – a beautiful central plaza that leads to sandstone churches and pretty streets. Be sure to take a look at the grandiose 18th-century **Catedral de la Immaculada** (Cathedral of the Immaculate Conception) with its ten fluted 5m columns. The cemetery chapel, the **Capilla de Jesús Resucitado** (Chapel of the Resurrected Christ), and its fascinating tombstones are also worth a visit, as is the restored **Iglesia de Santa Bárbara** (Church of St Barbara) and the **Capilla de San Antonio** (Chapel of St Anthony). The colonial house of the former president, the **Casa de Aquileo Parra Gómez** (Home of Aquileo Parra Gómez), has been opened up to the public on Carrera 2. A small Guane pottery exhibition and fossil display is housed at the **Casa de Cultura** (House of Culture) on Calle 5 (✎ *726 7002*) – admission is just 500COP. Up at the top of the town you'll find a free-to-visit sculpture garden with views over the valley and if you are up for it strike out on the 2-hour hike from here to Guane.

Guane (*Telephone code 7*) Guane may be a tiny little one-horse town but it offers visitors expansive views, lying 10km northwest of Barichara. A rather handsome plaza centres on a very pretty church – the **Iglesia de Santa Lucía** (Church of St Lucy) – that dates back to 1720. Guane is also notable for its marvellous collection of fossils and artefacts at the **Museo Paleontológico y Arqueológico** (Museum of Paleontology and Archaeology). A curator offers guided tours 08.00–17.00 daily (closed noon–14.00). The town has a peaceful, almost sleepy air and is a nice place to simply shoot the breeze. A couple of rustic restaurants serve homemade *sabajón* – a sweet non-alcoholic drink that tastes just like Bailey's Irish Cream. Good, inexpensive lunch menus offer soup, goat meat, rice and yucca. Guane is an important site of indigenous heritage and was first discovered by Martín Galeano in 1540.

Getting there and around Just a couple of **buses** a day connect Guane with Barichara – one leaves at 11.30 and the other leaves at 17.00 and both stay only 15 minutes, Monday to Friday and Sunday only. A rather nice trail out of Barichara dates back to the conquistador era. It's been well maintained since being declared a National Monument in 1997 and is easily navigable year-round. Those who do decide to walk this 'Camino Real' will find it takes around 1½ hours; to avoid the trek back simply tout for a lift in town. It's common practice and costs around 1,000–2,000COP.

Where to stay Although local residents sometimes open up their houses to bed-and-breakfast guests, Guane has only one official place to stay. The brightly coloured **Hostal Santa Lucía de Mucuruva** (✎ *732 0163*; **$**) is nothing special but offers clean, basic rooms in an old colonial home.

BUCARAMANGA (*Telephone code 7*) As a major commercial hub in the northeast of Colombia and the capital of Santander, Bucaramanga plays a significant role in trade with Venezuela. The city is expanding rapidly with very little evidence of its colonial past amongst modern buildings and commercial districts. Bucaramanga was founded in 1622 and was used by Simón Bolívar as a strategic stopping-off point *en route* to Caracas during his campaigns. The original part of the city is today the Parque García Rovira (García Rovira Park) where Bucaramanga's first church can still be seen. An ideal base for exploring, Bucaramanga offers easy access to the surrounding mountains and colonial villages. It is also close to seven rivers and creeks rich in fish. Although it isn't brimming with tourist attractions, the city does have a handful of museums and a small botanical garden – along with a good stock of decent hotels and plenty of great places to shop and eat.

Getting there and around Arrivals by **air** benefit from marvellous views on the approach to Bucaramanga's Palonegro Airport. Frequent flights connect the city with many of Colombia's main hubs, including Bogotá, Medellín, Cúcuta, Santa Marta and Yopal. There are also international flights with Copa to Panama from here. Bucaramanga's modern **bus** station (La Terminal de Transportes de

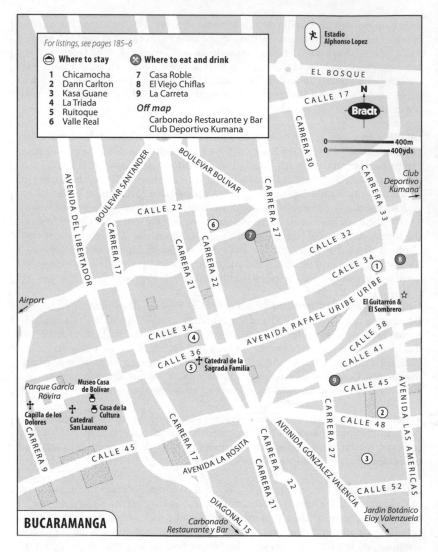

For listings, see pages 185–6

Where to stay

1 Chicamocha
2 Dann Carlton
3 Kasa Guane
4 La Triada
5 Ruitoque
6 Valle Real

Where to eat and drink

7 Casa Roble
8 El Viejo Chiflas
9 La Carreta

Off map
Carbonado Restaurante y Bar
Club Deportivo Kumana

Estadio Alphonso Lopez

EL BOSQUE

CALLE 17

N

Bradt

0 — 400m
0 — 400yds

CARRERA 30

CARRERA 33

Club Deportivo Kumana

BOULEVAR BOLÍVAR

BOULEVAR SANTANDER

CALLE 22

AVENIDA DEL LIBERTADOR

CARRERA 17

CARRERA 21

CARRERA 22

CARRERA 27

6

7

CALLE 32

CALLE 34

1

8

Airport

AVENIDA RAFAEL URIBE URIBE

El Guitarrón & El Sombrero

CALLE 34

4

CALLE 38

CALLE 41

CALLE 36

5 † Catedral de la Sagrada Familia

Parque García Rovira

Museo Casa de Bolívar

† Capilla de los Dolores

† Catedral San Laureano

Casa de la Cultura

CALLE 45

9

AVENIDA LAS AMERICAS

2

CALLE 48

CARRERA 27

3

CARRERA 9

CALLE 45

CARRERA 17

AVENIDA LA ROSITA

CARRERA 21

AVENIDA GÓNZALEZ VALENCIA

22

CALLE 52

Jardín Botánico Eloy Valenzuela

BUCARAMANGA

DIAGONAL 15

Carbonado Restaurante y Bar

Bucaramanga) in the southwest of the city links to a large number of cities across the country as well as Venezuela, Peru and Ecuador. Locally, several public and private transit companies cover almost all of the metropolitan area (Bucaramanga, Girón, Floridablanca and Piedecuesta) with hourly buses connecting the airport to the city centre. Numerous *colectivos* (shared taxis) also nip back and forth across Bucaramanga all day long (5,000COP). **Taxis** (✆ *633 0781*) to the airport cost around 50,000COP with the largest taxi rank stretching along the Parque de Santander. The city's Metrelinea *public transit system* opened in 2009 and has gone some way to alleviating the city's standstill rush hour traffic.

Tourist information and tour operators Bucaramanga's central tourist information booth is located on the Parque de Santander (Santander Park) where there is also a tourist police office stocked with free city maps and brochures.

Where to stay *See map, page 184.*

As a major regional hub of commerce and a tourist base, Bucaramanga has numerous hotels and other places to stay. Signs for *cabañas* for rent can be seen by the roadside less than 10 minutes from the airport on the road into the city centre, including the **Mirador Cabañas** at 20,000COP per person. The city's cheapest accommodation is centred on the Parque Centenario although some places double as brothels so these aren't the safest or most salubrious choices.

Hotel Chicamocha (200 rooms) Calle 34, No 31–24; \634 3000; e reservas@solarhoteles. com; www.solarhoteles.com. Part of a Colombian chain, this hotel offers single, twin, double, triple & family rooms, as well as a few suites. Rooms are bright, clean & pleasant but vary considerably in size & style. Each comes with AC, cable TV, a minibar, safe & telephone. Amenities include a swimming pool, steam bath, sauna, gym, bar & restaurant. **$$$**

Hotel Dann Carlton (133 rooms) Calle 47, No 28–83; \697 3266; e reservas@ dannbucaramanga.com.co; www. dannbucaramanga.com.co. In an atmosphere of plush grandeur, guests enjoy stunning views from a rooftop terrace at the 5-star Hotel Dann Carlton where waiters attend to their every whim beside a kidney-shaped pool. The gorgeous AC suites contain a minibar, security safe, fax, cable TV & internet connections. On-site amenities include a jacuzzi, sauna & gym as well as a very good restaurant & bar. This place is very popular with international visitors & tends to get packed out when there's a conference in town. **$$$**

Hotel La Triada (59 rooms) Carrera 20, No 34–22; \642 2410; e reservas@hotellatriada. com; www.hotellatriada.com. Choose from elegant rooms & 7 suites in this classy 5-star option where in-room facilities include free internet use, telephone, cable TV, fax, security safe & minibar. A mainly business clientele enjoy 24hr room service & a speedy laundry service in a nice, central location. Rates include a buffet b/fast. Other amenities include a sauna & gym. **$$$**

Hotel Ruitoque (35 rooms) Carrera 19, No 37–26; \633 4567; e reservas@hotelruitoque. com; www.hotelruitoquebucaramanga.com. Although this place is pretty basic, rooms are meticulously clean & excellent value for money. As a result, it is important to book in advance of arrival. Rooms come with AC, fridge, TV & minibar. Convenient central location & staffed by an efficient, friendly bunch. **$$**

Hotel Valle Real (sleeps 50) Carrera 22, No 28–72; \645 2922/3179; e Hotelmivallereal@ hotmail.com; www.hotelmivallereal.com. This uninspiring sludge-brown building may look like a 1970s office block, but it houses a very nice set of rooms that can accommodate up to 50 guests. On-site facilities include a small pool & a couple of meeting rooms. There's a tariff for large group bookings of between 12 & 50 people. **$$**

Kasa Guane (6 rooms) Calle 49, No 28–21; \657 6960; e info@kasaguane.com; www.kasaguane.com. As the only hostel in Bucaramanga, the Kasa Guane is located in the most exclusive part of town on the border of the areas of Cabecera & Sotomayor. The area is within walking distance of most of the best bars, clubs & restaurants. What is more, it is safe to walk around at any time of day or night. Offering dorms & private rooms, comfortable terraces with a bar, pool table & various evening activities, your hosts Milo & Tim are a wealth of information about the city. It's worth noting that this hostel runs a highly regarded social project called Goals for Peace (*www.goalsforpeace.com*), which accepts volunteers from the hostel wishing to pitch in for a good cause. **$**

Where to eat and drink *See map, page 184.*

Umpteen local eateries, fast-food outlets and different ethnic foods can be found in Bucaramanga. Many are located in the city's various entertainment zones and along the airport road.

Expect standard local fare and grills at the **Restaurante Club Deportivo Kumana** and the **Carbonado Restaurante y Bar** on the Vía Aeropuerto with a similar menu available at **Casa Roble** on Calle 31. Numerous street vendors sell *arepas* and drinks around the Centro Comercial with vegetarian restaurants, health-food

MAIZE HAZE

The word *chicha* is thought to derive from the verb meaning 'to sour a drink' and this bitter-tasting fermented maize drink certainly packs a powerful punch. Originally concocted by the indigenous people prior to the arrival of the Spaniards, the manufacture of *chicha* was outlawed in 1948 by the Colombian government, to great dismay. The ban was lifted in 1991 and in celebration a 'Festival of the Chicha, Maize, Life and Joy' takes place each year in the Barrio La Perseverancia in Bogotá. Today, various recipes offer alcoholic potency to different degrees using a fermentation of concentrated broth. Original *chicha* requires maize grains to be chewed to transform the starch with saliva enzymes. Once a sugary consistency is achieved the mixture is then placed into a container where it's left to ferment in the shade for several days or weeks. Once fermented, the *chicha* is strained and bottled for later consumption. In some parts of Colombia maize is substituted by rice, yucca or potatoes and can contain cannabis or coca leaf. Although it is drunk in large quantities at celebrations as a stimulant, *chicha* is considered a source of nutrition in some Colombian communities. A person who produces good *chicha* is a highly respected member of society and the tradition of *chicha*-making has spread to Colombia's non-indigenous population, despite being served in some city bars. It remains very much the cheap drink of the poor rural communities and varies in colour depending on how long the *chicha* has matured. It's usually a pale straw-yellow with a slightly milky appearance, but can be a more mature mustard-colour; beware of this, it's fearsome and highly potent and can blow your head off at 20 paces.

shops and juice bars along Calle 36. Santander's famous fried ants (see box, page 187) are sold in bags in delicatessens and shops during March–May. On Carrera 33, **Restaurante El Viejo Chiflas** (✆ *632 0640*) serves particularly good grilled meat with the *parrillada viejo chiflas* (a mixed meat platter), a delicious signature dish at 18,000COP. For something a little more upmarket head to the **Restaurante La Carreta** (✆ *643 6680*) on Carrera 27. Gastronomes rave about this 45-year culinary tradition and the menu in this lovely old Bucaramanga building is deserving of the hype with fine food at well under 20,000COP a head.

Entertainment and nightlife For a medium-sized city of 600,000 people Bucaramanga boasts a lot of places to eat, drink and be merry. Most after-dark nightlife is concentrated in the Zona Rosa de la Aurora in the northeast of the city but there is another string of lively bars and restaurants in the Centro Commercial and Zona Oriental in the east and in the west by the airport. For salsa music head to **Calison** in the Zona Rosa de la Aurora in front of the Chicamocha Hotel where Betos specialises in *vallenatos* and New York old classics. **Mi País** in the Centro Commercial district is popular with a young and lively party crowd while **Babilonia**, **Candelaria** and **Africa** are all happening bars on the Vía al Aeropuerto. Two of Bucaramanga's most famous venues are live-music joints **El Guitarrón** and **El Sombrero**. Both have *mariachi* bands every night from 22.00 to 02.00 – find them on Carrera 33 but be prepared to queue.

Shopping Bucaramanga's downtown shopping district and Cabecera retail zone fill with crowds at weekends – and the city is renowned as one of the best in

Colombia to buy shoes. Numerous shoe factories are based around the outskirts of the city, so the range is vast and prices low, with Bucaramanga synonymous with good leather and high-quality manufacturing. Several roadside stalls sell ceramics on the way into town from the airport with other vendors selling *dulces* (sweets) and desserts every mile or so.

Other practicalities Banks (with ATMs) can be found around the Parque de Santander with a couple of money changers located along Calle 34 near the Centro Comercial La Triada. International phone calls can be made from **Click & Play** (◊ 642 2882), also on Calle 34. There are numerous internet cafés throughout the city, including **Telenet** (◊ 670 5850) on Calle 36.

What to see and do Bucaramanga has a number of churches. The oldest in service is **Catedral San Laureano** (St Laureano Cathedral) on Parque García Rovira and the **Catedral de la Sagrada Familia** (Cathedral of the Holy Family) facing the Parque de Santander is the largest and most impressive. It took nearly 100 years to complete, between 1770 and 1865, and the result is a vast piece of religious architecture with statuesque twin towers and fine stained glass. The **Capilla de los Dolores** (Chapel of Our Lady of Sorrows) on the Parque García Rovira is the oldest surviving church in the city. It was built in 1748 but is no longer serving as a place of worship.

The rather nice gardens at **Jardín Botánico Eloy Valenzuela** (Eloy Valenzuela Botanical Gardens) (⊕ *08.00–17.00 daily; admission 2,000COP*) are located on the old road to Floridablanca in Bucaramanga's Bucarica suburb. They were created by Luis Arango Restrepo – an avid orchid collector – who was keen to design a space in which he could exhibit regional flora. Shaded terraces, vibrant blooms, a small pool and a Japanese tea garden make for a pleasant afternoon stroll. It's a nice place to escape the heat with a book and there's a frequent bus from Carrera 15.

Bucaramanga's **Casa de la Cultura** (House of Culture) (*Calle 37;* ◊ *642 0163; ⊕ 08.00–18.00 Mon–Fri, closed noon–14.00, 08.00–noon Sat; free admission*) is housed in a character-packed old building and contains plenty of collections of paintings and crafts by local artists. It also houses exhibitions of indigenous history and Colombian art.

Of the city's many fine museums the **Museo Casa de Bolívar** (Bolívar House Museum) (*Calle 37;* ⊕ *08.00–18.00 Mon–Fri, closed noon–14.00, 08.00–noon Sat;*

FAT-ASSED ANT, ANYONE?

The name translates as big-butt or (fat-assed) ant, and *hormiga culona* is Santander's beloved snack. Once in the mouth, they crackle and crunch like popcorn but these snacks aren't crisps or candy – they're fried giant ants. Typically bitter in flavour and full of toasted juices that coat the tongue, these invertebrates also have hairy legs that tickle the back of your throat on the way down. Inhabitants of northern Colombia believe eating *hormigas culonas* is an aid to good health, curing all manner of ailments from sexual dysfunction to Alzheimer's disease. Bags of the inch-long ants are sold at special roadside stalls in and around Bucaramanga and are a snack much relished. In 2006, the UK was given the opportunity to enjoy entomophagy for itself when a businessman exported more than 350kg of fried queen ants to London. Today, many of these have been hand-dipped in Belgian chocolate and are being sold in swanky department stores such as Fortnum & Mason, priced at £4 for a half-dozen.

admission 2,000COP) is probably the most significant as it is housed in a building where Bolivár stayed for eight weeks in 1828. At this strategic planning point during journeys to Venezuela he would replenish supplies and plot campaigns from this colonial mansion. Today the museum contains lots of historical displays depicting the era along with a large number of Guane artefacts, including weapons, utensils and crafts.

AROUND BUCARAMANGA
The road to Chicamocha National Park
The 54km drive from Bucaramanga to the Chicamocha National Park offers some of the most outstanding views in Colombia. As it cuts through the mountains and begins to climb slowly, silver-pink rocks take on a golden tinge and are tufted with green scrub. Woodlands and palm thickets covered with purple and red flowers lie in the valleys below. Needle-thin cacti form a line along the roadside as the gradual 600m ascent begins. The route takes in coffee fields and truly fearsome drops down to distant rivers. Travelling along this road is one of those genuinely memorable experiences when the backdrop becomes so breathtaking you almost want to drink it in.

The route also passes a lot of places to stop and eat *en route*. Grilled-meat restaurants start flanking the roadside just 10km out of Bucaramanga and continue pretty much to within 5km or so of the park – look out for the British-style blue-and-white signs bearing a knife and fork. A road toll approximately 40km from Bucaramanga is alive with fried-ant vendors touting bags of *hormigas culonas* to passing traffic. Look out for a scattering of camping and *cabaña* signs – it means you're almost there.

Parque Nacional del Chicamocha (Chicamocha National Park) (*www. parquenacionaldelchicamocha.com;* ⊕ *until 20.00 daily; admission 15,000COP*)
This magnificent 264ha expanse of mountains and canyons a little over 50km from Bucaramanga opened to the public in December 2006. The cable car across the canyon is the most popular attraction but there is far more tourism infrastructure in place. Costing US$20 million, the park currently includes a typical Santandereano village, viewpoints, footpaths and picnic areas. Piped *guanvinas* music adds an ethereal ambience to some of the park's most atmospheric lookout points. In its first week of opening, the park attracted 15 walking clubs and 12 mountain-biking clubs with more than 800 people walking the mountain paths from one club alone each Sunday now. Eight well-maintained trails vary in difficulty and total 55km across spectacular honey-coloured rocky peaks. Contoured grassy knolls, trees and cacti are home to bears, snakes and iguanas while park rangers plan to restock rivers left depleted from centuries of over fishing. A number of local tour operators operate out of San Gil to serve the Parque Nacional del Chicamocha.

Paragliding
Paragliding has really taken off – excuse the pun – in recent years in Bucaramanga and the surrounding areas. The best and most reputable outfitter is Richie Mantilla of **Colombia Paragliding** (*www.colombiaparagliding.com*). Mantilla has his own Fly Hostel up next to the paragliding school so those wishing to immerse themselves in intensive courses can remain up here in Ruitoque just outside of Bucaramanga. Mantilla also takes flights in the Chicamocha canyon and other parts of Santander.

Rock climbing
If you are interested in rock climbing outdoors then look no further than the Mesa de Los Santos just 40 minutes outside of Bucaramanga. The rock-climbing area is referred to as La Mojarra and there are two hostels there,

both owned by climbers: the first is called **Juan Palitos** (m *300 268 2316*) and the second is **El Refugio de la Roca** (The Rock Refuge), (*www.refugiolarocacolombia. com*). The two are 100m apart and both offer great facilities: check out both and see which you prefer. The turn-off is well signposted and known by the bus drivers in the region.

GIRÓN (*Telephone code 7*) Much like San Gil and Guane, the town of Girón (*www.giron-santander.gov.co*) is full of picturesque cobbled streets and colonial buildings that are seemingly stuck in time. Founded in 1631 as San Juan de Girón on the banks of the Río de Oro, it was declared a National Monument in 1963. Significant restoration work has centred on the central plaza and a lot of Girón looks much as it did more than 350 years ago. The town's laid-back character makes it a popular centre for authors, academics and intellectuals and Girón has an established avant-garde arts scene. At just 9km from Bucaramanga, the town has become popular with weekending urbanites and is emerging as a popular second-home destination.

Getting there and around From Bucaramanga, pick up one of the frequent **buses** to Girón from Calle 15 and Calle 33 – it'll drop you half an hour later at the back of the main plaza. Girón itself can be easily explored **on foot** although **taxis** can be found around the Parque Principal.

Tourist information

i **Secretaría de Cultura y Turismo** Calle 30, No 26–64; ☎646 3030; ⏲ 08.00–18.00, closed noon–14.00

i **Tourist Police** Cnr Calle 30 & Carrera 27; ☎630 2046

Where to stay

🏠 **Girón Chill Out** (6–10 rooms) Carrera 25, No 32–06; ☎646 1119; e info@gironchillout.com; www.gironchillout.com. This stylish boutique-style hotel is a former colonial mansion house & boasts lots of wonderful old character, from its reed roof & authentic thick walls of mud to carved wooden beams. Decorated in plain & simple style using natural materials & eye-catching sculpture & art, the Chill Out is just that – relaxing, ethereal, beautifully cared for & blessed with peace & quiet. Added extras include gourmet b/fasts & spa therapies. **$$–$$$**

🏠 **Hotel Las Nieves** (24 rooms) Calle 30, No 25–71; ☎646 8968; www.hotellasnievesgiron. com. Simple courtyard colonial-era rooms offer single, double & triple accommodation with private bathrooms which have been lovingly cared for by the Valdivieso family for almost 20 years. For views across the plaza ask for a balconied room at the front of the building – they're large with a TV. An on-site restaurant, Mansión del Fraile (see below) serves some of the nicest budget food in town with simple meat-&-rice dishes from 15,000COP. **$$**

Where to eat and drink

Food vendors congregate along the river at weekends while many of Girón's finer dining establishments can be found around the plaza. Two of the best are listed below.

✗ **Restaurante Mansión del Fraile** Calle 30, No 25 27; ☎646 5408; ⏲ lunch & dinner. This grand mansion house, now Hotel Las Nieves (see above), is one of the finest buildings in Girón with a restaurant & craft shop (⏲*noon–19.00*). A small but promising menu offers plenty of local flavour

with soups & grilled-meat dishes. **$$**
✗ **Restaurante La Casona** Calle 28, No 28–09; ☎646 7195; ⏲ noon–18.00. Generous helpings & charming surroundings are trademarks of this local eatery. Expect hearty meals of grilled goat, chicken & *carne a la plancha*. **$**

Other practicalities There's a **bank** with an ATM on Carrera 25, and an internet café called **el port@l.net** (☏ *646 9878*) nearby that's open 08.00–23.00 weekdays only. In the centre of town there are a number of **pharmacies** and small **supermarkets**.

What to see and do Most visitors head to Girón to explore its tiny cobbled streets and the most striking sightseeing attractions are the town's beautiful whitewashed colonial homes. Small stone bridges lead to shaded leafy gardens and grand mansions. Some of Girón's most notable fine architecture includes the **Mansión del Fraile** (Friar's Mansion) on Calle 30 and the **Catedral del Señor de los Milagros** (Cathedral of Our Lord of Miracles) on the main plaza. Two smaller plazas – Plazuela Peralta and Plazuela de las Nieves – are equally pleasing on the eye.

BARRANCABERMEJA (*Telephone code 7*) Barrancabermeja (population 200,000) is a bustling refinery town catering to a fluid population of engineers and their families, drawn in from all over the country by offers of work. The real reason to visit, though, is to use this city as the embarkation point for river travel. The temperature is constantly tipping 30°C and at first the city may not seem like it can offer a great deal but remember, this is the sixth-largest economic hub in country owing to the petroleum bonanza. There are plenty of places to stay, ordinarily offering convenient deals over the weekends when the engineers return to their home towns and occupation is low. Barrancabermeja is not a town generally on the tourist trail but it is not without its charm and the surrounding countryside and *cienegas* (or lakes) are often weekend picnic destinations for families in the region. For those interested in the city's petroleum history, you can take in the **Cristo Petrolero** (*Petroleum Christ* sculpture) and the **Museo del Petróleo Samuel Schneider Uribe** (*10 minutes outside town*), which provides a good background to the history of the region, the growth of the city as first a hub for Tropical Oil which then became Shell and then was turned over to the state-run EcoPetrol company.

Getting there and away Colombia's Magdalena River needs no introduction but it is worth mentioning that for those souls eager to get out there and experience some distinctly non-touristy forms of travel, the river is indeed navigable for passengers on fluvial public transport. In theory you can actually start journeying by river from La Dorada, Caldas, and make the journey from here through the sweltering lowlands of Puerto Boyaca, Puerto Berrio and to Barrancabermeja, Santander. At the Puerto el Yuma you can travel with one of two companies: **San Pablo** and **Contransfluviales**, both with offices at the port (🕐 *06.00–noon Mon–Sat*) by **boat** along the Magdalena River up towards the Caribbean coast. Leaving at 06.00 (be there at 05.30), you can make the journey to El Banco, Magdalena (5 hours) to then connect to the town of Mompóx. Passing through backwaters and overlooked towns such as Cantagallo, San Pedro, Gamarra and so on, you'll be on front-row view of riverine Colombia, until recently out of bounds because of the conflict. This is just transport; expect no luxuries or bathrooms on the *chalupas* (boats), and pack snacks and drinks. Barrancabermeja is served by once-daily **flights** from Bogotá to Los Yariquíes airport with Avianca and Easyfly. There are several **buses** daily between both Bucaramanga (3 hours) and Medellín (6 hours) with Copetrans and Omega from the terminal building.

🏠 Where to stay

🏠 **Hotel Pipaton** (53 rooms) Av del Río 47–16; ☏ 602 0250; www.hotelpipaton.com. Without doubt Barrancabermeja's most stately hotel option, the pink-walled hotel rises mansion-like over the banks of the Magdalena River. Rooms are uncomplicated & spacious & the swimming pool will provide a welcome relief from the soporific heat here. **$$$**

🏠 **Hotel San Cristobal** (40 rooms) Calle 50, No 12–36; ☏ 622 4346. Should you find yourself in need of decent, economical & clean digs look no further than the Hotel San Cristobal. Located just off the main drag of bars & restaurants & walking distance from the Yuma port, you could do a lot worse. AC is provided. **$**

🍴 Where to eat and drink
Dining options are largely restricted to grill houses and chicken eateries but you can find respite from the heat and bustle at the new **Centro Comercial San Silvestre** which has some fast-food joints and a multi-screen cinema.

NORTE DE SANTANDER

This region on the Venezuelan border offers a varied geography with rugged, mountainous areas, patches of desert, cool plateaus, muggy plains and gently sloping hills. The department's municipalities sit at varying altitudes surrounded and divided by a criss-crossing of rivers, streams and lagoons. The magnificent peaks of the Cordillera Oriental meet the steamy savannahs that roll lazily into Venezuela with three great river basins, the Río Catatumbo, Río Magdalena and the Orinoco. Owing to its frontier location, Norte de Santander boasts a large number of Venezuelan influences that are evident in its dialects, culture and gastronomic tradition. The capital city of Cúcuta has a sizeable number of émigrés from Venezuela and its strategic position has ensured its status as a hotbed of contraband activity.

HISTORY The land that constitutes modern-day Norte de Santander played an important role in Colombia's independence from Spain. The department was created by the expedition of Law 25 July 1910 by territorial division, at which time the Norte de Santander was born.

PAMPLONA (*Telephone code 7*)

The snow ceased quickly, like music.
Birds and green come across the cold. ...
But I just want to burn like a red sun in your white body.

From '*Quiero Apenas*' (*I Just Want*)
by Pamplona-born poet Jorge Gaitán Durán (1925–62)

Despite a major earthquake in 1875, this delightful colonial town in the deep Valle del Espíritu Santo in the Cordillera Oriental still contains some exceptionally old

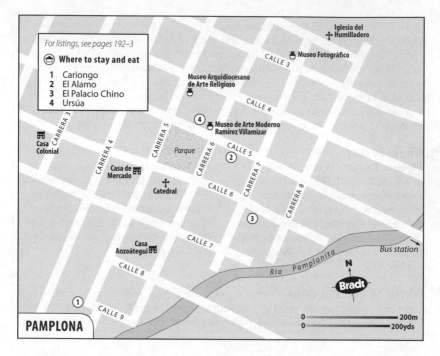

For listings, see pages 192–3

Where to stay and eat

1 Cariongo
2 El Alamo
3 El Palacio Chino
4 Ursúa

Iglesia del Humilladero

Museo Fotográfico

CALLE 3

Museo Arquidiocesano de Arte Religioso

CALLE 4

Casa Colonial

CARRERA 3

CARRERA 4

CARRERA 5

Parque

CARRERA 6

CALLE 5

Museo de Arte Moderno Ramírez Villamizar

Casa de Mercado

Catedral

CALLE 6

CARRERA 7

CARRERA 8

Casa Anzoátegui

CALLE 7

CALLE 8

Río Pamplonita

Bus station

N

CALLE 9

Bradt

PAMPLONA

0 200m
0 200yds

buildings in its narrow streets. Restoration projects conserved what wasn't totally razed but a great deal of modern construction was required to meet the city's needs. Today Pamplona is a key centre for commerce and political administration and has a number of important religious buildings. It is also an academic hub and is home to a growing number of schools and colleges as well as the Universidad de Pamplona. A sizeable student population gives Pamplona a laid-back campus feel and the city has a developed culture scene. It earned the nickname 'Patriotic City' as described by Simón Bolívar on account of its staunch support of the New Granada revolution. The city was founded in 1549 by Pedro de Orsúa and Ortún Velasco, making it the oldest in the region. Pamplona is the birthplace of one of Colombia's greatest poets, Jorge Gaitán Durán.

Getting there and around Numerous **buses** pass through Pamplona as it's on the main Bucaramanga–Cúcuta route – the trip takes about 1½ hours to Cúcuta (15,000COP) and 4½ hours to Bucaramanga (25,000COP). Pamplona's modern bus terminal is a very short walk southwest of the main square. However, those with luggage can grab a **taxi** for the 600m journey for 5,000COP.

Where to stay and eat *See map, above.*

Hotel Cariongo (85 rooms) Cnr Calle 9 & Carrera 5; ✆ 568 1515; www.cariongoplazahotel. com. This is a tired-looking business hotel at the back of the main plaza. Shabby rooms are comfortable but in dire need of TLC & come equipped with TV & cold-water bathrooms. Attracts a convention crowd with meeting rooms & exhibition space. **$$**

Hotel El Alamo (sleeps 69) Calle 5, No 6–68; ✆ 568 2137. Every room has a private bathroom in one of Pamplona's best budget options where pocket-sized rooms are basic but clean – & b/fast is just 10,000COP. **$**

Hotel Ursúa (sleeps 80) Calle 5, No 5–67; ✆ 568 2470. There's a 10,000COP premium for

a room with a TV at this 400-year-old period property on the main square where interior walls are adorned with bric-a-brac, curios & folksy art. $
✖ **El Palacio Chino** Calle 6, No 7–32; ☎ 568

1666; ◷ noon–19.00. This functional oriental diner serves up a fusion of Colombian–Chinese dishes at pleasing prices, including sweet-&-sour veg-&-rice & seafood noodles. $$

Other practicalities Find the **post office** on Calle 6 – it's open weekdays only, 08.00–18.00 (closed noon–14.00). Most of the **banks** with ATMs are clustered around Calle 6 and there are at least half-a-dozen **internet cafés** around Calle 5.

What to see and do Pamplona has a number of museums and the **Museo de Arte Moderno Ramírez Villamizar** (Ramires Villamizar Museum of Modern Art) (*Calle 5;* ☎ *568 2999;* ◷ *09.00–18.00 Tue–Fri, closed noon–14.00, 09.00–18.00 Sat/Sun; admission 5,000COP*) is one of the finest, containing extensive works by Eduardo Ramírez Villamizar. He was born in the town in 1923 and this beautifully restored 16th-century home offers considerable insight into this great artist's career from his expressionist era to his geometric abstract sculpture. Others in Pamplona include the quirky old photograph collection at the **Museo Fotográfico** (Photographic Museum) on Carrera 7 and the **Museo Arquidiocesano de Arte Religioso** (Archdiocese Museum of Religious Art) (*Calle 4, Carrera 5;* ☎ *568 1814*) where a rather fine collection of religious objects can be found.

Many of the town's old historic mansion houses and ten churches are also open to the public. Check out the 19th-century **Casa de Mercado** (Market House) on the corner of Carrera 5 and Calle 6 and the **Iglesia del Humilladero** (Church of Humility) by the cemetery. **Casa Anzoátegui** (Anzoátegui House) on Carrera 6 is the former home of heroic Venezuelan general, José Antonio Anzoátegui, who fought in the Battle of Boyacá and died in Pamplona three months later at the age of 30. One of the town's oldest buildings now houses a collection of pre-Spanish objects. **Casa Colonial** (Colonial House) is on Calle 6 and is open 08.00–17.00, closed noon–14.00.

Festivals
Fiestas del Grito de Independencia (June/July) The city plans all year ahead of the 'Fiestas de Pamplona' and the result is a jam-packed two-week calendar of musical concerts, street processions, marching bands, bullfighting, beauty pageants and general merriment in a wide variety of venues across Pamplona.

CÚCUTA (*Telephone code 7*) The most populous city in the region is the capital Cúcuta (*www.cucuta-nortedesantander.gov.co*), a bustling trading point bordered to the east by Venezuela. Rapid population growth has seen the city sprawl since the 1960s and today the so-called City Without Borders has a burgeoning mix of Venezuelan and Colombian inhabitants. More than a million people reside within the metropolitan area, with 650,000 living within Cúcuta's inner core. Vast temperature disparities separate the wet and dry seasons with 28°C when the rains come and highs of 35°C in the summer. December–March are the driest months. The wettest are April, May, September, October and November with August's wind attracting kite-fliers to Cúcuta in their droves.

More than 300 neighbourhoods form the city's urban network with the wealthier suburbs of the north and northeast leading to the less affluent communities in the south and the slums in the southeast. Although the city has a reputation as a rather uninspiring grubby hubbub Cúcuta proudly proclaims that it has more green zones than many other cities in the nation. In fact, this urban lung benefits

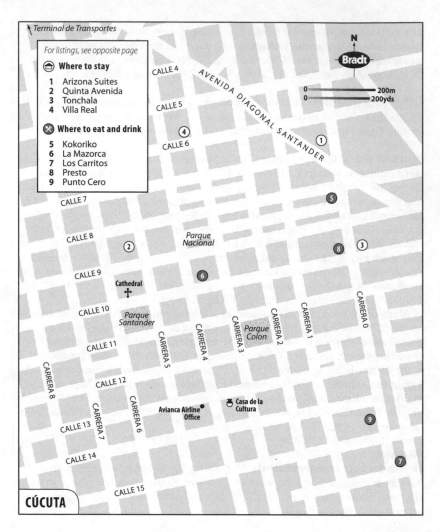

For listings, see opposite page

Where to stay

1 Arizona Suites
2 Quinta Avenida
3 Tonchala
4 Villa Real

Where to eat and drink

5 Kokoriko
6 La Mazorca
7 Los Carritos
8 Presto
9 Punto Cero

Terminal de Transportes

CALLE 4
CALLE 5
CALLE 6
CALLE 7
CALLE 8
CALLE 9
CALLE 10
CALLE 11
CALLE 12
CALLE 13
CALLE 14
CALLE 15

AVENIDA DIAGONAL SANTANDER

Parque Nacional
Cathedral
Parque Santander
Parque Colon

Avianca Airline Office
Casa de la Cultura

CARRERA 8
CARRERA 7
CARRERA 6
CARRERA 5
CARRERA 4
CARRERA 3
CARRERA 2
CARRERA 1
CARRERA 0

N
0   200m
0   200yds

CÚCUTA

from less pollution than many would expect due to its proliferation of trees. These were planted by Francisco de Paula Andrade Troconis after an earthquake partially destroyed the city in 1875.

History Originally a pre-Hispanic settlement, Cúcuta was founded by Juana Rangel de Cuellar on 17 June 1733, becoming a small village with a church and growing to a modern-day population in excess of 45,000. In May 1875, a large earthquake almost completely wiped out the city and also seriously damaged others in the region, including several across the border. The construction of a railway in the 19th century prompted a fresh spurt of economic growth. However, the railway company went bankrupt in 1960 and the line closed and fell into disrepair.

Getting there and around Cúcuta's Camilo Daza Airport is on the northern outskirts of the city and is served by a regular **bus** service. Numerous **taxis** nip back and forth for a 6,000COP fare. **Flights** from the city connect to most major Colombian cities, although do not always go direct. There are no direct flights to Venezuela from Cúcuta – these leave from San Antonio del Táchira, 12km from the city. Avianca has an office in the centre of town (page 196) and frequent shared **minibuses** and taxis serve the airport at around 2,500 COP per person.

Travellers heading to Cúcuta's chaotic 'Terminal de Transportes' should keep their wits about them as it is notorious as a hotbed of scamming and deceit. However, public transport within the metropolitan area of Cúcuta includes a massive public transit system with numerous buses serving Bucaramanga (6 hours, 40,000COP) and Bogotá (16 hours, 130,000COP) each day. The highway to Bucaramanga was greatly improved at the beginning of 2007 and connects Cúcuta with Bogotá, Medellín and Cali; the highway to Barranquilla, Cartagena and Santa Marta; and across the border to the road to Caracas. To ensure safety, avoid travel after dark.

🏠 Where to stay   See map, page 194.

Like most big cities, Cúcuta has its fair share of hellhole hotels, especially around the red-light district in the five or so blocks surrounding the transport terminal. Most of these double as brothels and are not considered safe.

🏠 **Hotel Tonchala** (102 rooms & suites) Cnr Av 0 & Calle 10; 🔌 575 6444; www.hoteltonchala.com. Choose from rooms & suites in a variety of styles & sizes in this upmarket casino hotel, from singles to large suites. Amenities include a restaurant, sauna, pool & gym with rates including buffet b/fast. **$$$**

🏠 **Hotel Arizona Suites** (77 rooms) Av 0, No 7–62; 🔌 572 6020; www.hotelarizonasuites. com. Room rates include b/fast at this pleasant contemporary hotel set behind a distinctive dark-glass façade. Conveniently located in the heart of the city, the Arizona has a bar, restaurant & a pool with each room equipped with AC, minibar, safe, cable TV & telephone. Choose from singles,

doubles & triples – each has a private hot-water bathroom. **$$**

🏠 **Quinta Avenida** (50 rooms) Av 5, No 8–32; 🔌 572 0086; e Hotelquintavenida@gmail.com; www.hotelquintaavenida.com.co. Nice, bright, cheerful AC rooms come with private, modern bathrooms & a fridge. B/fast inc. There's also a swimming pool. **$$**

🏠 **Villa Real** (44 rooms) Av 6, No 14–24, Centro; 🔌 582 2333; e hotelvillarealcucuta@gmail. com, www.hotelvillarealcucuta.wordpress.com. Most of the rooms at this reasonable dirt-cheap option are triple bed but there are some singles & doubles – all with fans or AC. **$**

✖ Where to eat and drink   See map, page 194.

There are lots of fried-chicken joints, burger bars and pizza places in and around town as well as a good number of local restaurants, bakeries and cafés – some of them 24-hour. For fast food check out the **Presto** (🔌 577 5596; $) on Avenida Los Libertadores, **Kokoriko** (🔌 572 2822; $) on the corner of Avenida 0 and Calle 8, and **Los Carritos** (🔌 571 0097; $) on Avenida 0. For some good, uncomplicated local food head to **Punto Cero** (🔌 573 01533; $) on Avenida 0 where a menu offers traditional dishes in a homely atmosphere – even the most expensive big-plate meal costs no more than 10,000COP. **La Mazorca**'s ($) fine Creole set meals and decent wines are also great value at 15,000COP. Find it on Avenida 4 and dine at a pleasant courtyard table.

Shopping   Cúcuta's many malls include a Unicentro on Avenida Libertadores, where an endless succession of shops include a Carrefour and a number of food outlets as well as a bingo hall and a casino. Ventura Plaza is the biggest shopping centre in the city, between Calle 10 and Calle 11.

Other practicalities Staff at the Avianca airline office (✆ 571 5161) can guide you through the complexities of the timetable from Cúcuta – find it downtown on Avenida 4. Numerous town-centre shops offer plenty of places to pick up essentials, with **banks** with ATMs on Avenidas 5 and 6 and a **post office** on Calle 8a. Travellers heading to Venezuela will need to visit the Migracion Colombia immigration post on the road to the border. The Venezuelan consulate is located on Avenida Camilo Daza *en route* to the airport, 3km from the city centre.

Safety and crime Large numbers of travellers in Cúcuta have reported encountering the city's well-organised fraudsters who operate in and around the bus terminal and appear perfectly legit. Foreigners are targeted almost exclusively, usually by English-speakers, who either offer to help with bus tickets or offer to insure your cash against theft. Most carry official-looking documents and a triplicate pad of receipts but the tickets they tout are forgeries. The insurance is also a scam to part you from your cash. They push the benefits of insurance by telling an alarming story about recent hold-ups by bandits on buses and urge you to protect your cash against theft. However, the paperwork requires details of the cash you are carrying and once you have entered the amount, the con artists ask to count the money for clarification. At this point there is an almost invisible sleight of hand and suddenly, lo and behold, the amount is halved before your eyes. It's also important to watch your luggage like a hawk.

What to see and do Cúcuta isn't blessed with a host of sightseeing attractions but a reasonably sized **Casa de la Cultura** (Culture House) (*Calle 13;* ✆ *571 6689;* ⊕ *08.00–18.00 Mon–Fri, closed noon–14.00; free admission*) houses year-round exhibitions of local handicrafts and art. For slightly more excitement grab tickets for a Cúcuta Deportivo home match – or head to a local bar to watch the game on television when you hear cries of 'GOOOOOLLLLLL' echoing through Cúcuta's streets.

AROUND CÚCUTA
Villa del Rosario (*Telephone code 7*) This town, located about 10km southeast of Cúcuta on the road to the Venezuelan border, is significant as the venue for the inauguration ceremony of Simón Bolívar as President and Vice President of Gran Colombia in 1821. Today the Parque de la Gran Colombia signifies the spot where the New Granada of Colombia and Panama, Venezuela and Ecuador was unified to form the new nation of Greater Colombia. The town was founded by Don Asencio Rodriguez in 1750 on the Río Táchira and today forms part of the metropolitan area of Cúcuta. In 1813, Simón Bolívar liberated the city in the Battle of Cúcuta *en route* to Caracas, killing 20 Spanish fighters and injuring 14.

Getting there and around At about 20 minutes from the Venezuelan border, Villa del Rosario is easily reached by **public transport** and **taxis** from Cúcuta and Pamplona. It is also easily criss-crossed **on foot** and has several local taxi firms for those weighed down with luggage.

What to see and do Villa del Rosario's main claim to fame is its Simón Bolívar connections and the **Parque de la Gran Colombia** (Gran Colombia Park) is the town's number-one tourism attraction. It's been built on the remains of the Templo del Congresso where congressional talks and Bolívar's inauguration took place. Pretty red-tile pathways are flanked by large numbers of trees. Although the church was almost wiped out in the earthquake of 1875, it has since been restored,

COLOMBIA'S CONTRABAND CAPITAL

One of Colombia's contraband epicentres, Cúcuta is powered by numerous criminal syndicates that flex considerable muscle within local circles. Under the watchful eye of the city's kingpin players, Cúcuta's underworld has a tentacle-like control of trade and commerce, smuggling vast quantities of petrol over the border to sell at up to ten times the Venezuelan price. Contraband is big business in this frontier town and is a commerce that runs like clockwork – with battered old trucks carting goods over the border in back-to-back trips. The border was closed by Venezuelan presidential decree on a couple of occasions in 2014 and 2015 to try and combat the flood of Venezuelan products being shipped over and sold in Colombia. Whether this really prevented the flow of contraband remains debatable as the criminal gangs and freelance operators can be seen routinely crossing the river on foot with their goods.

albeit not sympathetically. In the newer section of the church there's a marble statue of Bolívar and a few other related mementos. The park is also the site of the **Casa Natal del General Santander** (*General Santander's Birthplace;* \ *570 0741;* ☉ *09.00–17.30 Mon–Fri, closed 11.30–14.00; admission 2,500COP*), former residence of Francisco de Paula Santander, and today it houses a small exhibition relating to his life, including some photographs and letters.

COLOMBIA ONLINE

For additional online content, articles, photos and more on Colombia, why not visit www.bradtguides.com/colombia.

5

Los Llanos

Ah my Llanura! Green enchantment, where the blue of the sky gets confused with the soil of your vast expanse. In the dawn, the sun kisses you from the lake to the moriche. The air is full of herons and the palms whisper for liberty!

Armulfo Briceño, 'Ay mi Llanura', Tributo Al Llano, 1999

Los Llanos – 'the flat plains' – is a vast grassland savannah that sprawls to the east of the Andes in northwest Colombia and Venezuela. These cattle-clad seasonally flooded lowlands cover over 50% of the country's total landmass, comprising rolling grassy knolls, scrubby pasture and prairies dotted with ranches. The region's main river is the Orinoco with gentle slopes that lead away from higher elevations, which barely rise above 200m. Herdsmen in Los Llanos raise mammoth droves of cattle over many thousands of acres with stud farms, horses and cow fields the lifeblood of Colombia's 'cowboy country'. Corralling, roping, ranging and lassoing are all-important skills in this rural hinterland where the nasal dialect of the Llaneros (plainspeople) remains peppered with phrases unchanged from the idioms of the first Spaniard settlers. The Llaneros are proud of their hard lives and are dedicated cowboys from cradle to grave, spending long days enduring extreme heat and high winds in the saddle. Having learned how to 'break' horses while young, these gaucho-like ranchers enjoy a provincial culture rich in folklore, legends and stories. It is hard to image a Colombian song more poignant than those of Los Llanos' heartfelt lilting lyrics to the melodic strum of the *cuatro* guitar or harp. A true Llanero is a legendary figure on the ranches of Colombia and these accomplished horsemen often wear the distinctive traditional working clothes of a poncho, straw hat and *cotizas* (rope-soled sandals).

HISTORY

Niklás Federman, a German conquistador, approached the *altiplano* of Bogotá from the savannahs of Venezuela, navigating an inhospitable area created by the waters of the Orinoco Basin. Los Llanos, as the hinterland region was referred to, remained neglected by settlers for more than 300 years in favour of coastal territory. Few ventured east for fear of its problematic geographical obstacles and oppressive heat. However, in the 1840s, a small group of farming folk moved from villages in eastern Bogotá to establish the settlement of Gramalote, which officially became the parish of Villavicencio in 1855. Inhabitants of the plains became known as the Llaneros and these formidable horsemen first fought for the Spanish royalists and then for the Venezuelan and Colombian rebels during the war of independence. It is said they crossed the Andes with Bolívar to take the Spaniards by surprise on Tunja's plateau, where they cleared the way for the taking of Santa Fé de Bogotá in August 1819. Villavicencio began to grow as the availability of medicine made this rural outpost more hospitable. Land was offered free to relocating farmers –

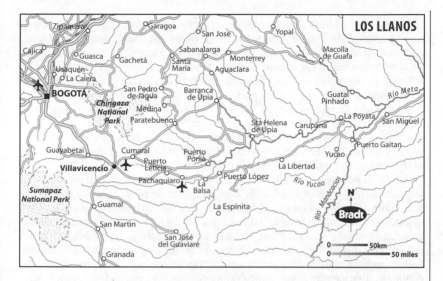

the construction of a simple mule track made it all the easier to navigate. Soon new colonisers were building roads that improved access to the extremes of Los Llanos, enabling farming communities to better ship their produce and cattle to the markets of Bogotá.

THE ECOSYSTEM OF LOS LLANOS

South America's savannah ecosystem covers a total of 269 million hectares. Most of it (76%) belongs to the *cerrados* of Brazil but about 11% forms the Venezuelan Llanos and 6% (16–17 million hectares) the Los Llanos region of Colombia. The plains of Venezuela and Colombia form a single eco-region, an area of extensive grasslands covered mainly by savannah vegetation. Geographically relatively young, at less than 10,000 years old, the region has experienced a major subsidence. The result is a striking landscape of dramatic alluvial plains and highlands.

The Llanos are some of the world's richest tropical grasslands, a diverse landscape of dry forests, grasslands, and seasonally flooded plains that teem with wildlife. It eventually disperses into a river delta of swamp forests and coastal mangroves as it approaches the Atlantic and harbours more than 100 mammal species and over 700 species of birds – around the same number of birds as found in the entire United States. Boasting the largest river flow on earth, the mighty Orinoco cuts through the heart of the Llanos landscape.

WILDLIFE AND BIRDS One of the most critically endangered reptiles on the planet can be found in Los Llanos, the endemic Orinoco crocodile. The species can reach a length of 7m in maturity but scientific reports suggest that fewer than 1,800 of these magnificent individuals remain in the wild. The Orinoco turtle, giant river otter, ocelot, giant armadillo, black-and-chestnut eagle and several species of catfish are also in need of conservation. The capybara, the world's largest rodent at around 0.5m high, resides in wet, flooded savannahs, as does the anaconda, the largest existing boa, at over 7m long. The jaguar, the largest American felid, has been severely hunted in the Llanos, for both sport and to protect cattle. The tapir was once prevalent in the region but is now drastically reduced.

In contrast, no bird species is at serious risk of extinction in Los Llanos, although some are vulnerable. These include the sharp-tailed ibis, found only in Los Llanos and Colombia's most scarce ibis species. Colombia has the richest avifauna of any country in the world at more than 1,700 bird species, although less than 40% is found in the region. At least 62 of the bird species in the Orinoco region are Neotropical migrants, accounting for nearly 40% of the migratory species found in Colombia and Venezuela. Indeed, the wetlands of Los Llanos are among the most important areas for Neotropical migratory birds, such as shorebirds like sandpipers and yellowlegs. Seasonal visitors to the region include the broad-winged hawk and swallow-tailed kite. There are renewed concerns for the future of the scarlet macaw as these are often captured and kept as pets.

Although relatively unaffected by negative human influences until recent times, the natural resources of Los Llanos have increasingly become important to the economies of both Colombia and Venezuela. Fire is used regularly to increase the quality of native grasses, while slash-and-burn tactics are used to increase pasture lands and natural plains are being replaced by introduced pastures. More than 1.3 million hectares of the Colombia Llanos are being used as introduced pastures with 15 million head of cattle in the region. This large-scale cattle production and commercial agriculture has seen the draining of sizeable expanses of wetlands. Rice and oil production have also damaged natural ecosystems. Dredging for ditches, dykes and ponds has destroyed habitat, with the widespread use of agro-toxins in pest control also a concern.

THE ROAD FROM BOGOTÁ

A modern road has shortened the driving time from Bogotá to 1½ hours, travelling east through Avenida Boyacá and passing the mist-shrouded peaks of Paramount Crux Verde. It cuts through Bogotá's notorious Sur Bolívar slum district, a distressing collection of shanty towns set back beyond the highway. Although dangerous, this stretch of 'no-go area' poses no danger to daytime drivers. Illegally constructed thrown-up shacks have no foundations, power or sanitation. Unsurprisingly, the nearby Río Tunjuelito is one of the most polluted stretches of water in South America. In the distance, the magnificent slopes of the mountains of **Sumapaz National Park** form a sharp contrast to the squalor in the foreground. Stretching 200km, the park's folds have effectively halted the continued growth of Bogotá's southern slums. Chickens peck at rotting garbage on the roadside by lotto-selling kerbside vendors while wealthy slick-haired urban cyclists on gleaming 100-million-peso bikes head out to do battle with the peaks.

A Mobil-branded petrol station on the left at the end of a tatty cluster of houses signifies the end of the city – and the beginning of the route into Colombia's southeast. The first of three tunnels along the route is the Argelino Durán and it is around this point that the town of **Caqueza** can be sighted on the right, although the actual entry point is 28km further along. On the roadside there's a *lácteos la delicia* (dairy vendor) selling smoked cheeses, creams and yoghurt drinks. The route starts to wind through lush green grassy verges with wood-and-wire fencing. A shabby sign hails the Tienda la Piacita on the left, a stopping-off point for snacks and cold drinks.

Soon, the second town of **Chipague** is just about in view as the road sweeps around to take in its shape. A small string of bars and shops has the rustic Restaurante PPC in its midst – a simple food joint where a plate of plantain, rice and grilled meat costs less than 6,000COP. Giant orange rocks and a mustard-coloured mudbank are to the right-hand side of the road. To the left, a truly vast, breathtaking drop forms a stunning valley clad with green palms. In this region of Colombia there is no shortage of roadside eateries, mostly the omnipresent *asaderos* – the nation's much-loved wood-fired local grill. Both the La Vara and the Estadero la Fonda typify this rustic gastronomic favourite, serving big slabs of beef at tables set just yards away from grazing cattle herds.

Next up is the pit-stop town of **Abasticos**, little more than a row of snack stalls on the left of the road. The Restaurante Donde Mireya may not look much from the outside but it is always packed with truckers and passers-by. Rumour has it the chorizo is worth stopping for even if time is tight.

Running alongside the left-hand side of the road beyond Abasticos is the Quebrada Blanco. Look out for Hollywood-style white lettering in the hillside above – although not as glamorous as its Californian inspiration, the sign for 'Drogas Casa Ortiz' (a family-run drugstore) made from white pebbles is worth a peek nonetheless. Next up is the La Vara Sasados on the right of the road, a big local diner serving fried fish, *arepa* and grilled meat. Opposite, the Restaurante Cafetería sits next to a petrol station. Further up the road, a stretch of tiny snack shops and kiosks (*tienditos*) sell bits and bobs, sodas and sweets.

At this point the rocky banks become more densely covered in the so-called spoon tree. Rope-tethered soot-coloured bulls graze on spongy verges by the Quebrada La Honda. Nearby are a couple of tiny grill joints and a handful of small white single-storey *fincas*.

Then, hurrah! It's the long-awaited La Petite Source (2) Restaurant – the first in this family-run duo of fine diners that are loved by tourists and locals alike. Look out for a pretty stone-built building with lots of wrought-iron detail, flying a patriotic flag with great aplomb. Inside, the place is spotlessly clean with tiled floors and square wooden tables. A decent menu has plenty of seafood, chicken and meat dishes served in typical style with rice or *patacones*. A well-stocked Panadería Típica sells packed goods to take away with numerous sugary treats perfect for a road trip. A wide range of beers, liquor, wine and fresh juices sits on rows of wooden shelves along with jars of preserved fruits.

Half a kilometre on the right, the Parador Punta offers snacks with stunning views. Then it's La Petite Source (1) – the original restaurant and a similar concept to its sister, although much smaller and less popular with large families and groups as a result. Don't miss the waterfalls to the left – they are spectacular but often hidden by foliage.

Next it's the Quebrada Blanca tunnel and on to the scrappy truck-stop town of **Guayabetal** where there's a small hotel, bakery, a handful of *arepa* stalls, some cell-phone minute vendors and a couple of local restaurants. The Rancho Grand is near to a drugstore, Claro phone shop and tiny kiosk while the Restaurante Don Pacho nestles between a couple of rickety beer shacks. Against a backdrop of Andean forests of red, black and green hues there is lots of water gushing down from the mountains – it's crystal clear and deliciously drinkable, according to the locals. At exactly 70km from Bogotá by a bright-yellow bridge, it's possible to spot the remnants of the old road – an impossibly narrow crumbling strip under magnificent cascades of tumbling water and emerald creepers. There's another spectacular water feature around 5km further along the road, but more by accident than planning or Mother Nature. A thin stainless-steel water pipe suspended across two high peaks hasn't been patched up in years and today spouts spray from at least half-a-dozen holes to create a ghostly apparition in the mist.

About 8km from Villavicencio, a handful of attractive plum-coloured *fincas* catch the eye just as an overpowering smell of chickens catches the breath. A steady climb leads to Alto de Buena Vista where, as the name suggests, the views are truly amazing. Pull in by the smallholding at the top on a clear day to look out across to Río Meta over a lush green valley – a true photographic opportunity. Nearby, there are a few shops for basics and snacks but not much more.

VILLAVICENCIO *Telephone code 8*

A sign on the edge of town proudly announces your arrival in Villavicencio, 'La Puerta al Llano' (The Gate to the Plains). Sitting on the historical path from the Colombian interior to the vast savannahs of the Colombian–Venezuelan plains between the Andes and the Amazon, Villavicencio is both a city and municipality and the capital of the Meta department. In a period of just over 40 years, this

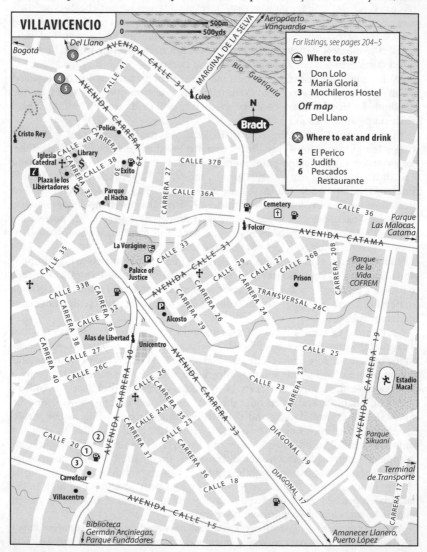

VILLAVICENCIO

For listings, see pages 204–5

Where to stay
1 Don Lolo
2 María Gloria
3 Mochileros Hostel
Off map
Del Llano

Where to eat and drink
4 El Perico
5 Judith
6 Pescados Restaurante

frontier outpost has been transformed from a hamlet of 30 people into a metropolis of more than 400,000. Dubbed 'Villavo' by its inhabitants, it lies on the banks of the Río Guatiquía in the footholds of the Andes range to the east.

Founded in 1840, it was named after Antonio Villavicencio, who was an early advocate of the struggle for independence from Spain. Today, Villavicencio serves as an important manufacturing and commercial centre for the plains and rainforests of eastern Colombia. Although its industries include a distillery, brewery, rice mills and saddleries, Villavo is primarily a cattle-raising centre. Today, a modern highway links the city to Bogotá 90km northwest, making Villavicencio a commercial hub for roads from the northeastern and southern parts of the Meta department. Although early morning and evening breezes from the mountains attempt to cool the city, Villavo is typically hot and muggy. Heat rises in a haze along a muddle of sun-parched streets that enjoy disorder born out of 40 years of crazed development. Unfortunately this expansion has been largely uncontrolled and poorly planned. Modern-day Villavicencio is not a pretty city. Many areas still lack clean water and decent sanitary systems, and its poorer neighbourhoods often lack even the most basic amenities, due to an electrical grid that fails to keep pace with demand. Concentrated clusters of colourful single-storey houses crowd highways, alleyways and plazas with makeshift markets, and retail zones slam up against swish residential streets. This manic development has encroached on the very outskirts of Villavicencio; a large roundabout with an Esso service station on the left denotes where the central urban spread begins in earnest. However, what it lacks in beauty it retains in importance and in the midst of a sprawling agricultural wilderness Villavicencio is a crucial commercial hub.

GETTING THERE AND AROUND Villavicencio's La Vanguardia Airport is served by Satena with frequent 30-minute **flights** to and from Bogotá. The 98km overland route is around a 3-hour drive from Bogotá – a far cry from a decade ago when the road was so bad it was a 10-hour haul. Several **minibuses** run from Bogotá including **Bolívariano** (✆ 1 424 9090; *www.bolivariano.com.co*), **Macarena** (✆ 1 425 4900; *www.flotalamacarena.com*), **Velotax** (✆ 1 429 6984; *www.velotax.com.co*) and **Auto Llanos** (✆ 263 0799). Costs range from 20,000COP to 50,000COP and some of the companies operate round the clock, departing every 15 minutes. **Taxis** are in plentiful supply throughout the city – and are the best way to get from A to B. Expect a cross-town journey to cost around 6,000COP.

TOURIST INFORMATION There are three PITs (Puntos de Informacion al Turista) in Villavicencio.

i **Terminal de Transporte de Villavicencio** María Ximena Sanabria; m 310 582 4411; ⊕ 08.00–noon & 14.00–18.00 Tue–Sun

i **Plazoleta los Libertadores** Ana Yisseth Torres Santos; m 314 524 6757; ⊕ 08.00–noon & 13.00–17.00 Tue–Sun

i **Villavicencio airport** Johanna Medina Esposito; m 310 885 3774; ⊕ 08.00–noon & 13.00–17.00 Mon–Sat

🏠 **WHERE TO STAY** *See map, page 202.*
Although there are plenty of shoestring places to find a bed for the night, the three nicest (and safest) hotels in the city are the most popular with foreign visitors. Those willing to chance a cheap joint will find umpteen throughout El Centro. The

The Huitoto ('*wuh-toe-toe*'), also spelt Witoto, are recent arrivals in Los Llanos, a region without any surviving indigenous tribes. One of Colombia's largest indigenous groups, the Huitoto hail from a principal territory in the La Chorrera of the Amazon jungle and have only had a presence in the region for a few years. Artistically talented, the Huitoto make masks, rattles and blowguns as well as a range of jewellery made from bark cloth, seed and nuts coloured with vegetable dye. Bark cloth is made from a palm tree beaten until it is paper-thin. Traditional clothing for both sexes consists of a short skirt. Women used to be bare-breasted but now often wear traditional dress for ceremonial occasions only.

The Huitoto believe they emerged from the earth with tails thanks to their god, Jitoma. A bee removed their tails with its sting – and the Huitoto tribe were born. The Huitoto proceeded to a lake to wash where they came across an anaconda. Hungry, the local people killed the snake, cutting it into four. This signified the birth of the tribe's four dialects.

However, over the years the Huitoto became increasingly marginalised until in 1990 the discrimination became intolerable for some. After first having contact with white rubber producers in 1980, the indigenous people suffered slavery. Then white missionaries attempted to convert them to Christianity, while the Colombian government made forceful inroads into eradicating Huitoto culture, language and beliefs. In 1999, the Huitoto denounced their oppressors, which by this time included drug-traffickers and guerrillas. Santiago Kuetgaje (✆ *578 664 8464; www. resguardoindigenamaguare.com*) found his voice on Chorrera FM 104.9. However, his outspokenness prompted death threats and Kuetgaje judged these sufficiently serious to flee the Amazon in 2004, under cover of darkness. He eventually settled in Los Llanos where the rest of his 16 family members joined him, earning money as guides at the local zoo and making handicrafts to sell. Realising that the success

following offer a combined room count of over 200 rooms but are often packed out so pre-booking is crucial.

🏠 **Hotel Del Llano** (116 rooms) Carrera 30, No 49–77; ✆ 671 7000; e reservas@hoteldelllano. com; www.hoteldelllano.com. Another bright, modern place that lacks a bit of soul but is perfectly adequate, catering for a mix of family vacationers, travelling merchants & overseas tourists. **$$$**

🏠 **Hotel Don Lolo** (57 rooms) Carrera 39, No 20–32; ✆ 670 6020; www.donlolohotel.com. This modern hotel has rooms that vary in size, ranging from some rather pokey singles to triples & quadruples. As one of Villavicencio's most popular resting places, the Don Lolo is packed to capacity during summer & public holidays, so be prepared to be disappointed if you turn up on spec. **$$$**

🏠 **Hotel María Gloria** (60 rooms) Carrera 38, No 20–26; ✆ 672 0197; e reservas@ hotelmariagloria.com; www.hotelmariagloria. com. This popular hotel has a wide range of rooms to choose from, so be sure to check out a few to compare. On-site pool & conference centre. **$$$**

🏠 **Mochileros Hostel** (dorms & private rooms) Calle 18, No 13–08, Balata, Villavicencio; ✆ 667 6723, e info@mochileroshostel.com; www.mochileroshostel.com. The only hostel in Villavicencio is a welcoming & organised affair offering all the information necessary on what to do in the area. Small dorm rooms & privates are available & b/fast is offered too. **$**

Those keen to give large modern hotels a wide berth will find plenty of little-known alternatives on the outskirts of town. A growing number of *fincas* are offering of their established community lacked an economic foundation, Kuetgaje travelled to speak to tribal leaders in Peru. He learned about indigenous tourism and the dynamics of this emerging sector in Colombia, winning first prize in a Corporación Andina de Fomento (CAF, Andean Development Corporation) initiative for indigenous talent. Kuetgaje's award was US$22,000, a sum he used to establish the Los Llanos project. The objectives are to maintain the Huitoto culture, ethos, traditions and language whilst giving visitors an insight into how they live and think.

Key traditions the Huitoto are keen to explain include a woven stick (*robaindias*) they use to catch a partner. There is also the 'human–nature' connection they call 'El Mambeo' – a ritual that involves ingesting ground coca leaf to link with god. Eaten with a spoon, the coca powder is a stimulant that the Huitoto view as the 'female' energy of their version of ying and yang. The tribe also ingest tobacco in a thick, black jelly form. It is eaten from a small earthenware pot with a small toothpick. This is the male energy to counterbalance the coca leaf.

In the past, the women were allocated to a potential partner at birth, wrapped in a palm parchment. Today, a man and woman can have a relationship after the girl reaches puberty. The Huitoto are a patriarchal society with the *cacique* (chief) the most important male. Part of their belief system is shape-shifting into animal form. After El Mambeo the chief can better 'see' where his people should hunt in the jungle and his men shape-shift to become one with the animals to improve their hunting chances.

The Huitoto settlement is less than half an hour from Villavicencio but visitors should not turn up on spec to experience the dance, rituals, food, drink and handicrafts of this fascinating community. Villavicencio's Huitoto are 100% reliant on tourism for their income. After such a turbulent recent history they have many tales to tell.

homestay programmes and bed-and-breakfast accommodation in pretty rural settings; many are located on working farms. Few advertise and as they tend to be set way back from the road they are often difficult to find without help. Independent tour operator **Raman Vergel** (m *311 281 9328*) is a good person to call regarding agro-tourism.

✗ WHERE TO EAT AND DRINK See map, page 202.

Diners are spoilt for choice in the upmarket areas of Villavicencio, such as El Barsal and El Caudal, as well as the city's two *zonas rosas*. Expect to find numerous juice joints, bistros and grills on Carerra 32 as well as some of the city's best after-dark hangouts.

Travellers on the move will find plenty of cheap, rustic food places on the edge of town. Some of the best include **Restaurante El Perico** and **Restaurante Judith** (on the right as you come into town from Bogotá) and the **Pescados Restaurante** on the left. In the heart of the city (as well as the outer edges), there are umpteen budget fast-food joints. Clusters of reasonably priced local restaurants can also be found around the Plaza de los Libertadores and around Carerra 39.

ENTERTAINMENT AND NIGHTLIFE Villavicencio's two *zonas rosas* (entertainment zones) are awash with bars, clubs and restaurants. Find them in the southwest and the north of the city – but don't count on having an early night.

Heartfelt lyrics typify *música llanera* with proclamations of love and declarations of pride at top-of-the-lung-volume singing. The cattle-herding Llaneros are loyal to their homeland and proud working people who yearn for romance. Harp-led melodies in traditional *joropo* style blend machismo with big-hearted passion in this folkloric musical tradition. Beautiful words and poetic prose capture the essence of these vast cattle- and horse-raising flatlands. Joyous, rhythmic, string- and percussion-based songs are crafted on a *cuatro* (small, four-stringed guitar) and harp. Other instruments include a *bandola* (a pear-shaped guitar), bass and maracas and the songs of Los Llanos are usually florid at a syncopated pace. Verbal contests called *contrapunteos* are often part of this musical tradition. Some of the famous *música llanera* artists include such greats as Alma Llanera, Cimarron, Luis Ariel Rey, Carlos Rojas, Sabor Llanero, Arnulfo Briceño and Orlando Valdemarra. Visitors will hear this toe-tapping, infectious musical style everywhere in Los Llanos. It forms a constant soundtrack to a journey through the savannahs, a melodic backdrop redolent of rural cattle-farming life.

☆ **Los Capachos** Carrera 48, No 17–87; 📞578 662 2079; e info@loscapachos.com; www. loscapachos.com. Colombians travel miles across country to get to this frenzied party venue – a booming, pumping & neon-lit bar-cum-nightspot that even Bogotanos consider oh-so cool. Expect big sounds & big drinking at Los Capachos, with non-stop dusk-til-dawn fun-fests every w/end that promise the ultimate in hedonistic merriment. Since it opened in 2002, Los Capachos has earned a formidable reputation for fun with a capital F. It's named after a set of rattle-style maracas used in Los Llanos created from hollowed gourd or *totumo* fruit & filled with *achirilla* or *curcuma* seeds – & after midnight in Los Capachos there are plenty of people shaking their maracas at this heaving wild night out.

SHOPPING At the time of writing, Villavicencio is still undergoing sizeable redevelopment in its retail sectors. The **Unicentro** (*Av 40, No 26C–10*) shopping mall opened in 2008, with several smaller shopping outlets recently opening in the surrounding area too including **Centro Comercial Centauros** (*Carrera 31, No 37–32*) and the **Centro Comercial Llanocentro** (*Carrera 40, con Cl 15*) to name a couple.

The city has all the usual large supermarkets, such as **Exito**, as well as numerous boutiques and small shops in El Centro. In the middle-class district of El Barsal there are umpteen cosmetic surgeries, salons and beauty parlours, many funded by dubious means.

Carrera 39 is Villavicencio's makeshift market area, a mile-long stretch of counterfeit goods, cheap electronics, discount clothes, sunglasses, CDs and designer knock-offs. Endless street vendors and stalls attract big crowds of people in a street renowned for its low prices and red-light low life.

OTHER PRACTICALITIES As you'd expect from a large trading outpost, Villavicencio has numerous **banks** and **ATMs**. It is also a great place to stock up on hardware items, get tents and equipment repaired, and replace worn-out boots and T-shirts.

SAFETY In the city's central Acacias district the Parque de Fundadores offers a pleasant collection of seating under shady palms. However, in the area's central tree-lined boulevard the ambience is less tranquil. Muggings have increasingly become a problem in this most unlikely spot. Travellers are advised to be vigilant when in Acacias – and to avoid carrying excess belongings, valuables or sums of cash.

WHAT TO SEE AND DO On the large Unicentro roundabout on Avenida 40 stands a rather handsome monument, called *Alas de Libertad* (*Wings of Freedom*), in honour of people who have been kidnapped from the region. Close by, on the Avenida del Llano Vía Restrepo, there is also a statue commemorating Villavicencio's bullfighting tradition, *Monumento Al Coleo*. On the Vía Marginal de la Selva a roundabout boasts a magnificent water feature with illuminated cascades designed to emulate harp strings accompanied by piped *música típica*.

About 15km from the centre of town is Villavicencio Zoo, complete with restaurants, souvenir stalls, vendors and taxis.

AROUND VILLAVICENCIO

CUMARAL This small town 10km from Villavicencio is named after the important palm '*cumares*', from which extracted fibre is used to make rope, hammocks and baskets. A wide main drag comprises a string of bars and restaurants serving excellent wood-fired grilled meats and a handful of essential shops. One of the finest local eateries in Cumaral is the centrally located **Asadero los Camares**, an on-the-street food joint with inside and outside tables. Expect the patron to rush out with a plate of meat to sample before you make a decision to eat. If you like what you taste, grab a seat. A handful of waiting staff dressed in matching bright-blue T-shirts attend to a dozen or so wooden tables, serving up hearty chunks of grilled beef, salted potatoes with boiled yucca washed down with an ice-cold beer.

SHAKER MAKER

Devilish little rebel pebble,
furious, fuzzy and vigorous.
Rumba rattle made of hollow gourd, with pebbles or lead shot inside.

Ramón Guirao, 'The Maracas', 1975

Maracas are one of the most recognisable percussion instruments on the planet and these rattles made from gourds are essential to Latin and South American music. Usually oval or egg-shaped, the maracas are filled with beads, beans or small stones, with a handle used for shaking. Traditional maracas are made from only natural materials including gourds or other plant pods, wood and leather. The word '*maraca*' is believed to have come from the Araucanian people of Chile, and players of maracas in South America favour different varieties. In Colombia, traditional-style maracas are preferred above newer models, with small *gapachos* popular in the Andes region filled with seeds from the gapacho plant. In Los Llanos, *clavellinas* similar to gapachos are played – and both these styles of maracas are heard in many forms of Latin music. This characteristic percussive sound is essential to traditional Colombian rhythms. Worldwide, maracas are often played at parties, celebrations and special events. Even rock and pop musicians have adopted the maraca, including Bo Diddley, Mick Jagger, and Bez from the Happy Mondays. The music of Los Llanos, *música llanera*, has maracas at its heart, accompanied by a harp and *cuatro* (a sort of four-stringed guitar).

Los Llanos AROUND VILLAVICENCIO

5

THE ROAD TO FINCA POTREOCHICO The road east towards Finca Potreochico near Paratebueno cuts through 65km of lush green fields, passing more local restaurants and cattle-breeding territories, vets, feed stores and farmers outlets. Fruit stalls dot grass verges scattered with maroon-coloured *fincas* on roadsides heavy with vegetation dominated by the *morishes* palm – a clear sign that water is close by.

Between Villavicencio and Pompeya, look out for landmark pineapple stall 'Papa Quiero Piña' – meaning 'Daddy, I want a pineapple' – a place dedicated to stocking the finest pineapple around. That the owner stole the name from a fellow trader in Córdoba in western Colombia doesn't seem to matter – if you've time, be sure to pull in to taste the sweetest, juiciest *piña* in town.

Pompeya (*Telephone code 8*) This small town 25km from Villavicencio hugs a 2km stretch of main road with a couple of simple *hospedajes*, a small supermarket, a petrol station, burger bar and a handful of drink kiosks as well as the inevitable half-dozen places selling '*minuto cellular*'. A favourite stop-off with heavyweight trucks journeying back and forth across the Venezuelan border, at the end of town soaring gas exploration towers and a radiating glow of an aerated diffusion flame can clearly be sighted.

Alcaravan (*Telephone code 8*) There are more power plants, drilling sites and energy companies at this tiny town 2km from Pompeya – a prime site of major US oil giant Harken Energy Corp. Harken Energy holds the largest net exploration acreage position in Colombia and is a driving force behind many of its so-called mega-projects. Beyond a thick-forested area lies one of the region's most important industrial shipping hubs, Puerta Porfía, a prime transit point for oil, and an industrial plant that is almost completely obscured from view. Harken Energy boasts the distinction of having former US president George W Bush as a director – a relationship not without scandal. During a high-profile crackdown on corporate fraud, Bush's own financial dealings came under scrutiny. This centred on his decision to sell 212,140 shares for US$848,000 just before the company announced a US$23.2 million loss, causing the share price to drop to US$2.375 from US$3. The next day, Harken returned to US$3, but fell to US$1 at the end of 1990. A flagrant breach of disclosure laws was cited as grounds for prosecution by many of Bush's harshest critics. Bush supporters say that he did fully disclose the transaction, and that 'half of corporate America was filing forms late at that time'. An irritated Bush himself said, 'There was an honest difference of opinion as to how to account for a complicated transaction. Sometimes the rules aren't as specific as one would expect, and therefore the accountants and the auditors make a decision.'

FINCA POTREOCHICO (*Telephone code 8*) The town of Paratebueno is actually 18 minutes from Finca Potreochico (m *310 325 0060*; e *cauchoparr@yahoo.es*), travelling northwest from Villavicencio. A frequent bus service connects Villavicencio with Potreochico where it is possible to get a taxi to the *finca*; just tell the driver you're staying with Rodrigo Echeverri. The *finca* sits at the end of a long unmade off-road track that leads to the owner's sprawling 260km² farmland where Echeverri has lived since childhood after his father left Bogotá for an alternative to city life. Today, his vast farm encompasses pasture, crops, cattle herds and jungle and enjoys a beautifully remote location in the heart of the countryside. Witty, charming and erudite, Echeverri is an engaging host who is enthusiastic about nature and adventure sports – especially cycling. His extraordinary stamina, skill and agility would put most men half his age to shame and he is a valuable source of local knowledge, tips

A DEVIL OF A PLACE

Ancient legend has it that the local children once swam in the river when the devil came to visit in human form. Over several weeks, he played with the youngsters and began to plot their demise, before being rumbled by the local priest. He exorcised the devil who was furious at the intervention and in an enraged state he decided to flood the river to wipe out the entire village. However, he'd been weakened by the exorcism and could only manage to create a crater – not the huge tidal wave he'd intended. This left Medina and its inhabitants unharmed 5km away. Today El Cañón del Diablo (Devil's Canyon) serves as a reminder of the villagers' good fortune and the triumph of good over evil.

and advice. His tours are highly popular with adventurous types, mainly Europeans. Echeverri prefers individuals and small groups and is basically up for anything, from madcap downhill mountain-bike rides to rappelling, rafting, caving and hiking. He likes nothing more than multi-day trips involving a bike, a boat and a tent, and advises guests to pack plenty of stamina – especially if they agree to do the eight-day 1,000km trip to the Río Orinoco. He operates under the name Wuajari Adventure Tours – and with Rodrigo Echeverri 'adventure' is just what you get.

On the farm itself, guests can horseride, cycle and hike across rubber plantations and through forests full of monkeys and grasslands with excellent birdwatching, fishing and numerous thermal springs. Echeverri embraces a management practice that involves educating locals in sustainable farming. He raises cows purely for organic fertilisers for the rubber plants and palm oil crops. He also promotes farming with great ecological focus over profit. White-water rafting is another of his passions on the Río Humea, Río Gasanta and Río Gasamumu.

Overnight accommodation is convivial with open-air lounges overlooking flower-filled trees and a lovely swimming pool – although guests should prepare themselves for plenty of wildlife. Frogs the size of sugar sacks hop around your feet. Farm rats scuttle along the rafters. Howls, shrieks, cries and yowls dominate the night air. Rooms are pretty basic but there's an outdoor shower in a space pod – yes, a space pod. Let's just say this bubblegum-coloured *finca* is truly unique.

An overnight stay at Finca Potreochico costs 120,000COP per person including breakfast, lunch and dinner – and the food is truly sublime.

MEDINA This small town 95km from Villavicencio was located elsewhere 50 years ago. After yellow fever almost wiped the whole population out the remaining half-dozen inhabitants relocated 10km to the north. Today, the 'new Medina' is a pleasant farming town of dusty muralled whitewashed walls and a good stock of shops for essentials, including a few small supermarkets, a hardware stall, a drugstore, bakery and grocers.

If you find yourself parched in Medina, be sure to pop into Los Centaurus, a pocket-sized beer-and-soda joint in the centre of town. It boasts the distinction of selling broom handles, root vegetables, bits of hardware and breakfast cereals at a makeshift counter. Choose from one of five plastic red chairs by a fully stocked candy rack and expect lots of loud *música típica*. At dusk this place is frequented by cigar-smoking, moustached *campesinos* in ponchos who drink quietly, with purpose, until they drop.

A rough unmade track leads out of the centre of town up to a place the locals call El Cañón del Diablo (Devil's Canyon) on account of an old local legend. Don't

They always put social experiments in the easiest, most fertile places. We wanted the hardest place. We figured if we could do it here, we could do it anywhere.

Gaviotas founder Paolo Lugari, 1976

Although it is rumoured to be totally impossible to find, Gaviotas (e *gaviotas@lists.greenbuilder.com; www.friendsofgaviotas.org*) – a small village of around 200 people – is one of the most unique communities on the planet. Set in the Vichada province in eastern Los Llanos, the settlement has redefined sustainability, developing revolutionary designs for power-collecting windmills and creating ground-breaking solar heating systems. Even their hospital has been hailed as 'one of the most important buildings on earth' by the *Japanese Architectural Journal*. This is no ordinary village – far from it.

In the late 1960s, Paolo Lugari encouraged a group of like-minded environmental engineers, scientists and researchers to join him in realising a vision of Colombian self-sustaining community. They arrived in Gaviotas and immediately began work, creating a reliable water supply in the inhospitable climate of Los Llanos, eventually designing a unique deep-soil water pump attached to a children's see-saw. The Gaviotan team also produced a sunflower-shaped windmill so effective that it is now found all over Colombia, thanks to their policy of not patenting their designs in order to ensure they are free to the world at large. The community's 16-bed hospital building is an elevated maze of glass skylights, steel columns and solar panels with an air-conditioning system that blends ancient wind ventilation techniques with modern technology. Although the hospital was closed by a shift in government policy, the building now provides a sterile environment for a new water- and tropical fruit juice-bottling operation. This fresh drinking water has reduced gastro-intestinal ailments and R&D staff have also designed a unique water bottle that children can assemble like Lego blocks. If the Gaviotan team have their way, an adjacent greenhouse looks set to contain one of the finest medicinal plant laboratories in the tropics. Even so-called failures have spawned ideas for future successes.

Other noteworthy achievements include the reforestation of the Orientales Llanos – a replenishment project that began in 1984 with the planting of hardy Caribbean pines in an area that had been barren for centuries. At the last count, Gaviotas has planted 8,000ha of Caribbean pines, creating a 10% rise in the area's precipitation. The resin produced has been harvested for conversion to colofonia, which in turn has been sold for use in a range of products, such as cosmetics and household paints. More than 325ha of palm trees have also been planted for oil to make bio diesel, enabling Gaviotas to be entirely fossil fuel-free since 2004. Methane from cow dung provides fuel for kitchen appliances with solar pressure cookers used for most of the cooking. They farm organically and every family in the community enjoys free housing, community meals and schooling. Unlike most Colombian towns Gaviotas has no weapons, no police force and no jail – there isn't even a mayor.

Gunter Pauli, head of Zero Emissions Research and Initiatives (ZERI) has cited Las Gaviotas as the world's premier example of sustainable development. The United Nations named the village a model for similar projects. Gabriel García Márquez has called Paolo Lugari 'the inventor of the world'.

The Llaneros are renowned throughout Colombia for their myths, legends and folkloric beliefs. Many remain intertwined with modern life in the plains and a powerful force within the local community, governing many unspoken social rules.

BOLA DE FUEGO (BALL OF FIRE) Many Llaneros report seeing balls of fire in the summer sun. Some, reportedly, have been of such ferocity that the balls have chased them into their homes. The locals believe that many balls of fire are successful in catching their victims and burning them and their homes to the ground. Llaneros view a small fireball as being close to them – and therefore presenting greatest danger. A fireball that looks large is far away and less of a threat. So what should you do if the fireball gets too close to you? Swear, apparently. Spilling your bad words and verbal poison will stop the fireball from burning you – but if the ball is tiny, you'd better be quick!

GENTE SIN CABEZA (HEADLESS HORSEBACK RIDER) According to local legend, the headless horseback rider only appears when the Llaneros gather together at night. Wearing black clothing and wielding a razor-sharp machete, the horseman tries to attack the locals. The Llaneros believe that if they get caught they will be decapitated in an act of revenge. This belief stems from Colombia's bloody La Violencia era in the 1950s when enemies would kill each other in their sleep with machetes – the ultimate cowardly act.

LEYENDA DEL DIABLO (DEVIL'S LEGEND) Llaneros believe that a man walking through the trees at night is exposed to the wrath of the devil. He appears, peering down from the leaves in the form of a witch. What does he want? The victim's soul in return for untold riches and all the women in the world. He can be highly persuasive, especially if the man has partaken of *aguardiente*.

be tempted to do this drive in anything other than a 4x4 as this craterous route is appalling. However at 5km another option is to tackle it on foot. Pass some big hibiscus shrubs past remnants of the old dry-stone walls favoured by the villagers centuries ago. At the top of a steady, sloping climb, the track turns to grass running between two fenced-off paddocks. Carry on until the end and walk 200m to a gap in a barbed-wire fence (don't worry, this is an 'official' cut through). Walk about 100m northeast towards an obvious drop – you can't miss it, it's vast.

PACHAQUIARO This 6km pit-stop stretch of rustic restaurants and small supermarkets is edged by expansive rice paddies. Pass by at dawn or dusk to spot feeding waterbirds in the low-lying sodden fields beyond. Pachaquiaro is blessed by a good paved single carriageway free from billboards. A spare scattering of trees enables great views across open fields over fragile wood-and-wire fencing.

LA BALSA One good reason to stop at this small horse-farm town is its excellent smoked meat. Set your milometer for 70km from Villavicencio and look out for private residential homes with fresh cuts hanging from the porch. Other than that, La Balsa has a few basic shops selling essentials, and a couple of cold-drink vendors. On a nice day, the views out to stud farms and cattle fields makes this a pleasant place to get out of the car and stretch your legs, with slender white ponies and herds of chocolate-brown cows.

PUERTO LÓPEZ Best described as a medium-sized small town, this modest portside settlement on the Río Meta is around 99km east of Villavicencio. Crossing the wide, sluggish coffee-coloured Río Meta allows colourful views of rusting cargo boats, tethered horses, cattle carriers and hulking oil tankers with agriculture and cattle ranching the town's prime industries. Travellers passing through will find Puerto López's restaurants well worth trying. Head for the roundabout in the centre of town to discover **Restaurante Tamanaco** (✆ *645 0630;* $$) – a first-class grill renowned for generous portions of good food. Other good options include the diner at the **Hotel la Prima** ($$) and the **Restaurante Mi Caseta** ($$) as well as the more basic **Asadero de la Mancheo** ($). Passers-by in a rush will also find plenty of places to eat on the hoof, including numerous fried-chicken joints, fish-

---

A COWBOY'S TALE

Llanero cowboy Luis Abetardo Nieve is a former *coleo* (cow roping) champion. He was just a small boy when he first started working with horses and cattle. Today, in his late 30s, cattle and horses are his life:

I started to help out with shoeing horses at the age of seven and soon learned the daily rhythm of work on the ranch. Today, I work full-time with cows and horses wearing the customary jeans, boots and a *sombrero llanero* (palm-woven cowboy hat) with a serrated knife in a holster on my hip (*cuchillo*). Horses mean a lot to me – they represent me as a Llanero. I am a man of the plains, so horses are my identity as well as my life. Today, I get up each day at 05.00 to milk the cows – a herd of cebú and criollo species. Another good Los Llanos working breed is pardo suito. Once this is done it is time to dedicate some time to the horses, so I get them ready to take out to graze on the grasslands after I have mucked out the stables.

After a quick lunch at home at 11.00 I train the new horses. I work with criollo as this breed is intelligent and good for speed. Other species in Los Llanos are more about brawn, not brains. First I use a rope and lasso to dominate the animal so that it eventually submits to being saddled. I use a stick-and-robe tool called a *muñeco* (meaning 'doll') and keep the horse still using rope ties. After about three days the horse loses its fear and accepts the saddle – and at that point it is ridden for the first time. Tied to the doll, I get the horse circling first anti-clockwise and then clockwise. At this point I start training a second horse as it is important to keep the momentum going. After another three days the horse is comfortable with being ridden and is six days into its training. Next, I teach the horse *quebrada* – how to move right and left. Also how to move at different speeds, from a trot and a gallop to a stop. Once the horse is happy with this instruction I attach the reins (*rienda*). Initially this is a double rein for strength but as the horse relaxes I remove the spare.

Once my work with the horses is finished, I return to the cows. I leave many of them out grazing overnight – after all, the more grass they eat the better the milk. However, I do bring the calves in by rounding them up on horseback and herding them back to the stalls. After the cows are settled I wash down the horses. At about 17.00 my day is done and I can think about going home. To relax, I practise *coleo*, or cow tailing – a horseback cattle-roping challenge when my skills are pitched against a strong wild herd. Every week there's a bull-roping festival somewhere in Los Llanos with an annual international fair in Villavicencio each year. This annual event attracts dozens of competitors from ten countries and is an incredible event that truly sets my blood pumping.

They chug along looking like crumbled milk-bottle tops on wheels but the Russian-built VAZ is the beloved vehicle of the Los Llanos campesino. A VAZ (the acronym of Volzhsky Automobilny Zavod) is better known to the rest of the world as a Lada but in Colombia the first model was a 1970 VAZ-2101. The VAZ factory is one of the biggest in the world with over 90 miles (144km) of production lines and is unique in that most of the components for the cars are made in-house. In Colombia, the original VAZ vehicle – a 'rugged' jalopy lacking in any comfort or luxury – is perfect for harsh terrain. In Los Llanos these workhorses of the road are dented, bruised and battle-scarred. Most lean markedly to the right because of long-term excessive overloading: cargo of cattle feed, straw bales, sacks of grain and boxes of potatoes teetering precariously under a spaghetti of bungee cords, and spewing black fumes out in clouds under great duress.

and-rice street stalls and snack kiosks. A few kilometres further along the road is Colombia's geographical heart – a mustard-coloured 100ft totem pole-like structure on a paved ledge of high land, the **Alto de Menegua**. A semi-permanent small market comprises vendors of woven bags, baskets, jewellery and carvings as well as some basic snack and drink options. Nearby, one of the nicest resorts in Los Llanos makes an excellent base from which to explore the region – the Lagos de Menegua Hotel & Resort not only benefits from breathtaking natural surroundings but is also spotlessly clean and an easy place to be based, especially off-peak. A programme of road improvement works has transformed the journey from Puerto López for 33km east. It has taken an army of manual labourers several years to complete sections of the 150km of paved road here – and parts still remain incomplete.

Where to stay and eat

Lagos de Menegua Hotel & Resort
(24 rooms) m 315 326 6070/645 0013/0193; e informacion@menegua.com; www. lagosdemenegua.com. This hotel has crisp, clean rooms with a bright-white, zen-like décor. Although the place has plenty of modern resort trappings these play second fiddle to the setting, an incredible 100ha spectacular of lakes, peaks, hills & rivers. Don't be fooled by the subdued plains immediately around the resort; greater magic lies beyond. Rounded hillocks form a rippling landscape of numerous shades of green that roll down to scrubby grasslands, which millions of years ago once lay underwater. Coralline rocks & fossils can still be spotted amongst the scrub. Modest plateaus are dotted with dense, small wooded thickets close to forests of skinny palms. Expect to see lone hawks soaring above the savannahs & to hear a cacophony of crickets at dawn & dusk. Lagos de Menegua is renowned for its truly awesome sunsets & sunrises, when the sky moves from tangerine to powder pink then baby blue & violet to inky midnight blue.

Tours at the resort range from gentle walks to full-on adventure hikes with birding, kayaking & horseriding. A loop of hiking trails overlooks large resplendent lakes & although camping isn't strictly on the menu, it can sometimes be accommodated in individual circumstances (although you'll need to demonstrate a responsible eco ethos). Standard accommodation can house 2–8 people & comprises white walls, white ceilings, white stone, terracotta floors, wooden beams, white linen, white drapes & white bedding. Rooms are equipped with towels, TV, minibar/fridge & AC. Showers are cold water but are big, clean & efficient. Communal amenities include an outdoor swimming pool, covered pagoda-style dining area, pool bar, ice-cream parlour, games room & large patio terrace. Guests can also use the internet although there are no telephones in the rooms. **$$**

Caño Cristales, a river sometimes described as a liquid rainbow and '*el rio mas bonito del mundo*' (the most beautiful river in the world), is a phenomenon of nature, otherworldly and breathtaking. It is located in the Llanos just a 75-minute flight almost directly due south of Bogotá. During his 2014 trip to Colombia, Prince Charles visited Caño Cristales and witnessed the blossoming of the telltale burgundy-and-red *Macarenia clavígera* plants found just beneath the water level. Until recently the river was off-limits to the public and was known to only a select few, although with increased security in the region, trips are becoming the norm. Perhaps what is most rewarding about the type of tourism being promoted here is that it is designed to benefit the local townspeople and you'll find that your obligatory guide is from the region, probably used to work as a *raspachin* (coca leaf picker), and is knowledgeable and enthusiastic. Visitor numbers have been steadily increasing, albeit restricted to one very high season when the river is in bloom and then dropping off completely outside of this period. As yet there are no real restrictions on travel here at the moment and this is something that needs to change to protect the park and the delicate ecosystem. But, for the moment the Macarenenses (as people from La Macarena are called) are more than content with this new industry.

CAÑO CRISTALES: WHAT YOU NEED TO KNOW You can fly all the way into the town of La Macarena from Bogotá with **Satena** (*www.satena.com*), saving you the journey from Villavicencio, or you can head down to the departmental capital and catch charter flights to La Macarena from there. The company **Aero Star** runs this route (✆ *664 8343*) and you can expect to pay in the region of 450,000COP for this short flight. Remember that you cannot bring luggage weighing above 15kg on these flights.

- The best time of year to visit is from June to November when the *Macarenia clavígera* is in full bloom.
- The park is incredibly secure with a very large presence of Colombian military all around.
- You do need yellow fever and tetanus vaccinations.
- If you plan on swimming in the designated swimming areas you are not permitted to use suncream due to its damaging effect on this fragile ecosystem.
- Given that the average year-round temperature is 30–35°C, dress appropriately for bugs, sun and hiking.
- Keep well hydrated as you would in any equatorial situation.

ADVICE FOR PHOTOGRAPHERS This river, El Río de Los Cinco Colores, is well known to photographers through Andrés Hurtado Garcia's famed images. If you've not seen them, search for them online.

- Photographing the river depends entirely on the weather. If the sun is not shining and the reflection is not going your way, be prepared to wait for that perfect shot.
- Check the weather forecast in the lead up to your visit. If it has been too dry water levels on the river fall, burning the plant life and altering its colour from

vivid red to a more subdued brown. Fortunately, the colours will return within a couple of days of rainfall, which allows new growth on plants.

* You are photographing a river and there's a great deal of reflection. Do not leave that tripod behind on a whim and pack those polarising filters. There are photography courses that take in Caño Cristales as a workshop now and this would be a fine option for those wishing to see a true marvel and learn more about photography at the same time. Tours can be booked through www.cano-cristales.com.

WHAT ELSE IS THERE TO DO? Aside from the obvious: amazing hikes, photographing this glorious river, bathing in the naturally formed pools carved out of the Guyanese shield over millennia, there is plenty more to see and do over a few days in the town of La Macarena.

* There are more than 400 species of bird in the *sierra* here.
* If you are lucky you'll spot primates and pink river dolphins on the trip along the Guayabero River.
* Enjoy traditional Llanero hospitality, complete with *joropo* dancing and delicious *carne a la llanera*.
* Take a charter flight in a two-seater plane over Caño Cristales for a bird's-eye view.
* Learn about Colombia's contemporary history when this part of the country made up part of the FARC demilitarised zone between 1998 and 2002.
* The preferred form of unwinding and passing time in La Macarena is to head to any one of a dozen pool halls in town.

The locally run **tourism agency** can be found at Calle 5, No 7–35, La Macarena (m *321 842 2728;* e *info@cano-cristales.com; www.cano-cristales.com*).

WHERE TO STAY There are six decent hotels in La Macarena; nothing luxury, but all comfortable and clean. Reservations are generally made through the information centre located in the airport or travel agencies such as De Una Colombia, The Colombian Way and Colombia Occulta.

Casa Hotel Real (45 rooms) Carrera 9, No 4–104 –110 Barrio el Centro, Frente al Parque Principal; m 313 292 9925; e casahotelreal@gmail.com. You are out in the wilds here in the town of La Macarena but the hotels on offer are clean, organised & secure. All rooms have TVs & en-suite bathrooms. **$$**

Hotel Mariana M (7 rooms) Calle 4, No 7–14–35 Barrio El Centro; m 313 8407658; e marianix0310@gmail.com. Another centrally located option, all the rooms are set on the ground floor & have TVs & en-suite bathrooms. **$$**

PRACTICALITIES Remember that the town of La Macarena is not on the national electrical grid and the power runs here from a large generator. The power is shut off at a certain time in the evening but most, if not all hotels, have their own independent generators.

Ask a Llanero what the distance is between one town and another and he'll rarely answer in kilometres or miles, for in Los Llanos the cigar-smoking moustached travelling cowboy measures distances in so-called 'tobacco miles' (*'millas de tabaco'*). This unique and unconventional measuring stick relates directly to the time it takes to finish a smoke. So, a 2km journey (at 20 minutes) is a 'one tobacco' trip while a 'six tobacco' slog would be a 2-hour trek requiring half a packet of Colombia's finest thigh-rolled – at least.

RÍO MANÁCACIAS This pleasant waterfront setting is a favourite with fishermen but is largely undiscovered by tourists at a 2-hour trip (108km) from Puerto López. Yet those prepared to explore the river will find plenty of boatmen ready to make it happen. Expect to pay about 20,000COP for a half-hour journey to the point where the Río Manácacias joins the Río Meta and Río Yucao. Pink river (boto) dolphins can be easily sighted here with plenty of places to picnic and chill out along the way.

YOPAL With only 150,000 inhabitants, the departmental capital of the Casanare, Yopal gives the feeling of a frontier town … because it is. Don't let this deter you as the Casanare department is coming into its own as an ecotourism destination for people interested in the natural environment, the ethnic tribes here and the beautiful and pristine vistas on offer. The surroundings of Yopal have an abundance of hiking trails, from dense jungles, to typical Llano plains with rich wildlife watering holes, to foothills of the Andean mountains with their wild rivers and waterfalls. This off-the-beaten-track destination is Colombian nature at its best. And if you needed any more impetus to come here, there are more than 400 species of bird that are permanent residents of Casanare. The town has a central park with cafés, juice stands and a big farmer's market with all the fruit you can imagine. Should you find yourself in the city for more than a few hours, check out the local-history museum and the statue of the **Virgin of Manare**, overlooking the city, where the locals go for their evening or morning pilgrimage. For the less religious, the hike up rewards with views across Yopal and Los Llanos (it's a bit like Yopal's version of Bogotá's Monserrate Mountain). On the way up are a bar and a restaurant, both with amazing views, especially at sunset.

Yopal's real attractions are culture and nature. The city has a range of fairs and festivals all year round featuring traditional *joropo* dancing, *música llanera* and *coleo* (cow-roping) but December is the ultimate festival month with the Feria Ganadera y Equina (livestock and equine fair) and Cimarron de Oro (music festival).

The area's natural attractions include the many natural pools in the rivers surrounding the city. The best known and most easily reached is Aguatoca and another called La Calaboza has a beautiful waterfall. A third, El Garcero, are so called due to the prevalence of hundreds of 'garzas' (white herons) that arrive to this copse in the early evening hours: it is a spectacle best watched from the bar/restaurant opposite. Aventur Eco Tours (see below) can organise hikes to all three pools.

Tour operator For reliable information, guiding in English, German and Spanish, look no further than **Aventur Eco Tours** (*aventurecotours.com*). Run by local Andrés and his German wife Julia, they offer guided bike rides, horseriding trips and hikes through the lesser-known areas of the region. The terrain is diverse, from dry prairie, to lush fields with waterholes, to tropical forests and streams. It's not uncommon to spot groups of monkeys, eagles, turtles, giant anteaters (*oso palmero*), foxes, alligators, anacondas, wild pigs and deer, as well as a huge array of birds.

Where to stay and eat You'll find plenty of options in Yopal but below are a few recommended places.

GHL Hoteles (58 rooms) Calle 29, No 28–14; ⊠634 5999; e reservas.yopal@ghlhoteles. com; www.ghlhoteles.com. Although part of a chain, the GHL is new & has been thoughtfully decorated with photos of Llano wildlife on each floor. Expect an airy, Swedish-style design with modern comforts. **$$$**

El Camoruco (30 rooms) Carrera 22, No 8–43; ⊠635 8046; www.hotelcamoruco.com. Yopal's most traditional hotel, very centrally located with a beautiful green patio, pool, gym & Turkish bath. **$$**

Finca Hotel Salem (Multiple rooms of 4, 6 & 8 people) Km2, Vrda Buena Vista baja; m 312 435 0467; e f.hotelsalem@gmail.com; www.fincahotelsalemyopal.com. Located in the countryside just outside Yopal on a hill with a lovely view. Owner Pascual calls his establishment a '*casa de paz*'. It's an oasis with a pool & lots of tropical green. They have *cabañas*, dorms/family rooms, double rooms – the whole range. **$$**

6

San Andrés Archipelago

Telephone code 8

San Andrés, how beautiful you are. San Andrés, how beautiful –
it is a privileged place where God put his hand; a privileged place.

Francisco Zumaque, 'San Andrés', *1991*

Colombia's only oceanic department – the West Indies department – is one of
the most isolated island regions in the Americas, located 800km northeast of the
Colombian mainland, just 150km from the Nicaraguan coast. Laid-back locals
pride themselves on being barefoot champions of leisure in a calypso culture that
is a world away from fast-paced Bogotá. Warm Caribbean waters are home to a
cluster of palm-scattered atolls, islets and cays in an archipelago where 300,000km²
forms the main constituent of a UNESCO Seaflower Biosphere Reserve (Reserva de
la Biosfera Seaflower). Fertile waters, grass beds and mangrove-clad lagoons host a

CONSERVATION EFFORTS

Although the combined landmass of the islands of the San Andrés Archipelago totals
less than 60km², the marine area is expansive and delicate. Declared a Protected
Marine Conservation Area as part of the Man and the Biosphere (MAB) programme
in November 2000, the reserve is recognised by the UN for its extraordinary
coastal ecosystems. With UN help, local projects are attempting to reconcile the
conservation of the biodiversity of the San Andrés islands with its sustainable use.
Trademark pristine sparkling waters and pastel-coloured underwater gardens have
survived threats of pollution and over fishing, thanks to the widespread efforts of
conservationists. Sedimentation and litter once saw the health of the coral reef
spiral into decline as the marine resources of the archipelago suffered at the hands
of industrial fishing vessels and poachers from the Colombian mainland, Central
America and many Caribbean nations. A ramshackle collection of shanty towns
became a prime source of coastal pollution due to inadequate sanitation, while
rising levels of tourism threw the islands into a waste management crisis.

Today, the picture-postcard islands of San Andrés, Providencia and Santa Catalina,
Bolívar Albuquerque and Cotton Haynes islets, Alicia and Bajo Nuevo sandbanks,
and Grunt Johnny Rose, Easy Cay, Roncador, Serena, Serranilla, Quitasueño, Brothers,
Rocky, Crab and Santander cays, are reaping the rewards of a decade-long forceful
ecological drive that has worked hard to promote the crucial linkages between the
biological systems of the islands – terrestrial, coastal and marine – with a healthy
social system. In support, the Colombian government has created a new officially
sanctioned and funded agency, **CORALINA** (Vía *San Luis;* 512 0080; *www.coralina.
gov.co).* Before CORALINA, native islanders played no part in the decision-making
process in environmental matters relating to the archipelago. CORALINA is charged
with a number of ecological responsibilities, including the preservation of the

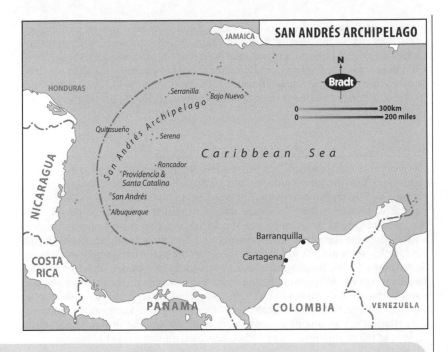

archipelago's fragile coastal and marine ecosystems. Article 37 of the 1993 Law 99 defines the responsibilities of CORALINA as including the safeguarding of the islands' resources in a way that 'promotes economic growth and improvements in the quality of life and social wellbeing, without depleting reserves of sustaining natural resources or damaging the environment, and preserving the right of the future generations to use and enjoy these resources'. Municipal tax revenues continue to fund a number of CORALINA environmental and community projects, striking a delicate balance between socio-economic pressures and the preservation of native trees, mangrove forests and other natural habitats. Achieving this equilibrium remains a challenge to the archipelago, where flower-filled marshlands and salty coralline outcrops attract large numbers of migrant birds. Improved sanitation and refuge systems have ensured the translucent waters around these remote oceanic castaway islands remain home to some of the western hemisphere's most highly productive coral reefs.

However, human activities remain poorly managed and a key cause for concern. Sand stolen from beaches on the South Island in the 1950s left it seriously depleted, a resplendent strip called Baby Beach now a tiny reminder of how idyllic it once looked. More than 100 tonnes of refuse is produced on San Andrés Island each day with an unmet escalating demand for water. Despite an annual average rainfall of 1,800mm the islanders suffer from severe drought. Studies by CORALINA have revealed that 70% of groundwater is polluted. Saline intrusion from over extraction and rising sea levels also pose a serious threat with rainwater collection on the island well below its potential. CORALINA's presence has undoubtedly furthered the archipelago's environmental goals. It has also brought this remote territory closer to the government administration in Bogotá, where the ecological needs of a group of islands many thousands of miles away are all too easily overlooked.

San Andrés Archipelago

6

magnificent array of bird species with isolated soft-sand beaches and undisturbed coral reefs rich in underwater flora and fauna. Three inhabited islands form the archipelago's geographical and spiritual heart, as immortalised in the lyrics of Colombian musician Francisco Zumaque's catchy chart-topper 'San Andrés'. Around them lie five uninhabited atolls to the north and two to the south with a liberal scattering of sandbanks and cays in between, including the submerged islet of Alicia Shoal.

HISTORY

For a petite cluster of islands, the San Andrés Archipelago has a colourful history, steeped in tales of pirate plunder and glory-seeking conquistadors. Although claimed by English Puritans in 1627, it was first discovered by Dutch colonisers at least three decades earlier. They were also often visited by Mosquito people from the coast of Central America to trap sea turtles and collect bird eggs and guano. Unsubstantiated claims that Christopher Columbus discovered the islands during his fourth voyage in 1502 add another theory to the pot. After quickly establishing San Andrés Island, the English chose Providencia as a preferred settlement for its advantageous lofty position and freshwater supplies. Slaves were shipped from Barbados and Jamaica to cultivate cotton and tobacco in 1633. Before long, Providencia became a pivotal centre for slave trading and a strategic hiding place for seafaring rogues touting contraband and pirates seeking shelter. The Spanish, furious at the prosperity of the English, launched an unsuccessful invasion of the island in 1635.

From 1670 to 1689, legendary buccaneer **Henry Morgan** established a base in Providencia from where he raided both Panama and Santa Marta. He is also reputed to have sacked Spanish galleons laden with gold, angering Spain and prompting another unsuccessful attack. According to local legend, Morgan buried his treasure on the island during such an invasion where it remains undiscovered to this day.

The battle for control of the islands continued for over a century with England and Spain equally determined to conquer. In 1793, the signing of the Versailles Treaty recognised Spain's sovereignty over the archipelago, yet the Spanish had already begun to lose interest in the islands. Groups of former slaves soon established communities in the archipelago, fusing cultural influences of their English 'masters' with the traditions of their African homelands. After independence from Spain in 1810, Colombia laid claim to the islands, a move fiercely contested by Nicaragua just 150km away. Colombia occupied the islands in 1822, although the United Province of Central America (a federation that comprised the states of Guatemala, El Salvador, Honduras, Nicaragua and Costa Rica) did not recognise this as legal and claimed ownership for itself. In turn, Colombia disputed the UPCA's occupation of the eastern coast of modern-day Nicaragua. After a civil war dissolved the federation, the resulting state of Nicaragua continued the dispute along with the Republic of New Granada (modern Colombia and Panama) that emerged from the collapse of Gran Colombia. In 1928, the signing of the **Esguerra–Bárcenas Treaty** between both governments resolved the dispute temporarily in favour of Colombia. However, when the Sandinista government assumed power in Nicaragua in 1980, the treaty was renounced – and the archipelago's ownership has been contested ever since. In 2012, a tribunal, made up of judges picked by the UN Security Council, decided to grant Nicaragua around 60% of the disputed area of the Caribbean that had been previously administered by Colombia, jeopardising the future of fishermen from the Colombian island of San Andrés, but granting new opportunities to Nicaraguan fishermen. The area in question measures more or less 200km wide by 450km long.

Until 1953, the archipelago was virtually ignored by the rest of the world. However, once the Colombian government designated San Andrés and Providencia as a Free Trade Zone, flights to the island brought an appetite for commercialism to the archipelago. It also encouraged immigration from other parts of Colombia

LOS RAIZALES (ROOTS PEOPLE)

When the Colombian government prompted a large influx of migrants to head to the San Andrés Archipelago from the mainland it had just one goal: to create a self-financing region without costly reliance on the capital. It paid little heed to the cultural concerns of a small, native population and failed to anticipate the dramatic effects of the marginalisation of the Raizal people. Following General Rojas Pinilla's declaration in 1953 that made the archipelago a free port, changes to the region's make-up were marked. The population began to swell, the new Duty Free Zone prospered and the island became linked to the mainland via frequent flights. However, by the 1970s, native islanders began to complain of a lost identity. They also protested against discrimination and grew fearful over their increasingly marginalised status. Insularity, they argued, may have had its economic problems but it was a crucial tool in preserving their ethnicity, grounded in food, architecture, literature, oral traditions, music, religion, art and language.

By the 1980s, the cultural and linguistic characteristics of the native islanders were seriously under threat from Spanish-speaking dominance. In 1995, the government of Colombia began to take steps to preserve, restore and protect the rights and way of life of the Raizal people and other indigenous peoples living in the country. In 1952, there were just 5,675 inhabitants in San Andrés, a number that 12 years later in 1964 had more than trebled to 16,731. In 1973, their population totalled 22,989. By 1988, it had almost doubled to 42,315. Today, the archipelago's indigenous population remains a minority at 25,000 people compared with 75,000 mainlanders, a significant demographic adjustment that has eroded many traditional ways of island life. Since the late 1990s, new human rights legislation has been enacted and institutional support for indigenous communities encouraged. The region has also been designated as an official department within the Colombian administration with a governor appointed from the Raizal population. Each of these measures has helped foster a better understanding of the importance of Raizal identity to the community's social web. However, despite strict government measures to limit migration to the islands, the issue regarding the diminished influence of Raizal culture remains one of contention.

In November 2004, the Raizal people marched the streets of San Andrés Island in a peaceful Prayer-Walk in support of their human rights led by Pastor Raymond Howard. From Mount Zion Baptist Church in Perry Hill the Raizales crossed the island, singing hymns of praise along the way. Howard carried a large Moses-style walking stick as he led a crowd of men, women and children, with many elders over 80 years of age. This peaceful protest by the Raizal community passed without incident, unlike a 2002 rally when heavy-handed Colombian troops fired tear gas into the crowd.

to the underdeveloped region, boosting economic activity through tourism and transforming the archipelago into a net contributor, rather than a drain on the government purse. However, this population explosion has done much to dilute traditional Raizal lifestyle, culture and language (see box, page 221), something that island-wide community initiatives are striving to correct. In 1993, the Christian University of San Andrés was founded by a coalition of Baptist congregations from the archipelago to spearhead the economic, cultural, political and environmental future of the islands from a community standpoint. The United Nations Development Program (UNDP) is also involving racial, social and religious projects with the island Raizal population. Politics in this small archipelago remains a hot topic.

PEOPLE

The culture of the San Andrés Archipelago is intimately linked to its people, who have diverse ethnic origins. Islanders form three main groups: the Raizal people of African and British origin who speak Creole and English; the Continentals who preserve the Colombian culture and speak Spanish as their mother tongue; and foreign immigrants (mainly from Israel and Lebanon). The English/Creole-speakers refer to themselves as 'natives' or 'islanders' in clear distinction from residents who migrated from mainland Colombia. In the new Colombian constitution, the native islanders are referred to as 'Raizal' (singular) or 'Raizales' (plural). Today, the modern-day inhabitants of the San Andrés Archipelago reflect its turbulent history and the diverse mix of races and cultures that have settled on the islands over the centuries. Strong English influences abound with English still the primary language on Providencia and names such as Mr Green, Mr Smith and Mr Brown commonplace throughout island communities. Many are devout Baptists, attending church in their Sunday best each weekend. Parlour games, afternoon tea and dancing the foxtrot are other tell-tale legacies of the archipelago's ties to a bygone England. Very, very different from the rest of Colombian society in every sense, the islanders remain linguistically, socially and culturally unique – a distinction that is heightened by the remote isolation of the archipelago's geographic location.

LANGUAGE

The Colombian Constitution acknowledges English as the mother tongue of the native islanders. It also grants the archipelago two official languages – English and Spanish. The Raizal people speak a Creole-English patois quite unlike any other Caribbean islanders. This mesolectal, middle-class linguistic hybrid – called Bendé or Wendé – is a wholly unique English lexifer, distinctly different from that spoken on the Caribbean and Pacific coasts of Colombia. It is also completely unintelligible to other patois or Creole-speakers, despite its use of a language syntax derived in parts from African languages and similarity to Miskito Coastal Creole. Spanish-speakers are also utterly baffled by the languages of the San Andrés Archipelago, a place that feels very 'foreign' to visiting Colombian mainlanders, even though it is home soil. Confusingly, variants exist along with the choice of language. Creole tends to be spoken in the home and during social interaction in public places, while Spanish is often used for business and government matters. English is the language used in the many Protestant churches, with Spanish spoken in the archipelago's Catholic places of worship. On San Andrés there is a greater use of Creole-English in the south while in the north social chatter is usually conducted in Spanish – even by native islanders. On Providencia, Creole-English is spoken as a primary language pretty much everywhere.

Descubra y disfrute el estilo de vida de los nativos
(Explore and enjoy the lifestyle of the island natives)

ECONATIVE, 2006

Keen to learn more about island culture? Then check out the archipelago's excellent homestay programme. Posadas Nativas has about 30 participants – each an owner of a traditional wooden island home. Accommodation includes hearty meals shared with the family. Rates vary, but start at around 80,000COP per night. All participants are members of the Asociación de Posadas Nativas del Archipelago (Native Lodging Association) and ECONATIVE. Both organisations are dedicated to the promotion of island culture and traditions in conjunction with FUNDESAP (Foundation for Development of San Andrés and Providence), SENA (Small Business Development Corporation) and CORALINA (Corporation for Sustainable Development of the Archipelago of San Andrés, Providence and Santa Catalina). ECONATIVE is constantly attracting new participating islanders You can contact them (✆ *512 1155;* e *fundesap@sol.net.co*) for a full list of places to stay.

UNDERSTANDING THE NATIVE ISLANDERS

greetins to aal da peepl av di worl	greetings to all the people of the world
wi lov unu	with love to you
chaka chaka	messy, disorderly, untidy
no badda mi	don't bother me
bampa	grandfather
bama/bam-bam	grandmother
pa	father
ma	mother
taanti	aunt
con	cousin
eda	brother
ta/tita	sister

FAUNA AND FLORA

MARINE LIFE The warm, fertile Caribbean waters that surround the islands are rich in marine life, including plentiful supplies of queen conch, spiny lobster, black crab, long spined sea urchins, sea turtles and large numbers of fish. Fish and lobster larvae from the archipelago's vibrant reef systems are believed to travel as far as the Florida Keys, fulfilling a critical role in restoring depleted stocks there. Some 57 species of coral (including brain, fire, lace, black star and stony) have been identified in the archipelago, including at least 24 species of sponge and octacoral. The 273 recorded fish species include spotted drum, snapper, grouper (including the endangered goliath), indigo hamlet, bluehead, parrotfish, surgeonfish, snow bass, striped cardinal fish, tuna, yellow-cheeked basslet, bar jack, puffer, balloonfish, white hamlet, white spotted filefish, spotted scorpionfish and the winged flying gunard. Eels, octopus, dolphin, nurse shark and spotted eagle ray are also spotted frequently. Whales are not common to the San Andrés Archipelago although migrant species are occasionally sighted.

San Andrés Archipelago   FAUNA AND FLORA

6

For a group of small coral outcrops, the San Andrés Archipelago is home to a lot of birds, attracting large numbers of migratory species from its location in the westernmost Caribbean Sea. This natural stopover point on the Western Flyway ensures the archipelago welcomes species *en route* to land further south from North and Central America. Many of Colombia's 150-plus hummingbird species can be found in the San Andrés Archipelago, along with large numbers of Neotropical migrants such as gadwalls, willows, alders and flycatchers. Birders can also expect to spot yellow-throated vireos and Nashville, Tennessee and Canada warblers. Green-breasted mangos and ruby-throats are also found on the islands along with the bananaquit (a popular sight around the islands and called a 'wish-wish' by the locals), black-faced grassquit and an endemic species of black-whiskered vireo. Many species of hummers such as the colourful puffleg and dusky starfrontlet can be found flocked around a pink-flowered species of unnamed leguminous vine. The **San Andrés vireo** (*Vireo caribaeus*) is the archipelago's beloved endemic but endangered species. It serves as a poster-child for ongoing conservation efforts and is now restricted to an area of 17km², where it is threatened by encroaching urbanisation, agriculture and coconut cultivation. Colombia's ornithological action group, ProAves, a non-profit organisation, is highly active within the archipelago. The San Andrés vireo favours inland mangrove swamps as habitat and feeds on arthropods and caterpillars in shrubby vegetation. Another endemic species under threat is the rainbird or 'old man bird', a bird steeped in local legend. A subspecies of the cuckoo, it also inhabits swamplands. Owing to the erosion of mangrove forests, the species has now become limited to a few localities on the southern half of San Andrés Island and is currently facing extinction.

REPTILES, AMPHIBIANS AND MAMMALS A wide variety of resident and endemic reptiles, insects and other invertebrates can be found on the islands, including iguana, lizards, caiman, snake (boa), gecko, salamander and frog. One of the archipelago's two endemic swamp turtles (known locally as a *swanka*) is an endangered species. Bats are the only reported terrestrial mammal species. Four species of turtles nest in the archipelago: loggerhead, hawksbill, green and leatherback. Beaches on the northern banks and southern atolls are especially important nesting habitats. Sporadic nesting also still occurs on the island of San Andrés along with regular nesting at several spots in Old Providence, most notably Old John and Mona bays on the northern coast of Ketlina.

Loggerhead turtles are the archipelago's most common nesters, favouring Seranilla Bank in June and July. Hawksbills also nest frequently on Serrana and Roncador banks during August. Sand mining remains a potential disruption to nesting and threatens the quality and size of some beaches in the archipelago.

TREES AND PLANTS Almost 400 plant species have been identified in the San Andrés Archipelago, 70% of them native and 25% classed as non-endemic. Indigenous beach vegetation includes sea grape, coconut palm, seaside mahoe and West Indian almond with shrubs such as bay cedar, beach bean, wild plantain, marigold and sea lavender. Although sizeable areas of woodlands have been cleared as grazing land for cattle, native trees can still be found in inland areas, mainly cotton tree, birch and cedar. Breadfruit, guava and citrus are also in good supply with numerous species of mangrove and large sea grass beds, including saltgrass and shoregrass species. This vegetation constitutes an important breeding ground for many invertebrates and provides an important habitat for turtles. More than 18 resident and 76 migrant bird species also rely on the mangrove forests, including two endangered species and several endangered subspecies found only in the archipelago. Rainbird (or 'old man bird') is an endemic subspecies of the cuckoo and the subject of local legend. It inhabits swamplands and is in danger of extinction.

PRACTICALITIES

CLIMATE Expect high humidity, plenty of sunshine and average temperatures of 26–30°C. Light tropical showers aren't uncommon year-round. May and June are the driest months with rains heaviest September to December.

PEAK SEASON Flights and accommodation are in short supply during the peak tourist season. Pre-booking is essential late December to late January and throughout the Easter week. Crowds also swell from mid-June to mid-July with rooms like gold dust at Carnival time (February/March).

SAFETY Tourists in the San Andrés Archipelago benefit from one of the lowest regional crime rates in Colombia, with just a few hundred reported crimes each year. However, don't be fooled by the laid-back atmosphere; petty theft does happen. Most visitors come a cropper on the beach when they let their guard down and leave belongings unattended. This is also the place where drug dealers often tout for trade, selling 'weed' in 50,000COP bags. Isolated muggings have been reported on the western side of the island between Morgan's Cave and the Blow Hole (Hoyo Soplador) where lone tourists have been targeted for expensive watches and jewellery. Female travellers should avoid walking alone late at night, especially in remote and unlit areas.

WHAT TO PACK Cut-off jeans, flip-flops and T-shirts are *de rigueur* in this oh-so-casual archipelago. Pack beach and swimming gear, snorkel and mask, water socks/shoes (some seabed areas are sharp), an underwater camera and plenty of sunscreen. Mosquito repellent is also essential, as are seasickness pills for those who don't travel on water well.

DIVING IN THE ARCHIPELAGO

As the home to one of the largest barrier reefs in the Americas, the San Andrés Archipelago is a true diver's paradise. Dozens of operators offer scuba and snorkelling in a destination still relatively unknown in diving circles, despite being accessible. Underwater visibility is remarkable at an average of 30m year-round and as much as 60m in some spots. Conditions are calm with minimal currents and water temperatures of around 27°C.

Most boat dives are within a half-hour travel time, with several only 5 minutes away. Steep walls, fine coral, sponges and sand shelves are often visible at about 70m. A spectacular 33km-long reef is the third-largest on the planet. Volcanic crags and sunken shipwrecks add further excitement. The reefs on both Providencia and San Andrés are famous for their abundant array of varicoloured sponges. Giant purple sea fans gently wave in time with the ebb and flow of the sea. Brains, fingers, pencils and pillars are clouded by a rainbow of small fish. Feather bush hydroids sway like windswept grassy meadows amidst dense coral growths. Divers are also likely to spot turtles, lobsters, rays, barracudas, groupers and red snappers.

Most dive-specialist operators are based on San Andrés and offer two single-tank dives each morning, departing at around 09.00 and returning at lunchtime. Many then run a single-tank dive in the afternoon subject to demand. Night dives are popular and organised to order, departing half an hour before sunset. However, as with all things in San Andrés, dive times are more a general concept rather than a fixed constant. Most operators will also offer tailored dive tours for individuals and groups. Costs vary, so it pays to shop around. Budget for 20,000COP for 1½ hours' snorkelling, including equipment hire. Scuba hire runs at about 160,000COP for a morning's dive, including equipment. PADI courses start at 750,000COP and rise to 900,000COP for the full Dive Master certificate. A night dive with equipment will set you back at least 120,000COP (about 100,000COP without equipment), with a set of mask, fins and snorkel 20,000COP per day and 70,000COP for a wetsuit. Sea urchins in the vicinity make water shoes a good idea.

Expect year-round water temperatures of around 27°C with visibility of 23–33m. Only a few sites carry currents that make them only out of bounds for non-advanced divers. Although winds are stronger during the dry season, January–June, these tend to be from the east. The position of the barrier reef makes it possible to dive the western wall and the internal patch during these windier months, with no tidal problems. The most popular sites in the archipelago have been buoyed by CORALINA in association with UNESCO and the Colombian government and include the following.

DIVE SITES

Anita Small coral caves surround this dilapidated wreck site, located on the outside of the reef opposite Crab Cay (Cayo Congrejo) at 10.5m. Although the site lacks maturity (the boat sank in 2001), there are large numbers of tarpon resident to the area along big pillars of stony coral.

Bajo San Félipe Just 1km offshore, this sand-bottomed dive site reaches 13.5m in parts along a vast coral patch, in a spot famed for its abundance of colourful sponges and coral formations. Excellent visibility makes this a popular night-dive site.

Blue Diamond According to San Andrés lore, the *Blue Diamond* sank in 1995 after being impounded by the Colombian government for running drugs. Today it is one of the most popular dive attractions in the archipelago – a fascinating wreck full of little nooks and crannies that beg exploration. Resting not far off the eastern shore of San Andrés in about 10.5m of water, this medium-sized freighter split as it sank, ensuring some decent gaps for adventuresome divers to swim through without running much risk of getting stuck or caught. A massive propeller is half-buried in sand while an open hatch in the bow leads to a passable hole in the side of the hull. Fans, corals and sponges cover the wreck – look for barracuda and other fish darting in and out of the cracks.

Canal The abundant nooks, crannies, holes and ledges of this twin-site contain plenty of underwater creatures and fish species, located either side of the navigation channel into Catalina harbour. On the outer edge, a sand bottom at 21m at the wall's base rises to plateaus. Expect a wonderful mix of dramatic pillar corals and a variety of hard and soft species.

Cantil de Santa Catalina Initially sand, this scenic dive reaches maximum depths of 24m along a 12m wall. Large coral mounds include a plentiful supply of healthy star species as well as visiting chubs, queen conchs, lobsters and green morays.

Confusion Divers can expect to encounter large numbers of blue runner jacks, yellow-tail snappers and horse-eye jacks as well as the Creole wrasse that hide along the wall. It starts out at 12m and is over a wall that plummets to the depths.

Connoly This enjoyable wall dive starts at 12m and has a site to the right where two walls of coral sit 9m apart. On the right, find three caves with two small caverns at 24m and a larger, swimmable cave at 27m that is home to nurse sharks.

Convento The edge of this coral-lined sand basin starts at 15m with a wall offering diving at any depth up to the recreational limit.

Cromis As the name suggests, this popular dive site is renowned for large numbers of blue cromis. It is usually dived in conjunction with the magnificent wall, Félipe's Place (see below).

Crystal A broken-down shipwreck sits on the edge of the reef in 11.5m of water, providing a good site for corals, sponges and a wide variety of fish. Expect to spot snapper and barracuda along with the occasional visiting nurse shark and a large number of chubs.

Dos Puntos Two Points consists of a duo of underwater ridges and starts at 18m, sloping to 26m depths. Leading to the outside southern tip of the coral reef, the site offers super vistas of healthy stony coral.

El Jardín Not always an easy dive due to moderate currents, The Garden is so named for its bountiful healthy coral, sand carpets, grass and large sponges. Starting at 23m, the dive takes in some big mounds of coral that are home to fish and moray eels with good visibility throughout.

Espiral This sizeable cavern opens at 42m and features a spiral-like staircase – hence the name. Exit the cave at 30m to spot dog snapper and grouper before following the wall to a height of 21m.

Félipe's Place One of the region's finest wall dives, the site starts at a depth of 10m on a coral ledge. A sand spur leads to 24m over a steep wall with a small canyon to the right that is jam-packed with colourful fish.

Hippies' Place This super little horseshoed site used to attract an outdoorsy flower-power crowd, hence the name. Small but perfectly formed, it is located on the east side of the island on the inside of the reef. Unusual coral formations on the deeper edge are home to large numbers of fish in a site that reaches maximum depths of 13.5m, 2m on top of the coral in parts.

Manta City Rather confusingly, despite the name, this site isn't home to manta rays but is a haven for southern stingrays – many of them with spans over 1.5m. It starts out over sand and hits a maximum depth of 13.5m around large patches of coral the size of a double-decker bus. Divers pass between coral mounds and sand over gardens of ghost feather dusters that are home to brown garden eels, a wide variety of fish, moray and lobster.

Nick's Place Numerous coral outcroppings are prominent features of this nice wall dive that starts at 15.2m, where visiting marine life includes turtles and reef sharks.

Nitrogen Excess (NX) Advanced divers adore 'NX' as it starts deep and becomes deeper to 60m or more. Although short, the dive is worth it for the truly spectacular views alone, but requires immersion to the recreational limit.

Paulino's Place Located close to Manta City on the island's south tip, this pleasant sand-bottomed dive site features boat anchors and vast coral patches to a maximum depth of 13m. Southern stingrays are a common sight here with occasional reports of juvenile hawksbill turtles spotted.

Planchon A sunken barge forms a dramatic 90m-long feature of this dive, set in 22.5m of water on a flat terrain. Inhabited by numerous species of fish, corals and reef creatures, the wreck contains deteriorating oil drums so cannot be entered, but is a fascinating experience nonetheless.

Snapper Shoal As the name suggests, this is an excellent site in which to see snappers and is also renowned for sleeping nurse sharks. Large jacks and spotted snake eels are also sighted in a site that has a maximum depth of 21m.

South Bank This submerged bank off the south end of San Andrés Island is located outside the reef and starts at 24m – often in strong currents. Popular with drift-drivers, a key attraction of this site is its vast number of very large snapper and grouper. An enjoyable if unpredictable dive that experienced divers will find rewarding.

Stairway to Heaven At 24m, this deep dive starts in a sand shoot that leads to a striking gorge from which small plateaus form steps – hence the name. A vertical wall provides plenty of colours, with stunning views on a clear day.

Table Rock Popular with snorkellers and scuba divers alike, this shallow site has a depth of 8m blessed with large areas where the light play can be magnificent.

Tete's Place Located less than 1km offshore, this site has a maximum depth of 13m and very little current. Initially sand, it starts at 9m, forming a short 3m wall. Over a sloping coral bed blessed with a wide variety of fish species in large numbers, it is possible to spot mid-sized goat fish, squirrel fish, grunts and school masters in a dive that is described as 'like swimming in an aquarium' by those in the know.

The *Andy* This broken-down wreck sits in 10.5m of water on the outskirts of the reef and boasts dozens of nooks and crannies. Reef and nurse sharks can be spotted on a sizeable coral and sand platform with good visibility.

The Bight Starting on a sand plateau at 18m, this wall dive is located on the point of the reef with a sand step at 45m. Dive at any depth up to the recreational limit to experience beautiful corals and multi-coloured sponges on the wall.

The Cave Plentiful colourful sponges are the appeal of this pleasant dive site characterised by a small cave at a depth of 33m and an array of resplendent orange, red, yellow, green and gold hues are not to be missed.

Timkam Channel At 10m this shallow dive leads through a cut in the reef in front of Manzanillo Beach, offering perfect visibility when conditions are right.

Tres Casitas Initially at 13.5m on the edge of the wall, a drop to 30m leads to a flat sand bottom where a large gap in the coral allows plenty of opportunity to spot big groupers, jewfish and hog fish.

Turtle Rock Frequently dived, this unique site has a strange structure that features a large rock on a short ledge separated from a wall. A rounded top and broad base give the rock the look of a turtle. Start at 18m approximately 45m from the wall to discover the top of Turtle Rock at 21m and its base at 36m. Follow the wall to rise to a small illuminated canyon with stunning views.

DIVE OPERATORS

Banda Dive Shop [234 C2] Hotel Lord Pierre, L–104, San Andrés; ☎ 513 1080; e dive@ bandadiveshop.com; www.bandadiveshop.com.

Luis Miguel & Gloria are a friendly husband-&-wife team with a dive centre that boasts a sterling reputation. International certification

LOOK, BUT DON'T TOUCH!

Responsible divers understand that experiencing the magic of the underwater world is a privilege granted by Mother Nature. As coral reefs around the world come under extreme threat it is vital to ensure that future generations will enjoy the same honour. To help preserve the ecology, health and beauty of the planet's coral reefs the following responsible diving tips should be considered:

- Anchors cause serious damage to reefs. Only dive with an operator prepared to ensure the reefs will not be damaged via a responsible tourism and diving policy. Visit www.responsibletravel.com for further advice on choosing an ethical tour operator.
- Check that the point of entry into the water is away from fragile corals. Practise your buoyancy over sand before moving towards corals and reefs and vulnerable organisms.
- Resist the temptation to feed fish and discourage others from doing so. Feeding marine life upsets the normal pattern of behaviours. It can also encourage aggression.
- Contamination from poorly treated waste and water systems causes damage to corals. Choose a hotel that manages grey water responsibly.
- Keep time spent in underwater caves to a minimum to reduce the likelihood of leaving air bubbles behind, as these can threaten organisms.
- Refuse to buy souvenirs made from corals, shells or hardwoods. Report any traders to Earth Dive via an online science log (*www.earthdive.com*).
- Be sure to take away all litter – collect any that you see, not just your own.
- Finally, look but don't touch! Never step on live marine organisms and be mindful that even the gentlest of touches can destroy robust-looking corals, sponges and polyps.

San Andrés Archipelago DIVING IN THE ARCHIPELAGO

6

in all levels of PADI, BIS & NAUI is offered, along with courses that range from a 3-day session to 20 days of Dive Master certification, using a modern 9.5m boat with 2 x 115hp motors, a Ford truck, GPS navigation equipment & a Mako 18.7cf compressor. A well-stocked shop offers a wide range of equipment & clothing for hire & sale, including TUSA & Oceanic accessories, Body Glove wetsuits & T-shirts. Visa & MasterCard accepted.

✈ **Caribe Azul Dive Center** [map page 231] Pepper Hill Rd, San Andrés; ☎512 3419; e ecoturismocaribeazul@gmail.com. Bilingual instructors offer a wide variety of adults' & children's packages at this popular dive outfit owned by Hugo Arboleda, who videos dives for posterity.

✈ **Karibik Diver** [234 D2] Av Newball, No 1–248, Edificio Galéon, San Andrés; ☎512 0101; e karibikdiver@gmx.com; www.karibik-diver.com. This German-owned diving outfit comes highly recommended with English, German & Spanish spoken.

✈ **San Andrés Divers** [map page 231] Av Cincurvalar, Km10, San Andrés; ☎512 5695; e info@sanandresdivers.com; www.

sanandresdivers.com. This specialist dive operator has a 1.5ha building complex in an idyllic palm-tree setting, bathrooms & lockers, new 2.25m³ tanks using yoke valve systems, a Bauer compressor, nitrox fill station, & full rental gear availability as well as dive accessories such as lights, cameras, etc, & a tabled dive briefing area, training pool & AC classroom.

✈ **Sharky's Dive Shop** [map page 231] Carretera Circunvalar, San Andrés; ☎512 0651; e buceo@sharkydiveshop.com; www. sharkydiveshop.com. Having clocked up 21 years of experience this outfit has grown in size & stature & now has a 9.5m boat with 2 outboard 4-stroke motors of 115hp to whizz divers out to sites at speed. Other equipment includes a Ford 150 pick-up truck; 2 Bauer compressors to fill 100 air tanks; 30 nitrox-enriched air tanks; 25 buoyancy control devices & 25 Aqualung scuba regulators. Sharkey's specialities include day & night dives & underwater photography tours.

✈ **Sirius Dive Center** [map page 244] Providencia; ☎514 8213; e info@siriushotel.net; www.siriushotel.net

ISLA SAN ANDRÉS *Telephone code 8*

Sea-horse-shaped San Andrés is the archipelago's principal island, an ancient volcanic landscape buffered with layers of coralline built up over many millennia. A small mountain range rises to 55m, criss-crossing the island from north to south and covered in lush coconut palms. Sharp ravines, limestone deposits, white clay and coral sand meet dark-red topsoil on a terrain characterised by farmland and rocky outcrops. Surrounding coral beds, particularly along the eastern shore, afford the water a beautiful array of oceanic hues described by the locals as 'The Sea of Seven Colours'.

Flanked by sandy beaches, San Andrés is the archipelago's largest island and prime tourism centre. Visitors arrive and depart from the airport and jetties, flying out to Providencia and the mainland and journeying to the surrounding cays. A congested town centre (El Centro) sits at the northwestern tip of the island's urbanisation to form the archipelago's commercial hub. A higgledy-piggledy jumble of duty-free shops, hotel blocks and restaurants occupy an austere collection of concrete buildings that are a vicious assault on the eyes. Vendors tout sunglasses, rice cookers, televisions, sports gear and perfume. Streets packed with tooting taxis, scooters and golf buggies spill down to the northern waterfront where the lion's share of boat launches and dive shops can be found.

In contrast, the brightly painted single-storey wooden houses of the local population sit amongst palms in the centre of the island. Rocking-chair porches overlook leafy, bloom-filled gardens in these fine examples of English–Caribbean architecture. A picturesque 30km paved road loops the entire island and is the main tourist trail for sightseeing and attractions. A tiny lagoon sits in the centre

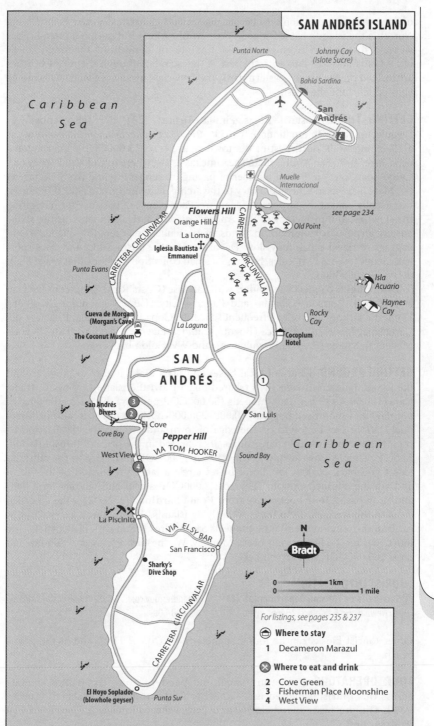

SAN ANDRÉS ISLAND

Caribbean
Sea

Punta Norte

Johnny Cay
(Islote Sucre)

Bahía Sardina

San
Andrés

Muelle
Internacional

see page 234

Flowers Hill

Orange Hill

La Loma

**Iglesia Bautista
Emmanuel**

Old Point

Punta Evans

**Cueva de Morgan
(Morgan's Cave)**

The Coconut Museum

La Laguna

**SAN
ANDRÉS**

Rocky
Cay

**Cocoplum
Hotel**

Isla
Acuario

Haynes
Cay

CARRETERA CIRCUNVALAR

CARRETERA CIRCUNVALAR

**San Andrés
Divers**

El Cove

Cove Bay

Pepper Hill

VIA TOM HOOKER

West View

San Luis

Sound Bay

Caribbean
Sea

VIA ELSY BAR

La Piscinita

San Francisco

**Sharky's
Dive Shop**

N

Bradt

| 0 | 1km |
| 0 | 1 mile |

CARRETERA CIRCUNVALAR

**El Hoyo Soplador
(blowhole geyser)**

Punta Sur

For listings, see pages 235 & 237

🏠 **Where to stay**

1 Decameron Marazul

⊗ **Where to eat and drink**

2 Cove Green
3 Fisherman Place Moonshine
4 West View

San Andrés Archipelago   ISLA SAN ANDRÉS

6

231

of San Andrés and is home to heron, pigeon and caiman. German Point (Punta Norte) is the island's palm-fringed northern tip. A handful of quiet, inland roads weave across the undulating terrain of the interior, connecting the sleepy towns of La Loma and San Luis with the rest of the island. Although the nicest beaches are located on the island's eastern flank, the first-class diving of San Andrés can be enjoyed all along the coast.

GETTING THERE Gustavo Rojas Pinilla Airport [234 F2] (also known as Sesquicentenario International); (\ 536 0187; *aeropuertosanandres.com/en/*) is a 10-minute walk northwest of the town centre (taxi 15,000COP). International departures from San Andrés incur the same tax as elsewhere in Colombia (page 67). Cargo boats carry a limited number of paying passengers to and from Cartagena but there is no fixed schedule. Entry to the archipelago incurs a 47,950COP tourist tax, usually paid at the airport of departure. Pack plenty of patience for navigating the slow-paced bureaucracy of San Andrés's airport arrivals process, as the sixth-busiest airport in Colombia in terms of passengers has lengthy queues – and baggage retrieval is painfully slow. Departing is more businesslike and the airport has a bank (with ATM), cafés, bars and a small collection of shops that make flight delays less of a bind.

Direct flights connect San Andrés with San José (Costa Rica), Montreal-Trudeau and Toronto-Pearson (Canada) and Panama City (Panama) – amongst others. Domestic airlines also offer a frequent schedule: Copa (Barranquilla, Bogotá, Cali, Cartagena, Medellín); Avianca (Bogotá, Cali, Cartagena, Medellín); Lan (Bogotá, Medellín); Satena (Bogotá, Providencia); and VivaColombia (Bogotá).

GETTING AROUND Plenty of local buses and taxis make it easy to move around the island. Numerous *colectivos* (shared taxis) trawl the island touting for trade. Cars (100,000COP per day), mopeds (50,000COP per day), bicycles (10,000COP per day) and motorised buggies (60,000–200,000COP per day) can also be hired. Fuel stations can be found on the edge of town and around the circular tourist trail. Higher fuel prices in San Andrés are reflected in the price of transportation. Expect a simple cross-town **taxi** ride to cost 4,000COP and a trip to the outskirts to set you back 20,000COP. Local **buses** circle a large proportion of the island and are the cheapest option. They cost 2,000COP a trip and operate on a hail-and-drop basis. **Tour boats** leave from **Punta Sardinas** [234 D2] – the so-called 'nose of the sea horse' – to travel to outlying islands. A **catamaran** service (*www.catamaranelsensation.com*) now connects San Andrés Island with Providencia. The journey takes 2½ hours, runs every Monday, Wednesday, Friday and Sunday, and costs 260,000COP for a return ticket.

TOURIST INFORMATION

Z Secretaría de Turismo Departmental [234 C2] Av Newball, No 6–30; \ 512 3466; www. sanandres.gov.co; ⊕ 08.00–18.00 w/days, closed noon–14.00.

Other tourist kiosks can be found at the airport (\ 512 1149) and at the town's beach.

TOUR OPERATORS Numerous small independent tour companies operate across this tourism-focused isle. Expect to find a tour desk attached to every hotel. On the basis of reliability and price, the following are some of San Andrés's best.

She is known throughout San Andrés as 'Lucy in the Sky with Diamonds' but this colourful, effervescent islander was born Lucy Trigidia Chow Robinson (◌ *513 2233;* m *311 808 9039;* e *lucytrigidia@yahoo.com*). Today she delights visitors with a mix of wisdom and wit, a bilingual guide extraordinaire with a considerable zest for life. Dressed in gold-and-tangerine robes this larger-than-life eccentric is a retired schoolteacher and unashamed 'island girl'. Lucy is excellent company and a very good source of historical and cultural information. Having her along for the ride is not only great fun; it also allows an opportunity to see the island through her eyes.

Flying Dolphin Servicios Turísticos Hotel Lord Pierre [234 C2], Av Colombia, No 1B–104; ◌513 1836; e contacto@flyingdolphins.com; flyingdolphins.com.co. A decent tour menu including the standard excursions such as pontoon boat tours, island hops & snorkelling.

Gema Tours [234 C2] Centro Comercial, New Point Plaza, No L1–106; ◌512 8666; e paologarcia@gematours.com; www.gematours. com. Large-scale award-winning tour company with offices across Colombia that benefit from a long-term presence on the island.

San Andrés Caribbean Tour Ltd Sunrise Beach Hotel; ◌512 3977 ext 1303; e sacatur530@yahoo. es. An affable woman called Gladys organises all manner of tours & services, including bicycle rental, boat tours around the islands, car hire & horseriding.

Semisubmarino Manatí [234 C1] Av La Playa; ◌512 3349; e semisubmarinomanati@hotmail. com; www.semisubmarinomanati.inf.travel. This 1½hr underwater tour provides a decent alternative to snorkelling or scuba diving. Large windows allow good views of the reefs around the island. Tickets (at 48,000COP pp) can be purchased from several outlets on the town's beach.

Regretfully, the island's tourist train – Tren Blanco – is actually a tractor-pulled vehicle in disguise, but its 4-hour circuit around San Andrés's key attractions is excellent value at 20,000COP per person. Climb aboard from the bus stop on the corner of Colombia and Hotel Bahia Sardina [234 B1] (m *317 509 4577*); it departs every morning at about 09.30.

WHERE TO STAY See maps, pages 231 and 234.

Accommodation in San Andrés tends to be pricier than the rest of Colombia. However, as new places open the competition gets fiercer – a great basis on which to haggle. In simple terms, hotels fall into three main categories: large-scale resorts, beach hotels and mid-town options by the shops. All-inclusive packages are popular in Colombia and no more so than in San Andrés. Visitors keen to interact with the locals should also check out the island's excellent homestay programme, Las Posadas Nativas.

Hotels

Hotel Aquarium Decameron (250 rooms) Av Colombia 1–19, Punta Hansa; ◌513 0707; www.decameron.com. Out of all of the five Decameron hotels on the island, this gets the best reports. Nicely located partially offshore, it sticks to the standard Decameron all-inclusive format. But despite this it manages to offer pretty *cabañas* in a very nice spot for diving enthusiasts. Rates include b/fast, lunch, dinner & all snacks, cigarettes & domestic drinks. Rooms come as twin or double & include cable TV, fridge, safe & AC. **$$$**

Hotel Casablanca (10 bungalows & 91 rooms) Av Colombia; ◌512 4115; www. hotelcasablancasanandres.com/en/. This orderly 4-star hotel was one of the first to open up on the island & prides itself on being a 'big small hotel'. Guest accommodation comprises

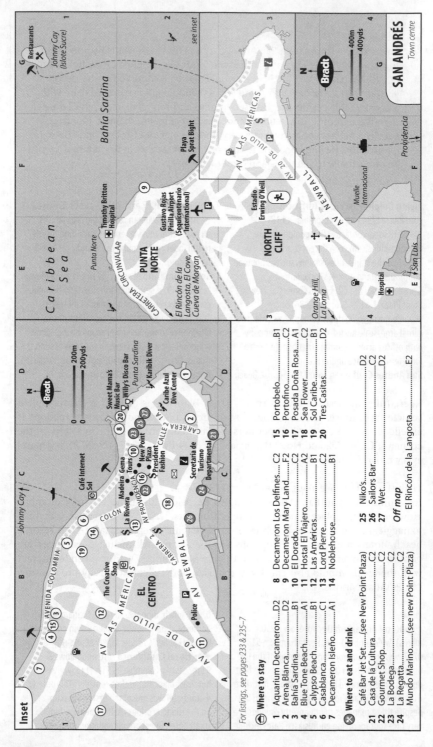

SAN ANDRÉS
Town centre

Inset

For listings, see pages 233 & 235–7

Where to stay

1 Aquarium Decameron....D2
2 Arena Blanca............D2
3 Bahía Sardina...........B1
4 Blue Tone Beach.........A1
5 Calypso Beach...........B1
6 Casablanca..............C1
7 Decameron Isleño........A1

8 Decameron Los Delfines..C2
9 Decameron Mary Land......F2
10 El Dorado..............C2
11 Hostal El Viajero......C2
12 Las Américas...........B1
13 Lord Pierre............C2
14 Noblehouse.............B1

15 Portobelo..............B1
16 Portofino..............C2
17 Posada Doña Rosa.......A1
18 Sea Flower.............C2
19 Sol Caribe.............B1
20 Tres Casitas...........D2

Where to eat and drink

21 Café Bar Jet Set......(see New Point Plaza)
22 Casa de la Cultura.....C2
23 Gourmet Shop...........C2
24 La Bodega..............C2
25 La Regatta.............C2
26 Mundo Marino.......(see new Point Plaza)

25 Niko's.................D2
26 Sailors Bar............C2
27 Wet....................D2

Off map

El Rincón de la Langosta..............E2

modern fully equipped bungalows along with large, comfortable rooms. Both the Casablanca Restaurant & Sea Watch Café have a fine menu, with the red snapper *au gratin* & seafood spaghetti both particularly tasty. **$$$**

🏠 **Hotel Decameron Isleño** (220 rooms) Av Colón Calle 3ra, No 6–106, Sector Spratt Bight; ✆ 513 4343; www.decameron.com. Located 3mins from San Andrés Airport & just a few blocks away from town-centre shops, this hotel offers terrace & balconies with ocean view along with 7 family *cabañas*. Amenities at this all-inclusive resort include 3 restaurants, 2 bars & a swimming pool. **$$$**

🏠 **Hotel Decameron Los Delfines** (36 rooms) Av Colombia, No 1B–86; ✆ 512 4083; www. decameron.com. This sweet little motel-style place sits right on the beach so some of its rooms have uninterrupted views out to sea. Minibars, AC & cable TV all come as standard. There's also a palm-edged central swimming pool from which to enjoy the vistas. **$$$**

🏠 **Hotel Decameron Marazul** (128 rooms) road to San Luis (4km); ✆ 513 2678; www. decameron.com. This all-inclusive hotel lies between the sea & the jungle in the Orange Hill district & is popular with a Canadian package-tour crowd due to its location right on one of the island's best beaches. Gym, 3 bars (*Bar el Duende* ⊕ *24hrs*), 3 restaurants, swimming pool, watersports, tennis, disco & volleyball are just some of the on-site amenities offered. **$$$**

🏠 **Hotel Decameron Mary Land** (65 rooms) Av Colombia 9–38; ✆ 513 1818; www.decameron. com. Another Decameron chain hotel, this time located on the North End close to the boat launch at Punta Sardina, not far from the airport at the very edge of the hotel zone. Rooms are twin beds & doubles, with a restaurant, 3 bars, swimming pool & the usual all-inclusive deal. **$$$**

🏠 **Hotel Las Américas** (72 rooms) Av Las Américas; ✆ 512 3949; e reservas@hotel-las-americas.com; www.hotel-las-americas.com. Choose from doubles, triples & suites in this 2-storey wooden hotel, centred on a garden terrace with pool. Rates include b/fast, with rooms equipped with AC, minibar & cable TV. On-site amenities include a perfectly reasonable buffet restaurant (with 24hr room service) & laundry. **$$$**

🏠 **Hotel Lord Pierre** (60 rooms) Av Colombia, No 1B–106; ✆ 512 7541; e reservas@lordpierre.

com; www.lordpierre.com. This central hotel has double & triple rooms plus 12 self-contained suites. Each has AC, tiled floors & colour TV. Amenities include a very nice outside pool terrace & safe sea bathing area with sunloungers & seating & a pool bar with stunning views. Expect perfectly reasonable fish, chicken & steak dishes at the on-site restaurant, Don Anibal. **$$$**

🏠 **Hotel Sol Caribe** (223 rooms) Av Colón, No 2–77; ✆ 512 3043; e reservas.scsa@solarhoteles. com; www.solarhoteles.com. This modern, white-&-glass hotel in the heart of downtown is well positioned for shopping within easy walking distance of the beach & a 5 min drive of the airport. 4 on-site restaurants offer seafood, themed buffets, grilled Caribbean food & an international menu. There are also 2 bars, a large swimming pool, gym, business centre, childcare services, solarium & a popular nightclub. Rooms come with cable TV, AC, fridge & phone. **$$$**

🏠 **Noblehouse Hotel** (15 rooms) Av Colón 380; ✆ 512 8264; e info@sanandresnoblehouse. com; www.sanandresnoblehouse.com. This 15-room 2nd-storey guesthouse close to the beach overlooks busy shops & restaurants. Friendly staff attend to guests well & respond well to requests for recommendations & tour tips in a well-run, professional, European-owned establishment. All rooms have a private bathroom, AC, minibar, satellite TV, safe & phone. Services includes tours, 24hr room service, rental car & motorcycle hire with b/fast & internet use included in the room rate. Credit cards are accepted. Italian, French, Spanish & English spoken. **$$$**

🏠 **Hotel Arena Blanca** (72 rooms) Calle 2, No 1–51; ✆ 513 1199; e info@hotelarenablanca. com.co; www.hotelarenablanca.com.co. The rooms include 6 large suites – all with balconies & sea views. Each is equipped with AC, cable TV, & a buffet restaurant, disco & swimming pool are just some of the on-site amenities. Discounts available for longer stays. **$$**

🏠 **Hotel Bahía Sardina** (42 rooms) Av Colombia, No 5A–29; ✆ 512 4783; e reservas@ bahiasardina.com; www.bahiasardina.com. Most of the quaint little rooms in this yellow-&-blue ocean-front hotel boast views over the water. Each comes with AC. **$$**

🏠 **Hotel Blue Tone Beach** (144 rooms) Av Colombia, No 5A–25; ✆ 512 4255. It's not hard to establish why this large, modern hotel is so popular with beach-going guests. Most of its rooms have balconies overlooking sand out to sea. Each comes with AC, colour TV & a safe. The hotel has a swimming pool, gym & very nice restaurant. **$$**

🏠 **Hotel Calypso Beach** (100+ rooms) Av Duarte Blum; ☎ 512 2045; e reservas@ hotelcalypso.com.co; www.hotelcalypso.com. co. This modern blue building sits on the ocean & has rooms equipped with AC, minibar & cable TV. There is a rooftop pool & restaurant with sea views. **$$**

🏠 **Hotel El Dorado** (63 rooms) Av Colombia, No 1A–25; ☎ 512 4056; e ventas@ hoteleldorado.com.co; www.hoteleldorado. com.co. A pleasant pool terrace is a nice feature of this mid-range hotel. Rooms have cable TV & AC – some with better views than others. An on-site restaurant serves a mix of international & local fare. **$$**

🏠 **Hotel Mary May Inn** (9 rooms) Av 20 de Julio, No 3–74; ☎ 512 5669; e info@marymayinn. com; www.marymayinn.com. Budget travellers rave about this cosy little place opposite a cheap fried-chicken joint. It's nothing special, but the ambience is relaxed & friendly. Each room has a bathroom & colour TV. A neighbouring café serves a hearty b/fast at a bargain price. **$$**

🏠 **Hotel Portobelo** (31 rooms) Av La Playa, No 5a–69; ☎ 512 7008; e reserves@ portobelohotel.com; www.portobelohotel.com. It may not look much from the outside, but this little town-centre hotel has a beach & rooms that overlook the sea. Each has AC, cable TV & minibar. Not a bad choice & a reasonable price. **$$**

🏠 **Hotel Portofino** (50 rooms) Av Providencia, No 1–115; ☎ 512 4212; e reservas@ portofinocaribe.com; www.portofinocaribe.com. Rooms are small but pleasant in this decent mid-budget hotel. All have AC & TV & rates include b/ fast & dinner. **$$**

🏠 **Hotel Sea Flower** (45 rooms) Av Las Américas, No 1B–36; ☎ 512 0325; e hotelsa@epm. net.co; www.solarhoteles.com. All rooms in this high-rise balconied hotel have AC & are a decent size. An on-site internet café & laundry are a boon although the restaurant has had mixed reviews. **$$**

🏠 **Hotel Verde Mar** (44 rooms) Av 20 de Julio, No 2A–13; ☎ 512 5525; e reservas@ hotelverdemar.com.co; www.hotelverdemar. com.co. This functional resting place couldn't be

closer to the shops. The rooms are basic but clean & equipped with AC, colour TV & telephone. A restaurant serves a respectable menu round the clock. **$$**

🏠 **Tres Casitas** (10 rooms) Av Colombia, No 1–60; ☎ 512 5813; e reservas@ apartahoteltrescasitas.com. This charming little blue-&-yellow wooden motel-style complex is popular with families as it faces the sea & has a safe, secure centrally located swimming pool. Each room has a colour TV, video, telephone, minibar, fridge, kitchen, water cooler & balconies. Rates include b/fast & dinner. **$$**

🏠 **Hostal El Viajero** (22 rooms) Av 20 de Julio, No 3A–122; ☎ 512 7497; www.sanandreshostel. com. The only officially registered hostel on the island & brought to you by the same team with hostels in Cartagena & Cali, this is everything you would expect in the way of being organised & well thought out. Just a short walk from the beach, this hostel caters to Argentinian backpackers seeking Caribbean sun & those on a budget & looking for the fun of a hostel. **$**

🏠 **Posada Doña Rosa** (8 rooms) Av Las Américas; ☎ 512 3649; www.posadarosa.blogspot. com. Lone shoestring travellers will enjoy the price of these dirt-cheap rooms. All fan-cooled rooms have private bathrooms. **$**

Homestay options

🏠 **Carson Hudson Martínez** 'Mistic's Place' (La Loma); ☎ 513 0352. **$**

🏠 **Cleotilde Henry De Montes** 'Cli's Place' (El Centro); ☎ 512 6957. **$**

🏠 **Emerson Williams** 'William's Place' (La Loma); ☎ 513 0395. **$**

🏠 **Ethel Corpus Jay** 'Ethel's Place' (El Centro); ☎ 512 4502. **$**

🏠 **Fitarda Henry Valbuena** 'Henry's Place' (El Centro); ☎ 512 6150. **$**

🏠 **Gladys Bolaños** 'Gladys's Place' (El Centro); ☎ 512 1229. **$**

🏠 **Inéz De Macariz** 'Macariz Place' (El Centro); ☎ 512 6356. **$**

🏠 **Justina Pérez** 'Justina's Place' (La Loma); ☎ 513 3174. **$**

🏠 **Maximiliano Hooker** 'Maxi's Place' (El Centro); ☎ 512 5441. **$**

🏠 **Reolicia Duke Santana** 'Licy's Place' (La Loma); ☎ 512 9679. **$**

WHERE TO EAT AND DRINK See maps, pages 231 and 234.

✘ **El Rincón de la Langosta** Carretera Circunvalar; ✆ 513 2707; e langosta@sol.net.co; www.rincondelalangosta.com. Located in between the museum & Morgan's Cave on the northeast side of the island. Charming patron Francisco Guzman has one of the most popular restaurants on the island, a waterfront seafood haven of great repute & a San Andrés tradition since 1994. Diners can eat in 1 of 4 different seated areas, including several indoor options & a breezy tropical outside dock-style terrace. Langoustine specials are the order of the day here along with a long list of fresh island fish. Choose from garlic octopus, stuffed crab, prawn thermidor with coconut & buttered lobster tail. However the gastronomic *crème de la crème* here is the lobster – it comes served grilled, steamed or roasted with a choice of 21 mouth-watering sauces. $$$

✘ **Gourmet Shop Restaurant** Av Newball, in front of Parque La Barracuda; ✆ 512 9843. Dine in style on wooden tables or reclaimed barrels, surrounded by an impressive cellar of vintages from all over the world. Walls racked with shelves are full of herbs, spices & bottled provisions in this sophisticated eatery. Expect beautiful glassware & good service in this true escape from Caribbean chaos. A menu of fine cheeses, smoked meats & foreign breads has a distinctly European feel. $$$

✘ **La Regatta Restaurante** Club Náutico, Av Francisco Newball, No 3–121; ✆ 512 3022; e info@clubnauticosai.org; www.clubnauticosai.org; ☺ lunchtime daily. The lobster, shrimp & crab dishes at the yacht club's lively on-the-water eatery are served under moody lighting

amidst bobbing yachts & fish-filled waters. Arrive hungry to make the most of an excellent seafood platter – a plate piled high with grilled shrimp, langoustine, snails, calamari, crab claws & fried fish. Curried lobster tails, conch in coconut sauce & seafood stew are also recommended. Dishes come with warm bread & a choice of salads, potatoes & rice. $$$

✘ **Cove Green Restaurante** El Cove, Carretera Circunvalar. *Ceviche* & fried conch are just some of the Cove Green's specialities. Enjoy a plate piled high washed down with an ice-cold beer. $$

✘ **Fisherman Place Moonshine Restaurant** El Cove, Carretera Circunvalar; ☺ lunch & dinner daily. Daily specials depend on what the boats bring back to shore, but fried fish with garlic & langoustine in coconut are staples at this rustic food joint. $$

✘ **Niko's Restaurante y Bar** Av Colombia, Punta Hansa, No 1–93; ✆ 512 7535; ☺ daily. This wooden single-storey diner has a strong nautical theme with walls adorned with nets & ropes & a seafood menu at least a mile long. Eat casually outside under umbrellas or in a more formal indoor setting. Highlights include a delicious crab soup, roasted crab & lobster in crab sauce. The squid in garlic is also sublime. $$

✘ **Restaurante West View** Carretera Circunvalar; ☺ lunchtime until 18.00 daily. Expect loud reggae music & a tourist crowd at this on-the-water diner next to La Piscinita (page 240). It serves seafood dishes & acts as an unofficial changing room for swimmers & divers who, in turn, buy bags of bread to feed the fish. $$

ENTERTAINMENT AND NIGHTLIFE San Andrés has a reputation as a lively party town – even the local cemetery is next to a sign that says 'Caribe dreams … enjoy yourself!' Venues have a relaxed, easy-going feel. Most can be found on Avenida Colombia and Avenida Newball with plenty of bars, restaurants, salsa clubs and live music also found in many larger hotels. The **Discoteca Blue Deep** can be found at the Hotel Sunrise (✆ 512 3977) with **Discoteca Extasis** at the Hotel Sol Caribe Centro [234 B1] (✆ 512 3043) and the **Discoteca Confetis** [map, page 231] at the Hotel Decameron Marazul (✆ 513 2678). Decent alternatives include **Willy's Disco Bar** [234 D2] and **Sweet Mama's Music Bar** [234 D2] downtown. Rustic rum shacks and thatched-roof seafood diners provide a real flavour of island life. These are a good fallback off-season when the more sophisticated venues have yet to reach full swing. San Andrés also has a lengthy cockfighting tradition. Breeding and fighting is a serious business on the island where night fights take place in cockpits in Black Dog and North Cliff.

♀ **Café Bar Jet Set** [234 C2] Centro Comerical New Point, Av Providencia. This small outdoor plaza bar has a decent daily happy hour (*17.00– 19.00*). Its little-known generous measures & great 2-for-1 deals may just be the best-kept secret island-wide.

♀ **Casa de la Cultura** [234 C2] Av Newball; ✆512 3405. Frequent Caribbean-themed food, music & dance nights attract a lively crowd each Fri. Expect polished renditions of numerous Bob Marley classics washed down with rum punch & bowls of crab stew.

♀ **Sailors Bar** [234 C2] Club Náutico, Av Newball; ✆512 3022; e info@clubnauticosai.org; www. clubnauticosai.org. One of the best drinks menus in San Andrés can be found at the yacht club's watering hole, where punters can enjoy happy hour (*17.00–19.00*) on a rustic dinghy dock overlooking the sea.

☆ **La Bodega** [234 C2] Av Colombia. This fantastic off-the-street salsa joint is next to Niko's (page 237). Video screens show MTV while a sound system emits Colombian classics at deafening volume. A small dance floor is packed after 23.00, but it's cool to arrive early to grab a table & a bottle of *aguardiente* while the place fills up.

☆ **Mundo Marino** [234 C2] Centro Commercial New Point Plaza; ✆512 1749; e Munmarino@ gmail.com. Join a mixed crowd of singles, couples & tour groups aboard this popular evening 'Morgan' party cruise. Live music has a reggae theme with accompanying dancers. Tickets cost 36,000COP pp; departs Tue, Thu & Sat at 20.30.

☆ **Wet** [234 D2] Av Colombia; ✆512 3287. This glitzy place looks a little out of place in laid-back San Andrés. Expect a menu of OTT cocktails at Manhattan prices. A dance floor has a sound system that is permanently cranked up to the max.

SHOPPING 'Retail therapy' is a San Andrés tradition and the island's duty-free shops are awash with mainlanders making their money stretch. **La Riviera** has several stores of different sizes dotted around the town. This duty-free specialist stocks a large range of designer perfumes and big-name cosmetics. Numerous other outlets offer sunglasses, electronic items, cameras and jewellery, including **Madiera** (✆ *512 5619*) and **President Fashion** (✆ *512 6579*), both on Avenida Providencia. Here, you'll find Lacoste, Polo, Ralph Lauren and Dior at 30% cheaper than in Europe. Sports goods such as Billabong, Speedo, Fred Perry and O'Neill are also inexpensive.

In recent years, the town has received a cash injection that has added new shops and malls. Local wine made from noni fruit and honey can be purchased from **César Palacío Santos** (✆ *513 2057*) in La Loma [map page 231]. For an extraordinary array of exquisite goods and produce head to the **Gourmet Shop** [234 C2] (✆ *512 9843*) on Avenida Atlántico where congenial patron Humberto Mejia truly knows his stuff. For hair-braiding look out for street hawkers outside the main hotels downtown. For a chance to buy leftover portions of dinner or extra baking look out for what the islanders call 'fair tables' by the side of the road.

OTHER PRACTICALITIES
Medical services The **Timothy Britton Hospital** [234 E4] (✆ *512 3443*) on the island of San Andrés is equipped with a hyperbaric chamber and is staffed by high-standard, bilingual medical professionals. Emergency medical attention can be sought here at an outpatients clinic. However, the archipelago's diving community prides itself on an excellent dive safety record. Injuries are rare, with sunburn and heatstroke the most common medical complaints from tourists. Find the hospital in the island's North End area in Sarie Bay next to the Hotel Decameron Mary Land. At last half-a-dozen pharmacies have premises in downtown San Andrés while the locals swear by bush rum as a cure for toothache.

Money As you'd expect in a Duty Free Zone, the island of San Andrés is well served by financial institutions and few establishments will turn a credit card away.

A decent handful of banks (with ATMs) and money changers can be found in El Centro and at the airport. Outside of town the options are much more limited. Travellers planning to journey further afield should therefore be sure to top up their wallet prior to departure. Given its remote location, the San Andrés Archipelago is more expensive than the Colombian mainland, as many goods are imported. To be safe, budget for at least 10–15% more than you would elsewhere. Transport and tours can also be pricey although food is generally good and cheap.

Communications Many of San Andrés's larger hotels offer internet services – at a price. However, local-rate internet connections can be found at a handful of places in the town centre. The **Creative Shop** [234 B2] (↺ *512 3416*) on Calle 4 and the **Café Internet Sol** [234 C1] (↺ *512 2250*) on Avenida Duarte Blum are two of the best and there are Wi-Fi hot spots at various points in town. The only post office in San Andrés is on Avenida Colón [234 C2] (↺ *512 9405*).

WHAT TO SEE AND DO
Playa Sprat Bight [234 F2] Also known as the 'town beach' or simply referred to as 'la playa', this sandy stretch in Bahía Sardinas is also the island's main beach. Proximity to the town centre means this 450m white-sand stretch can get crowded. Despite this, those in the mood to let off steam will find it a fun place to hang out. Expect hair-braiding, volleyball, frisbee-throwing and picnicking families. Those looking for sand to relax on in tranquillity should head to the island's eastern shore.

Cueva de Morgan (Morgan's Cave) [map page 231] This water-filled rocky cavern is steeped in legend and is where the locals believe Captain Henry Morgan buried his treasure. Every island tour and bus will make a stop here, although the grotto itself is secondary to the souvenir stalls and vendors that surround it. As the cave is waterlogged, entry is impossible. However, guides will take you through a historic narrative as you peer into the depths.

Coconut Museum [map page 231] For a chance to browse a collection of old artefacts and tools from the days of the coconut boom head to this bumper house of coconuts where plenty of coconut-related souvenirs range from carved shells to bizarre painted fronds – find it next to Morgan's Cave (⊕ *09.00–17.00 daily*).

Johnny Cay [234 G1] This tiny coral islet is no larger than a football pitch 1.5km north of the coast of San Andrés. Sometimes called Islote Sucre, it's covered in coconut palms and edged by a beautiful white-sand beach. Most people visit to hang out and picnic on the sand – as a popular day trip Johnny Cay can often be deluged with tourists far beyond its capacity during peak season. However, in its quieter guise, the island is a fun place to spend the day. In the 1960s, Marlon Brando was spotted sunbathing here during a break from filming the movie *Burn* in Colombia. This gritty tale of slave revolt on an early 19th-century Caribbean island is arguably Brando's finest performance. The film won acclaim for using a cast of amateurs other than Brando and Rento Salvatori – along with 20,000 extras. General Prada was played with wit and aplomb by a Colombian lawyer, while a British Petroleum employee starred as Mr Shelton. Johnny Cay was Brando's choice as a place for R&R away from the intensity of the film set. However, he got bored with Colombia and parts of the film ended up being shot in Morocco, Rome, St Malo, and the Virgin Islands. Johnny Cay has a handful of restaurants selling fish and rice dishes, beer and cocktails.

Saturday is horseracing day in San Andrés, a time of great excitement. Small crowds gather on the sand, their pockets stuffed with pesos. Although the prize is officially honorific, bets are placed in hurried secret exchanges. Expectations are high. But first the beach must be blessed according to *Obeah*, a type of voodoo witchcraft prevalent throughout the archipelago (see box, page 247). Spells are cast to give a horse extra power or weaken the competition. The ground is also checked for signs of evil or trickery, such as a buried dead dog or voodoo doll. Often just two horses race for the Saturday purse. Riders mount bareback, but such is the pace of this rousing exuberance, the race is over almost before it begins.

Isla Acuario [map page 231] Tours to Aquarium Island are often packaged with a trip to Johnny Cay. Littered with tourist huts, it sits in chest-high water next to Haynes Cay, off the east coast of San Andrés. Snorkelling gear can be hired from a dive shack. Other facilities are pretty rudimentary, but include toilets and a collection of small lockers for rental by the hour. Glass-bottom boats offer tours and jet skis are also available for hire. As a popular spot with holidaying families, Aquarium Island is packed to capacity at weekends and can all too easily become a hellish mix of screaming, sunburnt kids and shrieking teens. Every fish is scared off by the racket and all the shade is taken, while lockers become like gold dust in the heat. Holiday weekends tend to be particularly unbearable, so stick to midweek if a more chilled-out vibe is your thing.

Haynes Cay [map page 231] This pretty, palm-covered isle is often part of a standard boat tour around San Andrés – usually as a half-hour stop-off for a spot of snorkelling in its shallow waters. Dense thickets of coconut trees provide plenty of shade not far from Acuario. Sharp exposed coral makes water shoes essential for swimmers and divers.

La Piscinita [map page 231] Located west of West View just a little further along the coast from El Cover, La Piscinita is described by the locals as a sea bath for its calm warmth. Waist-high translucent waters are home to a rainbow of fish. A nearby restaurant (Restaurante West View) serves as a changing room and snorkel-rental joint (page 237).

El Hoyo Soplador [map page 231] Every self-respecting holiday isle should have its own funny little natural phenomenon and this blowhole geyser is San Andrés's. A spurting jet of seawater blasts out of the coral rock in the southern tip of the island when the winds and tides collude – reaching heights of up to 15–20m and drenching onlookers in spray. Several enterprising locals have set up souvenir stalls and a restaurant to cater for the many tourists that visit. However, other less desirable instances of free enterprise have been reported at Hoyo Soplador; belongings have been stolen from tour buses and hire cars, and some so-called free drinks haven't been quite as free as they seemed.

La Loma [map page 231] Most visitors head to the town of La Loma to visit its pretty Baptist church – the first to be built on San Andrés, in 1847. This red-roofed whitewashed building wouldn't look out of place in a sleepy English village and the Iglesia Bautista Emanuel (Bautista Emanuel Church) is very much at the centre of La Loma's daily life. The spire once served as a landmark for sailors – a kind of unofficial 'lighthouse' that guided ships into San Andrés. Islanders wear their best outfits on Sunday to attend church services. Despite being partially rebuilt in 1896 the building still provides a fine example of the traditional architecture of the island.

Festivals San Andrés plays host to a Coconut Carnival in November each year to celebrate the birthday of the island and its coconut culture. Festivities abound during this three-day event, a loud, pulsating affair that requires earplugs and stamina. Christmas, Easter and Carnival are also big parties on the island. The 20 July celebration (Colombian Independence Day) sees processions of schoolchildren, military personnel, officials, brass bands and dancers take to the streets dressed in special costumes. A Pentecostal choir festival celebrates the island's choral history in musical merriment at the end of September each year. In May San Andrés hosts an International Triathlon on Johnny Cay. Other key festivals are the Battle of Boyacá celebrations in San Luis on 7 August and Columbus Day on 12 October in La Loma.

SAN LUIS [map page 231] Visitors seeking a quieter alternative to the tourist-focused capital of San Andrés will enjoy San Luis. Located on the east coast, the so-called town is really just a hamlet – a simple string of houses. This former coconut-shipment port is notable for its traditional wooden island architecture. San Luis has a nice, relaxed feel and also some fine white-sand beaches and superb snorkelling. Despite having no real town centre, San Luis has a scattering of shops, restaurants, dive shops and hotels. Keen prices and fewer tourists are increasingly appealing to shoestring travellers and holidaymakers keen to interact with the locals. Frequent buses connect San Luis with San Andrés via a 15-minute journey.

Where to stay and eat As San Luis slowly establishes itself as a tourism centre, a growing number of enterprising locals are opening bed and breakfasts and simple food joints. On occasions it is also possible to rent a small house or apartment through word of mouth. **Karibik Diver** opposite the Cocoplum Hotel has a nice place that sleeps four people – ask at the office for rates as these vary throughout the year.

Hotels

Decameron San Luis (323 rooms) 'Km17, San Luis'; ☏ 513 0300; www.decameron.com. As 1 of 4 vast Decameron all-inclusive beach resorts on the island, this is pretty much true to form, although the use of authentic island-style architecture gives it a nicer feel. Rooms are set amidst palm trees & native trees with b/fast & lunch buffets & à la carte dinners & all snacks, cigarettes & domestic drinks included in the price. A show wows the punters at 20.00 each night. On-site amenities include tennis, volleyball, windsurfing, kayaking, snorkelling, 3 restaurants (including Japanese), 4 bars, 3 swimming pools, laundry & a disco. Rooms come as twin or double &

include cable TV, fridge, safe & AC – but no phone. However, several female guests at this resort have expressed concerns regarding personal safety. Beach vendors can also be a nuisance, singling out women & flogging coconuts for cash. **$$$**
Cocoplum Hotel (42 rooms) Carretera San Luis, No 43–39; ☏ 513 2121; e informes@ cocoplumhotel.com; www.cocoplumhotel.com. This comfy beach hotel has its own stretch of sand shaded by palm trees & offers good access to the snorkelling in nearby Rocky Cay. At the hotel itself, watersports include snorkelling, diving, sailing, kayak & jet skiing. Typical island architecture is painted in vibrant dayglow aqua & lime with 24 double rooms & 18 family suites, bar

service, swimming pool, beach chairs, hammocks, massage & a nice terrace. A decent restaurant can accommodate 80 people & serves casual fish-&-rice meals all day long. **$$**

🏠 **Ocean Beach Resort** (26 rooms) ☎ 513 2866. This all-inclusive deal enjoys a magnificent palm-clad beachfront spot a short walk from the Cocoplum. Shoestring travellers shouldn't be put off by the advertised rack rates – in the off-season rooms are let go at a discounted price. **$$**

🏠 **Villa Verde** (sleeps 8) Tom Hooker, No 1a–24; m 315 770 0785; www.temporadasanandres.com. This splendid green-roofed traditional wooden home enjoys a peaceful location in a leafy palm-filled garden, just 5mins from the beach,

& is one of the nicest places to stay in San Luis. It can be hired in full, or part & sleeps 8 people. A large lounge has a tiled floor & gorgeous wooden furniture. 3 bedrooms, 2 bathrooms & a kitchen come with large wooden balconies & porched terraces overlooking lush vegetation. The house has partial AC, cable TV, swimming pool, maid service & optional car. Rates vary depending on the length of stay – haggling is expected. **$$**

Homestay options

🏠 **Caselita Forbes** 'Monica's Place'; ☎ 513 2209. **$$**

🏠 **Vicenta Livingston** 'Centa's Place'; ☎ 513 0183. **$$**

ISLA PROVIDENCIA *Telephone code 8*

> In de Caribbean de very best, is de beautiful island of Prov-ee-dence.
>
> Willy B, Providencian musician, 2001

The word 'idyllic' is often over used, but in Providencia the beaches live up to the hype. Empty stretches of powder-fine palm-scattered white sand are lapped by languid waves. The water is warm and azure-green – and often occupied by a sole bobbing wooden boat and a couple of wild horses frolicking in the lazy afternoon sun. In fact pretty much everything seems to move in slow motion in sleepy Providencia – an island with a laid-back energy. A handful of old Chevrolets pass by at walking pace, fulfilling the role of taxi, an absence of paintwork and door handles a testament to their advancing years. Calypso-shrouded open-sided restaurants care little for world-class service. Food comes served with a generous helping of good humour. Life unfolds at a leisurely pace. Friendly smiles lead to unhurried conversations. Time is an unimportant detail in this true get-away-from-it-all location – a place where it is impossible not to chill out and kick back.

Providencia's beaches are small, beautiful and often deserted. Bahía Manzanillo (Chamomile Bay) is the most popular, and there are other fine ribbons of sand at Bahía Aguadulce (Sweetwater Bay) and Bahía Suroeste (South-East Bay). Numerous other tiny white-sand bays and idyllic stretches can easily be found dotted around the shoreline.

HISTORY Providencia's colourful history is intertwined with that of neighbouring San Andrés, attracting the first human settlers at the beginning of the 17th century. Traditionally known as Old Providence, the island is now commonly known under its Spanish guise. It is the second largest in the archipelago at 17km² and lies 90km north of San Andrés. Unlike its younger, coralline neighbour, Providencia is a mountainous island of volcanic origin. Occupied and besieged by pirates throughout its history, including Dutch buccaneer Edward Mansvelt, Englishman William Dampier, Welsh privateer Henry Morgan and Frenchman Louis Michele Aury, the island is steeped in myth and legend. Like San Andrés, Providencia is rumoured to have been a final resting place for Morgan's buried treasure. Aury captured the island on 4 July 1818, establishing a settlement with a thriving economy based on plundered Spanish cargo. He unsuccessfully tried to rebuild good relations with

Bolívar before being thrown from a horse and killed in August 1821. However, his death gave rise to a number of conspiracy theories that prompted some sources to claim he was alive and living in Havana in 1845. Aury dredged a channel between Providencia and Santa Catalina. Today, the two islands are united by a 100m floating bridge called 'Lovers Lane' or 'Bridge of the Enamoured'.

GETTING THERE AND AWAY At present, there are no direct **flights** into Providencia's El Embrujo Airport other than those that connect it to San Andrés. Tickets for the 20-minute jaunt cost around 300,000COP or thereabouts, depending on demand and the season, through a single airline, Satena Airways. Strict weight restrictions apply on these tiny little planes: just 10kg is allowed for luggage before charges of 1,000COP per extra kilo apply. Seats can be scarce during high season but most passengers turn up on spec so pre-booking online (*www.satena.com*) should be OK. Be warned; it is imperative to reconfirm a return flight to avoid your seat being given away.

Few tourists are even aware there are **boats** to Providencia as these cargo carriers lack facilities and comfort. If this option appeals, head down to the Maritime El Cover del Muelle on Avenida Newball and ask for a boat called the *Doña Olga*. At the time of writing an unreliable schedule favoured a Wednesday and Friday. Pack a mattress, water and food and expect to pay 40,000COP apiece.

GETTING AROUND It's easy to rent a car or moped and drive around the island's 20km circuit of roads. Ask for car rental at the airport on arrival or head to the hamlet of Aguadulce on the west coast – the centre of the island's tourist industry, a 15-minute taxi ride away. Mopeds can be rented privately almost everywhere. *Colectivo* transport (shared minibuses) can also be found at the airport. Cycle hire is a good option for visitors keen to explore off the beaten track. The *chiva* is an easy way to circumnavigate the island's tourist trail. Tours by *lancha* (small boat) depart from Aguadulce. The chief settlement is Isabel village in the north of the island, close to the southeast of Santa Catalina Island. Other villages are San Félipe on the west coast and La Paz in the southeast.

🚗 **Muitas Rent a Car** Av Newball, Edificio Galéon; ☎ 512 4590. Expect friendly & efficient service from Jorge & Carlos Alberto García at this family-run firm. A small fleet of buggy-style open-sided jeeps are clean & well maintained. Costs range from 160,000COP in low season to 200,000COP in high season.

TOURIST INFORMATION AND TOUR OPERATORS

ℹ️ **Fundo de Promoción Turística Providencia y Santa Catalina** Santa Isabel; ☎ 514 8054; www.providenciaespasion.com. A useful website for info about Providencia.

Body Contact Bahía Aguadulce; ☎ 514 8283. This small, independent tour specialist offers a wide range of services, from kayak trips (25,000COP) & horserides (25,000COP) to hikes to El Pico (20,000COP) & boat excursions (20,000COP pp). It also rents out bicycles (20,000COP per day) & snorkel gear (12,000COP per day) & handles flight reservations & currency exchange.

Rodolfo Bahía Suroeste; ☎ 514 8626. Superb tours on horseback are this tour company's forte. Most last a couple of hours (15,000COP) & follow a mix of beach & mountain trails.

🏠 **WHERE TO STAY** *See map, page 244.*
As a tiny island, Providencia isn't blessed with umpteen hotel choices, and accommodation tends to be more expensive than San Andrés as a result. A couple of upmarket options offer some luxurious touches but most hotels are mid range or simple,

rustic affairs. Like San Andrés, Providencia offers visitors homestay accommodation as part of the archipelago's highly recommended Posadas Nativas project.

Hotels

🏠 **Hotel Deep Blue** (12 rooms) Maracaibo Bay; ✆ 514 8423; e info@hoteldeepblue.com; www.hoteldeepblue.com. As Providencia's only 'boutique' hotel the Deep Blue unashamedly wins – for all the right reasons – all the praise for luxury digs on the island. Built on a hillside with views out over the water towards Crab Caye, everything has been constructed with a careful eye for detail. The restaurant is located on a dock over

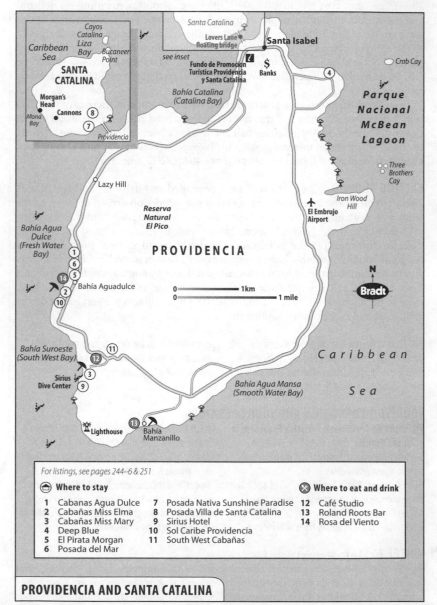

For listings, see pages 244–6 & 251

🛏 **Where to stay**
1 Cabanas Agua Dulce
2 Cabañas Miss Elma
3 Cabañas Miss Mary
4 Deep Blue
5 El Pirata Morgan
6 Posada del Mar
7 Posada Nativa Sunshine Paradise
8 Posada Villa de Santa Catalina
9 Sirius Hotel
10 Sol Caribe Providencia
11 South West Cabañas

✖ **Where to eat and drink**
12 Café Studio
13 Roland Roots Bar
14 Rosa del Viento

PROVIDENCIA AND SANTA CATALINA

above   Lago Yahuarcaca is the place to see giant lilies in abundance (SW) page 271

right   A young boy from the Amazonian Tukano tribe dressed up for a festival (SS) page 257

bottom   Leticia's market provides a good introduction to this bustling town in the heart of the Amazon (SS) page 257

left   Medellín's streets and squares are adorned with a number of sculptures by the city's favourite son, Fernando Botero (SW) page 326

below   Simón Bolívar was buried at Santa Marta Cathedral in 1830 but his body was later moved to Caracas (JK/S) page 438

bottom   Cartagena was declared a UNESCO World Heritage Site in 1984 (JK/S) pages 403–19

right The Valle de Cocora is famous for its soaring palmas de cera, Colombia's national tree (UR/DT) page 378

below National Park Tayrona is one of Colombia's most easily accessible national parks (HBS) pages 444–6

bottom The mountainous Los Nevados National Park is a popular walking destination (JK/S) pages 361–3

above   The crater of the Volcán de Lodo El Totumo is full of thick, warm mud, making this a popular spot for visitors seeking a mineral-rich natural bath (MB/S) page 421

above left   The best beaches on Isla San Andrés are on the east coast (JK/S) pages 230–42

left   A bombastic festival consumes the city of Barranquilla in the run-up to Lent; locals claim that it is second only to Rio de Janeiro's Mardi Gras (UR/DT) page 430

below   The islands of Providencía and Santa Catalina are united by a 100m floating bridge (SW) page 250

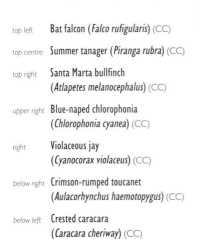

top left	Bat falcon (*Falco rufigularis*) (CC)
top centre	Summer tanager (*Piranga rubra*) (CC)
top right	Santa Marta bullfinch (*Atlapetes melanocephalus*) (CC)
upper right	Blue-naped chlorophonia (*Chlorophonia cyanea*) (CC)
right	Violaceous jay (*Cyanocorax violaceus*) (CC)
below right	Crimson-rumped toucanet (*Aulacorhynchus haemotopygus*) (CC)
below left	Crested caracara (*Caracara cheriway*) (CC)

above **Squirrel monkeys (*Saimiri sciureus*)**
(TM/MP/FLPA)

right **Jaguar (*Panthera onça*)** (FL/FLPA)

below **Streamer hogfish (*Bodianus diplotaenia*)** (WF/A)

the water where you can also laze on a sunlounger & clear your mind of the hassles of the day-to-day existence in paradise. **$$$$**

🏠 **Cabañas Agua Dulce** (24 cabins) Bahia Aguadulce; ☎ 514 8160; www.cabanasaguadulce. com. Set back from the beach but located in a charmingly painted enclave, perhaps in need of a little refurbishment, these 24 cabins cater to families & couples seeking a little more privacy. Decent restaurant on site & a short walk from the shops & other restaurants in Bahia Aguadulce. **$$$**

🏠 **Hotel El Pirata Morgan** (30 rooms) Bahia Aguadulce; ☎ 514 8528; e morganhotel@hotmail. com; elpiratamorganhotel.org. Undoubtedly one of the best mid-budget hotels on the island & has the added benefit of being close to a decent supermarket with a terrific rooftop pool, good restaurant & lovely terrace. **$$$**

🏠 **Sol Caribe Providencia** (approx 10 rooms) Bahía Aguadulce; ☎ 514 8036; www.solarhoteles. com. This charming hotel located in a bright & breezy blue-&-orange-painted 2-storey building is a real delight. Built in traditional architectural style, the exterior wooden terraces are adorned with palm-filled pots & wind-chimes while shuttered windows boast stunning views across leafy gardens. All-inclusive deals favour 3-night stays. Cheerful rooms have AC, colour TV, fridge & phone. **$$$**

🏠 **Cabañas Miss Elma** (4 rooms) Bahia Augadulce; ☎ 514 8229. A handful of fan-cooled rooms & suites with AC are comfortably furnished & right on the beach. A restaurant is a little pricey, but good nonetheless. Opt for the lobster if you feel like a splurge. **$$**

🏠 **Cabañas Miss Mary** (8 rooms) Bahia Suroeste; ☎ 514 8454. Highly recommended on the basis that it sits on a jaw-dropping palm-scattered beach, Miss Mary also has a fine seafood-&-rice restaurant as well as basic rooms with AC, right on the sand – request 1 of the 4 with gorgeous sea views. **$$**

🏠 **Posada del Mar** (30 rooms) Bahía Aguadulce; ☎ 514 8168/628 0000; e inforeservas@posadadelmarprovidencia.com. Almost all rooms in this Decameron-affiliated beach-facing hostel have pleasant balconies slung with hammocks. It's clean, comfortable & a good budget option close to restaurants & bars. **$$**

🏠 **Sirius Hotel** (7 rooms) Bahia Suroeste; ☎ 514 8213; e info@siriushotel.net; www. siriushotel.net. Swiss-Colombian owned, relaxed & good value, the Sirius has been set up for those wishing to opt out & escape on a diving holiday. **$$**

🏠 **South West Cabañas** (30 rooms) Bahía Suroeste; ☎ 514 8221; e info@southwestbayhotel. com; www.southwestbayhotel.com. Although it's not right on the beach, this place is only a 5min stroll away & is highly popular with a mixed crowd of vacationers. Choose from 14 rooms & 16 larger self-contained suites that are ideal for longer stays on the island. Discounted packages for 1 week plus. **$$**

Homestay options

🏠 **Christine Huffington** 'Christine Huffington's Place' (Bahía Aguadulce); ☎ 514 8361. **$$**

🏠 **Josefina Huffington** 'Miss Elma's' (Bahía Aguadulce); ☎ 514 8953. **$$**

🏠 **Joyce Hooker** 'Joy's Place' (Bahía Agua Mansa); no phone (just ask around). **$$**

🏠 **June Marie Mow Robinson** 'Miss June's Place' (Lazy Hill); ☎ 514 8953. **$$**

🏠 **Rosa María Fortune Archbold** 'Posada Fortune' (Bahía Agua Mansa); no phone (just ask around). **$$**

🏠 **Victoria Bernard** 'Miss Vicky's' (Bahía Suroeste); ☎ 514 9152. **$$**

✖ **WHERE TO EAT AND DRINK** *See map, page 244.*

In addition to the restaurants listed below, many of the hotels have good dining options.

✖ **Café Studio** Bahía Suroeste; ☎ 514 9076; ⊕ 11.00–21.00 Mon–Sat. This coffee-&-cake joint is owned by a Canadian expat & almost everyone sipping espressos is a traveller far from home. However, the menu is exceptionally good with unsurpassed traditional favourites that include seafood & rice, pesto spaghetti & roasted crab. **$$**

✖ **Restaurante Rosa del Viento** Bahía Aguadulce; ☎ 514 8067; ⊕ for b/fast at 07.00, this pleasant eatery serves food until early evening. Find it behind the Hotel El Pirata Morgan & expect a decent plate of fried fish, coconut rice, salad & *patacones*. **$**

THE FOOD OF THE ISLANDERS

Native cuisine represents an important part of the island's culture and Providencia dishes have a strong Afro-Caribbean flavour. Islanders adore *rondón* (meaning 'rundown'), a stew of conch, yucca, plantain and dumpling cooked in coconut milk. The island's sweet-fleshed crab is prepared in numerous ways, from a delicious soup served in deep terrines with sweet bread rolls and fried crab patty to simply cooked with butter in its shell. Fresh fish fried in coconut oil comes served with coconut rice and plantains with lots of conch and lobster dishes and fish meatballs. Another firm favourite is baked *po* (roasted pork). Islanders also have a very sweet tooth and so baked cookies, cakes and sweets are in good supply, including mango pies, Johnny cake and coconut bread. Meals are often accompanied by the home-distilled rum known as 'bushy'.

✕ Roland Roots Bar Bahía Manzanillo; ☏514 8417. This atmospheric open-air hangout is shaded by coconut palms & drenched in the sound of reggae rhythms from noon until dawn. Roland & his late-night revelry are legendary in Providencia. Before the serious drinking starts the bar also serves a decent menu. They serve some tasty fried fish & seafood dishes. Roland also has a room for rent – but earplugs are a must. $

ENTERTAINMENT AND NIGHTLIFE Night-owls will discover that Providencia is a simple place after dark. A dozen or so bars and a few open-air nightclubs are frequented by a mix of islanders and tourists while groups of local musicians often perform on the beach. Those lucky enough to arrive on a full moon can join in the celebrations at Manchineel Bay or Southwest Bay. A bonfire is lit to the pulsating sounds of loud reggae music. Rum flows like water until the party ends at dawn.

Wherever you are in Providencia, you are sure to hear the loud slap of dominoes. Islanders play with great gusto on rickety wooden tables in the street, under the glare of a street lamp.

The music and dance customs and traditions of the island reflect the heritage of its inhabitants' mix of European, indigenous and Afro-Caribbean roots. European influences can be clearly found in *schottische*, polka and *mazurka* dances. Indigenous music known as 'string' is played using a washtub bass, fiddle, mandolin, maracas and the jawbone of an ass. A *mento* comes from the Antilles and reggae from Jamaica. The island's calypso tradition stems from Trinidad, with guitar *pasillos* from Spain. An entertainment known as 'rhyme' uses extemporaneous rhyming to poke fun at those present, an African tradition. North American country music can also be found in Providencia along with Colombian salsa, *merengue* and *vallenato*. **Roland Roots Bar** (see above) in Bahía Manzanillo is a popular place to hang out listening to reggae into the wee small hours.

Storytelling remains an important part of Providencia's lengthy oral tradition and some of the best historic tales of the island's former days come from Virginia Archbold, a former mayor of Providencia. Virginia's family were one of the first on the island. She often conducts historical tours and is happy to chat to visitors. To seek out this fountain of knowledge, just ask around.

SHOPPING Souvenir stalls and street vendors sell a diverse range of artwork and tourist tat, but some of the nicer handicrafts are the bright Caribbean paintings and woven baskets. A browse around Bahía Aguadulce's excellent Arts and Crafts is worth it for meeting the French owner alone. 'El Frenchie' is a great source of local information for travellers, and whips up a mean fresh-fruit smoothie to boot. Local homemade fruit wine (tamarind and plum) can also be purchased. On Sundays, look out for stalls of freshly baked pies at the roadsides island-wide. These melt-in-the-mouth local delicacies (*tortas*) are truly delicious. Choose from cocoa, lemon, mango, pumpkin and papaya – at 2,000COP each.

OTHER PRACTICALITIES

Money and banks Visitors are strongly advised to sort out cash and currency ahead of arrival as Providencia isn't blessed with facilities. Two banks in Santa Isabel are open from 08.00 until 13.30 Monday to Thursday. They extend the hours by 30 minutes on Friday and have an ATM. Other, unofficial, money changers operate on the island but most will only trade dollars – and rates are dire. Credit cards are not widely accepted.

Internet and communications In Santa Isabel, **Net Crawler** (✆ *514 8956*) is open 08.00–21.00 (closed noon–14.30) each day. Although this is Providencia's only dedicated internet facility, **Body Contact** (page 243), offers chargeable internet access in times of need. Be warned; connections on the island can be frustratingly slow.

Medical Dr William Burbano offers a clinic to visitors 14.00–17.00 on weekdays in Aguadulce (✆ *514 8912*).

WHAT TO SEE AND DO

Hiking Providencia's craggy rise-and-fall volcanic terrain makes it a pleasant place to explore on foot. Several guides operate out of Casabaja and Aguadulce

---

SPIRITED AND SPELLBOUND

Ha I'm the Obeah woman, above pain
I can eat thunder and drink the rain
I kiss the moon and hug the sun
And call the spirits and make 'em run.

Nina Simone, 'Obeah Woman', It is Finished, 2004

Obeah is a style of Afro-Caribbean shamanism that uses ancient occult powers handed down orally over the centuries through the generations. Today, this aged spell-craft is practised throughout Africa and the Caribbean. In the San Andrés Archipelago it is prevalent, albeit in a watered-down form. Purveyors of present-day *Obeah* use traditional witchcraft, sorcery, shamanism, voodoo, *palo, santeria*, rootwork, hoodoo and tribal magic– yet it remains shrouded in secrecy. Islanders believe that *Obeah* is a potent force – a deadly and dangerous power in the wrong hands. Grown men believe they can be weakened by the spells of *Obeahman*. Those committing ill deeds render themselves powerless to the strength of *Obeah*. Nothing is free – there is always a pay-off somewhere at the hands of the spirits, they say. Spells relate to both black and white magic using charms, talismans, luck and mysticism. *Obeah* also came to mean any physical object such as a talisman or charm that was used for evil magical purposes. However, despite its fearsome reputation, *Obeah* is also used to good purpose. Like many other forms of folk magic it contains traditions for healing and bringing about luck in love and money.

and will usually offer a hike to the top of El Pico (page 249) or along the mangrove coastal path to the west for 20,000–30,000COP. The highest hills on Providencia are remnants of a carapace of felsic lava flows and domes. Trails lead through lush vegetation containing flocks of varicoloured birds. Stunning views and lots of small animals offer plenty of points of interest. An absence of poisonous snakes makes a walk in the wild non-hazardous although hikers should remain vigilant of mosquito swarms and biting ants.

Snorkelling Apart from the sites around the offshore belt near the islets of Cayo Tres Hermanos (Three Brothers Cay) and Cayo Cangrejo (Crab Cay), most of Providencia's finest dive spots are located on the island's western flank. Here, the coral reefs are even more remarkable than those around San Andrés with brightly coloured sponges and pristine fingers and brains. Snorkelling and scuba tour companies primarily operate out of Aguadulce, with most offering boat dives and instruction with a choice of half- and full-day tours. Crystal-clear waters make underwater photography popular – and even novices should pack a disposable waterproof camera to capture Providencia's stunning seabed views.

Fishing Islanders are practised masters of fishing and never come to shore empty-handed, even from the most difficult of waters. Little wooden boats bob close to shore in the early morning with larger vessels departing for deeper water at dusk. Many local fishermen offer one-to-one or small group tours, using nets and hooks and free diving in search of lobster, sea snail, bream, grouper, turtle, crab and other reef species. Ask around at Aguadulce – the guys at tour operator Body Contact (page 243) usually come up trumps.

Parque Nacional McBean Lagoon (McBean Lagoon National Park) (*admission 20,000COP*) On volcanic terrain shaped by ancient streams, this 990ha conservation zone at the northeastern end of the island was declared a national park in 1995. Underwater gardens account for more than 360ha with a terra firma segment that encompasses a 150m volcanic peak, Iron Wood Hill, and flat expanses of mangrove swamps. These complex marshland forests contain a predominance of red, yellow and white mangrove – an important breeding site for several species of turtles, fish, molluscs and birds. Shallow lagoon waters contain Crab Cay and Three Brothers Cay protected by sand bars and coral reef.

The vegetation on Iron Wood Hill is dry forest with cockspur the dominant species and a natural habitat for an aggressive biting ant. Pactá palms and several species of

---

COOK WITH AN ISLAND GIRL

Flamboyant islander Lucy Trigidia Chow Robinson (\ *513 2233*; m *311 808 9039*; e *lucytrigidia@yahoo.com)* (see box, page 233) is also an accomplished cook in the traditional style of San Andrés. She adores food and her enthusiasm for all things culinary is evident in the cookery schools she hosts. Packed with fun and gastronomic insight, Lucy takes students shopping for ingredients at the local fish and fruit markets. She introduces them to indigenous herbs and ancient cooking styles – and then they get to eat the results. Lucy's workshops cost from 50,000COP (excluding ingredients). She can accommodate a maximum of five would-be chefs at a time.

We should praise the Lord for that we can be making so much crabs soup. All because of He bountiful goodness. We rich. He give us plenty crabs.

Mr Williams, Providencia resident, 1991

Islanders have a strong connection with the black land crab (*Gecarcinus ruricola*), an important symbol of native cultural identity and valued source of protein. Generations of islanders have celebrated the link between crab and human through story, folklore and song. An annual crab festival also honours the island's unusual relationship with this magnificent species of crustacean. Yet it is in April and May each year that the black land crab really makes its mark, journeying from the cool inland forests to the sea to spawn in a vast moving carpet. After two perilous weeks in the ocean, the young make the return trip, crossing treacherous paths and roads back to the relative safety of the woodlands. This extraordinary mass migration lasts a good two weeks and brings traffic to a halt in Aguadulce and Suroeste. Roads are covered so densely with crabs on the move that it is impossible to cross from side to side without decimating their ranks.

cactus and scrub can also be found on the slopes of the hill. In Crab Key (Cayo Cangrejo) vegetation is mainly coconut palm while in Three Brothers Cay (Cayo Tres Hermanos), the picus tree provides an important nesting place for frigatebirds. Several extensive areas of sea grass surround the lagoon including a large prairie of marine phanerogams with coral outcrops on a rocky coastal strip home to several algae species. Sizeable numbers of multi-coloured lizard and bird species can be easily spotted throughout all areas of the park environments, including 56 migrant bird species from the western Caribbean. Birders will enjoy a slow meander along the 800m-long eco-path that winds through the mangrove systems.

Reserva Natural El Pico (El Pico Natural Reserve) Don't forgo a chance to tackle the 1½-hour ascent to the top of El Pico, the highest point of Providencia at 360m above sea level. It not only offers spectacular panoramic views across a stunning seascape but also provides a chance to enjoy some beautiful leafy bird-filled trails. Most people begin the steady climb in Casabaja although several paths criss-cross upwards. It's no hard slog, more a leisurely hike. However, it is recommended that tourists use a guide to avoid getting lost. Most charge 20,000–30,000COP and can be booked through a tour operator or the tourism office. Making an early start is worth the effort to avoid the heat of the day. Take plenty of water for the trip as there are no shops or facilities along the way.

Festivals Providencia has a lengthy horseracing tradition with regular meetings on the beach. Cat-boat racing and domino tournaments are also staged year-round by the islanders – look out for the posters and ask around the bars for details of the venues or follow the crowds. The locals of Providencia are renowned for their love of tombola, carnivals and national and religious holidays. A potent local brew makes each festival or celebration a lively affair (see box, page 246).

Providencia's main annual event is a week-long cultural festival in June. Dancing, live music and parades culminate in an iguana beauty contest – well, what else?

San Andrés Archipelago   ISLA PROVIDENCIA

6

Now put your shirt on. You look much too naked for a decent English gentleman.

'Captain Sir Henry Morgan' – *The Black Swan* (1942)

Much has been written about Henry Morgan's seafaring exploits and maritime battles with the Spanish. In 1666, Morgan commanded a ship to seize the islands of Old Providence and Santa Catalina. He then took the well-garrisoned town of Portobelo, using captured Jesuits as human shields when attacking the fortress. After escapades in Jamaica and Cuba, Morgan recaptured the island of Santa Catalina in 1670, from where he planned the sacking of Panama's capital city. It was a bloody raid that saw Morgan leave with riches beyond his wildest dreams. As he departed, he burnt the city to the ground, massacring thousands. Morgan returned to the San Andrés Archipelago with his plunder and settled on Santa Catalina where islanders are convinced he buried gold and treasure. So are the locals on Providencia, who swear his booty lies in Cueva de Morgan.

However, this sacking of Panama violated a peace treaty between England and Spain. Morgan was arrested and returned forcibly to England in 1672 where he was able to prove he had no knowledge of the treaty. He was knighted in 1674 before taking up the post of lieutenant governor until his rowdy behaviour and drunkenness caused him to be replaced. Morgan's health steadily declined until his death in 1688.

Today he is immortalised in many diverse ways. Morgan is depicted in an array of films and books including John Steinbeck's 1926 novel *Cup of Gold* and Bob Marley and the Wailers' song 'You Can't Blame The Youth'. In 1942, cinema goers watched Anthony Quinn in *The Black Swan*, a film that drew on the life of Sir Henry Morgan. Each year in early summer, Colombia's boating scene honours Wales's own menace of the seas. Mariners, boaters and cruisers complete a 400-mile race to Providencia in a good-natured battle that attracts a motley potpourri of sailing crafts. Morgan's Run (La Ruta de Morgan) takes place over several days, making landfall at Bajo Nuevo in the northernmost corner of Colombia before heading to Serrana and Low Cay. Providencia comes out in force to welcome the flotilla to the island before hosting a madcap rum-soaked award ceremony befitting of a man who liked his drink. On Providencia, several bars bear the name of Morgan. Santa Catalina has a Hotel El Pirata Morgan while a volcanic rock battered by the sea is said to resemble his face. Morgan is also the figurehead for Captain Morgan's Spiced Rum – an ironic legacy for a man whose alcoholism brought about his death from liver failure.

ISLA SANTA CATALINA *Telephone code 8*

A brightly coloured 100m 'floating' bridge links this islet to neighbouring Providencia and exploring Santa Catalina on foot starts with a crossing. Green hills and rocky cliffs typify the landscape. Hidden caverns lie tucked away in volcanic outcrops edged by tiny soft-sand beaches. Santa Catalina has no roads. Some steep steps to the west of the bridge lead to a picture-pretty rocky beach, a decent spot from which to snorkel to spot octopus, lobsters and sea crabs.

On the southern flank of the island a small settlement contains a handful of fish-and-rice restaurants. From here, a short walk leads to Morgan's Head and the ruins of Fort Warwick – complete with cannons. History has ensured that Santa Catalina remains inextricably linked with Henry Morgan and several sites on the island are attributed to the Welsh buccaneer. Morgan's Head is a volcanic boulder carved by the breeze and now said to resemble the privateer's face. Under the rock, a natural pool is home to large barracudas; many thrill-seeking travellers jump from the rock straight into the depths. Santa Catalina's wild vegetation and rugged nooks and crannies are home to boa constrictors, iguana and numerous black crabs.

WHERE TO STAY AND EAT *See map, page 244.*

Posada Nativa Sunshine Paradise
(2 suites) 514 9031; m 311 2270 333; e franciscarobinson@yahoo.com; www. posadasunshine.com. Lovely 'island-style' suites comprise a sitting room with garden table, bedroom & private bathroom (b/fast extra). Located just a few minutes from the bridge to Providencia, the building boasts super views across the island. Owners Francisca & Fredy are warm, chatty & welcoming. **$$$**

Posada Villa de Santa Catalina (7 rooms)
514 8400. This pretty, private home is owned by Francia de Armas. Leafy gardens surround this statuesque cream-painted wooden house with breezy terraces overlooking palms & lush shrubs. Sra de Armas opens her family home to tourists keen to learn about native island traditions. Typical dishes are served at mealtimes & cultural rituals observed. Rates vary, depending on the season. From **$**

SEND US YOUR SNAPS!

We'd love to follow your adventures using our *Colombia* guide – why not send us your photos and stories via Twitter (@BradtGuides) and Instagram (@bradtguides) using the hashtag #colombia. Alternatively, you can upload your photos directly to the gallery on the Colombia destination page via our website (*www.bradtguides.com*).

7

Amazonia

Our land is special, a spiritual place. It's the lungs of the world, a rich botanical store-cupboard. I believe that the Earth gave us life. Our magnificent territory is sacred. Blessed by Mother Nature.

Ticuna Amerindian elder, 2007

Few places in the world are as untamed and wild as the Amazon Basin, an isolated region swathed in vast, impenetrable jungle covering almost one-third of the Colombian territory. Exhilarating, humbling and awe-inspiring, the watershed is roughly the size of Germany, spanning 643,000km² and covering some 40% of South America as the largest lowland in Latin America. The river starts as a tiny trickle atop the snow-capped Andes Mountains and flows across the South American continent until it enters the Atlantic Ocean at Belém, Brazil. Reaching 40km in width at the height of the rainy season the mighty River Sea (as it is often referred to) can flood up to 350,000km² of land. Stretches of the Amazon River are deep enough to accommodate ocean liners. Sections are fast-flowing and debris-scattered fed by over 1,100 tributaries, 17 of which are more than 1,000 miles long. This mammoth watershed contains over two-thirds of the earth's fresh water in its rivers, streams and tributaries. From the headwaters of Peru's Ucayali-Apurímac river system the river flows for 6,400km to Brazil via Colombia, a distance slightly shorter than the Nile River but roughly the equivalent of a journey from New York City to Rome. Tiny wood-and-thatch villages hug emerald vine-tangled riverbanks to the cacophony of squawking crimson parrots, chattering monkeys and whining insects in the treetops overhead. Piranha, crocodiles and dugout canoes navigate the waters of the mighty Amazon River and its many tributaries. Indigenous tribes hostile to strangers hide themselves away in the rainforest, living much as they did before the arrival of the Europeans, hunting, fishing and eating a diet of berries, plants and fruit. Giant blue butterflies and water lilies the size of serving trays are just a couple of the highlights in this magical, surreal land. Hot, sticky conditions complete with vast swarms of hungry mosquitoes and reddish glue-like mud prevail along this brooding river stretch of inky green.

As a region, the Amazon is home to at least 7,500 species of butterfly, 1,800 birds, 800 insect species and almost 2,000 species of reptile and amphibian. It contains 3,200 species of fish and is home to a staggering 10% of all species found on the planet. Botanists have recorded 51,220 species of plant, but doubt they will ever be able to catalogue everything in the lifetime of the world. In a single acre of forest, as many as 100 arboreal species have been counted. Up to 121 million litres of water per second are generated by the Amazon River with an average of three million tonnes of sediment deposited each day near its mouth. The annual outflow from the river accounts for 20% of all the fresh water draining into the entire world's oceans.

COLOMBIAN AMAZON

While the Colombian Amazon is, in reality, a small sector of the whole basin region, it is nonetheless complex and varied. Quite, quite different from the rest of the region, it plummets from the Andes to low, forested plains. Extensive lowlands flank the river and its many tributaries (*várzeas*). Rapids and cascading waterfalls make Colombia's Amazonian waterways tricky to navigate but they are worth the effort nonetheless. Annual flooding is significant so soil is richer than the savannahs with areas dotted with coarse igneous rock. Local tour operators generally include bits of Peruvian and Brazilian territories into their itineraries. Although this throws a mobile-phone signal into confusion, it does allow a greater chance to observe the astounding wonder of this unique environment. In some small way it also helps to capture the essence of scale in the Amazon's vast wilderness.

Today, despite the concerted efforts of humankind to dominate the natural resources of the Amazon region, this vast drainage basin remains intact. Carbon dioxide is absorbed at a phenomenal rate by this enormous, resplendent biomass – just one of the many environmental reasons that the Amazon is an important ecological component of the planet. Unlike the crude destruction of the forest in Brazil, the watershed remains a remote and undisturbed landscape in Colombia, primarily because it is inaccessible and foreboding. Razor-sharp machetes often struggle to slice a trail for even the most modest of treks through the Amazon's dense, multi-layered forest. These small clearings re-establish themselves relatively quickly. Unlike the commercial logging in Brazil, Colombia's indigenous communities rarely embark on large-scale deforestation, felling only single trees for their own small-scale needs.

Amazonia

7

Formed in the Palaeozoic period, somewhere between 500 million and 200 million years ago, the Amazon region boasts untold riches in geological terms. Once, the Amazon River flowed westward, possibly as part of a proto-Congo (Zaire) river system from the interior of present-day Africa when the continents were joined as part of Gondwana. When the South American and Nazca plates collided 50 million years ago, the Andes were formed, blocking the river and causing it to create a vast inland sea. Over time, the water became marshland and freshwater lakes, prompting the evolution of marine life to adapt to this new saline-free environment. Some ten million years ago, the Amazon experienced its next geological milestone as the water forced its sandstone borders to begin the flow eastward, leading to the birth of its forested areas. Mammals migrated, plants flourished and species spawned subspecies to create an incredible array of flora and fauna. During the Ice Age the levels of the great Amazon Lake dropped to become a river.

Isolated, inhospitable and riddled with disease-carrying biting insects, it is hardly surprising the Amazon was largely ignored by the civilised world until its discovery by Vicente Yáñez Pinzón in 1502. However, early European explorers were daunted by the tangle of dense vegetation through which they were forging and soon realised that it offered little in the way of fresh supplies of food. Pinzón ascended to a point about 50m from the sea, naming it the 'Río Santa María de la Mar Dulce'. He fast became known throughout the world as the first explorer to discover an estuary of the Amazon River. Yet it is Francisco de Orellana who is credited with giving the Amazon River its name. Born in 1511 in the town of Trujillo in the Spanish Extremadura province, Orellana was the son of a prominent family. The conquistador was hardly more than a boy when he first went to sea. He cut his teeth fighting Manco Inca but was tempted to venture further into South America in 1541 by tales of a land rich in gold – El Dorado. He had heard that the ruler of these lands dusted himself with gold each day and Orellana was keen to meet this fabled Golden Man. He joined an expedition to a remote region east of Ecuador, trekking across rain-drenched mountains and hacking through native rainforest for seven months in desperate conditions. Eventually, the men arrived at the banks of a wide river, but not before some 4,000 of Orellana's comrades had died, with many too sick or hungry to continue. The expedition set about building a boat to ferry the sick and dying upstream and soon the *San Pedro* was ready to sail. The men soon realised that the land ahead was vast and uninhabited, offering little in the way of food to help them survive. Orellana suggested that he take the boat and some 60 men downriver in search of supplies as an alternative, agreeing to return within 12 days. However, the current was so strong that Orellana had no choice but to sail downriver with no hope of return.

During the terrifying journey Orellana's party survived several attacks by Amerindians, encountering a fierce tribe of warriors he swore were female. So strong and fearless were this tribe, Orellana compared them to Amazon women from Greek mythology, so when his crew made it through alive despite near-starvation Orellana is said to have given the river its name. Historians now argue that the women were more likely long-haired male native fighters, although few alternative theories exist on how the river got its name. However, Orellana faced mixed fortunes on his return to Spain. Instead of being hailed a hero, he was widely viewed as a turncoat for deserting the rest of the expedition. Indeed he became known as the infamous 'One-Eyed Traitor' in certain circles, having lost an eye early in his career during one of many hand-to-hand battles. Francisco de Orellana returned to the Amazon region in 1549, where he died. Today he is credited with the distinction of having been the first man to have navigated the entire length of the Amazon River, thus bringing recognition of its immensity to the world. He is honoured in Leticia by a park bearing his name.

ECOLOGICAL CONCERNS

The drum will be my home, the cradle my canoe
The river my road, the jungle my science
The land my base, the sun my reach
The air my lungs, the blood my sap.

Francelina Muchavisoy, Inga Amerindian song, the Amazon, 2006

Even conservative estimates suggest that rainforest deforestation will destroy almost half of the world's ten million species of plants, animals and micro-organisms or see them severely under threat within the next 25 years. Some 137 plant and animal species are lost every single day – a staggering 50,000 species a year. Serious conservation concerns exist in relation to the Amazon's role as one of the planet's most complex chemical storehouses. For, although rainforests across the globe today provide sources for 25% of all modern medicines, a massive amount of untapped potential remains. Scientists are confident that some 70% of rainforest plants have some anti-cancer properties. However, at the current rate of deforestation, many of these plants will be extinct before studies can be carried out. The National Institute for Space Research (INPE) shows more than 25,000km² of forest were cleared in one year – with vast swathes of land logged to grow crops. Moderate figures suggest that in the last 15 years, more than 243,000km² of the earth's forests have been destroyed. Just 100ha of Amazon rainforest can contain up to 1,500 different plant species, as many as in the whole of the UK.

A broader fear among ecologists is that deforestation and slash-and-burn has seen greenhouse gases increase. Other concerns include the impact of deforestation by the coca cultivation trade on the Amazon's ecosystem. In some of Colombia's key biodiversity hot spots vast quantities of glyphosate have been sprayed as part of a government initiative. Although figures suggest drug production has been slowed, it is far from eradicated. However, serious concerns surrounding the effects of the sprays continue to fuel protests from the local indigenous peoples, who claim surfactant chemicals and herbicides have penetrated the foliage of plants vital to their traditional medicines and diet. According to a survey by the Food and Agriculture Organization of the United Nations (FAO), deforestation in the Amazon rainforest suffered the largest net loss of forests between 2000 and 2005. However, in 2006, a WWF report suggested that deforestation rates in the Amazon were in decline, but warned that ranching, logging and agricultural activities were continuing to degrade the jungle, especially in the Brazilian Amazon, where 17% of the natural vegetation has already been lost. A report released in 2011 revealed that between 1990 and 2010, Colombia lost 3.2% of its forest cover, or around 2,020,000ha and the most recent UN report shows that Colombia loses nearly 2,000km² of natural forest every year. Colombia's forests contain 6,805 million metric tons of carbon in living forest biomass.

In a bid to protect their land, some indigenous tribes are using Google Earth, global positioning system (GPS) mapping and other technologies to combine traditional rainforest knowledge with Western technology to better conserve the Amazon's forests. The initiative is designed to help the Amerindian communities preserve their ecosystem and medicinal plants through an enhanced understanding of their location and its threats. It is led by the **Amazon Conservation Team** (ACT)

(+1 703 522 4684; e info@amazonteam.org; www.amazonteam.org), a US-based non-profit organisation working with a number of indigenous communities to help nurture a better understanding of conservation in the Amazon whilst protecting its biodiversity and rainforest culture. ACT was founded by Mark Plotkin, an accomplished author and renowned ethnobotanist, who has spent much of the past 20 years with some of the most isolated indigenous groups in the world.

PEOPLE

Six *departamentos* (provinces) make up the Colombian Amazon region: Putumayo, Caquetá, Amazonas, Vaupés, Guainía and the Guaviare. The local Amerindian population is large and extremely diverse, although it represents a thin spread (0.33

A RUMBLE IN THE JUNGLE

Colombia's history of domestic warfare equipped it well to deal with its conflict with Peru. A powerful riverine fleet proved crucial in defending Colombian borders when the two nations went head to head over the control of the harbour town of Leticia in 1932. It wasn't the first time this Colombian Amazon settlement had been at the centre of a battle as Leticia had been up to its neck in boundary wrangles since the colonial era. An 1829 bilateral treaty was drawn up using the principle of *uti possidetis* (possession at end of war), but this failed to specify with true geographic accuracy the precise co-ordinates of the colonial boundary. A second agreement in 1930 was dismissed by Peru as biased towards Colombian interests with four subsequent treaties in 1906, 1909 and 1911. However, despite arbitration the opposing sides failed to agree on the nitty-gritty. Troops from both countries moved into the region and in 1911 things turned ugly. After Peruvian soldiers attacked the tiny Colombian garrison town of Puerto Córdoba both countries agreed a treaty limiting the number of troops in the area. In 1922, a further treaty officially recognised the legitimacy of Colombia's boundary. However, Peru refused to ratify this agreement for six years. In 1928, the pact was finally signed and sealed with both parties confirming that the lengthy border wrangle was resolved. In 1930, Colombia took formal possession of its territory although Peru took until 1932 to fully withdraw its troops.

Then, lo and behold, trouble flared up again when over 300 armed Peruvian civilians seized the town of Leticia in a bloody show of strength that saw arm-to-arm combat in the streets. Infuriated, Colombia immediately mobilised 1,500 soldiers to repel the invaders, prompting the Peruvian government to switch tack. Within a flash, it stopped openly criticising the actions of its unruly citizens and began speaking out in support of their protest. In early 1933, a Colombian river fleet was sent up the Amazon to Leticia to reclaim the town from the invaders. Months of diplomatic spite followed before both parties agreed on how to end the dispute. Brokered by the League of Nations, a provisional peace treaty was signed in May 1933, followed by yet another bilateral agreement in June 1934, when Leticia was formally returned to Colombian control. Peru issued an apology for the 1932 invasion, while Colombia pledged a non-aggressive future relationship based on mutual goodwill and bilateral co-operation. The agreement was ratified in September 1935 with relationships between the two cordial ever since.

inhabitants per 1.6km²) across a territory that is still remarkably unexplored. Many of Colombia's ethnic and linguistic groups have their home in the world's largest rainforest, accounting for several hundred tribes and more than 100 languages and dialects.

The Tukanos, Gwananos, Taiwanos, Kubeos, Karapanás, Dsanos, Barasanas, Makunas, Sionas and Koreguajes all use the Tukanoan family of languages, while Witotan is spoken by the Boras, Witotos, Muinanes, Andokes and Mirañas. Many indigenous groups speak languages belonging to the Arawakan family, including the Yukunas, Tamimukas, Matapies, Kuripakos and Baniwas. A tiny population of Karibs speak a Karib derivative while numerous groups of nomadic Makús use a language that remains unclassified. Few large congregations of people exist outside of the administrative capital of Leticia. Unsurprisingly, this isolation has appealed to Colombia's narco-traffickers and leftist rebels who continue to seek sanctuary in the Amazon's secluded leafy depths.

Many Amazonian people simply want to be left alone and care little for interaction with tourists. In Nazareth, a small tribal settlement just off the Amazon River, the villagers have told local tour operators to stay well away and have banned curious outsiders. With 35,000 tourists visiting the region each year, some communities have become fed up with people disrespecting their heritage and hospitality in what they wear, what they say and by how much rubbish they leave behind. The issue of sensitivity when it comes to taking photographs (page 108) has also led to communities saying enough is enough.

Further information can be obtained from the following organisations.

Fundación Gaia-Amazonas Carrera 4, No 26B–31, Bogotá; www.gaiaamazonas.org. NGO set up to strengthen indigenous conservation in the Colombian Amazon.

Indians of the Amazon e info@amazon-indians.org; www.amazon-indians.org. US-based educational resource for photos & videos of native indigenous people of the Amazon rainforest.

LETICIA *Telephone code 8*

Providing a gateway to the Colombian Amazon, Leticia (*www.leticia-amazonas. gov.co*) sits on a narrow strip of land stretching south of the Putumayo River, at the point where the borders of Colombia, Brazil and Peru meet (Tres Fronteras). Hot, steamy and often oppressively humid, Leticia retains the air of an isolated outpost despite good flight connections with Bogotá. Arrive on a small, low-flying plane to enjoy hours atop the rainforest canopy with no sign of human settlement. For a frontier town engulfed in wild, inaccessible jungle Leticia is actually remarkably pretty – and a welcome sight for new arrivals after several hours skimming across the Amazon's broccoli-like jungle. More than 800km from the nearest Colombian highway, it boasts a kaleidoscopic mix of restaurants, cafés and painted houses, set on grid-system streets that are parched in the dry season and boggy in the wet. Leticia and Tabatinga (in Brazil) remain joined as a single city in many ways, with easy pedestrian and vehicular access and no clear border or patrol.

Leticia has grown considerably in the last decade to support increased levels of **tourism**. As the capital of the department of Amazonas, Leticia is home to the only major port on the river, although at first glance this seems a rather grand title for a muddy stretch of riverbank in Colombia's southernmost town. But while the port is nothing special, the atmosphere certainly is, amidst dozens of vendors and market stalls selling all manner of fruits beside a brightly coloured children's playground. Expect to find a mishmash of travellers sat patiently on their haunches – fresh-faced Scandinavian backpackers, American biologists and lone birdwatchers –

This potent jungle brew is known by at least 42 indigenous names in the Amazon and is used by more than 70 of the region's several hundred indigenous tribes. Though widely separated by distance, language, culture and societal values, these very different communities each have this hallucinogenic tipple in common, be they in the jungle settlements of the Peruvian Amazon or the fishing villages of Ecuador, Colombia, Bolivia and Brazil. Called *yajé* (or *yagé*) in Colombia, *ayahuasca* in Ecuador and Peru and *caapi* in Brazil, the drink is made from vines boiled with leaves from plants that include *Psychotria viridis* or *Diplopterys cabrerana* – to name just a couple. The result is a brew that is powerfully hallucinogenic, thanks to alkaloids harmaline, harmine, d-tetrahydroharmine and often N,N-dimethyltryptamine. Indigenous groups throughout the Amazon use *yajé* as a medicine to enter the sacred supernatural world, to heal, divine and worship. Psychic effects vary depending on the amount imbibed but typically include brilliant visions in bright colours, macropsia (objects appearing larger than real life), or seeing multiple people or animals, such as anacondas and jaguars. Nauseatingly bitter, *yajé* is frequently drunk during dance ceremonies and generally causes vomiting and diarrhoea to the uninitiated. In recent years, the Western world has become increasingly curious about *yajé*, prompting a growing number of indigenous tour guides to tout it to pseudo-New Age/spiritual tourists. Some have reported extreme out-of-body-type experiences and an intense altered state of consciousness (ASC). Others report a sense of spiritual awakening or a strong (non-visual) acoustic 'psychedelic' trip.

The Unión de Médicos Indigenas Yageceros de la Amazonia Colombiana (Union of Yajé Healers of the Colombian Amazon, UMIYAC) (e *amazon@ amazonalliance.org*) was established in 1999, as a result of a gathering of 40 of the Colombian Amazon's most prominent shamans in Yurayaco, Caquetá. Seven tribes were represented in a meeting designed to share ideas relating to the future conservation of their forest, their medicine and their people.

beside gently bobbing boats, and an army of local Amerindians loading up giant sacks of maize, bananas and fish on to needle-thin dugout canoes.

Founded in 1867, this remote settlement of 55,000 people was originally christened San Antonio. Until 1932, it was part of Peru (see box, page 256) and because of this heritage and tri-border location, Leticia boasts plenty of linguistic, cultural and gastronomic influences born out of its past – and present. Leticia's melting pot of migrants includes umpteen ethnic fusions made up of Colombians from Cali, Medellín and Bogotá; Amerindians from at least several-dozen jungle tribes across the Amazon; Peruvians; Brazilians; and those of a racial mix. However, few language barriers exist with a style of local 'Amazonian Spanish' generally spoken, littered with linguistic influences from Peru, Brazil and many indigenous cultures. Typical food also often fuses a myriad culinary traditions, combining the hearty *sancocho* (soup) of Colombia with some fine Brazilian *churrasco* (barbecued meat) washed down with a glass of ice-cold Peruvian Cristal beer. However, around the town little has changed in generations. Indigenous tribesmen hunt and gather along the river while children swim and women wash in the shallows by the banks.

Today, like much of Colombia, Leticia is enjoying much-improved **safety**. In the 1970s, the narcotics trade had an economic grip on the fortunes of the city.

Trafficking became a new, fast way to make money in the region, along with shady contraband deals. Drugs were reportedly bought and sold in broad daylight with entire communities involved in the shipment of narcotics to some degree. For a time, Leticia basked in unprecedented prosperity as rich drugs cartels established themselves in the town. Vast sums of money were ploughed into big houses and river transportation. Bombarded with wealth, villagers chose to watch their brand-new televisions instead of gathering rubber plants. Prostitutes from Cali, Bogotá and Medellín worked two-week shifts in Leticia's three brothels, making enough money in a six-month period to return home and live a life of luxury. Drugs were ferried along the Putumayo River to avoid the scrutiny of air carriers. Work also started on an ambitious 70km highway from Leticia to the Peruvian town of Tarapacá before the arrest of cartel members halted construction at the 12km mark. In a bid to eradicate the drug trade, a zero-tolerance police presence was installed in Leticia in the 1980s, followed by a significant investment in military strength.

Now, this gateway to the Amazon is calm, safe and growing in confidence as a tourism destination. At sunset and dawn the town's Parque Santander becomes a cacophony of sound and colour as several thousand screeching *pericos* (small parrots) fill the skies in a magnificent, almost choreographed, display. Much has been made of the region's potential for tourism but there has been little action by the political class. The sad fact is that Leticia is an all-too-easily overlooked jungle community. OK, it may be a metropolis by local standards, but it's a world away from the government bigwigs in Bogotá, and easily forgotten.

GETTING THERE All foreign arrivals are liable for an entry tax of 19,000COP.

By air There are now daily flights from Bogotá with both Avianca (*www.avianca. com*) and LAN (*www.lan.com*) to Leticia's tiny Vásquez Cobo Airport. From Brazil, a number of airlines connect Tabatinga with Manaus, including Rico Linhas Aéreas (` +55 92 3625 1164; www.voerico.com.br`). It has a main base at Eduardo Gomes International in Manaus (MAO). Both Leticia and Tabatinga airports are served by a flurry of *colectivos* (communal taxis) that meet every flight and run back and forth all day. At the time of writing there is a twice-weekly (*Monday and Friday*) service provided by small Peruvian airline ATSA PERU (*www.atsaperu.com*) from Leticia to Santa Rosa and on to Iquitos.

By boat As the only significant community for several hundred kilometres, Leticia may not be accessible by road but it does boast regular river connections with Iquitos (Peru), Manaus (Brazil), Florencia (Caquetá department) and other jungle towns.

To **Manaus**, the super-fast express boat leaves from Tabatinga every day except Monday. The journey takes around 10 hours and costs upwards of 150,000COP. For a more leisurely pace opt for the three-day, four-night trip departing Tabatinga Wednesday, Friday and Saturday. Expect a 14.00 departure (but like most things on the Amazon River this can be wide of the mark) and a cost of around 105,000COP – this is a real adventure if time isn't an issue. Additional boats sometimes run, so be sure to check this if a Tuesday, Thursday, Monday or Sunday departure is more preferable – you never know. Boats are likely to be packed out so be sure to board early in order to find a spot to hang your hammock (for sale everywhere in Leticia and Tabatinga at around US$8). The best spot is the space behind the control room towards the front of the boat as you will be shielded from the night-time wind. Although food is included in the ticket price, bring plenty of bottled water and snacks for the journey as well as some toilet roll, a good lock for your luggage (theft on board can be a problem) and plenty of mosquito spray. Expect to pay around

Tourists seeking to experience yagé themselves may well inadvertently be jeopardising the autonomy of the indigenous people and their sacred practices. Rather than detail the intensely personal and deeply introspective experience to which I was subjected in Iquitos, Peru, some years ago when I was persuaded to accompany a friend in the ritual, perhaps we should be opening a debate about yajé and the commercialisation of an ancient and sacred indigenous ceremony and the potential dangers for those people who embark on this journey without knowing the risks they are taking.

I was initially against the whole exercise and then started researching yajé. It was easy to find convincing texts from 'experts' all over the world and references to the works of Huxley, Ginsberg and Burroughs. Eventually, I decided that taking part in a ceremony wouldn't do me any harm; I was going to be there as support and as a precaution because there had been reports of participants in other regions being raped under the influence.

But it wasn't as simple as paying a fee and slugging back a supposed hallucinogen. The whole process involved in the creation of the yajé (known as *ayahuasca* in Peru) potion is sacred, knowing and respecting the shaman is important too, as well as feeling comfortable with those who will be participating in the ritual with you. The shaman has the final say over whether you are deemed an appropriate candidate for the ceremony, and you must follow a strict diet in the days leading up to your experience.

In Colombia you can find yajé retreats in towns surrounding Bogotá as well as in jungle departments but this is not a tourist activity and it should never be regarded as such. The people of the Amazon are conditioned to the resulting effects. The yajé brew is potent and has been known to produce unexpected chemical imbalances in some people. Tragically, a gap-year traveller from the UK died from causes stemming from yajé ceremonies in Putumayo in 2014.

US$65 if you are bringing a hammock, or US$240 for a double cabin. The upstream trip from Manaus to Tabatinga takes a day or so longer and costs about US$110 (hammock) or US$330 for a double berth.

To **Iquitos**, the best way to travel from Tabatinga is on a high-speed passenger boat, departing in the early hours on a Sunday, Friday or Wednesday morning. The 10-hour trip costs about US$70 in either direction and includes breakfast and lunch in the price. Obtaining an exit stamp at Leticia's airport a day prior to departure is crucial. Another consideration is onward transport from Iquitos into Peru as there are no roads, just riverboats (these take a week to reach Pucallpa). Another option is connecting flights.

GETTING AROUND The Colombian Amazon's difficult topography and isolation can make travel expensive, as it is practically impossible to navigate the region without a guide and a boatman. Many of the most reputable local independent tour operators are part of Fondo de Promoción Ecoturística del Amazonas (page 262). Hiring a member of this organisation brings with it some guarantees in regards to quality and safety. It also avoids being ripped off on the basis of price and 'unforeseen' added costs and demands, a very good reason to resist the temptation to engage the services of a man on the street. Most visitors arrive by plane from Bogotá and feel

Antonio Cruz is a rarity in Leticia, a worldly traveller who once lived in California but was born to a traditional Amazonian family. Twenty years of guiding have equipped him with considerable knowledge. This, combined with a great enthusiasm for his homeland, makes spending time with Cruz difficult to beat. His approach to guiding is simple: he gives visitors the experience they want, rather than foisting on them what's simple. With flawless English and impeccable manners Cruz is also a plain-talking, easy listening guy. Ask about the Amazon and its problems and he'll provide a wealth of intelligent insight into the challenges it faces. Antonio Cruz can organise anything in the Amazon Basin, from an exhilarating four-day wildlife trek or ecotour to a sedate cruise along the river. He owns **Amazon Jungle Trips** (page 263) and is a founder member of the Fondo de Promoción Ecoturística del Amazonas (page 262). He also speaks Italian and Portuguese. Cruz prefers working with groups smaller than half-a-dozen people and relishes trips that take him to the small nature reserves along the Río Yavarí.

an urgency to start exploring immediately. However, it's worth holding back from striding around Leticia as soon as you arrive in this quirky rainforest town – in the Amazon region there is no substitute for proper planning. Settle in slowly and see what's what at a nice, lazy pace. As with all jungle-based exploration, weather conditions play a major part in what is possible. Expect heavy rains from February to April when water levels can rise as much as 15m. Navigation is often easier in the dry months of July and August. The river peaks from May to June and is at its lowest levels from August to October.

Communal taxis (*colectivos*) nip backwards and forwards between the towns of Tabatinga and Leticia. Many visitors also travel between the two on foot or by local bus. Opposite lies the small Peruvian island of Santa Rosa. Frequent boats provide a shuttle service throughout the day. Several bike-hire shops and scooter-rental yards are open seven days a week in Leticia. Expect to pay 30,000COP a day for a scooter (plus petrol) and around 25,000COP for a bike.

IMMIGRATION Moving between Leticia and Tabatinga is free from immigration formalities with no visa requirements or passport control. However, those planning to travel further into each country will need to meet normal immigration criteria, such as clearing passport control, getting an entry stamp and undergoing standard checks. This can be done at Leticia's airport or at the Policía Federal in Tabatinga on Avenida da Amizade 650 (closed noon–14.00). In Leticia, the Brazilian consulate is open 08.00–16.00 Monday to Friday (closed noon–13.00). Travellers should be sure to check visa requirements for entering Brazil from Colombia, especially those from Canada, the US and Australia who will need an ID photo and yellow fever vaccination certificate and will almost certainly be charged a fat fee. Crossing into Colombia from Brazil tends to be less bureaucratic. Visit the Colombian consulate on the Avenida da Amizade Manaus in Tabatinga to check if in any doubt. Those travelling to or from Iquitos should pass through the Policía Internacional Peruviano (PIP) office on Santa Rosa to obtain an exit or entry stamp. Leticia's Peruvian consulate is open Monday to Friday, but only from 09.00 to 14.00.

Moving around the Amazon provides an excellent opportunity to add extra stamps in a passport, even for those on a flying visit.

WHY IT'S BEST TO CROSS YOUR LEGS IN THE JUNGLE

I felt like urinating. I stood up. It was then it attacked me. It went deeper and deeper inside.

Silvio Barbossa, *candirú* victim, 2006

Forget the Amazon's predatory packs of carnivorous piranhas, prowling jaguars or giant anacondas, there are few more treacherous pastimes in the jungle than taking a pee in the river. Just uttering the word 'candirú' (*Vandellia cirrhosa*) can make a grown man wince. No, this isn't some mighty fearsome mammal with teeth the size of pitchforks, but rather a tiny vertebrate the size of a toothpick – sometimes known as the 'willy fish' in the Western world thanks to its loathsome reputation born out of its fondness for entering the human body via the urethra, the tube inside the penis. Once in, the barbs of the candirú jam it firmly into place. Squirm.

Removal of this bloodsucker is a tricky procedure, that's if the patient survives the excruciating pain. Thankfully, only a handful of people have suffered a candirú invasion, but these isolated tales serve as a cautionary reminder to those caught short in the bush. Leg-crossing stories about the candirú have been horrifying men in the Amazon for generations, earning it the local name of 'vampire fish'. One Amazonian fisherman reported being attacked as he waded naked in shallow water. The candirú swam towards him and forced its way at speed inside his penis. The man had tried to grab the fish but it was too slippery and fast.

Local shamen advise treating a patient with the xagua plant and the buitach apple. This does the trick, apparently, via insertion into the affected area (if space is tight, use an extract). Once the candirú is killed and dissolved it can be removed. There is no evidence the fish can survive once inside a human body.

TOURIST INFORMATION

i **Departamento Administrativo de Fomento Ecoturístico** Calle 8, No 9–75; ☎592 4162

i **Fondo de Promoción Ecoturística del Amazonas** Av Internacional, No 6–25; m 310 229 9456; www.fproturismoamazonas.com. This self-regulating tourism association was established to raise standards across the local tourist industry. More than half of all businesses involved in tourism are now members. All work to a mandate of truthful service, customer focus & a spirit of co-operation.

i **Secretaria de Turismo y Fronteras** Calle 8, No 9–75; ☎592 7569

TOUR OPERATORS Every hotel and backpacker joint will have umpteen tour guides they are happy to recommend. Taxi drivers at the airport will try their best to introduce visitors to a cousin or friend. Tourist information offices will also be able to point you in the right direction. Owing to recent reports of unscrupulous behaviour by guides touting for business, using a member of the Fondo de Promoción Ecoturística del Amazonas (see above) is highly recommended over a hustler on the street. Proper, registered Colombian tourist guides need a licence to operate legally. Cheap options are invariably a waste of money and unlike a registered, licensed outfit there is no recompense via a formal complaint. A guide who knows about red tape is also totally invaluable in the Amazon, given the complexities of negotiating a tri-country bureaucratic system that has more twists, turns and dead ends than the river itself.

Amazon Jungle Trips Av Internacional, No 6–25; ☏592 7377; e contacto@amazonjungletrips.com. co; www.amazonjungletrips.com.co. Visitors are spoilt for choice by an array of Leticia-based jungle tour companies, but this is one of the best. Punctual, reliable & multi-lingual (English, Italian, Spanish & Portuguese), this bunch are well organised. Opt for a standard 1-day tour or a more complex 3–4-day option. Good, knowledgeable guides – & nice people that care about what they do.
Paraíso Ecológico Carrera 11, No 6–106; ☏592 5111; e paraisoecologico@hotmail.com. www. paraisoecologico.com.co. This small, independent tour company is run by the highly efficient Diva

Maria Santana Smith, a founder member of Leticia's Fondo de Promoción Ecoturística del Amazonas. She organises tour programmes for groups or individuals & comes highly recommended. Although she speaks very little English herself she can engage bilingual guides on request.
Yurupary Amazonas Tours Calle 8, No 7–26; ☏592 6529; e viajesyurupary@hotmail.com; www.exploreturismo.com. Reports are mixed about the standard of tours from this agency, based in the Yurupary Hotel. Programmes include Amerindian villages, dolphin spotting & trips to the Jardín Zoológico Departmental.

Amazon tour itineraries
Don't be fobbed off by a 'one-size-fits-all' tour package if it really doesn't appeal. The following itineraries are all pretty much standard, but can be easily tailored to a specific theme, such as birding or trekking.

Four days
Day 1 Leticia – Lake Yahuarcaca – Isla Santa Rosa (Peru) – Tabatinga (Brazil) – Leticia
Day 2 Isla de los Micos – Yagua and Ticuna villages – Leticia
Day 3 Benjamin Constant (Brazil) – Leticia
Day 4 Leticia and Tabatinga city tour

or

Day 1 Leticia – Tarapacá
Day 2 Isla de los Micos – Yagua and Ticuna villages – Reserva Natural Paraná
Day 3 Full day at Reserva Natural Paraná (kayaking, birding, hiking) – night safari
Day 4 Leticia and Tabatinga city tour

Five days
Day 1 Leticia – Reserva Natural del Zacambú (kayaking, birding, wildlife) – night safari
Day 2 Marajá Lagoon – jungle wildlife tour – Zacambú Lodge
Day 3 Full jungle tour – night safari (optional jungle camping)
Day 4 Indigenous villages (Río Chítá) – Zacambú Lodge (hiking and wildlife spotting)
Day 5 Leticia and Tabatinga city tour

or

Day 1 Leticia – Tarapacá
Day 2 Isla de los Micos – Yagua and Ticuna villages – Puerto Nariño
Day 3 Lake Tarapoto – Insituto OMACHA – Reserva Natural del Zacambú – night safari
Day 4 Marajá Lagoon – jungle wildlife tour in Parque Nacional Amacayacu – Zacambú Lodge
Day 5 Benjamin Constant (Brazil) – Leticia

Seven days

Day 1 Leticia – Tarapacá

Day 2 Benjamin Constant – Reserva del Zacambú – night safari (optional jungle camping)

Day 3 Full day in the jungle (kayaking, birding, hiking and wildlife spotting)

Day 4 Islas de los Micos – Yagua and Ticuna villages – Puerto Nariño

Day 5 Full day in Parque Nacional Amacayacu (kayaking, birding, hiking and wildlife spotting)

Day 6 Full day in Parque Nacional Amacayacu (kayaking, birding, hiking and wildlife spotting)

Day 7 Return to Leticia (via Lake Tarapoto and Lake Yahuarcaca)

WHERE TO STAY *See map, page 265.*

Leticia has dozens of small hotels that offer good value for money. Most are clustered in the centre of town, by the park or near the border. Unless you are an especially hardy soul, don't scrimp on a room without air conditioning or a particularly efficient fan.

Decalodge Ticuna (28 rooms plus cabins) Carrera 11, No 6–11; 592 6600 ; www. decameron.com. Visitors keen to enjoy the finest accommodation the Colombian Amazon has to offer should check out this luxury option. Top-notch thatched-roof cabins offer space, style & elegance overlooking a palm-edged terrace & pool area. Cabins suit 1-4 people with either king-size or 2 double beds. Cocktails are served in a huge open-air bar by an army of smart-suited staff while a restaurant menu offers gourmet dining Amazonian-style. **$$$**

Amazon B&B (6 cabins & 4 double rooms) Calle 12, No 9–30; 592 4981; www.amazonbb. com. Offering a variety of bungalows & single-storey villas ranging in size from 2-person singles & doubles to a 4-person mix of singles & doubles, this lodge-style accommodation is set in lush, tropical gardens & includes a good b/fast in the rate. Run by multi-lingual staff, the property offers guests bike rental, ecotours, laundry services & Wi-Fi. There is also a coffee & juice shop on site. Accepts MasterCard & Visa. **$$** (per cabin)

Amazonas Hotel Yakuruna (14 rooms) Calle 8, No 10–32 (office), Km5.5 vía Leticia – Tarapacá; 592 7125. This rather bland green-painted building with yellow signage is located next to the very reasonably priced Restaurant Viejo Tolima, opposite the Panadería y Pastelería la Sevillana, one of Leticia's finest bakeries. Rooms have AC, TV, phone & private bathroom. There's also a bar, laundry, restaurant & a small swimming pool. **$$**

Hotel Anaconda (50 rooms) Carrera 11, No 7–34; 592 7119; e reservas@hotelanaconda. com.co; www.hotelanaconda.com.co. Past guests include Michael Palin & a host of Hollywood stars, & the bright AC rooms in this well-located hotel are difficult to beat. Each has a large private bathroom & is clean, spacious & equipped with a minibar, telephone & TV. Electrical plug sockets are also in good supply. Recent expansion has maximised the outside pool area to include a larger bar & restaurant. Ask for a room at the front of the building for balcony views across the Francisco de Orellana Park & out to the river (room 301 has 3 singles & a huge bathroom) – perfect for those keen to be right in the thick of it during fiesta season. **$$**

Hotel La Frontera (16 rooms) Av Internacional, No 1–04; 592 5600; e fronterahotel@hotmail.com. Drive too fast across the Tabatinga–Leticia border & you'll miss this nice little hotel. The AC rooms include a good mix of doubles, triples & family-sized accommodation & are meticulously clean. Views of both Brazil & Colombia can be enjoyed from a breezy rooftop terrace bar & restaurant. Look out for the huge painted mural-style ad for this place as you wait patiently in the heat by the luggage carousel at Leticia's Aeropuerto Internacional Vásquez Cobo Airport. **$$**

Hotel Yurupary (30 rooms) Calle 8, No 7–26; 592 4743; e hotelyurupary@hotmail. com; www.hotelyurupary.com. This good-value option is well located 50m from a cheap 24hr

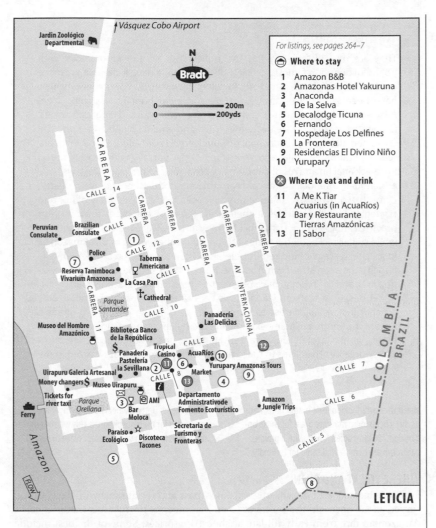

Map labels (Leticia):

↑ Vásquez Cobo Airport

Jardín Zoológico Departmental

N

Bradt

0 ——— 200m
0 ——— 200yds

CARRERA 10

CALLE 14

CARRERA 9
CALLE 13
CARRERA 8
CALLE 12
CARRERA 7
CALLE 11
CARRERA 6
AV INTERNACIONAL
CARRERA 5

Peruvian Consulate

Brazilian Consulate

Police

Taberna Americana

Reserva Tanimboca
Vivarium Amazonas

La Casa Pan

Cathedral

Parque Santander

CALLE 10

Panadería Las Delicias

Museo del Hombre Amazónico

Biblioteca Banco de la República

CALLE 9

Panadería Pastelería la Sevillana

Tropical Casino

AcuaRíos

Yurupary Amazonas Tours

Uirapuru Galería Artesanal

Market

CALLE 7

Money changers

Museo Uirapuru

CALLE 8

Tickets for river taxi

Parque Oreliana

AMI

Bar Moloca

Departamento Administrativo de Fomento Ecoturístico

Amazon Jungle Trips

CALLE 6

Ferry

Amazon

FLOW

Paraíso Ecológico

Discoteca Tacones

Secretaria de Turismo y Fronteras

CALLE 5

COLOMBIA
BRAZIL

LETICIA

For listings, see pages 264–7

Where to stay
1 Amazon B&B
2 Amazonas Hotel Yakuruna
3 Anaconda
4 De la Selva
5 Decalodge Ticuna
6 Fernando
7 Hospedaje Los Delfines
8 La Frontera
9 Residencias El Divino Niño
10 Yurupary

Where to eat and drink
11 A Me K Tiar
Acuarius (in AcuaRíos)
12 Bar y Restaurante
Tierras Amazónicas
13 El Sabor

---

diner & has large, clean brightly furnished rooms (singles, doubles, triples, quadruple) set around a picturesque, leafy courtyard. The hotel's substantial buffet b/fast costs just 15,000COP with lunch & dinner options from 12,000COP & a well-stocked bar. Only 1 drawback: the staff rarely smile & aren't exactly welcoming – a real shame. Look out for the red-&-yellow sign set back from the road. **$$**

Hospedaje Los Delfines (9 rooms) Carrera 11, No 12–85; 592 7488; e losdelfinesleticia@hotmail.com. This friendly family-run small hotel has a handful of simple courtyard rooms that come with a fan & private bathroom. No frills, but good value. **$**

Hotel de la Selva (11 rooms) Calle 7, No 7–28; 592 7616; e hoteldelaselvaleticia@gmail.com; www.hoteldelaselva.com. Doubles, triples & quadruple accommodation may be small & sparsely furnished but each room has AC, private bathroom, TV, telephone & minibar. An on-site restaurant & laundry are also a real boon for those on the go. A reliable & popular option with a loyal clientele – look for the painted green entrance. **$**

Hotel Fernando (15 rooms) Real Calle 9; 592 7362. Simple fan-cooled rooms are without frills but OK nonetheless. Located a few doors down from the Tropical Casino opposite the A Me K Tiar Restaurant. **$**

Residencias El Divino Niño (9 rooms) Av Internacional, No 7–23; 592 5594. www.divinoninohotel.com. Shoestring travellers rave

They are undoubtedly among the ugliest fish on the earth today with powerful dentition famous for a lethal bite. Piranha have a sizeable presence in the waters of the Amazon, forming carnivorous congregations that have been known to attack livestock and even humans. Hatching from microscopic eggs, piranhas come into the world armed and dangerous, feeding on small crustaceans, seeds, fruits and aquatic plants. Their physical characteristics vary with location, population and age. Generally piranhas are reddish-orange ventrally and silver-grey-green dorsally with a black dorsal fin, black anal fin and reddish-orange pectoral fins. Short, powerful jaws have a triangular, interlocking row of teeth that are not dissimilar to razor blades. Once they grow in size, piranha hunt in packs, using a wide array of hunting strategies to kill and devour their prey. Piranhas eat other fish and also practise cannibalism and infanticide. They also prefer to feed on their victims while still alive. Feeding frenzies can churn up the waters of the Amazon as in an effervescent blood-red bubble and when the piranha attack with true ferocity they can strip flesh from the bone within seconds. More than two-dozen species of piranha have been catalogued in the Amazon so far.

Yet despite a fearsome, aggressive reputation, as portrayed above, only a handful pose any threat to human life, such as the red-bellied piranha, *Pygocentrus nattereri*. Many experts, in fact, believe the ferocious reputation of the piranha is totally unwarranted. However, uncorroborated reports claim 300 people lost their lives to these toothy fiends when a boat capsized in the Amazon in the 1980s.

about this tatty-looking little border hotel because its dirt-cheap room rates are great for those on a budget. 20 fan-cooled rooms with a private bathroom are clean & well cared for by kindly housekeeper Betty. Owners Karen & Edgar are renowned for their hospitality & this warmth makes the El Divino Niño a very pleasant place to stay. **$**

✖ WHERE TO EAT AND DRINK *See map, page 265.*

Leticia is blessed with dozens of good cafés, bars and restaurants with decent food served as the norm. In the centre of town a number of no-fuss local eateries serve Amazonian fare from early till late at shoestring prices. Some of the best include the Amazon Sazón Restaurante, Restaurante Viejo Tolima, Restaurante Los Paisano and Restaurante Marina where a daily menu of fresh fish (usually *gamitana* or *pirarucú*), rice and plantains comes in at under 6,000COP. Other good options are as follows.

✖ Bar y Restaurante Tierras
Amazónicas Calle 8, No 7–50; ☎592 4748; ⏰ 11.30–late. Don't be put off by the fact that this quirky food haunt is aimed squarely at the tourist – the menu is as terrific as the Amazonian clutter hanging from the rafters. Jungle bric-a-brac & Amerindian artefacts adorn every inch of wall space in this wooden-clad diner. Huge tropical ceiling fans whir slowly over bench-style tables with mezzanine & streetside seating when the restaurant gets full. A wooden menu has soups, juices, grilled meats, fish, chicken dishes a mile long as well as numerous cocktail options – beware the potent *caipirina limón* as it really packs a punch. **$$**

✖ A Me K Tiar
Carrera 9, No 8–15; ☎592 6094; ⏰ noon–midnight. This popular grilled-meat joint attracts a mixed crowd of locals & tourists with low prices & a good menu. It's always packed out. **$**

✖ Restaurante Acuarius
Carrera 7, No 8–12; ☎592 5025; ⏰ 07.00–21.00. Serving some of

the best fish in the city, the Acuarius is celebrated for its pan-fried *pirarucú* & *gamitana* & is a nice place to grab a bite in the open air. $
✗ **Restaurante El Sabor** Calle 8, No 9–25; ☏592 4774; ⊕ every day. The 24hr cheap, tasty food makes this a popular backpacker hangout. Hearty chicken-&-rice meals include an unlimited refill of fruit juice. Other menu items include salads, vegetarian burgers & fruit pancakes. $

ENTERTAINMENT AND NIGHTLIFE Some of Leticia's most innocuous buildings transform themselves into lively salsa bars and drinking dens after dark. Many are clustered along Calle 8 with some in Calles 11 and 10. During peak tourist months the Bar y Restaurante Tierras Amazónicas (page 266) is the place to party when the staff crank up the volume on the CD player and the salsa doesn't stop until dawn. Numerous impromptu fiestas take place in the Parque de Orellana while many of Leticia's larger hotels host live music during the busiest months. Leticia's only legal gambling joint is the garish-looking **Tropical Casino** on Calle 9, a hotbed of local gossip and scandal and an *en vogue* place to be seen.

♥ **Bar Moloca** Carrera 11, No 7–34; ☏592 7119. For a sundowner away from the hubbub of Leticia's street noise, head to the open-sided poolside bar at the Hotel Anaconda. Cocktails, beer & wine (by the glass, half-bottle or bottle) are served to salsa classics on an aged jukebox while flocks of *pericos* screech overhead.
♥ **Taberna Americana** Carrera 10, No 11–108. Few places in Leticia can boast as much *aguardiente* consumption as the Taberna Americana. Swaying glassy-eyed men burst into song to the distorted sounds of salsa emitting from the speakers. For a night of drink-soaked camaraderie this rustic booze-joint has a certain charm.
☆ **Discoteca Tacones** Carrera 11, No 6–14; ☏592 7719. This rather uninspiring nightspot is the place in Leticia to let your hair down. A decent dance floor is heaving in peak season when a sea of sweaty bodies strut their stuff to raunchy Latino beats.

SHOPPING Leticia has a reasonable range of shops geared to tourists passing through, but is far from being a retail paradise. T-shirts, souvenirs and trinkets are sold from stalls along the street with some interesting artefacts and rustic art for sale in some scruffy-looking makeshift galleries opposite the Parque Orellana (Orellana Park). Those stocking up on food supplies ahead of a day in the jungle should be sure to pay a visit to one of Leticia's many excellent bakeries. **La Casa Pan** on Calle 11 is highly recommended, as is **Panadería Las Delicias** on Calle 9 and the first-class **Panadería y Pastelería la Sevillana** on Calle 8. Leticia's biggest souvenir and handicraft shop is the **Uirapuru Galería Artesanal**, an open-fronted place on Calle 8 (☏ 592 7056). Expect to find all manner of indigenous knick-knacks, some more authentic than others, including hand-woven hammocks, spears, tablemats, pottery and jewellery made from seeds and nuts.

OTHER PRACTICALITIES
Emergency numbers
Police ☏112/592 5066

Banks and money As you'd expect in a commercial triple-border town, Leticia is blessed with dozens of places to change money. Most are around Calle 8, Carrera 11 and the market, where it is easy to obtain US dollars, Colombian COP, Peruvian soles and Brazilian reais. Rates vary dramatically so be prepared to shop around if clinching the best deal in town is important to your pocket. Leticia's three banks are located on the corner of Calle 10 and Calle 7. All have ATM facilities but are loath to change dollars and have unpredictable policies regarding travellers' cheques. Both

Amazonia LETICIA

7

reais and COP are generally widely accepted in Tabatinga and Leticia, especially by larger businesses and hotels.

Internet Internet cafés continue to spring up across town. Expect to pay about 2,000COP per hour, possibly as much as 3,000COP in the newer, swanky places. However, one thing is certain: wherever you choose to log on in Leticia the connection is sure to be painfully slow. Some of the better options include **Indio. net** at the Centro Commercial AcuaRíos on the corner of Carrera 7 and Calle 8 and **AMI** on Carrera 10. Both offer printing, photocopying and other sundry services and sell a limited stock of consumables.

Laundry, supplies and repairs Leticia's good handful of drugstores and pharmacies are mostly centred on Calle 8 with almost every hotel offering laundry services at competitive rates. At the Hotel Anaconda, one of Leticia's most expensive hotels, a whole set of clothes can be laundered for about 6,000COP – that's a shirt, a pair of shorts, socks, underwear and a pair of jeans. Laundry at the Hotel Amazonas is slightly cheaper with the cost of laundering the entire contents of a suitcase unlikely to exceed 55,000COP. At the Lavandería Aseo Total on Calle (✆ *592 6051*) a kilo of

CLOSE ENCOUNTERS WITH THE BIGGEST SNAKE ON EARTH

You can't scream if you can't breathe.

Anaconda (1997)

Hunting its prey with considerable stealth before crushing it into a breathless state, the mighty **green anaconda** (*Eunectus marinus*) is revered by Amazon Amerindians and Hollywood film-makers alike. Reaching 10m long and around 130kg in weight, the world's largest snake lives both in water and on land, hunting in the rainforests and river systems of the Amazon amongst swamps and sluggish streams. Olive green in colour with black blotches down the length of its body, it has a narrow head with distinctive orange-and-yellow stripes on both sides and high-set eyes. It can survive for around three months on a sizeable kill, using its powerful muscular body to coil and constrict birds, reptiles and mammals. Although large anacondas may occasionally consume large prey like deer, caiman, tapir and capybara, such large meals are rare.

Exaggerated tales of anaconda attacks on humans frequently do the rounds in the Amazon, but can rarely be proven. Strikes are rare and are generally attributed to self-defence. However, this hasn't prevented the green anaconda from becoming one of the most exaggerated animals on earth in regard to tales of its size. Unconfirmed reports abound about sightings of beasts up to 40m, with the Brazil–Colombia Boundary Commission claiming an anaconda of some 27.5m in 1933. In 1948, a 30.5m-long anaconda was reportedly killed in Fort Tabatinga, giving rise to the sorts of fearsome jungle myths of which films are made. In the 1997 blockbuster film *Anaconda,* some of the terror that this vast reptile can create unnerved cinema goers across the globe. Yet despite starring Jennifer Lopez and rapper Ice Cube the movie failed to impress the world's herpetologists owing to the script's many fundamental errors. Not only did the film portray the anaconda's speed, reproductive habits and feeding rituals incorrectly, in one scene the animatronic anaconda shorted out and can clearly be seen out of control in the final cut. An ill-conceived storyline of an ill-fated *National Geographic* expedition also took a bit of swallowing, as did as the egg-hatching scene – anacondas don't lay eggs; they give birth to live snakes. Unsurprisingly, this modest washing costs US$1.50. Travellers in need of twine, tent pegs, tarpaulins, mallets and machetes will find at least three hardware vendors in the centre of town. There's also a camera-repair shop and a couple of places that will mend boots and shoes.

SAFETY Leticia is a calm and safe town posing few problems for travellers. On the river, all prime points of interest can be visited without concern. However, long treks deep into the jungle require careful planning, as forested areas can be inaccessible and also unsafe. Advice from the British Foreign Office at the time of writing is not to visit Putumayo or Caquetá. Putumayo, close to the Ecuadorian border, has become a prime focus of the government's coca-plant crop-spraying programme in accordance with the US$44 billion US-sponsored anti-drug effort, informally known as Plan Colombia II (pages 31–3). It also has a history of leftist FARC guerrilla activity, right-wing paramilitary units and regular Colombian military forces. Caquetá is also a drug-trafficking centre where left-wing insurgents remain strong.

WHAT TO SEE AND DO
Jardín Zoológico Departmental (Regional Zoological Garden) (*Av Vásquez Cobo;* ⊕ *08.00–17.00 daily, closed noon–14.00; admission 2,000COP*) Located near

box office hit was critically panned, garnering six nominations in the 1997 Golden Raspberry awards. Many critics sniped that the CGI (computer-generated imagery) snake had also upstaged other cast members.

The green anaconda is not officially registered as threatened, but it is protected by the **Convention on International Trade in Endangered Species** (CITES) (☎ *+41 (0) 22 917 81 39/40; www.cites.org*). Further information is available from **Come Back Alive** (☎ *+1 800 504 0640; www.comebackalive.com*), author and adventure traveller Robert Young Pelton's live-dangerously stay-safe site, and the **Adopt an Anaconda Programme** (℮ *jesus@anacondas.org*), an independent funding initiative for anaconda conservation worldwide.

FACED WITH AN ANGRY ANACONDA? The US government Peace Corps Manual suggests that its volunteers in the Amazon jungle do the following to survive an anaconda attack:

- Do not run. The snake is faster than you are.
- Lie flat on the ground, put your arms tight against your sides and your legs tight against each other.
- Tuck your chin in.
- The snake will begin to nudge and climb over your body.
- Do not panic.
- The snake will begin to swallow your feet first.
- You must lie perfectly still. This will take a long time.
- When the snake reaches your knees, reach down, take your knife, slide it into the side of the snake's mouth between the edge of its mouth and your leg.
- Quickly rip upward, severing the snake's head.
- Be sure you have your knife.
- Be sure your knife is sharp.

the airport, the place has a rundown, ramshackle air – and although it has just a measly entrance fee it isn't an attraction for those who truly love wildlife. A reasonable collection of Amazonian animals look forlorn and listless.

Museo del Hombre Amazónico (Men of the Amazon Museum) (*Carerra 11, No 9–43;* ✎ *592 7729; www.banrepcultural.org/leticia;* ⊕ *09.00–14.30 Mon–Fri, 09.00–13.00 Sat; free admission*) This small collection of artefacts contains some household items and implements gathered from a small number of indigenous communities in the region.

Museo Uirapuru (Uirapuru Museum) (*Calle 8, No 10–35;* ✎ *592 7056;* ⊕ *09.00–noon & 15.00–19.00 Mon–Sat, 09.00–noon Sun; free admission*) This backroom collection is at the rear of Leticia's biggest handicraft and souvenir shop, the Uirapuru Galería Artesanal. If, like me, you like your wildlife to be alive, this

THE BARDS OF AMAZONIA

> Neither whisper, sweetest, soft from the peaceful springs that slip away across the
> meadow fair;
> nor the howl a forest downpour brings,
> those through the thickness to the ear supplied;
> nor starlight splendours vivid flair,
> beacons hanging up on high when sparkling, beauteous, in midair, amidst the mists of
> dark night's sky,
> have not ever terrible deep marks produced,
> those unnameable impressions in me loosed like when I gaze upon your course's pitch
> and roll Oh! I feel you, sacred river! in my soul.
>
> Fabriciano Hernández, Amazonian poet, 'Hymn to the Amazon', 1868

Although many of the native tongues of the Amazon are without a written form, the region has produced many generations of poetry, song and verse. Most have their roots in the myth, history, geography and cultures of the Amazon. Many centre on the power of the river as a crucial life force. Indeed, the Amazon's vast water system unifies much of the work of these wordsmiths through the rich colours of the poetry, stories and verses of the Amazon's traditional indigenous groups. Many themes explore the dismay felt at the threat to their survival or look at the complex relationship between humans and nature. Some describe colonial and neocolonial exploitation of the land and its inhabitants by bards who frequently assumed the role of spokesperson for social justice. One story born out of the myth of the magical boto (pink river dolphin) tells of its metamorphosis into human form. Another recounts the origins of the Amazon River through the inconsolable and torrential weeping of a beautiful love-struck girl. Jungle life has provided the Amazon tribesfolk with an extraordinary number of folk legends evoking numerous magnificent legacies that honour one of the world's most important river cultures.

Further information can be obtained from the Centre for Amazonian Literature and Culture (CALC) (e *nsuarez@sophia.smith.edu; www.smith.edu/calc*) and Poets and Writers Against the Destruction of Amazonia (PWADA) (*www.smith.edu/calc/pwada*).

depressing range of dusty stuffed animals, snakeskins, turtle shells and pickled birds will fail to impress.

Biblioteca Banco de la República (Republic Bank Library) (*Carrera 11, No 9–43;* ⊕ *09.00–15.00 Tue–Sat; free admission*) Housed in this modern orange-coloured building is a fine (if small) collection of artefacts including masks, instruments and pots gathered from the Ticuna and Huitoto peoples. It is funded by the Banco de la República as a lobby showpiece. A guide is obligatory, but speaks Spanish only.

Reserva Tanimboca Vivarium Amazonas (*Km11, vía Tarapacá;* 592 7679; ⊕ *08.00–16.00 daily*) Located a short bus ride out of town, why not conquer your fear of snakes and head to the vivarium here to see the critters on show. In addition to snakes there is a good collection of frogs and lizards too. For those wishing to make a day of it, pay 120,000COP per person and sign up for all the activities at Tanimboca including a kayak trip, zip line and a jungle walk.

Birding around Leticia Birdwatchers in the Amazon have reported sighting a wide range of birdlife in the forested areas immediately surrounding the town centre. These include the white-vented euphonia, purple-throated fruitcrow, grey antbird, spot-winged antbird, ochre-bellied flycatcher, black-spotted barbet, cinereous antshrike, reddish hermit, black-throated hermit, violaceous trogon, ocellated woodcreeper and brownish twistwing.

AROUND LETICIA

LAGO YAHUARCACAS This picturesque lake island is edged by multi-coloured heliconias and palms dotted with parrots, but it is for its giant lilies (*Victorias regias*) that most people visit. Easily reached via a short jaunt from Leticia, this natural collection of the world's largest water lily (named after Queen Victoria) is a favourite with local tour guides, many of whom will explain its 93-day life cycle and the co-existence role it supposedly plays with piranha. Try to pluck the lily from the water and you're likely to sustain a scratch from a thorn, attracting piranha from far and wide with the smell of blood.

PARQUE NACIONAL AMACAYACU (AMACAYACU NATIONAL PARK) This 293ha expanse of rainforest is located about 75km upriver from Leticia, occupying a large part of the Amazon trapezoid. Jointly run by the municipalities of Leticia and Puerto Nariño, this stunning protected stretch of wilderness is accessed by an exhilarating boat ride up the Amazon River to the Quebrada Matamata at the edge of the park. The name 'Amacayacu' means 'Hammock River' in Quechua, the most widely spoken Amerindian language in the world today. In 1542, the Spanish conquistador Francisco de Orellana discovered Kahuapanas, Jeberos, Boras, Kotuenes, Jiduas, Muinanes, Mirañas, Andokes, Huitotos, Omaguas, Yaguas, Cocamas, Otucunas and Ticunas in this part of the Amazon Basin. Today only the Tikunas remain in their ancestral land.

Amacayacu's terrain has two very different landscapes: the rolling and relatively dry scrubland that supports vegetation and the swampy marshes of the floodlands. A spectacular array of trees can reach up to 30–40m high on drier terrain. Mammoth ceiba trees need up to 30 people to fully encircle their girth. Other species include red-and-white cedar, mahogany, rubber, balsam, caoba and uvo. In the boggy

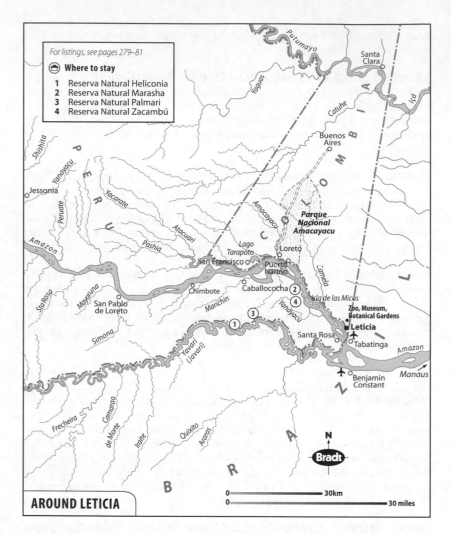

For listings, see pages 279–81

🏠 **Where to stay**

1. Reserva Natural Heliconia
2. Reserva Natural Marasha
3. Reserva Natural Palmari
4. Reserva Natural Zacambú

AROUND LETICIA

| 0 | 30km |
| 0 | 30 miles |

wetlands the spectacular Victoria lily, capiron and munguaba trees are typically found along with 150 mammals and dozens of reptiles and snakes. Species range from caiman, boa snake, anaconda, danta, jaguar, otter, pink dolphin (boto), black alligator, coral snakes and monkey (including the small but resplendent golden lion tamarin) to the jabuti, the world's largest freshwater tortoise. More than 500 species of birds include flocks of brightly coloured parrots. Short-tailed swift, thrush-like wren, screaming piha, yellow-browed antbird, yellow-browed tody-flycatcher, rufous-bellied euphonia blue-throated piping-guan, red-throated caracara, scarlet macaw, chestnut-fronted macaw, black-spotted barbet, lettered aracari, cuvier's toucan, fasciated antshrike, striped woodcreeper, Amazonian umbrellabird, chestnut woodpecker, scarlet-crowned barbet, black-fronted nunbird and dusky-chested flycatcher have also been sighted here, while parcucú and piranha are among the park's rich abundance of fish.

With the aid of a guide, the Río Yavarí is the perfect arterial route for a four–seven-day trip. Look for anaconda with a torch at night or learn the art of basketry from an Amerindian craftsman. Sling a hammock to escape the ferocity of the afternoon heat after dining on palm-wrapped fish, rice and plantain.

Excursions into the wilds of Amacayacu begin at the confluence of the Quebrada Matamata and this is where every birder, hiker and kayak launch departs. Every visitor is assigned a local guide for a range of tours that include night safaris, camping, fishing and visits to Amerindian villages. Prices vary but entry for non-nationals starts at 35,000COP per person with group rates and discounts that change depending on the season. Most people allow a good couple of days to do Amacayacu justice. Book at the Aviatur office on Calle 7, near Carrera 11 (*www. grupoaviatur.com*).

Further information may be had from **Territorial Amazonía–Orinoquía** (*Calle 14, No 8–79, Piso 2; Bogotá;* ✆ *243 1940;* e *amazonia@parquesnacionales.gov.co; www.parquesnacionales.gov.co*).

Getting there and away The best way to reach the park is to catch one of the several daily passenger **boats** from Leticia to Puerto Nariño (Leticia–Parque Amacayacu: 08.00, 10.00, 14.00; Parque Amacayacu–Leticia: 07.30, 11.00, 16.30). It passes by the Amacayacu Park visitor centre so simply ask to be dropped off on the way. To be sure of a seat, don't leave things to chance. Book in advance at 20,000COP for a journey that will take about 2 hours. For the return trip, a certain amount of patience is required, unless you have found a way to secure a seat. Try enlisting help from staff at the visitor centre as they are usually prepared to flag a boat down at around about noon and 16.00 each day.

Where to stay At the time of writing the Decameron resort was no longer in service so please check with tour agencies and at the PNN Amacayacu office in Leticia regarding places to stay in this national park (*Carerra 9, No 6–100, piso 2, Leticia;* ✆ *592 4872/7124*).

PUERTO NARIÑO (*www.puertonarino-amazonas.gov.co*) This tiny pedestrianised jungle town has a population of fewer than 6,000 with quiet sleepy streets that make even Leticia feel like New York's urban sprawl in comparison, albeit just 75km away. At the heart of the community is a dual-use basketball and football court, flanked by the might of the river one side and a raised wooden boardwalk on the other. Young boys clad in Brazil football shirts hone their keepy-uppy skills while women braid hair and sew in the shade. Billiard games, dominoes and idle gossip centre on this hub of town in weathered open-fronted buildings. After dark every resident of Puerto Nariño, young or old, seems to descend on the wooden bench seats overlooking the courts, from giggling toddlers and love-struck teens to groups of wrinkled elders.

Neat, paved footpaths divide Puerto Nariño, characterising the town as improbably tidy. Cars are banned, apart from a battered VW van that collects the rubbish. Puerto Nariño is also the only place in Colombia to embrace recycling as a citizen-led initiative, an idea that on the face of it seems more likely in an urban centre than a small jungle outpost. Yet the residents of Puerto Nariño are surprisingly well versed in environmental matters, possibly as a result of the many biologists, ecologists and conservationists that pass through (see box, page 276). A piece of rogue litter would probably be seized upon within minutes, if not seconds. Rubbish bins are in plentiful supply, gardens are well maintained and neighbourhoods seem to positively burst with community pride. This neatness is challenged a little when the rainy season arrives and its children's playground resembles a paddling pool; even more so when the population swells to accommodate entire communities seeking sanctuary from rising tides. Kids attempt to play five-a-side in murky knee-deep water while men wade through thick mud with giant crates of yam and yucca. Yet most fresh arrivals will be greeted by Puerto Nariño's pseudo-suburban scene of a green public park on a backdrop of turquoise-painted single-storey wooden houses edged by lush garden palms. It has freshly swept pavements and an electricity supply that ceases with an abrupt clank at 22.00.

Getting there The easiest way to reach Puerto Nariño from Leticia is by booking a seat with one of the handful of **boat** companies that run a daily weekday schedule of passenger services there. This is easily organised via all Leticia-based hotels and hostels or can be booked direct with the boat operators in offices on Calle 8 near the riverfront. Departures are at around 09.30 and 13.30 but are often affected by the water levels of the river and weather conditions. Pre-booking a ticket (about 25,000COP) is a wise precaution as these boats are often full. Try Expreso Tres Fronteras, Transporte Amazónico or Expreso Líneas Amazonas. Another alternative is to book one of the umpteen tour companies that include Puerto Nariño as a final port of call on its full-day itinerary. Chartering a vessel can be an expensive option at 120,000COP unless there are others in a similar predicament prepared to chip in and share the cost.

Getting around As a tiny, pedestrian town Puerto Nariño is easily navigable on foot. To visit local points of interest along the river simply head down to the riverfront. You'll find several local boatmen waiting to ply their trade as well as other travellers keen to share the cost.

Tourist information
⛱ Puerto Nariño Informacion Turística
m 313 268 8901

🏠 Where to stay
🏠 **Casa Selva** (12 rooms) Carretera 6, No 6–78; m 311 212 6043; e casaselvahotel@ yahoo.es. www.casaselvahotel.com The comfortable rooms in this fine wooden 2-storey building are without a doubt Puerto Nariño's most luxurious option. Each has a private bathroom & fan or AC with shuttered windows & a small balcony. Simple, wooden furniture, white linen & white towels give the place a monastic elegance. A decent restaurant seats 40 people at yellow-clothed tables & offers excellent value for money. A bar serves beer, water & soda. Guests can lounge around in the hotel's communal hammock lounge or grab a seat in a pleasant leafy courtyard. Pre-book & a member of staff

will meet you off the boat to save you lugging your gear 2 blocks uphill. **$$**
🏠 **Hotel Paiyu** (12 rooms) m 313 237 0840. Budget travellers highly recommend this small family-run hotel. Simple rooms are small but clean & equipped with a fan. Look out for a single-storey wooden building with a red tin roof opposite the Casa Selva. **$**
🏠 **Maloca Napu** (8 rooms) Calle 4, No 5–72; m 315 607 4044; e reserva@malocanapu.com;. www.malocanapu.com. With 8 clean & simple rooms & a couple of *malocas* to rent for family-sized groups, the Maloca Napu has opened up competition in town. They offer tours & will help out with logistics. Highly recommended. **$**

✕ Where to eat and drink
As you'd expect from a small jungle town, Puerto Nariño doesn't have many gastronomic hangouts, but a couple of places a block from the riverfront serve decent fish-and-rice meals. Both **Las Margaritas** and **Doña Francisca** are open for lunch and dinner with a set soup-and-main-course option costing under 9,000COP. Domino-playing men mainly populate a handful of drinking holes with the **Granero Bodega** and **Alvear** two of the best. Both overlook

the basketball courts and have a few plastic chairs on the boardwalk, a perfect spot from which to people-watch at dusk with an ice-cold *cerveza con limón*.

What to see and do

Mirador Nai Pata (*admission 5,000COP*) The charge is a small price to pay for the breathtaking views this lookout affords from the west of the town. Gaze out over the river, lakes and Puerto Nariño from this wooden purpose-built tower set atop the town's highest point, built in 2004.

San Martín A number of walking trails lead in and out of this Ticuna village, where tourists are welcome to learn about traditional medicine, indigenous plants, local customs and the history of the community. All hotels offer tours out to the village (or can point you in the right direction). Walk out of the town along a leafy path bathed in sunlight. Artisans in San Martín offer visitors plenty of opportunity to buy Ticuna crafts on arrival.

A Catholic church stages Mass on a Sunday when it is visited by a famous Amazonian *fraile* called José Rivera. This community-spirited monk opens his home to travellers and is renowned for his genuine hospitality. If you bump into him expect a fund of stories. He is also a great source of tips and information on how best to interact to get the most from local life. Ask anyone in Puerto Nariño for directions to the 'Fraile's place' and you'll be guided by scribbled maps and wild hand signals from a host of helpful passers-by. **Fraile José Rivera's *cabañas*** are a welcome sight after a sweaty hour-long hike from the town centre, high above a flooded forest by the riverbank amidst palms and coloured blooms. As you'd expect from a monk, the *fraile* is a rather unique host in the wilds of the Amazon. However, this remarkable fountain of knowledge is a superb source of information for travellers as he was posted to the region many years ago. He left once, at the Church's suggestion, but returned to build a home after missing the jungle so much. Today, the *fraile* works with local communities, taking in travellers that take the time to pass by. Simple, wooden *cabañas* are without any home comforts but up to 12 guests are welcome to a jungle retreat that has a dining area and a rustic cold shower. Verandas are slung with hammocks where the only distraction is birdsong and jungle chit-chatter. A viewing tower affords truly magnificent views and is a big hit with birders who make it this far. The *fraile* is respectful of traveller independence but is happy to arrange boat trips and local guides for those who need them. He also has a couple of wooden kayaks for guests keen to explore the river.

San Francisco For a chance to explore some wildlife-rich trails close to Río Loretoyacu ask a guide in Puerto Nariño to take you on a stomp around San Francisco. Eminent traditional herbalists reside in this pretty indigenous Ticuna village and may also accompany visitors on a tour around the trails' vast array of curative plants.

Lago Tarapoto This large, magical expanse of water is edged by ficus trees and is a famous location in which to spot pretty rose-coloured dolphins (boto) and admire the vast *Victoria amazonica* (giant lily). Located about 9km west of Puerto Nariño and 80km from Leticia, the lake is accessible only by boat via the river, with trips costing about US$25 (for four people) for a half-day. Canoes can also be hired from the local Amerindian settlements that dot the lake for about US$8 per day. Most full-day tours from Puerto Nariño will take in Lago Tarapoto, with a host of local boatmen prepared to depart from the riverbank every day. In 2002,

AN EDEN FOR ECOLOGISTS

As you might expect, the Colombian Amazon attracts dozens of ecologists and conservationists, keen to observe the region's extraordinary biodiversity and unique habitat. Some establish study bases in the jungle or along the river. Others operate on a more nomadic basis throughout the region as a whole. Many choose to centre themselves in the town of Puerto Nariño, because it enjoys a location close to Lake Tarapoto (Lago Tarapoto) and Parque Nacional Amacayacu. One such organisation is the OMACHA Foundation (+57 1 256 4682; e info@omacha.org; www.omacha.org), a non-government and non-profit organisation created to study, research and protect the Colombian Amazon's fauna and aquatic ecosystems. Since 1987, OMACHA has worked closely with local communities in the Putumayo, Caquetá and Apaporis rivers and tributaries to devise programmes for the sustainable development of aquatic resources. The biological station and laboratory opened in 1993 to focus on two species of river dolphins that inhabit the Amazon region: the boto (*Inia geoffrensis*) and tucuxi (*Sotalia fluviatilis*), both of whom face possible threat. Other studies have concentrated on the fish population, especially the largest fish species in the Amazon, the cucha (*Pterygoplychthes multiradiatus*) and the pirarucú (*Arapaima gigas*).

In recent years, OMACHA scientists have begun studying river wolves (*Pteronura brasiliensis*) and otters (*Lontra longicaudis*) in Puerto Nariño. It also rehabilitated an Amazonian manatee calf (*Trichechus inunguis*) following the capture and death of its mother at the hands of local fishermen. Whilst raising and observing the behaviour of the calf (named Airuwe, meaning 'manatee' in the Ticuna language), OMACHA began a series of studies on the Amazonian manatee in conjunction with native Ticunas, Yukunas, Tanimucas and Macues along with the mixed-race fishermen from Puerto Nariño and the Caquetá and Apaporis rivers areas. The Florida-based Sirenia Project fitted the manatee with a belt and radio to enable researchers to monitor it via telemetry techniques. The Amazonian manatee is the smallest of the living sirenians and the only manatee species to live entirely in fresh water. An educational project was launched within local communities where manatees are hunted as a food source. National and international film-makers followed the project, making documentaries about the pioneering nature of the manatee conservation efforts. In 2002, the OMACHA Foundation and the Puerto Nariño community returned Airuwe to the wild at three years eight months old, in Lake Tarapoto, a fertile manatee feeding area. OMACHA's manatee project captured the hearts and minds of many people Colombia-wide and has since furthered the Amazon's conservation profile to a large degree.

Visitors will find the Fundación Omacha centre right on the riverfront. It is open to the public and has a small exhibition space. Pop in to learn about the projects and Adopt a Dolphin programme or to lend much-needed volunteer support.

Lago Tarapoto was the site chosen by the OMACHA Foundation and the Puerto Nariño community (see box, above) for the return to the wild of a three-year-old Amazonian manatee. The lake is a well-established manatee-feeding area and a sacred place for many local people, many of whom believe it has special powers. Myths are important to the Amerindian communities of the Amazon and centre

Many of the pinprick-sized riverbank communities in the low-lying Colombian Amazon are used to abandoning their homes during the wet season. A cyclical climate makes this necessary as close to 3m of rain can pound the land each year. Yet this dousing isn't viewed as a flooding disaster zone, but rather simply the Amazon's way. Rising river levels can see the water increase by up to 15m. Entire wood-and-thatch villages are engulfed, with huge tracts of jungle immersed and only the highest *ceiba* trees able to peek out above the surface of the water. Once the rains subside and water levels fall, villagers return to reclaim their homes for the dry season. Much of the Amazon lowlands is richer and more fertile after this prolonged soaking thanks to plant matter decomposition and nutrients from the river. Fish feed on berries and seeds from the forest ahead of reproduction.

Generally speaking, river swelling occurs between the end of December and the end of June, with levels reaching their highest level in March to the beginning of June. During this rainy season the volume of the Amazon River increases, flooding the forest. Large lagoons and swamps are formed to provide ideal areas for observing birds, caiman and *Victorias regias* (water lilies) and fishing for piranha. Ebb tides begin in mid-July and last until the beginning of December, reaching their lowest levels in July–November. During this time, sandbanks are formed at the river borders. Turtles nest and lay their eggs, local people plant rice on exposed beaches and fishing is at its most popular.

on integration with nature. At Tarapoto, legends relate to a strange green light that illuminates the night sky, an eerie glow that has prompted many fishermen to return home after setting their nets. Rumours say that those who choose to fish overnight under the light have been found dead and headless in the lake in the morning. Some say pirates ascend from the water's depths, killing unsuspecting fishermen as the light shines. Others say the body parts are harvested for research purposes by scientists from the United States.

Birding around Puerto Nariño Visiting birdwatchers prepared to explore in and around Puerto Nariño and San Martín are likely to spot numerous species in the many walks that loop the town. Recent sightings include the black-tailed tityra tui parakeet, white-bearded hermit, rufous-breasted hermit, rusty-fronted tody-flycatcher, spotted tody-flycatcher, yellow-bellied dacnis, glittering-throated emerald, scarlet-crowned barbet, bare-necked fruitcrow, campo oriole, dark-breasted spinetail, plain-breasted piculet, maroon-tailed parakeet, hooded tanager, lesser yellow-headed vulture, sapphire-rumped parrotlet and white-eared jacamar.

EXPLORING THE YAVARÍ RIVER

This mighty, winding tributary reaches into large unbroken stretches of rainforest, meandering into some of the most magnificent areas in which to observe Amazonian wildlife first-hand. An increasing number of small private reserves have sprung up along the Yavarí River, to offer adventure activities with the services of a guide, such as night safaris, alligator spotting, birding, jungle hikes along old Amerindian

Unfortunately, many of even the Amazon's most seasoned guides are hopelessly equipped. Many carry torches with low-watt bulbs, even if they plan to hike the jungle overnight. Few have binoculars, waterproof matches or a basic first-aid kit. Others don't have any firm ideas of what they'd do in an emergency. Don't be afraid to request a full briefing ahead of even the most straightforward itinerary to check that you pack what you need. As a rule of thumb, always wear boots – even in the dry season. Light baggage is the way to go as you'll probably have to lug it on and off boats and along unmade roads. Choose lightweight clothing that includes swimming gear, long trousers, long-sleeved shirts and waterproofs. Be sure to pack a hat, sunglasses and sun block as protection against the harsh equatorial sun. Candles and matches are also advisable as most lodges only have electricity 18.00–21.00 each night. Be sure not to forget your binoculars and camera and be sure to wrap them to avoid problems with moisture – there is nothing more disappointing than a set of pictures plagued by condensation. Carry water and lots of mosquito repellent and keep a mobile phone (a quad band works best) close at hand.

trails, and jaguar trekking. Simple accommodation tends to be basic at best, usually in the style of mud-and-thatch cabins with rudimentary, communal washrooms. Food is generally included in the cost of your stay, with tours and transfers extra. Those travelling in a group will find there are plenty of discounts up for grabs on accommodation and tours. The Yavarí stretches from the border between Brazil and Peru's Loreto department, flowing northeast for 870km. It joins the Amazon River near the Brazilian outpost of Benjamin Constant, so enquiries regarding visa requirements for each territory should be made prior to travel.

Journeying the Yavarí River allows plenty of opportunity to spot the Amazon's pretty pink river dolphins (boto) as well as the silver-coloured tucuxis (*Sotalia fluviatili*) – start scanning the water from the moment you leave downtown Leticia. In the virgin rainforest swatches within reach of the river, expect to find common squirrel monkey, black-mantled tamarin, black agouti, Amazon dwarf squirrel, pygmy marmoset, night monkey, brush-tailed rats and white-fronted capuchin. Other possible sightings include red howler, titi monkey, woolly monkey, monk saki, short-eared dog, collared peccary, tapir, oncilla, giant armadillo, sloth, jaguar, ocelot and giant otter. Foliage along the riverbank runs an entire spectrum of green, from garish paintbox-green ferns and black-green mangroves to olive-green reeds, yellow-green palms and a tangle of lush emerald-green creepers. The colour of the river also alters dramatically from a creamy swirl of thick vanilla to a deep brick-red. Ichthyologically speaking, the Amazon and its tributaries are some of the most exciting on the planet. Even on a slow day, fishermen can expect to find cardinal tetras, discus, angel cichlids and armoured pleco catfish with thin-nosed tube-snout knifefish, freshwater dogfish, motoro, tooth-lip knifefish, tiger stingray, Faulkner's stingray, Harald Schultz's cory, arowana, American lungfish, hatchetfish, giant peacock bass, tambaqui and goliath pirarucú. Piranhas are omnipresent as are electric eels and river stingrays. Since 1960, more than 50 species of fish have been discovered, named and catalogued in the Amazon each year. The number of identified fish species currently stands at 3,200 but experts agree that the true figure is likely to exceed 4,000 – at least.

Many of the eco-lodges in the Amazon region prefer their guests not to use the hard stuff. Citing health concerns relating to high chemical content as well as the damage it is said to cause the environment, there is also a joke in the Amazon that Western sprays seem to attract more mosquitoes than they repel. An increasing number of herbal insect repellents can be found on the market. Many are 100% natural, contain no chemicals, are organic and fully biodegradable. Some are safe enough to use even in pregnancy and suitable for people of all ages, including children and babies.

Many eco-conscious travellers swear by citrus essential oils in the Amazon, liberally applied to clothes, hair and skin. Citrosa geranium has up to 40% of the repellent power of DEET, great when added to crushed lemon thyme (*Thymus citriodora*), which itself has over 60% of DEET's repellence.

In the Amazon, many indigenous tribes have developed their own ecological repellent for the use of whey-skinned bug-bitten tourists. Each has been designed for multiple use in generous drenching quantities to cope with the prevalence of mosquitoes in the region. The following recipe comes highly recommended:

Mix alcohol with menticol in equal measures in a jug. Add a chopped bar of nopikex soap and six camphor tablets. Pour into a blender to make a paste. Add three tablespoons of 10% eurax (for every 300ml of alcohol) with 30cc of citronella essence and four tablespoons of Johnson's Baby Oil. Mix well before pouring the liquid into a bottle, preferably with a pump spray attachment. Use the lotion to spray clothing ahead of travel to the Amazon, repeating this process for a good three or four days. Before direct exposure, apply liberally to the skin (taking care to cover the head, hairline, ear lobes and other 'forgotten' areas). Douse the outer edges of bedding, sleeping bags, hammocks and mosquito netting. The mixture is also effective in reducing pain and inflammation from existing bites.

WHERE TO STAY AND EAT *See map, page 272.*
Yavarí River

Reserva Natural Heliconia (21 rooms) Book at the Reserva Natural Heliconia office; Calle 13, No 11–74, Leticia; 601 8709; m 311 5085 666; e info@amazonheliconia.com; www. amazonheliconia.com. Located on the Yavarí River amidst palms & trees that exceed 100m in height, the wood-&-thatch cabins of the Reserva Natural Heliconia sit on 15ha of beautiful, preserved jungle. Only environmentally friendly materials are used in the running of the lodge. The reserve's philosophy also extends to a number of conservation projects in the Amazon in conjunction with non-profit groups, including a protection programme for the native cultures that inhabit the surroundings of the lodge. A wide range of boat & hiking tours including dolphin watching, kayaking, fishing & canopy exploration. Birding tours have become something of a speciality of the lodge with observation towers & on-site guides. Rates vary depending on the tours chosen & the season but it is well worth taking advantage of a transfer from Leticia airport & the assistance Heliconia staff offer in regards to immigration arrangements with Colombian & Brazilian authorities, Migracíon Colombia & federal police. **$–$$$**

Reserva Natural Palmari (100-person capacity in hammocks, floor mattresses, rooms & lodges) Contact the multi-lingual owner Axel Antoine-Feill at his Bogotá HQ; 610 3514/610 3517/236 3813; www.palmari.org. Dolphin views abound from this sprawling wooden lodge with a viewing tower that ensures prime vistas from a lofty vantage point. Rooms have private bathrooms while a circular communal building is hung with dozens of hammocks. A decent restaurant serves

7

hearty meals & the lodge has a number of guides. Tours include hiking, birding, kayaking, night safaris, camping & trips to Amerindian villages. The reserve is a fully fledged research facility so the focus is ecological. Guests can also swim in natural springs, fish in the surrounding waters, dolphin watch, have a temporary pigment tattoo applied by local tribesfolk, & learn about Neotropical flora in the lodge's purpose-built library on a complimentary basis. More than 541 species of bird from 62 different bird families have been recorded in & around the environs of the reserve with 7 of the species classed as 'unknown' (& awaiting classification). Guests are forbidden to bring any manufactured insect repellents to the lodge. Ecological recipes are allowed (page 279). **$$**

🏠 **Reserva Natural Zacambú** (30 rooms) Book accommodation & tours through Amazon Jungle Trips; Av Internacional, No 6–25, Leticia;

📞 592 7377; e amazonjungletrips@yahoo.com. Overlooking Lake Zacambú & on a tributary of the Río Yavarí, this mangrove-flanked lodge offers simple, earthy rooms with mosquito nets & hammocks but without private bathrooms. An all-in price includes meals of fish & yucca in a setting where you can actually hear dolphins frolicking in the water. Canoeing in the lake is easy from a boardwalk dock from where caimans can be spotted up to a few metres in length. Machete-wielding patron Jorge is fond of after-dark caiman hunting using a powerful flashlight strapped to his head. He utters strange guttural sounds to emulate the call, sweeping a beam of light along the shore. Walking trails are limited around the reserve with almost every excursion by boat. However the chirping of frogs, humming insects & local anteaters has a certain charm. Birders are sure to sight egrets, kingfishers & parrots on the shores of

MOUNTING YOUR OWN EXPEDITION

By Peter Hutchison, co-author of *Amazon: the Bradt Travel Guide* (third edition, August 2007) with Roger Harris.

The most important requirements for a successful trip are to have a purpose and a plan. Your expedition must have a definite goal, otherwise you will just drift from place to place. Ask yourself why you want to mount your own expedition. If it's so that you are free to go where you want when you want, to stay away as long as you wish and to be in total control of your own destiny, then to achieve that much freedom you will need to finance it yourself. If you are sponsored, commissioned or under contract to carry out some sort of research you won't have complete choice in where you go and what you do.

Most expeditions use local guides, porters and boatmen. For a first-time independent jungle trip, travelling, camping and daily chores will take up most of your time and all your energy; you would need experience to be able to carry out project work as well. If you plan to write a book when you return home or make a film while you're there, then you will have to compromise your freedom. The main things you need to concentrate on are as follows.

GETTING TO KNOW YOUR DESTINATION The more information you can gather about your destination the better equipped you will be to handle any unforeseen circumstances that arise – and arise they will. Buy the best maps and plan your route, then start doing the detective work. Contact embassies, ministries, tourist boards, but make your enquiries concise.

GAINING PERMISSION Whether or not you need a visa to enter the country itself, make thorough enquiries about requirements to enter the area you will visit. Some officials are sensitive if there is logging or mining activity. To travel in a national park, a protected area or the home of indigenous tribal people may take the lakes, with piranha fishing as easy as throwing a piece of string into the water. **$$**

Amazon River

🏠 **Reserva Natural Marasha** (50-person capacity) Office in Leticia: Carrera 10, No 7–55; 📞592 6700; www.reservamarasha.com. The boat drops arrivals on a muddy riverbank ahead of a good hour-long trek through the jungle, but the Marasha Reserve is worth the effort – even in the rainy season. For a start, the people who work there are a breath of fresh air – dedicated, friendly & prepared to go the extra mile. Secondly, the setting makes a great base for some deeper exploration into the wilds. Set on a sparkling lake & surrounded by peaceful waterways, the reserve is blessed with wildlife-rich trails full of monkey, sloth, toucan, eagle, owl & butterflies. Stay overnight in simple, slung hammocks along with a resident pair of parrots, a couple of titi monkeys & a curious coati who thinks he's a cat. Overhanging branches are festooned with creepers & bromeliads with the Marasha's oldest giant ceiba tree, over 400 years old. A wide range of day & night jungle excursions range in price depending on the number of people but it is worth budgeting at around 85,000COP for a full-on full-day trip (lunch included). **$$**

BENJAMIN CONSTANT

This small Brazilian river town is named after Benjamin Constant Botelho de Magalhães (1836–91), a military man and political thinker. Like many Amazon settlements it

six months or longer to gain permission. Be patient, polite and persistent and remember that some of the most interesting places cannot be visited on a whim.

WHEN TO GO In the dry season the rivers will be low, sometimes so low that the riverbed is exposed, making river travel arduous. But in the dry season you will see lots more wildlife and camping is more pleasant because it's not raining all the time. In the rainy season it rains nearly every day and river levels are high. Rivers will be flowing fast and the jungle may flood. Clothes that get wet take ages to dry, while mould grows on camera equipment and film. But the rainy season does have its compensations, particularly if you are visiting a waterfall.

CHOOSING YOUR BOAT Dugout canoes are the most common means of travel on Amazonian rivers. They are strong, and respond well under power, but they are heavy and sit low in the water. Sometimes the sides are built up with planks, which makes them more stable but even heavier. Fibreglass, plastic and aluminium canoes are light, fast and responsive under power, but they are not so readily available and are much more fragile than dugout canoes. Take this into consideration if your river is a rocky one. If you choose this type of boat you will probably have to take one from your home country. Inflatable boats are excellent, particularly for the novice. They rarely capsize even when punctured or full of water; they bounce off rocks, carry enormous weights and are repairable and comfortable to sit on day after day. But on fast water they slide, they spin, they are slow and almost impossible to paddle. However, for a first trip my choice would be an inflatable powered by an outboard engine light enough for one person to carry.

WHAT TO TAKE It may be possible to buy most of the things you will need in larger towns, but if an item is essential take it with you.

isn't blessed with endless attractions, but the town's compact **Magüta Museum** has some interesting artefacts relating to the region's endemic tribes, including books in the Ticuna language. All in all, Benjamin Constant could probably be walked from end to end within 30 minutes. Dominated by a cathedral and a timber mill, the town is a popular refuelling point with boats travelling to and from Manaus. A handful of decent restaurants and bars also make it a good place to stop off for lunch.

Benjamin Constant is one of the oldest agricultural frontier areas in eastern Brazil with a population of small-scale farmers practising subsistence agriculture. Relying on the existence of secondary forests, the local communities use 135 plant species to survive, producing food, tubes, latex, oils, fibres, resins, gums, balsams, condiments, candles and cellulose from their natural environment. In 1988, the town gained international notoriety following the mass slaughter of Ticuna people at the hands of logger Oscar Castelo Branco. Some 14 Ticuna were shot to death with 23 wounded, in a brutal attempt to prevent them from reclaiming their traditional forestlands.

The **Ticuna** are one of Brazil's most populous indigenous groups, with some 95 villages mainly scattered along the banks of the Upper Solimões River and its tributaries. Despite being home to more than 50% of the world's Ticunas (Colombia and Peru also have Ticuna peoples), Brazil has only recently started to invest in native language education. Brazilian Ticunas now have written literature and an education provided by the Brazilian National Foundation for the Indian (FUNAI) and the Ministry of Education. Ticuna is a tonal language similar to Chinese with the meaning of a word varying greatly simply by changing the tone.

PARQUE NACIONAL CAHUINARI (CAHUINARI NATIONAL PARK)

This 575,000ha expanse of lowland tropical rainforest lies in the western region of the Amazon Basin where the Cahuinari and Bernardo rivers meet, with the Caquetá River forming its northern border. Characterised by a high degree of both terrestrial and aquatic biodiversity, the park also overlaps two of Colombia's legally declared indigenous territories: the Predio Putumayo and Miriti-Paraná. Brackish rivers, sparkling creeks and alluvial plains provide a wide variety of ecosystems with a mix of lowland forest and flooded forest covering about 90% of the land. Soaring trees reach 40m entwined with vines and epiphytes. However, a history of intensive fishing and hunting of black caiman, otters and various primates has seriously depleted wildlife numbers. Rare and endangered animals found in Cahuinari include jaguar and the magnificent giant river otter, for which the lower Río Caquetá is a last remaining habitat. Another species under severe threat is the endemic Charapa river turtle. Other inhabitants include the white-lipped peccary and tapir with very little research conducted into bird species, which include the nocturnal curassow, grey-winged trumpeter and blue-and-yellow macaw.

Accessing the park is problematic, with the area subject to safety concerns owing to its remoteness, but many of those who have made it there have been mightily impressed. Cahuinari is certainly a landmark in the conservation of Colombia's indigenous patrimony. Traditional cultures have been preserved and the lessons of conservation offer considerable potential to other communities in educational terms. One of the best-preserved forests in the Colombian Amazon, the park is of great importance to the 1,500 indigenous people who live within its boundaries. Rubber exploitation was threatening to devastate the land and people. Today, the park protects the indigenous groups that survived and the amazing tropical rainforests in which they live.

Before visiting the Parque Nacional Cahuinari be sure to check on the latest safety advice on the ground. At the time of writing, **accommodation** seems to be limited to a couple of basic cabins and an undeveloped camping area. Visitors must pre-book ahead of arrival at a Parques Nacionales office (*call the Bogotá Ecotourism office for details;* ✆ *353 2400*). Entry is prohibited to anyone who hasn't engaged the services of a recognised guide, with permits awarded on a discretionary basis only if the park isn't in use for community projects.

Further information can be obtained from **Territorial Amazonía – Orinoquía** (*Calle 14, No 8–79, Piso 2, Bogotá;* ✆ *353 2400 ;* e *amazonia@parquesnacionales.gov. co; www.parquesnacionales.gov.co*).

TABATINGA *Telephone +55 (Brazil) +97 (Tabatinga)*

Leticia's Brazilian twin town lacks the charm of its Colombian neighbour but it does serve as an alternative base for those keen to swap salsa for samba. Hotel accommodation tends to be much pricier than in Leticia but Tabatinga has a good range of decent restaurants and some lively bars. Travellers planning to board an early-morning launch to Iquitos may find staying overnight in Tabatinga makes good logistical sense. Locals often refer to crossing over 'Checkpoint Charlie' when describing the Leticia–Tabatinga border. However there is no distinguishable boundary, no guards or passport check, and no immigration red tape.

GETTING AROUND Exploring Tabatinga on foot is easy enough, with taxis in good supply. Hail one on the street or head to the port where you'll find a number waiting for trade, including a fleet of Faz Freet taxis. Citywide, the streets are a swarm of motorbikes and scooters with plenty of places to hire by the day or hour. Down by the river, dozens of boats and wooden dugouts vie for position under the pale, stone-terraced steps of the portside. Goods and chattels form ugly piles in ready-to-board preparedness while backpackers catch 40 winks on rolled-up hammocks by sacks of bananas. All boats leave Tabatinga from this launch point, be they hulking great grey cargo ships or leisurely dolphin cruises.

WHERE TO STAY Much like Leticia, Tabatinga is blessed with umpteen hotels and budget hostels but is rather light on luxury options. Most of the dirt-cheap options are clustered around the border area. Others can be found a stone's throw from the port.

Hotel Takana (24 rooms) Rua Oswaldo Cruz 970; ✆ 3412 3557; e takana@takanahotel. com.br; www.takanahotel.com.br. Although this hotel is on the outskirts of town, those looking for something swish will find that it is Tabatinga's most upmarket option. Spruce, AC rooms boast a pleasing décor surrounded by mature leafy courtyard garden with a restaurant & swimming pool. **$$$**

Hotel Bela Vista (6 rooms) Rua Marechal Rondón 1806; ✆ 3412 3846. Just a few steps from the port, this cheap-&-cheerful resting place is a popular option with shoestring travellers. It's nothing much to look at, but the location is unbeatable & the rooms have AC. **$$**

Pousada do Sol (7 rooms) Rua General Sampaio 50; ✆ 3412 3987. The decent-sized rooms have AC, a fridge & private bathroom & are within easy walking distance of the launches for Iquitos & Manaus. It's close to a handful of good local restaurants & also has a courtyard garden & a small swimming pool. **$$**

WHERE TO EAT AND DRINK Tabatinga has numerous places to eat, from sizzling food stalls and fried-chicken joints to funky kerbside cafés and seafood diners.

When Slovenian Martín Strel (*www.martinstrel.com*) announced plans to swim the entire length of the Amazon River in 2007, the world thought he was mad. For not only did Strel's route stretch a gruelling 5,268km, the river is also a proverbial soup of piranha, crocodiles and other predatory water-borne beasts. The Slovenian also chose to conduct his mammoth swim during the rainy season between February and April. Rising water is at its most hazardous at this time of year with the river scattered with fast-moving debris from the flood-ridden jungle. Strel's goal was to average 85km per day, departing Atalaya Peru on 1 February 2007. He entered Colombian waters after 26 days in the water and on 11 April a huge party welcomed Strel to the riverbanks of Belém where he finally limped ashore. During his arduous trip, the Slovenian swimmer became a legend throughout the Amazon with every small village dispatching a flotilla of dugout canoes packed to the gills with awestruck indigenous people as he passed their way. After suffering chronic sunburn on the stretch of river approaching Colombian territory, Strel donned a mask fashioned out of an old bedsheet and wore a floppy sun hat. Proceeds from the charity fundraising marathon swim have helped numerous indigenous communities along the Amazon River, improving sanitation and basic living conditions (*www.amazonswim.com*).

Guinness Book record-holder Strel is no stranger to challenge. He swam the Danube in 2000, the Mississippi in 2002, the Paraná in 2003 and the Yangtze in 2004. A documentary about the Amazon swim (Big River Man) was broadcast in Latin America in 2007 to much acclaim. Strel's slogan for his repeated feats of endurance is 'Swimming for Peace, Friendship and Clean Waters'.

Typical Brazilian fare is easy to find, such as *feijoada* (black beans) and *coquetel de camarão* (shrimp cocktail) and, of course, Brazil's delicious Skol beer.

✗ **Blue Moon Restaurante** ✎ 3412 2227. Located right on the side of the port, this cream-coloured single-storey restaurant may not look much, but there are few better places to dine while waiting patiently for a boat. Brightly coloured hanging baskets give the place a cheery feel but it is the prices that truly put a smile on your face at less than US$5 for a big plate of chicken & rice. $

✗ **Churrascaria Tia Helena** Rua Marechal Mallet 12; ✎ 3412 2165. The décor may be functional but the food is cheap & hearty – with an all-you-can-eat option that's a budget traveller's delight! Melt-in-the-mouth meat is brought to the table on skewers from the grill on demand. It's then carved in true flamboyant Brazilian style with flashing blades, with much aplomb. $

✗ **Restaurante Tres Fronteiras do Amazonas** Rua Rui Barbosa; ✎ 3412 2341. Dine in style in this pleasant thatch-roofed open-sided restaurant where a simple menu of grilled chicken, fish & meat dishes rarely disappoints. $

OTHER PRACTICALITIES Very much a town designed for travellers passing through, Tabatinga has everything for people on the move. Supermarkets, mini markets and kiosks can be found in abundance with the excellent Mini Mercado Baratinho a popular fallback for backpackers dashing to board the boat. A large permanent market is a great place to pick up spare T-shirts, flip-flops, hammocks, boots, hats, sunglasses and replacement luggage. Public toilets can be found on the portside just a short walk from a row of shops that includes a drugstore, mobile-phone shop and internet café.

SANTA ROSA

A big blue sign welcomes arrivals to Santa Rosa with 'Bienvenidos al Perú' on arrival, but most visitors are simply passing through. Dozens and dozens of boats zoom in and out hurriedly for a visa stamp. Passengers who do disembark are usually party goers from Leticia, arriving in Peru to make the most of its cheap beer and *chicha* bars. Larger boats that berth are crammed with pigs, chickens, lumber and electrical goods and, of course, backpacking tourists. Santa Rosa's local population is a mix of Peruvian government administration, immigration officers and local farming folk.

A cluster of decent bars and restaurants hug the shoreline and Letician townsfolk eagerly cross the river on the basis of Santa Rosa's excellent *ceviche* and ice-cold Cristel. Music is teeth-rattlingly loud at the Bar El Delfin Enamorado while the wild parties at El Paisa are rumoured to rage until dawn. However, during daylight hours Santa Rosa is a much more sedate place to be. Expect to see border controllers washing their clothes at the water's edge while their colleagues snooze on benches in the shadows. Sleepy dogs roam the dusty streets, and the only action is the frenzied refuelling of passing boatmen on the move.

SEND US YOUR SNAPS!

We'd love to follow your adventures using our *Colombia* guide – why not send us your photos and stories via Twitter (@BradtGuides) and Instagram (@bradtguides) using the hashtag #colombia. Alternatively, you can upload your photos directly to the gallery on the Colombia destination page via our website (*www.bradtguides.com*).

8

The Southwest Interior

Colombia's inner southwest region is home to some of the country's most diverse topography amidst a dizzying array of altitudes and contrasting terrain. Impenetrable folds of jungle stretch to snowy mountain peaks with patches of arid desert leading to dusty country towns. Dramatic green valleys give way to rugged highlands and magnificent rolling hills. Delve into the countryside to discover the southwest's host of pretty *pueblitos* and fine colonial cities along with some of the most important pre-Columbian sites in the Americas. The region is also home to the nation's third-largest city, Cali, Colombia's ultra-modern urban hub. Renowned as the salsa capital of Colombia, Cali boasts a lengthy dance tradition and this hot, rhythmic musical pulse has made the city famous worldwide. Expect hundreds of sweaty, sexy salsa joints and sassy movers in a city devoted to partying hard – a sharp contrast to the region's genteel religious centres and pilgrim prayer sites.

VALLE DEL CAUCA

That an entire department is named after a single valley reflects the importance of the Valle del Cauca to the region where fertile soils produce bountiful crops of sugarcane, tobacco, maize and cotton. Wedged between the Cordillera Occidental and Cordillera Central, the Valle del Cauca's 22,140km² terrain is riddled with nourishing rivers. Emptying into the mighty Río Cauca, these mountain waters have nurtured the region's prosperous agriculture-based economy in which sugarcane remains the fiscal bedrock. Cotton, tobacco, soy and coffee are also grown, alongside *bagasse*-based (sugarcane fibre) pulp and paper mills and a growing number of cement works. Good access to Buenaventura port on the Pacific coast enables the efficient import and export of goods to the rest of Colombia – and beyond. Despite Valle del Cauca comprising large swathes of countryside, more than 80% of the population live in cities or towns. The coverage of public services is among the highest in the country.

PRACTICALITIES Personal safety in some areas of the Valle del Cauca department is a major priority, especially in the rural areas near the cities of Pradera and Florida. Once the stronghold of FARC rebels, safety is much improved in many areas, although pockets of guerrilla and military remain. In June 2002, the kidnapping of 12 local politicians grabbed the world's headlines. After being held for five years by FARC to pressure a prisoner exchange with the Colombian government, guerrilla leaders suddenly announced that 11 had been killed, despite recently releasing so-called live video footage of the hostages. FARC claimed that the deaths occurred after the group became caught up in crossfire during an attack by an 'unidentified military group'. The only hostage survivor was Sigifredo López, who for security reasons was travelling in another group of FARC operatives. In September 2007,

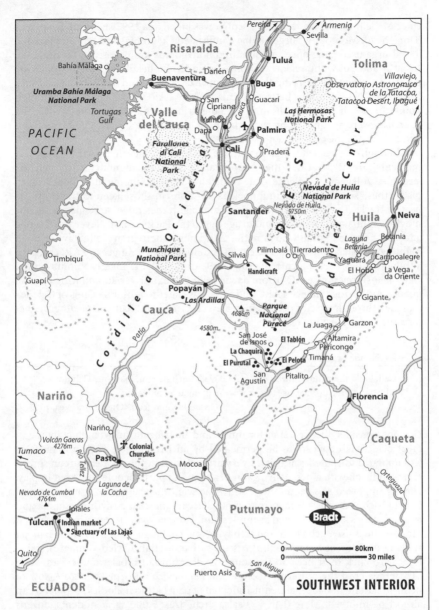

the Red Cross was allowed to recover the bodies and return them by helicopter to their families. In the same year Diego Montoya, who ranked alongside Osama Bin Laden on the FBI's ten most-wanted fugitives list, was arrested at a small farm in the Valle del Cauca, following a nine-year manhunt. As one of Colombia's most powerful and dangerous drug barons, Montoya is thought to have been responsible for 80% of the cocaine in the United States and Europe. Even conservative estimates value his exports since 1993 at 500 tonnes of cocaine worth more than US$10 billion. The FBI had offered US$5 million for information leading to the arrest of Montoya and his capture has been hailed as the biggest victory in the drug war since Medellín cartel leader Pablo Escobar was killed in a 1993 shootout. Known as 'Don Diego', Montoya is alleged to have infiltrated Colombia's military and boasted a well-organised gang of several hundred bodyguards known as the 'macho men'. In 2013 and 2014, the region was once again in the headlines due to the FARC guerrilla strategy of harrying the towns of Inza, Suarez and Toribio in Cauca. In November 2014, tensions between locals and the FARC reached an all-time high point when two members of an indigenous tribe were killed by the FARC. The guerrillas were sought out by the indigenous authorities and captured, tried and handed over to the relevant authorities.

Although the security situation in the Valle del Cauca makes these types of incidents rare, the fact that they happen at all is a stark reminder of the region's struggles. A legacy of violence, drug trafficking and kidnapping in Valle del Cauca places these small, isolated rural pockets off-limits to those keen to travel off the beaten track. The troublesome regions are highly desirable strategic routes for moving combatants, weapons and drugs out to the Pacific coast. Never travel alone and use a trusted guide who is native and knows the region well. Stay on main highways, especially at night. The city of Cali itself is no stranger to FARC activity, although it has been much reduced. On 9 April, 2007, a 45kg car bomb gutted Cali's five-storey police HQ before dawn, killing a taxi driver and injuring over 30 people. Authorities blamed FARC and three days later tens of thousands of Caleños marched through the city's streets in protest carrying giant banners reading 'I reject terrorism' and 'Death to fear'.

CALI *Telephone code 2*

In Cali, look, they know how to enjoy. By day it's burning sun, make my Cali hot …
Let the band tune up, because this year we're going to explode!
Orquesta Guayacán, 'Oiga, Mira, Vea', 1992

Caleños consider their passion for music and their beautiful women a source of great pride. Cali appears to be permeated by an irrepressible rhythmic pulse as Colombia's undisputed 'salsa city'. Every arterial road in this modern urban sprawl seems to throb with a percussive Latin beat as Cali's party people come out to play. Having imported salsa and other Latin American musical genres from Cuba and Puerto Rico, Caleños are rapturous about staccato *merengue* rhythms, samba and rumba classics and syncopated ta-tum-ta-tum *bossa nova* beats. Even on a weekday, hip-swaying *salseros* can be found sashaying and snaking through downtown *arepa* stalls bound for downtown *salsotecas* (salsa bars). High-heeled women in skin-tight garb click their heels to the sound of drumming timbales and claves while car stereos emit the powerful boom of *tumbao, cuica* and *cavaquinho*. A row of neon-lit basement dancehalls emit a cocktail of pan-Latino melodies so sweet it can almost be imbibed. More than 130 salsa orchestras, 5,000 salsa students, dozens of music stores and instrument makers, over a hundred *salsotecas* and numerous conga, bongo and maracas players give Cali its character – along with an energetic nightlife that requires plenty of stamina. Cali is also home to a week-long salsa festival – the largest on the planet – that celebrated its 50th anniversary in 2007. This kaleidoscope of music and dance is not for the faint-hearted. Indeed, it's as hot, claim the Caleños, as the women of the city and its year-round sultry heat.

In Glynis Anthony's travel narrative *Colombia: Land of Tomorrow* a tale is told of a Cali taxi driver who is transporting a newly arrived French businessman across the city. Cali born and bred, he is boasting of the city's progressive stance

CITY OF SALSA CHAMPIONS

We have received from our ancestors the passion for salsa dancing. We live it with all intensity and we have transmitted this passion outside Colombia – all the energy and speed that we have in our hearts and that runs through our blood.

Viviane Vargas,
Cali resident and Word Salsa Federation Champion 2005 and 2007

Cali is home to a number of world-champion salsa aficionados, including the dance troupe Swing Latino (winners of the Team Division 2006), John Vásquez and Judy Aguilar (winners of the Cabaret Division 2006), and Viviane Vargas and Ricardo Murillo (World Salsa Federation Champions 2005 and 2007).

Vargas and Murillo also performed at the Festival Encounter Latino in London in July 2006, the Carnaval Del Pueblo, Europe's largest free Latin American fiesta, and Birmingham's Latin American Festival in 2007. In 2009, Cali's own Jenny Rodriguez and Jonathan Landa won the World Salsa Championship (now known as the World Latin Dance Cup); 2011 saw five-time World Cup winners John Vásquez and Judy Aguilar embark on a worldwide tour, including venues in the USA and UK.

Further information can be found online: World Salsa Championships (*www.worldsalsachampionships.com*); World Salsa Federation (*www.worldsalsafederation.com*); Carnival Del Pueblo (*www.carnavaldelpueblo.com*); and Latin American Festival (*www.abslatin.co.uk*).

and developments and asks his passenger if it was really true that Parisians still lived in houses that were over 400 years old. The Frenchman, rather mystified by the question, confirmed that this was true. Aghast, the taxi driver proudly asserts that Cali, whilst not as famous as Paris, doesn't have a building dating any further back than 1990 – all the older structures having been torn down. This is a slight exaggeration, but it isn't *that* wide of the mark, with Cali's architectural make-up largely modern. Some interesting colonial buildings can be found hidden amongst the skyscrapers, flyovers and shopping malls, with some nice, leafy pathways along the Río Cali.

HISTORY Before the arrival of the Spanish, the land on which Cali now sits was inhabited by a number of indigenous tribes, including the cannibalistic Morrones and large Calima communities. Fiercely protective of their fertile valley, the indigenous peoples offered stiff resistance when Sebastían de Benalcázar and his men arrived fresh from founding Quito and Popayán and conquering the Incas. However, he was able to establish a settlement in 1536 – dubbed Santiago de Cali – and shipped in thousands of African slaves to work the sugarcane plantations. In 1540, Santiago de Cali fell under the jurisdiction of Popayán's political and economic administration after Benalcázar decided a cooler climate would aid governance. The settlement continued to grow and by 1793, Cali had a population of over 6,500, of which more than 1,100 were slaves. Strategically positioned for trade among the mining regions of Antioquia, Chicó and Popayán, Cali soon spawned a trail for mules and horses to the coast at Buenaventura. However, it was the arrival of the railway in the early 20th century that brought true prosperity to Cali as it enabled the fast and efficient movement of goods to world markets. By the 1940s, the city had witnessed explosive growth to become a dynamic, industrial centre. Today

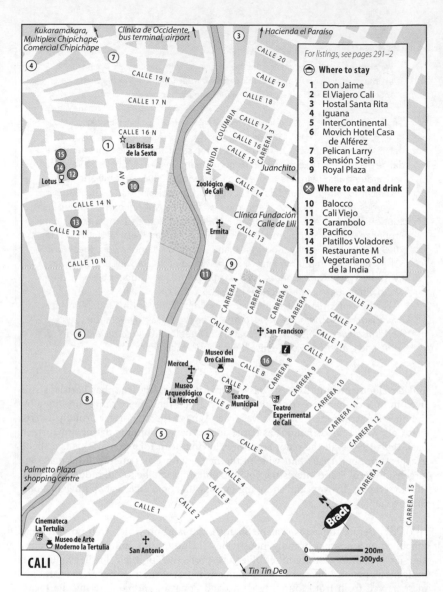

CALI

it is Colombia's third-largest urban settlement after Bogotá and Medellín and is the prime trade and commercial hub in the nation's southwest. With a population of around 2.6 million, Cali is home to more than half the people of the Valle del Cauca. It continues to grow in size and girth on a grid-based layout, neatly divided by the Río Cali. The locals describe the city as 'La Sucursal del Cielo' – meaning 'The Branch Office of Heaven'.

GETTING THERE AND AWAY Palmaseca International Airport (*www.aerocali. com.co*), also known as Aeropuerto Internacional Alfonso Bonilla Aragón, is an important national and international hub and Colombia's second-largest airport in terms of passengers serving much of Colombia's southwest region. Located 16km northwest of the city, it has daily international **flights** to and from the US, Spain, Ecuador and Panama – amongst many others. Minibuses between the airport and the bus terminal run every 10 minutes (5,000COP, 40 minutes) until mid evening. A **taxi** into Cali will cost you upwards of 50,000COP depending on the time of day. Avianca operate frequent flights direct throughout the day to Bogotá as well as a number of other Colombian cities, including Cartagena, Medellín, Pasto and San Andrés. American Airlines has flights to the US.

Long-distance **buses** arrive at and depart from the city's bus terminal, a 25-minute walk northeast of the city centre – or a 10-minute taxi ride. Frequent buses run regularly to Bogotá (85,000COP, 12 hours), Medellín (45,000COP, 9 hours) and Pasto (35,000COP, 9 hours). The Pasto bus also serves Popayán (15,000COP, 3 hours) as do **minibuses** (18,000COP, 2½ hours).

GETTING AROUND In 2009, Cali launched its own, brand-new mass transportation system, the US$405 million Masivo Integrado de Occidente (MIO; *www.mio. com.co*). The six-line articulated bus system runs along 243km of dedicated lanes and serves over 95% of the city. The MIO provides over 70% of Cali's public transportation needs and connects poorer areas once 'out on a limb' with the amenities, businesses, colleges and hospitals of the city centre. Routes are served by custom-built fuelling stations, terminals, rest stops, station buildings, pedestrian bridges and parking areas. Each truncated bus can carry 160 passengers while the conventional rigid buses in the fleet have capacity for up to 100. Fares have been set at an affordable 1,700COP.

TOURIST INFORMATION

Secretaría de Cultura y Turismo Carrera 7 (between Calle 9 & Calle 10); Edificio Palacio de San Francisco; ✆886 0000; ⊕ 08.00–14.00, closed 12.30–14.00

City website www.cali.gov.co
Department website www.valledelcauca. gov.co

TOUR OPERATORS Numerous tour operators offer tours around the city and outlying areas with day trips to Popayán and Buga a popular option – the tourist office has a good range of leaflets and maps. A great little after-dark *chiva* bus tour runs at the weekend at 35,000COP per person, subject to demand: **Viajes Oganesoff** (✆ 892 2840; *www.viajesoganesoff.com.co*).

WHERE TO STAY *See map, page 290.*

Hotel InterContinental (300 rooms) 2–72, Av Colombia; ✆882 3225; www. intercontinental.com. Expect top-notch amenities at this high-end option, including a swimming pool, tennis courts, a trio of restaurants, bar & gym. **$$$$**

Movich Hotel Casa de Alférez (60 rooms) Av 9N, No 9–24; ✆521 5050; movichhotels.com. An elegant lobby sets the scene at this luxurious property where the rooms are superbly appointed with a stylish décor that oozes with colonial grandeur. Amenities include cable TV, Wi-Fi & a fitness centre together with a range of upmarket restaurants & bars serving cocktails & the finest

Asian & Mediterranean gourmet cuisine. **$$$$**

Hotel Pensión Stein (25 rooms) Av 4N, No 3–33; ✆661 4927; www.hotelstein. co. Another Swiss-owned option, the Stein is a rather fine small hotel that has offered top-notch accommodation in a grand stone building for over 50 years. Expect simple, clean rooms that are high in demand with good-value rates that include b/ fast. **$$$**

Hotel Don Jaime (30 rooms) Av 6N, No 15N–25; ✆286 8455; www.hoteldonjaime.com. Choose from a range of comfortable AC rooms in this nicely presented mid-range hotel, popular with visiting blue-collar workers & conference executives. B/fast is offered at an additional cost of 7,000COP. **$$**

🏠 **Hotel Royal Plaza** (60 rooms) Carrera 4, No 11–69; ☎883 9243. Although the rooms could do with some TLC, views from the upper storeys across the Plaza Cayecedo are rather nice. Located 20km from the airport with free Wi-Fi, a restaurant & bar & rooms with cable TV, minibar & private bathrooms. **$$**

🏠 **El Viajero Cali** (15 rooms) Carrera 5, No 4–56, San Antonio; www.elviajerohostels.com/hostel-cali. Another in the Uruguayan El Viajero chain, expect efficiency & plenty of activities in this made-to-measure hostel with dorms, private rooms, salsa lessons & bar. **$**

🏠 **Guest House Iguana** (sleeps 30) Av 9N, No 22N–22 ; ☎382 5364; m 313 768 6024;

e iguana_Cali@yahoo.com; www.iguana.com.co. This great little Swiss-run budget traveller's lodge is excellent value with large, clean rooms (single, double & dorm beds), a shared kitchen, laundry & internet access in a quiet backstreet close to the thick of it. Staff are friendly & helpful & will organise guides, tours & salsa lessons – that the owner speaks fluent English, Spanish & German is the icing on the cake. **$**

🏠 **Pelican Larry** (7 rooms) Calle 20N, No 6AN–44B; ☎382 7226; e jpierre@hostelpelicanlarry.com; www.hostelpelicanlarry.com. The Pelican Larry Hostel opened in 2008 & offers all facilities backpackers need: hot showers, big & comfy beds, high-speed internet, Wi-Fi, big flat-screen TV, kitchen & a helpful staff. **$**

✕ **WHERE TO EAT AND DRINK** *See map, page 290.*

Dining out in Cali is rewarding and well priced with numerous restaurants, cafés and diners offering a very wide range of cuisines. Visitors looking for cheap eats will not be disappointed, as Cali's rustic local food joints offer simple meat-and-rice dishes for well under 8,000COP.

✕ **Platillos Voladores** Av 3 Norte, No 7–19, Barrio Centenario; ☎668 7588; www.platillosvoladores.com; ⊕ lunch & dinner. Expect an experimental fusion-style menu at this fashionable eatery with oriental, European & Colombian influences mixed to glorious effect using the freshest local produce. **$$$**

✕ **Restaurante Cali Viejo** Arboledas Santa Teresita; ☎521 5140. Upmarket & situated in a sprawling old colonial *casona* a stone's throw from the zoo, this is the place to come & try out the region's traditional dishes such as *champus*, *Aborrajados* & delicious *empanadas vallunas*. **$$$**

✕ **Restaurante Carambolo** Calle 14N, No 9N–18; ☎667 5656; ⊕ lunch & dinner. Tables of power suits & media types at this slick dining establishment, where an ultra-funky ambience & neat eats are as stylish as the punters. **$$$**

✕ **Restaurante M** Av 9N, No 15N–39; ☎660 1787; ⊕ noon–21.00. For a splurge book a table

at this opulent upmarket eatery set in a grand mansion house where a rather fine menu of Asian-fusion food has wowed the critics. **$$$**

✕ **Pacifico** Av 9, No 12N–18, Granada; ☎653 3753; www.pacificorestaurante.com. For many visitors to Colombia Cali may be the closest that they get to the Pacific coast here & so we have included one of the most traditional seafood restaurants in the city in this list. Be sure to enjoy the *ceviche* & the local delicacy of the *piangua atollao* clam. **$$**

✕ **Restaurante Balocco** Av 6N, No 14N–06; ⊕ lunch–early evening. Choose from a tiny menu of simple hearty local fare at this super little family-run restaurant. **$**

✕ **Restaurante Vegetariano Sol de la India** Carrera 6, No 8–48; ☎884 2333 ⊕ w/days lunch only. A menu of mild curried vegetable-&-rice dishes make this a good cheap vegetarian option – the breads & deep-fried *pakoras* are particularly good. **$**

ENTERTAINMENT AND NIGHTLIFE With so much going on throughout the city it is worth swotting up on Cali's 'what's on' listing in *El Pais* newspaper. There's also a decent entertainment section online at www.terra.com. It's hard to go wrong when heading for a night on the town in Cali as Caleños could turn a visit to the dentist into *la rumba* (partying) on a grand scale. After an early-evening beer in the city's *zonas rosas* on Avenida Sexta and Calle 5, the pace begins to quicken as cocktails are downed and punters begin to move to a host of Latino beats. At around midnight (but not before) the crowds head to the Juanchito district 12km to the east of the centre (20 minutes by taxi, about 10,000COP). A slim selection of what's on offer is listed below but the best way to discover Cali's excellent salsa-infused nightlife is to just throw yourself in – feet first.

Bars and clubs

♀ Fanaticos Sports Bar Palmetto Plaza Shopping Center; m 300 600 2637. This lively sports bar is open 7 days a week & is popular with college students & young professionals. Expect dead-cheap beer, loud music & flat-screen TVs.

♀ Lotus Calle 15, No 9N–27; ✆681 5906; ⏰ from 19.00 Thu–Sun. Chill-out music & moody, glowing walls attract Cali's style-setters in this decent early-evening option. First-rate cocktails.

☆ Kukaramakara Calle 28N, Bis–97; ✆653 5389. Famous throughout the city for the beautiful women it seems to attract, this simple watering hole often has live music & is located in the north of the city. To get a table, order a bottle of liquor

or a half-bottle to sit at the bar. That there isn't a dance floor doesn't seem to matter as everyone climbs on the table tops after about 23.00.

☆ Las Brisas de la Sexta Av 6N, No 15N–94; ✆661 2996. This popular hangout is one of the largest bar-cum-discos in Cali. The cocktails are strong & the music deafening in this hot & steamy *salsoteca*.

☆ Tin Tin Deo Calle 5, No 38–71; ✆514 1537. Expect ear-splitting Música del Pacífico (African-Colombian music from the Pacific coast) at this crowded bar, which attracts an easy-going mixed-age crowd.

Juanchito The Juanchito district south of Cali's city centre contains at least 30 salsa bars and *salsotecas* with new places opening up – and closing down. Two of the best-known salsa nightspots are both located on Juanchito's legendary Vía Cavasa. **Changó** (✆ 662 9701) is a classic Juanchito nightclub that heaves with crowds of gorgeous, sexy movers in a smoke-filled atmosphere that positively sizzles with body heat. Not as swish, but still highly charged, is neighbouring **Agapito** – a popular dance hall that plays the salsa fast and loud until 06.00.

SLANG OF THE CITY

Like all Colombian cities, Cali has its own distinctive dialect and local vernacular with numerous homespun jargon not found elsewhere.

como fue que?	What's up? What's going on?
malandro	bad person or criminal
chino/chinaso/parcero/pana	friend
flacha veloz	fast arrow (meaning slow-witted)
cabeza de motor	big head
no me coja de destrabe	don't mess me around
pa las que sea!	I'm up for anything!
prendido	tipsy
bolqueta	drunk
bochinchero	somebody who fabricates stories
que destrabe	having a good time
ruñidera or *ruñiendo*	a two-faced backstabber
sisas	yes
todo bien	all good

Theatre

🎭 **Teatro Experimental de Cali** (TEC) Calle 7, No 8–61; ☎ 884 3821. Cali-born Enrique Buenaventura, one of Colombia's most successful dramatists, poets & theatre directors, founded this innovative company. It has since won considerable national & international acclaim for its ground-breaking drama & adaptations.

🎭 **Teatro Municipal** Carrera 5, No 6–64; ☎ 883 9106. Cali's oldest existing theatre dates back to 1918. It offers a year-round calendar of varied performances from classical concerts to opera & ballet.

Cinema As with Colombia's other two major cities, Cali has a number of multiplex commercial cinemas. One of the most popular is the **Multiplex Chipichape** (*Centro Comercial Chipichape, Calle 38 Norte, No 6N–35;* ☎ *659 2199; www.chipichape.com*), a large facility screening Hollywood offerings. The **Cinemateca La Tertulia** (*Museo de Arte Moderno, La Tertulia, Av Colombia, No 5, Oeste–105;* ☎ *893 2939; www. museolatertulia.com*) is Cali's best art-house option. It's located in a fine building established in 1536.

SHOPPING Cali has at least half-a-dozen shopping malls of which the Comercial Chipichape on Avenida NN, No 39N–25, is one of the best. Expect plenty of fashion brands, electronic shops, CD stores, perfumeries, handbags, and shoe shops. For a full listing, visit www.chipichape.com.

OTHER PRACTICALITIES Cali has everything a traveller could need, from numerous banks with ATMs and dozens of great shopping malls to internet cafés, pharmacies, large supermarkets, hardware stores, camping shops, drugstores, camera shops, international payphones and **fuel** stations. The biggest concentration of **internet cafés** can be found along Avenida Sexta where most charge around 2,300COP per hour. The Bancolombia on the corner of Calle 15N and Avenida 8N is a favourite with foreign visitors as it offers cash advances on credit cards and changes currency. Medical centres are in good supply with a 24-hour city ambulance service (☎ *123*). Good hospitals include **Clínica Fundación Calle de Lili** (☎ *331 9090*) and **Clínica de Occidente** (☎ *660 3000/608 3200*) – both are open round the clock.

WHAT TO SEE AND DO

Zoológico de Cali (Cali Zoo) (*Cnr Carrera 2A, Oeste & Calle 14 Oeste; www. zoologicodecali.com.co;* ⊕ *09.00–16.30; admission 14,000COP*) With an excellent collection of species native to Colombia and a magnificent host of lush, green gardens, Cali's zoo is easily the nation's finest. Spread across 10ha around lakes and mature shrubs, the zoo is home to about 1,200 animals, representing some 180 species – from armadillos and condors to bears and butterflies. A key centre for research and conservation studies, the zoo's flower-filled picnic areas along the picturesque Río Cali make this an extremely pleasant place to spend the day.

Museo Arqueológico La Merced (La Merced Archaeological Museum)

(*Carrera 4, No 6–59;* ☎ *885 5309; www.museosdelvalle.com/museos/museo-arqueologico-la-merced;* ⊕ *09.00–13.00 & 14.00–18.00 Mon–Sat; admission 4,000COP*) Cali's oldest existing building dates back to around 1538–40 and was formerly La Merced Convent, but today houses an archaeological museum containing a fine collection of pre-Columbian pottery. All of central and southern Colombia's ancient cultures are well represented, including Calima, Tierradentro, San Agustín, Quimbaya, Tolima, Nariño and Tumaco.

Iglesia de la Merced (La Merced Church) *(Cnr Carrera 4 & Calle 7;* ⊕ *06.30–10.00 & 16.00–19.00; admission by donation)* The first foundation for Cali's oldest church was laid in 1545, just nine years after the founding of the city, and it was built in the best Spanish colonial tradition. A beautifully whitewashed exterior masks a rather simple interior of wood and stucco containing a long, narrow nave and a gilded, Baroque high altar.

Iglesia de San Antonio (San Antonio Church) *(Colina de San Antonio;* ⊕ *07.00–16.00; admission by donation)* The nuns at this pretty little hilltop church keep it in tip-top condition. Built in 1757, it contains some highly valuable *tallas quiteñas* from the 17th century – a rather fine set of Quito carved-wood statues of saints. It's an easy 10-minute walk westward from the old town centre. There's also a little stall selling religious art.

Museo del Oro Calima (Gold Museum) *(Calle 7, No 4–69;* ☎ *684 7754;* ⊕ *10.00–17.00 Tue–Fri, 10.00–17.00 Sat; free admission)* This small collection of Colombian gold is rather modest. There is also some pre-Columbian pottery made by the ancient tribes of Calima.

Iglesia La Ermita (La Ermita Church) *(Cnr Av Colombia & Calle 13;* ⊕ *mornings; free admission)* This early 20th-century construction, inspired by Cologne Cathedral, Germany, contains an 18th-century painting *El Señor de la Caña (Lord of the Sugarcane)* that is said to have produced many miracles.

Museo de Arte Moderno la Tertulia (La Tertulia Museum of Modern Art) *(Av Colombia 5, Oeste–105;* ☎ *893 2941;* ⊕ *09.00–19.00 Tue–Fri, 10.00–17.00 Sat; admission 2,000COP)* Home to the city's best art-house cinema and a range of fine temporary exhibitions of contemporary paintings and photographic design, this fine collection is located just outside the centre of the city.

Iglesia de San Francisco (San Francisco Church) *(Cnr Carrera 6 & Calle 10; free admission)* This 18th-century Neoclassical church is next to the Convento de San Francisco and Capilla de la Immaculada and stands opposite a fine example of Mudéjar art, the Torre Mudéjar bell tower.

Hacienda el Paraíso (El Paraíso Hacienda) *(Vía Santa Elena, El Pomo;* ☎ *514 6848;* ⊕ *09.40–16.30 Tue–Sun; admission 3,500COP)* A number of old sugarcane plantations outside Cali are now open to the public. One of the best is the Hacienda el Paraíso about 40km north of the city. Numerous tour operators run half-day trips and it is a fascinating way to see how the 19th-century Colombian elite lived. Today, this lovingly restored mansion is a well-stocked museum containing beautiful furnishings, paintings and books from a bygone Cauca era. The manor house also boasts literary connections as the setting of Jorge Isaacs's romantic period novel *María*.

Football The first Colombian city to host the Pan American Games in the 1970s, Cali is home to two of the nation's most successful soccer clubs, **Deportivo Cali** (*www.deporcali.com*) and **América de Cali** (*www.america.co*), although the latter has fallen on less impressive times of late being relegated to the local second division. Two vast stadiums – Estadio Deportivo Cali (built in 2007, capacity 58,000) and Estadio Olímpico Pascual Guerrero (built in 1937, capacity

45,625) – cater to Cali's enthusiastic soccer nuts. Deportivo Cali is the older club, founded in 1912 with América de Cali established 15 years later. Fierce rivalry exists between the two, which are divided by clear class distinctions. Deportivo Cali is mainly supported by the affluent upper class with fans of América de Cali primarily working class from poorer outskirts of the city. Bad vibes have existed since the early 1930s when after a local derby América de Cali's players accused the referee and Deportivo Cali of fixing the match. In 1982, 24 people were killed and 250 injured during another bad-tempered clash after a stampede at the Pascual Guerrero stadium. At the time of writing, Deportivo Cali has the edge, having won 19 of the 39 league derby matches played in the last decade. The team plays in a green-and-white strip, while the América de Cali team kit is all red.

Festivals and events

My mother used to tell me that when I wasn't even one year old I would grab the bars of my baby bed and dance to the rhythm of Noel Petro's song Cabeza de Hacha.

Carlos Molina, Cali musician, 2010

Feria de Cali (December) (*www.feriadecali.com*) Cali is famous throughout Latin America for its long-established Feria de Cali, Colombia's biggest festival. It runs from Christmas to New Year and pulls crowds from all across the region, filling up every bar, venue, park and salsa hall citywide. Expect lots of music, dancing and *aguardiente*-drinking in party-loving Cali plus a host of events that range from beauty pageants and *cabalgata* (parade of horseriders) to bullfights, processions and salsa competitions.

Fiesta de Salsa (July) This week-long free summer salsa festival includes concerts by the world's great salsa musicians and dancers. Expect flamboyant costumes and '*melomano*' competitions in which salsa connoisseurs try to outdo each other by digging deep to discover long-lost salsa classics.

AROUND CALI

DAPA (*Telephone code 2*) Located 13km outside of the city, this little settlement sits amidst cool mountain trails and cloud-shrouded peaks. Once too dangerous to visit due to guerrilla and military activity, Dapa is now becoming a popular place for urbanites visiting at the weekend. A paved road winds up a mountain from the city, passing little food kiosks on the way. Stream-fed natural bathing pools attract Caleños keen to escape the heat of the metropolis – they dip to cool off while eating *arepa* and chorizo on a Sunday. Crisp breezes fan the mountains with temperatures dropping dramatically the higher you climb. Fields and fields of coffee plants lead to vast stretches of forest and meadow. A popular area for kite-flying and horseriding, the area around Dapa is also popular with people keen to slide down the side of the mountain on a piece of cardboard – an exhilarating pursuit that draws the crowds. Peaceful walking trails delve deep into the heart of the mountains past creeks, wild poinsettias, rivers, ice-cold lagoons and hanging vines (*bejucos*) that are strong enough to swing on, Tarzan-style. The town itself has a handful of friendly, local restaurants selling beer and simple meat-and-rice dishes. More and more makeshift roadside signs are also advertising *cabañas* and places to camp. Several local guides offer treks out across the rocks to Dapa's Cueva del Indio (Indian Cave).

Where to stay and eat

El Rincón de Dapa (sleeps 30) 521 8191. This charming *casa de campo* is owned by the patrons of the Juana de Farra (see below), a young Colombian couple called Juan & Adriana. A comprehensive set-up offers guests every conceivable option, from a simple overnight camping stay to a full set of outdoor pursuits that include horseriding, rappelling, fishing, hiking, buggy tours & hotel accommodation. Juan is an energetic, enthusiastic guide who enjoys nothing more than heading out into the mountains to set up camp by the river & cook freshly caught fish over a fire. 4 brand-new cabins offering luxury accommodation have recently opened. Options range from 10,000COP to camp to 250,000COP for a *cabaña* that sleeps 4. **$$**

Hostel Mochileros (5 rooms) Carretera a Dapa, Km7, Calle de las Flechas, Villa Lucy; m 315 4200 315; e hostelmochileros@gmail.com; hostelmochileros.googlepages.com. Run by extreme-sport nut Fernando Urzuz, this cheap option is fine for those used to roughing it, offering empty rooms for backpackers equipped with a sleeping bag. A simple, clean wooden house designed around a large feature window affords magnificent views across the mountains. Urzuz runs rock-climbing tours, hikes, camping trips & horseriding – & has plans to expand the hostel into an upgraded facility. A local bus connects the hostel with the centre of Cali at 2,000COP pp. **$**

Entertainment and nightlife

Juana de Farra 613 0289; m 300 774 3592; e juanadefarra@hotmail.com. This ultra-stylish open-sided bar sits right in the upper side of a mountain, wedged in amongst some stunning countryside & offering truly memorable views. Even on a dreary day, Juana de Farra's outlook is totally captivating – but in clear, dry, sunny weather it'll draw an involuntary intake of breath. A huge drinks menu offers numerous cocktails, liqueurs & beers with a wooden bar & seating illuminated by candle lanterns. Expect atmospheric ambient music & a relaxed star-gazing crowd. Find it 7km from Cali on the Dapa road – look out for the sign.

Shopping You'll find numerous small handicraft stalls and vendors along the Cali–Dapa road selling an array of bags, jewellery, woven crafts, scarves and knick-knacks. In Dapa itself, there is a small market of baskets, beaded bracelets and carved woods.

YUMBO (*Telephone code 2*) Heavily industrialised with large paper-pulp factories, metalworks and one of Colombia's largest breweries (a US$55 million Bavaria plant), Yumbo offers very little to tourists, apart from the usual practicalities for those passing through. Numerous fuel stations, car-repair shops, restaurants and hardware stores can be found on the town's outskirts as well as several small supermarkets and snack kiosks. Those keen to stop overnight will find a number of billboards for *hospedajes* and hotels on the approach road.

Tourist information

Local government website www.yumbo.gov.co

Yumbo city website www.yumbovalle.com

THE ROAD TO BUGA From Yumbo the road north towards Buga offers some extraordinary views from a winding mountain road that climbs and plummets in rolling waves. Startling green meadows lie permanently cloaked in haze with stud farms, haciendas and sugarcane fields as far as the eye can see. The occasional *poker* (beer) kiosk and rustic diner sits by the side of the road until at about 7.5km from Yumbo the *areá de servicio* – complete with restaurant, toilets and showers – appears on the right. At about 18km from Buga on the left amidst cattle fields and horse farms you'll see the Restaurante Taypa, a fine-looking wooden building set high above the road that can't be missed. Further along, a string of juice vendors, snack stalls, watermelon sellers and a small kiosk sit opposite the Restaurante Fogonaza as you enter an area dubbed 'Little Switzerland' on account of its pine-clad slopes, flower-filled gardens and chalet-style houses.

BUGA *Telephone code 2*

Founded in 1650, the agricultural town of Buga (*www.buga.gov.co*) sits on the Pan-American Highway and on a main route between Bogotá and Buenaventura. An important hub for trading cattle, rice, tobacco and sugarcane, the town has a population of 145,000. Despite pleasing temperatures that average 23°C year-round, it is Buga's famous El Señor de los Milagros (Miraculous Christ of Buga) that prompts three million people to visit the town per annum. This vast basilica totally dominates the plaza and attracts numerous pilgrimages throughout the year. In recent years, Buga has undergone a sympathetic beautification project to smarten up its streets and to give the main square some TLC.

Until just a few years ago, the town was considered off-limits due to guerrilla and paramilitary activity. In 2001, the United Self Defence Forces of Colombia (AUC) executed 24 people in Buga at point-blank range. Cancer victim Andrés Félipe Perez (aged 12) also earned the town worldwide media attention when he repeatedly appeared on Colombian television news. Perez was calling on rebels of the Revolutionary Armed Forces of Colombia (FARC) to free his kidnapped father, policeman Norberto – but died after his appeals were ignored.

Today, Buga (formally Guadalajara de Buga) is making more cheery headlines and is enjoying vastly improved safety. The town stages a highly popular agricultural fair each July and celebrates Festibuga in August.

GETTING THERE AND AROUND Guadalajara de Buga can be reached by a 40-minute **minibus** journey from Cali's main bus terminal. It may also be possible to cadge a lift

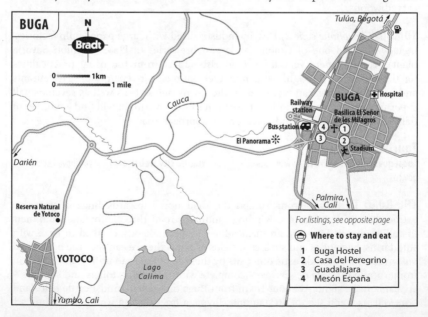

from the steady stream of Bugueños who travel back and forth, usually for around 12,000COP. Buga-based bus, coach and *buseta* companies include **Trans Calima** (✆ *227 7853*), **Coop Ciudad Señora** (✆ *237 0522*) and **Montebello** (✆ *228 3111*). **Taxis** are easy to find, with **Cootaxbuga** (✆ *227 9495/237 4949*) and **Unitax** (✆ *227 7931*) two of the most reliable firms. Cross-region buses include **Expreso Palmira** (✆ *227 6586*) and **Expreso Trejos** (✆ *227 1171*). From Cali, the Tren Turistico Café y Azúcar **steam train** connects with Buga via a seasonal schedule. Pick up a timetable from Cali's central station or contact the reservations office (*Av Vásquez Cobo, No 23N–47, Piso 2;* ✆ *666 6899/620 2324;* e *trenturistico@ert.com.co*).

By bus Buses run from Cali to Buga early till late seven days a week, every 20 minutes or so. Expect to pay around 9,000COP for a one-way journey in a comfortable minivan. Services run 05.00–20.00 from Buga and 04.30–21.00 from Cali. Buses to Darién from Buga depart every 90 minutes, costing around 8,000COP.

By taxi A cab across Buga will cost around 3,000COP, rising to 6,000–8,000COP for trips to the outskirts. Expect to pay around 85,000COP from Buga to the airport in Cali, where frequent flights connect to Bogotá and Medellín.

🏠 WHERE TO STAY *See map, page 298.*
Buga's small budget hotels are clustered on or around the main plaza and include the **Mesón España Hotel** and the **Hotel Casa del Peregrino ($$)**. For considerably more style, head to historic **Hotel Guadalajara** (*Calle 1, No 13–33;* ✆ *236 2611; www.hotelguadalajara.com.co;* **$$$**), where 67 elegantly appointed rooms (including 18 suites) overlook a stunning courtyard garden. On-site amenities include a Turkish bath, jacuzzi, swimming pool and sauna. For budget travellers there is the very comfortable **Buga Hostel** (*Carrera 13, No 4–83;* ✆ *236 7752;* e *bugahostel@yahoo.com; www.bugahostel.com*), which has dorms and privates and even the Holy Water Ale Café on site serving their own freshly brewed ales.

✕ WHERE TO EAT AND DRINK *See map, page 298.*
A string of local restaurants edge the right-hand side of the basilica, almost all serving grilled meats and *rapido comida*, including the **La Merced** (**$**). The nicest place to dine is by far the restaurant at the grand colonial **Hotel Guadalajara** (see above) where delicate fish-in-sauce dishes are served by tuxedo-clad waiters (**$$$**). Try the **Buga Hostel**'s Holy Water Ale Café for pizzas and other inexpensive comfort food (**$**).

SHOPPING Dozens of small stores and vendors around the Basilica sell religious artefacts, from necklaces and charms to statues and paintings.

WHAT TO SEE AND DO Buga's only tourism attraction is the vast **El Señor de los Milagros basilica** (e *info@milagrosodebuga.com; www.milagrosodebuga.com*) on the main square. It boasts a stunning interior with lavish use of carved wood and gilt.

Outside the town, the **Lago Calima** (Calima Lake) is a popular day-trip excursion. Expect windsurfing, fishing, boating, kite surfing, paragliding, waterskiing, jet skiing and diving around this hydro-electric reserve. Temperatures around the lake rarely exceed 17°C and the fact that the national kite-surfing championships are staged here is indicative of how windy it is. Depending on the season, it is also possible to camp here overnight – look out for the road signs by the side of the road for *cabañas* and *zona de camping*. The road out to the lake climbs up to a magnificent lookout, known locally as **El Panorama** – a great spot for a photo.

On the road between Cali and Buenaventura, alight the bus at the town of Cordoba where you can gain access to the '*Brujita*'. Not for the faint of heart, the *Brujita* is a skilfully engineered motorcycle hybrid attached to an old railway track and used to transport locals and now tourists from Cordoba down to San Cipriano. Negotiate the price (expect to pay in the region of 8,000COP return per person) beforehand and then hang on tight as health and safety are not a consideration. The journey, which whips you through humid sub-tropical forest, takes you down to a region of Afro-Colombian settlements and beautifully chilled rivers and waterfalls. You may even catch sight of a toucan or two on the way. Return before nightfall or expect to stay in some cheap but rustic options in San Cipriano.

Reserva Natural de Yotoco (Yotoco Natural Reserve) This important state-managed 559ha woodland reserve is central to numerous conservation projects and studies and contains many of the region's 3,000 orchid species. It is also home to over 1,000 howler monkeys. Several high-profile behavioural studies by eminent international scientists have centred on the community of monkeys and their feeding, breeding and social characteristics. Other research projects include how the health of butterflies and insects in the reserve has been affected by changing weather patterns from the Pacific Ocean. Unfortunately, at the time of writing, a plan to enlarge a stretch of road looks as if it may impact the reserve to detrimental effect – although well-organised objectors have managed to keep construction crews at bay to date. Two trails – Sendero el Corbón (1 hour) and Sendero el Cedar (1 hour) wind through mosses, pine, cedar and bamboo. Visitors to the reserve need to seek permission ahead of arrival (❨ 228 1922; www.cvc.gov.co). It is also possible to camp overnight and meet resident biologist, Pablo Emilio Florez Brand (e pablo-emilio.florez@cvc.gov.co).

AROUND BUGA

DARIÉN (*Telephone code 2*) This pleasant little town was founded in 1912 and is a nice place to explore on foot with neat streets and a pretty little plaza – and plenty of useful shops. Dozens of tiny restaurants, bars, kiosks and a bakery flank the main square, where the locals park their cars in haphazard style. There's also a pizza joint, laundry, doctor's surgery, dentists and a hardware store. There are a handful of small budget hotels just off the plaza, including the **Hotel Casa Blanca**, **Hotel Leyenda Calima** and **Hotel Calima Plaza**. For good local food, try the **Café Monalva** and the **Restaurante Porvenir**. Darién's major tourist attraction is the **Museo Arqueológico** (Archaeological Museum) on the edge of town (⊕ *08.00– 17.00 Tue–Fri, closed 13.00–14.00, 10.00–17.00 Sat/Sun; admission 2,500COP*). It contains an impressive collection of pottery from the Calima culture.

HUILA AND CAUCA

For many years these two adjoining departments were too dangerous to visit due to a strong rebel presence that ruled all travel out. Today, the region is once again 'open for business', allowing a growing number of tourists to discover for themselves the treasures of the triangular route connecting the colonial gems of Popayán, San Agustín and Tierradentro's pre-Columbian marvels – each real 'must-sees'. Bordered by the departments of Tolima, Cundinamarca, Meta and Caquetá, the neighbouring regions of Huila and Cauca are wedged between the Eastern and Central cordilleras (mountain ranges). Both are rich in water resources, oil and minerals such as phosphate rock, natural gas, gold, silver and quartz. Well-nourished farmlands produce coffee, cocoa (for chocolate), cassava and livestock while, at 5,365m, the great Nevado del Huila volcano ranks as Colombia's highest active volcano. Before the arrival of the Spaniards in the 16th century, the region was populated by three of Colombia's most formidable warrior tribes: the Pijaos, Paeces and Yalcones. Today the modern population is predominantly Spanish descent or *mestizo* (a racial mix of indigenous and Spanish descent).

NEIVA *Telephone code 8*

Although its full name is Nuestra Señora de la Limpia Concepción del Valle de Neiva, most people just call this hot, dusty town 'Neiva'. As the capital of Huila with a population of almost 500,000, this modern regional hub sits amidst some of Colombia's most folkloric heritage where old traditions are upheld with pride. Lying close to the Equator, this lowland terrain averages temperatures of 30°C year-round. Enriched by the fast-flowing butterscotch-coloured Río Magdalena, the region is an important source of rice, corn, beans, cotton, potatoes, sesame, tobacco and bananas surrounded by vast cattle plains and with the snow-capped peaks of the Nevado del Huila rising to the west.

Most tourist arrivals in Neiva don't plan to stay, as they are hot-footing it to Popayán, San Agustín and Tierradentro or the cacti-scattered Tatacoa Desert. However, Neiva is an important town as a gateway to Bogotá (and the world beyond) for the region's oil, coffee and vegetable farm community. Aside from the city's role as an economic lifeline to the region, Neiva also stages three colourful annual fiestas, the Festival Folclórico, Reinado Nacional del Bambuco and Muestra Internacional del Folclor, and plays an important part in upholding a pride in Colombian traditions. Neiva is particularly devoted to its song and dance traditions of *sanjuanero*, *rajalena* and *bambuco*, with the townsfolk famous for their use of the phrase '*Péguese the rodadita!*' (hit the road), an expression that urges anyone listening to come and join the party.

DANCING QUEEN

Although few will openly admit that Neiva's Reinado Nacional del Bambuco (National Queen of Bambuco) is crowned during the town's St Peter festivities in order to 'liven up festivities', that is exactly what it does. For now the Fiestas del San Pedro – an old festival of religious significance – centres on a beauty queen pageant at which the Reinada Nacional del Bambuco is decided and much beer and liquor consumed. According to olden folklore, only unmarried childless Colombian-born females who have resided in the region for over a decade are eligible to enter. Other requirements are a college education and an age between 18 and 25. However, it is the entrants' dance skills and natural beauty that are all-important in this crowded, merry party.

Sanjuanero folk dance is revered in Huila and the locals place great emphasis on the purest form of *bambuco* rhythm using the *bandola*, the *tiple*, and the guitar. Marks are awarded for the choice of music, costume (layered skirts) and the choreography of the dance as the town erupts into booze-fuelled applause during raucous parades and processions.

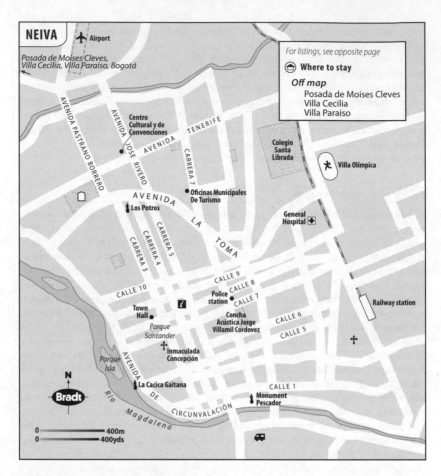

GETTING THERE AND AROUND Avianca flies thrice-daily from Bogotá to Neiva's Benito Salas Vargas Airport with regular direct connections to half-a-dozen other Colombian cities. A *colectivo* departs every 30 minutes or so from Bogotá's main bus terminal (25,000COP, 9 hours). **Driving** from Bogotá to Neiva takes about 6 hours.

TOURIST INFORMATION

Oficinas Municipales De Turismo Calle 16, No 7–45, Antigua Estación del Ferrocarril; ☎867 1300; www.huila.gov.co

Secretaría De Turismo y Cultura Departamental Cnr Carrera 4 & Calle 8; ☎871 4472
Neiva town website www.alcaldianeiva.gov.co

AROUND NEIVA

TATACOA DESERT This vast expanse of scrub, rock and sand is rich in fossils and is a base for several scientific teams from universities in America. In recent years some exciting discoveries have been made, including some well-preserved crocodile skulls, fossilised ground sloths and other endemic South American mammals. In-depth studies have served to highlight the striking bio-geographic differences between the tertiary faunas of Colombia and the country's near-neighbours. Today, fossils are still found daily of molluscs, turtles, mice and armadillos – sure evidence that this arid, inhospitable region was once a well-nourished lush area rich in trees and plants. The **Desierto de la Tatacoa** (Tatacoa Desert) (*www.tatacoacolombia. com*) is located around 50km north of Neiva and ranks as the second-largest dry area in Colombia after the La Guajira region on the country's northern tip. Covering an area of 330km², Tatacoa is characterised by rust-coloured sand punctuated by bizarre wind-sculpted cacti and isolated trees almost charred by the heat of the sun. Sprouting plant species – hardy and brittle – poke through the sands like extra-terrestrial beings. Temperatures soar in this desert to reach 50°C on the most exposed cliffs and gullies. Elsewhere you'll find deep fissures that plunge to depths of 20m clad by thorny flora that are home to rattlesnakes, scorpions and eagles.

Getting there Some 10km outside lies the charming village of Villavieja, the main access point for the Tatacoa Desert. Located about an hour from Neiva, Villavieja claims to be the centre of Colombian palaeontology and provides a natural gathering point for travellers with a penchant for fossils. Follow signs to a cactus forest called **Bosque de Cardon** (Cardon Woods) and the route to the desert is waymarked from there. Visitors to the Tatacoa Desert will find plenty of locals willing to act as guides. Make an early start before the heat of the day sets in, pack plenty of water and dress in light, cotton clothing. Apply lots of sunscreen – the conditions can be quite harsh on all the many trail options, from a 60-minute walk to a full-day hike.

Many visitors to Tatacoa are there for the **Observatorio Astronomico de la Tatacoa** (Tatacoa Astronomical Observatory), a state-of-the-art facility built close to the equatorial line. Dry, clear conditions lend themselves perfectly to stargazing. People journey great distances for a chance to observe meteor showers in a spot that is moisture- and cloud-free with zero light pollution. Inside the observatory building regular lectures and workshops take place in classroom-style rooms. Astronomer Fernando Javier Restrepo runs the show at the observatory and is justifiably proud of the facilities. Visitors can make good use of several telescopes set up along an open terrace or witness bedazzling constellations and orbiting satellites with the naked eye.

Opposite the observatory, a *mirador* (lookout point) provides some truly dramatic views across the desert at sunset, with crimson, orange and amber glows set against black shadows and the pale light of the moon.

Where to stay and eat *See map, page 302.*
The following rustic options are all in Villavieja.

Posada de Moises Cleves (2 rooms)
m 313 305 6898; e moisestatacoa@yahoo.es.
Rustic wooden cabins sleep 2 & 3 respectively
& are conveniently located a 5min drive from
the observatory. Meals are cooked by a friendly
housekeeper who will try to cater for special diets

on request. **$$**
Hotel Villa Cecilia (4 rooms) Calle 5, No
4–42; m 313 237 4528. **$**
Hotel Villa Paraiso (4 rooms) Calle 4, No
7–69; m 301 559 4651/321 234 5424;
e hotelvillaparaiso@yahoo.es. **$**

THE ROAD FROM NEIVA TO SAN AGUSTÍN This 5-hour drive makes for a superb road trip through dry, dusty farming towns hemmed in by rice paddies and vegetable fields. First, pass through the rice-growing village of **Campoalegre**, a gritty working place with a few simple food joints serving breakfast for 4,500COP, before hitting **La Vega da Oriente**, famous for its *alfarería* pottery. At the humble carrot-farming town of **El Hobo** there are numerous sizzling food stalls around a small plaza as well as a handful of local restaurants and a fried-chicken joint. A string of roadside banana stalls and ceiba trees hail the approach road to **Gigante**, a busy little chocolate-making town. A couple of restaurants and a hotel sit on the left tucked amongst the trees, with a small tourist information office by the main square – look out for green signs. Around the plaza you'll find a bakery and half-a-dozen restaurants, as well as an 'El Gaucho' beer shack on the right of the road exiting the town. A kilometre on, on the **Quebrada la Honda** (Honda Creek), there's a nice open-sided wood-and-thatch grilled-meat place. Then it's past some particularly charming rose-coloured *fincas* by the **Río Oro**. The town of **Garzon** is notable as the first Catholic settlement in Huila and has become an important religious centre, attracting pilgrims in their droves. It's also a town of considerable hubbub with numerous shops, banks, drugstores, restaurants and cafés – and also boasts a 1km stretch of cheap-food stalls. Leaving the town behind to pass tethered mules and scrawny chickens by the roadside, the road snakes into cattle-grazing country dotted with smallholdings to **La Juaga**. This handicraft centre is famous for its bags, mats and jewellery boxes made from *figue* (palm fibre). The town is also reputed to be the home of Las Brujas (witches), slow-speaking long-haired women with mystical powers who are said to curse. At **Altamira**, 75km from San Agustín, the Amnesia Latin Club makes a decent place to stop for a drink – it's open dawn until dusk; look out for a bright-orange building.

A terrifying hairpin bend heralds breathtaking views of the **Río Magdalena** (Magdalena River) at a point used as a suicide spot by ancient Amerindians in the village of **Pericongo**. Vast cliffs overlook the fast-flowing river, a reminder that Huila means 'Mountain with life' in the language of indigenous tribes. In the horse-and-trap town of **Timaná** you'll pass cute little single-storey houses in pastel hues. The main square has a rather fine pinky-red brick cathedral with a handful of basic amenities nearby. Huila's second city **Pitalito** is famous for its coffee, a rich, full-bodied and distinguished coffee with citrus acidity and a tart undertone. Cows nibble on the verges that edge the city's outskirts alongside a necklace of stalls selling milk, cheese and vegetables. Farmers ferry their crops across town in *zorras* (horse-pulled carts), careering around a busy main plaza edged by cycle shops, hardware stores, bakeries, drug stores and local restaurants. Founded in 1818, Pitalito has around 150,000 inhabitants and is 188km from Neiva. The city averages daily temperatures of around 19°C and is served by Contador airport, located 6km outside of town on the road to San Agustín. The road out of Pitalito is edged with brightly coloured gardens selling plants, shrubs and flowers. Sombrero-wearing *campesinos* walk their prize bulls to market past fields of sunflowers and vegetables and hedges of violet bougainvillea. Soon wooded slopes and gushing streams soften dramatic views of the mountains. Lush, green thickets of vegetation mean that San Agustín is nearing – fast.

SAN AGUSTÍN (*Telephone code 8*) Tourism has more than doubled here since the safety situation began to dramatically improve around seven years ago, and today San Agustín is fast becoming one of Colombia's most-talked-about attractions. City-dwellers from Bogotá visit at weekends and during *puentes* (extended weekend breaks) to stroll around its pleasant streets and leafy plaza. Although the town itself is nice enough, it is San Agustín's fascinating archaeological zone that people come to see, 2.5km to the west: a truly resplendent collection of standing stones, carved monuments and burial chambers that was awarded UNESCO status in 1995.

Getting there and around Regular **minibuses** run from Neiva (15,000COP, 5 hours), and there are also **buses** from Bogotá (45,000COP, 12 hours) and Popayán (20,000COP, 8 hours). Battered **taxis** nip back and forth around San Agustín's tree-lined streets but most attractions can be reached on foot.

Tourist information

ℹ Tourism office Cnr Calle 3 & Carrera 11–55; ☏ 837 3080; ⊕ 08.00–16.00 Mon–Fri, closed noon–14.00

San Agustín town website www.sanagustinhuilacolombia.com

Tour guide There will be dozens of people offering their services in San Agustín. **Fabio Burbano** clearly relishes every aspect of San Agustín's mysterious history and as the owner of **World Heritage Travel** (☏ 837 3940; e *viajespatrimoniomundial@ yahoo.es*), offers a range of archaeological tours to the area's 18 sites. Prices vary with itineraries arranged to suit individual needs. **Teofilo Salcedo** (m *313 449 5484*; e *humbertoguiadeturismosanagustin@yahoo.com*) is another good option.

🏠 **Where to stay** There are dozens of places in San Agustín from which to choose and you shouldn't encounter too much difficulty in procuring accommodation outside of Colombian national holidays. Touts do a brisk business for a commission (your hotel price will increase as the establishment will need to cover this cost) as you alight the bus so it pays to know more or less where you want to lay your head.

🏠 **San Agustín International Hotel** (sleeps 72) m 310 754 8144; e inturcol@gmail. com. www.hotelsanagustininternacional. com. More likely to appeal to domestic tourists than international visitors, this global-themed collection of 6 individual houses seems a little out of place. Each has been built to a unique design & reflects American (à la New England), Mediterranean, Arabic, Oriental, Scandinavian & traditional Colombian architecture. Houses can be shared or hired & can accommodate 8–12 people. It's located just slightly outside the town. **$$$**

🏠 **Hotel Yalconia Vía al Parque Arqueológico** (30 rooms) ☏ 877 3831; e hotelyalconia@hotmail.com. This old-fashioned boxy motel has OK rooms & an OK restaurant about 1km from the centre of town. A reliable option, close to the archaeological park. **$$**

🏠 **La Casa de Francois** (4 private rooms, dorms & camping) ☏ 837 3847; e info@ lacasadefrancois.com; www.lacasadefrancois. com. Set about beautifully tended gardens this charming hostel/B&B is relaxing & welcoming. French owned & run, the staff are always on hand to provide up-to-date information about where to eat & what to do in San Agustín. **$$**

🏠 **Casa de Nelly** (sleeps 22) ☏ 837 3221. Rooms are configured as guests arrive in singles, doubles & family sizes. As one of the town's original countryside backpacker hostels, Casa de Nelly is French owned & has been run by Nelly since 1982. With its beautiful gardens & gorgeous views, the property is a wonderful place to spend time in a gently swaying hammock. Choose from accommodation in cabins or in the main house. Casa de Nelly is located on the edge of town to the west (a 4,000COP taxi ride from the town centre). **$–$$$**

🏠 **Finca El Maco** (sleeps 22) ☏ 837 3437; m 320 375 5982; e info@elmaco.ch; www. elmaco.ch. Lovely Swiss-owned guesthouse, ideally located close to the archaeological site (although the property is often tricky to access other than on foot during the wet season because of muddy conditions). Amenities include a communal kitchen (a range of home-grown organic produce is sold on site). Owner Réné Sutter is a fountain of knowledge on great places to seek out locally. He speaks English, French & German & is renowned for his friendly, relaxed style & passion for ecological farming. Camping also available. **$–$$**

✕ **Where to eat and drink** There are numerous eateries around town, including lots of small, inexpensive places. In the centre there's everything from burgers and pizza to Chinese. However, **Donde Richard** (*Vía al Parque Aqueológico;* m *311 809 3180*) is the best value and the most consistent restaurant in San Agustín. It serves up big plates of fish, pork, sausages and chicken from a pleasant open kitchen with wooden tables and chairs on a tiled floor.

Entertainment and nightlife San Agustín is not renowned for its party scene, but there are a handful of bars and a couple of clubs in the centre of town, including the **Santelmo Disco Bar** and the **Casa de Tarzan**.

Other practicalities There are a number of **banks** but none reliably offers anything other than cash withdrawal – and even then there is only a single ATM at the **Banco Ultrahuilca** (*Calle 3, No 12–73*). There's a reasonable internet café opposite the tourist office: the **Internet Galería Café** (⊕ *08.00–22.00*).

What to see and do
Parque Arqueológico (Archaeological Park) (⊕ *08.00–16.00 year-round; admission 20,000COP*) Declared a UNESCO World Cultural Heritage Site in 1995, the site is shrouded in mystery as almost nothing is known about its exact origins or purpose. An incredible array of carved monumental stones of varying shapes, styles and sizes are believed to have been erected to honour the dead. That they have remained so perfectly untroubled and intact is almost impossible to rationalise, given the history of unrest in the region. However, it is easy to fathom why an ancient civilisation would choose this stunning setting as consecrated ground – it is a beautiful and other-worldly spot. Without a written language to go on, experts have applied scientific guesswork to unravel the history of the site – but why or how the entire culture was wiped out nobody knows. Set amidst 78ha of massifs and canyons, the ceremonial stones symbolise continuity, birth and evolution and are thought to date from the 2nd century BC to the 10th century AD. Megalithic tombs, small temples, sculptures and anthropomorphic figures span a wide range of themes, both human and beast. The monuments were first discovered by Juan de Santa Gertrudis in 1758. He wrote a book, *Wonders of Nature*, prompting a thorough investigation by German Koonrand Theodor Preuss.

Educated guesses by archaeologists conducting studies in San Agustín have added some credible theories to the wild speculation that abounds about the origins of the monumental stones, megalithic tombs, dolmens, caryatids and burial chambers. Most are considered to represent reincarnation themes in a wide variety of depictions that characterise the afterlife, including the following:

Eagle grasping a snake with its claws Depicting a large anthropomorphic figure delivering a child, this oversized example is said to represent power and the political hierarchy. Featuring El Partero (the male midwife) and El Obispo (the bishop), the stone stands 4m tall and weighs several tonnes. Mysteriously, El Partero looks to the east – in the direction of the rising sun, believed to be symbolic of a life reborn.

La Fuente de Lavapatas (The Foot-Washing Fountain) More than just a location, La Fuente de Lavapatas is a sophisticated work of Agustinian sculpture set along a babbling stream, thought to be a foot-washing area. Reached by steps, the monument is complex, containing a maze of small pools and channels etched deep into the bed of the riverside. With a large number of carved stones of a wide variety of shapes and sizes, the site depicts a range of reptiles – such as lizards, snakes, salamanders, iguanas, toads, chameleons and turtles – with human attributes and include a birthing chair. Water flows through the channels to represent the journey of life in what is believed to be a sacral ceremonial bathing site. A path winds up to the **Alto de Lavapatas** (Feet-Washing Hilltop), where the oldest archaeological site is located. As well as some magnificent statue-guarded crypts, there are astounding views.

The double self Represented by a being with conjoined heads and a dual soul, this carved stone is said to hold strong shamanic powers. One of the site's most intriguing monuments, the double self combines masculine and feminine elements and is believed to represent a guardian or warrior.

At the entrance of the park the **Museo Arqueólogical** (Archaeological Park) contains some of the artefacts discovered on the site.

Other archaeological attractions More can be found at the **Alto de Los Idolos** (Idols On High), located 4km southwest of San José de Isnos on the other side of the Río Magdalena. It is notable for the largest ceremonial stone in the San Agustín area, and many visitors choose to access the park via a very pleasant 3-hour walk across the Magdalena Gorge. **Alto de las Piedras** (Stones on High) is 7km north of Isnos and contains a distinctive collection of stones dyed black, red and yellow. **El Tablón, La Pelota, El Purutal** and **La Chaquira** are often visited in a single trip as they are situated quite close together, a 5-hour hike or 4-hour horseback trek. Other lesser-known archaeological sites include **Naranjos, El Jabón** and **La Parada**. Appointing a specialist guide is highly recommended (page 305).

TIERRADENTRO (*Telephone code 2*) This remote little town is notable for its remarkable catacombs and funeral sites in which the world and the afterlife appear to be honoured in an extraordinary collection of burial chambers. Although the exact origins of the catacombs remain a mystery, it is clear that they were created by a civilisation that anticipated death and planned for it in quite a magnificent way. As the lesser-visited of Colombia's two main archaeological sites, Tierradentro is located in a fittingly remote spot that it is often difficult to access in or after wet weather. However, those who do manage to navigate the waterlogged muddy approach road are sure to marvel at the town's mysterious subterranean chambers and other-worldly standing stones, which were awarded UNESCO Cultural Patrimony of Humanity status in 1995. Tierradentro's statues depict human forms while the chambers offer a palpable sense of ancient history with their vivid crimson-and-black daubed etchings on crumbling rock of half-moon symbols, lizards and faces. The site appears to date back to the 6th century although historians admit to not knowing much for sure about the exact origins of the mammoth underground burial caves that reach up to 12m in width. Decorated with geometric motifs and pictures of birds, animals and symbols, Tierradentro's catacombs mainly face west and plunge to depths of up to 8m. Looming stone statues of various shapes and sizes can be found at four main archaeological zones: **Alto del Aguacate** (Avocado on High); **Alto de Segovia** (Segovia on High); **Alto del Duende** (Spirit on High); and **Alto de San Andrés** (St Andrew on High). Alto de Segovia is the most visited because it is located close to the entrance of the park and therefore offers easy access to 25 decorated tombs. Expect some extraordinary examples of subterranean funerary chambers. The park's two fine museums offer visitors plenty of archaeological and ethnographic artefacts and speculation.

In many ways the tiny village of **San Andrés de Pisimbalá** has been absorbed by Tierradentro as it serves as a base from which to explore the archaeological park and surrounding countryside. At least two walks can be enjoyed from the village – one winds its way to Alto de Segovia and one to Alto del Duende. Hundreds of tombs have been recovered so far, but archaeologists expect to unearth more in the future as numerous studies are ongoing in this ancient rocky volcanic terrain set amidst verdant, mist-cloaked hills.

Getting there and around   At least three **buses** pass El Cruce de San Andrés de Pisimbala, a 15-minute walk from the museums, on their way to Popayán (15,000COP, 6 hours). Two direct buses connect with Bogotá and San Agustín with a more frequent service from Pitalito, a 45-minute *colectivo* journey away. **Drivers** should take the road from Neiva via la Plata and San Andrés de Pisimbalá – a route that contains 130km of paved road and 50km of rough unmade track in its final stages. From Popayán the road goes vía Inza and San Andrés de Pisimbalá with just 50km of road paved and 53km unmade. Be warned: the journey can be long and slow in wet weather with roads often waterlogged and impassable due to deep puddles and mudslides. Bridges can often close as routes erode during and after the rainy season while buses can simply give up hope.

Where to stay and eat   Accommodation is scarce and simple in and around Tierradentro – but the good news is it's cheap. Close to the museums and the path to the Alto de Segovia, the **Hotel El Refugio** (✆ *824 0220;* m *321 811 2395;* e *albergueelrefugio@gmail.com; $$*), is the most comfortable option and has a swimming pool, sauna and restaurant in lovely gardens. Choose from 19 ground-floor rooms, all with private bathroom. A restaurant serves perfectly decent food although if the owners added some warmth to the service this place would have greater appeal. The best shoestring hotel is the nearby **Hospedaje Pisimbalá ($)** – though conditions are very basic.

Other practicalities   Most hotels are happy to arrange guides, horses and maps in the absence of a dedicated tourist office. Temperatures average 18°C and it can be damp at times. When visiting the tombs, pack a torch – but don't bother with a camera as photography is forbidden. You'll need to carry several changes of clothes and wear a decent set of waterproofs as the conditions can be very muddy.

What to see and do   Most people head to museums first as most attractions lead off from this part of town. A combined ticket offers admission to both museums over two consecutive days and also includes entrance to all archaeological sites. Decorated pottery forms the centrepiece of the collection at the **Museo Arqueológico** (Archaeology Museum) while the **Museo Etnográfico** (Ethnographic Museum) houses an exhibition of Páez Amerindian artefacts. Both are open 08.00–16.30 daily.

To explore burial sites and tombs, walk for 15 minutes north uphill to **Segovia** where there are 28 catacombs and some of the best preserved. From Segovia, walk another 15 minutes uphill to the four tombs of **El Duende** before heading to the five tombs of **Alto de San Andrés,** two of which are perfectly intact. Close by, **El Tablón** comprises ten elaborate stone monuments, like those found at San Agustín. The 30-plus tombs at **El Aguacate** are a 2-hour walk from the museum high on an isolated mountain ridge. All have been raided so are something of a disappointment, although the walk itself offers magnificent views.

LAGUNA BETANIA   (Betania Lagoon) Approached by a giant causeway 9km from El Hobo, this vast water reserve has become a sport-fishing and fish-farming centre. Developed as a hydro-electrical resource by the Colombian government in 1997, 80% of the energy generated is sold to Ecuador. The reserve is now Chilean-owned. Fish stocks at the Laguna Betania were severely affected in April 2007 after an estimated three million died after a four-month drought. Water levels fell so drastically – 25m in just a few months – that there was insufficient oxygen in the lake to sustain its dozens of hatcheries. More than 1,320 tonnes of tilapia floated to the surface during soaring temperatures. The local fish industry, which exports the tilapia as fillets to the United States and Europe, lost more than US$2 million after burying and incinerating the dead fish. To protect consumers from the threat of contaminated fish, Colombia's government placed a temporary ban on the sale of fish produced in Betania's hatcheries. It pledged US$700,000 in federal subsidies to help fishing stocks recover and asked Spanish power company Endesa SA to help restore the reservoir's water levels by scaling back production of electricity at the dam.

Views around this 541-megawatt hydro-electric facility are well worth enjoying. A number of tourist facilities have begun to spring up around the shores of the dam, including kayaking and fishing boats. There are also usually a handful of taxis and local *colectivos* hanging around.

YAGUARÁ (*Telephone code 8*) A sculpture of a bull and *campesino* in the ultra-neat Parque Ángel María Paredes forms the centrepiece of this small farming town. Founded in 1623 as a cattle-breeding centre, 49km southwest of Neiva, Yaguará was largely neglected until 2005 after being effectively cut off by rebel violence. Today mass investment has put the town back on the map and given its 9,200 population some swanky amenities. Along a once-neglected waterfront stretch of wasteland you'll find a pleasant tree-lined promenade. The US$30 million, 1.2km regeneration project has revitalised Yaguará and the town's gleaming tourist information booth reflects the townsfolk's optimistic outlook for the future. Today visitors to the boardwalk can enjoy live music in a stone-built open-air auditorium or rollerblade, cycle and jog along paths with superb views over the lake. A couple of very nice restaurants serve great fish dishes close to the launch point for cruise boats and water taxis. In the fullness of time a further 2.8km will be added to the main drag to include a conservation area complete with ecological trails. There are also plans to construct a bridge from the promenade to the other side of the lake – a beautiful body of water created by the Betania Dam.

Getting there and around Frequent **buses** and *colectivos* connect with Neiva and the surrounding area, with Yaguará's many **taxis** huddled around the square.

Tourist information
⚡ Yaguará Secretaría De Turismo Calle 4, No 3–91, Alcaldía Municipal; **☎** 838 3066;
e contactenos@yaguara-huila.gov.co; www. yaguara-huila.gov.co

🏠 **Where to stay and eat** Look out for signs on the approach road into town advertising rooms for rent and campsites; they come and go but often line both sides. Yaguará also has a small number of mediocre budget hotels, including the

---

VERY MUCH STILL ALIVE

After lying dormant for over 400 years, the snow-capped Nevado del Huila volcano suddenly sprung to life in 2007. At 5,365m, the highest volcano in Colombia produced 7,000 minor seismic events between February and April, prompting the region into a high state of alert – and justifiably so. It erupted twice on 18 April 2007, causing avalanches of snow into the Río Paez, which in turn saw water levels rise along the Río Magdalena. Incredibly, although more than 4,000 people were forced to flee their homes, no casualties were reported. Later that month the volcano showed further signs of seismic threat, prompting more than 1,500 Nasa indigenous families to abandon their sacred territories and permanently relocate.

Hotel el Largo and a Hotel Savarin, but expect the choice to broaden once tourism comes to town. For simple local food head to the Restaurant Doña Anita and Palo Verde – be sure to order the delicious local fish, *mojarra Chichayaco*.

What to see and do No visit to Yaguará is complete without taking to the waters of Largo Yaguará (Yaguara Lake), an extraordinarily beautiful expanse set amidst lush, green rolling hills. Ferries depart at the weekends at 15.00 for 4-hour trips around the lake's most scenic spots. Costs vary, but expect to pay around 10,000COP with food and drink extra from the café on board. Another option is to hire a boat for around 120,000COP – they typically seat about six passengers and come with two drivers. Highlights include the Bahía de Chichayaco (Chichayaco Bay), where the water reaches a depth of 15m, and the Quebrada de Chichayaco (Chichayaco Creek), which runs into the lake. This is where Yaguará's plentiful stocks of freshwater mojarra Chichayaco are found and on the surrounding hills a growing number of deluxe mansions owned by Colombia's affluent business people reflect the growing popularity of the area with second-homers. One such area is the Costa Brava, a stretch that overlooks rice fields and offers outstanding lakeside views. At the beautifully contoured Punta Catalina (Catherine Point), thick folds of vegetation form a patchwork of different shades of green. Santa Helena used to be a simple farm, but is now a Mecca for watersports enthusiasts with boats, jet skis and kayaks for hire amidst former chocolate fields. Two particularly undulating mounds, known as Las Tortugas (The Turtles), denote another prime spot to fish. An Italian construction team working on the dam named the Cuevas del Amor (Caves of Love) in 1988. These Tolkein-esque labyrinths hewn from towering pink rock became a favourite spot for the workers to engage in a bit of romantic activity – and it remains popular with courting couples today.

There are some rather fine houses in the street beyond the promenade where the buildings were once home to families and their livestock. Vast wooden doors are a common characteristic of these aged properties as the entrance needed to be big enough to accommodate both man and beast. Now beautifully restored, this fine-looking street – dubbed *la calle de puertas* (the street of doors) – makes for a pleasant stroll as it is Yaguará's most historic quarter. It begins at the church on the plaza and heads right down to the water.

POPAYÁN *Telephone code 2*

Renowned throughout Colombia as 'La Ciudad Blanca' ('The White City'), Popayán is an architectural treasure, joining Villa de Leyva, Barichara, Mompóx and Cartagena as one of the nation's most handsome colonial cities. Surrounded by the undulating Valle de Cauca, Popayán (at an altitude of 1,737m) was once a strategic stop-off between Quito and the Caribbean coast, a transfer point for riches bound for Spain. It was founded in 1537 by conquistador Sebastián de Benalcázar but takes its name from the indigenous *po* (meaning 'two'), *pa* (meaning 'straw') and *yan* (meaning 'village') – a reflection of a time when Popayán was just a couple of straw-roofed villages. Although very little is known about the pre-Hispanic history of the town, Popayán has an ancient Amerindian pyramid known as El Morror de Tulcán. The structure was already abandoned when the Spanish first arrived in the city but is thought to have been a burial site. Local legend has it that the inner structure holds treasure and gold.

Uniformity abounds in the charming streets of Popayán, with one gorgeous whitewashed street connecting to another. Numerous churches reflect the town's religious importance and Popayán's many monuments, cobbled paths and pretty plazas are a true delight.

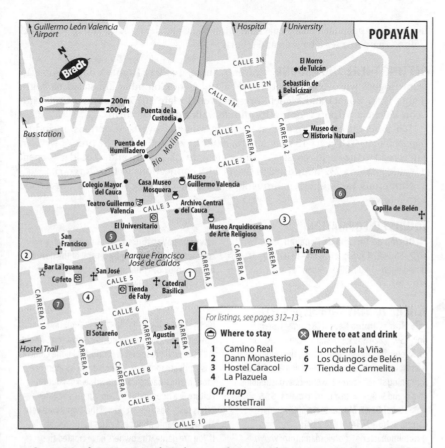

Guillermo León Valencia Airport

↑Hospital ↑University

CALLE 3N

CALLE 2N

El Morro de Tulcán

Sebastián de Belalcázar

0 ——— 200m
0 ——— 200yds

Bradt

N

Bus station

Puente de la Custodia

CALLE 1N

CALLE 1

Río Molino

Puente del Humilladero

CALLE 2

CARRERA 3

CARRERA 2

Museo de Historia Natural

Colegio Mayor del Cauca

Casa Museo Mosquera

Museo Guillermo Valencia

Teatro Guillermo Valencia

CALLE 3

Archivo Central del Cauca

El Universitario

San Francisco

CALLE 4

Museo Arquidiocesano de Arte Religioso

3

Capilla de Belén

6

La Ermita

2

Bar La Iguana
C@feto

San José

CALLE 5

Parque Francisco José de Caldos

i

1

CARRERA 5

CARRERA 4

CARRERA 3

CARRERA 10

Tienda de Faby

Catedral Basilica

CALLE 6

4

7

El Sotareño

San Agustín

CALLE 7

CARRERA 6

CARRERA 7

CARRERA 9

CALLE 8

CARRERA 8

CALLE 9

Hostel Trail

CALLE 10

For listings, see pages 312–13

🛏 **Where to stay**   ✗ **Where to eat and drink**

1 Camino Real   5 Lonchería la Viña
2 Dann Monasterio   6 Los Quingos de Belén
3 Hostel Caracol   7 Tienda de Carmelita
4 La Plazuela

Off map
HostelTrail

On 31 March 1983, an earthquake caused massive devastation moments before the city's much-celebrated Maundy Thursday procession was set to depart. It was a highly destructive 18 seconds, causing widespread damage to much of Popayán's historic core. The quake measured 5.4 on the Richter scale, killing about 250 people and injuring 1,500. More than 2,400 homes were completely destroyed with another 6,900 suffering major structural damage. Also destroyed were streets, schools, health facilities, shops, commercial and office buildings, rural infrastructure and bridges. The damage made it difficult for the government to function as public utilities needed major repair. The loss of electric power greatly complicated initial disaster relief efforts, such as providing emergency shelter. The resulting restoration took more than two decades to complete but the results are stunning with very little sign of any destruction evident today. Historically, Popayán has suffered major earthquakes at intervals of around 80 years – a cyclical pattern that will no doubt worry residents in 2063.

Popayán is famous throughout Colombia for its cultural and political life. It was once the nation's capital and boasts the distinction of producing more Colombian presidents than any other city – 17 to be precise. Popayán has also played an important role in the arts as the home of poets, painters, playwrights and composers and is synonymous with enlightened, progressive thinkers keen to lead and effect change. Today the city's sizeable student population enjoys some of the oldest academic establishments in the country, giving the town a youthful vibrant feel. The city's traditional colonial-era layout of neat linear narrow streets has a quirky peculiarity: two curved roads – the Calle del Banano and the Calle del Caiho – named after a banana and a horn.

GETTING THERE AND AROUND Currently there are three **flights** a day to Popayán from Bogotá with Avianca and EasyFly, and Viva Colombia are slated to begin flights from Bogotá and Medellín respectively in late 2015. Popayán's Guillermo León Valencia Airport is only a 15-minute walk from downtown.

Ten different **buses** provide an excellent range of overland options, including departures to Cali every 15 minutes (18,000COP, 2½ hours). At the time of writing, a new road to the Pacific coast is still under lengthy discussion and, should it happen, it would enable a 2½-hour drive to Guapi with connections to Isla Gorgona.

Numerous **taxis** operate throughout the city, charging 4,000COP for a ride across town.

TOURIST INFORMATION

i **Oficina de Turismo de Popayán** Calle 3, No 2–85; ☏ 824 2251; ☉ 08.00–18.00 Mon–Fri, closed noon–14.00, 09.00–noon Sat

www.popayantours.com This website, a collaborative project run by several of the hostels in town, provides information on independent tours available locally.

⌂ **WHERE TO STAY** *See map, page 311.*

⌂ **Hotel Camino Real** (28 rooms) Carrera 5, No 5–59; ☏ 824 3595; www.hotelcaminoreal.com. co. As one of Popayán's finer hotels, the Camino Real is a resplendent landmark: a fine colonial building containing stylish rooms & world-class gastronomy on a grand scale – with a tariff to match. **$$$**

⌂ **Hotel Dann Monasterio** (47 rooms) Carrera 4, No 10–14; ☏ 824 2191; e hotelmonasterio@hotelesdann.com; www. hoteldannmonasteriopopayan.com. This former Franciscan monastery has plush rooms (a mix of suites, singles & doubles) set around a vast courtyard & a host of top-notch amenities, including a swimming pool. **$$$**

⌂ **Hotel La Plazuela** (19 rooms) Calle 5, No 8–13; ☏ 824 1084; e laplazuela@hotmail.com; www.hotellaplazuela.com.co. This handsome whitewashed colonial mansion is packed with character, from its lovely arcaded courtyard garden & hulking wooden doors & fountains to its tiled lobby adorned with antiques. A restaurant serves good food, including delicious home-baked rolls. Family-run, spotlessly clean & well located with balconies that overlook the Holy Week processions. Check-in/out formalities are frustratingly slow. **$$**

⌂ **Hostel Caracol** (7 rooms & 4 dorm beds) Calle 4, No 2–21; ☏ 820 7335; e info@ hostelcaracol.com; www.hostelcaracol.com. Bright & clean, well organised & comfortable, the Caracol has 7 private rooms & 1 4-bed dorm & caters to a more mature backpacker crowd seeking out the culture & a good night's sleep. An on-site café offers tasty pastries & cakes & the owners are very knowledgeable about activities in the region. If you are game, the owners have created the Coconuco Downhill Cycle Trip. **$**

⌂ **HostelTrail** (14 rooms) Carrera 11, No 4–16; ☏ 831 7871; e popayan@hosteltrail.com; www.hosteltrailpopayan.com. Owned & run by a friendly couple from the UK, this clean & modern place to stay has free Wi-Fi, fast computers & an inexpensive laundry facility. Tony & Kim realised Popayán's potential in 2007 & have contacts with other hostels in South & Central America – a boon for anyone looking for tips & forward bookings. Rooms include an 8-bed dorm, singles, doubles & twin rooms with a mix of shared & private bathrooms. A fully equipped self-catering kitchen is also available along with free tea & Colombian coffee every morning. Cold beers, soft drinks, juices & water are sold 24/7 (via an honesty system). There is a comfortable TV area & lockers. **$**

✕ **WHERE TO EAT AND DRINK** *See map, page 311.*

Restaurants are easy to find in and around the historical centre and are well supplemented by street vendors selling *tamales*, juice and the local specialities, *empanadas de pipián* (a delicious empanada recipe using peanuts and potatoes), and a refreshing drink made from rice and lulo fruit, *champús*.

✕ **Lonchería la Viña** Calle 4, No 7–79; ✆ 824 0602; ⊕ early until late, daily. This family-run diner is rather schizophrenic in character with a restaurant section featuring a collection of nicely laid tables & suited waiters accompanied by a blaring TV, vending machine & take-away service. However, it is open when everything else is shut & serves decent food. $$

✕ **Los Quingos de Belén** Calle 4, No 0–55; ⊕ 08.00–19.00 daily. It's just a simple little local food joint but the Kingos de Belén serves up generous portions of regional fare with a choice of set meals & snacks. $

✕ **Tienda de Carmelita** Calle 5, No 9–45; ✆ 824 4862. This scruffy little snack shack serves cheap & delicious *empanadas de pipián* & cold drinks, but is – rather annoyingly – closed at lunchtime. $

ENTERTAINMENT AND NIGHTLIFE For a student town, Popayán has a distinct lack of nightlife. Try **Bar La Iguana** on Calle 4, No 9–67, for pumping salsa and cheap beer. For a night of retro tango head to **El Sotareño** on Carrera 6 – a Popayán institution renowned for its passé style, vinyl records and faded décor.

OTHER PRACTICALITIES Popayán has a decent handful of **banks**, all with ATMs. As with most student towns, it also has numerous **internet cafés**, including the **El Universitario** on Carrera 6, No 3–47, and **C@feto** on Carrera 9, No 5–42. Both charge 2,000COP per hour. Lone travellers seeking to hook up with others should head to **Tienda de Faby** on Calle 5 to check out its well-used noticeboard.

WHAT TO SEE AND DO Popayán's historic centre is home to all of the city's main sites of interest with narrow streets set within ten blocks that are easily navigable on foot. Almost all of the churches are open daily at around 08.30 and 17.00 for Mass. Wear comfy shoes and prepare to put in some leg work to see the lot within a single day. A stop-off at the leafy **Parque Francisco José de Caldos** (Franciso Jose de Caldos Park) makes a pleasant spot for respite amidst shoe-shiners and domino-playing elders. A statuesque **clock tower** bears a clock face donated by the British embassy in 1983 after the earthquake.

Popayán's largest colonial church is the **Iglesia de San Francisco** (San Francisco Church; *Cnr Carrera 9 & Calle 4*), a very handsome building with a stunning high altar. The **Iglesia de San Agustín** (San Agustín Church; *Cnr Carrera 7 & Carrera 6*) and the **Iglesia de San José** (San José Church; *Cnr Calle 5 & Carrera 8*) are other fine churches to visit. As the oldest church in the city, the **Iglesia La Ermita** (La Ermita Church; *Cnr Calle 5 & Carrera 2*) dates back to 1546. On Parque Caldos, the Neoclassical **cathedral** is Popayán's newest religious building, built between 1859 and 1906 after an earthquake destroyed the previous church.

Museo Arquidiocesano de Arte Religioso (Museum of Religious Art) (*Calle 4, No 4–56;* ✆ *824 2759;* ⊕ *09.00–17.00 Mon–Fri, closed 12.30–14.00, 09.00–14.00 Sat; admission 2,000COP*) Housed in an attractive colonial building set around a courtyard, this large collection of religious art reopened in 1989 and includes some magnificent silver items. Artefacts have been gathered from churches all over the region and include jewel-encrusted altarpieces, communion vessels, paintings and statues, many from the 17th century but some dating to 1580. Only a small proportion of the entire collection is on display at any one time – the rest of the time it's housed in eight vast vaults that are protected by an automatic locking

system that opens twice a year only. The building itself dates back to 1763 and today it also plays host to a number of important religious congresses.

Museo de Historia Natural (Natural History Museum) (*Carrera 2, No 1A–25;* ☏ *820 9800;* ⊕ *08.00–17.00 daily, closed noon–14.00; admission 3,500COP*)
This sizeable collection contains a much-acclaimed array of insects, stuffed birds and butterflies.

Casa Museo Mosquera (Museum of the Mosquero Homestead) (*Calle 3, No 5–14;* ☏ *820 9916;* ⊕ *09.00–17.00 daily, closed noon–14.00; admission 3,500COP*)
Once home to General Tomás Cipriano de Mosquera, Colombian president between 1845 and 1867, this colonial mansion contains an interesting collection of personal artefacts relating to his life. After suffering face wounds during a battle in 1824, Mosquera was forced to wear a metal prosthesis. This earned him the nicknamed 'Mascachochas' by his critics.

Museo Guillermo Valencia (Guillermo Valencia Museum) (*Carrera 6, No 2–69;* ☏ *820 6160;* ⊕ *10.00–17.00 Tue–Sun, closed noon–14.00; admission 2,000COP*) This sizeable collection of period furniture, paintings, documents and old paintings relates to the Popayán poet who lived in this gorgeous 18th-century building. Guillermo Valencia's son, Guillermo León Valencia, was Colombian president 1962–66.

Other sites To the north of the historic centre on the Río Molino, two bridges can be seen. The **Puente de la Custodia** (Monstrance Bridge) is the smaller of the two and was built in 1713 as a crossing point for priests to enable them to administer to the city's poorer outlying areas. The larger bridge, **Puente del Humilladero** (Humble Bridge), was constructed 160 years later alongside it to provide a more robust crossing – and this rock-solid 178m structure is still used today. It is overlooked by the majestic slopes of the **Cerro del Morro**. Close by, in the **Archivo Central del Cauca** (Central Archives of Cauca), over four million ancient documents contain the history of the city dating back to 1541 in rows and rows of dusty tomes stored in vast oak cabinets.

Don't pass up an opportunity to poke your head into the doorway of the **Teatro Municipal Guillermo Valencia** (Guillermo Valencia Municipal Theatre) – the 900-seat auditorium was restored in 1987 but retains a retro style. Opposite, spot the fabulous wrought-iron gates of the **Colegio Mayor del Cauca** (Cauca College) English school.

The tiny, old hillside place of worship **Capilla de Belén** (Belen Chapel) offers magnificent city views just east of the centre. Thought to be an ancient burial site, **El Morro de Tulcán** also affords stunning vistas and is home to a statue of the town's founder, Sebastián de Benalcázar. Sadly, in sharp contrast to the pristine historic centre, this is graffiti-adorned and littered with rubbish.

Festivals Crowds of some 20,000 people descend on Popayán for the city's famous **Semana Santa** (Holy Week) when stunning night-time processions snake through the streets. In 2011, the event celebrated its 455th anniversary, having taken place every year since 1556. Each year's procession is so complex it takes 12 months of meticulous planning and follows a route of 54 stopping points across the city during a colourful and poignant five-day event. Vast religious wooden figures of elaborate design and gleaming gilt are carried by townsfolk as part of the procession. Each weighs over 500kg and requires eight bearers who will then have to take the strain for over 4 hours across 20 blocks, from 20.00 to midnight. Every icon is assigned a *síndico* between each year's event who is required to painstakingly maintain and restore it. The procession itself is bound by tradition with townsfolk walking alongside the icons carrying flickering candles (*alumbrantes*) in a solemn fashion, their chests swollen with pride, such is the privilege of participation. As the second-largest Easter celebrations in the world, Popayán's Holy Week contains five processions devoted to Mary, Jesus, the Cross, the Laying in the Tomb and the Resurrection.

Central participants fulfil the roles of incense burner, the runny nose, Ruler, El Pichón, Knights of the Holy Sepulchre, banner-bearers, group singers and lighting fixers. The physical responsibility is huge, with statue-bearers often sustaining bleeding wounds from sheer weight of icons laid on their shoulders for hours and hours. Children, choir boys and flower carriers ferry brightly coloured garlands whilst dressed in flowing capes and robes.

Locals consider the following rituals the most poignant part of the Holy Week celebrations:

Palm Sunday procession Beginning with a blessing in Belen's chapel, this deeply moving ceremony involves parishioners waving white flags in a proclamation that Jesus is King on the pretty cobbled streets of Popoyán.

Holy Tuesday procession Lit by candles and moonlight, this ambient evening procession involves four ecclesiastical statues being transported in a ceremonial procession from San Agustín Church to the city centre for a Requiem Mass by a spectacular cortege of bearers in blood-red robes carrying bells and following a vast wooden crucifix.

Good Friday procession Representing Jesus before his crucifixion, the centrepiece of this event is the image of death as a skeleton. A deeply moving and symbolic procession, Holy Friday sees an all-male cortege bearing chisels, axes and hammers to reflect the withdrawal of Christ's body from the Cross.

Other major Holy Week and Eastertide events include the Procession of Our Lord of Veracruz on Holy Thursday, the Procession of Our Lord Jesus Christ Resurrected on Holy Saturday and the Procession of Remembrance and Legend on Easter Monday.

During Holy Week Popayán holds a **religious musical festival**, a modern tradition that was launched in the 1960s by Edmundo Troya Mosquera. The event draws many choral performers, soloists and orchestras to the city with a host of venues staging a world-class celebration of religious music. Further details on Holy Week can be found at www.semanasantapopayan.com.

A **Gastronomic Festival** in early August is another major tourist draw, with food stalls, markets and cook-offs throughout the city.

AROUND POPAYÁN

PARQUE NACIONAL PURACÉ (PURACÉ NATIONAL PARK) This 83,000ha reserve 45km southeast of Popayán contains some heavenly hiking trails amidst a geothermal wonderland of hot springs, waterfalls and grasslands – as well as an inactive volcano from which it derives its name. Created in 1961, the reserve sits at an altitude of between 2,500m and 4,750m above sea level, so offers plenty of geological biodiversity, rising from boggy, humid jungle to the snowy chill of rugged peaks. More than 50 lakes and a dozen creeks are home to many species of frogs, birds, butterflies and insects. The black-and-chestnut eagle, rainbow-bearded thornbill and yellow-bellied chat tyrant are all resident in the park. The volcano itself is a pleasant 4-hour trek along a leafy trail that climbs up from the visitors' centre. The park's Cascada del Bedón (waterfall) and major lake (Laguna de San Rafael) are an 8km hike from the road from the nearby village of Pilimbalá. Less than 2km from the falls you'll find the hot springs of the Termales de San Juan, in what is a scenic 15km round trip. Other trails lead to caves (Cueva de los Guácharos) and smaller lakes, including the Laguna de la Magdalena (Magdalena Lagoon). A striking characteristic of the landscape is its defined patches of colour.

Visitors can stay overnight in three rustic *cabañas*: each sleeps six and there is also camping in four tents that accommodate five apiece. Entrance is 18,000COP with a dorm bed 13,000COP per night, plus 15,000COP for three square meals. Visitors need a permit to enter the park from the Parques Nacionales Naturales de Colombia (Colombia National Parks) and should prepare for sharp temperature variations as these can range from 12°C to 20°C. A very helpful ranger has maps and route plans for most of the trails – find him in the visitors' centre.

LAS ARDILLAS Located 8km south of Popayán, this private nature reserve is popular with adventure sports fans who enjoy a host of extreme eco-adventures, from climbing walls, hiking and trekking to treetop zip wires. Try tube-riding on the rivers and trekking out to waterfalls after whizzing through the forest at speed on the canopy wire to enjoy a bird's-eye view. Suspension bridges stretch over ravines and the Río Honda while nature trails weave through wetland conservation zones renowned for their species of birds, frogs and butterflies. Package rates include activities with optional accommodation. Visit www.canopylasardillas.com for further information.

SILVIA Should your trip to Popayán include a Tuesday, don't miss the opportunity of travelling to the highland town of Silvia where the Guambiano people hold their weekly market. Colourfully dressed indigenous people come in their dozens to trade and barter, selling all sorts of traditional foods. Hidden away at 2,620m in the southern Andes, this important cultural event has managed to maintain an authenticity rarely found in other indigenous markets of Latin America.

NARIÑO

Colombia's most southwesterly department boasts a chequerboard terrain, from blankets of thick jungle to towering Andean peaks. An array of indigenous cultures and strong Ecuadorian influences ensure the cultural make-up of Nariño is quite unlike any other part of the country. Some of Colombia's finest ceramics and textiles are produced in the region, where a strong artistic tradition prevails. Pasto's Carnaval de Negros y Blancos (Black and White Carnival) is one of the nation's most riotous, while the region's hybrid ethnicity ensures the food is a wholly unique fusion of flavours.

However, the Nariño has become synonymous with many of Colombia's ills as a centre for coca production and cross-border conflict in recent years. The jungle geography and the rivers along the Colombian–Ecuadorian border make it perhaps one of the continent's most complex regions to patrol. It remains a hotbed of guerrilla activity with petroleum plants, including the San Miguel de Orito pipeline, relentlessly targeted by FARC. In times of upheaval, the region has also experienced massive flows of displaced people. Drug traffickers frequent the border, which is notorious for a steady flow of contraband. Goods are ferried in and out in vast quantities by any means possible, from human couriers and trucks to mules, buses and bicycles. Some of the most toxic and dangerous agrochemicals in the world are also shipped for use in cocaine production. In a single haul, the authorities seized over 1,093 tonnes of solid supplies and 182,000 gallons of liquid substances used for the purpose. Corruption is said to have permeated all levels of the military and government on both sides of the border.

As Colombia's largest drug producer, Nariño is prolific: conservative estimates put the number of hectares planted with coca plants at 13,875 – but the reality is that it is almost certainly much, much more. Figures closer to 70,000ha are often quoted by the local population. Official figures reckon that 44 tonnes of cocaine are produced in Nariño each year – much of it bound for the US via Ecuador. Amidst this scenario, Colombia's Washington-supported aerial spraying of coca crops has caused considerable cross-border tension. Although coca has been grown in Nariño for more than 25 years, the amount of crops has increased markedly since the late 1990s. Official reports suggest that 103,343ha of illicit crops are sprayed in a six-month cycle alone. A highly toxic herbicide containing glysophate is used in Colombia's anti-narcotics aerial-spraying programme and this has sparked fierce complaints from farmers on both sides of the border who claim it has seriously affected human health and poisoned livestock and vegetables. Demands by the Ecuadorian government for a 10km no-spray zone have failed to impress the Colombian authorities who remain committed to their programme. So far, it has failed to meet its goal of eliminating 50% of illicit crops in the country, despite an investment of nearly US$1.2 billion. More than four times the initial area of coca has been sprayed.

Both the United Nations and the US government have reported an increase in the area covered by illicit coca crops. A BBC investigation has also revealed that just eight weeks' production in a single Nariño coca production plant can amount to £800 million worth of cocaine in UK street prices. At the time of writing, the security situation in Nariño is best described as 'patchily turbulent'. Mixed reports from travellers crossing the border from either side suggest the situation is potentially volatile with months of calm suddenly becoming 24 hours of turmoil overnight. The British Foreign Office advises against all travel to Nariño with the exception of the border town of Pasto. Visitors should only travel during daylight hours and never cross the city after dark.

PASTO *Telephone code 2*

Most visitors to Pasto are simply travelling through, hopping on or off a bus to Ipiales to cross the border to Ecuador or boarding a plane to Bogotá – or beyond. Like most transportation hubs, Pasto lacks any real beauty, despite having several rather fine colonial buildings. An earthquake in 1834 destroyed many of its oldest buildings, leaving Pasto without a great deal of character. As Nariño's administrative and political capital, the city has a busy commercial centre. Despite its reputation for shady dealings, Pasto is a friendly place to be during daylight hours. It was founded in 1537 by Lorenzo de Alana and sits at the eastern base of the volcano La Galera at an altitude of 2,530m. Pasto is famous throughout Colombia for its *barniz de Pasto*, a glossy vegetable resin used to decorate wooden artefacts, and numerous examples of these colourfully decorated bowls, mats and boxes can be seen throughout the city.

GETTING THERE AND AROUND *Colectivos* nip back and forth to the airport 33km to the north of the city every 45 minutes (6,000COP) from Calle 18 at Carrera 25. Get your hotel to pre-book this for you and the driver will pick you up. Both Avianca and Satena run **flights** to Cali and Bogotá with connections to other cities.

Frequent **buses**, **minibuses** and *colectivos* connect with Ipiales (8,000COP, 2 hours), Cali (30,000COP, 9 hours), Popayán (25,000COP, 6 hours) and Bogotá (100,000COP, 22 hours). The bus terminal is 2km south of the city, a 5,000COP **taxi** ride away.

TOURIST INFORMATION

Oficina Departamento de Turismo de Nariño Calle 19, No 23–28; ☏ 723 5003; http://turismo.narino.gov.co; ⏰ 08.00–18.00, closed noon–14.00

WHERE TO STAY There are plenty of hotels in the city, but choose one with a restaurant to avoid having to cross the city after dark.

Hotel Agualongo (60 rooms) Carrera 25, No 17–83; ☏ 723 0606. e reservas@hotelagualongo. com; www.hotelagualongo.com. Pasto's most luxurious central hotel contains large modern rooms & top-notch private bathrooms overlooking the Plaza de Nariño – with the high-rise 1980s structure forming a striking contrast to the olden charm of its immediate surroundings. Modern wooden floors & contemporary furnishings give the hotel & airy feel with guest amenities that include a health centre, business centre, restaurant & café. **$$**

Hotel Concorde (25 rooms) Calle 19, No 29A–09; ☏ 731 1193. Located close to the Plaza de Nariño, this basic option isn't big on style but represents good value near to all central amenities. **$**

Hotel Rey del Sur (approx 12 rooms) Carrera 9, No 15A–10; ☏ 730 0114 . This inexpensive hotel near the city's bus terminal 2km outside of the centre is modern & clean. Expect simple rooms with private bathrooms & cable TV. **$**

Koala Inn (15 rooms) Calle 18, No 22–37; ☏ 722 1101; e hotelkoalainn@hotmail.com. This lively backpacker haunt comes highly recommended & is a popular choice with travellers crossing to & from Ecuador. It has all the usual budget travel amenities, from a book exchange & noticeboard to a laundry & shoestring restaurant. Choose from a collection of spacious rooms set around a courtyard, some with a private bathroom. B/fast is extra – if you're seriously hungry, opt for the large American plate. **$**

WHERE TO EAT AND DRINK

Caffetto Calle 19, No 25–62; ☏ 729 2720; ⏰ noon–late. One of the city's upmarket options, which has an international menu of salads, soups, sandwiches, juices & milkshakes. **$$**

Picantería Ipiales Calle 19, No 23–37; ⏰ 09.00–21.00 Mon–Sat, 10.00–18.00 Sun. Choose from a simple menu of delicious home-cooked meals, including fish-&-rice & grilled chicken, as well as plenty of fast food & snacks. **$**

Restaurante Tierra Colombiana Chipichape Calle 18, No 27–19; ☏ 772 8992; ⏰ 07.00–21.00 Mon–Fri, 07.00–15.00 Sat. This cheerful diner serves simple local chicken-&-rice dishes & decent b/fasts. **$**

Salón Guadalquivir Pl de Nariño; ☏ 723 9604; ⏰ 08.00–19.30 Mon–Sat, closed noon–14.30. Expect plenty of Colombian staples at low prices in this bustling little place, such as meat-filled *empanadas* & crispy *tamales*. **$**

OTHER PRACTICALITIES Almost every bank, internet café, *casa de cambio* and international payphone is centred on the Plaza de Nariño. Those crossing to Ecuador should change their money here rather than rely solely on Ipiales.

WHAT TO SEE AND DO
Museo Taminango de Artes y Tradiciones (Museum of Taminango's Arts and Traditions) (*Calle 13, No 27–67;* ☏ *723 5539;* ⏰ *08.00–18.00, closed noon–14.00;*

admission 2,000COP) Dating back to 1623, this is one of the city's oldest houses, a large restored mansion that houses an eclectic mishmash of antiques and books.

Museo del Oro (Gold Museum) *(Calle 19, No 21–27; ☏721 9108; ⏲ 08.30–18.00, closed noon–14.00; free admission)* This small collection of pre-Columbian gold and pottery from the indigenous cultures of Nariño is actually pretty impressive.

Iglesia de San Juan (San Juan Church) *(Pl de Nariño)* Check out the largely restored city church's lavish gold interior décor and ornate colonial Baroque detail. The building itself dates back to the 16th century but had lots of 18th-century attention.

Festival
Carnaval de Negros y Blancos (Black and White Festival) (January) Be prepared for lots of up-tempo processions and music during this two-day festival, celebrated since the time of Spanish rule. The city fills with the rhythmic sounds of beating drums and dancers in colourful garb and painted faces. It's a madcap high-energy event that goes back to the days of slavery and culminates in a messy merriment of black-and-white paint, flour and talc.

AROUND PASTO

VOLCÁN GALERAS The hiking trail from Pasto to the summit of this vast brooding volcano takes about 4½ hours and climbs up to 4,276m along some beautiful scenic paths past farms and meadows. Although it was active as recently as 2006, several guides offer treks along the 9km trail – including those employed by the tourist board. Views from the top take in a spectacular panorama across the city and beyond. An eruption in November 2005 threw smoke and ash across Pasto and surrounding villages, prompting 8,000 to evacuate their homes. In March 2009, Galeras erupted twice in a single day, although no injuries were reported. A mass evacuation in January 2010 was the tenth in a 12-month period. It was followed by less explosive activity in August of the same year and several weeks on 'high alert' in January 2011. Fortunately it has been less active in recent years.

LAGUNA DE LA COCHA (LA COCHA LAGOON) Everybody raves about the beauty of this lake and cloudforest – and it more than lives up to the hype. Located 30 minutes east of Pasto, the Laguna de la Cocha is a peaceful and resplendent place in which to fish for trout. An offshore island reserve (La Corota) offers magnificent views across the water and can be reached by boat. At 75m in depth and 20km long by 5km wide, the lake is one of the largest in Colombia and is an important scientific research centre under the auspices of the University of Nariño. *Colectivos* from Pasto serve the lake from the front of the church on Pasto's main square. The 20km trip will cost around 5,000COP.

IPIALES *(Telephone code 2)* Located 5km from the Ecuadorian border, Ipiales is every inch the ugly frontier town: grimy, seedy and functional with very little soul. Everyone is on the move to somewhere more inspiring with zero effort made to entice them to stay. That there is little to see or do in this mist-shrouded town makes it all the more dreary – a transit hub that people visit as a necessity, not for joy. Set on the banks of the Río Guáitara at 2,897m above sea level, Ipiales was founded in 1585 by Spanish missionaries and has a population now of around 75,000.

Set 45km above the river, and surrounded by plaques of prayer, the truly beautiful Gothic basilica of Santuario de Nuestra Senora de las Lajas (Shrine of Our Lady on the Rocks) dates back to 1926 and is set on a bridge spanning the Guáitara River. Today, the Shrine of Our Lady of Lajas attracts Catholic pilgrims from all over Colombia to this out-of-town verdant valley where an elaborate twin-arched bridge straddles water and rocks. Since the 18th century, there have been four buildings on the site – the current is a truly refined grey-and-white structure with elegant spires and stained glass. An illuminated image of the Virgén del Rosario (Our Lady of the Rosary) is the centrepiece and draws hundreds of thousands of visitors to a simple stone slab. Pilgrims journey for up to 12 hours on foot on a trio of religious holidays – 15 and 16 September (the date of onset), Holy Thursday (Easter) and during Christmas and New Year. Yet, every Sunday the church welcomes regular worshippers to its sacral splendour – you'll see the parishioners walking from Ipiales up to the bridge. In 2007, the basilica was voted as one of the seven wonders of Colombia by the readers of Colombian newspaper *Time* (the Salt Cathedral in Zipaquirá polled first place; see pages 152–3).

The miracle relating to the Sanctuario de Nuestra Señora de Las Lajas dates back to 1754, when a young woman called María Meneses de Quiñones was making the six-mile walk from her village of Potosi to Ipiales. As she approached a bridge over the Guáitara River at Las Lajas, a terrible storm erupted, prompting a terrified María to seek refuge in a roadside cave. To calm her nerves, she knelt in prayer, only to feel someone lightly touch her back. Fearing someone had joined her in the cave, she turned around shaking – only to find she was still alone. She fled the cave and ran home to her family.

Days later, María retraced her steps with her daughter Rosa – a child who couldn't hear or speak. On reaching the cave María sat down on a rock to rest when, suddenly, Rosa began to cry out: 'Mama, Mama, there is a white lady with a child in her arms!' Rosa had spoken for the first time yet María couldn't see a white figure. Frightened by what had happened she gathered up her daughter

Although it has long lost its original good looks, grace and beauty, Ipiales isn't totally bereft of charm – each Friday a market brings colourful textiles, beads and trinkets to the town. Ipiales is also a base for religious pilgrims on their way to visit the **Santuario de Las Lajas** (Shrine on the Rocks) – a stunning Gothic cathedral built on a reputed site of miracles located about 7km outside of town (see box, above).

Getting there, away and around   Avianca flies to Bogotá with connections to other cities but there are no flights from Ipiales to Ecuador. Ipiales airport is 7km northwest of the city, a 20,000COP taxi ride. The **bus** terminal is new and efficient, and is located 1km northeast of the centre. Frequent buses connect to Bogotá (150,000COP, 25 hours), Cali (50,000COP, 10 hours), Popayán (30,000COP, 8 hours) and Pasto (10,000COP, 2 hours). Numerous *colectivos*, **taxis** and **minibuses** serve the border at Rumichaca (1,000COP) – cross on foot before jumping in a taxi for the 6km trip to Tulcán, where there is a small airport.

Where to stay and eat   The city has a number of hotels as befitting a busy frontier post; some are better than others but most represent decent value. Room availability can make staying here a challenge, however, so try to book in advance.

and rushed to Ipiales, where she told relatives and friends what had happened. Later that same day, on the return journey to Potosi, María passed the cave with Rosa once again. The child pulled away from her mother and burst into the cave yelling: 'Mama! Mrs White is calling me!' Unable to see what her child referred to, María grabbed her daughter's hand – and ran home.

Over the days that followed, word began to spread of what had occurred in the cave. Then, a few days later, Rosa disappeared from her home, prompting a widespread search by friends and family around Potosi and beyond. Eventually, the search party arrived at Guáitara and María could see her daughter kneeling in front of a white woman who was playing with Rosa with a great warmth and familiar love. María felt the woman's divine and sublime tenderness and fell to her knees before her. She recognised that she was in the presence of the Blessed Virgin and wept with happiness.

In the weeks that followed, María paid frequent visits to the cave, filling it with posies of wild flowers and candles over time. One day, Rosa fell seriously ill and grew progressively sicker. Nursing her attentively, María could feel her child slipping away until her little body went limp in her arms. Distraught, María carried Rosa's lifeless frame up to the cave and begged the Blessed Virgin to bring her daughter back.

Overwhelmed by the sight that befell her, the Virgin reawoke Rosa. An overjoyed María ran straight to Ipiales. She roused her friends and family and relayed the miracle as the church bells began to peal and crowds began to gather. At first light, the townsfolk formed a procession and journeyed to the cave, arriving as the sun began to rise. There was no doubting the miracle as the cave was drenched in an extraordinary light while an image of the Virgin Mary was forever etched on a stone wall.

Today visitors to the Santuario de Nuestra Señora de Las Lajas can arrive by *colectivo* from Ipiales (3,000COP, 15 minutes); they leave from Carrera 6 at Calle 4. Taxis can also be hired for the round trip for around 20,000COP.

For a good choice of restaurants head to the Plaza de la Indepencia – you'll find everything from burger bars and French fries to fish-and-rice and *empanadas*.

🏠 **Hotel Metropól** (60 rooms) Calle 14, No 7–30; ✆ 773 3851. Conveniently located opposite the bus terminal, this modern hotel has simple, but comfortable rooms, each with private bathroom. B/fast not inc. **$$**

🏠 **Hotel Belmonte** (5 rooms) Carrera 4, No 12–111; ✆ 773 2771. This little cheapie favoured by backpackers has basic hot- & cold-water bathrooms. Friendly, clean & family run with decent-sized rooms. Cash only. **$**

Crossing the border Ipiales's Puente Internacional de Rumichaca border with Ecuador closes 22.00–06.00, so be sure to arrive with plenty of time for the all-too-slow border-crossing formalities. At the time of writing the British Foreign Office are continuing to advise travellers to use this frontier with caution. The recommendation is not to stop *en route* between the border and Pasto, while the wider route between Cali and the border with Ecuador is also described as 'volatile'. Travellers crossing into Colombia from Ecuador should ensure that their passport is stamped by the immigration authorities – both as they exit Ecuador and enter Colombia. Failure to do so may result in a fine. In the event that the immigration office on the border is closed, travellers are advised to seek assistance at the Migracion Colombia office – there is one in Pasto and another in Ipiales.

Other practicalities
The city's **internet cafés** are notoriously slow; head to **Internet** (*Calle 16, No 6–51*) for the speediest connection. Several **banks** are clustered around the Plaza la Pola, some with ATMs. None changes travellers' cheques or offers currency exchange but there are a handful of money changers nearby.

What to see and do Ipiales is renowned for being the home of the stunning **Santuario de Las Lajas** (see box, pages 320–1), but this popular pilgrim destination of great religious significance is actually located 7km outside of the city, not in the centre of town, so you'll need to organise local transport to reach it or ask about walking trails.

9

The Northwest Interior

> Our home, our mountains, our family for those we toil. Our hearts, our God, our pride for those we sweat. País Paisa for ever... our homeland.
>
> Anon, 'País Paisa', 1958

Colombia's northwest interior region is a landscape of two distinct characters, deftly defined by the majestic peaks of the Andes range. Sharply rising terrain soars up from steamy flatlands to cooler, verdant highlands and snow-capped mountaintops. Fertile valleys clad with thick, lush vegetation are home to folds of coffee, plantain and banana crops set in nutrient-rich soils. Pretty wooden haciendas sit enveloped by rolling meadow overlooked by fog-cloaked forests atop scrub-covered hills. Horseriding *campesinos* cart sacks of coffee beans to market while oxen plough the fields. The region's aged colourwashed colonial settlements are some of Colombia's most inviting with cobbled streets, flower-filled baskets and sleepy plazas seemingly lost in time. Tangled clumps of sky-high ferns form uniformed lines on plump, waterlogged terraces. Winding lanes are shaded by palm leaves the size of bath towels aside rocky rivers.

ANTIOQUIA

Spanning 63,612km², the department of Antioquia occupies the central-northwestern part of Colombia with a narrow strip that borders the Caribbean Sea. Comprising some of South America's most mountainous terrain with deep lush valleys and fast-flowing rivers, Antioquia's population of just over six million are true country folk. These so-called 'Texans of Colombia' have a strong cultural identity linked to the geography of the region, a territory isolated from the rest of Colombia from the 17th until the mid 19th century when the Antioquia expansion began. Many Antioqueños are known as Paisas (a shortened version of the Spanish '*paisano*' meaning 'countryman'), although strictly speaking Paisa Country (País Paisa) is a larger region made up of Caldas, Risaralda, Quindío, the north of Valle del Cauca and the northwest Tolima and just 80% of Antioquia. Paisas are true country folk who relish their strong cultural identity linked to the mountainous geography of the region. Isolated from the rest of Colombia until the mid 19th-century expansion, Antioquia's remoteness plays a crucial role in the make-up of the Paisa psyche – proud, resolute and self-sufficient. Alternately the butt of jokes and the object of envy for many Colombians, what makes Paisas stand out is their rugged individualism and nose-to-the-grindstone hard-work ethic. This reputation stems from the mid 19th century, when Antioqueños seized the government's carrot of free land and cleared their hinterland for agriculture. Huge progress ensued, earning them a certain status throughout Colombia. Soon, they became synonymous with industriousness, thriftiness and skill at turning a profit. Today that reputation persists with the term 'Paisa' meaning anything related to,

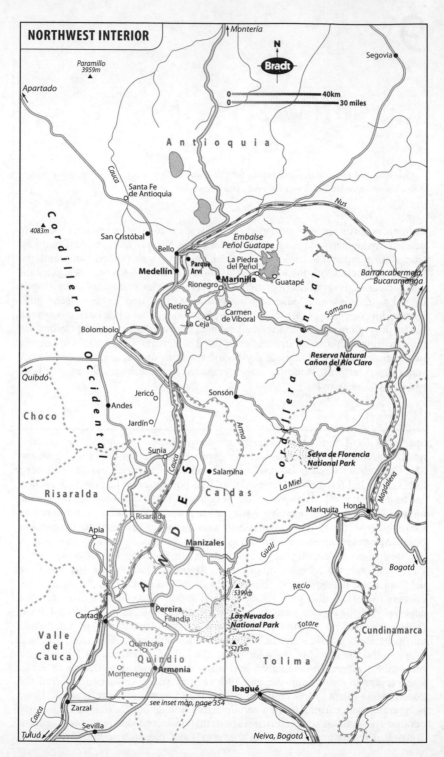

NORTHWEST INTERIOR

↑ Montería

N

Bradt

0 _____ 40km
0 _____ 30 miles

Segovia ●

Apartado

Paramillo
3959m ▲

A n t i o q u i a

Cauca

Santa Fe
de Antioquìa

Nus

▲ 4083m

San Cristóbal ●

Bello

Embalse
Peñol Guatape

Barrancabermeja,
Bucaramanga

Medellín ●

Parque
Arvi

La Piedra
del Peñol

Marinilla

Samana

Rionegro

Guatapé

Retiro ●

Carmen
de Viboral

Bolombolo ●

La Ceja

Reserva Natural
Cañon del Río Claro

Quibdó

Jericó ○

Sonsón ●

Choco

Andes ●

Arma

Jardín ○

Selva de Florencia
National Park

Sunia ●

Cauca

R i s a r a l d a

C a l d a s

Salamina ●

La Miel

Magdalena

Risaralda

Mariquita

Honda ●

Apia ●

Manizales ●

Guali

Bogotá

A
N
D
E
S

C
o
r
d
i
l
l
e
r
a

C
e
n
t
r
a
l

C
o
r
d
i
l
l
e
r
a

O
c
c
i
d
e
n
t
a
l

▲ 5399m

Recio

Pereira ●

Los Nevados
National Park

Cundinamarca

Cartago ●

Filandia

Totare

V a l l e
d e l
C a u c a

Quimbaya ○

Q u i n d i o

▲ 5215m

T o l i m a

Montenegro ○

Armenia ●

Zarzal ●

Ibagué ●

Cauca

see inset map, page 354

Tuluá ◀

Sevilla ●

Neiva, Bogotá ▶

or originating from, the region – with perhaps the biggest Paisa contribution to Colombia being its coffee. At the very heart of Paisa country is the mushrooming metropolis of Medellín – Colombia's former murder capital – a city now transformed into one of the nation's most progressive. Lush, rolling coffee fields lie scattered with pretty *fincas* and Paisa homesteads, encircling the cities of Manizales, Armenia and Pereira in the Zona Cafetera de Colombia. Unknown even to native Colombians until the first decade of the 21st century, the 'Coffee Zone' is a place where visitors can harvest coffee beans, learn about crop yields, discover the history of coffee growing and sample an array of rich, dark aromatic Colombian varieties. It is also an excellent base from which to explore one of Colombia's most exceptional national parks, the magnificent **Parque Nacional Los Nevados** (pages 361–3).

HISTORY By the 18th century, almost all of Antioquia's indigenous people had been wiped out by disease or Spanish settlers. They belonged to the Caribe ethnic group, which in its turn was divided into three tribes and families: the ferocious Catíos (who inhabited Urabá and Chocó), the fearsome Nutabes (located between the Cauca and Porce rivers) and the peaceful Tahamíes (who lived between the Porce and the Magdalena rivers). Fighting the Spanish with bows and arrows, often laced with poison, the Amerindians slowly lost their territory, eventually surrendering to slavery and ultimately to death.

The first Basque families from northern Spain began arriving in the 16th century, establishing small homesteads in what is now eastern Antioquia. The terrain, similar to that of the mountainous northern Spain region, soon had numerous settlements of family units. That these were not just communities of single men made a big impact to the local culture. Close-knit and hard-working, these early Basque pioneers began to shape the identity of Antioquia. To this day, Paisas speak using a distinct Castilian-sounding 's', with Basque less commonplace. They also tend to be more conservative than other Colombians with a clear devotion to family life. But above all, Antioqueños have a formidable settler's drive – and a strong and determined will.

MEDELLÍN *Telephone code 4*

The city of Medellín used to be synonymous with Colombia's deadliest drug wars and was also a critical hub for guerrilla activity. However, the city's security situation has been transformed since the early 21st century leaving the next major battle the reparation of its tarnished reputation. Many of Colombia's largest drug cartels – once a powerful fixture in Medellín – have long since dismantled, with the city's left-wing warring factions significantly reduced in size and clout. The Colombian former president Álvaro Uribe is a home-grown Antioqueño and was widely praised for cracking down on crime via a series of measures. Medellín is now a city of considerable elegance with high-end restaurants, swanky bars, chi-chi boutiques, iconic street art and diverse festivals and shows. It's also a burgeoning business destination in South America and was named as the world's 'most innovative city' in 2013.

Today, it is hard to believe that stylish, cosmopolitan Medellín was once under the violent control of drug lord Pablo Escobar, Colombia's most deadly cocaine baron, who ruled his empire by savage means. In the 1980s, Escobar's leadership saw Medellín become one of the most murderous cities on the planet. After his death at the hands of the police in 1993, Medellín entered a new era. It now ranks amongst the safest metropolises for tourists in Latin America – although spates of crime and violence remain. Part of the city's development has seen a rapidly changing skyline with new museums, metro links, expansive plazas and new road systems in the pipeline. The city's 2.5 million inhabitants are fiercely proud of their innovative metropolis – and justifiably so. As the second most populated city in Colombia after Bogotá, Medellín is a leading industrial centre as well as a cultural hub of international repute. Heavy urban development is evident throughout the city with Medellín's construction of new skyscrapers outpacing all other major Colombian cities. Medellín is also home to 34 higher-education establishments and universities, including some of Colombia's most important public and private educational bodies such as the Universidad de Antioquia, Universidad EAFIT and Universidad de Medellín.

The 121st most populous urban area in the world, Medellín was founded in 1616 by Francisco Herrera y Campuzano but was first discovered by Spanish explorer Jerónimo Luis Téjelo in 1541. It was originally named San Lorenzo de Aburra though this was changed in 1675 to Villa de Nuestra Señora de la Candelaria de Medellín but has also been known as San Lorenzo de Aná, Valle de San Bartolomé, Aburrá de los Yamesíes, San Lorenzo de Aburrá, Villa de la Candelaria de Medellín and Medellín over the years. In the 1960s, Medellín's now infamous drug cartels turned the city into a violent battleground and the world's cocaine capital. Bloodthirsty gangs roamed the streets, extortionists preyed on residents who feared for the lives of their families and narcotics traffickers attacked the police. It was a bleak era for Medellín with seemingly little hope of change. However, change did come thanks to a city blessed with true Paisa grit and determination. A large-scale clean up transformed huge areas of Medellín in an urban regeneration project unprecedented in Colombia. Decaying hovels used by drug dealers, hookers and hit-men have been turned into swish new office complexes stylishly renovated in upmarket mews. Educational parks have been built all over the city. In 2005, a 2,800m² convention centre opened to much acclaim and now hosts a dozen international congresses each year, an enterprise that alone generates over US$100 million in investment and business deals. Medellín's fashion industry is one of the largest in Latin America; its medical sector a leader in organ transplants, AIDS and cancer research. The city's universities attract over 150,000 students each year. Pleasant open-air settings are adorned by the sculptures of Medellín-born artist Fernando Botero (page 56), replacing a seedy red-light district and tatty open-air street market.

That the city is now a living renaissance of peace and hope is due in no small part to the vision of former mayor of Medellín, Sergio Fajardo – a man considered instrumental in the rebirth of the city. His evangelical enthusiasm for spearheading what he calls 'From Fear to Hope' captured the hearts and minds of Colombia. On taking office, he pushed ahead with a programme of rehabilitating the homeless and continued to eradicate street crime during his mayoral tenure (2003–07). Fajardo also effectively closed down Medellín's most notorious no-go areas. Turning blight into beauty, leafy parks and statues have replaced dimly lit scrubby wastelands and rubbish-strewn alleyways – a regeneration symbolised by the city's iconic central mural 'Horizontes' in which two Paisas are depicted looking forward and beyond.

But Medellín remains a place with an underworld that engages in turf wars and petty street crime, which ranges from random acts of desperation to well-organised gangs of pickpockets and bag snatchers. The centre of the city remains one of the most notorious places for pickpockets, especially around San Antonio metro station and Plaza Botero. Prostitution and drug problems persist in the central parks of Periodista and Bolívar. In the poor Comunas surrounding the city, serious violence, extortion, displacements, child prostitution and drug trading exists. In fact, certain areas remain hubs for international drug trafficking and have had

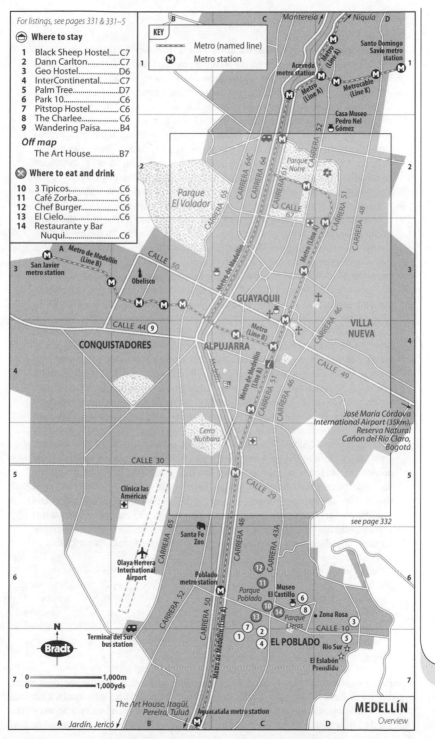

ESCOBAR TOURISM

To the chagrin of Colombia's tourist chiefs, the world-famous drug lord Pablo Escobar continues to prove a major tourist draw. In 2011, a dedicated tour package was launched for travellers keen to trace Pablo Escobar's life in Colombia. The 'Pablo Escobar is History' tour, arranged by operator **See Colombia Travel**, includes visits to the notorious drug lord's house, the home where he was killed in a shootout in 1993 and to the grave in the cemetery where he was buried. Created to provide a unique insight into the man and his life as the head of Medellín's drug cartel, tours centre on the Antioquia region. At his most powerful, Escobar was believed to have controlled up to 80% of the world's cocaine market. In 1989, *Forbes* magazine even listed him as the world's seventh richest man with a personal wealth of close to US$25 billion.

Escobar tourism has, unsurprisingly, caused controversy in a country that is keen to leave the darkest days of drug wars behind it. Some of the most popular 'Escobar sights' include his grave just outside Medellín and his birthplace in the village of Rionegro. In addition, there is **Hacienda Nápoles** (*www.haciendanapoles.com*), a lavish country estate in Puerto Triunfo, halfway between Medellín and Bogotá, where Escobar established a large private zoo of hundreds of exotic wildlife species. After his death, the Colombian government took over the running of the wildlife park and appropriated some of the land to disadvantaged families in the area. A running story since has been the whereabouts of Escobar's African hippos. In 2006, two were spotted near the Magdalena River in wetlands 100km from home. In 2014, reports of numerous sightings 250km away raised the question of what to do with the hippos. At the time of writing no decision had been made. Today the 1,500ha Hacienda Nápoles ranch is a theme-park attraction. Visitors enter under an archway on to which Pablo's private jet is embedded and drive into 'El Patron's' old stomping ground complete with lush green hills that were once roamed by lions, elephants and giraffe. The hippos are still there, wallowing in a muddy lake, with other animals that include zebras, ocelots, ostriches and buffalo. Other attractions at the park include Escobar's 500-seat bullring, which is now an African Museum, a garage full of the burnt remains of Escobar's classic car collection (they were torched by Escobar's rivals, the Cali cartel), and the airstrip used to deliver cocaine to the US. On a hilltop, overlooking the attractions, Escobar's once-opulent mansion is now a dilapidated ruin after it was ripped apart by looters. Inside is an anti-crime museum with newspaper cuttings of politicians and policemen murdered under Escobar's watch.

For tour information try:

www.medellincitytours.com
www.pabloescobartour.com.co
www.palenque-tours-colombia.com
www.seecolombia.travel

reported links with Mexico's Sinaloa Cartel. But while the drug trade continues, murder rates have plummeted after a ceasefire between the two main criminal underground organisations was agreed in 2013. The Medellín mafia, known as the Oficina de Envigado, and narco-paramilitary invaders, the Urabeños agreed a nonviolence pact after a meeting in a mansion in the town of San Jerónimo, just outside Medellín. Despite reports of cracks emerging in the agreement, statistics in June 2014 showed the lowest murder rate in Medellín since the days of Escobar and his drug cartel cronies.

CLIMATE Medellín's location 1,500m above sea level equips it with pleasantly warm year-round weather with an average annual temperature of 22°C and minimal variations. This agreeable 52-week spring-like climate has earned Medellín the nickname of 'La Ciudad de la Eterna Primavera' (City of the Eternal Spring), with weather that is more characteristic of a humid sub-tropical zone than that of a tropical region.

GETTING THERE AND AWAY

By air International flights arrive and depart via Medellín's José María Córdova International Airport (MDE) [off map, 332 D5] (*www.aeropuertojosemariacordova. com*) in the Rionegro suburb, 35km from the city, with daily flights to and from Miami, New York, Caracas, Quito, Panama City, Madrid, Lima and many other cities worldwide. Domestic flights are available too and are often inexpensive. Viva Colombia is a budget airline that services Barranquilla, Bogotá, Cali, Cartagena, Monteria, San Andrés and Santa Marta. Medellín's inner-city airport, Olaya Herrera Airport (EOH) [327 B6] (*www.aeropuertoolayaherrera.gov.co*), serves mainly regional flights, commuter, charter and light aircraft. It was once the city's only airport and ceased handling international flights once José María Córdova was built. Aerolínea de Antioquia (ADA) (✆ *361 4577*) operates flights to Acandi, Armenia, Apartado, Bahía Solano, Barranquilla, Bucaramanga, Cali, Cartagena, Caucasia, Corozal, Cúcuta, El Bagre, Manizales, Monteria, Nuqui, Pereira, Quibdo, Saravena and Tolu. Satena (✆ *605 2222*) offers frequent flights to over 20 destinations including Apartado, Bahía Solano, Bogotá and Quibdo.

By bus Medellín has two **bus** terminals, conveniently named Terminal del Norte [332 B1] and Terminal del Sur [327 B7]. The northern terminal serves all destinations to the north, east and southeast and is located 3km from the city centre (an 8,000COP taxi ride or 8-minute metro journey). The southern depot is 4km southwest of the city centre (8,000COP by taxi) and handles all traffic to the south and west of Medellín. Frequent services connect to most major cities, including Barranquilla (74,000COP, 15 hours), Santa Marta (74,000COP, 16½ hours), Bogotá (65,000COP, 9 hours), Cali (52,000COP, 9 hours) and Santa Fé de Antioquia (8,500COP, 3 hours). Shuttle buses run back and forth from José María Córdova Airport to the city centre every 30 minutes or so – the journey takes about 45 minutes and costs 8,600COP.

Small *busetas* operate throughout most of the metropolitan area until around 23.00 and are clearly marked. There is also a Metroplús network linking the metro line and many areas of the city. This bus service has an exclusive road route to allow faster transit and operates much like Bogotá's TransMilenio system. Tickets for both the Metro and the Metroplús can be purchased in every station. On-going work on the lines aims to extend services and alleviate traffic and pedestrian congestion. Avoid peak times as the queues become lengthy.

By taxi Taxis are also in plentiful supply Medellín-wide – a cross-town trip will set you back about 15,000COP with an airport run around 45,000COP. Taxis are metered and clearly show the exact fare, unlike Bogotá. The smartphone easytaxi app helps locate available taxis in the area and is a safe way to get a ride.

It may have cost the city over US$1.6 billion, but in societal terms the debt of the Metro de Medellín is worth its weight in gold. Sure, it will take at least 60 years to pay off, but it's a small price for a ground-breaking feat of modern engineering that has revolutionised the social fabric of a city. Before the Metro de Medellín and its cable cars, vast swathes of the city's outlying neighbourhoods were only accessible via an arduous trek across the mountains on foot. Today, these once isolated ramshackle suburbs may still cling desperately to the slopes but they are just a few minutes from Medellín's commercial centre – not a gruelling day-long hike. Not only has this improved employment prospects and fostered better social interaction; it has also opened up economic participation.

Medellín's complex urban transport system has transformed the city from a provincial town to a world-class commercial centre, crossing the metropolitan area from north to south and from centre to west. After the inaugural journey at 11.00 on 30 November 1995, the Metro of Medellín soon became a symbol of the city, heralding the unification of its remote, poorer and marginalised neighbourhoods with affluent areas. An absence of graffiti, chewing gum and litter in its pristine carriages is testament to how much the system is adored by the locals. That it is clean, efficient, safe and respected is a real source of Paisa pride. Genteel, patient, orderly queues are very much the norm.

At the time of its launch, the Metro had 25 stations – today it has more than 30. Two main lines run at ground level, while three cable-car lines, with over 90 cable cars, shift 20,000 people per day at a rate of ten per cart. The cable-car route climbs up a steep hillside and offers magnificent views frighteningly close to the rooftops. These communities are now fully employed – once an impossible dream due to their ostracised locations.

In every way, the Metro of Medellín continues to redefine the city, spawning dozens of plazas, galleries, restaurants, libraries, parks and recreational zones along its route, awarding new vision and fresh cultural dimensions to the communities in Colombia's burgeoning second city.

GETTING AROUND Medellín is divided into six metropolitan zones and these are subdivided into 16 communes that are in turn split into *barrios* and urban areas. The city contains more than 230 *barrios* (districts) and five *corregimientos* (subdivisions) and is divided north to south by the **Medellín River**. Medellín's six zones are defined as the Northwestern (Castilla, Doce de Octubre and Robledo); Northeastern (Aranjuez, Manrique, Popular and Santa Cruz); Southeastern (El Poblado); Southwestern (Guayabal and Belén); West Central (Laureles, La América and San Javier); and East Central (La Candelaria, Villa Hermosa and Buenos Aires). Streets are laid out according to the Cartesian grid system with *calles* running from east to west and vice versa, with numbers increasing south to north (except in upmarket El Poblado where numbers increase north to south). However, most locals refer to certain streets by colloquial names, not numbers – and this can be confusing. That aside, Medellín's compact city centre is easy to navigate around the Parque de Bolívar with almost all of its first-class nightlife and restaurants found along Calle 10.

Medellín is rightly proud of its public transportation system, a pioneering joined-up network of diesel buses, cable cars and an urban train referred to as the Metro de Medellín that connects the city with outlying areas. Line A departs from La Estrella to Niquía, while Line B goes from San Antonio to San Javíer. Line K comprises a cable car, locally known as Metrocable, and serves a sprawling, ramshackle neighbourhood on a mountainside that was once geographically remote. Line K begins on Acevedo station on Metro Line A, and continues uphill, ending in Santo Domingo Savio. Line J connects San Javíer with La Aurora. A later addition, Line L, operates from Santo Domingo Savio and continues further uphill to El Tambo in Arví Park near Guarne (serving tourists keen to travel the lake, again by cable car). An intermediate station has been added near Calle 67 Sur with the final station close to Calle 77 Sur. The **Metro de Medellín** (*www.metrodemedellin.gov.co*) operates from 05.00 to 23.00 Monday to Friday, and from 07.00 to 22.00 Sunday and public holidays, with a train every 3 minutes during peak hours and tickets costing 2,000COP.

Using public transport is highly preferable to attempting to navigate the roads of Medellín. Traffic is chaotic as the number of vehicles continues to exceed the capacity of local highways. Impassable gridlocks are common and even short journeys are arduous. Those mad enough to try it will find hire-car agencies throughout the city and within each airport.

TOURIST INFORMATION

i **La Alpujarra Administrative Center** [332 B5] Calle 44, No 52–165; ☏ 444 4144; ⊕ 07.30–17.30 Mon–Thu, closed 12.30–13.30, 07.30–16.30 Fri. There are information huts located around the city offering maps, advice & an information booklet. These are located at the North & South terminals, both airports, Plaza Major, Pueblito Paisa, Parque Arvi & Plaza Botero.

TOUR OPERATORS Dozens of local companies offer day trips around the city, from self-guided open-top buses to tailored itineraries for singles or groups. Medellín's excellent **Turibus** service (☏ 371 5054; *www.turibuscolombia.com*) journeys from sight to sight across the city. It picks up and drops off at numerous points from its main departure points at Parque Poblado and Plaza Botero for a day ticket (35,000COP) 09.00 to 17.00, Tuesday to Saturday. A more turnkey tour solution is provided by **Las Buseticas** (m 314 632 6453; *www.lasbuseticas.com*) – a professional outfit that offers a range of flexible itineraries to suit individual needs from 100,000COP, including an English-speaking guide and food throughout the day. **Palenque Tours** (☏ 312 8965; *www.palenque-tours-colombia.com; see also pages 396–7 & ad on page 322*), a socially and environmentally responsible tour operator based in Medellín, offers a great variety of personalised trips to the region, including city tours, eco hikes, and coffee tours. To enjoy Medellín's spectacular views from a bird's-eye vantage point, contact **Parapent Medellín** (☏ 427 2157; *www.parapentemedellin.com*) – flights are available for around 100,000COP including a video and photographs. A new gastronomy tour began in 2014 whereby tourists are taken around the city to sample true Paisa cuisine. The English-speaking guides explain the joys of street food, tropical fruits and the next generation of Latin flavours during this 2–3-hour tour. **La Mesa Food Tours** offers private and group tours for around 100,000COP (m 304 619 8657; e info@delamesa.com; www.delamesa.com).

⌂ WHERE TO STAY *See maps, page 327 and 332.*

Medellín has many places to stay and offers reasonably priced accommodation, from the shoestring hostels in El Centro to El Poblado's grand five-star hotels.

⌂ **The Charlee** (42 Rooms) Calle 9a, No 37–16, Parque Lleras; ☏ 444 4968; www. thecharlee.com. A fusion of modern art & lavish living has made the Charlee one of, if not *the*, most fashionable places to stay in Medellín. 4 types of rooms are adorned with Malaysian &

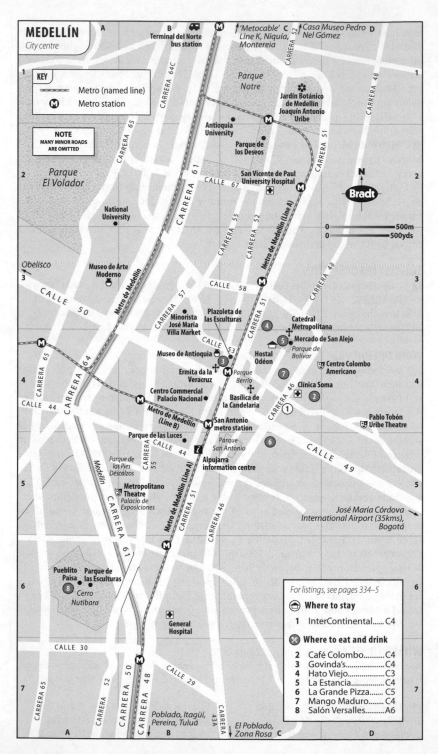

MEDELLÍN
City centre

KEY
- ┅┅┅ Metro (named line)
- Ⓜ Metro station

NOTE
MANY MINOR ROADS ARE OMITTED

Terminal del Norte bus station

'Metocable' Line K, Niquía, Montereia

Casa Museo Pedro Nel Gómez

Parque Notre

Jardín Botánico de Medellín Joaquín Antonio Uribe

Antioquia University

Parque de los Deseos

San Vicente de Paul University Hospital

Parque El Volador

National University

N

Bradt

Obelisco

Museo de Arte Moderno

Metro de Medellín

Metro de Medellín (Line A)

CALLE 50

CALLE 58

Minorista José María Villa Market

Plazoleta de las Esculturas

Catedral Metropolitana

Mercado de San Alejo

Parque de Bolívar

Museo de Antioquia

Hostal Odéon

Centro Colombo Americano

Ermita da la Veracruz

Parque Berrio

Basílica de la Candelaria

Clínica Soma

Centro Commercial Palacio Nacional

Metro de Medellín (Line B)

Parque de las Luces

San Antonio metro station

Parque San Antonio

Pablo Tobón Uribe Theatre

CALLE 49

Parque de los Pies Descalzos

Alpujarra information centre

Metropolitano Theatre
Palacio de Exposiciones

José María Córdova International Airport (35kms), Bogotá

Pueblito Paisa

Parque de las Esculturas

Cerro Nutibara

General Hospital

CALLE 30

CALLE 29

Poblado, Itagüí, Pereira, Tuluá

El Poblado, Zona Rosa

0 ———— 500m
0 ———— 500yds

For listings, see pages 334–5

🛏 **Where to stay**

1 InterContinental...... C4

🍽 **Where to eat and drink**

2 Café Colombo............ C4
3 Govinda's.................. C4
4 Hato Viejo................. C3
5 La Estancia................ C4
6 La Grande Pizza....... C5
7 Mango Maduro........ C4
8 Salón Versalles.......... A6

Balinese furniture, natural stone showers & 42" plasma TVs. Selected rooms have balcony jacuzzis or teppanyaki grills for a private chef to cook your desired dish. A 2-floor gym overlooks the palm-tree-laden Parque Lleras, while the rooftop bar, with a swimming pool centre, is a hugely popular party spot at w/ends. Recommended for couples rather than families. **$$$$**

🏠 **Hotel Dann Carlton** (200 rooms) Carrera 43A, No 7–50; ☏ 444 5151; www.danncarlton. com. Without doubt one of the most upmarket hotels in the city, the Hotel Dann Carlton offers every 5-star amenity you'd expect in a privileged location in El Poblado. Large, luxurious rooms (doubles, twins & triples) & suites are equipped with safety deposit boxes, TV with cable, phone, internet, iron, minibar & AC with on-site restaurants, bars, pool, spa, business centre & a gym just some of the many top-notch guest amenities. Its smaller, sister property, Hotel Belfort, can also be found in El Poblado, slightly less conveniently located, but a great choice for something equally decadent but quieter with less of a business feel. **$$$**

🏠 **Hotel InterContinental** (294 rooms, 38 suites) Calle 16, No 28–51; ☏ 319 4450; www. intercontinental.com. Located about 30mins' drive from the international airport, the InterContinental enjoys stunning views across the city & valley beyond & offers a range of sumptuous rooms & suites. Facilities include a business centre, tennis courts, 9-hole mini golf course, heated swimming pool, health club, restaurants, bar, cocktail lounge & laundry. The hotel is also connected to a commercial arcade with drugstore, travel agency, hair salon. Rooms come with a safe, TV (cable), en-suite bathroom & 24-hr room service. **$$$**

🏠 **Hotel Park 10** (55 rooms) Carrera 36B, No 11–12; ☏ 310 6060; e reservas@hotelpark10.com. co; www.hotelpark10.com.co. This rather showy & fancy 5-star place is geared up for midweek business executives – with prices to match. Travellers on a budget will find w/end discounts make this a more affordable option. That aside, the location of this postmodern hotel is nigh-on perfect with the Parque Lleras just a stone's throw away with its art galleries, restaurants, bars & boutiques. **$$$**

🏠 **The Art House** (5 rooms) Transversal 34, Sur 33–39, Apt 301 La Magnolia, Envigado; ☏ 270 5331; m 313 58 358 34/312 266 6712; e arthousemedellin@yahoo.com; www.

arthousemedellin.com. So named because of the owner's passion for art & photography, this budget boutique hotel comprises 5 large rooms, with a choice of private or shared bathroom. Choose from single, double or queen-sized beds (all come with quality sheets & pillows). Prices run from nightly rates to a weekly tariff with seasonal variances. Clean, stylish, comfy, modern & well run with a great little terrace chill-out area with mountain views & hammocks. Extras include communal kitchen, 24hr hot water, salsa dancing, Wi-Fi, 42" plasma TV with hundreds of new movies & weekly barbecues. Located in a nice suburban neighbourhood close to bars, restaurants & shops just a few mins from El Poblado, universities, the metro & numerous hiking trails. **$$–$$$**

🏠 **Black Sheep Hostel** (sleeps 80) Transversal 5A, No 45–133; ☏ 311 1589/1379; www. blacksheepmedellin.com. Well located in a quiet part of El Poblado, this Kiwi-owned hostel has won rave reviews since opening in 2005. Spacious rooms & communal areas offer plenty of places to hang out, with a garden, kitchen, barbecue, TV room (with cable), hammocks & internet for guest use. With El Poblado's nightlife just a 15min walk this is a good option for anyone keen to make the most of Medellín's excellent bars & restaurants. A metro station is also just 8mins down the road. Everyone speaks English here so it's also a boon for those with iffy Spanish & owner Kelvin is a congenial host. A choice of dorm rooms contains 4, 6, 8 or 10 beds with 11 double rooms available. En-suite bathrooms are equipped with hot power showers & extra-long European-style beds (great for those over 5ft 8in). On Sun the owners throw an all-you-can-eat barbecue party with sausages, steak, chicken, salad & potatoes. Kelvin's wife, Yadira, is the on-site Spanish teacher & has a reputation of excellence. **$**

🏠 **Wandering Paisa** (7 rooms) Calle 44a, No 68A–76; ☏ 436 6759; www.wanderingpaisahostel. com. Best hostel in Laureles with agreeable staff & welcoming atmosphere. There are 5 dorms with privacy dividers on each bed & 2 private rooms. On Tue salsa classes offer a taste of the surrounding party streets, Calle 70 & 33; Thu when foreigners & locals meet for a language exchange evening. **$**

🏠 **Geo Hostel** (8 rooms) Carrera 35, No 8A–58; ☏ 354 2945; www.geohostel.com. Good little option with 4 private & 4 dorm rooms that are clean well appointed & decorated with simple charm. B/fast, Wi-Fi & free use of the computers included. There is a laundry service & common area with a table-tennis table. **$**

🏠 **Palm Tree Hostal** (sleeps 30) Carrera 67, No 48D–63; 📞260 6142; e palmtreemedellín@ yahoo.com; www.palmtreemedellin.com. A highly popular backpacker option located in a residential area northwest of metro Estadio, the Palm Tree is just 3 blocks from the metro that connects to any part of the city. Painted bright orange, the building is just a few metres from a large Exito supermarket, & offers a collection of private rooms & dorm beds. Communal facilities include hot showers, laundry service, bar, book exchange, barbecue, TV room (cable), DVD movies, internet & free all-day coffee. There is also a fully equipped kitchen for guest

use & a chill-out lounge with hammocks. B/fast of eggs, yoghurt & toast included. Discounts are available for long-term stays. **$**

🏠 **Pitstop Hostel** (22 rooms) Carrera 43e, No 5–110, Patio Bonito; 📞352 1176, m 314 657 6390; e admin@pitstophostel.com; www. pitstophostel.com. With its beautiful garden strewn with hammocks, a swimming pool & poolside bar, pool table & big-screen TV, basketball court & small gym, this Irish-owned hostel prides itself on having 'better facilities than any other hostel in South America'. Choose from a range of rooms (ask to see a couple as they vary) with dorm accommodation, singles, doubles & family rooms. Events run from fancy dress parties to poker nights & generally centre on a well-stocked bar. **$**

✕ **WHERE TO EAT AND DRINK** *See maps, pages 327 and 332.*

Medellín has a burgeoning international-cuisine scene entwined with traditional food joints strewn across the city. Standards are high and prices low with plenty of inexpensive Paisa dishes found in the city centre. For more upmarket dining options head to El Poblado and Envigado where you'll find every type of international cuisine, from sushi and soul food to tapas and maize. The best way to discover the many excellent eating places in El Poblado is to stroll around the Zona Rosa perusing menus and sussing them out. Numerous restaurants offer all manner of dining options, from Brazilian steakhouses and Japanese noodles to Tex-Mex and fish and chips, almost all with outside seating. There's also a really nice open-fronted Juan Valdez coffee shop in Parque Lleras, just outside El Poblado. Most of Medellín's fast-food outlets are clustered around the streets that make up El Hueco. Expect to find snack bars, fried-chicken joints, diners, burger vendors and pizza places in abundance. Like most of Colombia, vegetarians aren't particularly well catered for, although there are a few suitable restaurants hidden away.

Central Medellín

✕ **Café Colombo** Carrera 45, No 53–24; 📞513 4444; www.colomboworld.com; ⏰ lunch & dinner Mon–Sat. You'll be distracted by the stunning views from this stylish 10th-floor restaurant located in the Centro Colombo Americano. Overlook the city & mountains in elegant contemporary-modern surroundings where the meals are as light & tasty as the décor. **$$–$$$**

✕ **Restaurante Hato Viejo** Carrera 47, No 52–17; 📞231 1108; ⏰ lunch & dinner. For great local meat dishes & traditional favourites this place is difficult to beat. Expect a menu of big-portion beef & pork dishes typically served with beans & corn tortilla, including the gut-busting Antioquian speciality Bandeja Paisa. **$$**

✕ **Salón Versalles** Pasaje Junín, No 53–39;

📞251 7416; www.versallesmedellin.com; ⏰ noon for lunch until early evening. Ask anyone about the Argentine-owned eatery Salón Versalles & its charismatic owner Leonardo Nieto & they're sure to mention the delicious *empanadas* they serve. Tables are in demand all day long – but especially at lunchtime when local office workers descend in their droves. Not cheap, but better value for snacks & desserts. **$$**

✕ **La Estancia** Parque Bolívar; ⏰ early until late. This cavernous diner packs in the locals with a simple lunch at shoestring prices. Don't expect anything fancy, but La Estancia remains unrivalled on the basis of cost – & is a good place to sit & watch city life unfold. **$**

✕ **Mango Maduro** Calle 54, No 47–5; 📞512 3671; ⏰ lunchtime until 15.00 Mon–Sat. Travellers wax lyrical about this wonderful little place that must be one of Medellín's best-kept gastronomic secrets. Funky, bohemian-style décor welcomes diners to 9 small tables at lunchtimes only for a single set menu. Expect excellent food that offers Colombian classics with a twist at incredibly low prices. Be prepared to scour the streets for this place as it's an inconspicuous above-street diner delightfully tucked away. Arrive early to grab a seat along with the academics, poets & artists who favour this great find. $

✗ **Restaurante Govinda's** Calle 51, No 52–17; ✆ 512 9481; ☺ lunchtime Mon–Sat. This cheery little upstairs restaurant is run by Medellín's friendly Hare Krishnas who serve excellent vegetarian fare. Great service. $

✗ **La Grande Pizza** Carrera 42, No 50a–34; ✆ 239 2621; ☺ noon–22.00 Tue–Sat. A popular pizza joint serving up the best calzones in town. Simple but tasty dishes at bargain prices. The only downside is they don't sell beer. $

El Poblado

✗ **El Cielo** Carrera 40, No 10A–22; ✆ 268 3002; www.elcielococinacreativa.com. Medellín's famed molecular gastronomy restaurant offers more than just great food. Dishes are separated into 'moments' & are all created by head chef Juan Manuel Barrientos & his team of designers in a food lab. Diners choose from either 10 or 15 'moments'. Each dish is created from Colombian ingredients & has a lifespan of 3 months, after which it is replaced by a new, vastly different dish. Expect to dine for 2–3hrs. $$$

✗ **3 Tipicos** Carrera 34, No 7–05, ✆ 312 3229; www.3tipicos.com. Located 4 streets up from Parque Lleras this open-sided restaurant may be quite expensive for local Colombian cuisine but the quality is unrivalled. Each dish is made using high-quality ingredients & the fruit juices are big & delicious. For a taste of Bogotá try the *ajiaco* – the best in the city. $$–$$$

✗ **Café Zorba** Calle 8, No 42–33; ✆ 580 4600; www.cafezorba.com.co. Vegetarian restaurant that has quickly become the best pizza spot in the city. Set in a seductive orchard, diners enjoy the intimate atmosphere with reasonably priced & delicious pizzas. The coconut milk is a particular delight as is the sangria & hummus starter. Live music is on Thu nights with a cover charge of 5,000COP. $$

✗ **Chef Burger** Calle 11A, No 42–05; ✆ 448 2378. It's hard to argue with their claim of serving 'the best burgers in town'. Several new restaurants continue to pop up around the city but the original close to Parque Poblado remains the most popular. Reasonably priced burgers range from a list of specials to regular cheeseburgers. Soft drinks are refillable & live music often entertains diners at the w/end. $$

✗ **Resturante y Bar Nuqui** Carrera 42, No 10–49; ✆ 312 3749. Located a block from Parque Poblado, this seafood restaurant is renowned for its top-quality menu of lobster, shrimp & squid dishes. The grilled *mero* & *langoustine* soup is also particularly tasty. Expect turquoise walls, red paintwork & a nautical theme. $$

NIGHTLIFE Cocktail-lovers and bar-hoppers are spoilt for choice in Medellín's **El Poblado** district [327 C7] where practically every place is alive with Martini shakers, slammers and flaming sambuca. Start at **Parque Lleras** [327 C6] and follow the crowds from beer joints and shot bars to neon-lit champagne lounges – there is no shortage of options with over 50 different watering holes to choose from in this up-tempo **Zona Rosa** [327 D6]. The El Rojo and Basilica are popular restaurants with people-watchers as they are positioned in a superb corner plot while Thaico is one of many bars offering regular 3–1 cocktails. Bogotá Beer Company is one of the few places offering beer on tap and is located a few streets up from the park near other chic hangouts such as El Social. When the lightweights head home those wanting to carry on the party head to the following clubs: Calle 9, an indie-house club open until 04.00; Blue, a popular rock bar reminiscent of a British university club; or El Deck, which plays deep house/techno and often hosts well-known DJs. If Parque Lleras is chic, fashionable and the trendy night spot, then **Parque Poblado** [327 C6] is its alternative sibling. Here punks and the indie crowd mix in a more down-to-earth manner. Tinto Tinteros overlooks the park and hosts DJs from overseas, open-mike nights and salsa evenings. Opposite are bars spilling into the park and a burgeoning party street where you can get absurdly cheap beer and watch sports at the likes of Costillas de Pedro.

Parque Lleras and Parque Poblado have crowds most nights of the week, although Thursday, Friday and Saturday are when it's standing room only. Bars close at around 03.00 but party goers with stamina congregate around the park until dawn to drink, smoke and chat the night away. Cigarettes, alcohol and street food can be bought from an army of vendors until the last person heads home. Close by is **Río Sur** [327 D7], a slightly more affluent and glamorous hot spot at the weekend. This slim mall hosts many high-end bars and is located on the so-called 'millionaire mile' on Avenida Poblado. Here Delaire Sky Lounge serves up delicious cocktails along with a sublime view of the city. Lower down is Sinko, another high-end bar with an extensive cocktail menu and for later on in the night, check out Sixttina nightclub. One of the last places to close in the city is Palmahia. Often host to huge international DJs, this multi-club venue is about a 10,000COP taxi ride from Parque Lleras and has a great salsa club next to it. Medellín boasts countless salsa bars and clubs to get intimate with a partner, and **El Eslabón Prendido** [327 D7] is among the very best. Every Tuesday night this small bar, located in the heart of downtown, bursts with locals and tourists dancing to a live band, often spilling out on to the street (taking a taxi is a must with safety in mind). There is an entrance fee of 6,000COP and it's better to go early for a seat or a section of wall to lean against. In Laureles, El Tibiri, a basement bar on Calle 70 close to the stadium, is a traditional salsa hangout with incredible dancers working up an even more incredible sweat. It's rather challenging to find so ask near the petrol station on Calle 70. Other salsa clubs are dotted around Calle 70 and its neighbour Calle 33, and offer a more traditional Colombian night out.

One of the major developments in the electro, dance music scene has been the emergence of Breakfest. Started in 2013, at a small *finca* outside of the city, this music festival has grown into a European-style event with artists such as Franz Ferdinand, Felix da Housecat and Hot Chip wowing crowds. Several events were held in Club Rodeo country club before it was relocated to Parque Norte opposite the Botanical Gardens. Although there is no set date for events they are usually held every three months so keep an eye on the Facebook page for news (*www.facebook. com/breakfestco?fref=ts*). Tickets usually cost around 50,000COP although prices on the gate will be higher.

ENTERTAINMENT Medellín plays host to numerous cultural shows, exhibitions, concerts, events and film festivals throughout the year in venues citywide. For a full list of what's on, pick up a Thursday edition of the daily *El Colombiano* newspaper (*www. elcolombiano.com*) – it includes a special weekend entertainment supplement and is Medellín's definitive listing. Monthly local entertainment magazine *Opción Hoy* varies in the quality of its content but is still worth a flick through – it's sold in newsagents throughout the city at 3,700COP. One of the best events is **Las Alumbrados** (mid-December–mid-January) – a must-see for anyone lucky enough to find themselves in the city over the festive period. Medellín's breathtaking Christmas lights are a real highlight and run all along the east side of the Río Medellín. The sheer quantity, size and vibrancy of the lights is simply astonishing. Take the metro to Industriales, and stroll down La Playa Avenue for countless varieties of glowing structures, wheels and decorative lights extending as far as the eye can see, interspersed with food and drink stalls aplenty. A tradition for over 50 years, each year sees Las Alumbrados more incredible than the last, bringing the city to light and generating over a thousand jobs for its residents. Don't forget to look up to Cerro Nutibara to see Pueblo Paisa illuminated against the hill, and be prepared for crowds.

Medellín's vibrant arts scene offers everything from black comedy and drama to experimental art-house cinema. A dozen or more theatres stage regular performances including alternative theatre at the **Teatro Matacandelas** (✆ *215 1010; www.matacandelas.com*), midstream plays at the **Teatro Pablo Tobón Uribe** [332 D4] (✆ *239 7500*), and musicals at the Teatro Metropolitano [332 B5] (✆ *232 4597*), home to Medellín's fine philharmonic orchestra. More than 20 commercial cinemas are mainly multiplexes although a handful of *cimematecas* offer more than just the usual blockbuster fare. These include the newly extended **Museo de Arte Moderno de Medellín** (Medellín Modern Art Museum) [332 A3] (✆ *230 2622*), the **Museo de Antioquia** (Antioquia Museum) [332 B4] (✆ *251 3636; www.museodeantioquia.*

FIRST FOR FASHION

As the home of Colombia's fashion industry Medellín is blessed with lots of home-grown creative talent, much of it nurtured in the city's prestigious Colegiatura Colombiana de Diseño. Wholesale clothing distributors, dress designers and bespoke fashion boutiques all have their base here in a sector that prides itself on being cheap and good in quality with manufacturing 100% sweatshop-free. ColombiaModa, Medellín's international fashion show, forms the heart of Fashion Week in the city in a dazzling star-studded display of glitz and glamour. Clothing buyers, style journalists, film crews and catwalk queens descend on Medellín from all over the planet to witness Colombia's latest fashion collections – a creative pool that is arguably South America's finest.

Designer Johanna Logreira is a bright example of Medellín's gifted fashion leaders, an independent designer who has been instrumental in showcasing individual talent. In 2005, she joined forces with others involved in fashion and textiles, forming a collective that soon had the backing of Medellín's mayor and ColombiaModa. They established a fashion district on Vía Primavera (*www.viaprimavera.com*), rejuvenating the streets with street lights, flowers and seating areas. Today, the collective has over 30 members, from boutique owners and couture specialists to fashion cafés and jewellery designers in a trendy, stylish urban space that attracts a growing number of style tourists. The group remains committed to being 100% Colombian-owned, using local materials and employing local people. Without any of the usual bitchy envy-based mistrust of fashionistas, the collective promotes a true sharing of talent, skills, ideas and resources. Each business is involved in education in the poor *comunas* including co-founder Nuria Canellas, who teaches sewing to women by recycling their own material. Nuria's store now lies on Carrera 37 after her first one was destroyed when a car bomb exploded in Parque Lleras in 2001 – a stark reminder of the city's troubled history. The success of the clothing scheme has been replicated in the streets leading up from the park and stores now cover three parallel streets. Another focus of the Vía Primavera fashion district is making sophisticated clothing styles available to the masses. In Medellín, women are extremely fashion-conscious but tend to stick to a uniform look, favouring tight jeans, bare midriff, high heels and a clingy top – regardless of age, shape or social group. By producing a broader range of clothing without astronomical price tags, Vía Primavera has widened Medellín's fashion scope at street level. Consumers have greater choice and are proud to buy a 100% Colombian item from a community-led business that is dedicated to giving something back.

co), and the **Centro Colombo Americano** [332 C4] – all of which screen foreign-language films and shy away from the Hollywood norm.

SHOPPING Medellín is one of Colombia's finest retail hubs with dozens of gleaming shopping centres, malls and markets selling all manner of items, from coffee and bric-a-brac to designer brands. Traditional flower markets throw their doors open at dawn while vendors start to ply their wares on the city's street corners well before 06.00. Medellín is also the nation's prime textile production centre and host of numerous fashion and clothing exhibitions, including the world-renowned **ColombiaModa** (*www.colombiamoda.com*) – a glittering three-day showcase event that features catwalk shows, retail booths and 470 exhibitors and is the most important annual fashion fixture in South America. It also has a dedicated fashion district, an impressive succession of colourful boutiques, dressmakers, designers and unique clothing stores (see box, page 337).

Medellín's prime shopping centres include the **Centro Commercial Palacio Nacional** [332 B4] (✆ *381 8144*) on the corner of Carrera 52 and Calle 48 in a pedestrianised bargain retail district nicknamed El Hueco (The Hole) by the locals. Here a plethora of stalls, independent stores, street sellers and shopping malls sell goods at shoestring prices. Literally you can find anything, and if not, tell a street vendor and they will run off and locate whatever you want. At the **Mercado de San Alejo** [332 C4] on the Parque de Bolívar a collection of handicraft stalls sell plenty of cut-price bags, paintings and jewellery on the first Sunday of the month. The vast covered daily market at the **Mercado Minorista José María Villa** [332 B3] on Carrera 57 and Calle 55 isn't for the faint-hearted with more than 2,500 vendors selling food, knick-knacks and clothing. Medellín is also the birthplace of one of Colombia's biggest supermarket chains, **Exito** (*www.exito.com*) – a retail institution with 26 outlets in the city alone. Once a small independent thrift store, the past few decades have seen Exito transformed into the symbol of Medellín's penchant for shopping. Look out for the bland brick and yellow buildings across the city with a rather garish sign. For the fastidious shopper, **Carulla**, also owned by the Exito group, offers more expensive, luxury goods like freshly watered glistening fruit.

OTHER PRACTICALITIES Medellín is a well-equipped big city that offers every conceivable convenience. Expect to find dozens of internet cafés in the streets that lead from the Parque de Bolívar [332 C4] (2,500COP per hour) as well as numerous pharmacies, banks (with ATMs), money changers, shoe-repair shops, payphones and luggage retailers. If you want internet access, **Colombo Americano** [332 C4] has a free Wi-Fi space on the second floor and a library with English books, newspapers and magazines on the first floor, located on Carrera 45. Elsewhere in 'El Centro' – the main artery at the heart of Medellín – there are dozens of clinics and drugstores. José María Córdova International Airport is well equipped with ATMs, cafés and international payphones and also has a newsagent that stocks a limited range of English-language magazines. For **medical attention** contact the city's ambulance service (✆ *123/235 3001*) or head to the **Clínica las Américas** [327 B5] (✆ *342 7070/341 2946*) and **Clínica Soma** [332 C4] (✆ *576 8400*) – both are open 24 hours.

SAFETY Transformed from murder capital to corporate boom town, Medellín has been hailed as a rare urban success story for neo-conservatism in South America. However, although the city is a much, much safer city than it was in the early 21st century, visitors should still exercise caution when walking after dark. Although the police have a presence in every neighbourhood, don't be tempted to venture into Medellín's poorer neighbourhoods without a local who knows the area well and can assure your safety. Care should also be taken in the crowded confines of the city's smaller backstreet parks, especially Parque Periodista and Parque Bolívar in the centre. The lively, popular districts of Poblado and Laureles are both safe and well patrolled, day and night, though taking a taxi together is recommended – the easytaxi app is a safe way to book a taxi. Use an ATM in a safe part of town and apply common sense – never flaunt cash and keep wallets out of sight. Single men should also be aware that Medellín has a large number of so-called *prepagos* (meaning pre-paids), generally stunningly beautiful middle-class girls who are often university students or professional models. *Prepagos* work secretly as prostitutes to fund their lavish 'it girl' lifestyles and commonly target foreigners in a blatant gringo-hunt – much to the annoyance of their regular punters, many of whom are of dubious, but powerful, pedigree.

WHAT TO SEE AND DO It is impossible to list everything worth seeing in Medellín. The city is fast evolving, thanks to multi-million-dollar investment, and change continues at a staggering pace. Medellín's parks are a particular highlight, with renovations occurring almost monthly – check out the new parks in Itagui and Envigado where many of the city's older generations congregate. Visitors with limited time will find the city easy to navigate with much of Medellín's attractions centred on the middle of town.

El Poblado (The Village) [327 C7] Occupying the southeastern corner of Medellín, on the cusp of a steep valley, the über-swish area of El Poblado is separated from Medellín's southwest by the river and stretches to Envigado (south), Santa Elena (east) and La Candelaria (north). Spanning over 143,258ha, this swanky neighbourhood is sometimes known as Las Manzanas de Oro (The Golden Apples) because it represents the fruits of the second-largest industrial and commercial Colombian economy; El Poblado marks the site of Medellín's founding in 1616. One particularly upmarket stretch of grand properties has been given the nickname Milla de Oro (Golden Mile) – property prices here are some of the highest in Colombia. Rather conveniently, El Poblado is also home to Medellín's financial centre so is also the city's wheeler-deal money hub. During the early 20th century, the district had become *the* place in which cash-rich families would build a country retreat. Once a road was built connecting Medellín with El Poblado, land prices soared as it ceased to be a rural outpost and became a part of the city.

A predominantly young neighbourhood, El Poblado falls almost entirely into the highest social stratum. A trio of metro stations – El Poblado, Aguacatala and Ayurá – serve this upwardly mobile community which is also served by Medellín's finest private schools, colleges and universities. Luxurious high-end shopping malls (Oviedo and El Tesoro) rub shoulders with gastronomic eateries, exclusive fashion boutiques and well-cared-for green space. The Parque Lineal La Presidenta spans over 20,000m² and links to Parque Lleras (the city's *zona rosa*) between calles 9–10 and carreras 36–42 – the setting for weekend partying on a grand scale. It contains a trio of bridges, streams and recreation and tranquil zones set amongst almost 50 species of trees.

El Poblado is also home to the medieval-style turreted **Museo El Castillo** (Castle Museum) [327 C6] (⊕ *09.00–11.00 & 14.00–17.00 Mon–Fri, 09.00–11.00*

Sat; admission 10,000COP). Built in 1930 and set in French-style gardens, the Nel Rodriguez-designed building was once a former private home. Today, as a museum, it is notable for its collection of European fine art and antiquities. Industrialist Diego Echavarría Misas bought the castle for his family, donating it to 'the people' in 1971. Those wishing for a romantic afternoon lunch can choose from one of its picnic packages and sip on champagne while gazing over the city skyline.

Central Medellín City planners have prohibited new construction in central Medellín that doesn't include public art within its blueprint and the result is a glorious outdoor gallery. At the very core of Medellín's centre are the much-photographed giant, rounded sculptures of Medellín's very own Fernando Botero (page 56), a prolific artist whose work is synonymous with the regeneration of the city. More than 100 sculptures have been donated to his home town, the most famous of which can be seen (and are also frequently touched) at the **Plazoleta de las Esculturas** (Little Sculpture Plaza) [332 C4]. More of Botero's work is displayed at the **Museo de Antioquia** (Antioquia Museum) [332 B4] in the resplendent **Palacio Municipal** (Municpal Palace) (*Carrera 52; No 52–43;* ✎ *251 3636; www.museodeantioquia. co;* ◷ *10.00–17.00 Mon–Sat, 10.00–16.30 Sun; admission 10,000COP*), where alongside Botero's fine donations are some magnificent pre-Columbian, colonial and contemporary works. His massive bronze of woman's torso, *La Gorda*, is sited outside the Banco de Berrío while in the Parque San Antonio three further pieces include the *Bird of Peace* (*Pájaro de Paz*); today, somewhat ironically, this symbolic piece is terribly scarred by a guerrilla bomb.

More fine monuments represent the work of Rodrigo Arenas Betancur, who wowed Colombia with numerous architectural/artistic triumphs until his death in 1995. In 1974, he unveiled the ultra-impressive *Monumento a la Vida* (*Monument to Life*) – a 14m-high twisted, semi-spiral structure in Centro Suramericana. His dramatic *Monumento a la Raza* (*Monument to the Race*) depicts the evolution of Antioquia at the Centro Aministravo la Alpujarra in a powerful, robust sculpture that represents the forces of good and evil.

Much of the **Parque Berrío** (Berrio Park) [332 C4] is dominated by the **Basílica de la Candelaria** (Candelaria Basilica) [332 C4], a structure that dates back to the early 1770s and was Medellín's cathedral from 1868 to 1931. The most important of the city's religious buildings, the basilica contains some beautiful, vivid interior decoration including an ornate ceiling with stunning recessed panels. Widely regarded as Medellín's oldest church, the **Ermita de la Veracruz** [332 B4] dates back to 1682 when the first brick was laid. Handsome and stone-built, it is located on the corner of Calle 51 and Carrera 52 and has a simple whitewashed interior adorned with wooden carvings and splashes of gold. However, it is the **Catedral Metropolitana** (Metropolitan Cathedral) [332 C4] overlooking the Parque de Bolívar that can claim to be Medellín's largest place of worship, having been constructed using more than 1.2 million bricks – as the locals are very keen to point out. A cavernous interior is adorned with paintings by Gregorio Vásquez de Arce y Ceballos while huge stained-glass windows glow in myriad vibrant hues. A number of architects played a part in creating this fine cathedral and this is reflected in an interesting hybrid of influences that contribute to a rather pleasing neo-Romanesque design.

Another not-to-be-missed sight is the ultra-modern **Parque de las Luces** (Park of Lights) [332 B5], a vast rectangular concrete plaza dotted pin-cushion-style with 300 needle-thin pillars that resembles a giant birthday cake when illuminated with white lights at night. At the nearby Zen-themed **Parque de los Pies Descalzos** (Barefoot

Park) [332 A6] visitors are encouraged to kick off their shoes to walk through a bamboo forest before dipping their toes in cascading water fountains and freshwater pools. Free concerts are often held here, especially during the festive season.

Southern Medellín Almost every visitor to the city feels compelled to visit **Pueblito Paisa** (Paisa Village) [332 A6], a rather well-constructed mock-up of a typical traditional Antioquian settlement in miniature form. Despite being aimed squarely at the tourist dollar, it is worth a trip as there is something rather charming about the little faux church, town plaza and mayoral residence atop Cerro Nutibara. At Christmas the whole place is illuminated by fairy lights and lanterns – a truly beautiful sight. Views from the summit of the 80m-tall hill are also magnificent. Pueblito Paisa is 2km southwest of the city centre and can be easily reached by taxi for 6,000COP – get the driver to drop you at the bottom of the slope to enjoy a short walk up a paved path to the top where a couple of nice bars and a restaurant serve good, hearty Paisa meals.

For some particularly fine abstract sculpture head to the **Parque de las Esculturas** (Sculpture Park) [332 A6] – it is also on the slopes of Cerro Nutibara and contains works by a whole host of South American artists, including Carlos Cruz Díez and Edgar Negret.

The grandiose **Museo El Castillo** (Castle Museum) [327 C6] (❀ 266 0900; ⏱ 09.00–17.00 Mon–Fri, closed noon–14.00, 09.00–17.00 Sat/Sun; admission 8,000COP) was once the home of a landowning family who spared no expense in creating a mock-Gothic castle fit for a king. Today this 1930s building remains a monument to that era and is open for guided tours and exhibitions. Each room is laid out with original furniture and furnishings and contains the family's belongings and personal effects. The museum is located in El Poblado on Carrera 9 about 5km south of the city centre – a taxi will cost around 10,000COP.

Northern Medellín A visit to the city's truly gorgeous **Jardín Botánico del Medellín Joaquín Antonio Uribe** (Joaquín Antonio Uribe Botanical Garden) [332 C1] (*Carrera 52; www.botanicomedellin.org;* ⏱ 09.00–17.00 daily) is highly recommended. Since opening in 1978, the garden has grown in size and stature and is now a wonderfully mature green space in which many urbanites choose to while away the hours. Botanists have collected more than 600 tree and plant species – including numerous orchids – and the gardens boast a thoughtful, contemporary layout that uses colour and textures to dramatic effect. At the weekends, choral and orchestral concerts are often staged in a small open-air auditorium to appreciative crowds sipping espressos at wrought-iron tables and chairs. Other attractions include a lovely lake, a herbarium and Orquideorama that houses a sizeable orchid display in March and April. It also hosts free yoga session every Sunday at 10.00. Expert instructors spilt everyone, often over 100 people, into two groups depending on the level.

Opposite the botanical gardens is the über-trendy **Parque de los Deseos** [332 C2], a concrete complex constructed along minimalist lines that is a popular place for many of Medellín's students to hang out. Sleek cafés/diners open out on to modern leafy garden areas designed to inspire hopes and dreams. There is also a planetarium, library, internet café and science building. The best time to visit is definitely late Sunday afternoon when hordes of people gather for the weekly movie beamed on to the planetarium. Hunger and thirst can be quelled by visiting the wandering street vendors.

Housed in the former home of Medellín's beloved Pedro Nel Gómez (1899– 1984), the **Casa Museo Pedro Nel Gómez** [327 D2] (❀ 233 2633; ⏱ 09.00–17.00

Mon–Sat; closed Sun) on Carrera 51B is wholly dedicated to the life and works of this most prolific artist. The highlight of the museum is a 2,000-piece collection of his murals, drawings, watercolours and sculptures. Find it 3km north of the city centre (6,000COP by taxi).

Festivals and events Paisas love to party and enjoy nothing more than dressing up to the nines to make merry all night long. Joining in this revelry is a rewarding way to get to Medellín's heart – there are numerous festivals ranging from artisan fairs to the world-famous flower festival. Some of the most important events include the following.

La Feria de las Flores (early August) The Festival of the Flowers is a key event in the Antioquian calendar, filling Medellín's streets with brightly coloured blooms and horse-drawn floral displays. The celebration has taken place every year since 1957 and culminates in a spectacular 500-strong procession of flower-bearing *campesinos* from the mountains in the Desfile de Silleteros (flower carriers' parade). The *silletas* (wooden frames laden with intricately woven flowers) are created in surrounding villages and are brought down on the backs of the *campesinos*, symbolising the end of slavery.

Festival de Poesia de Medellín (July; *www.festivaldepoesiademedellin.org*) This headline-grabbing poetry festival was the recipient of the 2006 Right Livelihood Award. In 2013, it attracted 60 poets from 45 countries from all continents during the ten-day event. The event is sponsored by the Municipality of Medellín and has financial support from prestigious institutions worldwide, and is dedicated to the pursuit of peace.

Parade of Myths and Legends (December) This exceptional fairy-lit event occurs every year on 7 or 8 December and features a pre-Christmas parade on deeply rooted traditional themes.

Feria Taurina de la Macarena (January/February) This event sees the bullring packed to capacity with 15,000 cheering fans as the Plaza de Toros La Macarena plays host to one of the most important bullfighting fairs in Colombia. A retractable rooftop ensures a rainproof event in this Moorish-style building on Autopista Sue on the corner of Calle 44. Expect large crowds, ticket touts and a riotous carnival atmosphere.

MedeJazz (September; *www.festivalmedejazz.com*) This week-long festival attracts jazz and salsa musicians from all over the world. The large auditoriums at Plaza Major and Teatro Metropolitano host the event where tables and chairs become surplus to requirements as dancing-fever envelops the entire crowd.

AROUND MEDELLÍN

The lush, mountainous areas to the southeast of Medellín seem to have been untouched by the modern world. Sleepy Paisa villages edge winding lanes that climb the slopes in the Circuito de Oriente where the rain-nourished Cordillera Central is rich with vegetation and sparkling streams. Most visitors embarking on a day trip to the region opt for a standard one-day itinerary that is offered by numerous local tour companies. Costs average 100,000COP per person – an excellent price for the opportunity to witness some truly memorable Antioquian scenery and towns. Those keen to go it alone can journey by bus from Medellín to connect to the following key day-trip attractions.

MARINILLA (*Telephone code 4*) This beautifully preserved city boasts some stunning Antioquian architecture, much of it dating back to the early 18th century. One of the oldest towns in the region, Marinilla is 45km from the centre of Medellín – a 1-hour journey by bus. Expect pretty whitewashed churches, leafy plazas and a little weekday market. A decent collection of local restaurants and budget hotels are clustered around the main square.

SAN CRISTÓBAL If you fancy getting away from the busy centre of Medellín, San Cristóbal makes for a great short half-day trip. Located in the west-central area of outer Medellín, this charming little village is known for its floriculture. There's a pretty church, plenty of places to stop for a snack and chat to locals, or watch *caballeros* on horseback through the streets.

Getting there is as much a part of the trip as San Cristóbal itself. Take the metro to San Javíer and then go up to La Aurora by cable car – a peaceful and fascinating trip up the mountainside, with wonderful views of the city. You will also see beneath you the densely populated poorer suburbs of Medellín, which sprawl out from the centre. Once you reach La Aurora, you can walk to San Cristóbal in around 40 minutes, or take a bus.

GUATAPÉ AND LA PIEDRA DEL PEÑOL Visiting Guatapé should be an essential part of any traveller's trip to Antioquia, and certainly to Medellín. Home to a stunning lake and one of the most charming, typical Antioquian *pueblos* in the region, it is an utterly unique place which really shouldn't be missed. Very popular with Colombian tourists, Guatapé is also attracting more and more backpackers. Its wonder and charm can come as a delightful surprise.

La Piedra del Peñol (*admission 10,000COP*) Meaning literally 'the stone' and commonly referred to as 'El Peñol', this 200m blackened-with-moss monolith rises from the banks of the lake, soaring 740 steps from the Emblase de Peñol. Those with plenty of stamina will find the climb rewards the effort with an astonishing and breathtakingly unusual view over the masses of islets, waterways and lakes of this manmade archipelago – a vast panoramic view stretching as far as the eye can see.

Guatapé (*Telephone code 4*) Whilst the main reason for visiting the area is El Peñol, it would be a crime to head back to Medellín without a stop in Guatapé itself. Walking around the village at times feels as though you are in a living museum. Brightly coloured, decorative houses with hanging baskets line the narrow streets and the beautiful *zólcalos* (the sculpted, painted designs of the lower parts of the walls) are in essence public works of art, with each house proudly displaying its own unique motif depicting the stories and culture of the region. Calle de los Recuerdos is the best street to see them. Many of the houses were repainted as part of Colombia's bicentennial celebrations in 2010, so are fresher than ever; you will stand in wonder at the charm of the detail. There is also a pretty church – Iglesia de Nuestra Señora del Carmen – on the main square, outside which you'll find the cheerful mini *chivas* parked up awaiting business.

Once in Guatapé try **La Fogata** for a great place to eat – the only restaurant with a terrace and a great view of the waterfront. Good value too, with typical

Paisa *almuerzos* costing 8,000–12,000COP and some great ribs and trout if you want something a bit different. They also have a couple of rooms upstairs and the breakfasts laid on won't disappoint.

At weekends the **Malecón** (waterfront) comes alive, bustling with local vendors selling food, drink and Paisa arts and crafts, and music coming from various stalls and boats. The **Flying Fox zipline** (or 'canopy') is higher than it looks, exhilarating, and with spectacular views of the lake beneath you, well worth a go at 15,000COP.

Getting there and away Buses to Guatapé leave every half-hour from Medellín's North Terminal and take 2–2½ hours (12,500COP). The buses pass La Piedra just before reaching Guatapé, so it's worth mentioning to the driver that you want to get off. From La Piedra you can jump into a mini *chiva* taxi which will take you into Guatapé for 3,000–4,000COP (these are far less frequent during the week). Buses back to Medellín leave from Guatapé's main plaza, where you'll also find the ticket office. It's worth booking your return ticket as soon as you get there, especially at the weekends when seats on buses back to Medellín are in demand.

Boat rides At the weekend, and especially when the weather is fine, lake trips are available on large boats stocked with plenty of beer and *aguardiente*. Board with a crowd and the deck is sure to fill with dancers swaying to salsa and Latin pop beats. Trips cost around 15,000COP per person, and take you around the lake for an hour or so, with no stop-offs but some lovely views, including of La Piedra (though a little way off).

Smaller, faster boats are another option, to take in more sites, costing around 100,000COP for up to eight people (total) – but you can certainly negotiate if there are fewer of you. These will take you out to the site of the old town, marked by 'La Cruz' – the memorial cross of the old church, now submerged. Boat trips can also include passing by one of Pablo Escobar's famous houses, 'La Manuela', and a visit to the Casa Museo – the only building from Viejo Peñol still standing, now a museum, giving an interesting insight into the history of Guatapé and Peñol. (It is also possible to reach Casa Museo by *chiva* taxi from Guatapé.) Most trips finish off with the Isla de las Fantasias (Fantasy Island), where there's a swimming area, a great little bar/shop and – if you fancy staying the night – *cabañas* for rent.

Where to stay and eat

El Descanso del Arriero (8 rooms) Calle 30, No 28–82; 861 0878; m 312 257 6953. A great, affordable option, ideally located just 1 block from the main square. *Arriero* means 'mule driver', & suitably this hostel has a real rustic charm about it, its architecture typical of the region, including lovely painted *zólcalos* of its own. Prices rise at the w/ends & even more so during high season (public holidays & festivals). **$$**

Hotel Guatatur (16 rooms) Calle 31, No 31–04; 861 1212; www.hotelguatatur.com. This fine hotel is situated just off the park in Guatapé. Catering mainly for getaway weekenders from Medellín, this modern option has all the creature comforts, with large windows (some overlooking the lake), jacuzzis in the suites, a restaurant & a bar

with a good selection of wines. The hotel can also organise various tours, including a trip out to see the local monastery set up against the hill outside Guatapé, boat trips, jet skiing & horseriding. **$$**

Lake View Hostel (8 rooms) 861 0079; m 311 329 9474; e patrongregorio@gmail.com; www.lakeviewhostel.com. This excellent hostel is a fantastic choice for travellers who choose to stay a bit longer in Guatapé. There is so much more to Lake View than its lovely rooms & great location a few mins' walk just outside the centre of the *pueblo*. Offering kayaking, mountain biking, guided fishing trips, horseriding, hiking to waterfalls & swimming holes, & even the option of Spanish classes & volunteering, this place really does have it all. All the rooms are clean, with appealing features such as tiled floors, exposed brick & decorative mirrors & furniture, some with plasma TVs. There is hot water, free Wi-Fi & a laundry service – a welcome relief for some! With friendly owners, games & DVDs on offer & a barbecue this is somewhere to unwind & really feel at home. It's only around 500m from the main square, along the Malecón, over the bridge & to the right, but if your backpack is heavy a *chiva* taxi will happily drop you there for 4,000COP. **$–$$**

🏠 **Mi Casa Guatape** (6 rooms) ✆ 861 0632; m 301 457 5726; www.micasaguatape.com. Located

a 5min walk from the road leading to the rock, this is one of the best hostels in town. Its owners are incredibly friendly, welcoming guests into their hostel as you would a close friend or family member. Rooms are clean & comfortable with 1 double looking out on to the lake. The back leads out to a terrace with tables & chairs overlooking the lake. During the day the owners will help you organise an array of activities & may even come along with you. At night, the midnight oil is often burned with a game of cards. **$**

RIONEGRO (*Telephone code 4; www.rionegro.gov.co*) This aged city has plenty of gorgeous buildings to wander around against a rural backdrop of rolling farmland and tree-lined meadows. Founded in 1663, Rionegro lies around 50km southeast of Medellín, and has a number of interesting museums and monuments, including the *Monumento a José María Córdoba*, a fine statue commemorating the War of Independence. Numerous Paisa-style buildings can be found just off the main plaza where the vast 200-year-old **Catedral de San Nicolás** casts its shadows. The backstreets are home to a handful of small hotels and restaurants. Frequent buses nip back and forth to Medellín, taking around 1 hour.

CARMEN DE VIBORAL (*Telephone code 4*) Most people come to this small Paisa town to visit its many ceramic stalls, pottery factories and workshops. Carmen de Viboral is renowned throughout Colombia for its fine ceramic industry, with most of its production still managed by hand. Buses connect to Rionegro 9km away every hour, taking 20 minutes. Half-a-dozen budget hotels are located around the plaza.

LA CEJA (*Telephone code 4; www.laceja-antioquia.gov.co/index.shtml*) This charming town centres on a handsome main plaza where balconied Paisa buildings adorned with brightly coloured flowers boast traditional Antioquian décor. Two gorgeous churches offer plenty of stunning religious art. A number of small handicraft stalls can also be found in the streets beyond the square. La Ceja has a handful of basic mid-range hotels and is served by an hourly bus to Medellín (1½ hours). Surrounding attractions include the **Hacienda Fizebald**, a lovely old mansion house dating back to 1825 that houses a collection of 150 species of orchids, and the **Salto de Tequendamita**, a stunning waterfall with a very nice restaurant at its base.

RETIRO (*Telephone code 4*) Prepare to be charmed by this pretty little cattle-ranching town, founded in 1800. Surrounded by emerald hills dotted with colourful haciendas, Retiro is one of the region's most scenic towns, with a beautiful main plaza edged by Paisa-style buildings. For a small town, Retiro also boasts a good stock of restaurants and hostels and makes an excellent stop-off for lunch. Buses to Medellín 41km away run every 35 minutes, taking an hour.

PARQUE ARVÍ Up in the mountains on the eastern edge of Medellín is Santa Elena, a great place to head to for a day trip from the city if you fancy a bit of hiking and good views over the valley. Parque Arví, next to Santa Elena, is an ecotourism nature reserve, designed – as part of the great transformation of Medellín over recent years – for the enjoyment of nature, biodiversity and regional heritage. There are wonderful walking trails and the chance to ride bikes or take horses through the park. A great spot is Piedras Blancas, a small lake within the park, where there is also a camping area. In the Comfama section a huge adventure park awaits those wanting to test their skills at manual zip lining and scaling vertical trees with the assistance of a harness. Basic training is given before guides suggest an appropriate level. You can reach Santa Elena and Parque Arví via cable car from Acevedo (metrocable lines K and L). It's also possible to get there by bus from Terminal del Sur (Southern bus terminal). You need to ask the driver to drop you off in a place called **El Silletero** where you would then catch another bus that takes you to Parque Arví. Cost-wise, it's better and easier to take the metro and metro cable.

JARDÍN (*Telephone code 4*) Unchanged for decades, Jardín is reminiscent of a different era and arguably one of Colombia's prettiest *pueblos*. The town lies at the foot of a valley, surrounded by stunning mountains and plentiful greenery. Its old colonial centre is beautiful, full of brightly coloured ancient houses and home to a stunning plaza (declared a National Monument by the Colombia minister of tourism in 1985) through which *caballeros* parade their Paso Fino horses. One of the most memorable characteristics of Jardín is the beautifully hand-painted wooden chairs you will see outside the various bars that line the plaza, each with unique paintings depicting local scenes of the region.

If your timings won't allow for a trip to Colombia's Zona Cafetera, then a visit to Jardín will give you a good taste of it. In fact, Antioquians often refer to Jardín as 'our coffee zone'. The valleys surrounding the town are covered in coffee plantations and there are one or two coffee farms around that you can visit. Jardín is also famous for its sugarcane milling (*molienda*) and plantain cultivation.

Getting there and away Buses from Medellín's South Terminal are regular (leaving almost every hour), and take 3–3½ hours. The first bus leaves at 06.00 and with a few more stops along the way, takes a little longer (4 hours). Tickets cost

JOURNEYING THROUGH PAISA-LAND

The **drive** to Jardín is interesting. You will pass through Caldas, a rapidly developing large *pueblo* just outside Medellín and through steep V-shaped valleys, the majority of which are cultivated from top to bottom regardless of their gradient. This is a uniquely Paisa undertaking; they are countrymen through and through and know how to maximise their land down to the very last square inch. Look out for the '*ojos de poetas*' (poet's eyes), the bright-orange wild flowers common throughout Antioquia. Another very typical Antioquian site is the (often red) painted *zólcalos* (lower part of the walls) of the decorative, flower-clad Paisa haciendas you will see dotted across the valleys.

If you have a clear day, you might be lucky enough to spot 'Cerro de Tusa', a marvellous pyramid-shaped hill, which protrudes out against the other rolling hills of the skyline (about halfway into the journey). A challenge for another trip could entail taking on the Cerro de Tusa climb. For this, you'd have to get a bus straight to Venecia from Medellín and find a local guide who will show you the way up once there.

As you near Jardín you will pass through Salgar – the birthplace of ex-president Uribe. This place holds great significance for Colombians for obvious reasons, with plaques and graffiti paying tribute to the great leader.

18,000COP one-way, depending on the size/speed of the bus. You could instead catch a ride in a *colectivo* taxi for 30,000COP per person – a faster option.

Buses back to Medellín depart from Jardín's small bus station, on the corner of Calle 8 Paez with Carrera 4 Bolívar. Buses leave at 06.15, 10.15, 14.15, 15.15 and 17.15, with an extra service on Sundays departing at 16.00.

If you are going on to the Coffee Zone from Jardín, you need to take a bus from Jardín's bus station to Andes, where you will change for buses to Pereira and Armenia. The ticket booth in Andes is located right next to where the bus from Jardín will drop you off. If travelling during busy periods (holiday, weekends), it's worth booking your onward journey from Andes ahead of time, through Flota Occidental (ask in Jardín). Buses from Andes to Pereira (32,000COP, c6 hours) and Armenia (35,000COP, c7 hours) depart at 07.00, 10.30 and 14.00.

Tour guide

Land Venture Travel m 321 769 9555; e landventuretravel@gmail.com; www. landventuretravel.com. Andrés Munera is an expert guide, with a staggering knowledge of Medellín, its surrounding areas & its history. His company, Land Venture Travel, was set up in 2010 & offers reasonably priced day trips (& some overnight trips) to Medellín's surrounding areas. A former cruise-ship worker, he has impeccable English & many a story to tell of times abroad (though with true Paisa loyalty, holds firm that through all his travels, there is nowhere that comes close to Colombia). Andrés is dedicated to showing the best of what Antioquia has to offer. He runs a wide variety of trips across the department bringing personal insight & energy into all aspects & introducing little hidden spots along the way. One of the best is his horseriding trip in Jardín (usually a 1-day trip). You'll go, with Andrés & a local *caballero*, right up into mountains that surround the town, with the most phenomenal view of the valley down beneath you & strong, well-trained horses who cope remarkably with the rough, steep terrain. He'll also get you access to a tiny, tucked-away *panela* factory, where sugarcane is processed, boiled & cooled into pats of *panela* which are then embossed with the factory's logo ready to be sold. A small, family business, the factory is operated by only a handful of old men who work day after day dedicated to the cause.

Where to stay and eat

Hotel Balandu (26 rooms) Jardín Río Sucio (500m north of Jardín) ☎845 6850/6848/6849; e comentarios@comfenalcoantioquia.com or Hotelhaciendabalandu@comfenalcoantiquia. com. The best, most expensive hotel in the area, Balandu has a great reputation & is worth splashing out on. A large, traditional-looking hacienda located just 800m outside the town centre, Balandu is quieter & has a more peaceful ambience than many of the smaller, central *posadas*. It has a large pool, offers attentive room service, stone showers, a good restaurant & also rents horses. **$$$**

Hotel y Restaurante Avalón (12 rooms) Km3, via Jardín Río Sucio; ☎845 5109. Many people miss this special spot as it's located 3km outside Jardín, which is a great shame as it's well worth the visit. Nestled on the edge of the Avalón Forest & right next to the river, it's a pretty, relaxing place to enjoy a lengthy meal (or even to stay overnight). Avalón has a great choice of food, most prominently the local speciality – *trucha* (trout). There is more to do here besides eating: there's a walking trail, & fishing is a popular activity (you can even catch your own lunch!). **$$$**

Hotel El Dorado (12 rooms) ☎845 5618. This place has a slightly more 'boutique' feel to it than other hotels in the town, but is still affordable & in a great location just off the main square. A 3-storey building, with a wide balcony overlooking the plaza & church, there are several rooms to choose from, all with hot water. El Dorado also has a very decent restaurant, again with reasonable prices. **$$**

Hotel Valdivia (16 rooms) Plaza Carrera 5, No 9–47; ☎845 5055; www.hotelvaldiviaplaza. com. A simple, clean hotel located on the main square. Several rooms have balconies looking out on to the spectacular church. Expect friendly staff, decent b/fast, hot water & free coffee. **$$**

✕ La Posada Right on the main plaza, with a little balcony from which you can stand and watch the goings-on of the world beneath you, La Posada is a great, cosy place to enjoy a meal. Roberto, the owner, is quite a character, full of enthusiasm & devotion to his guests & will always have time to stop for a chat. La Posada also has accommodation – lovely, simple rooms with various options for number of beds-per-room & hot water. It's worth haggling a little over the rates. $

✕ Zodiac Calle del Medio; ☎ 845 5616. Facing Hotel El Dorado, just off the main square, this is an excellent choice for quick service & good food. The menu is simple, offering tasty typical Paisa meals. The *chicharrón* is cooked perfectly with the correct balance of meat, fat & crispy skin. Note that service can be slow so you need to be patient. $

What to see and do Walking around the centre of Jardín, taking in the architecture and strolling through the main plaza (where you'll find the church, painted chairs and numerous restaurants, cafés, bars and shops), simply watching the world go by, is an activity in itself. **Dulces de Jardín** is a family-run sweet shop in the centre of the town, which sells a variety of mouthwatering local confectionery and tubs upon tubs of various sorts of *arequipe*. The business was set up by owner Mariela Arango Jaramillo in 1995, who turned a passionate hobby into a profession and has since won numerous awards and recognition across the country (much of which can be seen on placards covering the walls of the *tienda*). Definitely worth a visit to stock up on gifts and travel munchies.

A visit to **Alto de las Flores**, just outside the town centre, will give you an exceptional view of Jardín and the surrounding mountains. One of the '*moto-ratónes*' (literally 'motor' – the small *tuk-tuk*-style taxis) will be able to take you. It's also possible to take longer *moto-ratón* tours around Jardín – they'll take you to all the main sites for a reasonable price.

The *teleférico* (gondola/cable car) provides a short 5-minute ride up to the top of one of the nearby mountains. The view from the top is breathtaking, taking in

---

ON THE HOOF

If you've spent any length of time in Colombia, the chances are you'll have seen a horse parade pass you, its rider seemingly motionless as beneath him his horse's legs are performing a strange delicate, rapid trot – knees and hooves lifted up higher than usual, in a sort of elegant 'show'. If so, you'll have been watching a Caballo de Paso horse – an iconic and treasured part of Colombia and its culture.

Paso Finos originated in Spain, and were first introduced to the Caribbean islands by Christopher Columbus on his second voyage to the Americas in the late 15th century. Since then, three breeds of Paso Fino have emerged – the Peruvian, the Puerto Rican and the Colombian – trained to perform best in each particular country's conditions. One of the defining characteristics of the Colombian Paso Fino is that aside from the usual Paso Fino trot (literally meaning the 'fine step'), Colombian Pasos also perform a diagonal ambling gait known as the '*trocha*'.

You are likely to see *caballeros* parading their Pasos Finos through the streets and plazas of small, countryside *pueblos* across Antioquia and also in other parts of Colombia. They are notably beautiful horses, well looked after and have recognisable friendly traits which make them great horses to ride. There are countless places to ride through Antioquia – if you're lucky you may just get given a Paso Fino and can try out its smooth, fine step for yourself.

Jardín below you and a striking view of the entire valley. There's also a restaurant – a great place to stop and have a bite to eat, taking in the scene (8,000COP for a round ticket).

La Cueva del Esplendor (Splendour Cave) is perhaps one of the most impressive natural phenomena you will see in Colombia. A good 3- to 4-hour round hike or horseride, it's not the easiest place to get to – the terrain is arduous and the last part includes a steep half-hour trek down quite a slippery, forested trail and along a river (uphill on the way back!) – but the reward is well worth the effort. You will reach an opening and see a cave in front of you with a huge torrent of water falling straight down into a pool from a hole in the roof of the cave, carved out by the water. A marvellous surprise at the end of a decent trek and a chance for a refreshing dip for anyone brave enough to take on the natural (cold!) plunge pool.

It's possible to drive or hire a Willys jeep via La Salada road to save 30 minutes of walking through the dirt road that takes you to La Escalera (another, smaller waterfall) *en route*. From there the hike is about 60–90 minutes to the la Cueva del Esplendor. The other way to get there is by taking Jardín's *teleférico* (cable car) to Cerro de Cristo Rey. From that point on, the hike begins and continues on alongside the creek basin until you reach la Cueva del Esplendor. This hike takes about 2 hours. Whichever option is chosen, a guide is needed to lead the way. Enquire in the town for information about guides. Ask for Don Jaime – an expert guide and *caballero* who can lead you to Splendour Cave either on horseback then foot, or solely trekking – as the options above describe.

If you are heading to Jardín for a day trip from Medellín, Land Venture Travel (page 355) incorporates this tour (on horseback) as part of the package along with a visit to the sugarcane mill, Jardín's sweet shop (220,000COP per person, including lunch and round trip to and from Medellín in the company's new jeep).

There are also several other waterfalls around Jardín, which any local guide or *moto-ratón* driver will be able to take you to. Alternatively, ask a local and they will be able to point you in the right direction if you feel like making a walk of it. There are three main waterfalls – La Cascada Escondida (Hidden Waterfall), La Cascada del Amor (Waterfall of Love), and La Escalera (Ladder), the last of which you can see during the trek to La Cueva del Esplendor.

JERICÓ This unique, truly Antioquian *pueblo* can compete with Jardín for its well-preserved colourful, colonial architecture, although it has to be said that Jardín's plaza is by far the winner, described by many as the most beautiful in Antioquia. Still, Jericó is itself a lovely, pretty place to visit, with a wonderful attraction – Las Nubes Natural Park.

A cable car from the town centre will take you up to the park, where you will find yourself above the clouds, marvelling over the sensational 360° view beneath you. The view stretches for miles, encompassing not just Jericó but also other *pueblos* around, and overlooking the great valley of the Cauca River (binoculars can be handy if you want a closer view). There are young, local guides who will take you around the park – some not even 16 years of age but bursting at the seams with talent and professionalism.

In Jericó itself your time is best spent strolling the streets, taking in the local life, eating *arepas con queso* and drinking a coffee or two. This *pueblo* has its heart and soul in coffee – it is the town's main source of income, allowing it to have grown and developed into the charming, thriving *pueblo* it is today.

EL REFUGIO, RÍO CLARO 'El Refugio', a diverse activity centre within the beautiful Reserva Natural Cañon del Río Claro, makes for an excellent two-day trip from

Medellín. This is a stunning area of marble rock, lush forest, abundant birdlife, all surrounding the gentle Río Claro, which provides the base for numerous activities.

Getting there and away Any **bus** from Medellín to Bogotá will take you to Río Claro El Refugio; just ask the driver and he'll drop you at the entrance. Expect to pay 30,000–35,000COP for the journey. There's a big sign which can't be missed. Just remember to call or email the centre ahead of time to book (☎ *268 8855; e rioclaroelrefugio@une.net.co; www.rioclaroelrefugio.com*).

⌂ **Where to stay and eat** There are several options for lodgings at El Refugio, the prices of which all include three meals. The *cabañas* range from 100,000COP to 190,000COP per person. All the accommodation is very reflective of the area – simple and natural. If you're just visiting for the day you can buy lunch at the restaurant – a nice, open area with decorative designs on the wooden pillars depicting the nature in the reserve, painted by the owner's wife.

What to do

Rafting The centre provides great white-water rafting facilities, with young but confident and experienced local guides who will take you through the calm level-one rapids, ducking waterfalls, with opportunities for rope swinging and bathing alongside the raft. Make sure you look beneath you at the glimmering marble riverbed, and try scratching off some of the moss to see the spectacular emerald-green shine emerge. The cost is 25,000COP for 2 hours, grade 1.

Canopy Have fun whizzing high above the river along three zip-lines (20,000COP for 1 hour).

Caving Any visit to Río Claro would be incomplete without experiencing its unforgettable caves. At 20,000COP, it's a bargain for the 3-hour trip, usually consisting of a 45-minute walk, 45 minutes in the cave and 45 minutes back. You will half-walk, half-swim through the pitch-black cave – an exhilarating experience, using torches to examine the miraculous cavern around you. But the most memorable, eerily wonderful part of the experience is the sound of the *guácharos* – bat-like birds that live in the cave and make a terrifying sound, stopping you dead in your tracks. This is a completely unique and certainly unforgettable experience, but perhaps not for the faint-hearted!

Since the majority of experiences involve the river, you will need to take swimming gear with you, shoes you can get wet, and a torch if you have one for the caves.

SANTA FÉ DE ANTIOQUIA *Telephone code 4*

A visit to this sleepy agricultural town allows a step back in time through handsome streets that have remained unchanged since the early 18th century. As the oldest settlement in the region, Santa Fé de Antioquia is also the most beautifully preserved, set in a low-lying steamy valley watered by the Río Cauca and Río Tonusco. Founded in 1541 by Jorge Robledo as Villa de Santafé on the western bank of the Río Cauca, the town received its shield of arms and the title of City of Antioquia from King Philip II of Spain in 1545 and was elevated to parish status in 1547 by the Bishop of Popayán. In 1584, it became the capital of Antioquia, a role it served until the government relocated to Medellín in 1826, 80km to the southwest. Since then, Santa Fé de Antioquia has remained totally overshadowed by its neighbour, and more than a little aggrieved by its diminished status. However, in rivalry terms, the town has little competition when it comes to its architectural core, with stunning single-storey pastel-coloured colonial houses along narrow streets and gorgeous courtyards and plazas. Elaborate carvings decorate each vast wooden doorway beside patios planted to capacity with a rainbow of flowers. Balconies and windows are also adorned with blooms in what must be one of Colombia's prettiest streetscapes. In 1960, Santa Fé de Antioquia and its charming maze of cobbled paths was declared a National Monument. The completion of the Tunnel of the West in 2006 has cut travelling time from Medellín to a lazy hour-long drive. This has stimulated a surge of renewed interest in Santa Fé de Antioquia as a weekend destination and today tourism is an economic bedrock of the town, along with maize, coffee and beans.

GETTING THERE AND AROUND The town is well served by a good, frequent **bus** service to and from Medellín (8,500COP, 2 hours) with another half-dozen **minibuses** (11,000COP) and an on-demand collective service. **Taxis** loiter around the main square and are the best way to cross town (3,000COP).

TOURIST INFORMATION
🏛 Oficina de Fomento y Turismo Plaza Mayor; ☏ 853 2314; ⊕ 08.00–18.00 Mon–Fri

WHERE TO STAY AND EAT Rates at many of Santa Fé de Antioquia's decent handful of hotels can double when there are festivities in town – so it is well worth booking in advance. The town is often deserted until the weekending urbanites arrive on Friday night, so it pays to haggle midweek. Almost every hotel has a restaurant with simple meat-and-rice dishes the norm.

🏠 Hotel Mariscal Robledo (37 rooms) Carrera 12, No 9–70; ☏ 853 1111/1563; www.hotelmariscalrobledo.com. This beautiful hotel is *the* place to stay if you want the best in town. Expect stunning décor, a big courtyard swimming pool with great views, sauna, Turkish bath, pretty rooms & understated elegance throughout. Rates may be Santa Fé's highest but it's a real bargain when you consider they include 3 meals & free drinks 15.00–19.00. **$$$**

🏠 Hostal Guaracú (30 rooms) Calle 10, No 8–36; ☏ 853 1097; www.guaracu.com. Look out for the orange sign for this mid-range tourist hotel, located just off the main plaza. Each room has AC & TV & is clean if a little soulless. Has a sister hostel in Medellín. **$$**

🏠 Hotel Caserón Plaza (32 rooms) Plaza Mayor; ☏ 853 2040; e info@hotelcaseronplaza.com; www.hotelcaseronplaza.com.co. Well located, right on the main plaza, this former private residence has an aristocratic past. Courtyard rooms are clean, cheerful & nicely appointed with a swimming pool, restaurant & pleasant garden. **$$**

🏠 Hospedaje Franco (13 rooms) Carrera 10, No 8A–14; ☏ 853 1654. Located just a block from the main plaza, this super hotel has simple, fan-cooled rooms centred on a leafy patio. Each is small & comes with a clean private bathroom, but there isn't a restaurant. Rooms are like gold dust here in Jan. **$**

✕ Restaurante Portón del Parque ☏ 853 3207; ⊕ lunch & dinner. More expensive than Las Carnes, but in a better location & even more beautiful, this restaurant is known to be the best place to eat in Santa Fé. The meals are traditional Colombian dishes, expertly cooked & presented. **$$$**

✕ Las Carnes del Tío Calle 10, No 7–22; ☏ 853 3385. Whilst the prices have recently risen & the increase in popularity of the restaurant means sometimes waiting a little longer for your food, this restaurant continues to be a great option for guaranteed good food & service. You can stay here too – the rooms are lovely. **$$**

9

✕ Restaurante y Hospedaje El Méson de la Abuela Carrera 11, No 9–31; ☏ 853 1053; ⏲ early–late. This decent local restaurant serves robust meals in an outdoor dining room. Expect generous b/fasts at a dirt-cheap price of 6,000COP, tasty lunches & dinners of fish, chicken & meat. Double rooms, costing 60,000COP, are basic but come with fans & a private bathroom around a plant-filled courtyard. $

SHOPPING Be sure to try the local *pulpa de tamarindo*, a mega-sweet candy with a touch of sour made from tamarind grown in the surrounding valley. Numerous vendors on Plaza Mayor sell it throughout the day from battered wooden stalls opposite the church.

WHAT TO SEE AND DO In reality, the biggest attraction in Santa Fé de Antioquia is the town itself – a stroll through the narrow streets is an absolute delight. Most people head for the impressive **Iglesia de Santa Bárbara** (Santa Bárbara Church) on the corner of Calle 11 and Carrera 8 and the **Catedral Madre** (Cathedral of Our Lady) on Plaza Mayor before heading to the 17th-century **Iglesia de Chiquinquirá** (Chiquinquirá Church) on the corner of Carrera 13 and Calle 10 and **Iglesia Church Jesús Nazareno** (Church of Jesus of Nazareth) on the corner of Carrera 5 and Calle 10. All are open for evening Mass and boast a fascinating array of religious artefacts. There are more sacred *objets d'art* at the **Museo de Arte Religioso** (Religious Art Museum) on Calle 11, No 8–12, including paintings by Gregorio Vásquez de Arce y Ceballos. It opens every day except Mondays and entry is free; next to Santa Bárbara church.

Out-of-town attractions centre on the **Puente de Occidente** (Bridge of the West), one of the first suspension bridges in the world. This metal-and-wood single-lane structure was built by the famous Colombian architect – and renowned big drinker – José María Villa (1850–1913). Villa trained in Hoboken, New Jersey, and helped build New York's Brooklyn Bridge. On his return to Colombia he built four bridges on the Cauca River. The Bridge of the West boasts a distinctive design with twin turrets on either end and took eight years to complete between 1887 and 1895, at a cost of 171,300COP. Most of the materials used were shipped from England to create this 291m feat of engineering. It carried traffic until 1978 when it was declared a National Monument, and is now used only by light vehicles. Buses connect to the bridge from Santa Fé or you can walk it in about an hour on the road to Sopetrán.

Festivals

Semana Santa (Holy Week) Crowds swell and room rates soar during this highly popular week-long festival. Expect numerous colourful processions steeped in traditional pageantry and half-a-dozen religious ceremonies and services.

Antioquia Film Festival (early December; *www.festicineantioquia.com*) This popular event attracts film-lovers from all across the country with a broad range of cinematic treats from Colombian studios and film-makers from all across the world. Usually lasting five days, film fever spreads throughout the town with screenings in plazas, school halls and even in a graveyard. To ensure a seat check the programme and head there early.

Fiesta de los Diablitos (Festival of the Little Devils) (end of December) Dating back to the colonial period, this festival has been celebrated with gusto since 1653. In the past, Spanish *fiestero* Don Manuel de Benavides laid on bullfights, dancing and parties. Today, things are much the same – but faster-paced and more crowded. Expect lots of food, handicrafts and a beauty pageant.

ZONA CAFETERA (EJE CAFETERO) (COFFEE ZONE)

Colombia's rugged and green Zona Cafetera (Coffee Zone) is the nation's principal coffee-growing area, annually providing half of the country's 732,000-tonne coffee production in a region that represents just 1% of the country's landmass. Rolling plantations and quilted terraced slopes are hemmed in by banana plants, shaggy coffee bushes, bamboo groves and vibrant heliconia thickets. Lush tufted grassy knolls and verdant valleys richly nourished by frequent rainfall are dotted with phosphorus hot springs and bubbling pools of mud. Expansive meadows are home to white-painted wooden *fincas* with red-and-green window frames, shutters and broad shady balconies. Narrow, winding lanes scattered with podgy chickens lead to the snow-capped peaks of the Andes and aged volcanic crags. Here, between the magical altitudes of 800m and 1,800m, about 7% of the world's coffee supply is grown. Since the plummeting prices of the 1990s, Colombia's coffee growers have woken up to smell a new crop – tourism. Today, coffee *finca* tourism is big business, offering a taste of plantation life to visitors, whilst supplementing the income of the region's 300,000 growers. Centred on three coffee-growing regions in the west of the country – Quindío, Caldas and Risaralda – more than 1,000 farmers have opened up their homes. There is even a highly popular Disney-style coffee theme park, complete with a Broadway-esque Show del Café cabaret that honours the Colombians' beloved beans.

HISTORY The Spanish didn't settle in the area that makes up the Coffee Zone until the mid 19th century, but once Antioquia began its phase of post-colonisation growth the region became ripe for development. By 1905, it was sufficiently large and populated to become a department in its own right, and Caldas was born. However, widespread economic differences prompted the department to divide into three smaller areas, namely Caldas, Risaralda and Quindío. Today, the Zona Cafetera is dominated by the cities of Manizales, Pereira and Armenia, each departmental capitals and not terribly inspiring places. Sombre architecture and gnomish buildings reflect the region's fear of recurring earthquakes. Both Pereira and Armenia – along with 33 smaller towns – were badly damaged during a devastating burst of seismic activity in 1999. Some 2,000 people were killed or badly injured and entire streets razed to the ground after a quake that measured 6.2 on the Richter scale. It left more than 200,000 people homeless and was the third earthquake in 20 years. Ninety aftershocks wreaked havoc across the region for almost 24 hours with poor construction codes and ageing buildings contributing to the carnage. Since then, international aid has helped rebuild and expand the city. Numerous new government buildings and highways have been constructed, with the subsequent rebuilding project costing more than US$500 million. The Coffee Zone's seismic vulnerability is due to the triple junction that occurs at the northwest corner of the South American plate where the Nazca, Cocos and Pacific plates converge. The 1999 earthquake had a sizeable impact on coffee production in the region, adding to the woes of growers facing falling prices worldwide.

PRACTICALITIES Until around 2007, the Coffee Zone lacked any specialist tour operators offering coffee *finca* tours, but today there are a growing number of tour companies serving the region as well as international operators running tours for international travellers. Some people visit independently under their own steam,

9

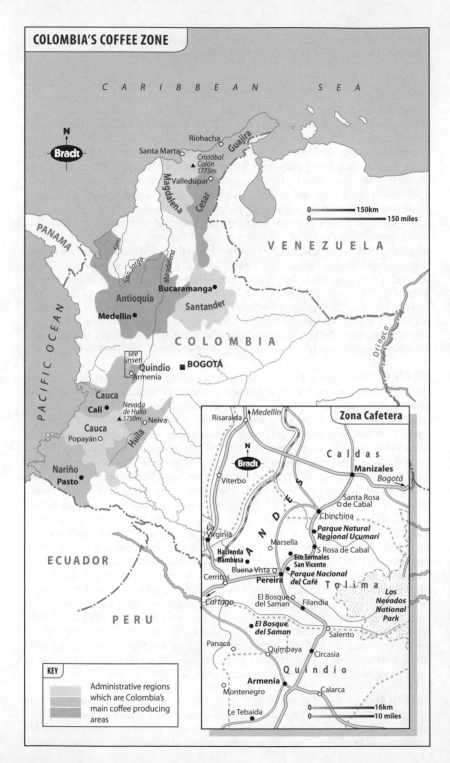

COLOMBIA'S COFFEE ZONE

N Bradt

C A R I B B E A N   S E A

PANAMA

Santa Marta
Ríohacha
Guajira
Cristóbal
Colón
5775m ▲
Valledupar

Magdalena
Cesar

VENEZUELA

0 ———— 150km
0 ———— 150 miles

Sinú
San Jorge
Magdalena

Bucaramanga ●
Antioquia
Medellín ●
Santander

C O L O M B I A

Orinoco

see
inset
Quindío ○
Armenia
Quindío
BOGOTÁ ■

PACIFIC OCEAN

Cauca
Cali ●
Nevada
de Huila
5750m ▲ Neiva
Cauca
Popayán ○
Huila

Nariño
Pasto ●

ECUADOR

Zona Cafetera

Risaralda
Medellín

N Bradt

C a l d a s
Manizales ●
Bogotá

Viterbo

Santa Rosa
de Cabal

La
Virginia
Chinchina ●

*Parque Natural
Regional Ucumarí*

Marsella ○
S Rosa de Cabal

**Hacienda
Bambusa** ●
**Eco Termales
San Vicente**
*Parque Nacional
del Café*

Buena Vista
Cerritos
Pereira ●

Cartago

El Bosque
del Saman
Filandia

T o l i m a

*Los
Nevados
National
Park*

*El Bosque
del Saman*

Salento

PERU

Panacá ○
Quimbaya ○
Circasia ○

Q u i n d í o

Armenia ○
Montenegro
Calarca ○

Le Tebaida ○

0 ———— 16km
0 ———— 10 miles

A N D E S

KEY

Administrative regions
which are Colombia's
main coffee producing
areas

354

using sites like www.clubhaciendasdelcafe.com to find the ideal *finca*. It lists coffee farms in Quindío that offer accommodation to tourists. Some have pools and all are traditional buildings with balconies, spacious rooms, gardens and coffee fields. Prices start at about 60,000COP per person per night, including breakfast. Another good reference is www.deunacolombia.com/zona-cafeteramedellin. It also lists a dozen or so *fincas* with descriptions in all three departments. Otherwise, contact one of the best tour companies in the area – **Land Venture Travel** (m *321 769 9555;* e *info@landventuretravel.com; www.landventuretravel.com*). Their day trips cost 180,000COP approximately and include door-to-door service with friendly English-speaking guides, horseback rides to waterfalls, a traditional lunch in Jardín, a coffee mill experience and visits to a sugarcane plantation and trout farm – plus lots of local history and stories about Antioquia's coffee area. There's also some useful information and links at the following websites:

www.paisatours.com/coffee_country.htm
www.turiscolombia.com/coffee_region.htm General guide to the area with some accommodation options.

MANIZALES *Telephone code 6*

A crucial part of the Colombian coffee-growing axis and the capital of the Caldas department, Manizales has long been an important commercial hub. Owing to a succession of devastating earthquakes and a terrible fire in 1925, the city has very little remaining historical character. Where grand period buildings would have once flanked the plaza there are now bland, concrete monstrosities: a dismal, grey reminder of Manizales's past despairs. Modern high-rise towers fail to add glamour – and finding charm requires considerable patience – yet the climbing streets that lead from the centre have a certain appeal. In the oldest part of the city, a vast cathedral is famous for its elaborate gold canopy and beautiful, large stained-glass windows – and is a rare structure of beauty. A large student population lends Manizales a European feel in part. Academics and scholars are omnipresent walking to classes or sitting in the many cosy little cafés along Avenida Santander or sharing notes in the Plaza Bolívar. Enter Manizales from Pereira to pass the city's vast white bullring on the right: venue of the Feria de Manizales.

HISTORY Founded in 1849, Manizales was born out of a desire by a group of Antioquian colonists to escape the ravages of civil war. At a height of about 2,153m, the land on which it is built offered relative sanctuary from the warring Liberal and Conservative factions. The original settlement is said to have comprised 20 families, including that of Manuel Grisales, after whom the new city was named. Manizales remained an isolated, fair-skinned settlement until other ethnic groups arrived in the early 20th century, once the universities were established and diluted the pure Spanish influences. The city's early development was seriously hampered by two earthquakes in 1875 and 1878. Prosperity came late to Manizales, once it became the capital of the newly created Caldas department and a pivotal part of the coffee trade.

GETTING THERE AND AROUND At the time of writing, Avianca and ADA were the only two **airlines** flying to Manizales from Bogotá and Medellín respectively. The city's La Nuba Airport is located about 8km southeast of the centre, just off the road to Bogotá (15,000COP by taxi). **Buses** from the main terminal on Avenida 19 northeast of Plaza Bolívar depart frequently to Bogotá (57,000COP, 8 hours), Cali

(38,000COP, 5 hours) and Medellín (30,000COP, 5 hours). Shorter hops are served by **minibuses**, including Pereira (9,000COP, 1½ hours), Armenia (17,500COP, 2½ hours), and Salamina (15,000COP, 2½ hours).

In 2009, the city's ultra-impressive mass transit system opened with the Cable Aéreo de Manizales (**cable car**) the major focus. Running 2km with three lines and cabins that hold ten passengers (eight seated, two standing), the system's docking station is beside the bus terminal. The service runs to the city centre and to the populated residential zones in the higher, more remote fringes of Manizales (Los Fundadores) via the middle station (La Fuente). It operates seven days a week from 06:00 to 22.00 with a fixed price of 1,500COP. For schedules, prices and updates check out the Manizales Transport Department's website (*www.cableaereomanizales.com*).

TOURIST INFORMATION

Oficina principal ventas Calle 56, No 23–16; 886 3300; 08.00–18.00 Mon–Fri, 09.00–18.00 Sat

Local government website www.manizales.gov.co

TOUR OPERATORS Most of the city's main tour operators offer day trips out to the Nevado del Ruiz, the highest volcano in the Parque Nacional Los Nevados, as well as longer stays in the park itself. One of the most established is **Ecosistemas** (*Carrera 21, No 20–45*; 880 8300; *www.ecosistemastravel.com.co*). Expect to pay around 200,000COP per person for a full-day package to Nevados park, including lunch. A more recent addition to the town has been **Colombia Eco Travel** (m *311 319 3195* e *tours@colombiaecotravelcom; www.colombiaecotravel.com*). Owned by US-born Daniel this company offers hikes up Nevado del Ruiz, coffee *finca* day trips, hot-air balloon rides, bike tours, rock climbing, Rio Claro Reserve trips, and day trips to towns in the region. Day trips start from 60,000COP for 3-hour city tours to 400,000COP for coffee *finca* visits on horseback. Daniel uses an array of local expert guides covering most of the cities and towns in the area. Longer trips are also available. Another fantastic place to while away time in the Eje Cafetero is to head out to the highly recommended **Hacienda Venecia** (*Vereda el Rosario, Manizales; www.haciendavenecia.com*). Hacienda Venecia is a working and award-winning coffee farm with every option for your accommodation tastes from backpacker to upmarket. Coffee tours and walking tours around the hacienda come very highly recommended in this verdant cornucopia just 15 minutes outside of Manizales.

WHERE TO STAY *See map, page 357.*

Hotel Carretero (100 rooms) Calle 36, No 22–22; 884 0255/1498; www.hotelcarretero.com. This nice mid-range upmarket hotel option attracts business travellers on a budget with decent rooms throughout the week. The hotel offers an excellent b/fast & clean, comfortable rooms, & huge beds. Try the presidential or junior suite for an extra lounge area. **$$$**

Hotel Estelar Las Colinas (65 rooms) Carrera 22, No 20–20; 884 2009; e ventas@hotelesestelar.com; www.hotellascolinas.com. Comfortable rooms come in a choice of doubles or large singles & are equipped with a desk, satellite

TV, minibar & private hot-water bathrooms. Other amenities on site include internet access & room service. **$$$**

Hotel Fundadores (sleeps 30) Carrera 23, No 29–54; 884 6490; m 318 747 9162; www.hotelfundadores.com. This faux-Paisa building offers reasonably sized rooms (single, double & family-sized) with decent beds & attractive, roomy décor. Rates include a good b/fast. **$$$**

Hostal Kaleidoscopio (6 rooms) Calle 20, No 21–15; 890 1702; www.hostalkaleidoscopio.com. Located in the historical centre of the city, this intimate hostel is clean, comfortable & is known to

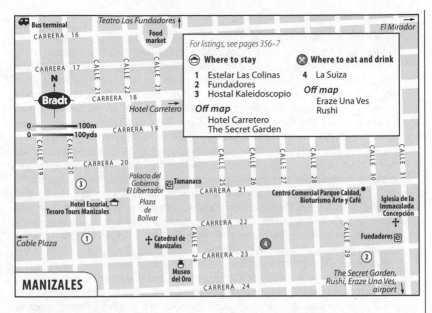

have extremely hospitable, kind owners. B/fast is included & is generous. **$**

🏠 **The Secret Garden** (3 rooms) m 321 770 3020; e stay@thesecretgardenmanizales. com; www.thesecretgardenmanizales.com. Located 30mins from the city centre, this hostel is the best option for visitors wanting a secluded stay surrounded by rolling fields & mountains. The double room has amazing views, with large windows & en suite. Owners Daniel & Eliesha are incredibly knowledgeable about the area; they will go out of their way to make your stay memorable. They also offer a plethora of tours in the coffee region & beyond. B/fast costs 12,000COP. **$**

✕ WHERE TO EAT AND DRINK *See map, above.*

✕ **La Suiza** Carrera 23, No 26–57; www.lasuiza. com.co. Located in the centre, La Suiza is the best when it comes to well-prepared international cuisine. Tasty hamburgers & piquant pastries are washed down with cups of fresh Colombian coffee in this 52-year-old restaurant. The homemade chocolates are delicious, as are the aromatic teas. **$$**

✕ **Rushi Restaurante** Carrera 23C, No 62–27; ☎ 881 0326; ⏰ noon–21.00. A vegetarian restaurant serving lunches & dinners with a splash of gourmet flair. Go at the w/end to see entertainment from harp players to local bands. **$$**

✕ **Eraze Una Ves** Puente de la Libertad (Liberty Bridge) ☎ 874 2484. Excellent late-night dining entwined with dancing is Once upon a time's forte. The decor is wild with brightly coloured chairs, heart-shaped lights & huge book-case walls. The food is both local & international, the service is refreshingly attentive & the late-night music is a real crowd pleaser. A Manizales jaunt wouldn't be the same without visiting Eraze Una Ves. Budget lunches are also available for 10,000COP. **$**

ENTERTAINMENT AND NIGHTLIFE The city has a **municipal auditorium** that stages a wide range of concerts, operas and classical music and boasts some decent nightlife along **Avenida Santander**. Here you will find many of the best discos and restaurants in Manizales, many of them aimed squarely at the city's vibrant student population. For three nights, Thursday to Saturday, the area is packed to the gills around the fast-food restaurants and pizza bars in the area. Dozens of clubs and discos serve up a powerful repertoire of R&B, house, trance, rock, salsa and tango music. The smaller residential neighbourhoods of Batallon and Milan in the south

COLOMBIA'S MAGIC BEANS

Unlike beans from other origins, Colombian coffee is 'washed' in style and it is this that gives it a distinctive rich taste and aroma. There are approximately 60 types of coffee trees in the world, but only ten are mass-cultivated. The most widespread are *Coffea arabica*, *Coffea canephora* and *Coffea liberica*. Of these, *Coffea arabica* is the most cultivated on the planet, representing 90% of the world's coffee production and the most valued of the species. Colombian coffee plants are grown in a nursery from selected beans that are sown close together. After about eight weeks, the seeds germinate and roots develop, and the healthiest plants are selected for nurturing. When the seedlings have grown to about 60cm in height, they are transplanted to the plantation, where they are carefully cultivated. An average coffee tree will take about four years to grow to full size and to blossom. The first fruit appears about six months later. Coffee trees bear ripened fruits and flower at the same time, with each tree producing around 455g of coffee per year. Coffee beans are ready for harvesting when they are a rich, red colour. They are picked individually, bagged up and loaded on to mules for transportation to the only mechanical part of the farming process – the de-pulping.

A machine removes the pulp from two seeds in the centre of each berry, leaving the beans encased in a tough parchment husk. These are put into concrete tanks where they are soaked in cold mountain water for 24 hours before being carefully washed. Twigs, debris and poor-quality beans are discarded at this stage before the good beans are placed in straw baskets. They are then spread out on open-air terraces to be dried in the sun before being sold at market. The beans are tested for aroma, colour, size, moisture and texture with only the best crops sold and distributed for export. Many Colombian growers sell their crops to the National Federation of Coffee Growers, an organisation founded in 1927. Beans are brought to the mill and fed into machines that remove the tough parchment husk and silvery skin. Different screening processes free the beans from impurities and sort them by size, weight and shape. After a final critical inspection to assess aroma, acidity and uniformity, they are packed into bags and sealed for export.

The Colombian Coffee Federation (FNC) is entirely owned and controlled by Colombia's coffee farmers (*cafeteros*), of whom there are over 550,000. Most growers only have around 2ha of land but by joining together they can benefit from the clout of a large organisation. All profits from the FNC are channelled back to the *cafeteros*, with the organisation providing a buffer against the volatile and unpredictable international coffee market. When the market took a dramatic dive in the early 1990s, this system served to compensate the farmers' US$1.5 billion shortfall.

of the city are home to a collection of rather fine dining options and upmarket bars. **Sector Cable** from Calle 63 to 67 on Carrera 23 is the most popular night hangout with trendy bars and clubs catering for students. Meanwhile **Calle del Tango** has been the Tango centre of Manizales since 1971 and has nightly shows – try Tiempo de Tango for lavish shows and Argentinian-style décor. For theatrical shows and art-house films, head to **Teatro Los Fundadores** on the corner of Carrera 22 and Calle 33 (✆ 878 2530).

SHOPPING While Manizales's food market, **Galleria**, remains popular with locals, visitors are well advised to avoid it completely as it is dirty and often dangerous. The **Cable Plaza** (*www.cableplaza.com.co*) on Carrera 23, No 61–11 is a trendy

Colombia's farmers are under no obligation to sell to the FNC as no commercial monopoly exists.

Colombians swear that the basic rule for making the perfect cup of coffee is to start with fresh cold water. Using two level tablespoons of 100% Colombian coffee, add six ounces of boiling water – the perfect quantities and ingredients for a truly splendid cup of coffee.

- There are more than 500,000 coffee producers represented by the National Federation of Coffee Growers of Colombia.
- A cup of coffee from a street vendor will cost around 300COP.
- Coffee is the second most popular drink worldwide; the first is tea.
- 90% of Colombians drink coffee daily.
- Globally, the coffee industry is worth over US$80 billion per annum.
- It takes 42 coffee beans to make an espresso. However, an espresso has one-third of the caffeine of a regular cup of coffee.
- Colombian coffee is grown across seven geographic areas and in 86 microclimates.
- Some Colombian companies actually import coffee from Peru and Ecuador due to the lower cost of beans.
- Brazil is the leading coffee producer, ahead of Vietnam, Indonesia and then Colombia.
- A Belgian living in Guatemala invented the first instant coffee in 1906 and later emigrated to the United States. His name, ironically enough, was George Washington.
- Coffee plants were first grown in Colombia around 1830.
- Starbucks opened its first store in Colombia in 2014; long first-day queues meant people waited in line for hours to be served.
- Vietnam is now the second-largest producer of coffee with the Netherlands the number-one consumer. Americans drink over 400 million cups of coffee per day.
- Some 25 million families worldwide are totally dependent on the coffee crop as their only source of income.

The official site of the Colombian Federación Nacional de Cafeteros (*www.cafedecolombia.com*) offers coffee industry news, yields, prices and statistics for the nation's various coffee-growing regions.

shopping mall which has a swanky supermarket, fashionable clothing stores, cinema, restaurants, bars and a nice view of the mountains.

OTHER PRACTICALITIES First-time visitors can be caught out by Manizales's cool year-round temperatures, which can feel like the Arctic for those fresh in from the Caribbean coast. Pack waterproofs, a thick fleece and dispense with the beach gear – especially during the rather bleak rainy months, March to May and September to November. Those planning to hike, trek or camp will need thermal clothing and cold-weather sleeping bags.

Thankfully, the city's large student population has caused numerous internet cafés to spring up citywide. Most charge around 2,500COP per hour. Some of the most central include the Internet **Café Tamanaco** (✆ *888 6290*) on the corner of Calle 23 and Carrera 21, and **Café Internet Fundadores** (✆ *884 2538*) on Carrera 23, No 30–59.

Almost all of the banks in Manizales have ATMs and are located in and around Calle 21 and Carrera 22, including the Bancolombia, Cambios Country and the Banco Unión Colombiano.

WHAT TO SEE AND DO At the heart of Manizales is the **Plaza de Bolívar** where, even on a dull, wet day, there are always plenty of shoeshine stands and vendors braving the relentless drizzle. In the middle stands an unusual statue by Rodrigo Arenas Betancur. It's dubbed *Bolívar-Cóndor* and depicts El Libertador as a bird. The plaza is flanked to the north by the **Palacio del Gobierno** (Governor's Palace), an attractive Neoclassical building dating back to 1927. On the south, the Gothic **Catedral de Manizales** (Manizales Cathedral) dominates the view and is the third church to occupy the site following earthquakes and fire. Two colourful murals decorate the wall under the cathedral steps and are as strange as the oddball assortment of decorative styles inside the church. The east and west of the plaza are edged by an eclectic array of nondescript shops and restaurants. East, the 20th-century **Iglesia de la Immaculada Concepción** (Church of the Immaculate Conception) has some fine woodcarvings to admire. A block south you'll find the **Museo del Oro** (Gold Museum) (✆ *884 3851; ☉ 08.00–18.00 Mon–Fri, closed 11.30–14.00; free admission*) on Carrera 23, No 23–6, where a small collection of Amerindian gold and ceramics help tell the history of the Quimbaya people.

Festivals and events
Feria de Manizales (January) One of Colombia's biggest events after the Barranquilla carnival, this annual party features parades, concerts, dancing and bullfighting – plus a beauty pageant to crown the Coffee Queen.

Festival Latinoamericano de Teatro (September) For over 40 years, this week-long festival has showcased some of Colombia's finest film-makers as well as the most cutting-edge cinematic talent in Latin America. Today it is arguably the nation's second most important film event, after the festival in Bogotá. Free concerts attract film fans from all over Colombia – and beyond.

AROUND MANIZALES

There's a fabulous lookout point offering astounding views about 18km from the city, on the Manizales–Pereira road. **El Mirador** (The Lookout) also has a rather nice restaurant, which as the name suggests also boasts to-die-for vistas. Swirling mists create ghostly shapes over emerald hills. Vultures sit poised on twisted palms ready to swoop into the valley below. Creeper-clad trees sprout up from tufted grass, shrubs and mile-high ferns.

The 70ha humid rainforest-cum-ecological theme park **Ecoparque De Selva Humeda Tropical Yarumos** (✆ *887 9700*) reopened in 2014, and lies to the west of Manizales and is divided into two zones: education and adventure. Supported by public funds, the park contains 60 plant species, numerous migratory and endemic birds, dozens of butterflies, monkeys, frogs, snakes, iguanas and at least 13 species of tree. Two separate manmade trails wind 1.5km and 2km along waterfalls and are used by scientists from the Alexander von Humboldt Institute for bird research.

In the sector devoted to adventure, there is a covered ice rink, a kids' playhouse, rappelling and a forest canopy ride – the highlight of the park. In the gardens, peacocks strut around a museum of stuffed animals and pickled exhibits. A very ethereal chill-out zone has been built on the roof of the museum building, featuring a vast stone-paved Zen-inspired plaza in which relaxing music is piped day-long. The park's sister attraction lies 10 minutes away to the north. Founded in 2002, **El Bosque de Popular** (Popular Woods) (✎ *887 9700;* e *bosquepopular.1@hotmail. com;* ⊕ *08.00–18.00 daily; free admission*) is a conservation and public space. One million visitors per annum use this picturesque 56ha parkland, a scenic spot with wooded and recreation zones. Close by, the National Coffee Federation-run **El Recinto del Pensamiento** (✎ *889 7073; www.recintodelpensamiento.com* (⊕ *09.00– 16.00 Tue–Sun*) has some nice gardens to visit that are home to almost 300 orchid species and a lake. A 1.5km trail skirts a museum devoted to Colombian rum past a butterfly house and out along a pretty, leafy path. The 179ha site also contains cable cars and a coffee-tasting pavilion. Admission is 17,000–19,000COP with a guide.

PARQUE NACIONAL LOS NEVADOS (LOS NEVADOS NATIONAL PARK) (*www. parquesnacionales.gov.co*) Travellers keen to hike through some of Colombia's most striking terrain will find this 583km² patch of the Andes fits the bill. Not only does this snow-caked range of volcanic peaks – topped by the 5,325m-tall Nevado del Ruiz – offer truly incredible views from trails that climb through cloudforest but it is also relatively easy to access and, most importantly, safe. However, it is very cold and the altitude can pose problems health-wise. On this basis, anyone not feeling 100% fit should give Los Nevados a miss.

A hike to the summit of the still-active Nevado del Ruiz takes about 3 hours. Varying altitudes ensure a collection of well-maintained paths wind through considerable diverse terrains, from humid thickets and cool highland scrubland to crisp, white snow and ice. The range comprises El Tolima (5,215m) at the southern end, followed by El Quindío (4,750m), Santa Isabel (4,950m), El Cisne (4,750m) and then El Ruiz in the north. The park attracts mountaineers from all over the world, many of whom traverse all four peaks. This takes about seven days to complete and is a highly popular challenge.

But it is not just the climbing that has made these mountains famous. On 13 November 1985, at precisely 21.08 Nevado del Ruiz erupted – with catastrophic results. Within four hours vast lava flows had travelled over 100km, leaving total devastation in their wake. More than 23,000 people were killed and more than 5,000 injured. The town of Armero (population 27,500) at the mouth of the Río Lagunillas canyon was hardest hit, disappearing entirely under the mud. Thousands of villagers along the Chinchiná, Gualí and Lagunillas rivers fled in fear as their homes surrendered to the lahars.

Earlier eruptions of Nevado del Ruiz occurred in 1595 and 1845, spewing melted snow and ice and forcing mudflows out into the surrounding valleys. However, when El Ruiz began showing clear signs of unrest in 1984 scientists feared the worst. A series of pyroclastic flows from the summit crater and phreatic (steam) explosions were an early-warning system but weren't enough to enable a firm prediction of when an eruption would occur. El Ruiz had been observed closely for a whole 12 months when, suddenly, pumice and ash began to fall in heavy rain. Within minutes, hot rock fragments melted about 10% of the volcano's ice cover, gouging channels 100m wide and up to 4m deep. A vast sluice of water, ice, pumice and rocks began to flow into the six major river valleys draining the volcano. In one river, the Azufrado, scientists found a 2m piece of ice over 3km from the crater. It is estimated that lahars reached speeds of 60km/h along the Río Guali and were up to 50m thick, quadrupling in size as they eroded soil, loose rock debris and stripped vegetation from the riverbanks. The eruption of Nevado del Ruiz remains the second most deadly in the 20th century. (Mount Pelée in Martinique was first, killing 29,000 people in its 1902 eruption.)

The volcano actually has three craters: Arenas, Olleta and Piraña. Arenas – the main one and the crater responsible for the 1985 disaster – is reached by a relatively easy trek on snow. Olleta has a soil-covered summit that is usually snow-free. It is also extinct, so after the climb to 4,850m many visitors opt to descend into the crater for an alternative view. For a superb meander through beautiful scenery, follow the 40km path to El Cisne and Santa Isabel, where the sparkling waters of the Laguna del Otún at 3,950m are a spectacular sight – and a great place for a spot of trout fishing.

Global warming continues to cause some ongoing shrinkage to the volcanoes due to decreasing levels of annual snowfall. According to a report entitled 'The Thawing of the Peaks' by the director of the Colombian Institute of Hydrology, Meteorology and Environmental Studies, this will have a devastating impact on the local population, severely affecting fresh water supplies within the next 100 years. The volcanoes have been relatively well behaved since 1985; however, since 2013 alerts have been raised causing restrictions to the hiking areas. As recently as 2014, there was a high alert meaning that anywhere above 4,000m was off-limits and El Ruiz was a complete no-go area. At the time of writing, El Ruiz was on yellow alert, meaning access up until Valle de las Tumba.

Spectacled bear (Andean bear), tapir, moose, deer, rabbit, puma, mountain lion, armadillo and squirrel are all found in the park along with sparrow hawk and eagle. It is also notable for its various species of bromeliads, fern and moss.

Practicalities Even when alerts are low it is only possible to explore the park with a registered guide costing 60,000–100,000COP. Visitors wishing to scale El Ruiz will enter the park via the northern access road, a gateway frequently used by those day tripping from Manizales. It's a long day, so be sure to allow at least 10 hours in which to reach around 5,100m and enjoy some truly magnificent views. Vehicles can only gain access via the northern access road so if your route involves the southern entrance you'll need to do it on foot. The northern road begins as La Esperanza just off the Manizales–Bogotá road and climbs up to 4,800m to the base of El Ruiz. It takes around 3 hours to ascend to the Arenas crater of El Ruiz at 5,350m and about 1½ hours to reach Olleta at 4,850m. Two trails offer access to the southern section of the park. One begins in Cocora and climbs up to the highlands and to El Quindío. The other links the Parque Ucumarí to the Laguna del Otún via a 15km uphill path. All visitors should pack boots (or durable trainers), gloves and thick, waterproof clothing and should be sure to stay close to their guide. As it is usual to stop off for a dip in the hot springs at the Hotel Termales, be sure to have a bathing suit with you too. Those staying overnight should be properly equipped with basic essentials, including cold-weather sleeping bags and a torch. Guides should have a satellite phone, emergency flares and a detailed map

When to go The park is open all year round with paths that are passable most days. However, it is more rewarding to avoid days shrouded with mist, fog and heavy cloud as they totally void the views, so plan your trip according to the local weather.

Getting there and around The park isn't served by public transport but most visitors will find that a transfer by **jeep** or **van** is included in the cost of a guide – be sure to double check. A milk truck offers rides out to the park bright and early each day for around 5,000COP – every hotel in town knows the driver, so just ask around.

Where to stay In 2013, the park had to close its Cisne cabin facilities due to concerning rumbles from the Ruiz volcano, meaning it is no longer possible to stay overnight in this part of the park. At the time of writing, there was no date for reopening so to keep up to date with the situation, visit www.parquesnacionales. gov.co, or ring ◥ 887 1611. However, those trekking the Tolima volcano or other peaks in the park can stay in privately owned cabins with basic amenities. For further information about visiting this area, contact the park's information service in Manizales (*Carrera 23, No 70A–44, Barrio La Camelia;* ◥ *887 1611/2273;* e *nevados@parquesnacionales.gov.co*).

Where to eat and drink Apart from the hotel restaurants the only other place to buy food is **El Refugio**, a simple shack selling drinks and snacks. As it opens and shuts on a whim it is wise not to rely solely on this option – to be on the safe side pack a picnic and bring plenty of water.

SALAMINA (*Telephone code 6*) This popular day-trip destination from Manizales attracts coachloads of devotees of the colonial era who visit Salamina to simply stroll through the town's genteel streets and breathe in the ambience of yesteryear. Streets of pretty buildings are dominated by a particularly fine cathedral, built in 1865 by an English architect. One of the oldest settlements in the Zona Cafetera, Salamina was founded in 1825 and has retained much of its original charm. A typical Paisa *pueblo* with a population of around 30,000, its houses boast lots of traditional architectural characteristics, such as ornately carved wooden doors and windows. A small handful of local restaurants and budget hotels can be found in and around the main plaza. Salamina was declared a National Monument in 1982. A frequent bus service connects it with Manizales (16,000COP, 2½ hours), with supplementary *colectivos* that nip back and forth throughout the day (18,000COP, 2 hours) – both pass through the town of Neria, another pretty colonial settlement.

PEREIRA Telephone code 6

With a population of around 600,000, Pereira is Colombia's sixth-biggest city and the largest in the Zona Cafetera – and as the capital of the department of Risaralda, it has coffee coursing through its veins. Founded in 1863, the city was named after Francisco Pereira Martínez, the former owner of the land on which it stands. Dubbed 'the Pearl of the River Otún', Pereira sits within a fertile valley at the very epicentre of the Coffee Zone and is equidistant from Cali and Medellín at around 230km. A succession of destructive earthquakes has dramatically reshaped the city over time. Today, much of Pereira is modern in construction with just a few telltale historic buildings in the city centre – but this hotchpotch of mismatched, patched-up architecture is undoubtedly part of its charm. Pereira is a growing tourism destination with diverse dining options and a few worthwhile sightseeing opportunities. Moreover, at the time of writing, a new eco-park was being built and, when it opens in mid 2015, it will be the biggest of its kind in South America. **Parque Temático de Flora y Fauna** (*http://parquetematicopereira.com*) will house wild African animals in vast enclosures, the biggest botanical park in Colombia and will have various museums and auditoriums dedicated to ecological research and education. The city is also renowned for its partying stamina and love of football, so expect plenty of passion and gusto (along with generous measures of *aguardiente*) when Deportivo Pereira kick off on home soil. Pereira is twinned with Miami and enjoys close links with the Floridian city.

HISTORY Before European colonisation, what became Pereira was the domain of the Quimbaya, a particularly fierce-fighting tribe of indigenous people. Although the Spanish established a small settlement in the area around 1540, the city itself wasn't founded until August 1863. On his death, landowner Francisco Pereira Martínez bequeathed the ground to the priest Remigio Antonio Cañarte for the specific purpose of building a city. Six days later, Pereira was inaugurated on what today is the Plaza de Bolívar. The settlement soon began to attract migrant farmers from Antioquia, ready to exploit Pereira's economically strategic location, fertile soil and good weather. In vast swathes of the mineral-rich volcanic soil of the Andes, they planted coffee crops, heralding the start of an era of prosperity. Over 140 years later, coffee remains the bedrock of the city and the dynamo that powers its economy.

GETTING THERE, AWAY AND AROUND Pereira's **Matecaña Airport** is located 5km west of the centre of the city. In 2014, Avianca began three weekly flights to New York with a 1-hour layover in Cartagena. The same company also flies regularly to Bogotá, while ADA and LAN have direct routes to Medellín. Viva Colombia flies to Cartagena and Santa Marta. At the time of writing, a major redevelopment of the airport was underway with a view to adding further routes from various US cities.

Pereira's **bus** terminal is on Calle 17, No 23–157, about 2km from the city centre. Numerous buses pass by and it's an easy 12-minute trip from the city. Here frequent departures serve Bogotá (55,000COP, 9 hours), Medellín (35,000COP, 5 hours) and Cali (22,000COP, 4 hours). Minibuses to Armenia (6,000COP, 1 hour), Marsella (4,000COP, 1 hour) and Manizales (9,000COP, 1½ hours) leave every 1½ hours.

The city's US$36 million mass transport system opened to much acclaim in 2006. The **Megabus** (*www.megabus.gov.co*) is modelled on Bogotá's hugely successful TransMilenio system and is a public–private partnership.

As of 2015, buses travel across dedicated transit lanes to 39 high-quality stations across the city, stopping on average every 5–7 minutes. There are three main lines – Ruta 1, 2 and 3. Ruta 1 (green) runs from Cuba to Dosquebradas via the west of the city, Ruta 2 (red) runs the same but through the centre, and Ruta 3 (blue) runs from Cuba but services just the centre. A one-way journey costs 1,700COP and runs 05.25 to 20.10. **Taxis** run on meters and the minimum fare is 4,000COP. To get from the bus terminal to the city centre costs 4,500COP.

TOURIST INFORMATION

☑ El Instituto Municipal de Cultura y Fomento al Turismo Office Centro Cultural Lucy Tejada; ☎ 311 6544; www.pereiraculturayturismo. gov.co; ⊕ 07.30–18.30 Mon–Thu, closed noon–14.00, 8.00–18.00 Fri closed noon–14.00

Local government website www.pereira.gov.co

🛏 WHERE TO STAY *See map, page 366.*

🛏 **Gran Hotel** (80 rooms) Calle 19, No 9–19; www.granhotelpereira.com. Despite its faded façade & tired décor, this massive Art-Deco building retains a certain charm. Expect large rooms with grand architectural flourishes. A rather slow restoration project has yet to gather pace – but here's hoping. **$$$**

🛏 **Hotel Abadia Plaza** (50 rooms) Carrera 8, No 21–67; ☎ 335 8398; e reservas.abadiaplaza@ ghlhoteles.com. This is a firm favourite with discerning domestic tourists from Bogotá due to its plush décor, upmarket funkiness & gorgeous bathrooms. Rooms are also fitted with soundproof glass so there is minimal disruption from the noise of the city below. **$$$**

🛏 **Movich Hotel de Pereira** (202 rooms) Carrera 13, No 15–73; ☎ 311 3333. This large, rather swish, modern hotel could be snooty & unwelcoming, but instead it has all the friendliness of a small family-run concern. A large, circular foyer boasts a sunken lounge with daily newspapers & a business centre. Large rooms are well equipped with modern private bathrooms with bath & shower, TV (cable), minibar, desk, phone, safe & room service. On-site amenities include an outdoor pool, spa, gym, 3 restaurants & bar. Highly recommended, if a little out of town. **$$$**

🛏 **Hotel Cataluña** (45 rooms) Calle 19, No 8–61; ☎ 335 4527. This great-value option is located close to the Plaza de Bolívar & has clean, cheerful rooms, some of which have balconies overlooking the street. **$$**

🛏 **Hotel Dann Soratama** (77 rooms) Carrera 7, No 19–20; ☎ 335 8650; www.hotelsoratama. com. Centrally located, this large hotel offers some of the most convenient & comfortable rooms in the heart of the city. Rooms are spacious & clean but the real highlight is the Sky Lounge on the top floor, complete with bar, restaurant & pool. **$$**

🛏 **Kolibri Hostel** (6 rooms) Calle 4, No 16–43; ☎ 331 3955; www.kolibrihostel.com. This highly rated hostel Is perfectly located at the top of Av Circunvalar. Rooms are clean with comfortable beds & are quiet at night. The owners, a Dutch man & his Colombian wife, speak perfect English & are extremely knowledgeable about the coffee region — whether it be a city tour, bike trip, coffee *finca* visit, advice on treks or just city info, nothing is too much trouble. There is a kitchen on the 2nd floor & a pretty balcony to read a book or plan your next excursion. Although b/fast is not included, the attached restaurant serves the best *migas de arepa* (crushed *arepa* with tomato & onion) in the city. **$**

🍴 WHERE TO EAT AND DRINK *See map, page 366.*

There are dozens of funky upmarket international-style restaurants in and around the Zona Rosa's Avenida Circunvalar and the city centre, from pizza joints and Chinese diners to French bakeries and vegetarian buffets. In the centre, restaurants largely serve typical Colombian dishes and Paisa specialities, and if you scratch beneath the surface you can find some diverse cuisine. There are more than a dozen unnamed restaurants in the centre, usually lurking above other shops. Try Calle 23 and 22, leading off Plaza de Bolívar for many of these secret locations.

🍴 **Kilaba** Calle 11, No 12b–27; m 300 275 8570; www.kilaba.com. Located just off Av Circunvalar, Kilaba serves typical Arabic food from falafels to *kibbe*. The owner's homemade bread is a real highlight – so much so that he often has orders from neighbouring towns & villages. **$$**

🍴 **Lenos y Parrilla** Carrera 12, No 2–78. If it's a hearty, succulent steak you desire then Lenos y Parrilla is the place to head. The service has a reputation of excellence as does the Argentine-style cuts of meat. The atmosphere is lively & clientele affluent – although prices are reasonable at 20,000–25,000COP for a steak. **$$**

🍴 **Govinda's Restaurante Vegetariano** Calle 15, No 6–58, 2nd floor; ☎ 333 9650; http://pereira. govindas.co. This Hare Krishna restaurant serves a

365

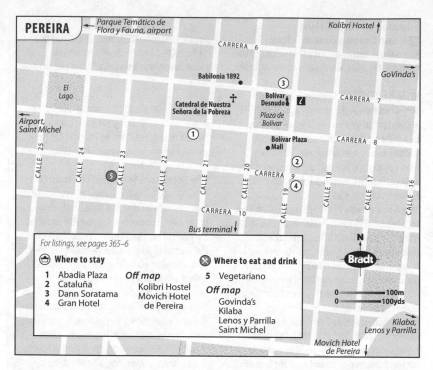

PEREIRA

— Parque Temático de Flora y Fauna, airport

Kolibri Hostel ↑

CARRERA 6

El Lago

Babilonia 1892

③

GoVinda's

Catedral de Nuestra Señora de la Pobreza

Bolívar Desnudo ✚ ℹ

CARRERA 7

← Airport, Saint Michel

Plaza de Bolívar

①

Bolívar Plaza ● Mall

CARRERA 8

CALLE 25 CALLE 24 CALLE 23 CALLE 22 CALLE 21 CALLE 20

CARRERA 9

②

④

CALLE 19 CALLE 18 CALLE 17 CALLE 16

⑤

CARRERA 10

Bus terminal ↓

N

Bradt

For listings, see pages 365–6

🛏 **Where to stay**

1 Abadia Plaza
2 Cataluña
3 Dann Soratama
4 Gran Hotel

Off map
Kolibri Hostel
Movich Hotel de Pereira

🍴 **Where to eat and drink**

5 Vegetariano

Off map
Govinda's
Kilaba
Lenos y Parrilla
Saint Michel

0 ———— 100m
0 ———— 100yds

Kilaba, Lenos y Parrilla →

Movich Hotel de Pereira ↓

filling, tasty lunch consisting of beans, rice, soya sausage, salad, a variation of hot & sweet sauces, organic tea & a sweet dessert. The restaurant is popular with locals & lunchtimes can get incredibly busy. The owners offer free yoga retreats for first-time visitors & are knowledgeable about treks & festivals in the area. $

🍴 **Restaurante Vegetariano** Calle 23, No 9–60, 2nd floor; ☎334 1402; ◷ 11.00–14.00 Mon–Fri. This is one of the best unnamed restaurants in the city offering vegetarian lunches for 7,500COP. Dishes

usually include rice, pasta, vegetables, soy cheese & organic chocolate. Portions are large & can often be shared between 2. $

🍴 **Saint Michel** Av Circunvalar, No 11–44; ☎333 4520; ◷ 08.30–19.00 daily. This petite French bakery is the perfect place to indulge in a puff pastry or cake. Mario the owner is Colombian & learned baking from a Frenchman in Bogotá. His glass cabinets are filled with inexpensive treats such as éclairs, tarts & biscuits. $

ENTERTAINMENT AND NIGHTLIFE The locals describe the city as 'Querendona, trasnochadora y morena' – meaning 'sleepless, loveable and dark' – as everyone in Pereira loves to party, from the city's 20-something student population to the aged grandparents. You'll find an ever-changing club scene that offers rumba, tango, salsa, rock and techno music along with numerous bars. Most of them are located on Avenida Circunvalar and the Turín-La Popa district, where typical Colombian bars and clubs with colourful décor and thumping music attract the hordes. Otherwise head to the centre and check out the bars near Plaza de Bolívar. One place of intrigue is **Babilonia 1892** bar (*Carrera 7, No 20–70*). This is the oldest building in the city and is famed for its great draught beers and three ghosts. The giant square next to Victoria Centro Comercial Regional often hosts concerts and cultural festivals.

SHOPPING Pereira's Bolívar Plaza Mall is conveniently located in the centre and is the most accessible of the city's seven shopping malls. As well as a cinema and paintball centre, it includes dozens of shops and a food court – and is a good place for sporting goods, mobile-phone consumables and clothing. Throughout Pereira you'll see makeshift markets and vendors selling goods laid out on blankets on the pavement. Much of it is knock-off; especially the sunglasses, watches and leather belts. On the outskirts of town on Avenida de Río there is a vast Carrefour superstore – you can't miss it.

OTHER PRACTICALITIES Pereira is home to dozens of internet cafés, many of which are centred on or around the main plaza. Most cost about 2,500COP per hour with **Cybernet** on the square (↳ 334 8840) open seven days a week. Similarly, all of the city's banks are clustered together. Most have ATMs, including the **Banco Unión Colombiano** and the **Bancolombia** on Calle 8. For laundries, head to Carrera 12.

WHAT TO SEE AND DO Much like Manizales, Pereira has a rather unusual monument to Simón Bolívar in the form of Arenas Betancur's *Bolívar Desnudo*. This 11-tonne 8.5m-high bronze sculpture of El Libertador naked on horseback was created in Mexico and then delivered, piece by piece, to Pereira in 1963. 'Naked the horse, naked the fire – as in the hands of Prometheus – naked the flags. Nothing else, nothing less than Prometheus,' Betancur, a teacher, wrote at the time.

Pereira's once-fine **Catedral de Nuestra Señora de la Pobreza** (Cathedral of Our Lady of the Poor) is a shadow of its former self, having been remodelled, rebuilt and repaired several times since the first foundation was laid in 1874. The interior, however, is said to be original and has skeletons in its walls.

Centro Recreativo y Vacacional Comfamiliar (Family Recreation and Vacation Centre) (↳ 313 5600; www.comfamiliar.com) This sprawling 44ha leisure
resort about 10km from Pereira is open for day trippers and vacationers and is popular with urbanites seeking some country fresh air. Hemmed in by a shallow forest, the park-style complex is centred on a wide range of sports and leisure attractions, including six swimming pools, half-a-dozen football pitches, tennis courts, hiking trails, fishing lakes, boating, basketball courts and cycle paths. It's all a bit formula-driven and borders on the tacky in places – but visitors at weekends top 3,000 a day with up to 40,000 people visiting each month. Accommodation options range from cottages and cabins to hotels, with six restaurants reflecting different regional styles of Colombian cuisine. Prices vary depending on the season and are around 100,000COP for a hotel room to 200,000COP for a cottage with outside jacuzzi.

AROUND PEREIRA

CERRITOS (*Telephone code 6*) You'll find the rural area of Cerritos just 5km outside the urban sprawl of Pereira city centre, past hammock stalls and springy grass verges. The Pereira–Cartago road has numbered milestones – look out for 'Entrance 4' on the left-hand side as it leads to a number of *fincas* open to tourists. This collection of large, old farmhouses has been tastefully converted into stylish hotels, bars and restaurants – all of them to great effect. Travellers seeking superb boutique accommodation away from the city should certainly consider the following options:

🏠 **Where to stay and eat**

🏠 **Finca Sazagua** (10 rooms) 8km via Cerritos Entrada 4, Urbanizacion Quimbayita; ↳ 337 9895; e info@sazagua.com, reserves@sazagua.com. A 15min drive from the city centre, this sumptuous

A sex strike may seem like a rather extreme method of persuasion, but for the women of Pereira it was a last-ditch effort in the name of peace. In 2006, every wife and girlfriend of gang members in the city called a sex ban in a bid to get their men to give up the gun. Hundreds took part in what the Colombian media called the 'strike of crossed legs', a protest backed by Pereira's mayor. In 2005, a total of 480 killings were reported in the city (90% of the victims were aged 14–25), prompting a disarmament scheme. However, many wives and girlfriends of gang members were worried that their partners were not handing over their weapons. They met with the mayor and came up with the idea of a sex strike as a clear message to disarm. Studies found that local gang members were drawn to criminality by the desire for status, power and sexual attractiveness, not economic necessity, Colombian radio reported. One of the women told Britain's *Guardian* newspaper: 'We want them to know that violence is not sexy.' The sex ban lasted ten days and attracted widespread global press coverage. In 2010, Pereira's murder rate saw the steepest decline in Colombia, down by 26.5%. In Naples, Italy, in 2008, women formed a similar strike, and another was held in Kenya in 2009. In 2011, Belgian Socialist senator Marleen Temmerman called for a sex strike inspired by the women of Pereira.

high-end former farmhouse looks like something out of *Architectural Digest*. Elegant furnishings adorn every one of the 10 stylish rooms in a property where no compromise has been made on the quality of the décor. Fittings, fixtures & drapes ooze good taste in rooms that overlook handsome gardens & a delightful outdoor pool. The *finca* is also home to a highly acclaimed restaurant & outdoor bar. **$$$**

⌂ **Hacienda Malabar** (7 rooms) ☎ 337 9206; e malabar@une.net.co. A neighbouring property 7km from Pereira. Offering a range of doubles & family suites with beautiful tiled floors & blood-red colourwashed walls, this aged *finca* has wooden shutters & chunky wooden furniture & ornate balconies overlooking flower-filled gardens. Huge baskets piled high with bananas flank the hallway, as do vast vases of birds of paradise. A rather good restaurant boasts a lime-green décor with exposed stone. Rooms start at 133,000COP for a double, and rates include b/fast. **$$$**

⌂ **Hacienda San Jose** (11 rooms) Km4, Vía Pereira – Cerritos, Entrada 16 Cadena El Tigre; ☎ 313 2612 /735 2321; www.

haciendahotelsanjose.com. It's worth taking a couple of days to experience this beautiful old, family-run farmhouse approx 6km outside Pereira. With stunning, perfectly landscaped private gardens, a pristine pool surrounded by flowers & large, decadent-style suites, it offers real respite at the end of a busy day coffee-touring. There's a remarkable 'Saman' tree – an icon of the hacienda – which is so large & majestic-looking you will stare in wonder. The owners have respected the history of the place, maintaining interesting elements like ancient saddles & old furniture. With only 8 suites, left unlocked, there's a calmness to the place, where time is passed reading, lazing by the pool & eating some of the most delicious food in the country. Juan Martin the owner will help organise fantastic day trips from the hacienda through Living Trips (*www.livingtrips. com*), including the Hotel Termales de Santa Rosa, the thermal baths at Balneario & San Vicente, El Bosque del Samán which has a 60m canopy over the coffee plantations, & rafting in the Río Barragan. **$$**

SANTUARIO OTÚN QUIMBAYA In the early 1990s, this 5km² of Andean forest was under threat. Today, its staggering biodiversity is beautifully preserved. Located 15km southeast of Pereira, and sitting at altitudes of between 1,800m and 2,400m, the Santuario contains several pleasant ecological trails, a lodge for overnight stays and a restaurant. Since 1996, it has been part of the Colombian government's national conservation programme. Rare plant species and vulnerable wildlife have been protected and the integrity of the natural environment restored. Today the area is used purely for ecological studies and ecotourism with five different well-maintained paths that climb through mountain forests where the average temperature is 16°C. Those wishing to combine a visit with a trip to the Parque Ucumarí can do so on foot in about 4 hours. Butterflies and birdlife are particularly rich along this wooded route.

Getting there and away Catch a *chiva* with the company Transportes Florida from Pereira towards El Cedral and get off at La Suiza at the entrance of the park. The *chiva* leaves at 07.00, 09.00 and 15.00 from La Plaza Civica Ciudad Victoria (✆ *334 2721*).

Where to stay and eat The reserve's only option is **Yarumo Blanco** (m *314 674 9248; www.yarumoblanco.co; $–$$*). Here three types of rooms are available: a double with private bathroom for 70,000COP; a room with two beds for 80,000COP, and a room with a shared bathroom for 32,000COP. Food is not included but isn't expensive with breakfast 7,000COP and lunch 10,000COP. A walk through the forest costs 40,000COP per group.

MARSELLA (*Telephone code 6*) Located 30km northwest of Pereira, this charming town is home to around 25,000 people and is totally surrounded by emerald carpets of coffee fields. Founded in 1860 by Antioquian farmers, Marsella is every inch the typical Paisa town. Most people visit to mooch around the tiny streets and the **Jesús María Estrada cemetery** before heading out for a stroll around the **Jardín Botánico Alejandro Humboldt** (Alexander von Humboldt Botanical Garden) (✆ *368 5233; ⊕ 08.00–17.00 daily*), where an hour-long trail along a cobblestone path winds through orchids, ferns and bamboo. Created in 1979 as an education and research facility, the gardens offer plenty of insight into the ecosystem of the Zona Cafetera. It contains a museum dedicated to promoting the protection of local bird species from the local region. The **Museo de la Cauchera** (Slingshot Museum) has actively sought to discourage local children killing birds with catapults – once a much-practised pastime.

Getting there and away Minibuses run to and from Pereira each day until around 19.00, every 15 minutes (5,000COP, 45 minutes).

SANTA ROSA DE CABAL (*Telephone code 6*) Tourism has become a focus of the town of Santa Rosa de Cabal, once a delightful one-horse pit stop that welcomed travellers *en route* to the surrounding thermal pools. Today, it has a handful of basic budget hotels, including the **Hotel Del Turismo** at 30,000COP per night, and is pushing itself forward as a destination to be reckoned with. Those who stay in the town can hop aboard a *chiva* that heads to the thermals three times a day for around 3,000COP each way. Times vary, so ask at the hotel for specifics. The hotel can also help you hire a driver and a jeep for around 40,000COP return trip.

The **Termales de Santa Rosa** (Santa Rosa Thermal Pools) (formerly Termales Arbeláez) (⊕ *08.00–midnight; day-guest admission 34,000COP*) are located 8km east of the town on the Pereira–Manizales road. A resort aimed squarely at tourists is totally engulfed by its natural surroundings in a truly stunning location that prompts audible involuntary intakes of breath. A 170m waterfall provides a formidable backdrop to the complex, where hot springs reach temperatures of

70°C but cool to around 40°C in the pool. Other amenities include a restaurant, bar and a hotel. Many choose to stay overnight at the very nice **Hotel Termales** (✆ *364 5500/1322*), where a wide range of accommodation offers something for every guest. Opt for the Casa Finca where rooms can comfortably accommodate up to seven people at 80,000–100,000COP per person, or stay in the newer **La Montaña cabins** (five to seven people) at 100,000–140,000COP per person and not including meals – it's not cheap, but it is worth the splurge.

ECO TERMALES SAN VICENTE (SAN VINCENT THERMAL POOLS) (*Telephone code* 6) Another popular thermal bath close to the Termales de Santa Rosa, this newer resort-style set-up is located 18km east of Santa Rosa de Cabal at the end of an unmade road. Leafy trails lead out to waterfalls and bloom-filled thickets on a complex that comprises a hotel, campsite, cabins and several thermal pools. There is also a place to take a mud bath and enjoy a massage. Packages range from a day-long visit (20,000COP) to a full-week stay.

Getting there and away The trip to the Eco Termales San Vicente takes just over an hour from Pereira. Transport departs daily from the Eco Termales San Vicente office at around 08.00 with the return leg at 17.00, and costs 10,000COP.

⌂ **Where to stay and eat** Accommodation at **Eco Termales San Vicente** (*www. sanvicente.com.co/*) ranges from a tent on its campsite (55,000COP) to a double room with or without a bathroom (100,000COP). Alternatively you can stay in a *cabaña* that sleeps six (100,000COP). Rates include use of the thermal pools. A restaurant serves lunch and dinner at around 12,000COP a head.

Other practicalities Visits to the Eco Termales San Vicente can be booked through the website www.sanvicente.com.co, or by calling ✆ 333 6157. The website offers full-day packages that include return transportation, lunch, snacks and full access to the pools at 65,000COP. Accommodation also needs to be booked in advance. Those wanting to camp need to bring their own equipment including tents, sleeping bags, towels and bathing costumes.

PARQUE NATURAL REGIONAL UCUMARÍ (UCUMARÍ REGIONAL NATURAL PARK) (✆ *314 1455*) A trail links this 43km^2 natural reserve with the Parque Nacional Los Nevados, winding along the Río Otún and through a magnificent gorge. Located about 30km east of Pereira, Parque Ucumarí was established in 1984. It offers a range of decent bird-filled hiking paths that rise up through forest-clad hillsides past waterfalls on to cloud-shrouded summits – some more gruelling than others. More than 185 bird species have been recorded here and the park is also home to a rich abundance of wildlife, including the spectacled bear. Rugged boulders and ice-cold streams pepper a rugged terrain covered in vibrant green vegetation. Mules and horses can be rented from the reserve's *refugio* – a worthwhile expense for those with camping gear, especially on the 8-hour trek to the Laguna del Otún.

Getting there and around From Pereira **bus** terminal, *chivas* will take you up the El Cedral, about 25km from the centre of town. It's a rough road but the scenery makes it a pleasant hour-long drive. From El Cedral (at 1,950m), the 5km uphill trek along the Río Otún to La Pastora will take around 2 hours. An enterprising local lad sometimes tethers his **horse** at the start of the trail to attract custom from those lacking stamina.

🏠 **Where to stay and eat** The reserve's Refugio La Pastora (**$$**) sits at 2,400m and can accommodate 22 guests in rooms that sleep four to eight. However, there is almost unlimited capacity for those prepared to sleep on mattresses around the campfire and there is also plenty of space for those prepared to pitch a tent for 5,000COP. A decent breakfast (6,000COP), lunch (9,000COP) and dinner (9,000COP) are served from a rudimentary kitchen. The *refugio* hires out guides at 80,000COP per day. It costs 18,000COP per person to stay overnight in a cabin.

Other practicalities Visitors need a permit to visit the reserve and will also need to pre-book and pre-pay for any accommodation. Both can be done via the Grupos Ecológicos de Risaralda (GER) office in the Centro Comercial Fiducentro Local A 119 in Pereira (✎ *325 4781;* e *grupos_ecologicos@yahoo.com*) – they can also help with transport, maps and guides.

ARMENIA *Telephone code 6*

Bearing the battle scars of earthquakes past, Armenia is not a city renowned for its beauty, with streets that have a rather makeshift, make-do feel. What hasn't been patched up seems to have been rebuilt in functional style. Construction born out of urgent necessity rarely wins awards for elegance and Armenia makes little pretence at that. However, the city does sit on some of the most beautiful countryside in the Zona Cafetera, between a luxuriant valley and the peaks of the Cordillera Central. Almost a third of Armenia's historic centre was razed by the region's 1999 earthquake. That it re-established itself with both speed and determination is testament to the gritty fortitude of the Armenian population, many of whom played an active role in literally piecing the city back together. Today Armenia is very much back in business and is dubbed 'Ciudad Milagro' (Miracle City), a bustling trade centre with coffee, bananas and plantains at its heart. This busy transportation hub seems permanently jam-packed with tooting cars, street markets, horses and carts, buses, taxis and shoeshine stands with cargo-laden highways that lead into the chaotic mix.

HISTORY Armenia was founded in October 1889 by hunter Jesús María Ocampo, a man whose success at trapping jaguars earned him the nickname 'Tigrero' (meaning 'tiger killer'). He bought the land for 100 pesos in gold coins and set about building a trade centre to serve the settlements that were beginning to spring up in the region. Within six months of its founding, Armenia's population had soared to 100 people, gaining it legal recognition by the government. Initially called Villa Holguin after the then president of Colombia, the name was changed to Armenia to honour the Armenian people murdered in the Hamidian massacres of 1894–97.

Armenia's rapid growth and expanding economy were hampered by poor transportation with mule trains used to traverse the mountainous terrain. The construction of an asphalt road in 1927 gave the city's prosperity further impetus and Armenia soon became a thriving distribution centre. In 1966, it became capital of the newly created Quindío department.

In 1999, disaster struck in the form of an earthquake. It measured 6.2 on the Richter scale and reduced large areas of the city to rubble. The devastation was immense and destroyed 70% of the homes in Armenia. More than 1,180 people were killed and 5,000 injured. Over 28,000 people were still living in '*alojamientos*' (multi-family spaces) in transitory camps two years after the disaster, placing enormous pressure on the provision of basic sanitary services, water supplies and food. A ten-strong team of search and rescue experts from Scotland helped

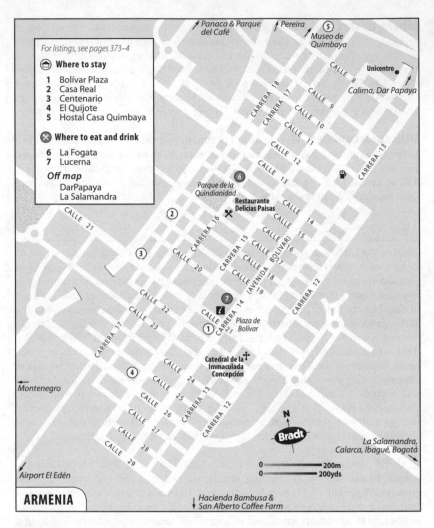

For listings, see pages 373–4

⊙ **Where to stay**

1 Bolívar Plaza
2 Casa Real
3 Centenario
4 El Quijote
5 Hostal Casa Quimbaya

⊗ **Where to eat and drink**

6 La Fogata
7 Lucerna

Off map
DarPapaya
La Salamandra

ARMENIA

to recover survivors. Volunteers from the International Rescue Corps (IRC) had previously been called upon after earthquakes in Afghanistan, Iran and Japan.

GETTING THERE, AWAY AND AROUND El Edén Airport is well outside the city, 20km southwest on the road to Cali. Avianca offers about half-a-dozen **flights** a day to Bogotá, where domestic and international connections can be made. ADA flies to Medellín and Spirit flies to Fort Lauderdale, US. The city's **bus** terminal is located on the corner of Carrera 19 and Calle 35 1.5km southwest of the centre. It is served by the many frequent buses that run along Carrera 19 and is a 5,000COP **taxi** ride from the centre of town. There's a good service to both Bogotá (53,000COP, 8 hours) and Cali (21,000COP, 4 hours), with **minibuses** serving Pereira (7,000COP, 1 hour), Manizales (11,000COP, 2½ hours), Filandia (4,200COP, 1 hour), Salento (4,000COP, 50 minutes), and the Parque Nacional del Café (2,500COP, 30 minutes) every 15 minutes. The terminal is well equipped with tourism stands and local companies offering trips to the coffee region and Parque Nacional del Café.

TOURIST INFORMATION

Armenia Cultura and Turismo Carrera 19A between Calles 26 & 29; 741 2991; www. armeniaculturayturismo.gov.co; ⏰ 08.00–18.00 Mon–Fri, closed noon–14.00

WHERE TO STAY See map, page 372.

In the city centre, there are a number of large hotels. Rates are competitive although very few look very much from the outside.

Hotel Bolívar Plaza (18 rooms) Calle 21, No 14–17; 741 0083; e hotelbolivarplaza@ telsat.com.co. As the city's most lavish accommodation, this hotel's major selling point is its stunning mountain views as its rooms are actually quite small. However, many look out on to the Cordillera Central – & some have balconies. Each has a private bathroom, cable TV & a minibar with on-site facilities that include a laundry, café/ bar & a very nice upper-floor restaurant, again with rather fine views. **$$$**

Hotel Centenario (35 rooms) Calle 21, No 18–20; 744 3143; www.hotelcentenario.com. Don't be put off by the rather synthetic façade of this central hotel as the interior is very nice. The rooms are clean & comfortable with cable TV, minibar & room service available in configurations that include 2 large family rooms & 48 doubles. The hotel's top-floor restaurant, Los Cristales, is widely praised & can accommodate 60 diners, offering a varied menu of delicious *comida típica* & international dishes until 22.00 each day. There is also an on-site gym & sauna. **$$**

Hotel El Quijote (16 rooms) Carrera 15, No 25–8; 744 0663. Offering some of the quietest rooms in the city, the El Quijote is set beyond the worst of the traffic & mayhem. It's nothing special, but rooms are modern & clean in this relatively new hotel. All rooms are doubles & come with private bathroom but b/fast is not included. **$$**

Hostal Casa Quimbaya (5 rooms) Calle 16n, No 14–92; 732 3086. The most popular hostel in Armenia is located just out of the city centre close to the university. The hostel offers basic but clean rooms with shared bathrooms, a nice garden, snack bar & kitchen. The cafe attached is a real highlight with delicious cocktails, shakes & food. **$**

Hotel Casa Real (19 rooms) Carrera 18, No 18–36; 741 4550; www.hotelcasarealarmenia. amawebs.com. This decent budget option has small, pokey rooms with mismatched furnishings – however, each has a private bathroom & is spotlessly clean & well equipped. Choose from single or double plus family options – each has cable TV. **$**

WHERE TO EAT AND DRINK See map, page 372.

On the main drag into town from the airport on the city's outer edge you'll find a number of cheap places serving good local food. Aimed squarely at the locals, none of them is particularly fancy. Otherwise the centre has coffee shops and restaurants for cheap *menu del dias*, as well as stalls in the middle of the street selling fresh fruit juices like *guanabana*. More upmarket places can be found near Parque de la Vida on Carrera 51d, No 62–42.

La Fogata Av Bolívar, No 14n–39; 749 5980; www.lafogata.com.co/es. A popular restaurant which serves excellent grilled meats & a spectacular *ossobuco*. The wine list is wide & they also sell draught beers from Bogotá Beer Company. A tad expensive, but worth the indulgence. **$$–$$$**

DarPapaya Av Centenario, Carrera 6la; 310 401 9995. Located in front of Calima shopping centre, DarPapaya is popular among locals thanks to a cool atmosphere, spectacular mountain views & a menu of well-priced international & Colombian

food. Varied fish dishes include grilled salmon, a shellfish *cazuela* & king prawns in a coconut & curry sauce. **$$**

Restaurante La Salamandra Carrera 6ta, No 6–80; 744 2880. This high-end restaurant serves international cuisine, & specialises in meat dishes. The portions are good & the service attentive. Stay around afterwards for a coffee on the terrace overlooking the mountains. There is also a separate restaurant decorated like a rainforest for children. **$$**

✕ Lucerna Calle 20, No 14–40. Located just off Plaza de Bolívar, this conventional café is a popular lunch spot among locals. Burgers & sandwiches cost 6,000–9,000COP. $

SHOPPING AND OTHER PRACTICALITIES On the road into the city from La Tebaida and the airport there are numerous vendors selling handicrafts and woven hammocks.

Armenia has several large shopping centres, the best of which are **Unicentro** and **Calima**. Both are filled with fashionable shops, restaurants and cinemas. Streets leading off Plaza de Bolívar are lined with shops for clothes, phones, electronics and furniture. The banks all have ATMs, including the **Bancolombia** on Calle 20, No 15–26, and there are several **internet cafés** in the centre. Most of the best money changers are housed within the Centro Comercial IBG building on Carrera 14, No 18–56, but they are only open during the week.

WHAT TO SEE AND DO Although there aren't many sightseeing opportunities amidst Armenia's urban sprawl, roads leading off Plaza de Bolívar (Bolívar Square) offer decent shops and restaurants. An elevated location atop a gentle slope affords good views of the mountains. As in Manizales and Pereira, the plaza in Armenia is also home to a rather eccentric monument to Simón Bolívar, in this instance the Rodrigo Arenas Betancur-designed *Monumento al Esfuerzo* (*Monument to Effort*). The rather grim-looking **Catedral de la Immaculada Concepción** (Cathedral of the Immaculate Conception) is also on the main square but is no object of beauty. Not surprisingly Armenia's centre is bursting with coffee shops and street vendors selling locally brewed cups of Joe. The **Museo de Quimbaya** (Quimbaya Museum) (✆ 749 8433; ☉ 09.00–17.00 Tue–Sun; free admission) on Avenida Bolívar is definitely worth a visit. A large collection of pre-Columbian artefacts includes about 400 gold objects, 104 pieces of anthropomorphic pottery and 22 stone sculptures and carvings mainly from the pre-Columbian Quimbaya civilisation. One of the most important pieces is a fine gold *poporos*, a traditional gadget for the chewing of coca leaves.

AROUND ARMENIA

LA TEBAIDA Armenia's airport is actually located in the small town of La Tebaida and as you journey towards the city you'll see numerous stalls on the right-hand side of the road selling milk, netted bags of oranges and great hands of bananas. There are also a couple of handicraft vendors, including the **Artisanas de Tebaida** and numerous snack kiosks and food stalls as well as the **Restaurante Paisa**, a rustic local eatery selling set meals for about 6,000COP. Just before you enter Armenia there are another couple of decent food joints, including the **Estación Paraíso** – a restaurant and coffee bar with outside seating and a children's playground.

HACIENDA BAMBUSA (*8 rooms;* m *300 778 8897;* **$$$**). Colombia is packed full of charming haciendas and *fincas*, but Hacienda Bambusa, 30km south of Armenia, is arguably one of the country's finest. If you are a nature-lover in search of somewhere to simply disappear and immerse yourself in the quietness of rural surrounds, this magical spot will not disappoint. After a 45-minute taxi ride from Armenia station, you'll reach the entrance to Bambusa's land, before driving for at least 10 minutes down the long track to the hacienda, taking in the abundant plantations of bananas, plantains and a whole variety of other fruits and vegetables growing all around.

Rooms are elegant, simple and rustic, some with balconies and private hammocks, where seeing hummingbirds flying around you showing off their vibrant colours is the norm. There's also a decent-sized pool.

There appears to be a Bambusa 'microclimate', meaning for most of the year it is warm and sunny there, even when 20 minutes down the road it might be pouring with rain, so eating alfresco is standard practice. Food is genuine Colombian cuisine with breakfasts filled with fresh fruit and delicious local coffee. Activities include spectacular birdwatching, visiting the nearby coffee plantations and, above all, embracing the natural stillness of Bambusa. In 2014, the Hacienda was taken over by English-speaking Oliver who oversees operations along with on-site manager Pablo.

SAN ALBERTO COFFEE FARM *(Buena Vista, Quindío;* \ *682 714 21;* e *terraza@ cafesanalberto.com; www.cafesanalberto.com;* ⊕ *daily)* Buena Vista, meaning literally 'lovely view', lies at 1,500m above sea level, with views over the Quindío Valley and Valle de Cauca. Just above the town, at 1,800m is the San Alberto plantation, an exceptional family-run coffee business offering a unique take on coffee production. The owner, unusually, spent some years in France working on vineyards, and on his return to Colombia decided he wanted to inject some of the finesse of wine growing and tasting into the world of coffee. As a result, San Alberto coffee is produced under a new and enlightening approach focusing on premium coffee. You'll have the opportunity to sample coffee as you might taste wine at a vineyard and will finish the tour with arguably the best cappuccino you'll ever taste.

PARQUE NACIONAL DEL CAFÉ (NATIONAL COFFEE PARK) (\ *753 6095; www. parquenacionaldelcafe.com;* ⊕ *depending on the season; admission fees reflect the number of rides you may want to go on, starting at 24,000COP & rising to 58,000COP for all)* On the face of it, a coffee-themed fun park may seem like an odd concept, but the National Coffee Park is one of the most visited tourist draws in Colombia. Building work on the park began in 1991 and since the Colombian Federation of Coffee Growers first threw open its gates in 1995 it has continued to attract crowds in their droves – 6,000 a day at its peak. Originally a 12ha site, it has since grown to 96ha, with every single square metre dedicated to Colombia's beloved bean. Disney it isn't, but that doesn't prevent the daily hordes from reaching fever-pitch excitement, especially during one of the highly popular 'Show del Café' musical extravaganzas. Multiple performances a day take place in a packed auditorium where the atmosphere is as highly charged as a boy-band concert. Clapping, whooping and hollering accompany a series of songs and dances that tell the story of how the coffee crop became the bedrock of the Colombian economy. It's a slick, well-choreographed visual production with beautiful costumes and catchy *bambuco* and *pasillo* music. Lyrics centre on the happy life of a Paisa *campesino* coffee picker with lots of machete-throwing dark-haired hombres in neckerchiefs. It's a real crowd-pleaser, and well worth the queue. Other attractions at the park include cable cars, buggy rides, go-karts, funfair rides, roller coasters (including 'krater' – a ride of 360 twists and vertical drops built in 2014), shops, dozens of restaurants and a number of ecological trails through coffee fields. Expansive gardens, lakes and pools lead to plazas and fountains. There is also a museum and, of course, places to buy and drink Colombian coffee. A food court offers Paisa dishes, pizza, fried chicken, Tex-Mex and sandwiches. The *cazuela de frijoles* at the Babor de mi Terra is highly recommended – but only for those with a big appetite.

Getting there and away The Parque Nacional del Café is located in Montenegro about 15km west of Armenia and is well served by **minibuses** from the city.

Where to stay and eat

El Delirio Quindío (10 rooms) \745
0405; m 310 438 9005; e casadelirio@hotmail.
com. Ignore the fact the gates are locked at this
beautiful old *finca* on the Montenegro road to
the Parque Nacional del Café – simply toot your
car horn or hang around expectantly & someone
will turn up to let you in. Set in stunning, mature
gardens, the property is a handsome farmhouse
in the truest sense & a fine example of the
Coffee Zone's rustic chic. Enjoy fine views across
immaculate grounds in stylish surroundings. A
handful of rooms can accommodate up to 18
people. Be sure to check the rooms before you
settle in as some are more private than others. **$$**

Finca Villa Nora (7 rooms & cabin);
m 310 422 6335. Conveniently located within
2.5km of the Parque del Café & 16km from
Armenia, the Finca Villa Nora seems to be from a
bygone era. Set off the road to Quimbaya on the
outskirts of a small village, this traditional red-&-
white painted wooden plantation home is truly
magnificent, offering lofty views across coffee &
banana fields amidst a cacophony of birdsong.
Although the present house was built in the early
20th century, the land has been in the same family
since 1892 & owners Nohora Londoño & Roberto
Echeverry are a mine of information on local
history & culture. Generous, attentive & friendly,
the couple genuinely enjoy inviting foreign guests
into their beautiful home. Acts of extraordinary
kindness appear to be very much the norm here,
be it a delicious menu of your personal favourite
Colombian delicacies or the loan of a car for the
night. Nohora & Roberto turned to agricultural
tourism in the early 1990s when coffee prices fell
to an all-time low. They still farm 15ha of guayaba,
bananas, macadamia nuts & cattle but have
worked hard building up a sterling reputation at
their *finca*. 6 traditional wooden-floored rooms
with solid oak furniture, rugs & throws each have
private bathrooms. A cabin in the grounds can
accommodate small groups. 3 very good meals are
included in the room rate. **$$**

PARQUE NACIONAL DE LA CULTURA AGROPECUARIA (KNOWN AS PANACA)

(\ 758 2830; e *panaca@panaca.com.co; www.panaca.com.co;* ⊕ *09.00–18.00 Tue–
Sun*) This agricultural attraction is part fun, part education, a complex with a strong
ecological ethos set up to showcase the importance of farming to Colombia. 'Without
the country, there is no city,' says the literature – and in the rural communities
of the Coffee Zone the locals are vehement that this is true. The park opened in
December 1999 and is privately funded by donations. A high proportion of visitors
to PANACA are wide-eyed urbanites with little idea of what agriculture involves.
Thematic displays explain exactly what is involved in getting milk to Bogotá in time
for the city to eat its cereal. They also detail the sheer hard work required to rear
livestock, grow crops and harvest. Visitors are transported by an old jalopy to eight
different farming zones that span 103ha to vast self-contained farms that centre on
individual species, such as poultry, cows, pigs, dogs and horses. PANACA produces
its own eggs, milk, meat and fruit for the half-dozen restaurants on site. The milk is
sold throughout Colombia under the brand name 'Colanta'. Everything on the farm
is organic and recycled with almost all of its fuel derived from manure. Visitors are
encouraged to feed, touch, taste and smell everything in interactive exhibitions and
live demonstrations. There are numerous picnic areas, lookout points, a medicinal
plant zone and a composting plant. A silk farm is one of PANACA's newest ventures
and there are already plans to make and sell sarongs, scarves and neckerchiefs.

The land in which the farms are set is extremely beautiful with rolling fields that
rise and fall in soft curves. Large thickets of needle-thin *guadua* (bamboo) provide
the raw materials for many of the buildings in the park – there is a plentiful supply
as this rampant species grows at a rate of 6cm per day. There are also numerous
birds, cacti and flower-filled hedgerows along well-maintained paths. Activities
include canopy rides, horseriding, ecological hikes, bull-roping, equestrian shows,
camping and sheep shearing. Each activity and show requires an entrance fee as

does entrance to the park, so the most cost-effective method is to buy the Pasaporte Terra ticket (59,000COP), which includes access to the nature walk, ten animal-and plant-stations, and entrance to five shows.

Getting there The park is located just outside of the town of Quimbaya on the Filandia road. The park isn't served by public transport but can be reached by *colectivo* or **taxi** from Quimbaya or Filandia.

🏠 Where to stay and eat

🏠 **Hotel Decameron Panaca** (125 rooms & 20 villas) ☏741 0505; www.decameron.com. This luxurious all-inclusive resort is the ideal place to stay when visiting Panaca. Located in front of the park, guests make the 5min journey between the two via a lovely bridge. Delightful antique furnishings & fittings are entwined with vibrant blooms giving a rustic/exotic ambience. The resort has a sauna, pool, 2 restaurants, 3 bars, tennis court, spa treatment room & English-speaking staff. Rooms are spacious, beautifully tiled, & have hammocks on the balconies. There are various tariffs available, but all include access to Panaca & Parque del Café. **$$$**

EL BOSQUE DEL SAMÁN (*24 rooms;* ☏ *336 5589;* m *315 543 4446;* e *reserves@ fincahotelbosque.com; www.bosquesdelsaman.com;* **$$**) This private reserve is located 15km north of Panaca park and is renowned for its forest canopy tours. Night tours are a particular highlight but must be booked in groups and in advance. At 2,000m, the views are incredible over surrounding village rooftops and open country. Overnight accommodation is offered in two separate buildings. An older, typical Antiochian *finca* has cheerful rooms complete with private bathroom and television, and there's also a new construction with larger rooms equipped with en-suite bathroom, television and balcony with hammock. Communal facilities include a lounge, two restaurants, outdoor terrace swimming pool, jacuzzi and sauna. A romantic plan is also available in a bamboo cabin with a private jacuzzi. Seasonal rates and special discounts apply.

FILANDIA (*Telephone code 6*) Established in 1878, Filandia (meaning 'daughter of the Andes') has an urban population that barely exceeds 6,500 in a town that has a collection of general stores, barbershop and a couple of bars well stocked with *aguardiente*. This small, well-preserved *pueblo* Paisa is legendary as the setting of popular RCN *telenovela* (soap opera), *Café Con Aroma de Mujer* (*Coffee with the Scent of a Woman*) – a series by Fernando Gaitán Salom, of *Ugly Betty* fame.

🏠 Where to stay and eat

Filandia is slowly beginning to make its way on to the tourist map and there are now ten hostels and hotels. Places to eat are overwhelmingly cheap and cheerful and you'll find several.

🏠 **Hostal Tibouchina** (8 rooms) Calle 6, No 5–01; ☏758 2646. This delightful option located in an unrivalled position on the corner of the Plaza de Bolívar & maintaining the original artistry of a traditional Coffee Zone house complete with brightly coloured balconies & decorative windows consists of 8 rooms ranging from shared dorms to private en suites. **$**

🏠 **Bidea Hostal and Camping** (6 rooms) Barrio La Cauchera; m 301 392 0542; e bideahostal@gmail.com; www.bideahostal.com. Basic yet clean & inexpensive, the Bidea is the no-frills option for travellers to Filandia. Located just 2 blocks from the main plaza, an ideal location for those on a budget. **$**

Getting there **Minibuses** from Armenia nip back and forth throughout the day (4,000COP, 1 hour).

SALENTO (*Telephone code 6*) This beautiful and colour-rich small town is packed with historic buildings and charming streets. The oldest settlement in Quindío, Salento was founded in 1850, and today provides a sharp contrast to the brashness of Armenia's architectural mêlée. With its fine, colourwashed traditional houses set around a charming main square, Salento is rich in aged character and bygone quaintness. Slim backstreets flow from the square and are lined with artisanal shops, cafés and restaurants. The main street, Calle Real, throbs with street musicians entertaining crowds. The scent of coffee and incense smoke seeps from handicraft and jewellery stores. At the weekend the town is descended upon by residents of neighbouring cities and towns for jovial parties often spilling out from the tented bars in the centre. Aim to go in the dry season, December to March and July to August, as most activities require good weather. And head there on a national holiday for a much more raucous atmosphere. A local tip is to organise activities when the moon is full, thus ensuring the driest weather.

Apart from strolling through the streets to soak up Salento's cosy ambience, most people arrive to visit the Valle de Cocora, a picturesque area famous for its concentrating wax palms (*palmas de cera*, see page 381), Colombia's national tree. The world's tallest palm tree reaches heights of 60m and from the lushness of the valley the views are quite breathtaking across skinny soaring tree trunks and out to snow-capped peaks. Take the path that leads from the end of Calle Real up the steps and to Alto de la Cruz – it is well worth the climb for views across the valley. An alternative option is to catch a jeep to the small neighbouring town of Cocora (3,000COP, 35 minutes) – or do the 11km on foot for a pleasant 2-hour walk. From here it is possible to hire a horse to explore the Valle de Cocora in depth or begin your organised trek up the mountains.

THE FACE OF COLOMBIAN COFFEE

Juan Valdez (*www.juanvaldez.com*) is Colombia's most famous name in coffee, an iconic brand and fictional character who has represented the country's coffee since 1981 and is more instantly recognisable to Colombian citizens than McDonald's. Wearing his poncho and sombrero, the moustachioed Juan Valdez stands alongside his faithful mule, Conchita, with Colombia's rugged mountains in the background. The brand was developed to reflect old-time Colombian *cafeteros*, the coffee-bean pickers of the nation's Zona Cafetero. The image was created to strengthen consumer loyalty to 100% Colombian coffee that has been inspected and approved by the National Federation of Coffee Growers of Colombia; the face of Juan Valdez guarantees that the coffee is wholly Colombian.

The National Federation of Coffee Growers of Colombia appointed the Doyle Dane Bernbach advertising agency to develop the brand. It chose the name 'Juan Valdez' because of its generic popularity on the basis that Latin America would readily identify with such common Hispanic names. Yet Juan Valdez isn't purely a logo; he is also a real live person – or three people to be more precise. Juan Valdez was initially portrayed by José F Duval in both print advertisements and on television until 1969. José Duval died in 1993 at the age of 72. In 1969, Juan Carlos Sánchez took over the role (although he was voiced by Norman Rose). In 2006, Sánchez announced his retirement after taking Juan Valdez to unprecedented heights across the globe. He was replaced by Carlos Castañeda, a grower from Antioquia, after open auditions nationwide.

Getting there and away Minibuses run to and fro every 15 minutes from Armenia (3,000COP, 50 minutes). There's also a scheduled public **bus** that departs Salento's main plaza hourly to Armenia (4,000COP)

Where to stay Salento is now a well-established tourist destination and there is no shortage of hotels and hostels.

Salento Pequeño Hotel (8 rooms) Carrera 3, No 8–23; m 313 743 5306; e inforeservas@ salentopequenohotel.com. This boutique option was a first for Salento & with just 4 *cabañas*, it certainly lives up to its name. This is a small, quiet, exclusive hideaway where you can catch up on some peaceful time & indulge a little. Each *cabaña* is fully equipped with kitchenette, private bathroom with beautiful blue-mosaic tiles throughout & large shower (if a little weak), minibar, safe, plasma TV & lovely wooden flooring. The double beds are king size & the sheets of high quality. Owners Francisco & Maria Christina have designed these delightful boudoirs with evident devotion; nothing has been missed. They are very attentive but equally respectful of their guests' personal space & privacy. A 5min walk from the centre, the *cabañas* are set back from the busy streets of Salento & may provide a welcome retreat for those travellers with a few extra pesos in their pockets. **$$$**

El Portal de Cocora (6 rooms) m 315 5919 141; e anaisabel@telesat.com. This out-of-town option is located on the Cocora road, about 500m from the centre. A rather nice restaurant offers super meals on a garden terrace. 2 *cabañas* have cooking facilities & stunning views across the Valle de Corora. **$$**

La Posada del Café (6 rooms) ☎759 3012; e info@laposadadelcafe.com; www.laposadadelcafe. com. Central, clean & spacious, this delightful old building boasts plenty of character & has a gorgeous courtyard garden, crammed with flowers & plant pots. The owner, Maria-Elena, will go out of her way to help & speaks great English. This place has a real home-away-from-home feeling; you'll feel like you're really being taken care of, & the b/fasts are a treat. There's also a cosy little 'sala' with a TV & games where you can curl up & relax after a tiring day of hiking. **$$**

Hostal Ciudad de Segorbe (8 rooms) Calle 5, No 4–06; ☎759 3794; m 320 283 6973; e hostalciudaddesegorbe@hotmail.com; www. hostalciudaddesegorbe.com. Enrique & Luis, owners of Segorbe, are personable, welcoming hosts who you're likely to pass time with chatting over a beer

in the small bar of this charming hostel in a great location in the centre of town. With an outside courtyard, lit in the evenings by lamp & candlelight to sit with a drink, a wide upstairs corridor & a lounge area (the 'sala Cocora'), this place has a spacious, relaxed & friendly vibe. The *sala* also has a decent selection of books & a good set-up for book exchange. All 8 private rooms have small Juliet balconies on to the streets, locally crafted lamps & hot water. B/fast & parking included. **$–$$**

Hostel Tralala (8 rooms) Carrera 7, No 6–45; m 314 850 5543; e tralalasalento@gmail. com. Another nice addition to the backpacker trail, Tralala is the perfect option for a relaxed, comfortable, good-value hostel. Catering for a maximum of 21 people, there's an intimate, calm feel to the place, & with 2 kitchens queues for cooking are out of the question. You can also hire rubber boots here & there is a handy laundry service (12,000COP per load). Dorm rooms & 3 double rooms available. **$–$$**

Plantation House (15 rooms) Alto de Coronel, Calle 7 No 1–4; ☎316 285 2603; e theplantationhousesalento@yahoo.co.uk. Located about 5 mins from the centre, Plantation House sits on the edge of town & is peaceful with a friendly vibe. Rooms are clean & the beds are soft with thick, fluffy duvets. There is also a well-kept communal area with kitchen facilities & book exchange. All bathrooms have hot water & Wi-Fi is available. The owners Tim & Cristina are walking encyclopaedias when it comes to Salento, offering advice, recommendations & even rides to surrounding towns & villages. Tim, an Englishman and Richard Attenborough lookalike, puts on a coffee tour for 20,000COP every morning at 09.00 to his coffee farm 15 mins down the valley. He also offers an airport pickup service & trips to the thermal baths in Santa Rosa. **$–$$**

Hostal de Lili (4 rooms) Calle Real m 300 612 3988; e lilianalopezbetancur@hotmail.com; www. hosteltrail.com/hostels/hostallacasonadelili. Perfectly located, just a block from the Parque Central, this stylish red, white & orange '*casona*', has been owned

9

by owner Lili since 2004. Painstaking refurbishment has transformed it from a shabby wreck to a beautiful, warm & tastefully decorated place where the welcoming aromas of home-cooked food greet every guest. Facilities include a fully equipped kitchen, laundry (6,000COP per load) & communal areas. Complimentary coffee bubbles away on the stove all day. Travellers also rave about Lili's great hospitality & eclectic music collection. Shared hot-water bathrooms are clean & well maintained. A couple of rooms also have a balcony overlooking lively Calle Real. A number of simple yet comfortable rooms offer single, double & triple accommodation. **$**

🏠 **Hostería Calle Real** (18 rooms) Carrera 6, No 2–20 ☎759 3272. This traditional Paisa home offers small, basic rooms but is clean & conveniently located – & run by a very friendly family. B/fast is optional at 5,000COP. **$**

✖ Where to eat and drink

✖ **Antorches** Just off the main plaza down the hill. Since one of the main reasons many people visit Salento is for the trout, it's not hard to find restaurants that serve it, but this place is worthy of a special mention. This large, open restaurant full of wooden tables is renowned as the best place in town for good-value trout. One of the cheapest dishes – simple *trucha con ajio* (trout with garlic) – is arguably the best. Whichever you pick, the portion will be big – a whole trout arrives covered by a giant *patacón* lid. **$$**

✖ **Balcones de Ayer** Calle 6, No 5–40; ☎759 3273. A local haunt, Balcones de Ayer has a real Colombian feel to it. A traditional old house, with pretty wooden tables & chairs, lit by candlelight at night, it has a certain buzz about it, & is one of the only places where you can get your hands on some good Argentine or Chilean wine (skip the Colombian). **$$**

✖ **Piccola Italia Restaurante** Carrera 6, No 1–10; m 315 410 1059. Known for its delicious homemade Italian pasta & pizzas served in a seductive atmosphere. The vegetarian pizza is a particular highlight as is the trout entrée. Located at the bottom of the stairs for the *mirador*. **$$**

✖ **Brunch** Calle 6, No 3–25; m 311 757 8082. Since opening Brunch has become a firm favourite in Salento. A menu of well-cooked American food including hot chicken wings, hamburgers, & delicious stacks of pancakes are complimented with perfectly made fruit juices & coffee with free refills. US-born Jeff, the owner, is always looking to extend his menu & is famed for his homemade peanut butter that is available to buy. Although not on the menu, ask for *poutine* for that Canadian twist. **$**

✖ **Rincon de Lucy** Calle Real. A typical Colombian *menu del dia* with a gourmet finish. Usually trout, sausage or chicken well cooked with vegetables, potatoes or salad. At 6,000COP it's the best-value lunch in town & a backpacker's paradise. The restaurant is not huge so it's a good idea to go early. **$**

☕ **Café Arte** Close to the middle of Calle Real; ⊕ 08.00–21.00. Artisanal café serving fruity aromatic teas, coffee, cocktails & beers. Sandwiches & cakes are available at bargain prices, although sometimes they run out. Classic 70s & 80s music gives this 2nd-floor café a chilled vibe especially for those seated on the 2 flower-laden balcony seats overlooking the bustling street. **$**

☕ **Tejadita de Salento** Directly opposite from Café Arte is a coffee shop/bar that looks like it has been carved out of a tree. Dim lights & thick tree-trunk tables give the place a chilled vibe; good then that live music is provided on busy days. **$**

What to see and do Outdoor activities usually mean leaving the town, although there are often street performances to keep you entertained while wandering around. The lookout point, the *mirador*, is reached by walking to the end of Calle Real and then ascending 250 steps to Alto de la Cruz. Here people just sit and stare at the spectacular 360° view of the Cocora Valley.

El Rancho (m 3105142694; e elranchodesalento@gmail.com; www.elranchodesalento. com) Only 5 minutes outside Salento, this is the closest working farm to the town, yet still has a wonderful feeling of remoteness. This is a quiet place for countryside- and nature-lovers, as it is devoted to ecotourism. Alberto, the owner of the ranch, is passionate about visitors to the *finca* really experiencing it, and encourages a wide variety of activities, including riding and fishing. Arguably the best way to pass time there is to explore the various walking trails which take you right up to the top of the hills with breathtaking views of the Río Quindío below. Alberto will pick you up from Salento's main square and drive you to his stunning, typical blue-and-yellow hacienda. The *finca* grows oranges all year round (delicious freshly squeezed juice is always on offer), and offers fantastic meals, costing 15,000COP. There are seven basic but decent rooms, all of which have private bathrooms and breakfast included.

Valle de Cocora (Cocora Valley) The Valle de Cocora is a 20-minute jeep ride from Salento's main square, leaving at 07.30, 09.30 and 11.30. However, the line of jeeps lining the square will go at whatever time you want, provided there are eight people or payment for eight people. Each journey costs 4,000COP per person. There are various options for walks, treks and horse rides once there but registered tour guides are becoming obligatory so it's a good idea to organise a trip with tour companies in Salento beforehand.

PALMA DE CERA

It may look like a towering spindle with an elaborate hairpiece on top but the mighty *palma de cera* (or wax palm) is a sight to behold in the high-altitude valleys of Cocora. An indigenous species native to the Andean highlands, the wax palm is endemic to northwest Colombia and was declared Colombia's National Tree in 1985. As such, the species is now protected: it is forbidden to cut a single tree down without a licensed permit – and a very good reason. Found at altitudes of over 1,000m, the wax palm is the tallest palm species and a tree of extraordinary and imposing beauty. But quirky good looks aren't all this skinny palm boasts – it is also blessed with strength and longevity, thriving in fertile, deep, well-drained mountainous terrain for up to 100 years. And its fruit is much appreciated by wildlife.

Wax palms provide a habitat for many unique life forms, often endangered species such as the beautiful yellow-eared parrot, who eat the fruit. This gregarious parrot travels in flocks and feeds on the fruit, bark, flowers and shoots of various trees, but particularly the wax palm. Once numerous, the yellow-eared parrot has declined dramatically in the face of hunting for food and habitat destruction. In 2008, the estimated number of birds had dropped to 144. Owing to co-operative conservation efforts the yellow-eared parrot and the wax palm have been given a new lease of life and are well on their way to recovery flying from the Critically Endangered list to Endangered – a remarkable turnaround.

The wax palm itself once faced extinction due to human action – the wax of the trunk was used to make candles (in high demand until the introduction of electricity to rural Colombia just a few decades ago). Thankfully, the wood of the palm is unsuitable for the timber industry but has been used as a cheap source of rudimentary conduit to carry water from rivers to the villages. Its leaves were once used extensively in the Catholic celebration of Palm Sunday, although this practice has ended thanks to a powerful campaign led by an alliance forged between Conservation International (CI), its partner Fundación ProAves and the Roman Catholic Church.

You'll find the image of the wax palm in all sorts of places as this very striking, very sparing tree works well in visual arts, photographs and paintings. All the graphic-design imagery and logos for the Colombian national parks bear the wax palm motif.

Paramo Trek (m *311 745 3761;* e *paramotrek@gmail.com*) is the best tour company and has a reputation of excellence among locals. Colombian owner Cristina speaks fluent English and will run you through the trip details in her office beforehand. A trek to Morro Gacho is a great one-day option, starting at the base in Valle de Cocora and reaching the 3,600m peak. The group is led by one of four biological expert guides – most of whom speak English fluently. The tour begins at around 06.30 and ends mid afternoon, depending on the fitness of the group. An array of birds and interesting vegetation will be explained along the way before you reach a forest-covered peak. Here you duck under trees, hop over branches and brush through thick vegetation before emerging at the peak, and the view of jagged mountains and swirling clouds below. Snacks and a picnic are provided as well as a beer and late lunch in Salento afterwards. Changing weather conditions requires trekkers to pack appropriately although waterproof trousers are provided. At the time of writing, Paramo Trek were the only company permitted to offer this trek. As well as this they offer multi-day treks to Nevado del Tolima and other peaks in Los Nevados park.

Fiesta de Salento The festival takes place in the first week of January and is the biggest party of the year. A stage is erected in the central square and for a week local groups and DJs entertain large crowds.

Honda Just 3½ hours outside of Bogotá, descending on the highway that eventually divides to take you along the Magdalena River valley or up to the Coffee Zone and Medellín is the once important colonial town of Honda (population 28,000) in the department of Tolima. As the last navigable point on the Magdalena River from transport coming from the Caribbean, Honda grew into importance as the point where all cargo coming to Bogotá would be then moved on to donkeys for the five-day trek into the *altiplano*. Honda was founded on 24 August, 1539 by Francisco Nuñez Pedroso and her 'golden age' was between 1850 and 1910. Known as the 'City of Bridges' due to the fact that Honda has some 25 of them spanning the Magdalena and the Guali rivers which run through here, Honda fell into decay once river travel was no longer the norm and the location became no more than a crossroads. Recently though, increased interest in the town has meant that refurbishments and restorations have taken place in the colonial centre making it a pleasant place from which to explore the region, the neighbouring historical towns of Mariquita and Amabalema, and to understand the importance of the Magdalena River in Colombia's growth.

Where to stay and eat There are numerous accommodation options in Honda but we recommend choosing from either of the upmarket options to fully enjoy your stay

Posada Las Trampas (8 rooms) Carrera 10a, No 11–05; ℡251 7415; www.posadalastrampas.com. Located in the historic area of town, the *posada* has been carefully restored. All rooms have AC, LCD television & en-suite facilities. There are great views over the town from the roof & a swimming pool to boot! **$$$**

Casa Belle Epoque (10 rooms) Calle 12, No 12A–21; ℡251 1176, www.casabelleepoque.com. The beautifully cared-for hotel is another standout option fully equipped to inform you of the must-see sights in Honda. There's a swimming pool & 1st-floor sun deck. **$$**

What to see and do The **Museo del Rio** (the Museum of the Magdalena River) (*Cuartel de la Ceiba, en la Calle 10, No 9–01;* ℡ *251 0507*) provides a fantastic insight into the importance of the town and its place in history.

10

The Pacific Coast

Magic days, golden nights, and the summer is forever. It's the endless summer... And I'm all about Pacific Ocean Blue.

Lyrics from 'Pacific Ocean Blue', 2002

The region known simply as El Pacífico is one of the wettest on earth, stretching for 1,300km along Colombia's western flank and lavished by an annual rainfall of up to 10m. Curved bays sit aside a jungle of extraordinary biodiversity with cliffs and beaches lined with mangrove forests criss-crossed by rivers of great girth. Outlying islands are renowned for their resplendent flora and fauna with fertile waters home to migratory whales *en route* from the Antarctic. Vast volcanic crags explode upwards from the sea amidst coral outcrops teeming with marine life.

El Pacífico is an important component of an eco-region known as the Chocó Biogeográfico, a key part of the Tumbes-Chocó-Magdalena ecological hot spot. This magnificent expanse of rainforest terrain runs from the Río Atrato near Panama to the Mataje River bordering northwestern Ecuador along the entire Pacific coast of Colombia and is bordered by Meso-America to the north and the tropical Andes to the east – a landmass larger than Costa Rica. Until recently the region's dense forest, abrupt mountains, deep gorges, marine flats and fast-flowing rivers stood in the way of so-called progress, dividing Colombia's key commercial centres from the western shore. However, this unique, moist ecosystem is now recognised as one of the richest lowland regions on the planet – a swathe of land blessed by isolation and inaccessibility and large volumes of freshwater run-off. Fertile coastal sediments have helped ensure an abundance of biologically distinct endemic plant, bird, amphibian and butterfly species. Today, despite multiple threats by commercial developers, much of El Pacífico is protected by conservation status. It remains a culturally rich region with numerous indigenous reserves (*resguardos*) and settlements as well as a burgeoning ecotourism and birding destination.

More than 85% of the population along the Pacific coastal stretch are Afro-Colombian – almost 60% are jobless and poor. Indigenous Emberá people account for 5% of the local people, living in reserves and communities by the Río Valle and Río Juná. The remaining 10% are *mestizo* (mixed race). Most inhabitants of the Pacific coast earn a living from subsistence farming, hunting, fishing, forestry and mining in terrain rich in mineral and natural resources. Since the early 19th century, large amounts of platinum and gold have been excavated in the region and sizeable deposits of zinc, nickel, tungsten, bauxite, manganese, tin, copper and chromium remain. It's little wonder former Colombian president Carlos Lleras Restrepo called this resource-rich, beautiful area 'our country's piggy bank'. Yet vast swathes of the Pacific coastal region remain untroubled by industry, commerce or modern technology. Cars are rare, electricity scarce and mobile-phone signals poor. Daily life continues much as it did in generations past with freshly harvested rice drying on hessian sacking while men fish silently in wooden dugout canoes. Children play in

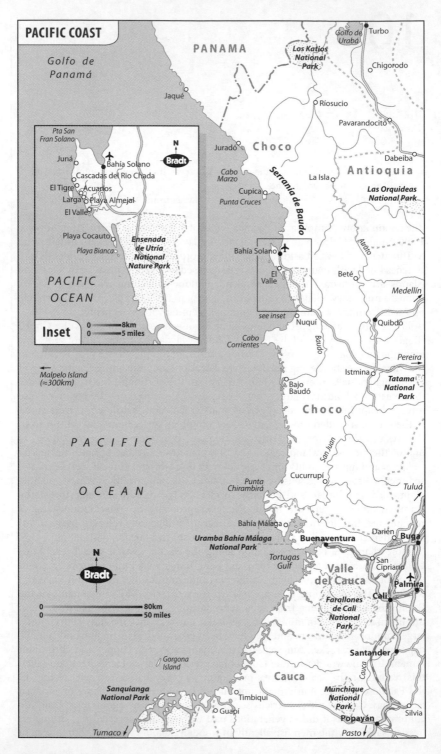

PACIFIC COAST

Golfo de Panamá

PANAMA

Golfo de Urabá

Turbo

Los Katios National Park

Chigorodo

Jaqué

Ríosucio

Pavarandocito

Jurado

Choco

Dabeiba

Antioquia

Cabo Marzo

La Isla

Las Orquideas National Park

Cupica

Punta Cruces

Serranía de Baudo

Bahía Solano

Beté

Medellín

El Valle

Atrato

Quibdó

see inset

Nuquí

Baudo

Pereira

Cabo Corrientes

Istmina

Tatama National Park

Malpelo Island (≈300km)

Bajo Baudó

Choco

P A C I F I C

O C E A N

Punta Chirambirá

Cucurrupí

Tuluá

San Juan

Bahía Málaga

Darién

Buga

Uramba Bahía Málaga National Park

Buenaventura

Tortugas Gulf

San Cipriano

Palmira

Valle del Cauca

N

Bradt

Cali

Farallones de Cali National Park

0 — 80km
0 — 50 miles

Gorgona Island

Santander

Cauca

Sanquianga National Park

Timbiqui

Munchique National Park

Silvia

Guapí

Cauca

Tumaco

Popayán

Pasto

Inset:

Pta San Fran Solano

Juná

Bahía Solano

N

Bradt

Cascadas del Rio Chada

El Tigre

Acuarios

Larga

Playa Almejal

El Valle

Playa Cocauto

Ensenada de Utría National Nature Park

Playa Bianca

PACIFIC OCEAN

Inset

0 — 8km
0 — 5 miles

384

shallow rivers while their mothers wash big bundles of clothes on rocks by the bank. Entire communities live in *tambos* (stilt mud-and-thatch huts) that teeter along the shoreline while stray dogs and chickens pounce on scuttling crabs on the sand.

FLORA AND FAUNA

The Pacific coast is home to eight species of mangrove in a region where expanses of forest over 20m in height extend up to 30km inland. Almost 3,000km^2 of mangrove thickets account for about 7.5% of Colombia's total Pacific exploitable forest, forming a complex drainage system in the region's hot, steamy lowlands. More than 70% of Colombia's mangroves are located along the Pacific coast and these evergreens play a vital role in the health of the seaboard's ecosystem, providing a component in the transition between land and sea. Mangrove habitat provides a breeding ground for 60% of the world's fish species with red, white, black and button mangroves found throughout El Pacífico.

Heavy rainfall and numerous rivers feed an abundance of lush vegetation with a rich network of tributaries running to the ocean. Conservationists estimate the number of plant species in the Tumbes-Chocó-Magdalena region at around 11,000, of which around 25% are endemic. More than 5,000 of these are found in the wet or pluvial forests of Chocó where more than 300 trees per hectare have been recorded, including the *níspero* (loquat) whose seeds are scattered by the Pacific's tidal currents. Although conservation status has protected large areas of forest in

BIRDING ON THE PACIFIC COAST

Ardent birders will be amazed by what the Pacific coast has to offer as one of the richest areas of avian endemism in the entire Neotropics. According to ProAves, the forests of the Tumbes-Chocó-Magdalena region contain around 900 bird species of which 14 are endemic and at least 110 can't be found anywhere else in the world. As Colombia's undisputed 'No 2 Birding Hot spot', the Pacific coast is second only in avian diversity to Santa Marta's El Dorado Nature Reserve and contains Endemic Bird Areas (EBAs) as defined by BirdLife International. The shoreline is a critical feeding, wintering and stopover site for millions of migratory shorebirds. The Chocó EBA has a total of 51 confirmed endemic bird species – the highest of any endemic bird area on earth. In 1991, a new species was discovered in the Colombian Chocó and was named in 1996 as the Chocó vireo (*Vireo master*) through an auction of its scientific title. Dr Bernard Master won the bid, paying 70,000COP to a fund for the conservation of threatened rainforest habitat along the Pacific coast. Rare, endangered or vulnerable birds found in the region include the esmeraldas woodstar, little woodstar, sapphire-bellied hummingbird, lava gull, ochre-bellied dove, banded ground-cuckoo, grey-backed hawk, plumbeous forest-falcon, blue-billed curassow, rufous-headed chachalaca, white-winged guan, bearded guan, tacarcuna wood-quail, brown wood-rail, long-wattled umbrellabird, slaty becard, Peruvian plantcutter, mangrove finch, medium tree-finch, tumaco seedeater, saffron siskin, hood mockingbird, cerulean warbler, tawny-chested flycatcher, great green macaw, grey-cheeked parakeet and Colombian tinamou. In 2007, more than 100 different bird species were spotted by birders on the Pacific coast in just 72 hours, including the fabled harpy eagle – the largest eagle in the Americas.

the Colombian and Panamanian portions of the Pacific coastline, the degradation in Ecuador continues – and is severe.

MARINE LIFE Coral reefs on the Pacific coast are small and scattered but provide important shelter for a wide range of marine fauna. Prime reef areas include Gorgona Island and Malpelo Island, both of which are protected national parks. Over 20 coral species have been recorded in Pacific waters. Dramatic volcanic extrusions rise from the ocean, seemingly undisturbed by sea spray, strong winds or tides. El Pacífico is home to an abundance of fish species and marine mammal populations. Regional fish production represents almost 50% of Colombia's national total – a figure that state officials believe is as little as 15% of its estimated potential. Whales breed in the warm Pacific waters during June–November each year. The Bay of Málaga, located about 50km northwest of Buenaventura, boasts one of the highest whale-calf birth rates in the world. It welcomes between 470 and 1,200 humpback whales annually – more than 25% of the total estimated whale population for the southeast Pacific region. A popular local song contains the lyrics 'they take care of their children and drive their husbands away' – a reference to the mating ritual of the whales who visit. It forms part of a chorus sung by the local women (*cantadoras*) after they have danced a *currulao* of African origin. Humpback whales are just one of at least a dozen species of marine mammals observed in the region.

GETTING THERE AND AROUND

Owing to its relative inaccessibility and absence of infrastructure, Colombia's Pacific coast is reachable only by **boat** and **air**. Only a single overland route links the interior to the commercial hubs of Buenaventura and Tumaco. **Buses** serve this 200km route but tend to do the journey overnight. Flights, usually in the morning, connect via Medellín to the tiny airports of Bahía Solano and Nuquí but often incur delays due to rainy conditions. Various new roads now link towns like El Valle and Bahía Solano, but journeying by boat is still a regular option. The road transport is still rudimentary: expect a decrepit old van without tyre tread, windows, shock absorbers or clutch to ferry you from the airport along craterous unmade roads to the nearest town. At the time of writing, there were plans to extend the region's airstrips, allowing for larger aircraft – though when this happens remains to be seen.

PRACTICALITIES

It rains a lot on the steamy Pacific coast where humidity frequently tops 90%. Be sure to pack waterproofs and plenty of lightweight clothes as the mud and rainfall will mean frequent changes. You'll also need a torch as few places have electricity and all paths are unlit. If you go during turtle season, September to January, use a red filter or red cellophane over your torch to avoid startling these reptiles when searching the beaches at night. Don't forget to pack a decent pair of binoculars if visiting during whale-watching season, from June to November. Arrive with enough cash (in low denominations) as few places accept credit cards and ATMs are scarce. Most of the department of Chocó is a malaria zone and some areas are affected by dengue. December to mid-March is the most prominent time for the spread of malaria, and mosquitoes tend to be most dangerous between 18.30 and 06.00. Although at the time of writing there were no reports of the spread of either disease, travellers should take proper precautions (pages 73–5) to minimise exposure to mosquito bites – with repellent and suitable clothing essential.

This steamy little jungle town has a population of about 10,000, most of them of African descent. Outlying indigenous Emberá communities are mainly located upstream along the river and comprise a handful of basic mud-and-thatch huts teetering on the banks. Local people eke a living from fishing and a small amount of tourism with boat owners adamant they can offer the best deep-sea fishing in the world. Bahía Solano usually has a small number of foreign tourists, while whaling season attracts lots of Colombians from all over the country. A recently built road connects the town to El Valle and a taxi should cost around 15,000COP for the 45-minute bumpy ride (*www.bahiasolano-choco.gov.co*).

GETTING THERE AND AROUND Satena and ADA **fly** daily direct to Bahía Solano's Aeropuerto José Celestino Mutis from Medellín. However, adverse weather and airport complications often mean neither can fly to the tiny airstrip of Bahía Solano, leaving just charter flights. To obtain a ticket on one of these jeep-sized aircrafts, ask your hotel to organise the flight. Alternatively call Jorge Casas (m *315 395 5272/314 888 9662*) – a pleasant Colombian who oversees **charter flights** between Medellín and Bahía Solano. At the time of writing, a charter flight costs 220,000COP each way, with payment made in cash at the airport. Another option is to travel **overland** to Buenaventura to catch a **fast boat** – it runs every Tuesday and returns on Saturday (150,000COP, 12 hours). There's also the **slower cargo boat** but it doesn't appear to adhere to any firm schedule (although it tends to leave on a Thursday or Friday at around 100,000COP) – the best place to get

STAYING SAFE ON THE PACIFIC COAST

Guerrilla forces and paramilitary groups were once highly active in parts of the region, targeting civilian communities who collaborated with the security services and occasionally kidnapping tourists for ransom. However, today over 4,000 marine troops patrol the Pacific coastline with a police force of 50–60 officers in Bahía Solano alone. Serious incidents impacting safety are increasingly rare and the Pacific coast is doing its utmost to consign the troubles of its past to history. Tourism continues to rebuild and visitor figures are increasing year on year and although some isolated pockets remain off-limits to tourists between Pasto and Tumaco, the coastline north of Buenaventura is considered safe. Towns like Bahía Solano and El Valle are strategic points for the Colombian army with a sizeable presence based there year-round. Travellers considering journeying on the Cali–Buenaventura road should check on the current safety situation as well as buses serving the Medellín–Quibdo and Medellín–Turbo routes. At the time of writing, the British Foreign Office warns against all travel to the port of Buenaventura. If you are visiting the port, check ahead of time about the security situation and consult the *Buenaventura* section (pages 394–6). Elsewhere, in 2014, major tourism operator, Aviatur, suspended routes to Isla Gorgona due to an alleged FARC attack that killed one policeman and injured six others. This means that, at the time of writing, the island is closed to tourists. As with a lot of areas in Colombia things can quickly change and no doubt the island will be serviced by official tourism companies in the near future. Check the website www.parquesnacionales.gov.co for the latest information.

The Pacific Coast   BAHÍA SOLANO

10

Bahía Solano's tiny airport is named after José Celestino Mutis (1732–1808), a Spanish-Colombian naturalist, physician and mathematician who assembled one of the richest botanical collections in the world at the time. He was born in Cádiz in Spain on 6 April 1732, but spent the last 48 years of his life in Bogotá after studying medicine and philosophy at the University of Seville. Using scientific subsidies from the Spanish government, Mutis visited Stockholm, where he worked alongside the great Swedish botanist Carolus Linnaeus. He then accompanied Viceroy Pedro Mesia de la Cerda to Bogotá in 1760 where he actively furthered botanical research for almost half a century. He was the first to explain Newton's theories in that part of America and gained membership of the Academy of Science of both Paris and Stockholm. His observational diary encapsulated discoveries in natural sciences from 1760 to 1790 and he was especially acclaimed for his studies of quinine. Mutis created the Botanical Mission in 1783 as a research centre for Colombia's flora and fauna and employed artists to prepare thousands of coloured drawings of the nation's many species. Mutis's magnificent collection of 24,000 specimens represents some 5,000 distinct species and the book he created remains indispensable to this day. In his later life, Mutis was ordained a priest. He died in his adoptive homeland of Colombia on 11 September 1808 and is buried in Bogotá. Today, the spectacular Jardín Botánico Botanico José Celestino Mutis (*www.jbb.gov.co*) on Carrera 66 con Calle 56 in Bogotá remains one of the city's premier attractions.

tickets is at the port from one of the tiny travel agent shops on Calle 1. **Buses** leave for Nuquí every Tuesday, Thursday and Saturday (70,000COP, 2 hours).

TOURIST INFORMATION

🛈 Oficinas Municipales de Turismo
📞 682 7418; www.bahiasolano-choco.gov.co

🏠 **WHERE TO STAY** The town and surrounding area has a variety of hotel and hostel options with additional 'unofficial homestays' prepared to top up during whale-watching season.

🏠 **Eco-Hotel Kipara** (10 cabins) Bahía Solano; m 311 634 4428; www.ecohotelkipara.com. Choose from 10 pastel-coloured cabins with terraces that overlook the jungle in a small complex close to the mouth of the river valley that offers numerous activities & tours, including whale watching, turtle conservation & birding. A large swimming pool, the only decent one in town, is edged by palm trees near a small snack kiosk & bar. Each cabin accommodates 4–5 people & costs 100,000COP pp, including 3 meals, airport pickup & walking tour. **$$$**

🏠 **Hotel Balboa Plaza** (27 rooms) Calle 2; 📞 682 7075; e hotelboap@telecom.com.

co. Famously once owned by Colombia's most notorious drug baron Pablo Escobar in the 1980s, this garish 4-storey hotel would have once been considered a swanky upmarket place to stay. Today, however, it forms a rather gauche yellow carbuncle with its glamour much faded & its glitz in tatters. Expect grotty furnishings, torn awnings & crumbling plaster work in a hotel that needs a lot of TLC. Prices are around 70,000COP for a double, not including food or tours. **$$–$$$**

🏠 **Posada Turistica Hotel Rocas de Cabo Marzo** (5 rooms) 📞 682 7525/7433; m 313 681 4001/312 895 8682; e bahiatebada@hotmail.com; www.posadaturisticarocasdecabomarzo.

com. This highly recommended B&B option is owned by a very friendly Colombian–American couple, Enrique & Nancy, who have lived in Colombia for more than 20 years. Rooms are clean & the open terrace with 2 hammocks & sofa is perfect for chilling & watching whale huffs in the distance. Fishing fans should note than owner Enrique is a knowledgeable deep-sea fishing & diving enthusiast who offers a wide range of tours including a sport-fishing tournament held on a nearby beach. 3 meals are included in the price, as are airport transfers, a walking tour & unlimited coffee. B/fast is traditional Colombian- or American-style; dinner is usually fish although delicious pizzas are available. Expect to pay around 110,000COP. **$$**

🏠 **Posada del Mar** (5 cabins & 5 rooms) 2km from the airport, 100m from the sea; m 314 630 6723; www.posadadelmarbahiasolano.com. This is a perfect location for backpackers as the rates are inexpensive, ranging from 30,000COP for shared rooms & bathrooms, to 80,000COP for a private cabin (all-inclusive rates are about 35,000COP extra). Rooms have a fan, mosquito net, Wi-Fi & comfortable mattresses. Food is delicious fish seasoned with local herbs & spices – though the real USP is the owner Rodrigo & his diving school. It's the only one in the area fully certified & Rodrigo himself offers 2 dives with all the equipment for 250,000COP. You can become certified by taking the course for 80,000COP. Rodrigo's wife, Estrella, will meet you at the airport & will happily arrange your flights. **$–$$**

✖ **WHERE TO EAT AND DRINK** There are a couple of open-fronted rustic local food joints near to the airport serving simple fish-and-rice dishes and cold beers. Hotel Rocas de Cabo Marzo's pizzeria **Oh Solano Mio** is a popular alternative. At the other end of town several local residents offer tourists seafood meals from their kitchens and there are numerous kiosks selling sodas, snacks and beers.

WHAT TO SEE AND DO There isn't a great deal to see in Bahía Solano itself. Most people use it as a base to explore outlying areas. A pretty, if muddy pot-holed road leads out of Bahía Solano, hugging the coastline on one side with a steep jungle bank on the other. Hidden beyond the palms are several beautiful waterfalls – you'll need to keep your eyes peeled as these are well camouflaged by thick jungle. Close by, a rustic coastal bar sells ice-cold beer – it's a popular watering hole with the military and a good place to let off steam. Migratory humpback whales arrive in numbers between July and November and local boatmen offer tours to the **Nacional Parque Ensenada de Utría** (Utría National Park). From the town take a three-wheel taxi to El Valle for 25,000COP, from there a selection of boats take you both ways for around 70,000COP, plus 37,500COP to enter the park. There are also plenty of local guys keen to rent out their boats for fishing trips for around 40,000COP for a morning on the bay.

Festivals
Festival de la Bahía (early August) The week-long festival celebrates Bahía Solano's local culture on and around the bay by bringing communities together with decorated boats, folkloric shows, processions, beauty pageants and dancing. The beat of loud drums and trumpets reverberate through the streets until the last day when a concert brings the festival to a close.

PLAYA ALMEJAL *Telephone code 4*

This silver-grey stretch of sand has its back to a jungle canvas and looks out to open sea. A handful of hotels have created a decent mini resort area aimed at ecotourists with gorgeous beach walks, gushing creeks and plentiful birdlife. The beach is quite beautiful and offers lots of crab-ridden trails from the sand out to waterfalls in the rainforest. Playa Almejal makes a nice base from which to explore the surrounding area. It's quiet, sleepy and very pretty – and some of the beachfront hotels are undoubtedly some of El Pacífico's finest. Stroll along the sand to discover vast volcanic boulders, some with wooden houses built precariously on top. Towering ferns and palms edge the seagrass-scattered beach with creeks that empty into the sea. Surfers can expect 3m waves when the season hits full pelt in September/October and February/March.

GETTING THERE AND AWAY Although Playa Almejal is only 16km or so from the centre of Bahía Solano the hard-going 1-hour **drive** can take twice as long in the rain. A deeply pot-holed unmade road winds, dips and climbs and is only the width of a single car. Thick jungle flanks both sides in a track that has literally been carved from the forest. Cloying pinky-brown mud and unpredictable boulders make a 4x4 the vehicle of choice. Grab one of the *colectivos* or haggle with a driver at the airport – the journey should cost no more than 15,000COP. El Valle is just 1.5km away. Boats out to Utría National Park and other attractions leave from La Bocana, a small riverbank dock a 20-minute stroll south along the sand.

TOUR OPERATORS Staff at the **El Almejal Eco Lodge** offer a wide range of different local tour options, the best of which include a Río Tundó tour (3 hours, 50,000COP) down the calm and seductive palm river, spotting birds and passing fishermen; a trip out to the waterfalls of Tigre and Chadó for 85,000COP, or a birdwatching tour with an expert guides for 70,000COP. And, from July to October, trips to see humpback whales for 85,000COP.

WHERE TO STAY AND EAT

Almejal Eco Lodge (12 cabins & upper *cabaña*) 230 6060 (Medellín); e almejal@une. net.co; www.almejal.com.co. Set in gorgeous tropical landscaping overlooking the ocean, the Almejal Eco Lodge opened in 1982. A fine collection of luxury *cabañas* have been built to an exceptional standard to combine rustic style with elegant touches. Each has a separate lounge & bedroom with a terrace looking out on to the beach. Private bathrooms are well appointed with owner César Isaza demonstrating a keen eye for detail where it counts. Expect wooden furniture & flower-filled vases with each cabin named after a local species of bird. Señor Isaza is a fanatical birder & an enthusiastic conservationist & paintings on the wall throughout the lodge depict flora & fauna from the Pacific coast. The food at the Almejal Eco Lodge is truly sublime – in fact a visiting 'celebrity chef' from Bogotá was astounded to learn that the cook was a self-taught mother of 3, not an academy-trained culinary virtuoso. After trying every possible form of bribery to acquire the recipe for a particularly good soup he had enjoyed, he finally accepted defeat – & promptly ordered another bowl. 12 wooden cabins are complemented by a large open-sided restaurant &

an upper *cabaña* with a double bed & bunk beds in the jungle high above the sea. Set on a terraced ledge, the cabin has a freezer & dining table & a deck with amazing sunset views, & binoculars to spot whale spouts in the distance. However, steep steps make this an unsuitable option for anyone unsteady on their feet. Rates range from 770,000COP pp for a 3-night, 4-day stay (all inclusive) to 1,640,000COP for a 5-night, 6-day stay with boat transport, airport transfers, meals & an expert guide part of the price. **$$–$$$**

Hotel Playa Alegre (5 cabins, 22 people) 451 1229. This sea-worn wooden hotel neighbours El Almejal but lacks any of its charm. However, it may suit travellers keen to secure cheap alternatives. Location-wise it's perfect & the grounds are spacious enough for a comfortable stay – but don't expect luxury. Fishing, whale-watching & waterfall excursions are available. Rates centre on multi-day packages, from 3 to 7 nights. Expect to pay from 180,000COP per night for all-inclusive stays with tours, meals, drinks & a guide. **$$**

Humpback Turtle Hostel (5 rooms, 1 dorm) m 312 756 3439; www.humpbackturtle. com. A budget hostel popular with backpackers & surfers. Located ideally on the beach, it has a restaurant, lively bar & area for camping. A surf school (30,000COP, 1hr) is offered in English for 6 months of the year. Surfing season lasts from Apr to Oct when waves break at 4m. Owner Tyler organises tours with locals to the waterfalls, Utría park & visits to local indigenous groups. B/fast is not included & costs 8,000COP; lunch & dinner are 12,000COP. There is also room for camping but tents are not provided. Those on a real budget can rent a hammock & mosquito net for the night. **$**

WHAT TO SEE AND DO If you can, visit the **Reserva el Almejal** (Almejal Reserve) behind the Almejal Eco Lodge – a magnificent 47,000km² private reserve established by César Isaza, patron of the hotel. A scenic trail contains fossilised ferns and winds through thick rainforest, *bosque húmedo tropical*, along a rocky creek. Halfway up is a natural pool for a refreshing dip and the tour guide, César himself, adds fascinating information along the way. There's also a short trail from the hotel along the beach to a small waterfall – turn right out of the entrance and look right after about 200m. El Almejal used to run a successful **turtle conservation project**, gathering eggs from the beach, taking them to a protected pen and then releasing the hatchlings into the ocean. The project bid to protect olive ridley sea turtles (*Lepidochelys olivacea*) from local poachers, scavenging dogs and hungry birds. From when it began in 1994 up until 2011, the project had seen 85,000 baby turtles released into the ocean with the help of volunteers, many of whom were guests of the lodge. However, in 2012 the Olive Ridley Project was halted due to a dispute with another local conservation group – Asociación Caguama. This team of around 20 local conservationists claimed the protection rights to all the eggs on this and surrounding beaches, and had the backing of the local government to do so. At the time of writing, El Almejal's owner César was hoping to resolve the situation with Asociación Caguama so they could work together. For now it's just the conservationists from Asociación Caguama who are permitted to take visitors on nightly searches for nesting sea turtles. The best way to locate a guide is to scour the beaches at night, or ask in local hotels. The group request a donation of around 20,000COP for a night tour.

Beaches Sandy beaches account for almost 25% of the 1,300km Pacific coast and some of the nicest can be reached from Playa Almejal. Playa Larga (Long Beach)

A LEADER IN ECOTOURISM

The World Tourism Organisation identified El Almejal as one of Colombia's most important ecotourism models in 2006 and its educational programmes have achieved considerable success. It was also named Colombia's best destination of sustainable tourism by the Ministry of Tourism in 2014. As well as its green practices such as vast organic waste heaps, herb and vegetable gardens, recycling schemes and campaigns to reduce water and energy, one of El Almejal's greatest success stories has been its education and business training schemes for local residents. The Río Tundó (river of palms) tour is a prime example. This 3-hour boat trip is run by an El Valle local Francisco and his wife Rosa. Having been given the opportunity by El Almejal to start his own company in 2012, Francisco takes up to eight people down the seductive Tundó River, pointing out the rich diversity of bird species before encouraging you to slip into the water and drift away with the current. When he is not preparing tours or looking after his large family in a tiny house on the riverbank, Francisco is trawling the Tundó in his new boat, picking up litter. At the time of writing, Francisco was working on a new night tour.

lies about 4km north and is accessible by boat or by a 2-hour medium–difficult hike through the jungle. A pretty 1.5km dark-sand beach has a waterfall close by. Playa el Tigre (Tiger Beach) is a 15-minute boat trip from Playa Almejal and this charming 200m soft-sand stretch has falls that cascade into the sea. Stretching 2km between waterfalls, Playa Chado (Chado Beach) lies north via a tricky half-day hike that takes you past lagoons and sparkling pools along some beautiful leafy tracks – those not feeling quite so fit can get there by a 20-minute boat journey. Playa Juná is the last in a succession of four beaches and offers golden sands and clear waters with magnificent views.

PARQUE NACIONAL ENSENADA DE UTRÍA (UTRÍA NATIONAL NATURE PARK)

(*Parques Nacionales Naturales de Colombia;* \ +57 1 353 2400; *www. parquesnacionales.gov.co*) This 777,750ha national park contains 18,850ha of marine fauna and waterways, including inlets, estuaries and creeks. Bordered by Corregimiento Valle to the north, Jurubira Nuquí to the south, the mist-shrouded Alto Baudo (at 1,200m) to the east and the Pacific Ocean to the west, the Parque Nacional Ensenada de Utría comprises three distinct ecosystems – rainforest jungle, mangroves (eight species) and coral reefs (hard and soft species). Sandy stretches provide important nesting sites for turtles while forested areas contain over 1,000 species of trees. Many of the park's 350-plus bird species are easy to spot along ten well-defined trails. Sendero Utría is the longest trail at 11km – it takes around 3 hours to hike and is medium-level difficulty traversing forest and mangroves to a pretty beach called Playa Cocalito. A community of Emberá people can be visited along a 2-hour trail. The Resguardo Boroboro is home to 21 families and this population of a little over 100 has plenty of handicrafts for sale. Another 1km track takes about an hour to complete during low tide or can be tackled in a canoe. It passes through seven species of mangrove and leads to a magnificent creek (Quebrada Estero Grande y Chocolate) where there are many birds. An abandoned scientific research station once staffed by conservationists from Natura Fundación lies derelict – a memento of a past era of troubles that saw 26 kidnaps in the park in a single day in 2002. Today, security is good in the area and that the park is once again (since 2006) open for business is a clear indication of safer times.

Many of the waterways are navigable by kayak, although visitors will need to bring their own equipment to the park. Marine fauna in the park is diverse and plentiful and includes 105 species of crustaceans and several species of whales, including the region's famous humpback. Other wildlife species include sting rays, turtles, fruit bats, insect bats, toucans and poison frogs. An education centre contains a small exhibition and there are also whale and dolphin skeletons at the entrance on the riverbank. On the park's southern limit, an area known as Morro Mico has water depths of 40m and is popular with free divers. There's also a protected coral garden that ranks as South America's largest. A liberal scattering of van-sized black volcanic extrusions reach up from the seabed on the outskirts of the park – a treacherous obstacle course for canoeing fishermen in the dark. Don't miss the trip to Playa Blanca – a 10-minute boat ride from the entrance of the park. Here you can swim and snorkel and grab lunch for around 16,000COP.

GETTING THERE The park is about an hour by **boat** from Nuquí and Bahía Solano, about 40 minutes from El Valle, and the trip is offered by almost every tour operator in both towns.

WHERE TO STAY AND EAT Stay overnight in *cabañas* for 160,000COP with three meals and walking tours. An on-site restaurant serves three meals a day. Contact the national park as detailed above.

OTHER PRACTICALITIES Permission should be gained from **Dirección Territorial Noroccidente** (\ *422 0833; www.parquesnacionales.gov.co*) in Medellín prior to visiting the park – your tour operator will organise this as part of the package price. Entrance is 37,500COP. Plastic bags, aerosol sprays, chemical products and litter are all prohibited in the park environs. Also note that few guides in the park speak English.

EL VALLE *Telephone code 4*

Around 4,000 residents make up El Valle's fishing and farming community. A rather nice shoreline contains a several-kilometre-long volcanic beach. Several big lava shoots sit amidst a magnificent stretch of jungle dotted with colourful flowers and huge blue morpho butterflies. On the Río Valle, a large partial-suspension bridge spans a slow-moving cloudy expanse. Tethered horses nibble from grain sacks on the riverbanks by a ramshackle collection of rustic wooden homes. Children giggle in huddles by lines of drying washing flapping in a warm, damp breeze.

GETTING THERE AND AWAY A regular *chiva* (open bus) connects Bahía Solano with El Valle and takes about 1½ hours to do the bone-shaking trip. Alternatively **taxis** and **jeeps** run regularly and cost around 15,000COP.

WHERE TO STAY

Hotel Valle (12 rooms) \ 682 7907. This family-run *posada* is clean, comfy & efficiently run. Double rooms have a shared bathroom (or pay 65,000COP for 1 of 7 that have private facilities). The price includes 3 decent meals. The food at the restaurant is renowned for its excellence throughout the village, while trips & tours can be booked at the reception. **$$**

Hotel Dasma (16 rooms) (No phone, just ask around town & pop in) Patron Domingo González offers 25 beds for around 50,000COP apiece, including 3 good meals a day. 7 rooms have a private bathroom – choose room 4 or room 1 at the back of the property for sea views & a balcony. **$**
Posada Villa Maga (3 cabins) m 320 777 4767; e magapacifico@yahoo.com.mx. This lovely

reasonably priced out-of-town option is run by Pepe Murillo & Carmen Lucía Gómez & is close to the beach. The centre of El Valle is a 10min walk along the sand. Each bamboo-&-thatch *cabaña* is nestled in jungle gardens with a small balcony & a sunken shower. It's conveniently located near Playa Respingue, close to La Bocana where all boats depart out to surrounding areas. 1 cabin has a private bathroom, the other is shared. B/fast is not included & costs 8,000COP. Lunch & dinner are taken in the village as part of Villa Maga's ecotourism drive. 3 meals cost 35,000COP at a variety of restaurants. Tours to waterfalls, whale watching & Utría Park are available for around 60,000COP. **$**

✕ WHERE TO EAT AND DRINK Almost all of the hotels and *posadas* in El Valle offer meals as part of their package, and there are a few hotspots offering delicious local fish like **Rosa del Mar** and **Donde Betty**.

SHOPPING There are many small shops and mid-sized supermarkets in the town. The main hub of activity is near the school where at lunchtime children scatter across the streets diving into internet cafés to check Facebook, and into shops for sweets and juices. There is one internet spot, with fans, opposite the school which is useful as Wi-Fi is non-existent in El Valle. The road from Playa Almejal into the town is a popular place for women selling bracelets, necklaces and other handmade items. Go in the evening and you will see groups sorting through trays of beads for sale the following day.

WHAT TO SEE AND DO Numerous boatmen in El Valle offer trips along the slow-moving creamy-green length of the Río el Valle. Bromeliad-clad trees and shrubs shade the water and are home to kingfishers, hawks, morpho butterflies and myriad purple, red and yellow flowers. Expect to haggle, with rates at about 35,000COP.

BUENAVENTURA *Telephone code 2*

As the Pacific coast's prime seaport, Buenaventura is a typical commercial hub – an ugly and grimy centre of freight and cargo that creeps along the shoreline. Roughly the size of Los Angeles's metropolitan area with a population of about 400,000, Buenaventura is a crucial distribution point for raw materials and goods for Colombia – and one of the Pacific coast's few metropolitan conurbations. Sadly, while many of the nation's larger cities have calmed down, Buenaventura has bucked the trend and today the city has a reputation as a breeding ground for drug trafficking and violence. In 2014, the UN called on Colombia to take urgent action to curb violence in the port but as yet little seems to have changed. Lying some 345km southwest of Bogotá, Buenaventura is also a key through-point for the cocaine industry – in some years more than 20 tonnes are seized in the city alone. In 2014, the media reported that US$13 million worth of cocaine was confiscated by police. Today the city's urban centre remains a dangerous place with criminal organisations engaged in a war over control of lucrative drug routes in and out of the port. The result has meant massive displacements, child recruitment and extreme violence.

Despite almost 50% of Colombia's exports passing through Buenaventura, the latest government figures suggest that some 80% of the population lives below the poverty line. And a reported unemployment rate of almost 40% means that many residents have little option other than crime. In a bid to quell the violence, special marine forces control the worst areas of the city where poverty and violence are rife. Although it's not a place that most visitors would choose to spend large amounts of time, Buenaventura does offer a transit point for travellers keen to head out to Bahía Málaga and Isla Gorgona (which at the time of writing was closed to tourists).

There are also some fine beaches a short boat ride out of the city centre while the Río San Juan is a great place to spot humpback whales and dolphins.

SAFETY As of 2015, Buenaventura remains a dangerous place for local citizens and all outsiders. Avoid taking buses as they can be hotbeds of crime, and avoid venturing away from Calle 1 at night. Although the violence is largely between neo-paramilitary organisations and local crime syndicates, tourists should avoid venturing away from Calle 1 and 2 at any time, especially on foot.

GETTING THERE Frequent **buses** and *colectivos* run from Cali's bus terminal. The 100km journey takes about 4 hours and costs 20,000COP, but before travelling overland be sure to check out the safety situation as the route is prone to security problems. Another consideration is that the road is often affected by landslides in the rains, resulting in a serious gridlock of traffic.

WHERE TO STAY AND EAT Buenaventura has numerous hotels throughout the city although anyone who values their personal safety should be sure to choose wisely. Don't be tempted to entertain any establishments that don't have soldiers in combat fatigues guarding the foyer. Proper security measures are paramount in Buenaventura so for a safe hassle-free overnight stay there is little sense in scrimping. On this basis, avoid the many cheap hotels near the bus station. Don't walk anywhere you don't need to. If you insist on venturing out to eat, **Leños y Mariscos**, on Calle 1 is the place to go, otherwise eating in the hotel is the best option. The following hotels are recommended.

Hotel Tequendama Inn Estación (74+ rooms) Calle 2, No 1A–08; 241 9512. This fine Neoclassical building was built in 1928 & has rooms that range from singles & twins to doubles, triples & suites. An elegant restaurant Las Gaviotas has plenty of ornate stucco & grandeur & serves a pan-Colombian seafood menu with plenty of international style. There's also a decent bar for cocktails, lunches & snacks. Rooms have central AC, cable TV, telephone, minibar & a safety deposit box as standard & start at 150,000COP. The hotel can help with diving & waterfall trips with a guide as well as a 3-day whale-watching package including accommodation & meals for around 800,000COP. For this ask at the reception or ring the travel agency (241 2826). **$$$**

Hotel Torre Mar (110 rooms) Calle 1, No 3–03; 297 8282; www.torremarbuenaventura. com. This luxury option ensures that you won't have to leave the hotel during your stay. Rooms are spacious with king-sized beds, AC, soundproof windows, electric locks, bathtub & plasma TVs. There is a fitness suite, jacuzzi, restaurant, bar & a nightclub, Amber, which is open till 02.00. **$$$**

FESTIVALS
Festival Folclórico del Litoral Pacífico (Pacific Coast Folkloric Festival)
(August) Musical concerts, dancing, street processions, religious services, beauty

---

FOOD FROM THE OCEAN

Traditional dishes on the Pacific coast centre on rich seafood stews and fried fish served with rice and plantain – and it's rare to be offered anything other than freshly caught produce from the sea. Don't miss a chance to sample a thin lentil soup with smoked fish and *piangua* (a clam-like mollusc) – it's absolutely delicious. Wash it down with a tropical juice and eat a dessert of sweet coconut milk and molasses as a finale.

pageants and art exhibitions celebrate Buenaventura's colourful mix of cultures across a wide range of venues in the city.

BAHÍA MÁLAGA *Telephone code 4*

This mixed community of black Afro-Caribbean and indigenous peoples is located around 20km northeast of Buenaventura amidst rocky outcrops and verdant jungle. The La Plata Archipelago sits in the middle of the bay and comprises more than 100 islands that form a maze of canals and boggy swamps. Hourly changes to this coastal area mark the tidal ebb and flow that covers islands and exposes beaches, charting the rhythm of the Pacific Ocean. Two of the great regions of the Colombian Pacific coast meet at Bahía Málaga, making it a superb spot for biological conservation. The mountains of Baudó and Los Saltos dominate to the north of this jungle-covered coastline where an enormous diversity of flora and fauna includes many species unique to the area. Bahía Málaga has 60 species of amphibians, 114 reptiles, 16 species of freshwater fish, 148 species of saltwater fish, 57 different marine birds and 360 terrestrial birds. Between July and November humpback whales arrive from the Antarctic to give birth to their young – the calves then grow up to 20cm per day.

The community of La Plata contains fewer than 70 wooden huts on stilts whose residents are keen to develop ecotourism to its full potential. WWF has been instrumental in furthering a strong environmental ethos in Bahía Málaga, helping to launch a migrations festival. The local community celebrates in October by playing traditional music on handcrafted wind and percussion instruments accompanied by lyrics that celebrate the beauty of the whales, birds and turtles and their natural habitat.

In 2007, WWF Colombia and its partner in the Colombian Pacific coast – the conservationist Yubarta Foundation – celebrated the decision of the Colombian government to become a member of the International Whaling Commission (IWC). Along with Brazil, Argentina, Chile, Mexico, Panama and Belize, Colombia is now a part of the 'Latin American Front' of IWC – an important coalition of countries who oppose reopening commercial whaling. During the migratory period (June–November), local communities in and around Bahía Málaga offer whale-watching tours to the tourists who visit. Guides have been tutored by staff from the Yubarta Foundation, which has not only developed environmental awareness campaigns with local people but has also established guidelines for ecological whale watching in the bay.

Other tours offered to visitors include boat trips around the mangrove swamps along the shoreline on a backdrop of low-lying jungle out to La Piscina, a natural pool at the mouth of a small river with a little waterfall and a leafy trail. Another highlight is La Sierpe, where two 50m waterfalls cascade into the bay and if you have time, head to the La Barra, which locals claim to be the best beach in the region. Local fishing boats can be hailed to the beaches where a few huts and houses offer overnight accommodation for around 20,000COP.

GETTING THERE AND AROUND Check with your tour operator regarding the current state of the road to Bahía Málaga before travelling. The journey is less than 20km but it pays to take local advice before making the trip to gauge the current level of safety – and hiring a guide could be a worthy investment.

One of the most rapidly growing and reliable tour operators is **Palenque Tours**, covering mainly Choco South (National Park Utría and Nuqui). This Medellín-based company offers all-inclusive packages from three to seven days with the premise of tourism that is beneficial to communities and indigenous groups. In conjunction with the Chocó Community Tourism Alliance, Palenque allows guests to immerse themselves in local life by joining community groups on a hike through tropical jungles or a canoe drive. Palenque is the only one of its kind to work officially with the Chocó community and it donates part of its earnings to the groups they work with. Prices start at around 1,000,000COP and include daily activities, transport, guides, food and accommodation. Accommodation will be a mix of comfortable beachfront cabins and local establishments, and owner Markus will happily tailor any trip to your needs. For contact details, see page 331; see also ad on page 322.

SAN CIPRIANO *Telephone code 2*

San Cipriano is a teeny-weeny settlement situated at 200m above sea level, hidden deep in tropical rainforest of the brightest green. It's an important area that generates much of the drinking water for the nearby port town of Buenaventura where vast expanses of the river's watershed are protected in order to maintain water quality with the thick surrounding jungle largely unspoilt.

Remote and almost inaccessible, San Cipriano has no roads and its fast-flowing river is too shallow to navigate easily. To overcome this problem, the locals have devised an ingenious transit system using a stretch of railway track. It runs past the village and consists of transportation known as *'Brujita'* (little witch) – there are various designs ranging from a wooden pallet with bearings as wheels and customised old mopeds, each powered by men the size of giants. These strange contraptions are pushed along with a pole in a style similar to punting with frightening speeds up to 50km/h achieved on downhill stretches. This journey is *not* for the faint-hearted as the single track makes little allowance for anything travelling in the opposite direction. The route is also still occasionally used by a cargo train. An absence of any safety measures and numerous blind bends and having just a shoe for a brake make this an exciting (but ludicrous) way to arrive. A sign seemingly in the middle of nowhere declares 'Bienvenidos a San Cipriano' – and this is certainly a welcome sight after the 15-minute white-knuckle ride that propels you into town.

GETTING THERE AND AROUND San Cipriano is at least 10km from the nearest road but **buses** from Cali (21,000COP, 2½ hours) or Buenaventura (15,000COP, 3 hours) pass by the entrance of neighbouring Córdoba. Here you'll find the guys who run the Brujita to San Cipriano – just walk over the suspension bridge down the hill and head for the railtrack. Expect to pay 5,000COP per person for the 15-minute ride into town, unless the *Brujita* operators relent and accept the local rate of 3,000COP.

WHERE TO STAY AND EAT There are plenty of accommodation and cheap restaurant options in town so no reservations are needed. Expect to pay around 15,000COP per person for a clean, comfortable but basic room in a simple wooden house. Some owners may also serve a cheap lunch, dinner and breakfast as well as soft drinks and beers. Try to avoid weekends or national holidays as this little town loses part of its charm with hordes of people.

OTHER PRACTICALITIES There's a very good reason why San Cipriano is so incredibly green – it is very wet. So pack a waterproof jacket, a change of clothing and a towel. Night falls in an instant and there are no street lights in town so a torch is essential. You'll also need swimming gear for tubing and messing about in the sparkling waters of one of the cleanest rivers on the planet. However, take heed of rising water levels – the river can swell alarmingly in seconds flat.

WHAT TO SEE AND DO Although the town itself is little more than two dirt roads lined with wooden huts, San Cipriano has a great atmosphere. A local population of about 500 is friendly and welcoming and there is something cathartic about being somewhere so isolated and removed from the outside world. Most visitors head out to hike into the jungle along a truly beautiful 1-hour trail out of town. Swimming in the river is another delight and there are some beautiful cascades and crystal-clear pools at a place called **Refugio del Amor** (Love Refuge). Ask the locals to show you the best spots – there are plenty of people prepared to guide for the day.

San Cipriano is also an excellent place for **birders** due to the unspoilt natural birding habitat in the area. Just follow the dirt track out of town to spot lesser swallow-tailed and grey-rumped swifts, white-thighed swallow, tawny-crested tanager, chocó toucans and dusky-faced tanagers, black-chested jay and spot-crowned barbet – it's also possible to hear plenty of golden-collared manakin. In a thick palm concentration there are purple-throated fruitcrow and chestnut oropendola with cinnamon and crimson-bellied woodpeckers in the trees nearby. Other species include the short-tailed pygmy-tyrant, half-collared gnatwren, blue-black grosbeak, white-ringed flycatcher, purple-crowned fairy, white-headed wren, masked tityra, buff-throated saltator, and rose-faced parrot. Look out for the bay-breasted warbler in the winter months.

NUQUÍ *Telephone code 4*

Colombian vacationers heading to the Pacific coast have long favoured Nuquí, a rustic but charming fishing settlement on the beautiful Gulf of Tribuga 50km south of Bahía Solano. This traditional Chocóan village has beautiful beaches surrounded by vine-tangled tropical jungle. Cascading waterfalls, stream-fed pools and rambling forest trails make this popular with a wide range of visitors, from serious ornithologists, divers, fishermen and hikers to artists, poets, beach bums and anyone who enjoys nature. Much like Bahía Solano, Nuquí serves as a base for whale watching from June to November and ecotours with numerous operators and eco-resorts offering a wide range of packages. July is a prime month for diving in Nuquí and is a great time to spot giant mantas and large numbers of dolphins. Nuquí's beaches and that of nearby Pijiba consistently rank amongst Colombia's finest in tourist polls. However, given their location the beaches are rarely crowded except at Christmas and New Year and during major surfing events when Nuquí's population of 8,000 can rise by at least 20% overnight.

GETTING THERE AND AROUND Nuquí's Reyes Murillo Airport is served, much like Bahía Solano, with frequent **flights** from Medellín (50 minutes on a small twin Otter plane carrying 20 passengers). Owing to changes in airstrip conditions, it is better to organise your flights through a hotel or tour company like Palenque (pages 331 and 396–7). **Boats** to and from Buenaventura depart to an unpredictable schedule at 130,000COP per person. The ticket price includes three simple meals and a bed.

TOURIST INFORMATION
☑ **Oficina de Turismo** ☏ 683 6005;
e contactenos@nuqui-choco.gov.co; www.nuqui-choco.gov.co/index.shtml

⌂ **WHERE TO STAY AND EAT** Many of Nuquí's nicest places to stay are out of town along the coast in the jungle where some particularly fine eco-resorts offer a wide range of adventure packages. Almost all offer an all-inclusive package, but if you do decide to eat elsewhere (or manage to negotiate a cheaper room-only rate off-season), try the **Restaurant El Paisa** and **Pola's Place** (ask around) – both serve good food for 7,000COP.

🏠 **El Cantil Eco Lodge** (7 rooms) ✆ 448 0767; e elcantil@elcantil.com; www.elcantil.com. This innovative eco-resort hosts a wide range of themed 1-week activities, from surfing vacations & jungle survival schools to diving, climbing, dancing & wellbeing weeks. From Jun to Oct it offers highly popular humpback-whale tours as well as year-round dolphin spotting, birding & fishing trips – the waters are full of sailfish, marlin, tuna, mackerel, wahoo & snapper in May & Jun. Dive masters offer 15 years' experience & a full equipment rental service. Established in 1998, El Cantil is located south of Nuquí near to Termales (a 35min boat transfer that's included in the price) & boasts a splendid spot right on the ocean with magnificent views. English-speaking guides can be arranged but notice must be given. 7 comfortable rooms with private bathrooms can accommodate 6 people each & have an ocean-view terrace. A communal area has a restaurant & sundeck & the resort is equipped with surfboards, kayaks & boogie boards. Prices vary but expect to pay around 400,000COP per night with reduced charges for more nights spent there. **$$$**

🏠 **Hotel Turqui Ecohotel** (5 cabins, sleeps 40) m 310 544 1107; www.hotelturqui.com. This lovely little eco-resort is located in the Cabo Corrientes (meaning 'end of the river current'), a 45min speedboat journey from the centre of Nuquí. Wood-&-thatch cabins sit inside the jungle overlooking the seashore & accommodate up to 40 people in a range of double & family-sized rooms, plus an area for hammocks. Communal space has decks over the beach, a fresh seafood restaurant, bar, diving centre & 7km beach. Fishing trips use 25ft Yamaha twin-engine fibreglass boats with 25 sets of diving gear, instructors & international diving experts, Bauer compressor, GPS, sonar & double tanks. Packages begin at 720,000COP for a 4-day, 3-night stay including fishing & all transport, transfers, meals, guides & tours. **$$$**

🏠 **Lodge Piedra Piedra** (9 cabins) Calle 10B, No 35–03; ✆ 204 0671; e info@piedrapiedra. com; www.piedrapiedra.com. This jungle lodge is 15km south of the centre of Nuquí between the tropical rainforest & the ocean. There are a total of 9 luxury cabins across 3 sites close to beaches, rivers, waterfalls, thermal springs & jungle trails. It gets pretty full during whale-observation months (*Jun–Nov*) & is also a popular base camp for birders. Dolphins & a great variety of fish can be seen in the surrounding waters with kayaking, fishing, surfing & swimming from a lovely wooden deck. An on-site restaurant serves 3 meals a day & there's a bar, communal lounge & laundry. Everyone eats around 1 large wooden table to give a family feel to the lodge. Rates start at 251,000COP for a basic 1-day, 2-night stay with meals, although 3–7-day inclusive packages offer better value for those keen to whale watch, fish & hike. Transfers are included. The lodge offers a budget camping option or a basic backpacker plan with no meals or activities. **$$**

OTHER PRACTICALITIES Bring enough money (in low denominations) as there are no ATMs in Nuquí. Pack rubber boots, waterproof clothing and plenty of bug spray. It's also advisable to bring a candle and matches (or a torch) as paths are unlit. The phone signal is poor and there is no Wi-Fi.

WHAT TO SEE AND DO Surfers, windsurfers and kite-surfers head to Nuquí's **Playa Olympica** west of the airport where the water is calm close to shore. The big waves happen about 100m out where they break to a height of 2.4m. Pick up some supplies, fresh fish and tinfoil from Nuquí before crossing the lagoon by canoe to set up a day camp on the beach. **Guachalito** is another popular tour and has some very nice sandy stretches an hour's boat ride south of Nuquí with whale watching, dolphins, sport fishing and diving all along the coast to the **Cabo Corrientes**.

A rather nice **birding trail** leads out of town along the river where a wide variety of species can be easily spotted. Expect to see purple-throated fruitcrow, chestnut-backed antbird, black-striped woodcreeper, southern nightingale-wren, mourning

Although much of the Pacific coast's natural habitat remains largely intact and undeveloped there remains widespread concern regarding proposed large-scale development in the area. In the name of progress, a number of public and private investors have pushed for roads, inter-oceanic canals, railways and hydro-electric dams in El Pacífico with slash-and-burn agriculture, logging and mining ever-present threats to the integrity of the region's forests. These state plans – known collectively as the Plan Pacífico – aim to tap into the local resources more systematically as part of a strategy for increased trade with the outside world.

Amphibian diversity offers more than 200 species in the Pacific coast region – 30 of them endemic. Scientists are struggling to keep up with the pace of new discoveries with shelves of specimens awaiting analysis at the National Herpetological Collection in Bogotá. However, several species remain under threat, with the Pacific horned frog, pink-sided tree frog, golden poison frog, green poison frog and Myers' Surinam toad endangered, critically endangered or vulnerable.

More than 285 mammal species have been recorded in the region – 11 of which are endemic. Species under threat include the spectacled bear, smoky bat, equatorial dog-faced bat, greater long-tailed bat, southern long-nosed bat, western nectar bat, Tacarcuna bat, Baird's tapir, silvery-brown bare-face tamarin, cotton-top tamarin, lemurine night monkey, red crested tree rat, Gorgas' rice rat and a giant anteater.

Scientists estimate that El Pacífico is home to more than 320 reptile species, of which nearly 100 are endemic. Poaching remains a problem in the Pacific region – multiple cases in 2012 saw boats intercepted while hunting for sharks. The Colombian and Costa Rican governments joined forces in the fight against illegal fishing along the Pacific coast and especially the act of shark-finning. In June 2014, the Colombian government reiterated its determination to stop the export of shark meat, most of which heads to Asia where fins are used in soup and seen as a delicacy.

warbler, blue-grey tanager, golden-hooded tanager, great-billed crimson-crested woodpecker, rufous-tailed jacamar, white-tailed trogon, ringed kingfisher, Amazon kingfisher, orange-chinned parakeet, blue-headed parrot, streak-throated hermit, purple gallinule, long-tailed tyrant, black-crowned tityra, seed-finch, buff-throated saltator, baudo oropendola, scarlet-rumped cacique, Wilson's plover, southern lapwing, roadside hawk, red-breasted blackbird, olive-crowned yellowthroat, dusky-faced tanager and great-tailed grackle – to name quite a few.

COLOMBIA ONLINE

For additional online content, articles, photos and more on Colombia, why not visit www.bradtguides.com/colombia.

11

The Atlantic Coast

Colombia's most accessible coastal stretch is also its most tourist-friendly with around 1,750km of palm-fringed coastline dotted with fine historic cities, Caribbean resorts and numerous attractions. Containing a vast range of ecosystems and six distinct sub-regions, the many contrasting facets of the Caribbean shoreline beg thorough exploration. From the Andean mountain range, a massif plain extends to the Sierra Nevada de Santa Marta and the Guajira Peninsula at Colombia's most northerly point. A criss-cross of rivers and the vast Ciénaga Grande de Santa Marta marshland lead to idyllic carpets of white sand on terrain bordered by Panama's impenetrable jungle swathe to the east and humble Venezuelan fishing villages to the west. From the windblown dry cacti-clad coastal desert in La Guajira and the steamy virgin rainforest of Parque Nacional Tayrona to the fine-looking colonial city of Cartagena and its exquisite UNESCO-listed architectural beauty, the Atlantic coast is steeped in history and legend. Myths continue to dominate modern culture, with many versions of La Llorona ('The Crying Woman') in existence. The region's nine million laid-back Costeños are mainly of African descent, renowned for their slow-paced lifestyle and pulsating *reggaetón, porro* and *champeta* Afro-Caribbean rhythms. The Atlantic coast is also synonymous with Colombia's wildest festivals, with the eye-popping Carnaval de Barranquilla an especially raucous affair. Various dialects of Caribbean-Spanish exist within each sub-region, along with several indigenous languages including Wayúu. La Guajira is also home to one of Colombia's concentrations of Middle Eastern émigrés in the border town of Maicao.

HISTORY

The Caribbean coast boasts the distinction of being the first conquered by the Spanish and contains Colombia's two oldest surviving cities: Santa Marta (founded in 1525) and Cartagena (1533). However, various indigenous groups inhabited the region long before the conquistadors' arrival. Two communities evolved into highly developed civilisations, with the Tayrona in the Sierra Nevada de Santa Marta and the Sinú in the region's southwest particularly industrially advanced. Both Santa Marta and Cartagena were important strategic shipping posts for vast riches amassed by the Spanish plunder. Mules ferried gold from besieged Amerindian tribes in the interior regions to galleons bound for Spain. As a consequence Cartagena was subject to sustained attacks and vicious assaults throughout its early years.

CLIMATE

Expect brutally hot, steamy conditions and temperatures that rarely drop below 28°C. Two rainy periods run from April to May and October to November with December to April and July to September typically dry. Cooling winds during December to January make this a pleasant time to visit.

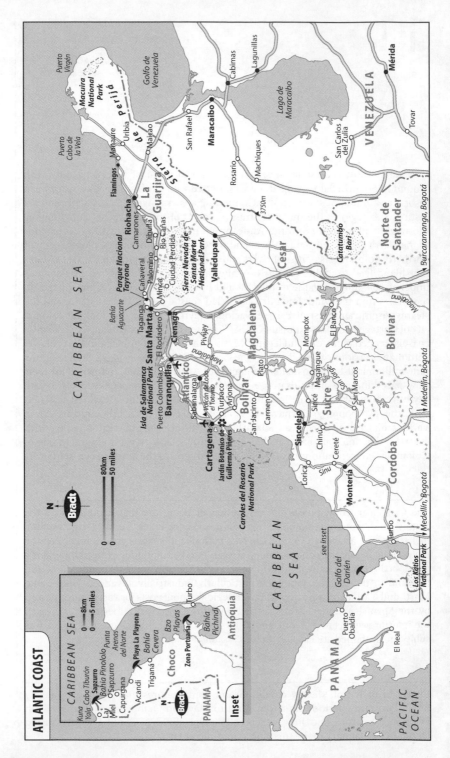

ATLANTIC COAST

CARIBBEAN SEA

N

Bradt

0   80km
0   50 miles

*Puerto
Virgén*

**Macuira
National
Park**

*Golfo de
Venezuela*

Cabimas

Lagunillas

VENEZUELA

Mérida

*Puerto
Cabo de
la Vela*

Manaure

Maicao

Uribia

Maracaibo

San Rafael

*Lago de
Maracaibo*

Tovar

Flamingos

Riohacha

Camarones

Dibulla

Rosario

Machiques

San Carlos
del Zulia

**Parque Nacional
Tayrona**

Cañaveral

Palomino

Minca

Ciudad Perdida

**Sierra Nevada de
Santa Marta
National Park**

Valledupar

**Norte de
Santander**

3750m

**Catatumbo
Bari**

↗ *Bucaramanga, Bogotá*

*Bahía
Aguacarte*

Taganga

Santa Marta

El Rodadero

Ciénaga

Pivijay

Magdalena

Cesar

**Isla de Salamanca
National Park**

Puerto Colombia

Barranquilla

Sabanalarga

Plato

Mompóx

El Banco

Magdalena

Bolívar

Magdalena

↗ *Medellín, Bogotá*

Atlántico

▲ *Volcán de Lodo
el Totumo*

Turbaco

Arjona

Magangué

Sincé

San Marcos

Cartagena

Carmen

San Jacinto

Bolívar

Sucre

San Jorge

**Jardín Botánico de
Guillermo Piñeres**

Sincelejo

Chinú

Cereté

San Marcos

**Corales del Rosario
National Park**

Lorica

Sinú

Montería

Cordoba

↗ *Medellín, Bogotá*

CARIBBEAN
SEA

Turbo

↗ *Medellín, Bogotá*

**Los Katios
National Park**

see inset

*Golfo del
Darién*

PANAMA

Puerto
Obaldía

El Real

*PACIFIC
OCEAN*

Inset

CARIBBEAN SEA

0   8km
0   5 miles

*Kuna
Yala*   *Cabo Tiburón*   **Sapzurro**

La
Miel   *Bahía Pinololo*   *Punta
Arenas
del Norte*

Capurgana   *Sapzurro*

Acandi   Triganá   *Bahía
Cevera*   ↗ **Playa La Playona**

*Bzo
Playas*

Turbo

Zona Portuaria   *Bahía
Pichindí*

Choco

Antióquia

PANAMA

N

Bradt

402

One of the most visited regions of Colombia, Bolívar extends from the coast at Cartagena near the mouth of the Río Magdalena before sweeping south along the river to a border with Antioquia. Pretty offshore islands and the resplendent colonial buildings of the walled city of Cartagena and the lesser-visited Mompóx make the department a major tourist draw. Much of its 25,978km² terrain consists of hot, humid, forested lowlands. Aside from tourism, Bolívar's economy relies on the production of livestock, sugarcane, tobacco, cotton, cereals, coffee and forest products. Cartagena's port has ensured the region is an important centre for commerce with strategic waterway connections via the Canal de Dique along the Río Magdalena.

CARTAGENA *Telephone code 5*

Abandon all thoughts of ticking off sightseeing attractions in Cartagena; simply take to the city's picture-perfect streets and meander through one of the greatest cultural treasures in the Americas. Stroll along an enchanting puzzle of cobbled paths complete with horse-drawn carriages past bloom-covered archways and fine colonial buildings painted a dazzling array of bold hues. Pristine leafy plazas adorned with vibrant bougainvillea and handsome palms lead to ancient fortifications with stunning sea views. Outdoor cosmopolitan cafés bustle with cappuccino-sipping tourists amidst street theatre, basket weavers and flower sellers. Facing the Caribbean Sea to the west with Cartagena Bay to the south, Cartagena was declared a World Heritage Site by UNESCO in 1984 as the region's true jewel box of Spanish colonial ostentation. Expect sweet, sticky heat in a city that seems to be in a permanent state of festival with plenty of unique historic 'character' of which slavery, sainthood and swashbuckling buccaneers are all a part.

HISTORY Founded in 1533 by Pedro de Heredia on the site of the Carib Amerindian settlement of Calamarí, meaning 'crab', Cartagena formed a vital part in the Spanish defence strategy. A walled military fortress was constructed to protect the city against plundering pirates from England, Holland and France. Cartagena's first buildings were destroyed when fire ravaged the city in 1552. Since then, only stone, tile and brick have been allowed in construction. As the main northern gateway into South America, Cartagena soon grew into a busy port used by the Spanish to store and ship looted Amerindian gold. Despite its robust design, the city was subjected to numerous attacks, with five violent assaults in the 16th century alone. Sir Francis Drake sacked the port in 1568, forcing the inhabitants to take refuge in the neighbouring village of Turbaco. He destroyed the nave of the cathedral and demanded a staggering 107,000 ducats (10 million COP) in ransom in return for agreeing not to raze the town to the ground. In a bid to better protect Cartagena, the Spanish engaged some prominent European military engineers to undertake the construction of a series of fortresses. In March of 1741, English admiral Edward Vernon and his troops attacked Cartagena with an enormous fleet of 186 ships and 25,000 men. Blas de Lezo (1688–1741), a Spanish officer who had already lost an eye and a leg in earlier fighting, had only six ships and 3,600 men. After weeks of intense fighting, the siege was repelled by the Spanish commander. He lost his remaining leg and died shortly after but is honoured by a statue outside the San Félipe fortress as the saviour of Cartagena. Vernon had not expected defeat and, before he attacked, overconfident of victory, had ordered medals bearing: 'True

British Heroes Took Cartagena, April 1741'. A statue of Vernon and a replica of this medal were erected as a permanent laughing stock. Never count your chickens, especially when fighting the Spanish and with incalculable amounts of treasure at stake. In November 2014, the UK's Prince Charles unveiled a plaque commemorating the fallen – of both sides – from this battle. A national furore resulted and the plaque was removed. What remains is the empty base of a plinth close to Blaz de Lezo's statue.

The first slave ship arrived in 1564 to send thousands of slaves all over the continent, prompting Cartagena to be granted shared monopoly (along with Vera Cruz in Mexico) of the Caribbean slave trade in the early 17th century. More than one million slaves were brought by ship to Cartagena during this era, forced to provide free labour to ensure the sustained growth of the Spanish Empire and becoming the greatest slave market of the New World. After an excruciating sea crossing, the surviving African captives were offloaded from their ships and taken straight to auction at the *feria de negros* (slave market) at the entrance of the old city. The slaves brought their culture, traditions, songs and dances from Africa and these soon became mixed with Catholic ritual with animist and Islamic rhythms. Today, Colombia's beloved *cumbia cienaguera* songs remain heavily laced with the influences of Cartagena's slavery in music that retains African beats and plenty of *sabor* (flavour) and *ambiente* (atmosphere).

In 1650, the construction of the Canal del Dique strengthened Cartagena's gateway role for ships heading to ports along the river. It continued to be one of Spain's most important colonial strongholds, serving as a warehouse for the wealth of the country before the riches were loaded on to boats for the journey to Seville. However, the self-rule movement began to gain momentum in Cartagena and in 1810, the city was one of the first to proclaim independence from Spain, signing a declaration on 11 November 1811. A four-month siege followed as the Spanish attempted to calm the revolt under the leadership of Pablo Morillo in 1815, during which time more than 6,000 inhabitants lost their lives. Although Simón Bolívar defeated the Spanish at Boyacá in August 1819, Cartagena wasn't liberated until 1820. Nationalist troops eventually freed the city by sea and it was honoured by Bolívar with the name 'La Héroica', 'the Heroic City'. 'Si Caracas me dio la vida, vosotros me desteis gloria', he declared – 'Caracas may have given me birth, but you gave me glory'.

Today, Cartagena's population has soared beyond one million and is growing. It is Colombia's number one tourist draw and continues to be a major destination for conferences, national and international tourism. Cartagena's literary prestige has flourished as the home of an overseas spin-off of the Hay Festival, bolstering its status as Latin America's essential detour for sun-seeking literati seeking also a new style of libertarian hedonism. This celebration of contemporary literature has a head start as the former home of 'Gabo', Gabriel García Márquez, author of *One Hundred Years of Solitude* and Colombia's Nobel laureate.

CLIMATE Owing to Cartagena's tropical location, the city's climate has little variation, with an average high of 32°C and an average low of 25°C throughout the year. Humidity is generally around 90% so it is permanently hot and sticky. A rainy season runs typically in October to November with the driest months December to April, although tropical showers occur year-round.

ORIENTATION The locals divide Cartagena into five distinct zones: Historic, Tourist, North, South and Residential. The Historic Zone (known by its original name Calamarí by the locals and also *centro histórico*) is, as the name suggests, the old quarter in the west containing the Ciudad Amurallada (Walled City) and the aged neighbourhoods of San Diego, La Matuna, Getsemaní and Santo Domingo. The Tourist Zone of Bocagrande, Castillogrande and El Laguito sits to the south of the old city in an odd-shaped peninsula that is home to the city's main beaches, with Cartagena Bay to the east and the Caribbean Sea to the west. Flanked by a succession of modern, high-rise Miami-esque hotels, the Avenida San Martín forms the backbone of this vibrant area renowned for its nightlife, shops and restaurants. The Rafael Núñez International Airport is in the North Zone in the suburb of Crespo. Cartagena's poorest residential neighbourhoods are in the city's southeast.

GETTING THERE AND AWAY

By air Cartagena's ultra-efficient Rafael Núñez International Airport (*www.sacsa. com.co*) is located in Crespo, 3km northeast of the old city, and handles more passengers than any other airport in the region. ADA, Avianca, EasyFly, Copa, LAN, Satena and Viva Colombia offer frequent flights to the Colombian cities of Medellín, Bogotá, Cali, San Andrés, Barranquilla and Pereira. The US, Panama and Venezuela (Miami, New York, Panama City and Caracas) are also well served with numerous seasonal operators serving Europe direct. The airport is serviced by frequent local buses with *colectivos* (shared taxis) departing to Crespo from the *Monumento a la India Catalina*. Arrivals at the airport can catch a bus to the centre (it's marked El Centro) for about 500COP. There is an official taxi office at the exit of the domestic arrivals area; expect to pay in the region of 11,000COP for a ride from here to the Historic Centre.

By boat At the time of writing, there was an infrequent ferry service from Colón, Panama to Cartagena with departures to Cartagena every Monday and Wednesday at 21.00 and arriving at 13.00 the following day with FerryXpress (\ *368 0000;* e *atencionalcliente@ferryxpress.com; http://www.ferryxpress.com/*). It is also possible to travel by sailboat from Cartagena to Panama – it takes around five days and is one of the great backpacker experiences. However, this is not a regular service so no schedules exist. We heartily recommend that you shop around and ask about reliable operators in Cartagena as most hostels will have secure contacts. Boats include the *Gypsy Moth, Mintaka, Cool Running* and others. Websites to visit regarding this journey include http://panamatravelunlimited.com, http://sailcolombiapanama. com and http://www.sailingkoala.com. The cost is roughly US$550 per person including food.

Passengers are dropped at the island of Porvenir, where a small airport connects to Panama City for around US$40. This is a preferable option to negotiating a place to hang a hammock on a passing cargo boat – safer, better equipped (with kitchen, etc) and not involved in contraband or drug smuggling.

By bus Cartagena's main bus terminal is on the eastern edge of the city and is served by Metrocar buses from the city every 10 minutes or so. Half-a-dozen daily buses run to Bogotá (120,000COP, 20 hours) and Medellín (100,000COP, 13 hours), with buses to Barranquilla (9,000COP, 2 hours) running every 15 minutes.

GETTING AROUND Numerous yellow taxis serve the Cartagena area with a ride across town costing 5,000COP, an airport run 11,000COP and a trip to the outskirts 8,000COP. To keep costs down, ask the driver to drive to the Green Church at Crespo rather than the airport – it's a simple walk across the road to the airport and

avoids incurring the expensive airport tariff. Taxis are not metered, so fix the price beforehand – for a full tariff, visit www.cartagenainfo.com/taxis.

The city's famous horse-drawn carriages operate around the historical centre and the tourist zones after 17.00 – ask for a general tour or give them a specific drop-off point for around 25,000COP. Please ensure that you choose a horse that is healthy and well looked after as there have been cases of animal cruelty and of horses collapsing and even dying from exhaustion whilst on these tours. A system of buses and *colectivos* serves all areas of the city and these are useful for getting to the beach at Bocagrande.

Cartagena's public transport has been invaded by 'mototaxis' – check out the many postings of harrowing footage on YouTube for a zillion good reasons why to give this cheap option a miss. At the time of writing, a multi-million-dollar mass transportation system was slated; for an update, visit www.cartagenadeindias.travel.

TOURIST INFORMATION Given that Cartagena is Colombia's eternal city of tourism, local authorities have ensured the prevalence of PITs (Tourist Information Points) around the city.

ℹ Main Office [407 B3] Plaza de la Aduana; ☎660 1583; e info@cartagenadeindias.travel; http://www.cartagenadeindias.travel; ☉ 07.00–23.00 daily
ℹ Plaza de la Paz ☉ 07.00–23.00 daily

ℹ Aeropuerto Rafael Nuenz (arrivals) ☉ 07.00–23.00 daily
ℹ Bocagrande [418 B7] Across from the Hotel Caribe; ☉ 08.00–13.00 & 14.00–17.00 daily

TOUR GUIDES
Marelvy Peña-Hall m 315 760 5034. Completely fluent in English, French & Spanish, a native of Cartagena, Marelvy combines the intimate knowledge of her home city with an enthusiasm for meeting new people.
Nico Medes ☎674 0336; m 315 710 8700. Expect an abundance of great historical facts & background from the likeable Nico, a quietly spoken, charming man who has been guiding in the city for 20 years. He speaks English fluently & is a popular man around the city. To explore Cartagena on foot is a genuine delight, such as his good-natured style & attention to detail. Nico has a regular tourism slot on Cartagena TV station C5.

TOUR OPERATORS Hop aboard a *chiva* (colourful, open-side traditional Colombian bus) for Cartagena's 4-hour city tour; they depart daily at 14.00 from Bocagrande. Another tour option is to take a horse-drawn carriage from Bocagrande for a trip around the walled city and along the waterfront. These operate from 17.00 each night and last about 1 hour. Numerous tour operators offer boat trips out to the islands, especially the Islas del Rosario. Cartagena also has lots of diving centres with a number located in the historic centre, including **Cartagena Divers** [407 C2] (☎ 664 0814; www.cartagenadivers.com), **Diving Planet** [407 B2] (m 320 230 1515; www.divingplanet.org), and **Tortuga Dive School** [418 B7] (☎665 6994; www.tortugadive.com) in Bocagrande.

To hire a captain and 52ft luxury yacht that can accommodate 15 people, complete with kitchen and bar, contact **Relax 2 Yacht** (☎664 1117; www.cartagenarelax.com). It costs 1,400,000COP for a full day on the ocean, with 48 hours' notice required.

⌂ WHERE TO STAY *See maps, pages 407 and 418.*
Cartagena has a positively enormous range of accommodation in every price bracket, but tends to be pricier than many Colombian cities. Getsemaní may have historically been the centre of backpacker hostels but is now gentrifying

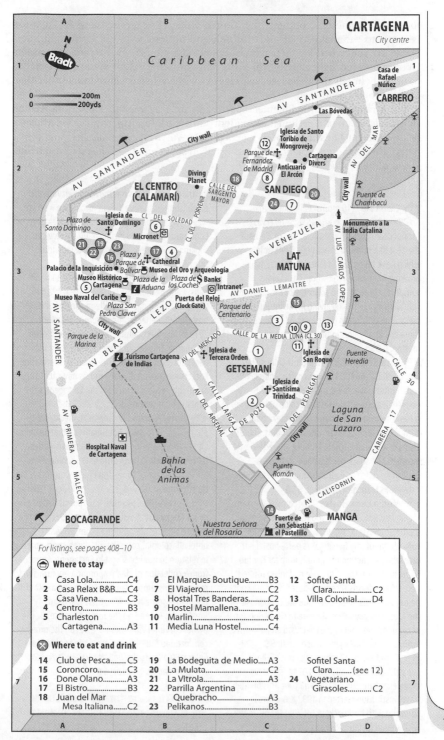

For listings, see pages 408–10

🏠 Where to stay

1	Casa Lola	C4	
2	Casa Relax B&B	C4	
3	Casa Viena	C3	
4	Centro	B3	
5	Charleston Cartagena	A3	
6	El Marques Boutique	B3	
7	El Viajero	C2	
8	Hostal Tres Banderas	C2	
9	Hostel Mamallena	C4	
10	Marlin	C4	
11	Media Luna Hostel	C4	
12	Sofitel Santa Clara	C2	
13	Villa Colonial	D4	

✖️ Where to eat and drink

14	Club de Pesca	C5	
15	Coroncoro	C3	
16	Done Olano	A3	
17	El Bistro	B3	
18	Juan del Mar Mesa Italiana	C2	
19	La Bodeguita de Medio	A3	
20	La Mulata	C2	
21	La Vitrola	A3	
22	Parrilla Argentina Quebracho	A3	
23	Pelikanos	B3	
	Sofitel Santa Clara	(see 12)	
24	Vegetariano Girasoles	C2	

to include some chic options; the Tourist Zone (Bocagrande and El Laguito) is home to the majority of mid- to high-end options while El Centro and San Diego are renowned for their upmarket boutique hotels. At the time of writing, Getsemaní's red-light activity still exists but, not to the extent of the past. On this basis, only hotels in the less sleazy parts of town are listed – but double checking on the ground is advised.

For a range of well-maintained apartments for rent contact **Colombia Rental** (*www.colombiarental.net*), an independent outfit run by an American called Michael or the efficient **Vacation Rentals Cartagena** (*www.vacationrentalscartagena.com*). Alternatively, there are plenty of places listed on convenient websites such as **airbnb** (*www.airbnb.co.uk*).

Getsemaní

Casa Lola (10 rooms) Calle Guerrero, No 29–108/29–118; ☎664 1538; e reservas@casalola.com.co; www.casalola.com.co. Perhaps the best of a number of boutique-style hotels which have taken full advantage of Getsemaní's growing bohemian reputation, Casa Lola is sumptuously decorated & worthy of the glossy full-spread coverage it is receiving in the international press. True comfort in this designer boutique; there are small pools in the cloister area & on the rooftop. **$$$$**

Casa Relax B&B (12 rooms) Calle de Pozo, No 20–105; ☎664 1117; www.cartagenarelax.com. Visitors rave about this French-run B&B housed in a beautifully restored colonial building. It has comfortable AC rooms (8 double/2 twin) with a TV & nice, clean private bathrooms. There's also a communal kitchen, laundry, shared lounge, internet, bar, snack bar & a pool. Staff speak English & French as well as Spanish. Rates include a delicious French-style b/fast. **$$$**

Media Luna Hostel (18 rooms) Calle de la Media Luna, No 10–46; ☎664 3423; e reservas@medialunahostel.com; www.medialunahostel.com. Undoubtedly Getsemaní's party hostel *par excellence,* attracting the hordes from far & wide to participate in the club-style hedonism offered here. Mixed dorms & cement-based beds may not be to everyone's liking but if you are checking-in at the Media Luna you are not here to sleep. Rooftop bar & paddling pool in the courtyard are attractive options in the Cartagena heat as well. **$$**

Casa Viena (9 rooms, 2 dorms) Calle San Andrés, No 30–53; ☎664 6242; e hotel@casaviena.com; www.casaviena.com. This budget travel institution started in 1992 & is a firm favourite with backpackers, offering simple rooms with shared facilities & a lot of practical help.

Austrian owner Hans has moved on leaving the establishment to his efficient local team who are well versed in tours, boats to Panama, treks, etc. Communal amenities include laundry services, cooking facilities, book exchange & individual safety deposit boxes. **$**

Hostel Mamallena (15 rooms, 31 dorm beds) Calle de la Media Luna, No 10–47; ☎670 0499; e Cartagena@mamallena.com; www.hostelmamallenacartagena.com. Opened in 2012 by the folks behind the Mamallena Hostel in Panama, this establishment delivers for the backpacker on location, price, tours & information. Lockers are provided, many rooms have AC & they are highly recommended for the Cartagena to Panama boat service. **$**

Hotel Marlin (24 rooms) Calle 30, No 10–35; ☎664 3507; www.hotelmarlincartagena.com. Choose from a range of pokey rooms with private bathroom in this cheap little backpacker option – ask to see a few as some don't have windows & are claustrophobic. **$**

Hotel Villa Colonial (30 rooms) Calle de las Maravillas, No 30–60; ☎664 4996; e hotelvillacolonial@hotmail.com; www.hotelvillacolonial.com. Potentially the best hotel in relation to quality & cost in Cartagena. Choose from a collection of clean, appropriately furnished rooms in this simple family-run hotel in a colonial building – some have AC, others just a fan. Breakfast is offered on the rooftop terrace. **$**. The owners of Hotel Villa Colonial also run the more comfortable & highly recommended Casa Villa Colonial (*Calle Media Luna, No 10–89;* ☎*664 5421; www.casavillacolonial.co*) **$$**

El Centro (Calamarí) & San Diego

El Marques Boutique Hotel (8 rooms) Calle Nuestra Señora Del Carmen, No 33–41;

📞 664 4438/7800; e elmarqueshotelctg@gmail.com; www.elmarqueshotelboutique.com. Classy furnishings & chic styling at this boutique hotel set within one of the nicest 17th-century colonial buildings in this part of the old city. A lavish restoration programme has equipped this fine historic property with a host of high-tech amenities in what was once the home of a famous New Yorker, Sam Green – boyfriend of Greta Garbo – who regularly entertained Yoko Ono & the Kennedy family. 6 luxurious rooms & 2 suites overlook an elegant courtyard garden with LCD-screen controls, cable TV, minibar & safety deposit boxes. El Marques also has a swimming pool, sushi bar & spa. A pricey option but an enjoyable extravagance nonetheless. **$$$$**

🏠 **Hotel Charleston Cartagena** (113 rooms) Plaza Santa Teresa; 📞 664 9494; www.hotels-charleston.com. 2 idyllic arcaded courtyard rooms & suites of tasteful décor at this elegant hotel. Guest amenities include a rooftop pool, 3 good restaurants & a gym. **$$$$**

🏠 **Hotel Sofitel Santa Clara** (180 rooms) Calle del Torno; 📞 664 6070; www.hotelsantaclara.com. Without a doubt one of Cartagena's classiest accommodation options, this landmark colonial building used to be the Convento de Santa Clara & dates back to 1621. No-expense-spared luxurious touches attract a well-heeled clientele with rooms & suites decorated in sumptuous grandeur. Amenities include a gym, business centre, 2 upmarket restaurants & a chic bar. The Santa Clara boasts its fair share of visiting Hollywood starlets, movie-makers & political leaders. Colombian Formula 1 star Juan Pablo Montoya had his wedding here & past lunch guests have included Bill Clinton. Worth a splurge. **$$$$**

🏠 **Centro Hotel** (16 rooms) Calle del Arzobispado, No 34–80; 📞 664 0461; e reservas@centrohotelcartagena.com.co; www.centrohotelcartagena.com. Just a few metres from the Plaza de Bolívar, the Centro is a good mid-range option with nice, clean AC rooms set around an open courtyard. Rates include b/fast. **$$$**

🏠 **Hostal Tres Banderas** (22 rooms) Calle Cochera del Hobbo, No 38–66; 📞 660 0160; www.hotel3banderas.com. This beautifully decorated alcohol- & tobacco-free hotel is drenched in colour. Rooms are larger on the 2nd floor & have a balcony. A stylish courtyard has waterfalls & palms beyond a bloom-clad tangerine exterior adorned

with a fine wrought-iron gate. **$$$**

🏠 **Hostel El Viajero** (20 rooms) Calle Siete Infantes, No 9–45; 📞 660 2598; www.hostelcartagena.com. Voted as the best hostel in Colombia in 2013, El Viajero is the only true hostel in this well-heeled district of Cartagena. The owner has taken the El Viajero chain from strength to strength in his native Uruguay & now runs 3 in Colombia (the others being in San Andrés & Cali). Everything you would expect from private rooms with AC, dorms with AC, activities, bar, free Wi-Fi & more. **$**

🏠 **Hotel El Viajero** (14 rooms) Calle del Porvenir, No 35–68; 📞 664 3289. Not to be confused with the aforementioned hostel by the same name, this good-value budget hotel has clean & comfortable AC rooms, a courtyard & communal kitchen. Excellent location. **$**

Bocagrande

🏠 **Hotel Caribe** (380 rooms) Carrera 1A, No 2–87; 📞 650 1160/665 0155; www.hotelcaribe.com. Grand, imposing & with a whitewashed stucco exterior, the palatial Caribe sits adorned with flags in lush, tropical gardens. Built in 1940, the hotel boasts ultra-posh rooms & self-contained suites. Expect top-notch service, with prices to match. **$$$$**

🏠 **Hotel Capilla del Mar** (200+ rooms) Cnr Carrera 1, No 8–12; 📞 650 1500; e reservas@capilladelmar.com; www.hotelcapilladelmar.com. This high-rise beachfront hotel's rooms are cheerfully decorated, spacious & well appointed with modern private bathrooms. Choose from a range of AC double rooms & suites with safety deposit boxes, telephone, minibar, cable TV & hairdryer. 3 restaurants, a pool & business centre are just some of the many amenities – it even has a slow-moving rotating 21st-floor bar offering panoramic views across the city. **$$$**

🏠 **Hotel Bocagrande** (30 rooms) Av San Martín, No 7–159; 📞 642 4513; e info@hotelbocagrande.com; www.hotelbocagrande.com. Comfortable, simple rooms come with AC & balconies at this tourist hotel close to the beach & are equipped with minibar, cable TV, private bathroom & telephone. Amenities include a restaurant serving a mix of fast food & Colombian specialities. **$$**

🏠 **Hotel Estrella del Mar** (9 rooms) Av San Martín, No 4–46; 📞 655 1349/6144; e estrella@

hotelesbarahona.com. Set a block or so from the
seafront; a fuss-free lower mid-range option,
popular with vacationing Colombians looking for

a cheap place to stay a short walk from the beach.
Basic AC rooms have a private bathroom & cable
TV. A place in which to recharge your batteries. **$$**

✖ WHERE TO EAT AND DRINK See map, pages 407 and 418.

Good food is easy to find in Cartagena, with an abundance of choice in the historic
centre and in and around Bocagrande in the Tourist Zone. Local specialities include
delicious small smoked meatballs (*butifarras*), deep-fried cheese sticks (*dedos de
queso*) and egg-filled fried maize (*arepas de huevo*) – all are sold throughout the
city by street vendors. There are way too many restaurants to list, but the following
will provide a starting point.

✖ **Club de Pesca** Fuerte del Pastelillo; ☎660
4594/5863/7065; e restaurante@clubdepesca.
com; ⊕ lunch & dinner. Cartagena's affluent
gastronomes like to eat at this great lunch spot
where chic tables are laid in grand style underneath
a giant tree on a patio overlooking a posh marina.
Expect a superb menu, fine wines & lots of designer
garb in Cartagena's oldest fort. **$$$**

✖ **Hotel Sofitel Santa Clara** Calle del Torno;
☎664 6070; www.hotelsantaclara.com;
⊕ lunch & dinner. It's difficult not to gush about
this truly gorgeous setting, amidst blood-red
paintwashed walls, hand-thrown tiles & towering
leafy palms. Rugged antiques, lavish drapes & fine
furnishings offer unabashed luxury. Choose from a
French menu at El Refectorio (the former convent's
dining area), snacks at El Corro (where the nuns
intoned their ecclesiastical chants) & El Caustro
Café (a relaxed outside brasserie-style lunch
spot) for some of the most memorable dining in
Cartagena's swishiest locales. **$$$**

✖ **Juan del Mar Mesa Italiana** Plaza San
Diego; ☎664 2782; www.juandelmar.com;
⊕ lunch & dinner. Choose from a menu of grilled
fish with basil, homemade mozzarella pizza &
pasta dishes at this charming place with indoor or
outdoor seating. **$$$**

✖ **La Vitrola** Calle de Bolaco, No 2–01;
☎664 8243; ⊕ noon–15.00 & 19.00–midnight
Mon–Sat. Routinely touted as Cartagena's best
restaurant, La Vitrola with her buzzing live Cuban
house band, elegant setting & mouthwatering
seafood dishes does not disappoint. Book in
advance to avoid disappointment. **$$$**

✖ **El Bistro** Calle de Ayos, No 4–42; ☎664 1799;
⊕ all day. Expect casual fare & light meals at this
pleasant German-owned backstreet café where
the travel tips for backpackers are as good as man-
sized sandwiches & pasta dishes. **$$**

✖ **La Bodeguita de Medio** Calle de la
Mantilla, No 3–32; ☎660 1436; ⊕ noon–
midnight. Coloured walls displaying rebel-rousing
posters supporting *la revolución* give it a studenty
feel with lots of hard-line political items relating
to Castro & Guevara. A small menu offers Cuban
bean-&-rice dishes & grilled meats. **$$**

✖ **La Mulata** Calle Quero, No 9–58; ☎664
6222; ⊕ b/fast & lunch Mon–Sat. This quirky
yet popular haunt serves set menus changing
every day at very reasonable prices. So, if you are
hankering for Caribbean cuisine look no further.
$$

✖ **Parrilla Argentina Quebracho** Calle de
Baloco; ☎ 664 1300; ⊕ lunch & dinner Mon–Thu,
all day Fri/Sat. Meat-lovers will die & go to heaven
at the sight of spit-roasted pig, huge slabs of steak
& chorizo sausage – washed down with a big cellar
of Argentine wine. **$$**

✖ **Restaurante Done Olano** Calle Santo
Domingo, No 33–08; ☎664 7099; ⊕ noon–23.00
Mon–Sat. A French-Creole menu offers some
interesting dishes a little different from the norm,
such as jambalaya & garlic fish. **$$**

✖ **Restaurante Pelikanos** Cnr Calle Santo
Domingo & Calle Gastlebondo; ☎660 0086;
⊕ 11.00–late. Superb value is the order of the
day at this chilled-out bohemian diner where a
set 6-course meal comes with limitless wine &
includes 4 mini appetisers. **$$**

✖ **Restaurante Coroncoro** Calle Tripita y
Medio, No 31–28; ⊕ 08.00–20.00. Expect simple,
filling local food at this inexpensive family-run
restaurant where most meals come in at under
8,000COP. **$**

✖ **Restaurant Vegetariano Girasoles** Calle
de los Puntales, No 37–01; ☎664 5239; ⊕ noon–
22.00. This San Diego meat-free joint offers tasty
beans-&-rice dishes & soups at budget prices. **$**

Bocagrande As you'd expect from a seafront tourist zone, Bocagrande offers plenty of vacation food, from hamburgers and pizza joints to indulgent family diners. Most of the restaurants are along Avenida San Martín. Menus don't tend to offer the sophistication or choice of the historical centre – the following are just a handful of what's around at the time of writing.

Enjoy first-rate beef kebabs at **El Otoyal** on Avenida 4 diagonally opposite the Carulla supermarket. For some of the most mouthwatering coconut macaroons head to **Pan De Bono**, while **El Kiosko de Bony** in front of the Hotel El Caribe is renowned for its excellent fried fish. Another **rustic seafood joint** is found opposite the Capilla de Mar Hotel on Carrera 1A in a blue-roofed hut on the sand. It boasts a sterling reputation for simple Caribbean-style seafood; simply sit at one of just a handful of tables and ask what's just been reeled in. A few doors down from the hotel on Carrera 1A, the **Ranchería Restaurante** (✆ *665 6163*) has a good 15,000COP menu of typical Colombian fare served at outside covered tables set back from the road. For great snacks head to the **Restaurante Crepes and Waffles** on Carrera 3, No 4–76. Other good dining options include the fabulous gaucho-style meat joint **Restaurante Dany El Churrasco Argentino** (✆ *665 4523*) on Calle 5, No 2–104, and the pasta specialists **Restaurante Granditalia** on Carrera 2, No 8–19 (✆ *665 6326*). Reviews of the lobster dishes at the **Nautilus Restaurante** on Carrera 2, No 9–145 (✆ *665 3964*) are consistently good.

ENTERTAINMENT AND NIGHTLIFE In Cartagena, music is everywhere, from the blaring radios of public transport and car stereos to the booming sound systems in bars, restaurants and even offices. Latin music dominates the local music scene, from *champeta* and *vallenato* to Latin rock and *reggaetón*. The retro salsa of the 1970s and 80s with its heroes like Hector Lavoe, Celia Cruz, Willie Colón, Ruben Blades and local lad Joe Arroyo is much adored. Cartagena's touristy nightspots are clustered around El Centro and Bocagrande with the bars on **Avenida del Arsenal** [407 B4] and the **Calle de la Media Luna** [407 C4] in Getsemaní at the heart of the backpacker scene. For real local nightlife check out the salsa bars and watering holes near Castellano – an area the locals refer to as Avenida de la Rumba (Party Avenue). A taxi from El Centro will cost 5,000COP, or catch a bus for 1,000COP. Nightly *chiva* tours are popular with both Colombian and foreign tourists and include live music, unlimited rum and Coca-Cola, some snacks, a stop at Las

CARTAGENA'S *CHAMPEDUROS*

Dirty-dancing *champeta* is Cartagena's most popular street music: a gutsy, sleazy rhythm born out of African beats. Musicians would lay down tracks at a rudimentary studio in Bazurto market. It was a rudimentary set-up, with local artists paid 10,000COP per song. Within hours the tapes had been passed round Cartagena's bus drivers. Copies were bootlegged, lyrics were learned, and the latest hot *champeta* hit was on the lips of every working-class *champeduro* citywide. Once considered scandalous and outlawed by Church elders, *champeta* caused some disapproving parents to seek police interventions, such was the lyric content. Today *champeta* is a more mainstream musical style but retains its earthy origins. In 2005, celebrated local *champeta* star John Gutiérrez Cassiani (aka 'El Johnky') was shot in gang violence. More than 8,000 dancing fans joined his funeral procession in a moving tribute that brought the streets of Cartagena to a standstill.

11

With its showbiz glamour, glitzy looks and big-screen presence it is little wonder Cartagena is a film star, a city that has many years of movie credits under its belt. OK, the Cartagena-based story of *Romancing the Stone* starring Michael Douglas was actually filmed in Veracruz, Mexico, but the film *La Quemada*, better known under the Brazilian title *Queimada* or the English translation *Burn*, put Cartagena on the cinematic map. During the filming of *Burn*, Italian actor Salvo Basile (*Once Upon a Time in the West* and *Chronicle of a Death Foretold*) liked Cartagena so much, he bought a house there and became a permanent resident. Since then Cartagena has made several cameo appearances in films, documentaries and travelogues. However, when Gabriel García Márquez finally agreed to bring his Cartagena-set romantic novel *Love in the Time of Cholera* to Hollywood, Cartagena became an A-lister overnight. Producer Scott Steindorff brought screenplay writer Ronald Harwood (*The Pianist*), British director Mike Newell (*Four Weddings and a Funeral, Mona Lisa Smile, Harry Potter and the Goblet of Fire*) and Oscar-nominated actors Javier Bardem and Giovanna Mezzogiorno to film in the city – to the jubilation of Cartageneros. Past movie productions have seen Robert de Niro, Marlon Brando, Jean Seberg and Klaus Kinski work in Cartagena.

Bóvedas, and free entry and a complimentary drink at the **La Escollera disco** [418 B6] in Bocagrande. At the time of writing Cartagena's best gay clubs are centred on **Centro Calle del Porvenir** [407 B2] and **Centro Calle de la Soledad** [407 B2]; visit www.guiagaycolombia.com/cartagena.

SHOPPING Cartagena has a sophisticated mix of small craft shops, antique stores and stylish boutiques. Elegant jewellery stores boast dazzling displays of emeralds while exclusive outlets offer Silvia Tcherassi creations that have graced the runways of Milan, Paris and New York. **Las Bóvedas** [407 C1] in the centre of the walled city stocks the biggest range of handicrafts and souvenirs, including Costeña dolls or Guajiran hammocks. Makeshift markets can be found all over Cartagena, especially in the Tourist Zone and the **Plaza de Santo Domingo** [407 A3]. A growing number of antique shops (many American-owned) have made Cartagena a popular place for collectibles. Try the **Anticuario Cartagena de Indias** (\ *664 9713*), **Anticuario El Arcón** [407 C2] (\ *664 5304*), **La Ruta de las Indias** (\ *664 9960*) and **Anticuario de Lupita** [418 C6] (\ *660 1067*).

OTHER PRACTICALITIES

Costs According to government statistical agency DANE, Cartagena is the most expensive city in Colombia, followed by Manizales and Villavicencio. Accommodation, food and tours are all significantly higher in price than in other areas – a consideration for those travelling on a tight budget. However, low-cost and efficient public transportation renders car hire unnecessary. Avoid the most touristy areas, where prices are heavily inflated and everyone has something to sell for cheaper eats and less expense.

Internet, post and telephone Many of Colombia's numerous **internet cafés** are open early until late seven days a week. Centro Uno contains half-a-dozen places alone, with a cluster opposite the Hotel Capilla del Mar in the Tourist Zone and lots in the streets around El Centro. Try the **Café Internet** (✆ *664 3003*) on Calle Roman, No 32–03, **Micronet** [407 B3] (✆*664 8409*) on Calle de la Estrella, No 4–47, and **Intranet** [407 B3] (✆ *660 0005*) on Avenida Daniel Lemaitre.

Numerous **payphones** can be found throughout the city and most internet cafés place international calls.

The office for the city's **postal service, 4/72**, is located on Avenida Concolón (✆*664 3173;* ⊕ *08.00–18.00, closed noon–14.00*). If sending mail to a local address, pay a bit more and use a courier service to ensure its safe arrival. International post is fine.

Medical services   Medical services are in good supply in Cartagena with two of the best healthcare centres found at the **Hospital Bocagrande** [418 C6] (✆ *665 5270/0873/5759*) and **Hospital Naval de Cartagena** (✆*665 5360–4*).

Money   Head to the historic centre for the largest concentration of *casas de cambio* in and around **Plaza de los Coches** [407 B3] and to Avenida Venezuela for Cartagena's numerous banks, including Davivienda, Bancolombia and Banco Colombiano – all have ATMs. Unlike other South American countries, there is no money-changing black market so do not be tempted to take up any 'great deals' offered on the street. This is almost certainly a scam involving fake bills or is a ploy to snatch your wallet. Some of Cartagena's larger businesses accept US dollars, but offer a poor rate of exchange.

In recent years, counterfeit Colombian currency has been a problem in Cartagena. Fakes tend to be passed off in taxis or dimly lit bars – check that yours has a watermark and a metallic thread running through. Coins are also counterfeited, especially the 1,000COP. These lead fakes are checked by hurling them on the pavement – if they don't bounce you've got a nickel-plated dud.

Safety   Cartagena has not been a violent city by tradition but it does have its seedy side – and with many locals earning around 5,000COP a day the threat of petty theft is real. Over 60% of the population live below the poverty line, with unemployment running at almost 20% – statistics that serve as a reminder to keep valuables out of the public glare. Muggings have been reported on the walls, Las Murallas, at night, and the road from the Convento de la Popa to Cartagena should not be walked at any time of day or night – catch a cab.

Like most Colombian cities, Cartagena has a criminal underbelly, although according to a report by the Colombian authorities this is largely contained. Its murder rate is lower than many Latin American cities with homicides concentrated in Cartagena's poorest suburbs. At the time of writing, there have been no reported violent incidents involving foreign visitors, with just two drug-related arrests since 1996, both relating to Italian citizens.

Street hawkers and hustlers can be an annoyance in Cartagena but generally back off when proffered a firm '*No gracias*'. Propositions centre on all manner of products and services, from island tours and sunhats for sale to uncut cocaine (*perico*) and prostitutes. Be wary of pushy vendors waving T-shirts in your face – this is often a distraction ploy to allow an accomplice to relieve you of a handbag or camera.

WHAT TO SEE AND DO   Cartagena's prime attraction is its beautiful *centro histórico*, comprising Calamarí, San Diego, La Matuna and Getsemaní. This large old city is packed with magnificent colonial architecture, beautiful churches, attractive plazas, mansion houses and cobblestone streets and forms one of the finest colonial cities in the Americas. Overhanging balconies draped in bougainvillea offer both colonial (wooden) and republican (stucco) styles. Vast leafy courtyards shaded by palm trees lie behind grand archways. Fetching monuments, resplendent towers and Baroque façades sit against ochre-coloured walls and houses of bubblegum pink. The following list details just some of the many gems to take in during a walk around town.

Las Murallas (City Walls) [407 A4] Construction of these thick stone walls began towards the end of the 16th century, after the city was subjected to a particularly costly attack by Francis Drake. Owing to pirate battles and storm damage the project took two centuries to complete. The walls were finally finished in 1796, just 25 years before the Spanish were eventually overthrown. Today Las Murallas remain in remarkably good condition with walkways that offer some breathtaking views. Some of the oldest sections of the walls date back to 1616 and contain cannons from a later date.

Puerta del Reloj (Clock Gate) [407 B3] This fine butterscotch-coloured tower is much photographed and signifies the entrance to the inner part of the walled city, Calamarí. Comprising three arched doorways, the central entrance once had a drawbridge that connected to Getsemaní. The outer doors were used as an armoury and a small chapel. Today the entrance houses a small booth selling maps for walking routes around the city. There is also a collection of stalls selling antique books and bric-a-brac. A four-sided clock and Republican-style tower were added in 1888. The Puerta del Reloj was originally known as the Boca del Puente.

Plaza de los Coches [407 B3] Cartagena's infamous slave market was once known as the Plaza de la Yerba, but today this triangular-shaped courtyard has a statue of the city's founder, Pedro de Heredia, at its core. An L-shaped collection of shops, restaurants and bars are housed in some handsome balconied houses as well as El Portal de los Dulces, a string of candy stalls.

Plaza de la Aduana [407 B3] A painstaking restoration has brought the old Royal Customs House back to its former glory and it now serves as Cartagena's City Hall. As the largest and oldest of the old town's plazas it was used for ceremonial events and as a military parade ground. A statue of Christopher Columbus takes pride of place in the centre surrounded by a plethora of banks with ATMs.

Plaza de San Pedro Claver [407 B3] This small rose-coloured tree-scattered tiled square is home to the **Museum of Modern Art** (✆ 664 5815; ⊕ 09.00–19.00 Mon–Fri, closed noon–15.00, 10.00–13.00 Sat; admission 1,000COP), a prestigious gallery with three sections containing the works of many avant-garde Colombian artists, including Cartagena-born Alejandro Obregón. An array of interesting wrought-iron sculptures outside the museum depicts traditional local trades. They were created by Eduardo Carmona and form a permanent display. Another dominant attraction is the **Convento de San Pedro Claver** (✆ 664 4991; ⊕ 08.00–17.00 Mon–Sat, 08.00–16.00 Sun; admission 4,000COP), formerly San Ignácio de Loyola, a Jesuit convent that dates back to the early 17th century and was renamed in honour of Spanish monk Pedro Claver (1590–1654). He took his vows aged 22, writing that he wished to 'do God's service, as if I were a slave'. He was ordained by Cartagena's bishop in 1616 at the age of 35 and worked with Father Sandoval, author of the book *Salvation and Catechising the Negroes*. Together they ministered to the slaves at the slave markets where Claver was appalled by the treatment they

received. On 3 April 1622, he wrote in his diary: 'Pedro Claver, slave of the slaves forever. He worked ceaselessly to care for the many unkempt, starved, diseased and frightened men, women and children that arrived by ship each day.' Over 40 years Claver baptised 300,000 slaves, ignoring all pleas to slow down. In his latter years he suffered from a degenerative disease that slowly rendered him bedridden. After his death, he was beatified in 1850, and canonised by Pope Leo XII in 1888. Part of the cloisters is open to visitors in this monumental three-storey building where a collection of graphic paintings tell the story of Claver's work with the slaves. In an adjoining courtyard a sundial commemorating the centenary of independence can be seen topped by a small 3.6m cannon. In 2001, a 2m statue of San Pedro helping an Angolan slave created by Colombian sculptor Enrique Grau was unveiled in front of the cloister. It has been set at ground level to enable it to be accessible to people on the street, just as San Pedro was in real life.

Next door, the **Iglesia de San Pedro Claver** (✆ 664 7256; ⊕ 06.45–07.15 Mon–Sat, 10.00–19.00 Sun) was completed in the early 18th century and boasts some magnificent stained-glass windows. The remains of the body of Cartagena's 'Slave of the Slaves' and 'Apostle of the Blacks' are housed in a glass coffin under the altar.

Other sights On Calle San Juan de Dios, the **Museo Naval del Caribe** [407 B3] (✆ 664 7381; ⊕ 09.00–19.00 daily; admission 3,000COP) opened in 1992 to commemorate the 500th anniversary of Columbus's discovery of the New World. A collection of models depicts ancient ships and maritime Cartagena with numerous historic artefacts relating to the Colombian navy.

Some of the city's finest colonial buildings flank the pretty **Plaza de Bolívar** [407 B3] with a statue of Simón Bolívar at its midst. Formerly known as the Plaza de Inquisición, the Plaza de Mayor and the Plaza de Catedral, it is a popular gathering point as numerous lively restaurants, street musicians, jugglers and mime artists are found in the surrounding streets. The park is also frequented by groups of locals playing draughts, dominoes and cards amidst shoe-shiners, scattered pigeons and swaying palms.

Opposite the park, a statuesque whitewashed building with a grand stone entrance houses the **Museo Histórico Cartagena** [407 B3] (www.muhca.gov.co; ⊕ 09.00–16.00 daily, closed noon–14.00; admission 16,000COP). Dating back to 1738, it boasts some particularly attractive balconies and contains an interesting array of historical documents and archaeological finds.

Witness fiercely fought board-game battles at Cartagena's *liga de ajedres* (chess league) housed in an open-sided building on the corner of Plaza Bolívar. A dozen or so tables and chairs have been set up in a beautiful colonial building with a large stone arch – just pop in.

One of Cartagena's most beautiful buildings, the **Palacio de la Inquisición** [407 B3] (✆ 660 6025; ⊕ 09.00–18.00 daily; admission 16,000COP) is worth a visit for its magnificent entrance hall alone. Once a punishment tribunal of the holy office, it primarily dealt with crimes relating to blasphemy and black magic. Culprits were anyone the Church viewed as heretic and the death sentence was issued on guilt with a resulting auto-da-fé. Around 800 people were condemned to death and executed between 1776 and 1821 and today a museum contains numerous instruments of torture. A small, barred window is the place where sentences handed down by the tribunal were announced to the public outside.

Cartagena's gold museum, the **Museo del Oro y Arqueología** [407 B3] (✆ 660 0778/0808; ⊕ 10.00–18.00 (closed 13.00–14.00) Tue–Fri, 10.00–17.00 (closed 13.00–14.00) Sat; free admission), contains a fine selection of riches from the Sinú tribes of the region. There is also a replica of a traditional Amerindian dwelling complete with household tools and utensils.

Although the construction of the plaza's **cathedral** [407 B3] began in 1575 the building work was partially destroyed in 1586 when the site was hit by cannons fired by Francis Drake. Work resumed in 1598 but was not finally completed until 1612 with further alterations made between 1912 and 1923 when it was given a terracotta-coloured stucco overhaul. A simple interior contains an 18th-century altar-ledge worked in gold leaf.

On the Calle de Santo Domingo the late 16th-century **Iglesia de Santo Domingo** [407 A3] is little-changed from colonial days and is the oldest church in the city. Architecturally, it has some quirky characteristics borne of construction imperfections. The bell tower is decidedly skewed but local legend has it this was the work of the devil, who knocked it in a fit of pique.

Facing the small Parque de Fernandez de Madrid, the **Iglesia de Santo Toribio de Mongrovejo** [407 C2] on Calle del Sargento Mayor is relatively small. The church was built between 1666 and 1732 and boasts some fine Mudéjar panelling and a pretty wooden altar covered with gold ornamentation. Although the building was hit by a cannonball during Vernon's assault on the city there were no casualties – despite it smashing through a window during a packed service. Today the ball is displayed in a glass container on the wall.

The 23 dungeons of the city walls, **Las Bóvedas** [407 C1], were built between 1792 and 1796 in stone 15m thick. During the Republican era they were used as a prison. Today they form a colourful succession of bunting-adorned handicraft stores, boutiques and tourist shops.

Just outside of Las Bóvedas in the Cabrero district, the historic green-and-white **Casa de Rafael Núñez** [407 D1] (✆ 664 5305; ◷ 09.00–17.00 Mon–Fri, 10.00–16.00 Sat/Sun; free admission) was the former home of the Colombian president, lawyer and poet. Cartagena-born Rafael Núñez was also the celebrated composer of Colombia's national anthem, creator of the Banco Nacional and mastermind of its constitution – and the only president of Colombia to be elected four times. Núñez was born in 1825, and was an elected congressman by 1853. He spent some time in Europe as a consul in Liverpool and Le Havre before returning to Colombia in 1875. This grand, old two-storey wooden mansion in Antillean Caribbean style built in 1858 was home to Núñez for 17 years. He died in Cartagena on 18 September 1894 and is buried alongside his wife Soledad in the Ermita de Cabrero, a small red-and-white church opposite his home. Today the property houses a museum commemorating his life, poetry and political thoughts. It contains photos, documents relating to the Delegates Council of 1886 (the basis of the Colombian constitution), his will and testament and a memorial poem by his contemporary Rúben Dario, entitled *Qué Se Je?* (Who Am I?). His famous motto is now painted above the doorway of the museum: 'Regeneration or Catastrophe' could not have been more apt, even with the benefit of hindsight.

Sculptor Eladio Gil's **Monumento a la Índia Catalina** [407 D2] was erected in 1974 to commemorate its pre-colonial past. It's located at the entrance to the old town in tribute to the Carib people, the indigenous group that inhabited the region before the arrival of the Spanish. This lovely bronze statue depicts the beautiful Amerindian translator who worked with Pedro de Heredia, a courageous warrior called Catalina. It stands by Puente de Chambacu in the middle of the traffic island. Smaller versions of this statue are coveted as distinguished awards presented during the annual Cartagena International Film and TV Festival held in March.

In the Getsemaní district in the northeast of the Old Quarter, the **Iglesia de la Santísima Trinidad** (Church of the Holy Trinity) [407 C4] was built in the second half of the 17th century but retains very little original character, having been modified without preserving its architectural style. A church-built school to the rear of the building was established to educate the poor and is still in use today.

To the east of the Holy Trinity, the **Iglesia de Tercera Orden** [407 B4] has an interesting wooden ceiling with ornate carved crosspieces in the central vault. Legend has it that heroic Don Blas de Lezo is interred here. Ask kindly and you may be permitted to see the plaque commemorating Blas de Lezo behind the altar.

North of Santa Orden Church is the leafy **Parque del Centenario** [407 C3], which was built to celebrate independence in 1912 and received an impressive makeover in 2006. However, despite being popular with families for its grassy areas, fountains, statues and ponds, it's also a hangout for bums, hookers and crack-heads – so be vigilant. It's just a few minutes' walk northwest of the Clock Gate.

To the west of Parque del Centenario, the **Iglesia de San Roque** [407 C4] was created in 1674 to celebrate the life of a saint who cared for plague victims. Legend has it St Roque was struck by the disease himself and so retreated to the wilderness to die. There he was befriended by a dog who brought him scraps of food, and was able to drink water that rose up from the soil. He recovered after the appearance of an angel and was able to continue his work.

No visit to Cartagena is complete without a visit to **Castillo de San Félipe de Barajas** [418 B2] (*Av Arévalo;* ☎ *666 4790;* ⊕ *08.00–18.00 daily; admission 10,000COP*), Colombia's largest and most impregnable colonial fort tower. Set on a 40m hill, east of the historic centre, it is the strongest fortress ever built by the Spanish in the colonies. The original, smaller fort was built between 1639 and 1657, but in 1762 extensive rebuilding work led by engineer Antonio de Arévalo enlarged it considerably to cover the entire hilltop. A matrix of complex underground tunnels enabled an efficient distribution of supplies. They were built to maximise even the smallest sound to allow approaching troops in the distance to be clearly heard in the fort. Today, a guided walk through these claustrophobic conduits is the highlight of a visit – and does much to explain why, despite many attempts, this powerful bastion was never taken by pirates. Cannons and an old military hospital also form part of this vast site.

Los Zapatos Viejos (*Old Shoes Monument*) [418 C2] was built in honour of Luis Carlos López (1883–1950), a famous Cartagena-born poet and satirical writer nicknamed 'One-eyed López'. Declaring that he loved Cartagena 'as much as he loves his own shoes' in a poem, López was honoured after his death by his friends and literary contemporaries with *Los Zapatos Viejos*, located at the back of the San Félipe Fort.

As one of Cartagena's first battle defences, the **Fuerte de San Sebastián el Pastelillo** [407 C6] is located at the western end of Isla Manga. Small and built in

---

HORN OF PLENTY

Visitors to Castillo de San Félipe de Barajas should look out for an entrepreneurial trumpet player at the entrance of the fort. As tourists pass he guesses their nationality and heralds them in with a rousing rendition of their very own national anthem – the reward is a 1,000COP tip. Although he occasionally gets it wrong, he has become highly skilled at distinguishing Costa Ricans and Peruvians from Panamanians and Nicaraguans, but scratches his head when a gringo comes to town.

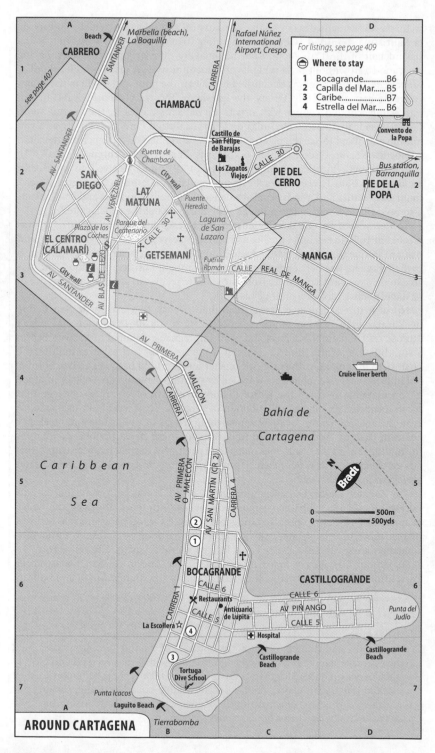

For listings, see page 409

⊝ **Where to stay**

1 Bocagrande............B6
2 Capilla del Mar......B5
3 Caribe....................B7
4 Estrella del Mar.....B6

CABRERO

Beach

Marbella (beach),
La Boquilla

Rafael Núñez
International
Airport, Crespo

CHAMBACÚ

Castillo de
San Félipe
de Barajas

Los Zapatos
Viejos

PIE DEL
CERRO

Convento de
la Popa

Bus station,
Barranquilla

PIE DE LA
POPA

AV SANTANDER

CARRERA 17

CALLE 30

Puente de
Chambacú

City wall

SAN
DIEGO

LAT
MATUNA

AV VENEZUELA

Puente
Heredia

Laguna
de San
Lazaro

MANGA

Plaza de los
Coches

Parque del
Centenario

EL CENTRO
(CALAMARÍ)

AV BLAS DE LEZO

CALLE 30

GETSEMANÍ

Puente
Román

CALLE REAL DE MANGA

City wall

AV SANTANDER

AV PRIMERA O MALECÓN

CARRERA 1

AV PRIMERA
O MALECÓN

Bahía de

Cartagena

Cruise liner berth

Caribbean

Sea

AV SAN MARTIN (CR 2)

CARRERA 4

N

Bradt

0 ——————— 500m
0 ——————— 500yds

2

1

BOCAGRANDE

CASTILLOGRANDE

CALLE 6

CARRERA 1

Restaurants

CALLE 5

Anticuario
de Lupita

AV PIN ANGO

CALLE 6

CALLE 5

Punta del
Judío

La Escollera ☆

4

Hospital

Castillogrande
Beach

Castillogrande
Beach

3

Tortuga
Dive School

Punta Icacos

Laguito Beach

Tierrabomba

AROUND CARTAGENA

see page 407

the 16th century, today there isn't much to look at. It is the home of the Club de Pesca marina and is just a short walk from Getsemaní.

Perched on a 150m hill known as La Popa (The Stern), and thought to resemble the back end of a ship, the 400-year-old **Convento de la Popa** [418 D1] (✆ 665 4798; ☉ 08.00–18.00, admission 8,000COP) lies about 1.5km from Castillo de San Félipe de Barajas. Officially named Nuestra Señora de la Candelaria, the convent was founded in 1607 by the Augustine order. It contains a beautiful image of La Virgén de la Candelaria, Cartagena's patroness, in the chapel. Superb views abound from this pleasant spot, but don't be tempted to walk here from the city as the road is dangerous – take a taxi (8,000COP).

The **Fuerte de San Fernando** and the **Batería de San José** guard the entrance to the Bahía de Cartagena through the Bocachica Strait. The Spanish strung a heavy chain between them to further strengthen defences. There used to be a second gateway to the bay, Bocagrande. After Vernon's attack it was blocked to ensure it was impassable – and it remains so today. Built between 1753 and 1760, the fortress is accessible only by boat, but much of the original structure can still be seen. Tours cost 35,000COP including lunch and admission. Boats leave daily from the Muelle Turístico at around 08.00 and return in the afternoon.

Festivals and events
Festival Internacional de la Música (January) (*www.cartagenamusicfestival. com*) Cartagena's long-standing celebration of classical music attracts musicians from all over the world with a host of performances and gala concerts citywide.

The Hay Festival (January) (✆ (UK) 01497 822620; *www.hayfestival.com*) Colombia's Hay Festival has captured the hearts and minds of Cartagena, attracting a high pedigree of Latin American literary greats and some high-profile international artists, including Gabriel García Márquez and Hanif Kureishi.

Festival Internacional de Cine (March) (*www.festicinecartagena.org*) The oldest film festival on the continent and the biggest cinematic event in Colombia, this glittering showcase of around 60 feature films includes movies competing for the India Catalina Awards.

Carnaval de Cartagena (November) This high-tempo week-long fiesta celebrates Cartagena's Independence Day (11 November) with an array of street processions, parties, parades and marching bands. The Reinado Nacional de Belleza – Colombia's national beauty pageant – paralyses the city. Although tickets to the judging and testimonial dinners sell out months in advance, the locals head to bars to watch it live on television.

AROUND CARTAGENA

ARCHIPELAGO NUESTRA SEÑORA DEL ROSÁRIO (*www.rosarioislands.com*) Cartagena's surrounding islands, the Archipelago Nuestra Señora del Rosário, sit amongst coral reefs and warm turquoise waters that make up the Parque Nacional Natural Corales del Rosário y San Bernardo 35km southwest of the city. Extending over 100ha, the islands were once inhabited by Caribe Amerindians who were slowly driven to the mainland after sustained attacks from pirates *en route* to test Cartagena's defences. The region contains important marine grasses, 113 plankton species, hundreds of crustaceans, 215 species of fish, five mangrove species, dozens of migrating seabirds, many seaweeds, 197 mollusc species and wildlife. Despite widespread erosion, many of the region's 52 coral species have been successfully spawned in an ongoing recovery effort. Some 30 coralline islands range in size, with the largest containing coastal lagoons, tourist facilities and dry tropical forests.

As the name suggests, **Isla Grande** is the archipelago's biggest island at around 200ha. A forested walking trail leads to a lagoon and sandy beach. Isla del Rosário is also popular with day trippers with the nearby **Isla de San Martín de Pajarales** home to a small aquarium containing sharks, turtles, rays and dolphins. **Isla de Barú**, which forms a part of the archipelago, is in fact a jutting spit of mainland 20km from the city. It offers one of the finest beaches around Cartagena with coral reefs close to the shore – so be sure to pack snorkel gear. Most tour boats take in three or four islands. Since the 1970s, many of the smaller atolls have been snapped up for private ownership. Even Colombia's most infamous drug lord, Pablo Escobar, got in on the act, ploughing his ill-gotten gains into real estate in this most scenic spot. Today this is home to some of Colombia's more exclusive second homes, with many islets home to a single luxury pad.

Getting there and around Tour boats depart year-round from Cartagena's Muelle Turístico at around 08.00 and return late afternoon. Choose from large, slow-moving cruisers that accommodate up to 150 passengers or smaller speedboats that seat fewer than a dozen – there are pros and cons for each. However, most boats follow a similar route past the old Spanish forts and out to Isla Grande, Isla del Rosario, Isla de San Martín de Pajarales and Isla de Barú. Expect to pay 70,000–90,000COP including lunch but allow an additional 20,000 for extras, such as drinks and snacks, entrance to the national park (5,000COP), tickets for the aquarium (20,000COP) and admission to the fort (4,000COP). A Sunday-morning **bus** departs early from Cartagena to the beach on the tip of Isla de Barú.

Where to stay and eat Staying overnight on the archipelago is becoming increasingly popular with a growing number of accommodation options springing up. These range from cheap hammocks on the beach and rustic camping to renting a house or booking a room in a plush boutique hotel. Many places are run by Europeans who offer boat tours, snorkelling trips and transfers from the mainland.

Hotel Agua (6 *cabañas*) Isla de Barú; 664 9479; e info@hotelagua.com.co; www.hotelagua.com.co. This striking boutique hotel opened in 2006 & offers the most upmarket accommodation on the islands, with trendy open lounges in contemporary style. A gorgeous bar area has inlaid pebble flooring, rattan swinging chairs, coralline pillars & oversized cushions. Gentle ambient mood-music plays from an upper terrace where wooden loungers look out on to open sea & palms. Staff in crisp white uniforms jump to attention under slowly whirring ceiling fans amidst chic décor. Luxurious *cabañas* sit in a staggered layout on a terraced slope & boast private pools. Room rates vary throughout the year but are not cheap – with an additional

180,000COP for the transfers to & from Cartagena. **$$$$**

Hotel Kokomo (sleeps 30) Isla Grande; 673 4072; e hotelkokomo@hotmail.com; www. hotelkokomo.com. This Norwegian-run budget set-up offers *cabañas* & hammocks as well as food. It also rents out snorkel gear & sells drinks & snacks. Cheaper rates for stays of a week or longer. **$$**

Campamento Wittenberg (sleeps 20) Isla de Barú; m 311 436 6215; e wittenberg2000@ hotmail.com. Run by affable Frenchman Gilbert, this place is a backpacker favourite with hammocks under a simple thatched roof & mosquito nets. He picks up once a week from Casa Viena in Cartagena & charges 6,000COP a night plus 12,000COP for the transfer. Meals are extra. **$**

LA BOQUILLA For a charming fishing village and exquisite fresh seafood take time to visit La Boquilla, 7km north of Cartagena, where fishermen work with *atarrayas* (round fishing nets) on the sand. Head to a collection of wood-and-thatch huts on the beach for ice-cold beers and delicious fish-and-rice dishes – this is also where locals sell handicrafts and wares. La Boquilla is a great place to hang out, enjoy a boat trip or take a canoe tour out through the mangroves amidst marine birds, and is best visited at weekends. The countryside around the village is a popular birding destination in the months of September to April when North American waders arrive. Look out for Wilson's plover; red knot, gull-billed and large-billed terns are regular. Also look for grey kingbird, lesser kiskadee, cattle tyrant, Wilson's phalarope, collared plover, least and semi-palmated sandpipers, solitary sandpiper and semi-palmated plover, black, least, brown-throated parakeet, Louisiana and little blue herons, reddish egret and ringed kingfisher.

Getting there and around Catch one of many frequent **buses** that run to La Boquilla from the monument of Índia Catalina in central Cartagena – they are clearly signed (2,000COP, 30 minutes).

🏠 **Where to stay and eat**

✕ **Restaurante y Hospedaje Marlene** (sleeps 6) El Paraíso; m 300 831 5704; ☉ 11.00–late. For friendly, family-run kitchens & accommodation this charming little beachside restaurant is well worth a visit. A simple palm-thatched open-fronted diner is hung with all manner of fishing paraphernalia, from nets to ropes & buoys. A menu offers a wide range of shellfish & fish dishes, from *pargo rojo* (red snapper) & *langostinos al ajillo* (garlic shell-on prawns) to *arroz de marisco* (seafood rice) & the house speciality *bandeja marisco* – a man-sized plate of mixed seafood. Chairs, tents & hammocks are offered free of charge to anyone who orders a decent meal. The owners also provide guided tours out to the mangrove swamps, passing through the *túnel del amor* (tunnel of love) & the *túnel de la felicidad* (tunnel of happiness) to Punta Icaco – all areas used as a film set for movie-makers shooting the García Márquez film. $

VOLCÁN DE LODO EL TOTUMO The crater of this 15m-high volcano is full of warm mud as thick as cappuccino and offers a therapeutic dip to visitors prepared to yield to this nutrient-rich natural bath. Located about 52km northeast of Cartagena, Volcán de Lodo El Totumo is the subject of considerable myth and legend. The locals swear that it once spewed fire, lava and ash but this was considered to be the work of the devil by a priest, who sprinkled it frequently with holy water and it slowly extinguished, drowning the devil in mud. A makeshift wooden banister leads the way to the top of the volcano. Visitors can bathe from dawn till dusk for 5,000COP with a neighbouring lagoon the perfect place for a post-dip clean-up. A massage is often part of the deal. Don't be surprised if local villagers turn up.

Getting there and around A growing number of tour companies are including the Volcán de Lodo El Totumo in their packages, so ask around. To visit independently, catch the hourly **bus** from Cartagena's main terminal bound for Galerazamba but ask the driver to drop you off at Lomita Arena (3,000COP, 1½ hours). The volcano is a 3.5km walk (45 minutes). Be sure to be back at Lomita Arena by 16.00 to catch the last bus back.

JARDÍN BOTÁNICO DE GUILLERMO PIÑERES This pleasant 8ha garden is planted with 250 coastal species of flora, including umpteen palms and grasses. Located 15km southwest of Cartagena on the outer edges of the city of Turbaco, it makes a nice half-day detour by bus – pick up the Turbaco service that passes the Castillo de San Félipe frequently (2,000COP, 45 minutes) and ask the driver to drop you off; the turn-off is a 20-minute walk from the park entrance.

MOMPÓX *Telephone code 5*

> Mompox does not exist... at times we dream of her, but it does not exist.
> Gabriel García Márquez, *The General in His Labyrinth*, 1989

An isolated colonial country town that was the setting for Gabriel García Márquez's literary classic *Chronicle of a Death Foretold* and potentially the inspiration for the Macondo of *One Hundred Years of Solitude*, Mompóx (also spelt Mompós) is an old-time settlement bearing much beauty from the past. Located 249km southeast of Cartagena amidst swampy rivers and thick vegetation, the city has all the hallmarks of remoteness. Much of its colonial character (*arquitectura Mompóxina*) remains unchanged from times gone by with a notable absence of many of the modern trappings of the 'outside world'. Founded in 1537 by Don Alonso de Heredia on the eastern branch of the Río Magdalena, Mompóx hasn't always been a sleepy backwater relic. Up until the 20th century, it was one of Colombia's most important commercial hubs as a port for the transportation of goods upriver into the country's interior. Mompóx even established a royal mint and became famous for its many goldsmiths. However, once the silt-laden Río Magdalena altered its course Mompóx

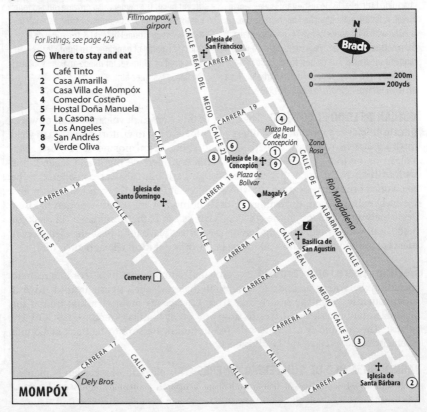

For listings, see page 424

🏠 **Where to stay and eat**

1 Café Tinto
2 Casa Amarilla
3 Casa Villa de Mompóx
4 Comedor Costeño
5 Hostal Doña Manuela
6 La Casona
7 Los Angeles
8 San Andrés
9 Verde Oliva

MOMPÓX

was left high and dry: a city isolated and much decreased in importance. Today it relies on a fledgling tourism industry hampered by the perils of isolation along with fishing and some commerce generated by raising cattle. The name Mompóx comes from the last *cacique* (Amerindian chief) of the Kimbay tribe that populated the region before the arrival of the Spanish. In 1812, Simón Bolívar gathered over 400 recruits to form the basis of an army to liberate Caracas, earning it the title Ciudad Valerosa, or Courageous City. UNESCO declared the city a World Heritage Site in 1995 on account of its historic splendour. Mompóx is famous throughout Colombia for two reasons, the first as the home town of singer Sonia Bazanta Vides, better known as Totó la Mompóxina (see box, page 425), and the second for its intricately made and beautiful filigree silver jewellery. Long-overdue restorations to the town and the October Jazz Festival are beginning to pull Mompóx from her slumbers.

GETTING THERE AND AROUND Getting to Mompóx appears a challenge but with direct daily **buses** from Cartagena and Barranquilla, the reality is a little easier. Unitransco/Caribe Express have departures from the aforementioned cities at 07.00 every day costing in the region of 50,000COP depending on the season, and taking roughly 8 hours but including an atmospheric ferry ride over the Magdalena River. These same buses return the following day, departing at 06.00. Transport exists from Valledupar (5 hours), Santa Marta (6 hours) Bogotá and Bucaramanga (via El Banco, 16 and 8 hours respectively) and for those short on time, the closest airport is at Corozal/ Sincelejo (3½ hours) reachable with Satena and ADA. There have been mutterings of a direct **flight** to Mompóx with Satena beginning mid 2015, so check with the tourist office (see below) before travelling.

Mompóx is easily navigable on foot and this is the best way to explore the town. If the oppressive heat gets too much, bikes can be rented to ease the strain at around 8,000COP per hour – head to **Café Tinto** on the corner of the Plaza de la Concepción to choose from a variety of bicycles. You can also hire the motorcycle/buggy hybrid vehicles known here as mototaxis for 18,000COP an hour to see the sights.

TOURIST INFORMATION
ℹ Punto de Informacion Turistica Calle San Agustín, just alongside the entrance of the Basilica   San Agustin; ⏱ 08.00–16.00 Mon–Fri

TOUR GUIDES A number of local guides offer walking tours around the streets of the colonial centre and along the riverfront. Recommended guides include Arnulfo, Jose and Yunis. Given that tourism is still emerging in Mompóx, and the arrival of an overseas visitor is still newsworthy, these guides will seek you out or ask at your hotel!

The best way of escaping the soporific heat of an afternoon is to sign up for one of the river trips through the wetlands and *cienegas* of the surrounding area. Departing at 15.00 daily (a minimum of four people are required) and taking roughly 3 hours, these tours give you an unrivalled view of the colonial architecture of the town as Simón Bolívar would have seen it from the river, before snaking along the pre-Columbian channels built by the original indigenous tribes of the area. Passing through forgotten rural communities and enjoying breathtaking scenery, birders will also get a kick from the quantity of local species on display. Howler monkeys, iguanas and, on rare occasions, a manatee have been spotted as well. Reliable and safe boats are organised by Fredy Lopez who knows the waterways well and prices should be in the region of 25,000COP per person. If the cost is suspiciously lower you are liable to have been signed up with someone who may well end up getting lost in the myriad channels found out here.

11

⌂ WHERE TO STAY AND EAT *See map, page 422.*

Almost all of the hotels in Mompóx are strung along the pretty Calle Real del Medio and the Albarrada in front of the river. Most represent excellent value and offer a good choice of rooms – but be sure to book in advance if you plan to visit during Holy Week (Semana Santa) or the Jazz Festival.

⌂ **Hostal Doña Manuela** (28 rooms) Calle Real del Medio, No 17–41; ☎ 685 5621. As hostels go, this is pretty plush with a pool & restaurant & prices to match. Choose from a fine collection of rooms set around 2 large plant-filled courtyards. At the time of writing, this building was undergoing a major refurbishment paid for by the Ministry of Culture & is expected to open in 2016. **$$$**

⌂ **Casa Amarilla** (11 rooms) La Albarrada, No 13–59; ☎ 685 6326; e lacasaamarillamompos@ gmail.com; www.lacasaamarillamompos.com. A lovingly restored colonial home belonging to a British journalist & his Colombian wife, the Casa Amarilla is the only hotel in front of the river, all rooms are en suite with Wi-Fi, cable TV, AC & prices include b/fast. An excellent value-for-money choice for those wishing to learn about Mompóx & enjoy the tranquillity of river views from the rooftop terrace. River trips & onward transport can be organised. **$$**

⌂ **Hotel La Casona** (12 rooms) Calle Real del Medio, No 18–58; ☎ 685 5307. Owned by Eucaris & Enrique Álvarez for the last 20 years, this is another excellent & inexpensive option with comfortable & well-appointed rooms in a 200-year-old colonial-era building & some nice communal areas – plus a fast, efficient laundry service. **$$**

⌂ **Hotel San Andrés** (12 rooms) Calle Real del Medio, No 18–23; ☎ 685 5886; e hotelsanandres@ hotmail.com; www.hotelsanandresmompox.com. This former budget choice is now a more luxurious option following a sympathetic restoration of the period property's exterior & interior features. Rooms aren't plush but are clean, comfy & well equipped with AC, TV & phone. Also a restaurant on site. **$$**

⌂ **Casa Villa de Mompóx** (8 rooms) Calle Real del Medio, No 14–108, ☎ 685 5208. Nicely appointed & rustic rooms situated along a corridor in a pleasant family-run atmosphere. Ideal for couples on a tight budget. **$**

✗ **Comedor Costeño** Calle de la Albarada, No 18–45; ☎ 685 5263; ⏲ 05.30–late afternoon. One of a few pleasant places to eat along the riverfront with nice views & decent *bocachico* fish-&-rice meals. **$$**

✗ **Verde Oliva** Cnr Plaza de La Concepción & Callejon de San Juan; ⏲ 17.00–23.30 daily. Verde Oliva serves decent pizza & local eats. **$$**

⌴ **Café Tinto** Cnr Plaza de La Concepción; ⏲ 17.00 until late daily). The best watering hole in which to enjoy a cocktail or ice-cold beer in the evening after a tough day of doing very little in the heat. Low music breaks from tradition on the Colombian coast & owner Onexi will make you feel welcome. **$$**

ENTERTAINMENT AND NIGHTLIFE Mompóx has a handful of local watering holes that serve beer until dawn – and beyond. Most are found on the streets leading off from the plaza outside the Iglesia de Santo Domingo and in the Plaza de la Concepción with the town's so-called Zona Rosa along the riverfront a pleasant place to enjoy a sundowner.

♀ **Los Angeles** La Albarrada & Plaza de la Concepción; ⏲ 17.00 until late daily. A new addition to Mompóx's nightlife scene in late 2014, Los Angeles is the creation of a collaboration between the Canadian-born son of a Momposino & the owner of the nearby & recommended restaurant, Verde Oliva (see above). Here you will find a greater selection of spirits & beers in an upbeat & friendly locale overlooking the Magdalena River.

SHOPPING For locally produced fruit wines head to **ViniMompóx** on Carrera 3, No 20–34, and choose from a range of flavours from banana and *guayaba* to orange and tamarind. You'll find stunning filigree work at a number of silver workshops around Calle Real del Medio and Mompóx's famous wooden rocking chairs are also in good supply. Recommended filigree shops include **Magaly's** and **Filimompox,** both located on the Calle del Medio. For those interested in the fabrication and artistry of this product, the workshops can be visited as well. Just ask a mototaxi driver to take you to the Taller Filimompox and at any moment you'll be able to see four or five young men and women weaving silver into earrings, bracelets and other collectibles.

WHAT TO SEE AND DO By far the best way to discover the delights of Mompóx is to wander aimlessly through this sleepy town, passing wrought-iron grilles, clay-tiled roofs, whitewashed walls, elaborate fronts, flower-shrouded balconies and pretty patios – it's a genuine journey back in time to an authentic Caribbean colonial town.

Mompóx has half-a-dozen churches, of which the **Iglesia de Santa Bárbara** (Church of St Barbara) is one of the finest, dating back to 1630 and situated on the Plaza de Santa Bárbara. Boasting a Mudéjar balcony, ornate moulding and Baroque figures, the church has an octagonal bell tower that ends in a crown-shaped dome. Others include the **Iglesia de San Francisco** (Church of St Francis), one of the oldest in Mompóx. The **Iglesia de la Concepión** (Church of the Immaculate Conception) is the largest local church, while the **Basilica de San Agustín** (Church of St Augustine) houses much of the richly gilded religious items at the heart of the Semana Santa processions. And don't forget to visit the town's ornate cemetery with tombs of famous Colombians such as General Maza who fought alongside Simón Bolívar in the war for independence from Spain and that of Candelario Obeso, the first black poet from South America.

FESTIVALS AND EVENTS

Semana Santa Mompóx honours Semana Santa (Holy Week) with several extraordinarily elaborate processions that bring the entire population out on to the streets on Maundy Thursday and Good Friday nights. From midday on the Thursday, the penitents leave to make a pilgrimage to all the churches and sacred sites of the town, amidst the mournful sound of trumpets and the tolling of bells. On Good Friday there are morning church services, afternoon sermons and a 6-hour evening procession from the Church of St Augustín to the Church of St Francis. Saturday sees a serenade in the Church of St Francis with a dawn procession of the Resurrected Christ. On Sunday morning, the procession of Minerva takes to the streets of Mompóx – a solemn and stately affair.

Jazz Festival Now perhaps a bigger event than Semana Santa, the annual Jazz Festival began in 2011 to rave reviews and attracts artists of international repute to play in the atmospheric plazas to an adoring public. This takes place in the first weekend of October and booking well in advance is required. Closing acts have included Totó La Mompóxina and ChocQuibTown.

ATLÁNTICO

Colombia's third-smallest department spans just 3,388km^2 but is home to a population of more than 2.5 million, making it one of the most crowded at over 670 inhabitants per square kilometre. Bordered by the Caribbean Sea to the north, the Río Magdalena to the east and the Magdalena department to the west, Atlántico sits on a coastal plain, earning its capital city the nickname 'La Arenosa' (meaning 'the Sandy City'). Almost 75% of the population lives in Barranquilla, one of Colombia's most active port cities and a major industrial centre. Large-scale cotton production, sesame crops, cattle rearing and fishing remain key areas of commerce as well as fluvial and maritime transportation. The department was established in 1905, boasts great economic diversity and is strategically positioned at the mouth of one of the continent's major rivers. Barranquilla is also known as Colombia's Golden Gate (La Puerta de Oro de Colombia).

BARRANQUILLA *Telephone code 5*

A chaotic concrete muddle that is quietly coming into its own, Barranquilla is proud to be home to South America's first airport, the Ernesto Cortissoz International, built in 1919. The world's second-oldest commercial airline was also founded in the city – and Scadta (Sociedad Colombo Alemana de Transporte Aéreo) is still in business today, now as Avianca. Scadta's first aerial transportation route pioneered civil aviation, with the Río Magdalena easily landed by seaplanes at almost any point. On 19 September 1921, the first scheduled service flew from Barranquilla and Girardot in what today is widely regarded as the most significant date in Latin American aviation history.

After Bogotá, Medellín and Cali, Barranquilla is Colombia's fourth-largest city. It is famous throughout Latin America for its wild four-day carnival. In 2003, UNESCO honoured the Carnaval de Barranquilla as a Masterpiece of the Oral and Intangible Heritage of Humanity, the only one of Colombia's most riotous festivals to have been recognised in this way. Barranquilla people are often referred to as *curramberos* (literally meaning 'party people'), a telling insight into the gregarious temperament of the city's fun-loving population. Nobel Prize-winning writer Gabriel García Márquez lived in Barranquilla during his early years as a journalist working at *El Heraldo*. Today his old bohemian literary hangout is an artsy-chic bar containing mementos relating to the intellectuals and philosophers who made up the Barranquilla Group (pages 52–3). Colombian-Lebanese pop sensation Shakira was born and bred in the city and has an apartment in the north. A massive six-tonne statue stands in her honour outside a school helped by the singer's Fundación Pies Descalzos (Bare Feet Foundation), founded in 2001. Other famous Barranquilleros include Dr César Carriazo, a home-grown ophthalmic specialist who pioneered Lasik eye surgery worldwide, and the voluptuous actress Sofia Vergara.

HISTORY Although no official records exist regarding the foundation of Barranquilla, the city is known to have been settled in 1629. However, modern Barranquilla was inaugurated in 1813 and it is this birth date that is commemorated citywide with gusto on 7 April each year. Barranquilla grew slowly in its early years before the city's Puerto Colombia – the nation's first port – began to handle both fluvial and sea vessels in the late 19th century. Barranquilla also welcomed large numbers of immigrants from Europe during the two world wars and a sizeable population of Middle Eastern and Asian migrants give the city a cosmopolitan cultural fusion. This ethnic mix differentiates Barranquilla from other big Colombian cities, with over half of the population of foreign descent. Gastronomic influences from Italy, Germany, China and Lebanon have fused with Hispanic traditions and Colombian cultures and makes for an interesting multi-racial mix. Unlike Medellín, Cali and Bogotá, the city also has large numbers of followers of non-Catholic faiths, including Protestants, Muslims and Jews. Barranquilla is home to the largest number of synagogues in Colombia, with Jews representing 1.1% of the city's population as well as kosher delicatessens and Ashkenazi and Sephardic cemeteries. The main wave of immigration took place during the Holocaust in 1944. Regardless of origin, those who hail from Barranquilla are known as Barranquilleras or Barranquilleros.

CLIMATE Barranquilla is dusty, hot and very humid with daytime temperatures that typically sit at around 32°C. January/February and June/July are the coolest months at around 25°C. April–June and August–November are the wettest periods with Barranquilla prone to flooding, often resulting in the loss of life. These deep fast-flowing torrents (*arroyos*) are the result of a lack of drainage in some sectors of the city – and render many streets out of bounds shifting vehicles as large as buses in their torrents after heavy rains.

GETTING THERE Some 10km south of the city, the Ernesto Cortissoz International Airport serves as both a domestic and international hub. Most of Colombia's domestic carriers serve Barranquilla, including **Avianca** (✆ *330 2255*), **ADA** (✆ *334 8253*), **Satena** (✆ *334 8019*), and **Copa** (✆ *360 9844*). About 1km from the southern edge of the city is Barranquilla's main **bus** terminal (*www.ttbaq.com.co*). A dozen buses connect with Bogotá (100,000COP, 18 hours), Bucaramanga (70,000COP, 10 hours) and Medellín (85,000COP, 14 hours) every day. Buses to Santa Marta (20,000COP, 2 hours) and Cartagena (15,000COP, 2 hours) leave every 15 minutes.

GETTING AROUND Barranquilla's layout is relatively simple. To the east the city is bordered by the Río Magdalena, with the remaining sector looped by a bypass called Circunvalar. A grid system divides the city using *calles* (streets north to south) and *carreras* (avenues east to west) with Barranquilla's downtown area located near the river on the city's eastern limits. Most tourists spend time in the district of El Prado, one of the city's most pleasant areas about 3km to the northwest of the centre. Barranquilla's Bogotá-style mass transportation system, called **TransMetro** (*www.transmetro.gov.co*), opened in 2010 to become the fifth Colombian city served by a sophisticated transit network (after Bogotá, Pereira, Cali and Bucaramanga). Based around a system of articulated buses that connect outlying metropolitan areas to the city centre, as well as serving inner-city areas, the network uses a smart card system with each vehicle equipped with GPS and electronic signage. Pre-recorded announcements indicate each stop with stations located every 500m. Services are colour-coded red, yellow and green to indicate centre, southbound and northbound with numbers that confirm the specific route.

TOURIST INFORMATION   As Barranquilla is emerging as a tourist destination and trying to tap into a tiny percentage of the tourist numbers visiting neighbouring Cartagena and Santa Marta, there are continual rebrandings of the city in an attempt to achieve this. Unfortunately, at the time of writing, there was no central information bureau for the tourist to Barranquilla so for the time being most information can be found on the Barranquilla local government's page (*www. barranquilla.gov.co*).

WHERE TO STAY   *See map, page 429.*
On the basis of safety not price, most travellers opt to stay in El Prado where pleasant streets can be walked without fear after dark. There has been a construction explosion in the city in recent years and travellers to Barranquilla will feel spoilt for choice – outside of Carnaval – for hotel options. Those happy to stay holed up in the city's cheapest options will find numerous shoestring choices clustered on and around Paseo Bolívar (Calle 34).

Hotel El Prado (200 rooms) Carrera 54, No 70–10; 330 1530; www.hotelelpradosa. com. Housed in a beautiful old national-heritage mansion house built in 1928, the hotel is set in palm-filled gardens bursting with colour. Once boasting the swankiest rooms in Barranquilla, although perhaps it could use a makeover, it does, however, offer plenty of space & elegance with a pool, internet, AC & hefty prices. **$$$**

Hotel Majestic (49 rooms) Carrera 53, No 54–41; 349 1010; e reservas@ hotelmajesticbarranquilla.com; www. hotelmajesticbarranquilla.com. Another top-notch option in a grand Moorish-style building renowned as one of the city's nicest places to stay, with a celebrated restaurant as in demand as the stylish rooms. **$$$**

Hotel Versalles Howard Johnson (80 rooms) Carrera 48, No 78–188; 368 2183; www. hojobarranquilla.com. This modern well-appointed hotel offers a range of double rooms & suites in widely differing décor as well as a rather nice French-styled restaurant. On-site amenities include a pool, spa, sauna, gym & business centre with internet. B/fast is included in the room rate. **$$$**

Hotel Colonial Inn (10 rooms) Calle 42, No 43–131; 379 0241; http://hotelcolonialinn. amawebs.com. This city-centre mid-range option isn't big on fuss but it does offer simple, comfortable rooms with AC, TV & private bathroom. **$$**

Hotel Sima (sleeps 30) Carrera 49, No 72–19; 358 4600; e hotelsima@enred.com. One of El Prado's best-value options offers clean, comfortable rooms including b/fast. Interestingly, this place is popular with visiting dignitaries. **$$**

The Meeting Point Hostel (6 rooms) Carrera 61, No 68–100; 318 2599; www. themeetingpoint.hostel.com. One of several hostels that have popped up in recent years in Barranquilla, the Meeting Point offers a relaxed & helpful atmosphere in an otherwise chaotic city. Well located. **$**

WHERE TO EAT AND DRINK *See map, page 429.*
Barranquilla isn't short of cheap dining options with dozens of cafés, fast-food outlets and shoestring eateries along the Paseo Bolívar. For more upmarket cuisine head to El Prado where you'll also find a good range of food-court fare in the district's shopping malls. Local delicacies include *arroz con coco* and *sancocho*

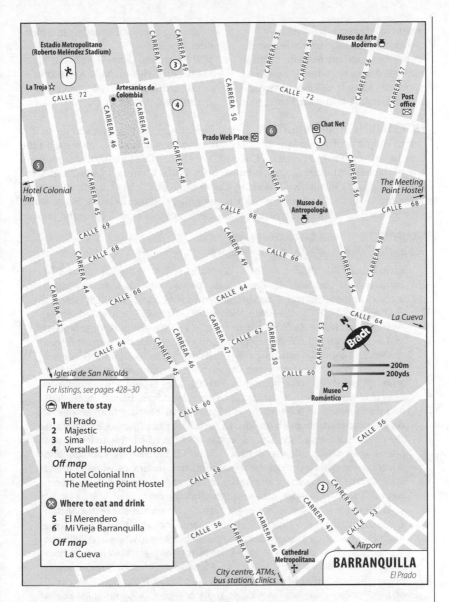

For listings, see pages 428–30

🛏 **Where to stay**
1 El Prado
2 Majestic
3 Sima
4 Versalles Howard Johnson

Off map
Hotel Colonial Inn
The Meeting Point Hostel

✖ **Where to eat and drink**
5 El Merendero
6 Mi Vieja Barranquilla

Off map
La Cueva

BARRANQUILLA
El Prado

de guandul (a soup of peas or '*guandules*' and meat), *bocachico frito* (fried fish from the Río Magdalena), *sancocho*, *arepas de huevo* (egg-filled fried maize), and *empanadas*.

✖ **Mi Vieja Barranquilla** Carrera 53, No 70–150; 🕾 360 2201/9592; ⏱ 11.00–15.00 & 18.00–22.00 Mon–Thu, 11.00–15.00 & 18.00–03.00 Fri–Sat, 11.00–16.00 Sun. This courtyard garden has been styled on a colonial plaza & is popular with local *vallenato* musicians. A good,

simple menu draws the crowds, as does the ice-cold Aguila beer. **$$**

✖ **Restaurante La Cueva** Cnr Calle 20 de Julio & Carrera 59; 🕾 379 2786; e reservas@ fundacionlacueva.org; www.fundacionlacueva.org; ⏱ lunch–late. Apart from being a fine monument to the so-called Barranquilla Group literary community, La Cueva is an exquisite restaurant in which diners can choose from terrace tables or a dark-panelled dining room amidst a gallery of memorabilia. A large menu & numerous special dishes offer seafood, pasta, salads & grilled meats in Colombian-European fusion style in an ambient atmosphere. **$$**

✗ El Merendero Carrera 43, No 70–48; ☎ 345 0956; ⊙ 11.00–midnight. A meat-lovers' paradise, with big plates of grilled steak in man-sized slabs & all the trimmings. **$**

ENTERTAINMENT AND NIGHTLIFE Barranquilla's nightclubs come and go so it is best to simply stroll around the city's Zona Rosa to see what catches your eye. At the time of writing, **Froggs Leggs** on Calle 93, No 43–122 (☎ 359 0709), is considered one of the best. Another local institution is **La Troja**, Carrera 44, No 72–263, for loud music and a distinctly Colombian Caribbean feel. Clubs generally open from Thursday to Sunday. Also popular are the city's many *estancos* – rustic liquor stores with battered tables outside where the music often comes from a car audio system.

COLOMBIA'S WILDEST PARTY

Curramberos like their pre-Lenten celebrations full-on hedonistic and at Barranquilla's Carnaval de Barranquilla (*www.carnavaldebarranquilla.org*) a truly explosive festival – declared an intangible and oral UNESCO World Heritage Event in 2003 – dominates the city for four days before Ash Wednesday. As the largest festival in Colombia, Barranquilla Carnaval is one of the biggest and best parties in Latin America – second only, the locals claim, to Rio de Janeiro, but arguably remaining closer to its roots in terms of the folklore and traditions. Everything stops in the city to make way for Barranquilla's revelry, a riotous event fuelled by more than 100,000 cases of rum and *aguardiente*. Streets fill with crowds of dancers, musicians, marching bands, processions and masquerades in a round-the-clock party that deviates from an official programme amidst boozy high jinks. La Battala de Flores (Flower Battle) starts the celebrations on a Saturday, a symbolic event in which the bullets of war are replaced with the flowers of peace. Colourful, bloom-filled carriages and floats surrounded by *cumbia* dancers kick off this endurance event in grand style. On the Sunday, many thousands of costume-clad people join *La Gran Parada* (The Great Parade) as it sweeps through the city.

This high-tempo showpiece event features drumbeat dances of African origin such as the '*torito*' (little bull) and the '*diablo*' (devil). With people wearing multi-hued wooden animal masks painted in black, red, white and yellow, it is a noisy, spirited affair that narrates the history of black slavery. A 24-hour concert of Caribbean music follows on Monday at El Festival de Orquestas before the conclusion of the Carnaval on Tuesday with the figurative burial of Joselito Carnaval. Joselito was, so the story goes, a Barranquilla coach driver who worked hard and enjoyed himself only on Tuesday. However, after drinking more that he was accustomed to one day, he lay down in the coach to sleep it off. In was carnival time, and merry-makers passing spotted Joselito slumped in a drunken state. As a joke, they took poor Joselito in his vehicle to the cemetery in a mock funeral cortege where crowds of 'mourners' were crying over the death of the coachman. 'Joselito has died, oh! Joselito! Why have you died? Why have you left us, Joselito?' Today these laments are re-enacted each year and signify the end of the Carnaval de Barranquilla – a time when Barranquilla can at last get some sleep.

Be sure to also try a *canelazo*, Barranquilla's local rum-laced cocktail that gives Brazil's potent *caipirinha* a run for its money.

♀ La Cueva Cnr Calle 20 de Julio & Carrera 59; ☏ 379 2786; e reservas@fundacionlacueva.org; www.fundacionlacueva.org. A one-time drinking den where Colombia's finest writers, journalists, poets, playwrights & philosophers hung out in the wild, hedonistic 1950s, La Cueva is a handsome corner-plot building that today houses a rather nice restaurant, bar, cultural centre & video theatre. The outfit behind this project also offers bursaries to young creative talent & has painstakingly restored this important part of Barranquilla's 20th-century literary heritage. Original photographs of Gabriel García Márquez, Álvaro Cepeda Samundop, German Vargas & Alfonso Fuenmayor, members of one of the most productive literary communities of that era, adorn the walls. Gunshot damage to one of the paintings on the wall is testament to the consequences of urinating in someone's drink. In an attempt to persuade the owner to open one day, artist Alejandro Obregon rode an elephant to the door – look out for a footprint at the entrance. La Cueva hosts a wide range of artistic events, talks, workshops, performances, recitals & book launches. Check out the website for a rolling calendar of evening events.

SHOPPING   For artisanal souvenirs head to the corner of Calle 72 and Avenida 46. This is where the largest collection of cheap handicraft kiosks are located as well as the more expensive **Artesanías de Colombia** store. There has been a boom in vast air-conditioned shopping malls so if you are interested in heading to the cinema or feeding your need for consumerism, head to the **Centro Comercial Buenavista**, Calle 98, No 52–115 (*ccbuenavistabarranquilla.com*). As a vast, heavily industrialised city, Barranquilla has plenty of basic essentials including drugstores and hardware stores.

OTHER PRACTICALITIES   Some of the fastest internet connections can be found at **Chat Net** (☏ 369 2600) on Carrera 54, No 71–111 and **Prado Web Place** (☏ 358 4577) on Calle 70, No 53–33 – both at 1,800COP per hour. The city's **Avianca Post Office** (☏ 330 2255) is located on the corner of Calle 72 and Carrera 58. Numerous **ATMs** are clustered along Carrera 53, including Bancolombia at No 68–69. A number of hospitals offer 24-hour medical care, including the **Clínica del Caribe** (☏ 334 6143) and **Clínica del Caribe SA** (☏ 378 6013/337 7226/356 4861).

WHAT TO SEE AND DO   Clearly the real attraction in Barranquilla is still the Carnaval period but little by little this business hub on the Caribbean coast has been making strong strides towards becoming a more socially inclusive and tourist-friendly city with some good museums, great food and a healthy emphasis on its cultural importance.

Museo de Arte Moderno (Museum of Modern Art)   (*Carrera 56, No 74–22;* ☏ *360 9952; www.mambq.org;* ⊕ *15.00–19.00 Mon, 09.00–19.00 Tue–Sat, closed 13.00–15.00; free admission*) Ferdinand Botero is just one of the many fine home-grown artists featured in this collection where works range from contemporary sculpture to photography and film.

Museo de Antropología (Anthopological Museum)   (*Calle 68, No 53–45;* ☏ *356 0067; www.maua.co;* ⊕ *08.00–17.00 Mon–Fri, closed noon–14.30; free admission*) Located on the second floor of the Universidad del Atlántico offices, this small collection of pre-Columbian pottery has been gathered from all across Colombia from a variety of indigenous communities.

Museo del Caribe and the Parque Cultural del Caribe (*Calle 36, No 46–66;* \ *372 0851; www.culturacaribe.org;* ⊕ *08.00–17.00 Mon–Thu, 09.00–18.00 Fri–Sun; admission 11,000COP*) The one museum on Colombia's Caribbean coast that can claim to be world-class, the Museo del Caribe was designed to showcase the Caribbean region's considerable cultural legacy. With rooms dedicated to Gabriel García Márquez, the nature, the people and the history of the region, this is the most complete collection for Colombia regarding *la Costa*. Perhaps more importantly than recognising the importance of the *costeno* culture and history, the museum and park – with spaces for open-air theatre and other events – was built in a less than salubrious area in order to stimulate regeneration and pride in the city.

Casa del Carnaval (*Carrera 54, No 49B–39;* \ *319 7616*) Constructed in 1929 by Luis Gutiérrez de la Hoz, this is ground zero for all things Carnaval-related in Barranquilla and so if your curiosity is piqued, a visit here is not without its merits to see the history of the event and of course some of the vulgar-shaped *marimondas* and other masks on display.

Museo Romántico (Romantic Museum) (*Carrera 54, No 59–199;* \ *344 4591;* ⊕ *09.00–noon & 14.30–18.00 Mon–Fri, closed Sat/Sun; admission 5,000COP*) Don't expect a homage to Casanova as this museum has a purely historical focus with exhibitions that tell the story of Barranquilla's founding and multi-cultural mix. It has a rather confusing name for what is a standard city collection, but it's a worthwhile browse nonetheless.

Catedral Metropolitana Maria Reina (Metropolitan Cathedral) (*Cnr Calle 53 & Carrera 46*) The interior of this ugly modern church designed by Italian Angelo Mazzoni de Grande has some pleasant surprises, including some beautiful stained-glass window designs and two wall mosaics using coloured German glass. Highlights include an over-the-altar 16-tonne, 16m-high bronze sculpture by Rodrigo Arenas Betancur.

Iglesia de San Nicolás (Church of St Nicholas) (*Cnr Paseo Bolívar & Carrera 43*) If you find yourself downtown in the epicentre of Barranquilla, take a peek inside this mock-Gothic building for its elegant altarpiece and handsome pulpit.

Festivals and sport Known as 'The Sharks', Barranquilla's beloved soccer team is Atlético Junior (*www.juniorbarranquilla.com*), also known as Corporación Deportiva Popular Junior. The pride of Colombia's Caribbean coast, the club enjoyed a golden age during the mid 1990s when Carlos 'El Pipe' Valderrama was instrumental in the championship wins of 1993 and 1995 (see box, page 439). The stadium holds 58,000, making it the largest in Colombia. It was built for the failed Colombian World Cup bid in 1986. The Colombian national team, the *cafeteros*, have chosen to play their World Cup qualifying games here given the nature of the partisan crowd and the stifling heat, both of which act as extra advantages to the home side.

CLOSE TO BARRANQUILLA

PUERTO COLOMBIA While Barranquilla is a coastal city on the Caribbean, it cannot be afforded the accolade of being a beach destination. Barranquilleros will hop into their cars and head to neighbouring destinations but those preferring to remain close will head to the historic destination of Puerto Colombia. Once regal and pleasing, Puerto Colombia has fallen on hard times with the pier (inaugurated in 1893) in a state of disrepair. But the beach and surrounding area are not without their charms and for a break from the bustle of Barranquilla, this makes for a convenient day trip. Fans of the works of Gabriel García Márquez will appreciate Puerto Colombia for the references made to it in his last piece of fiction, the laconic *Memory of my Melancholy Whores*, 2004.

CIENEGA GRANDE AND THE SALAMANCA ISLAND NATIONAL PARK Just 30 minutes outside of Barranquilla on the road towards Santa Marta is one of Colombia's least-visited yet most accessible and rewarding national parks. The Salamanca Island Park which makes up part of a huge body of water called Cienega Grande – protected from the sea – by a thin strip of land where the highway runs, consists of a collection of mangrove swamps, coastal scrub, islands, lagoons, ponds and waterways. Birders will get a thrill at the quantity of egrets on show but there are also endemic species in the area such as the rufous-winged chachalaca and sapphire-bellied hummingbird. Tours can be taken in dugout canoes for an hour or longer; expect to negotiate and pay in the region of 50,000COP per person. Contact De Una Colombia (page 66) for information and booking.

See also box, pages 16–17.

MAGDALENA

> Overcome by your moving temple, overcome by this holiest of altars. So pure, so rare
> to witness such a lovely goddess. I bear witness to this place, this lair, so long forgotten.
> So pure, so rare…
>
> A Perfect Circle, '*Magdalena*', Mer de Noms, 2000

A relatively small department at approximately 23,188km², Magdalena (*www. magdalena.gov.co*) is beautiful nonetheless, with a territory blessed by genuine contrasting landscapes that a wide variety of ecosystems bring. Powder-fine beaches and coastline in the north leads to the snow-covered peaks and swamplands in the west. Inland cloudforest and grasslands edge urban centres surrounded by farmlands and arid shrubby desert on a backdrop of valleys and rocky rivers. Four drainage basins are fed by dozens of lakes, lagoons, marshlands, creeks and waterways of which Río Magdalena is the most important. Bordered to the north by the Caribbean Sea; La Guajira to the northeast; the department of César to the east; and edging Atlántico in the northwest and Bolívar in the west and southwest, Magdalena is divided by Río Magdalena to the west. Thick jungle, fine national parks and peaks that soar 5,700m offer excellent hiking trails in a region that is undoubtedly one of Colombia's most picturesque.

SANTA MARTA Telephone code 5

Hot, sticky and with its colonial grandeur now partially restored, the waterfront city of Santa Marta is steeped in history as the place where El Libertador Simón Bolívar died. As a popular domestic tourist destination, Santa Marta is a byword for relaxation. Most Colombians visit to enjoy plenty of beer, rum and sun along with the leisurely delights of the beach. As the capital of the Magdalena department, the city is an important maritime port, although tourism is increasingly important to the local economy. In recent years Santa Marta has attracted large numbers of migrants displaced by conflict, drastically increasing the city's population. At the time of writing, restoration of Santa Marta's colonial streets is a work in progress. The city's mix of old architecture and modern beachfront complexes offers considerable past-and-future contrasts. Open-air reggae bars and palm-edged cafés make Santa Marta a pleasant place to spend time and from which to explore the local area. Exotic tropical fruit stalls adorn every street corner. Fruit can be bought whole or whipped up into a smoothie by vendors who hotwire electricity pylons into blenders all over town. Families huddle around disco-sized speakers listening to blasting *vallenato* at several million decibels as impromptu parties break out on the city's beach.

HISTORY The land on which Santa Marta was founded was populated by people Indians before the arrival of Spanish explorers who inaugurated the city in July 1525. On naming it after St Marta, Spanish conqueror Rodrigo de Bastidas planted a flag accompanied by some 200 of his men. Spanish colonisation began in earnest as the surrounding lands were conquered. Bastidas had previously reconnoitred the area and using this intelligence was able to pinpoint where the region's gold-rich indigenous settlements were located. Santa Marta's strategic location at the base of the Sierra Nevada de Santa Marta served the Spanish well and allowed the efficient transportation of untold treasures to the Old World via the Caribbean Sea. Fierce resistance from the natives prompted sustained attack that saw the Tayrona peoples decimated by the end of the 16th century. It was from Santa Marta that Jiménez de Quesada and his troops set off to march the Magdalena Valley in 1536, an expedition that later led to the founding of Bogotá.

During the colonial era, Santa Marta lost its importance to the nearby port city of Cartagena, a more dynamic commercial centre and better fortified. In 1871, the city became a university town when the University of Magdalena was founded, initially with law and medicine faculties. The export of coal and bananas gave Santa Marta's sluggish port trade a boost in the 20th century but was hit by industrial unrest in 1928. When the Colombian army was sent in to dispel banana plantation workers campaigning for improved pay and conditions in Gienga, near Santa Marta, the situation turned ugly. Troops opened fire in what has become known as the Massacre of the Bananeros. The official death toll was 47 but the reality was much worse. In 1961, the Atlantic Railway connected Bogotá with Santa Marta, and in 1968 the government decentralised the port authority, giving Santa Marta more autonomy. Today, Santa Marta is still a busy trading port although tourism is the economy's fastest-growing sector in this city of 600,000. The date of Simón Bolívar's death in Santa Marta on 7 December 1830 after liberating six Latin American countries is honoured nationwide.

CLIMATE Temperatures in Santa Marta can top 30°C but fall dramatically during the climb up the surrounding peaks of the Sierra Nevada de Santa Marta. During the stormiest months, Santa Marta's streets can become rivers due to rainfall and flooding from the sea.

SAFETY Santa Marta and the surrounding areas are generally safe for tourists despite being home to some *paracos* (ex-paramilitaries), a few FARC operatives, some *narcos* (narcotics traffickers) and a handful of drug labs, often referred to as the BACRIM (band of criminals). Saying that, incidents of tourists being caught up in this murky underworld are extremely rare, but do happen and downtown backstreets should be avoided after dark.

A six-day trek or an extortionate helicopter ride are the only ways to the ancient settlement of Ciudad Perdida, the so-called Lost City, which was built around 500AD but only discovered in 1976. The trek is an arduous but rewarding affair along muddy trails across a seemingly endless succession of mountains. For details on the Lost City and how to get there, see pages 448–9. Since the last edition of this guide was published, the numbers of visitors journeying to Ciudad Perdida has increased significantly and Britain's Foreign Office no longer warns of travelling there, although a warning still appears to be in place from the US government as a result of an unprecedented kidnapping of eight travellers to the site by ELN guerrillas in 2003. The hostages were treated well by their kidnappers and eventually released, the last after 102 days.

Since then the threat of kidnappings has been a recurring topic of discussion between hikers considering the trek. Some feel it was a one-off occurrence and others feel concerned that in such a remote spot the risk is just too great. The ELN said the purpose of the kidnapping was to draw attention to the problems faced by local communities in the Sierra Nevada. No kidnapping attempt has been reported since then. Today the people of Santa Marta consider the trek to be safe for tourists.

The Ciudad Perdida is cared for by the indigenous people who still live in the area. They have linked up with a number of local guides (page 449), who are authorised to take tourists to the Lost City. Of the total fee charged to tourists, 35,000COP is paid to the ICANH (Colombian Institute of Anthropology and History), 30,000COP to the indigenous communities and 30,000COP to small farmers in the region.

GETTING THERE AND AWAY The 98km stretch of **road** between Barranquilla and Santa Marta passes through numerous one-horse towns and villages once it leaves the city's zillions of car-repair shops in the industrial outskirts behind. A frenzied riddle of garages, workshops and tyre-fitting centres populated by tooting, gridlocked traffic gives way to fuel stations, roadside vendors, kiosks and grilled-meat joints. It then becomes much less frenetic as the road becomes much slower paced. Essentials are easy to find *en route* with water sellers plying for trade at junctions and windscreen washers at each toll. Mudflats and drier, dustier terrain turns to palm-fringed wetland expanses as the tropical resorts of Santa Marta come into view.

Santa Marta's **El Rodadero Airport** is easily reached by well-marked city buses, 16km (45 minutes) south of the city on the Barranquilla–Bogotá road. Avianca (↘ *421 4018*), Copa and Lan service Santa Marta, with direct flights to/from Bogotá and Medellín.

Frequent **minibuses** connect with the main bus terminal on the southeastern outskirts of the city. **Buses** run daily to Bogotá (120,000COP, 16 hours), Bucaramanga (80,000COP, 9 hours) and Barranquilla (20,000COP, 1¾ hours) – some stop at Cartagena (35,000COP, 4 hours). Daily buses from Santa Marta serve Maracaibo in Venezuela (85,000COP, 7 hours) where passport formalities take place in the border town of Paraguachón.

GETTING AROUND Buses and *colectivos* run along the seafront on Carrera 1C (Avenida Rodrigo de Bastidas) with frequent minibuses serving Taganga (15 minutes), El Rodadero (15 minutes) and Mamatoca (20 minutes).

Santa Marta is easy enough to navigate on foot with taxis widely available between *carreras* 1 and 5. Although illegal, motorbike taxiing is a highly popular form of local transport – and cheap. It costs 4,000COP to cross the city and is the fastest way to negotiate the traffic, albeit a little scary.

TOUR OPERATORS

Atlantic Divers Calle 10C, No 2–04; ☎ 421 4883. This decent little dive school offers a number of tour packages, from half & full days to night dives.
Poseidon Dive Center Calle 18, No 1–69, Taganga; ☎ 421 9224; e info@poseidondivecenter.com; www.poseidondivecenter.com. Highly recommended & efficient German-owned dive school in Taganga.

Turcol Calle 13, No 3–13, CC San Francisco Plaza L 115; ☎ 421 2256; e turcoltravel@gmail.com; www.turcoltravel.com. Every hotel in town offers tours out to Ciudad Perdida through this outfit, one of Santa Marta's longest-established specialists, & the best.

🏠 WHERE TO STAY See map, page 437.

Now that downtown Santa Marta's colonial district has been lovingly restored, the quality of hotels on offer ranges from the über-plush to high-end *hostals*. In short, there's something for every budget and all within walking distance from good restaurants and lively bars. Generally speaking, finding a room isn't difficult in the city unless it's during Carnaval, Christmas, New Year or Easter, when it is imperative to book ahead. Signs at the entrance to town advertise camping and cabins.

🏠 **Casa Carolina Boutique** (6 rooms) Calle 12, No 3–40; ☎ 423 3354; www.hotelcasacarolina.com. One of a new breed of boutiques that have sprung up in the restored colonial centre offering top-quality accommodation, service & the modern comforts that the more refined visitor has come to expect. Stylishly decorated rooms are well appointed around the central swimming pool. Don't miss the rooftop spa! **$$$**

🏠 **Casa de Isabella** (8 rooms, 2 suites) Carrera 2DA, No 19–20; ☎ 431 2082; www.kalihotels.com. This beautifully renovated colonial-era hotel, just around the corner from Ouzo (page 438), combines the beauty of Mudejar architecture with top-quality modern comforts including Wi-Fi, i-Pod radio & Apple TV, A/C, & free telephone calls to 40 countries around the world. **$$$**

🏠 **Hotel Irotama** (300 rooms) Vía Ciénaga, Km14; ☎ 432 0600; e reserves@irotama.com; www.irotama.com. This super resort-style complex boasts ultra-friendly staff & top-notch facilities & boasts spectacular views from a 12th-floor rooftop bar & restaurant complete with jacuzzi. Located a 5min drive from the airport & set across 23ha, the Irotama is surrounded by lush, tropical gardens & numerous exotic birds & edged by a 1km sandy beach. Spacious modern rooms in condo-style units have tiled floors, a lovely private bathroom, TV, minibar & balcony. The complex also has a collection of cabins, villas & suites. On-site amenities include business centre with internet, swimming pool, gym, spa, restaurants & bar. Travellers who have roughed it for weeks will

enjoy the splurge. Rates vary with a wide range of packages available with significant discounts for 7-day stays off-peak. **$$$**

🏠 **Hotel Yuldama** (54 rooms) Carrera 1, No 12–19; ☎ 422 9332; e hotelyuldama@reservashoteleras.com.co; www.hotelyuldama.com. For mid-range accommodation with AC, TV, Wi-Fi internet, refrigerator with minibar, telephone & sea views this is a decent choice popular with Colombian families; rates include b/fast. **$$$**

🏠 **Hotel Zuana Beach Resort** (185 rooms) Carrera 2a, No 6–80; ☎ 436 6111; www.zuana.com.co. This huge tropical-style resort complex has large, cheerful rooms with tiled floors, wicker furniture & brightly coloured décor. Amenities include pools, bars, snack bars & a buffet-style restaurant. **$$$**

🏠 **Aluna Casa and Café** (15 rooms) Calle 21, No 5–72 ☎ 432 4916; e info@alunahotel.com; www.alunahotel.com. Popular due to its ideal location in the historic centre of the city, just a few blocks from the beach, boasting comfortable rooms, excellent information about activities & day trips & with an on-site café, Aluna is based in a lovingly restored 1920s Spanish-style villa. Highly recommended. **$$**

🏠 **Hotel Nueva Granada** (21 rooms) Calle 12, No 3–17; ☎ 421 1337/0685; www.santamartahotelnuevagranada.com. Expect good value for money from this friendly mid-range option in the centre of town. Small rooms are simple but clean – but only some come with

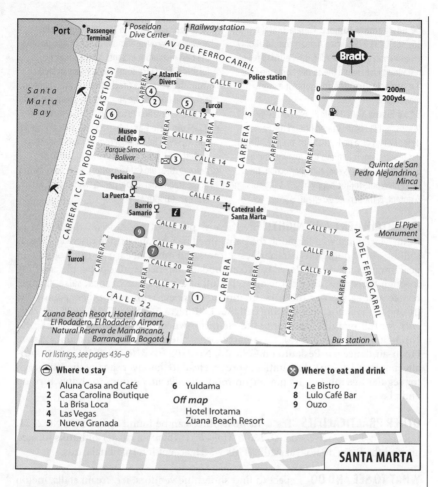

For listings, see pages 436–8

Where to stay

1 Aluna Casa and Café
2 Casa Carolina Boutique
3 La Brisa Loca
4 Las Vegas
5 Nueva Granada
6 Yuldama

Off map
  Hotel Irotama
  Zuana Beach Resort

Where to eat and drink

7 Le Bistro
8 Lulo Café Bar
9 Ouzo

SANTA MARTA

much-needed AC & a few have very little natural light. There's also a flower-filled courtyard where b/fast is served & a small swimming pool. **$$**

🏠 **Hotel Las Vegas** (15 rooms) Calle 11, No 2–08; ☎ 421 5094. Rooms lack style, but do have AC with streetside balconies & basic bathrooms. **$**

🏠 **La Brisa Loca** (sleeps 82) Calle 14, No 3–58; ☎ 431 6121; e labrisaloca@gmail.com; www.

labrisaloca.com. In this sprawling & beautiful downtown mansion just off the main plaza in Santa Marta, 2 brothers from California have set up party central in the Brisa Loca & singlehandedly changed the rhythm of the city. Multiple dorms, a lively bar, rooftop club & activities galore make this a destination for the more raucous crowd & with good reason. **$**

✗ WHERE TO EAT AND DRINK *See map, above.*

Santa Marta has a lot of little food joints serving inexpensive meals as well as fast-food bars and upmarket cafés. Meander along *calles* 11 and 12 or trawl the beachfront – and simply follow your nose. There is a sizzling 2km string of ramshackle food stalls along the PanAmerica, from meats grilled in makeshift oilcan barbecues to freshly fried *empanadas* and cauldrons of stew. Dozens of fruit vendors sell an excellent array of fresh produce citywide. For more refined options check out the area around the Parque de los Novios for the best options in the city.

✗ Restaurante Lamart Carrera 3RA, No 16–36; ☏ 431 0797; http://lamart.com.co. Highly recommended by one reader, this Peruvian fusion restaurant just around the corner from Lulo Café Bar (see below) may be pricey, but it is worth the money. $$$

✗ Le Bistro Calle 19, No 3–68, Parque de los Novios; ☏ 421 8080. Located just off the Parque de los Novios on a pedestrianised street, Le Bistro has brought unpretentious top-quality dining to Santa Marta. Meat is cooked to perfection, the cocktails (come for the happy hour!) & flavoursome & potent, & the service excellent. $$

✗ Ouzo Carerra 3, No 19–29, Parque de los Novios; www.ouzosantamarta.com. Quite possibly the best restaurant in Santa Marta & look no further if you fancy some Mediterranean food. Wood-fired pizzas & Greek offerings in addition to a seafood linguini are amongst the favourites here. Make a reservation to avoid disappointment. $$

▭ Lulo Café Bar Carrera 3, 16–34, Callejon del Correo; www.lulocafebar.com. For those seeking something lighter than your average *caldo de pescado*, the Lulo Café Bar offers some fancy twists to the traditional *arepa*, panini sandwiches, wraps & greats smoothies. $

ENTERTAINMENT AND NIGHTLIFE There is plenty of nightlife on the streets of Santa Marta; just wander along the palm-lined beachfront strip to discover crowds spilling out of numerous bars and restaurants and music at ear-splitting volume. In peak months, roads are closed to accommodate the sheer traffic of people crawling through the streets. Expect the air to be full of a heady mix of rock, salsa, techno, reggae and calypso as the bars attempt to compete with each other. Follow the throng to the innocuous-looking hangout **La Puerta** on Calle 17, No 2–29 (⊕ *Tue–Sat*), for full-on salsa music or to the Flemish-owned **Barrio Samario** on Calle 17, No 3–36 (m *310 710 9649*), for a party atmosphere that doesn't end until dawn. Open-air dance bar **Peskaito** on Calle 16, No 2–08 (m *310 729 4818*), opens mid-afternoon and doesn't close until daybreak. Head to the silver sand of the city beach for regular live music – it's not uncommon for *vallenato* groups to simply turn up and play.

OTHER PRACTICALITIES The **4-72 post office** can be found at Calle 22, No 2–21, Local 7 (☏ *430 6762*; ⊕ *08.00–18.00 Mon–Fri*). There's a cluster of **banks** located around the Plaza de Bolívar with ATMs which accept international cards.

WHAT TO SEE AND DO Expect to find shoeshine vendors, ice-cream stalls, melon sellers and balloon stalls in the Parque de Simón Bolívar (Simón Bolívar Park) along with elderly card-playing women and children playing happily. There's a backdrop of fine colonial buildings complete with vast wooden doors and ornately decorated balconies.

Museo del Oro (Gold Museum) (*Calle 14, No 2–07;* ☏ *421 0953;* ⊕ *08.00–11.45 & 14.00–17.45 Mon–Fri; free admission*) A decent collection of gold from the Sierra Nevada is housed in Santa Marta's Gold Museum in a fine, renently renovated colonial mansion known as the Casa de la Aduana (Customs House). It contains some rather fine Tayrona objects and some pottery from the Kogi and Arhuaco cultures in rooms set off a circular lobby.

Catedral de Santa Marta (Santa Marta Cathedral) (*Cnr Carrera 4 & Calle 17*) Ignore claims that Santa Marta's hulking great whitewashed cathedral is Colombia's oldest church – construction didn't finish until 1766. The ashes of the town's founder, Rodrigo de Bastidas, are contained in a vault by the entrance. Simón Bolívar was also buried here in 1830 but his remains were returned to his birthplace in Caracas in 1842.

Monumento Carlos 'El Pibe' Alberto Valderrama Palacio (El Pibe Monument) (*Eduardo Santos Stadium*) This 7m bronze statue of Colombian football legend Carlos Valderrama captures the great man perfectly, right down to his wild, frizzy hair. It was created by Colombian artist Amilkar Ariza and attracts tourists from all over the country. Find it outside the stadium, a 23,000 capacity complex built in 1951 that is home to the Unión Magdalena squad.

Quinta de San Pedro Alejandrino (San Pedro Alejandrino's Country Home) (*4km east of the city, a 20min bus journey from Santa Marta's beachfront strip or a 10,000COP taxi ride;* \ *433 1021;* ⊕ *09.30–16.30 daily; admission 10,000COP*)

Meaning the '*quinta* of St Peter Alexander', this grand hacienda was built in the 17th century and was the estate where Simón Bolívar spent his final days. He died in 1830 as the guest of the Spanish owner, Joaquín de Mier, a loyal supporter of Bolívar's push for Colombian independence. The hacienda produced rum, sugarcane and honey and had its own mill. Now a shrine and museum honouring Bolívar, this magnificent homestead contains a number of fine monuments to the liberator. Works of art in the Altar de la Patria have been donated by artists from all of the countries in Latin Ameírica freed by Bolívar's campaigns. A vast white marble memorial built in 1930 contains a centrepiece statue that offers a trick of the eye. Look at it head-on, and Bolívar is standing proud with a swagger. Step to

SANTA MARTA'S MOP-HAIRED HERO

He may not win any medals for his poorly dyed mop of hair, but Carlos Alberto Valderrama Palacio is a god in Colombian football circles. A Santa Marta local, he was born on 2 September 1961 and was skilful with a ball as a small boy and began his career at Unión Magdalena in the Colombian First Division in 1981. He was dubbed El Pibe ('The Kid') and became as famous for his bush of blondish-orange hair as for his adept passing whilst later playing for the Millonarios and Deportivo Cali. He then joined Montpellier in 1988. Valderrama captained Colombia during the 1990, 1994 and 1998 world cups, earning 111 caps and hitting the back of the net 11 times for his country. He played a memorable role in setting up Freddy Rincón's 1994 goal through the legs of German goalkeeper Bodo Illgner – it tied the match at 1–1 and sent Colombia into the second round of the World Cup for the first time in its history.

Today many of Colombia's sporting pundits consider him the nation's finest footballer of all time. After playing for Independiente Medellín then Atlético Junior from 1993 to 1996, Valderrama played the last games of his career in the US. The midfielder played for the Tampa Bay Mutiny (1996–97, 2000–01), Miami Fusion (1998–99) and the Colorado Rapids (2001–02). In 2005, he was added to the Major League Soccer All-Time Best. Valderrama ended his 22-year career in a tribute match at Barranquilla's Metropolitan Stadium in the company of Argentine legend Diego Maradona. He boasts the distinction of being the only Colombian to feature in FIFA's 125 Top Living Football Players listing. Valderrama was also honoured as a French Cup winner (1990), South American Footballer of the Year (1987, 1993), Colombian Championship winner (1993, 1995), MLS Player of the Year (1996), MLS All-Time leader in assists and MLS All-Star game MVP and is a Member of the FIFA Century Club.

the right and he is a generation older, wizened and visibly weaker. Stand to the left and he is younger and looking forward into the distance, wearing a knowing smile. The house, the Museo Bolivariano and the monuments can each be visited and the grounds are well worth a stroll.

Natural Reserva de Mamancana (Mamancana Natural Reserve) *(Not far from the Hotel Irotama just off the road to the airport out of Santa Marta;* m *317 220 8020;* e *info@mamancana.co; www.mamancana.co)* Eco-centre and adventure sports complex, a Mecca for downhill cyclists, Mamancana played host to Colombia's national competition in 2006 and offers a host of canopy rides, hiking trails and mountain-bike routes as well as a climbing wall and extreme sports, including paragliding. Sailing, kayaking and fishing take place on a large lake with 4x4 off-road tracks and 600ha of thick forest. A lofty lookout point offers breathtaking views out to the coast amidst springs, cactus, palms, ravines, rocks and nesting birds. A large open-fronted wooden lodge has to be one of the funkiest in Colombia with a part-canvas sail-style roof and a tasteful restaurant that transforms into a bar at weekends, complete with DJ. Wildlife in the park includes monkeys, foxes and wild cats. It is also home to numerous species of butterflies and migratory and indigenous birds. Guests can stay overnight in dorm beds (14) or double rooms and can handpick a range of activities. Rates include breakfast (**$$$**).

Festivals and events
Las Fiestas del Mar (mid year) Santa Marta's Festival of the Sea is celebrated during peak season and is a modern concept aimed squarely at tourists. Expect beauty pageants, parades and parties under the festival's slogan 'Santa Marta, la magia de tenerlo todo' (Santa Marta, the magic of having it all).

Festival de la Cumbia (July) An annual celebration of dance and song in tribute to the native tradition of *cumbia* with colourful processions and non-stop merriment and lots of stalls.

AROUND SANTA MARTA

EL RODADERO *(Telephone code 5)* Once a sleepy little seaside town, El Rodadero is now practically a beachside suburb of Santa Marta, with white sands surrounded by contoured scrub-clad slopes. Popular with volleyball players, and with calm waters for windsurfing, swimming and diving, El Rodadero is located 5km south of downtown Santa Marta. All the main resort amenities are clustered close to the beach with modern hotels, rental apartments, open-sided restaurants, dive schools, campsites, supermarkets, discos, casinos, a post office and a couple of internet cafés easily accessible on foot. Sunloungers and sunshades can be hired for the beach along with kayaks and paddle boats. Popular with Colombian holidaymakers, El Rodadero can get very crowded at weekends and during public holidays. It is also quite lively after dark when a host of beachfront bars fill with the sound of salsa, *vallenato* and *cumbia*.

Getting there and around All **buses** heading south of Santa Marta will drop off at El Rodadero. A **taxi** will cost around 10,000COP.

Tourist information There's a small tourism booth on the beachfront. It offers maps, hotel reservations, tour bookings and is open 08.00–18.00 daily.

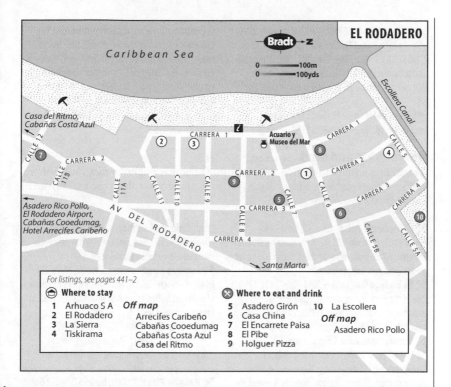

Caribbean Sea

Casa del Ritmo,
Cabañas Costa Azul

Asadero Rico Pollo,
El Rodadero Airport,
Cabañas Cooedumag,
Hotel Arrecifes Caribeño

Acuario y
Museo del Mar

Santa Marta

Escollera Canal

For listings, see pages 441–2

🏨 **Where to stay**
1 Arhuaco S A
2 El Rodadero
3 La Sierra
4 Tiskirama

Off map
Arrecifes Caribeño
Cabañas Cooedumag
Cabañas Costa Azul
Casa del Ritmo

🍴 **Where to eat and drink**
5 Asadero Girón
6 Casa China
7 El Encarrete Paisa
8 El Pibe
9 Holguer Pizza
10 La Escollera

Off map
Asadero Rico Pollo

🏨 Where to stay *See map, above.*

El Rodadero has dozens of hotels that offer similarly styled vacation accommodation, many in high-rise blocks. Look out for signs around the beach and on the approach road advertising cabins and camping. Some of the larger family-run restaurants also rent out rooms in peak season. Numerous outfits offer *cabañas* sleeping four to ten in and around El Rodadero, including **Cabañas Costa Azul** (*Calle 18, No 2–48;* \ *422 9749;* **$$**) and **Cabañas Cooedumag** (*Calle 21A;* \ *422 5650;* **$$**). A number of private individuals offer apartments for rental in and around the beach area of the town, including the following options. The apartment-rental agency **Vista Mar Colombia** (\ *422 3890;* m *315 446 8028/312 757 2535;* e *reservas@ vistamarcolombia.com; www.vistamarcolombia.com*) has a number of seafront units in and around El Rodadero.

🏨 **Hotel Arhuaco S A** (59 rooms) Carrera 2, No 6–49; \ 422 7166; e reservas@solarhoteles.com; www.solarhoteles.com. One of the best hotels in the area, the Arhuaco boasts a gleaming, ultra-swish lobby & spotless swimming pool. Rooms range from standard double to triple, each with TV & AC. There is also a laundry service, a couple of restaurants & indoor & outdoor bars. **$$$**

🏨 **Hotel Arrecifes Caribeño** (27 rooms) Calle 19, No 6–54; \ 422 3028/3265. This archetypal El Rodadero 4-storey hotel is modern & close to the beach with a range of different-sized rooms (2–6

people), some better than others. Prices double in high season. **$$$**

🏨 **Hotel El Rodadero** (74 rooms) Calle 11, No 1–29; \ 422 8323; www.hotelesrodadero.com. A large beachfront hotel with pool, restaurant, café & games room & modern rooms with AC & private bathrooms. **$$$**

🏨 **Hotel La Sierra** (74 rooms) Carrera 1, No 9–47; \ 422 7960; www.hotelasierra.com. Another much-of-a-muchness to look at, but a popular option nonetheless, close to the action with good amenities & first-class views from a

The Atlantic Coast AROUND SANTA MARTA

11

441

decent collection of AC rooms with balconies. **$$$**

🏠 **Aparta Hotel Tiskirama** (8 aptms) Carrera 2, No 5–159; ☎ 422 7903. This perfectly acceptable budget option has functional suite-style rooms that can accommodate larger groups or families. **$$**

🏠 **Casa del Ritmo** (3 rooms & 10 dorm beds) Calle 18, No 2–59; ☎ 420 5152; e info@ casadelritmo.com; www.casadelritmo.com. For those wishing to avoid downtown Santa Marta & enjoy more of a traditional beach retreat, the Casa del Ritmo is a delightful, Colombian-owned-&-run establishment just a few blocks from the beach in Rodadero. Tastefully & tropically decorated, you can find no better digs in this part of Santa Marta for the money. **$$**

✖ Where to eat and drink *See map, page 441.*

As befitting a touristy seaside resort, El Rodadero has plenty of fast-food options and ice-cream parlours. Places come and go so take a stroll along the beachfront to see what takes your fancy.

✖ **El Encarrete Paisa** Calle 12, No 2–04; ☎ 422 2063; ⊕ noon–23.00. A menu of traditional Colombian fare from many regions, including some great Caribbean fish plates. **$$**

✖ **La Bodeguilla** Calle 6, No 1–26; ☎ 421 3735. One of the best restaurants in Santa Marta, this Italian across the road from El Pibe (see below) is known for its seafood risotto. **$$**

✖ **Restaurante Casa China** Carrera 3, No 6–43; ☎ 422 8069; ⊕ lunch & dinner. El Rodadero's best Chinese diner has a reasonable choice of menus, from seafood noodles & sweet-&-sour shrimp & rice to spicy stir-fried octopus. **$$**

✖ **Restaurante El Pibe** Calle 6, No 1–26 L–101; ☎ 422 7973; ⊕ noon–midnight. Named in honour of Santa Marta's home-grown footballing talent Carlos Valderrama (see box, page 439), this restaurant has a good ambience & has posters of the midfield virtuoso on the wall. **$$**

✖ **Asadero Girón** Carrera 3, No 7–20; ☎ 422 0143; ⊕ lunch–23.30 Mon–Sat. Expect big plates of delicious grilled meat & plantain at this decent family-run food joint. **$**

✖ **Asadero Rico Pollo** Carrera 4, No 19 A–09; ☎ 422 4727; ⊕ all day. The speciality here is chicken – & it's cheap & good. A good choice for generous portions & lunchtime deals. **$**

✖ **Holguer Pizza** Calle 8, No 2–57; ☎ 422 6861; ⊕ 11.30–midnight. People rave about the pizza from this place. It can be ordered whole or by the slice with all manner of toppings. **$**

Entertainment and nightlife After dark it gets lively in El Rodadero with two of the nicest options the upmarket club and restaurant **La Escollera** (☎ 422 9590; ⊕ *Wed–Sun*) with its fun open-air bar, and the funky **Latino Café** (☎ 422 7089).

What to see and do

Acuario y Museo del Mar (Aquarium and Museum of the Sea) (☎ 422 7222; *www.mundomarinoacuario.com.co*; ⊕ *09.00–16.00 every day; admission 14,000COP*) Founded in 1966, this aquatic complex contains an aquarium which is home to sharks, dolphins, seals, turtles and other species of marine life. A dolphin show takes place when the audience is sufficiently large to warrant it. An adjoining museum houses an eclectic assortment of local artefacts. The aquarium can be reached by hopping on any bus heading northwest.

TAGANGA (*Telephone code 5*) This tiny fishing village is much favoured by visiting backpackers and alongside nets and boats you'll find ramshackle stalls selling hippy paraphernalia. Set on a horseshoe-shaped bay, Taganga divides opinions. Some visitors describe it as paradisiacal and wax lyrical about its simplistic beauty. Others are horrified by Taganga's many flaws. Dabbling in some of Colombia's illicit crops is certainly a popular pastime here, so if this isn't your scene opt for the beach-life in El Rodadero. Although some upmarket boutique hotels have sprung up, Taganga remains very much the domain of body-pierced, hair-braided, guitar-strumming ganga-smoking gringos. Most drop by *en route* to Venezuela after trekking to the Lost City. Many get caught up in Taganga's simple vibe and end up spending several months there, idly swinging in hammocks and making the most of cheap beer. Unfortunately, a once-idyllic palm-scattered beach is now in dire need of a clean-up. Describing Taganga as 'rubbish-on-sea' (as one French visitor did in 2007) may be a little unkind, but the main drag has now been worked on and is certainly more pleasant than previously . For a picturesque stretch of sand walk 20 minutes northwest of Taganga to the Playa Grande (or take a boat for 10,000COP), where beachside restaurants are pleased to see you and serve plates of delicious fish and rice.

Getting there and around Taganga is easily reached from Santa Marta's beachfront with numerous **minibuses** nipping back and forth throughout the day (2,000COP, 15 minutes).

Tour operators Taganga offers some of the best-value scuba diving in Colombia and a number of operators run PADI/NAUI courses. Standards vary enormously, so ask around for recommendations.

Where to stay There may be close to 40 places to stay in Taganga, all of varying quality. The following is a list of those we recommend:

Hotel La Ballena Azul (27 rooms & 4 suites) Carrera 1Cl, No 18; ☏ 421 9009; www. hotelballenaazul.com. A fine upmarket option on the main drag, the Blue Whale offers a mix of different styles of accommodation, from minimalist contemporary suites with sunken baths on ultra-chic terraces, to homely rooms that look in need of bringing up to date. There's also a bar & internet. **$$$**

Casa de Félipe (30 rooms) Carrera 5A, No 19–12; ☏ 421 9120; e info@lacasadefelipe.com, www.lacasadefelipe.com. Nice, friendly & well run by Frenchman Jean Philippe, this is a firm favourite with European backpackers & has grown considerably from a 5-room hostel to possibly the most complete establishment in Taganga. Excellent information is provided here by an able staff & guests can choose from dorms, private rooms, studios with a kitchenette & even *cabañas*. There's a snack bar & a recommended French restaurant on site too. **$$**

Hotel Casa Holanda (12 rooms) Calle 14, No 1B–75; ☏ 421 9390; e info@hotelcasaholanda.com. Clean, comfortable rooms with a good view near to the restaurants & bars in Taganga. Friendly staff. **$$**

Hostal Techos Azules (17 rooms & 3 *cabañas*) Sector Dunkarinca Cabaña 1–100; ☏ 421 2512; e contacto@techosazules.com; www. techosazules.com. Located just as you descend into the bay of Taganga the Techos Azules is easily distinguishable by its blue rooftops. Offering dorms, private rooms & *cabañas*, this long-time Taganga favourite is recommended for couples perhaps seeking a little more privacy off the main drag. **$**

La Tortuga Hostal (12 rooms) Calle 9, No 3–116; m 320 258 9677; e tortugahostel@ hotmail.com; www.tortugahostel.com. Set in an imposing building with unrivalled sunset views from the rooftop bar, the Tortuga is the young upstart calling out to an active clientele booking in for a week-long course in diving & staying for months. You can choose from dorms & private rooms all with en-suite bathrooms. **$**

✗ Where to eat and drink

✗ Asados Al Carbon y Comidas Rapidas Yiu Nu Sagu Taganga Calle 13, No 2A–86; ☏ 421 9137; ⊕ early until late. A popular place to grab a lunchtime bite & take-away food, this grilled-meat

café is excellent value but lacks service-with-a-smile. **$**

✗ Restaurante Las Velas Carrera 1, No 18–95; ☏ 421 9072; ⊕ early–late. Las Velas serves tasty,

inexpensive fish-&-rice dishes. $
🖵 **Los Baguettes De María** Calle 18, No

3–47; ✆ 421 9328; 🕒 until late afternoon. Offers sandwiches, juices, shakes & salads. $

Entertainment and nightlife Of the open-sided bars in Taganga, the liveliest is **El Garaje** (✆ 421 9003; 🕒 Wed–Sat), a popular gringo hangout that plays salsa and *reggaetón* until the early hours.

Other practicalities Although a couple of local shops stock a few tourist essentials, don't rely on this if you plan to stay. Bring everything you need with you, from sunscreen and cash reserves to over-the-counter medicines. Taganga also has a couple of **internet cafés** and a poorly stocked drugstore.

PARQUE NACIONAL TAYRONA (TAYRONA NATIONAL PARK) (*Admission 38,000COP; horse 25,000COP. Visitors travelling by road pay a toll of 11,000COP*) One of Colombia's easily accessible and most popular national parks, Tayrona offers some stunning beaches set within deeply contoured bays and hemmed in by coconut trees. Bordered by the Bahía de Taganga in the west to the mouth of the Río Piedras 35km to the east, Tayrona was once home to the indigenous Tayrona community. Today all that is left of their ancient civilisation are ruins of the pre-Hispanic town of Chairama (or Pueblito in Spanish). Today, Tayrona's gorgeous sandy stretches are edged by large coral reefs in an expanse that can be explored on horseback or on foot. Rocky ravines edge gushing rivers amidst dense rainforest and cacti-clad arid slopes. Wildlife includes wild pigs, spider-monkeys, lizards, frogs and snakes with parrots, vultures and crows. Spider webs the size of tablecloths stretch from tree to tree above a crocodile of mules piled high with rice bound for the park's Amerindian villages. Surrounding fertile waters are home to grouper, red snapper, octopus, mackerel, shark, lobsters, squid and eels. A hand-shaped terrain has its fingers round the coves of Concha, Chengue, Gairaca, Neguange, Cinto, Guachaquita and Palmarito. More than 15,000ha include 5,000ha of mainland and 1,200ha of coastal waters. Bathers should take precautions at beaches with strong currents, including Arrecifes and Cañaveral. The safest waters are found at La Piscina.

Neguange can be reached by the road to Palangana, which also goes to Gayraca and Playa Coralina. Through Cañaveral you can walk to the beautiful beaches of Arrecifes and El Cabo, or go to Pueblito to see the old Tayrona settlement, Chairama. Los Naranjos can be accessed from Cañaveral along some leafy trails amidst dense vegetation, or from a path leading out from Bahía Concha. From Los Naranjos there are numerous tracks to the mouth of the Piedras al Mar River, Playa del Muerto, Playa Coralina, Bonito Gordo, Concha Bay, Chengue Cove, Gayraca Cove, Cinto, Guachaquita. From Arrecifes, a half-hour trail connects with La Piscina, a deep bay with waters that are calm enough to swim and snorkel. A 20-minute walk leads on to the stunning beaches of Cabo San Juan de la Guía where a one-hour trail climbs up to Chairama (Pueblito). Tayrona's park rangers can provide details and maps of these and other trails. El Zaíno heralds the entrance to the park 34km east of Santa Marta, where a 4km paved road connects to Cañaveral. At Cañaveral there's an administrative centre and a place to organise horses and a guide. Be sure to check about routes that are off-limits due to bad weather or high seas.

Getting there and away To get to Cañaveral take a **minibus** from Santa Marta to Palomino and get off at El Zaíno (10,000COP, 1¼ hours) – they leave every half-hour from downtown. A **jeep** ferries passengers (every half-hour) between El Zaíno and Cañaveral (5,000COP, 10 minutes) with the walk taking about 45 minutes.

Where to stay and eat In Cañaveral, 11 park-run hillside thatch-roofed *cabañas* called **Ecohabs** (*www.ecohabsantamarta.com*) enjoy magnificent views out to sea. Each can accommodate two to four people and have been designed to reflect Tayrona style with wooden floors and simple beds cooled by coastal breezes. A two-bed cabin costs 600,000COP per night.

Below the staggered collection of Ecohab buildings there is a rather nice open-sided **restaurant** (**$$**) that serves excellent meals, such as seafood rice, lobster and grilled fish.

Cañaveral is also the venue for the park-run **campsite** (8,000COP per person). You'll need a tent, a mattress, sleeping bag and torch along with food and cooking implements should you not want to eat in the restaurant. The place is very, very basic and only for hardened backpackers with little regard for comfort. Book through the Parques Nacionales de Colombia website (*www.parquesnacionales.gov.co*).

BEACH RESORTS TO ESCAPE FROM IT ALL

Tayrona's beaches are rightly famous and you might want to try out the boutique-style resorts which have been popping up along the coastline from Santa Marta into the Guajira department.

For the moneyed bohemian crowd we can recommend the **Playa Koralia** (*Km47; www.koralia.com; $$$*). A dozen or so comfortable *cabañas* are situated along sand paths and set back from the beach, each decorated with a different culture in mind. The idea here is a holistic all-inclusive exclusive retreat with spa and locally sourced food. Rumour has it that the Playa Koralia is a long-time favourite of Shakira's.

Also along the coast you'll find the **Costeño Beach** (*Km36; www. costenosurf.com; $$*), owned by two Canadian brothers Colm and Brian. This establishment is aimed at a more youthful crowd and it does not disappoint. Costeño Beach is the only surf camp and eco-lodge operating on the Caribbean coast of Colombia with five beautiful rooms built from the finest local wood by skilled artisan builders. All rooms have private bathrooms, ocean views, comfortable beds, and solar-powered electricity. There are beach huts and hammocks available. Delicious meals are served on their on-site restaurant (based on the chef's daily menu), and there are surfboard rentals (18 to choose from) and surf classes if needed. Another high-quality boutique offering on the beach close to the town of Buritaca is the **Hotel Merecumbe** (*Km47; www.merecumbehotel.com; $$$*) with 11 beautifully equipped *cabañas*. But if you are looking to get back to nature try the **Cabañas Los Angeles** in its glorious palm-fronded rusticity (*Km33; www.cabanasantamartalosangeles.com; $*).

As the road to Venezuela winds its way along the coast you'll come to a truck-stop of a town known as Palomino. Palomino itself is not particularly interesting but it's the beachfront hotels which have injected life into this region found just within the departmental border of the Guajira. Take your pick from the highly recommended **Reserva El Matuy** (*www.elmatuy. com; $$$*), the **Eco Sirena Hostel** (*www.ecosirena.com; $$*), **Playa la Roca Ecohotel** (*www.playalarocaecohotel.com; $$$*), or the **Dreamer Hostel** (*www.thedreamerhostel.com; $$*).

Getting here is easy enough. Just catch any of the buses heading along the coast to Riohacha or Venezuela from Santa Marta and remind the driver at which km you need to get off!

In Arrecifes, there are two accommodation options. **Finca El Paraíso** (m *310 691 3626*; **$**) sits close to the beach and offers cheap rustic cabins, covered hammocks and camping. **Rancho Lindo** (**$**) is on the approach trail to the beach and offers the same basic accommodation. Both have simple restaurants that serve freshly cooked inexpensive meals as well as snacks and drinks.

Further west, a 10-minute walk along the beach, is the rustic lodge **Bucarú** (**$**). Basic *cabañas*, hammocks and camping are also offered here; again it's pretty cheap. It's owned by the same people as Finca El Paraíso.

At the end of the trail in Cabo San Juan de la Guía you'll find a cheap little backpacker haunt with **hammocks** at 10,000COP apiece.

Just before the park entrance, a string of small rustic restaurants offer local dishes, including grouper soup at 5,000COP.

Other practicalities There is rarely any mobile-phone signal in the park, so don't rely on this. Two small kiosks – Refresqueria Anita and Refresqueria Abril – are located immediately outside the entrance. Both sell bottles of cold water, sodas and snacks. Pack plenty of bug spray and drinking water.

MINCA (*Telephone code 5*) Located at 650m on the slopes of the Sierra Nevada de Santa Marta, the town of Minca may only have a population of 600 but it is the centre of one of the most exciting birding regions in the world. Birdwatchers from all over the world visit Minca, a mountainous settlement that makes a great base to explore the surrounding birding paradise. Surrounding forests are also home to indigenous Kogui tribes who fled higher into the mountains and have managed to remain isolated to this day as the only tribe unconquered by the Spanish. This reclusive group of about 12,000 people have a deep distrust of cultures born out of the Spanish invasion (pages 26–7). However, Kogui culture is evident throughout the town and is highly respected.

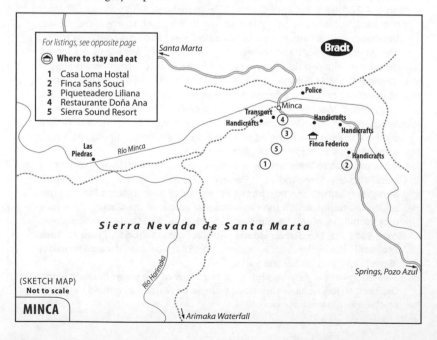

For listings, see opposite page

🏠 **Where to stay and eat**
1 Casa Loma Hostal
2 Finca Sans Souci
3 Piqueteadero Liliana
4 Restaurante Doña Ana
5 Sierra Sound Resort

Things are still done the old-fashioned way in flower-filled Minca, including the cultivation, harvesting and roasting of the local coffee. MinCafe is made entirely by hand from the planting under thick cloudforest to picking on the steep slopes. The town has three grades of MinCafe which is sold throughout the town along with aromatic herbs and shrubs. The town itself is full of lovely old clay houses, and has a beautiful old church with a friendly padre. There are no ATMs, so it is essential to bring cash.

Safety In the mid 1990s, Minca suffered at the hands of paramilitaries. Peace was restored to the area in 2000, although the town remained under peaceful paramilitary control until March 2006. It was then that the forces demobilised in a deal with the Colombian government. Today Minca is becoming a favourite destination for many mountain bikers, bird enthusiasts and hikers.

It is not advisable to attempt to photograph a Kogui tribe member without asking permission – they may not have seen a camera before and could believe it to be a weapon. Even Kogui who are familiar with photography may believe that taking an image is stealing their soul. Minca is surrounded by Kogui history and trails around the Río Minca contain shards of Amerindian pottery. In the event that any objects are spotted, it is not advisable to touch or remove them. This could be construed as an act of theft or grave robbing.

Getting there and around Minca is reached by an hourly **pick-up truck** from Santa Marta for 7,000COP. To find transport to Minca take a **taxi** to 'La Bomba' (petrol station at the entrance to Minca) or to 'la Linea de tren en Yuca' in Santa Marta; from here you can take a private taxi for around 30,000COP or a motorcycle for 7,000COP.

Tour guides Numerous locals offer guide services to birding spots and trails; just ask at the **Sans Souci Restaurant** (m *310 590 9213*) in the centre of town.

Where to stay and eat See map, page 446.

La Loma (2 private *cabañas* & camping) m 313 808 6134; e info@lalomaminca.com; www.lalomaminca.com. Brought to you by the same owners of the Casa Loma (see below), this offshoot has been designed for those seeking out a bit more privacy & to really get back to nature. Set in the verdant environs of the Sierra Nevada hills just a bit beyond the hostel, you can switch off, enjoy yoga classes, a massage & even participate in Spanish lessons. There's a vegetarian restaurant on site too. **$$**

Sierra Sound Resort (15 rooms) m 311 600 1614; www.mincahotelsierrasound.com. This sweet little *finca* offers nice, clean rooms with private bathrooms as well as a terrace restaurant that serves traditional Colombian & Italian cuisine. There is also a TV room & a very pretty garden containing lots of mature fruit trees. **$$**

Casa Loma Hostal (5 rooms, camping & hammock space) For contact details see *La Loma*, above. From Minca, walk past the church & turn left past Chiqui's Pizzaria. Follow the path for 2mins until you see a sign on your left. Follow the path to the top, around 10mins. Up above the town you'll find the Casa Loma, a stylishly bohemian, friendly & attractive place from which to base yourself for treks, birdwatching & relaxation in nature. **$**

Finca Sans Souci (sleeps 20) m 310 590 9213; e sanssouciminca@yahoo.com. Simple rooms & good food make this smallholding a decent base in Minca – there's even use of the kitchen for those who prefer to self-cater. The German owner is also a good source of local info & will organise mountain bikes, horseriding & local guides. It is also possible to pitch a tent here in the grounds. **$**

✕ Piqueteadero Liliana ✎421 9911. Expect fried chicken, pork, *empanadas* & *arepas* at this little food joint along with a good selection of *jugos naturales* (fresh juices). **$**

✕ Restaurante Doña Ana ✎421 9977. Try a bowl of delicious *sancocho de gallina Criolla* (soup) at this town-centre restaurant to taste it at its very best. **$**

What to see and do

Birds The Sierra Nevada de Santa Marta has about the same number of bird varieties as can be found in the whole North American continent. More than 620 known bird species inhabit the region, including the yellow-billed toucanet, Santa Marta warbler, white-lored warbler, Santa Marta sabrewing, vermilion cardinal, Santa Marta woodstar, coppery emerald, white-tailed starfrontlet, rufous-browed conebill, streak-capped spinetail, blue-knobbed curassow, Santa Marta antpitta, slender-billed inezia, sapphire-bellied hummingbird, buffy hummingbird, tyrian metaltail, bronze-brown cowbird, yellow-crowned whitestart, Santa Marta bush-tyrant, black-fronted wood-quail, chestnut-winged chachalaca, bearded helmetcrest, band-tailed guan, white-tipped quetzal, chestnut piculet, Santa Marta parakeet, black-backed thornbill, black-backed antshrike, brown-rumped tapaculo, Santa Marta tapaculo, white-whiskered spinetail, rusty-headed spinetail and Santa Marta wren – to name many. Over 70 migratory species from the US and Canada journey to this Endemic Bird Area (EBA B08), including red-tailed hawk, broad-winged hawk, orange-billed nightingale-thrush, Swainson's thrush, chimney swift, common nighthawk, yellow-billed cuckoo, olive-sided flycatcher, eastern wood pewee, black-throated blue warbler, bay-breasted warbler, cerulean warbler and grey catbird.

Las Piedras (The Stones) A 15-minute walk from the centre of Minca leads up to this large rock formation where freshwater pools offer an inviting spot to take a dip. The warm waters of the Río Harimaka meet the colder Río Minca and create natural whirlpools. To reach this stunning spot take the road out past the church and follow the signs to the Buruake and Doña Ana restaurants. Continue for about 500m beyond Doña Ana to the confluence of the two rivers.

Pozo Azul (Blue Pond) A 45-minute hike from Minca takes you to a pristine area of natural swimming pools and waterfalls. Pass the first shallow pool and head to the deeper one to submerge yourself completely.

Viña Victoria Located on an original coffee plantation up here in the Sierra Nevada, the owners will show you around the antique machinery used in the production of coffee. Here you can learn the process, get involved and try some of this exportation-quality brew (5,000COP per person).

La Cascada Arimaka (Arimaka Waterfall) Heading east out from Minca, the beautiful 45-minute walk along a leafy trail from the centre of Minca leads to a hidden waterfall that was once a sacred location for the Kogui people. After the Kogui fled to higher ground they used other sites for ceremonial rituals, and today the Arimaka Waterfall is used purely as a place to swim. Dark, craggy rocks and deep cool pools are surrounded by clay thought to have curative qualities.

El Dorado Bird Reserve Just a 90-minute jeep ride up the Sierra Nevada from Minca, the reserve is popular with birders from all over the world. For more information see box, page 8.

CIUDAD PERDIDA (LOST CITY)

One of the largest pre-Columbian archaeological sites discovered in the Americas, Ciudad Perdida lay undiscovered on the remote northern slopes of the Sierra Nevada de Santa Marta until 1972. A series of stone steps led treasure-hunter (*guaquero*) Florentino Sepúveda and his two sons to the abandoned city believed to have been built between the 11th and 14th centuries but with origins dating to the 7th century. They named it 'Green Hell' due to the extraordinary effort it had required to reach it through thick mountain jungle. Officials revealed the site's existence in 1975 when its gold figurines and ceramic urns began to appear on the local black market. Fights broke out as people rushed to loot it, resulting in a military crackdown in 1976. Archaeologists were sent in to study and survey the entire city.

It appears the site was once a major political and economic centre, housing 2,000–4,000 people over 2km². Known as Teyuna by its indigenous inhabitants, Ciudad Perdida sits on the Río Buritaca at an altitude of 950–1,330m. It consists of a series of 169 terraces carved into the mountainside with a network of tiled roads and small circular plazas. The entrance to the city is a climb of some 1,200 stone steps through dense jungle. Today the Lost City is partially overgrown but this seems to add to its character. It was apparently abandoned during the Spanish conquest and although local Arhuaco, Kogui and Assario tribes knew of its existence, they told no-one.

Getting there and around It is not possible to do the trip out to Ciudad Perdida alone, and there are a number of tour operators in Santa Marta authorised to take tourists to the Ciudad Perdida: **Expotur** (*Calle 18, No 2A–7 Taganga;* \ *421 9577; http://expotur-eco.com*), **Magic Tours** (*Calle 14, No 1B–50;* \ *421 9429; http:// magictourcolombia.com*), **Turcol** (*Calle 13, No 3–13 San Francisco Plaza;* \ *421 2256; http://turcoltravel.com*) and **Guias y Baquianos** (*Hotel Miramar, Calle 10, No C1C–59;* \ *431 9667*). The cost is around 700,000COP per person, which includes the charges made for ICANH, indigenous communities and small farmers (page 435). Porters are part of the deal too but only carry the cooking gear, not backpacks. Travellers should be sure to pack waterproof clothing, a torch, insect repellent and a water bottle. They should also bring a medical kit. Although the Lost City is just 40km from Santa Marta as the crow flies, the journey has to make allowances for an absence of access roads to navigate thick, impenetrable jungle and impassable mountains. It is a hard slog across muddy terrain that begins with a three-day arduous trek uphill. Tour groups are usually four–12 people with departures almost daily, owing to its popularity.

VALLEDUPAR *Telephone code 5*

Located in the department of Cesar, southeast of Santa Marta and almost directly south of Riohacha, Valledupar (population 500,000) is a lesser-known important city which is coming into her own as a burgeoning tourist destination. Founded in 1550 by the conquistador Hernando de Santana, the city is strategically located at the southern base of the Sierra Nevada Mountains and alongside the Guatipuri and Cesar rivers. The city grew as an important agricultural and livestock hub and then subsequently enjoyed greater riches as the mine of El Cerrejon produced more and more coal. Through the 1980s, 90s and early 2000s, Valledupar suffered from the violence and political unrest that was strafing Colombia at the time. The armed conflict brought to the region an increase in guerrilla activities in the region causing many people to flee their lands and move to other cities. Later, the United Self Defense paramilitary group (AUC) took control of these lands, forcing out the guerrillas but instilling their own form of terror. Times have changed now, though, and Valledupar could claim to be the most organised of Colombia's Caribbean cities. Most visitors here immediately note the lack of rubbish strewn around, as found in other regional hubs, in addition to the well-maintained pavements and roads, and the proliferation of tree-lined avenues. The principal reason to visit Valledupar would be to attend the raucous and whisky-soaked Vallenato Festival (see box, page 107), but outside of this date, the city can be enjoyed too. Visitors can swim in the cool waters of the Guatipuri River, take trips out to the immense boulders at the nearby town of La Mina and explore the rhythms of the accordion-heavy *vallenato* music that finds its roots here.

WHERE TO STAY AND EAT

Casa Rosalia (5 rooms) Calle Grande (Calle 16), No 10–10; 574 4129; www.lacasarosalia. com. By far & away the top-end boutique option in Valledupar, the emphasis here is on the details in the 5-room Casa Rosalia. Guests will be enchanted by the tranquillity & design of the establishment which offers a real escape from the bustle of downtown Valledupar. **$$$**

Aqua Hostal Valledupar (sleeps 30) Carrera 7, No 13a–42; 570 0439; www. aquahostalvalledupar.com. The Aqua Hostal is perhaps best described as offering the 'boutique' *hostal* experience in that it is very well thought out, is well located & oozes charm. **$**

Provincia Casa de Huespedes (8 rooms) Calle 16A, No 5–25; 580 0558; www.provinciavalledupar.com. Your best-value accommodation in Valledupar is undoubtedly the Provincia which is located 1 block from the central plaza, is fully equipped with private rooms & dorms & is a Mecca for information about activities & sites in the region. **$**

Restaurante Bar Café Plaza Mayor, Carrera 6, No 15–66, Plaza Alfonso Lopez; 580 9267. Popular due to its location on the main plaza, this bar/café is seductive with her open areas & offering of live music on w/ends. Food is a mix of steaks & Caribbean cuisine but if you don't fancy eating, just enjoy a cocktail in the ample back patio. **$$**

Terraza Calle Grande, Carrera 7, No 1–85; 570 5757. Offering your standard tasty Colombian platters you could do a lot worse for a decent meal & chilled drink in Valledupar. The patrons know what visitors come here for & it is undeniably the unrivalled views over the city. **$$**

LA GUAJIRA *Telephone code 5*

(*www.laguajira.gov.co*) Colombia's most northerly department is populated mainly by Wayúu Amerindians and their descendants and is distinctly different from any other region – from the guttural language and dialects of the Guajiros and their walnut-coloured skin to the coloured robes adorned with pom-poms and face-blackening to protect the skin from the fierceness of the sun. Dry, arid deserts dominate the peninsula, bounded by the Caribbean Sea to the north and west and the Gulf of Venezuela to the southeast. Although much of this sparsely populated peninsula lies in Colombia, La Guajira extends into Venezuelan territory.

Approximately 120,000 Guajiros have lived in the region since before the Spanish conquest. After the Spanish arrival, the Guajiros adopted horses and cattle from them and lived a pastoral lifestyle. They also acquired weapons from the Spanish and built temporary wattle-and-daub huts in the inhospitable barren desert – but were far from isolated. Many became involved in trade and smuggling and much later lived a life of co-existence with pick-up trucks and wage labour on Venezuelan farms. In the late 1990s, large-scale mining began in La Guajira, severely disrupting the livelihoods of the Guajira people and placing their culture and lifestyle under threat. However, under the leadership of Governor José Luis Gonzalez – himself a Wayúu Amerindian – the department has positioned itself as Colombia's centre of cultural tourism. Considerable investment has gone towards the preservation of sacred sites and conservation of local cultures and traditions. La Guajira people also have a greater political voice and are intent on ensuring their rituals survive. As a result, visitors will find it easy to access some of the seven indigenous groups that inhabit the province, including the Wayúu and Kogui peoples. La Guajira is also an excellent place to buy high-quality woven crafts, including hammocks, basketry and shoulder bags (*mochilas*). A growing number of folkloric festivals also allow tourists to learn more about the region's unique ethnic roots, language, societal structures and proudly upheld traditions.

THE ROAD TO RIOHACHA Riohacha is the riverside capital of the La Guajira department; a former pearl-diving settlement and still a regional maritime hub. The 166km journey northeast to Riohacha on the road from Santa Marta initially skirts the palm-flanked foothills of the magnificent **Sierra Nevada de Santa Marta**, a terrain of lush vegetation so rich and fertile the locals say a rusty nail could sprout green shoots. A successive string of flower-filled towns sit surrounded by carpets of emerald foliage with even the most humble dwelling blessed with a garden of healthy crops. Vast banana plantations tumble down to the sea from roads hemmed with vegetable stalls and fruit. Cattle, horses and tunic-clad Amerindian farm workers dot large, verdant fields. Sausages hang in every doorway of the little village of **Pericoaguardo**, a community with a strong livestock tradition. Then it's on to **Palomino**, a town that signifies the border between the departments of Magdalena and La Guajira, 42km from the coast. Stand by the **Río Palomino** on a clear day to enjoy fine views of the Sierra Nevada's highest peak, Pico Cristóbal Colón (5,775m). It's a good spot to stop for breakfast at a little roadside joint, **La Saga** – a plate of *arepas*, grilled ham, juice, eggs, toast and steak washed down with sweet coffee costs less than 5,000COP. A little further up the road just before Río Ancho there's another good-value stop-off, **Restaurante Glario**, close to a sign advertising *cabañas* for rent.

After crossing the Río Caña into the bustling agricultural hub of **Mingueo** with its permanent food market and fresh-fish stalls, you'll see a ramshackle wooden food joint that appears to be nearing collapse. Parada doesn't look much but it offers good rustic food at low prices amidst palms, pecking chickens and the sound of a crackling transistor radio. After a stretch of waterlogged pasture and grazing mules, enter the fruit-growing village of **Dibulla**, 53km from Riohacha, where the ground is suddenly drier and yellow rather than green. A brand-new paved road takes over at **Pelucha** as the surrounding forest gradually becomes less tropical and more scrub. At about 20km from Riohacha, take a left-hand turn down a mangrove-flanked road signed to the village of **Camarones** (meaning 'prawns'). Cross a small bridge past saltpans and freshwater lakes that are home to flamingos and seabirds hunting for shrimp (see box, page 455). Every little kiosk and restaurant in Camarones sells prawns in one guise or another – try the mural-covered **Restaurante Mira Mar** right down on the beach for good local dishes and incredible, uninterrupted sea views. After the detour rejoin the road to Riohacha, a stretch that becomes uglier the closer you get and passes numerous stalls selling knock-off Venezuelan petrol in cola bottles.

RIOHACHA *Telephone code 5*

After decades of living in the past and letting the present die, Riohacha is finally beginning to look more like a department capital. The city's once mournful central streets and grubby buildings have had a cheery facelift. Spotless pastel-coloured plazas have been built where filth and decay once prevailed. Riohacha still has its neglected, rundown areas but it can now, at least, hold its head up high. Founded by Nicolás Federman in 1535 as an important pearl-trading port, Riohacha has another commercial focus today, namely contraband from Venezuela. The city's post-colonial fortunes have been mixed, but largely depressing, the result of a distinct lack of interest by Colombia's central government. In the early 1900s, Riohacha had a fishing fleet of 150 but just 40 years later this had dwindled to fewer than half a dozen. Most of the inhabitants are 'in the trade' today as it is easier and more lucrative. The result, however, is that few people are prepared to work hard to develop local resources. In its darkest days, Riohacha's dirty, rubbish-strewn streets were home to neighbourhoods of single-storey hovels – many containing Scandinavian fridges, Italian coffee-makers and piles of boxed electronic goods and designer brands unseen in Bogotá.

Riohacha was inhabited by La Guajira's Wayúu people when the territory was sighted by Spanish sailor Alonso de Ojeda in 1498 from the sea. During its time as a major pearl-shipment centre it was the subject of many attacks, including one led by Francis Drake in 1596. It became the capital of the newly created La Guajira department in 1964. A rather nice palm-scattered beach, some interesting historic buildings and a strong handicraft tradition form the backbone of Riohacha's tourism ambitions.

GETTING THERE AND AROUND The city's Aeropuerto Almirante Padilla (✆ 727 3855) is located just west of the town and is well served by local taxis and *colectivos*. Twice-daily Avianca (✆ 727 3914) **flights** to and from Bogotá are the only option at the time of writing. Bogotá departures are at 10.15 and Riohacha flights leave at noon.

Much of Riohacha can be covered **on foot** with the town's **cyclotaxi** fleet a cheap and fun option. The city's motorised taxis are easy to spot along the main drag (✆ 728 5555) – expect to pay 300COP for a cross-town trip and 10,000COP to the airport.

TOURIST INFORMATION
ℹ Riohacha Oficina de Turismo Calle 2, No 8–38; ✆ 727 2333; ⏲ 08.00–noon & 14.00–18.00 Mon–Fri

Riohacha city website www.riohacha.gov.co

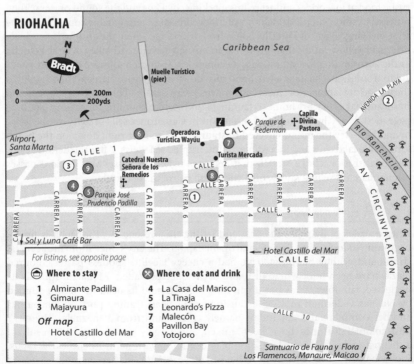

RIOHACHA

Caribbean Sea

Muelle Turístico (pier)

Airport, Santa Marta

Operadora Turística Wayúu

Parque de Federman

Capilla Divina Pastora

Turista Mercada

Catedral Nuestra Señora de los Remedios

Parque José Prudencio Padilla

Sol y Luna Café Bar

Hotel Castillo del Mar

AVENIDA LA PLAYA

Río Ranchería

AV CIRCUNVALACION

Santuario de Fauna y Flora Los Flamencos, Manaure, Maicao ▶

For listings, see opposite page

⌂ Where to stay
1 Almirante Padilla
2 Gimaura
3 Majayura
Off map
  Hotel Castillo del Mar

✗ Where to eat and drink
4 La Casa del Marisco
5 La Tinaja
6 Leonardo's Pizza
7 Malecón
8 Pavillon Bay
9 Yotojoro

TOUR GUIDE AND OPERATORS Although a guide isn't necessary for Riohacha itself, it is imperative to engage someone with a 4x4 and some local knowledge if travelling further north. Much of the journey is through inhospitable desert where an absence of defined tracks means getting easily lost is a genuine threat. On the basis of reliability, good humour and musical taste, **José Barros** (m 315 749 1431) at Tourismo Ecológico comes highly recommended. Not only does he navigate the ever-changing desert trails with ease and a smile but he also dances as he drives. Also recommended are the good people at **Kai Eco Travel** as well, who run their offices in Riohacha at the Hotel Castillo del Mar (*Calle 9A, No 15–352*; m *311 436 2830*; e *info@kaiecotravel.com; www.kaiecotravel.com*).

A growing number of large- and mid-sized tour companies operate out of Riohacha, including **Aviatur** (\ 728 7523), **Guajira Magica** (\ 728 5758; e *guarijamagica@hotmail.com*), **Guajira Tours** (\ 727 3385), **Guajira Viva** (\ 727 0607; e *guarijaviva@hotmail.com*), and **Sol-Era Viajes y Turismo** (\ 727 2317; e *sol-eraviajes@yahoo.es*).

🏠 **WHERE TO STAY** *See map, page 452.*
Riohacha's hotels are located near the beach on Avenida la Playa or in the streets that lead off it, but the city isn't known for its fine accommodation, so be prepared to shop around.

🏠 **Hotel Almirante Padilla** (30 rooms) Carrera 6, No 3–29; \ 727 2328; e hotelalmirantepadilla@hotmail.com. Expect clean but bland rooms at this high-rise hotel, just a block or so from the beachfront main drag. It's got a restaurant & bar, & rooms have AC & TV. **$$**

🏠 **Hotel Gimaura** (42 rooms) Av la Marina; \ 728 6656. This hotel sits on the banks of the Río Ranchería adjacent to the beach & over the Río Ranchería Bridge. Expect the best service in town & comfortable AC rooms close to the pier, restaurants & tourist office. **$$**

🏠 **Hotel Majayura** (32 rooms) Carrera 10, No 1–40; \ 728 8666. This reasonable mid-range hotel is set back from the beachfront strip at the opposite end of the pier, 100m from the shoreline. Rooms are clean & have TV & AC but the staff are indifferent. A restaurant serves decent food but has a blaring TV – try the little bars & restaurants opposite for a more enjoyable ambience. **$$**

🏠 **Hotel Castillo del Mar** (25 rooms) Calle 9a, No 15–352; \ 727 5043. At one end of town, this hotel has been here for more than 30 years & perhaps shows it. However, you'll be staying here if you sign up with Kai Eco Travel for a trip into the Alta Guajira. **$**

✖ **WHERE TO EAT AND DRINK** *See map, page 452.*
Typical dishes can be found in plentiful supply in the town's numerous rustic local eateries, including rice-and-shrimp, grilled goat, goat stew (*friche*) and a minced shrimp-and-onion meal (*salpión de camarones*). Opposite the pier you'll find a string of fast-food, fried-chicken and pizza joints, including **Leonardo's Pizza**. Try the nearby **Restaurante Malecón** (\ 727 6762) opposite the park for something a tad more refined, the neighbouring upmarket **Yotojoro**, the seafood joint **La Casa del Marisco** next door or fish specialist **La Tinaja**. The consistently good **Pavillon Bay y Restaurante** (\ 727 5555) is four blocks north. Candy sellers on the beach boast an array of sticky-sweet treats typical of the region – listen out for the singsong cry from women who carry vast pots on their heads.

ENTERTAINMENT AND NIGHTLIFE Rather surprisingly, the typically machismo town of Riohacha also has a highly evident community of transsexuals. They don't don girly garb but wear typical Colombiano male attire – whilst sporting a full face of make-up. For a more mainstream night, head to the **Sol y Luna Café Bar** on the main drag opposite the beach – it serves up good, cheap cocktails and light bites. For a lively full-on noisy fun-fest head to the **Restaurante Malecón** after 23.00 – once the diners are finished this place rocks till daylight. Some funky little tequila bars and grilled-meat joints can be found along Calle 10 opposite the Hotel Majayura.

SHOPPING There is no shortage of vendors, stalls and hawkers selling cheap handicrafts around town, with bracelets, bags, hammocks and beaded jewellery the most popular crafts. The tourist office also has a small craft retail section but this tends to be pricey. One of the best-stocked independent stores specialising in Wayúu crafts is the **Operadora Turística Wayúu** on Calle 1, No 4–35 (✆ 728 7720; e operadoraturisticawayuu@hotmail.com). Another good option on the main drag is the **Turista Mercada** (✆ 728 3684; e turismoyelisgomez@hotmail.com), a small shop packed high with sombreros, Wayúu crafts and bags, run by helpful Yeliz Solano.

OTHER PRACTICALITIES Most of Riohacha's **banks** are set back a block from the beach in a long succession of buildings with ATM booths outside. A couple of **internet cafés** are located on the main drag near to the tourist office.

WHAT TO SEE AND DO There are not a huge number of sightseeing attractions as such in Riohacha but a few points of interest are worthy of a closer look, including the **Catedral Nuestra Señora de los Remedios** (Our Lady of the Remedies Cathedral), the city's principal church. Close by, the **Muelle Turístico** (Muelle de Santa Lucía) – Riohacha's 1,200m, 70-year-old wooden pier – is a popular promenade with strolling, ice-cream-eating families, hand-holding teens and snoozing elders. Thrill-seeking children jump into the water below amidst much shrieking and laughing. The pier fell into disrepair 50 years ago and began to rot into the sea. Today it has been restored to its former glory and is the tourist centrepiece of the main drag and a great place for a *paseo de la playa*. Nearby, the old **Capilla Divina Pastora** (Divine Shepherd Chapel) sits in the **Parque de Federman** (Federman Park). A stretch of pavement adjacent is inlaid with symbols and flanked with six fine columns adorned with mosaic designs and images relating to the Wayúu belief system connected to Mother Earth.

Festivals and events
Fiestas Nuestra Señora de los Remedios (February) Riohacha's main festival brings crowds of locals out on to the streets in celebration of its patron saint – and sees hotel prices soar.

Feria Comercial Artesanal y Turística de la Guajira (July) This artisan extravaganza showcases the region's rich handicraft tradition.

AROUND RIOHACHA

SANTUARIO DE FAUNA Y FLORA LOS FLAMENCOS (FLAMINGO FLORA AND FAUNA SANCTUARY) At Boca de Camarones 20 minutes south of Riohacha, the sanctuary is a nesting ground for large numbers of small salmon-pink flamingos. Large numbers of birds build mud nests in this oppressively hot 7,682ha mangrove forest around the areas of Manzanillo, Laguna Grande, Ciénaga del Navío Quebrado and Tocoromanes. Gondola-style canoes are hired for 50,000COP (with a boatman) from the visitor centre for the 45-minute journey out to the nesting zone. Boarding the boat requires wading out into the water across very slippery weed-covered sandbanks. The sun is also incredibly fierce out on the open waters, so pack plenty

The village of Camarones is rich in birdlife with rufous-vented chachalaca easily spotted in the early morning when they feed on the maize thrown down for the chickens. In the surrounding countryside, just beyond the village, Orinocan saltator, Caribbean hornero, bare-eyed pigeon, green-rumped parrotlet, scaled dove and brown-throated parakeet have been sighted. Thick, cactus-rich scrub is the preferred domain of the black-crested antshrike, vermilion cardinal, straight-billed woodcreeper, buffy hummingbird, red-billed emerald, pileated finch, chestnut piculet, white-fringed antwren, crested bobwhite and red-crowned woodpecker. Beyond the dry scrubland is a seasonally flooded flat plain favoured by terns, cormorants, herons, egrets and Ibis. It's also a good place to sight wood stork, roseate spoonbill and greater flamingo. White-rumped sandpiper has been recorded here.

of water, sun block and a hat – and binoculars are a must. Shrimp farmers fish the lake with all surrounding communities 100% reliant on this economically. Eagle-eyed tourists have spotted frogs and snakes in the mangroves, including large boa. Look out for flying fish in the Laguna Grande.

CENTRO DE EDUCACIÓN E INVESTIGACIÓN DE TORTUGAS (TURTLE EDUCATION CENTRE) (06.00–17.00 daily; free admission) Attached to the flamingo sanctuary is a small turtle-conservation centre complete with hatcheries, nurseries and clinic. Since 1977, it has collected approximately 40,000 turtle eggs from local beaches. Today it draws almost 5,000 visitors a year and regularly hosts conservation talks and workshops.

SALINAS DE MANAURE (MANAURE SALT MINES) With its charming waterfront and stunning views, it's difficult to believe that the pretty little seaside town of Manaure is home to the most important and extensive salt mines in Colombia. More than 700,000 tonnes of salt are mined here each year across 4,200ha and these vast silvery mounds are quite astounding and can be seen on the coastline beyond the beach. A pleasant plaza is just a 50m walk from the waterfront where children skip the lazy waves. Local boat owners sometimes ply for tourist trade near hammock-strung *cabañas*. Try the *chicken a la plancha* with *frijoles*, rice, plantain and salad ($) at **Restaurante y Panadería** in the centre of town.

RANCHERÍA EGNOTURÍSTICA WAYÚU UTTA (m 312 687 8237; e reservas@ rancheriautta.com; www.rancheriautta.com; admission 20,000COP, must be pre-booked. Overnight stays accommodated in rustic cabañas for 60,000COP pp, including all meals. There are 11 cabañas & space for around 120 chinchorros or hammocks.) This small Wayúu community have opened up to tourism and offer talks, tours and demonstrations to provide an insight into the origins of their beliefs and culture. Utta means 'Star of Spring' and the settlement is run along traditional lines. In this matriarchal society, the oldest woman has the greatest power and is highly respected. She has the final word and wears black pom-poms as a symbol of her status. When a girl is born there is much merriment. Once married, a woman is the controlling force with the husband joining her family. Domestic issues are also resolved within the community. If a wife fears infidelity on the part of her husband she seeks help from the *piache* (medicinal leader) who then concocts a potion using plants and herbs to win him back. Negative

thoughts and insecurity are banished by the wearing of a stone in the waistband. Women are schooled in marriage from seven years old. During ceremonies and celebrations the Wayúu drink a potent liquor made from fermented trupillo fruit. Visitors are plied with the mega-strong *chirrinchi* during their tour and are also treated to dancing, singing and traditional food.

THE TURTLES OF LA GUAJIRA

For many people, the closest they will ever get to a sea turtle is the creature gliding through a tank in their local aquarium. Adult sea turtles are elusive at best, and the majority of hatchlings crawl from their beaches and into the surf, disappearing from human radar. Adult sea turtles spend most of their lives in the water migrating, foraging or mating. Females will return to the beach in order to lay eggs, and males will occasionally leave the water to 'bask'. With the use of radio-tracking devices and international tagging, researchers have created a map of migration routes and better understand the sea turtle's life at sea.

Female sea turtles lay their nests in sand and never return, leaving their offspring to hatch, evacuate the nest, avoid predation and find the ocean all by themselves. Once the hatchlings emerge, they instinctively move into the water as quickly as possible. After the initial arduous journey ends, the turtles become very passive, drifting in the water instead of actively swimming. Their carapaces (shells) are still quite soft, leaving them defenceless, so hatchlings are a snack for predators, including sharks, large fish and sea birds.

In their first nesting season, sexually mature sea turtles migrate into poorly defined courtship/mating areas, which are generally much closer to the nesting beaches. After insemination male turtles return to their foraging areas and females move into nesting sites in the same region as their birth. The belief that a turtle has an uncanny ability to return to the exact beach where it was born is an exaggeration. Sea turtles do in fact return to the region of their birth (impressive considering their foraging habitats could easily be 1,000km away) but not necessarily the beach where they hatched. Within her birthing region, a female turtle selects a nesting beach (utilising an unknown selection process) and returns to that very precise area for her successive nesting seasons approximately every three to five years.

Sea turtles nest at night, although there are specific exceptions to that rule, including but not limited to *arribadas*. However, it is still important to note that as cold-blooded reptiles, the majority of turtles nest during the cooler night-time hours, because of a decreased risk of overheating under the hot sun. A female crawls ashore, a laborious process during which she may change her mind and return to the sea for no apparent reason. She may also select a nesting site (habitat choice is varied by species – green turtles and leatherback turtles lay in open sandy areas, while hawksbills often lay under trees and shrub cover), often facing away or parallel to the water. After selecting a site, she clears a surprisingly deep body pit with long, sweeping movements of her front flippers. When the pit is cleared sufficiently, the turtle begins digging her nest hole. This amazing process begins by her first easing one rear flipper into the sand, scooping up a 'flipper-full', and tossing it to the side. Then, she immediately places the flipper on top of the loose sand, effectively keeping it from sliding back into the nest. This process is continued as she alternates flippers while digging. This is a lengthy procedure that eventually results in a flask-shaped nest. The turtle will keep digging until

THE ROAD TO CABO DE LA VELA The road to Cabo de la Vela (Sail Cape) crosses the Ahuyama Desert and is not for the feeble or fragile. Unmade, unmarked, treacherous desert trenches are hard going for the toughest 4x4 on the last stretch to the cape (known as Jepira in the language of the Wayúu). It's relentlessly bumpy but exhilarating; just check the vehicle has decent shock absorption and air conditioning.

her flippers cannot reach any more sand and never turns around to check on the progress of her nest.

When the turtle is ready to lay her eggs she positions herself directly over the top of the nest chamber. It is at this point in her nesting process that most permitted researchers will tag, measure and gather data since the turtles become much more tolerant of noise, light and other distractions. Once all of her eggs are deposited, the turtle begins a methodical process of covering them. She scoops up sand with one rear flipper, places it on top of the eggs, and taps it down. This continues until the eggs are totally covered.

Although her eggs are covered, she is not yet ready to return to the sea. As she moves forward slowly, she will stop and use her front flippers to sling massive quantities of sand behind her before advancing. This returns the beach environment surrounding the nest to its original condition, and, as researchers late in marking their nests have found out, it also serves as an effective camouflage. She then slowly makes her way back to the sea. Females create nests, deposit their eggs, and return to sea multiple times in a single nesting season. Although it is extremely variable among and between species, this process is commonly completed as often as every two weeks but usually no more than four times in total.

Six to 13 weeks after laying, the hatchlings begin to emerge in a brief period of intense activity, termed 'a hatchling frenzy'. This consumes most of the resources provided by the egg yolk and their instinct is to immediately get to the water. Environmental cues, such as sand temperature, light reflection and the slope of the beach are significant tools that prompt ascending from the nest and aid in orienting their advancement towards the ocean.

Marine turtles can be traced back to the Jurassic era, over 150 million years ago, evolving and adapting to include modifications to the forelimbs, shell and rear limbs for swimming.

La Guajira is one of the biggest nesting grounds for loggerhead turtles in Colombia. Turtles migrate thousands of miles through warm-water oceans and, according to experts, cry real tears. In La Guajira stories are told of when beaches were so full of turtles, men could not manoeuvre their boats out to sea. Today, all of Colombia's marine turtles face extinction and conservation groups now use volunteers to walk the beaches each night during the season in order to protect, tag and monitor those that arrive. Conservation groups throughout South America now collaborate on recorded data and research – a vital move as turtles vary nesting patterns over the years. Marine turtles are also threatened by fishing wire and nets, which cause many to drown, as like all reptiles they need to breathe air. Visitors can help stop the illegal poaching of turtles by refusing to buy eggs, meat or shell, if offered it. Sadly many tourists are still tempted by claims that the eggs act as an aphrodisiac. While locals are slowly responding to education concerning the threat to turtles, many believe that they will simply never die out.

Another essential is plenty of water. Initially, a wide stretch of paved road runs parallel to a stretch of train track, cutting through dark-orange sand flanked by scrub. Birds of prey perch on a large billboard advertising Cabo de la Vela. At this point you are 17km from the cape – and just about to enter the undulating desert. This barren terrain of cactus-edged rugged sands is an alien land to the uninitiated – much like the most remote areas of the Australian Outback. As it is totally unlit and poorly drained, this sand expanse should not be attempted in bad weather or after dark.

CABO DE LA VELA (*Telephone code 5*) In 1499, Spanish explorer Alonso de Ojeda named this rocky outcrop El Cabo de la Vela after spotting what he thought was a white sail from his ship. Today this rustic little fishing village on the tip of the peninsula is home to a friendly Guajira community, thought to be the inspiration behind the tribe featured in Henri Charrière's *Papillon*. Women clad in brightly coloured flowing *yonnas* serve as a reminder that Cabo de la Vela is 99% Wayúu. Distinctive palm-thatched huts and battered fishing boats are the predominant features in the beachfront settlement of El Cabo, an idyllic spot with an 8km sandy stretch. Shallow waters form a theatrical contrast to the surrounding desolate tract and give it an oasis feel. Sparsely populated at just 800 people, it's an easy place to hang a hammock and simply shoot the breeze.

Getting around Several local **boatmen** offer their services to tourists, including Machorrito (m *312 630 637*). Expect to pay 60,000COP for a return trip to the lighthouse and 100,000COP for the salt mines at Pilón.

Where to stay and eat Most of Cabo de la Vela's dozen small, family-run hotels are little more than hammock-strung huts – and almost all are on the beach at El Cabo. However, one of the nicest places to stay is a few kilometres along the main drag. Beachfront **Refugio Pantu** is run by friendly owner Claudia and her two young daughters, Kelly and Katiara. Two rustic *cabañas* have small private bathrooms and open up right on the sand at 60,000COP, including breakfast – just ask someone around town to point you in the right direction. Other options in central El Cabo include the **Ranchería Jarrena** (m *310 603 2517*), **Ranchería Jeke'Tumana** (m *311 416 4004*) and **Restaurante y Hospedaje Mahannain**. Many will also allow camping.

Many of the local restaurants also rent out rooms (*usually* **$$**). Try **Restaurante y Hospedaje Jarrinapi** (m *311 683 4281*), **Restaurante Utta** (m *310 644 4450/311 415 3933/300 825 0133*), **Mar y Sol**, **Restaurante Mauicha**, **Restaurante Bonita**, **Restaurante Calamar**, **Restaurante Salaaima** and the **Restaurante Cabo Mar**. Local dishes tend to revolve around seafood, especially snapper, prawns and lobster – but goat is also on the menu. Food is generally served 07.00–21.00 each day with restaurants supplemented by vendors selling *empanadas* and sodas on the beach.

It is worth noting that you will engage is some pretty serious haggling for places to stay and for meals if you decide to come out to La Guajira independently. This can be time-consuming and trying. If you are short of time, book an all-inclusive tour as this will save you the effort and ordinarily, what is offered by reputable travel agencies is of a higher quality.

Shopping A couple of souvenir shops have opened up along the seafront. Most sell shells and local handicrafts, including *mochilas* (woven bags).

Other practicalities As a simple, rustic place without electricity or running water, visitors should expect accommodation and services to be basic. A bucket of water per person constitutes a bath with all generators switched off at 22.00. Pack a torch, bring a book and maybe a card game – and bring snorkel gear, etc. If you can, buy mineral water in Riohacha as this is in short supply.

What to see and do Most visitors simply hang out on the beach eating fresh seafood before napping in a hammock and enjoying a swim in some of Colombia's bluest waters. However, those keen to do some sightseeing should take in the **Faro de la Vela** (lighthouse) – it's high up on an out-of-town headland that offers some truly magnificent views. The area also has a salt pile (**Pilón de Azúcar**) that is worth a peek. Both are covered by local tour guides.

SOUTHERN ATLANTIC COAST

The sprawling department of Chocó just manages to stretch to the Atlantic coastline and is the only Colombian province able to boast that it is also bordered by the Pacific Ocean. Set within the northeastern part of the Gulf of Urabá, this tiny ribbon of land is home to some rather nice seaside towns on a backdrop of yucca plantations, maize crops and plantain trees. It is also perfectly placed for jungle treks, tours to Kuna Yala (San Blas islands) and hikes across the border into neighbouring Panama and is flanked to the west by the mighty Serranía de Darién.

CAPURGANA *Telephone code 4*

This small coastal settlement of 2,800 inhabitants is carved out of the jungle on the northwestern Atlantic coast. Nudging the Darién Gap just a stone's throw from the Panamanian frontier, Capurgana overlooks the Gulf of Urabá where the waters of the Río Atrato run into the ocean. Two simple but gorgeous beaches attract a fledgling tourist crowd that more than doubles the local population in high season from December to January. Outside of high season, the sands are empty and utterly idyllic and are a great place to witness gorgeous sunrises as the sun slowly emerges from the ocean, flooding the water with an amber glow. The northern beach is famed for its crystal-clear waters, so is a popular spot to watch the surf or snorkel in near-perfect visibility, especially during the rainy season when the water is calm. Although pebbly, the southern beach is an exciting place to spend time listening to the roar of the crashing waves against the shore. Island hopping, diving and kayaking are the prime occupations. It's also a great place to enjoy some superb seafood dishes at candlelit tables looking out across the ocean. Traffic-free and largely Afro-Colombian, Capurgana has a funky laid-back beach-town vibe.

GETTING THERE Three daily **flights** depart from Medellín during high season, arriving at the tiny Aeropuerto Narcisa Navas in about 75 minutes. Regional airline ADA (Aerolínea de Antioquia) operates a fleet of small 19-seater aircraft that fly to Capurgana. Departure times from Medellín are highly dependent on weather conditions so the timetable is best described as 'fluid' – it's worth preparing for possible delays. On arrival, passengers will discover a **quirky taxi fleet** primed for action. *Coches* – Capurgana's makeshift pony and trap – transport luggage and passengers to hotels across town for 5,000COP. Those arriving during the rains will find themselves serenaded by a zillion croaking frogs – they live in large numbers in the jungle behind the airport and hit high volume every time it showers.

GETTING AROUND Compact Capurgana is easily navigable on foot. Without roads or motorised vehicles (apart from a single motorbike) the only other option is the local horse-and-cart transport (*coché*) – plastic garden chairs with their legs removed have been roped to the hulk as seats and, other than a wheelbarrow, this eccentric taxi is the best way to get luggage to/from the airport at a cost of 5,000COP.

TOUR OPERATOR Small tour operator **Excursiones Ecológicas** (*\ 682 8789*) has an office opposite the park. It runs snorkelling trips and organises horseriding and jungle treks and will lend a hand with hotel bookings.

WHERE TO STAY Capurgana's first hotel opened 33 years ago. Today, a number of large hotels and a good handful of smaller places offer rooms to rent – often with meals thrown in. Shoestring travellers will also find some camping options and a youth hostel – all within a 10-minute walk of the beach. However, those keen to stay near the park should pack a pair of earplugs unless they are immune to loud music and revelry 24 hours a day.

Hotel Almar (49 rooms) \ 436 6262; e almar@epm.net.co; www.almar.com.co. This beachfront hotel opened 30 years ago & is one of the most popular all-inclusives in Capurgana. On-site amenities include a, bar, spa & TV lounge. AC rooms aren't particularly plush but are comfy with white wooden balconies that overlook pretty hedged tropical gardens. Buffet-style meals include seafood, meat, chicken & salads with beer, wine & cocktails & snacks all part of the all-inclusive package. **$$$**

Hostal Marlin (8 rooms) m 310 593 6409; www.hostalmarlin.com. This big wooden building located at the end of the main drag overlooking the bay has large balconies & is notable for its sizeable carved marlin over the porch. Prices include meals but rooms vary so be sure to ask to see a few. **$$**

Tacarcuna Lodge (35 rooms) \ 412 2552; www.hotelesdecostaacosta.com. This beautiful wooden orange-&-blue building oozes style with terracotta floors & inlaid rocks adorned with flower-filled tubs & planters. Hanging baskets brim with varicoloured blooms under a wood-&-thatch roof hung with shells, molas & wind chimes. Rooms offer single, double & triple accommodation at 105,000COP pp all inclusive – but don't stay here unless you have a high noise tolerance as this hotel is right, smack bang in Capurgana's local party zone. **$$**

Cabaña Daruis (7 rooms) m 314 622 5638; e joeysilver8@yahoo.com; www.dariuscapurgana. es.tl. Delightful, clean & only 30m from the water's edge, this is another good choice for your downtime in Capurgana. **$**

Hostal Capurgana (8 rooms) \ 824 36111; www.hostalcapurgana.net. This charming *pensionado* is located opposite the Tiende y Restaurante Don Blas. Room rates include b/ fast & dinner – with lunch available for an extra 25,000COP per night. Rooms are set around a leafy courtyard where wooden tables & chairs enjoy a cooling breeze amidst palms, trees & flowers. In low season the hotel offers rates of 20,000COP pp room only & is open to negotiation regarding discounts for longer stays. **$**

La Bohemia Hostal (6 rooms) 50m back from the Playa de Piedras. Cheap & cheerful & aimed at the shoestring traveller, La Bohemia offers shared dorms for 17,000COP per night & private rooms for around 25,000COP per night. Great value. **$**

Posada del Gecko (5 rooms & 3 bungalows) Calle del Comercio 2; m 314 525 6037; e posadadelgecko@hotmail.com; www. posadadelgecko.com. Beautifully crafted wooden rooms, private bungalows & a good restaurant make this a firm favourite in Capurgana. Shared rooms cost from 22,000COP per night, privates from 57,000. **$**

WHERE TO EAT AND DRINK The beachside **Restaurante y Marisqueria Josefina** (*Playa Caleta, nr Hotel Almar; ⊕ for dinner daily; $$*) serves up arguably the finest seafood dishes in town. Choose from prawns in coconut, red mullet in garlic, fish soup, squid and langoustines.

Visitors rave about the quality of fishing in and around Capurgana. Today, the town generates 90% of its revenue from tourism with just 10% from fishing, ensuring there are plenty of fish in the sea for enthusiastic amateurs. Large numbers of marlin, prawns, tuna, jacks, needle fish, angel fish, queen fish and red snapper can be found in the surrounding waters. Numerous boatmen offer fishing trips out around the bays and islands for around 50,000COP per person.

On the edge of Playa Caleta, near the bridge that connects with the town, the **Luiz de Oriente** (✎ *824 3719*; **$$**) has a distinctive Asian décor. Red lanterns hang around the wooden frontage in a restaurant adorned with bamboo, lacquered fittings and teak. Yet, rather confusingly, the menu appears to be 100% Spanish-influenced with paella a speciality. This place also has rooms (see *Where to stay* above) and a cocktail bar.

For a tiny kiosk, the **Cocteleria Emilyn** ($) drums up a lot of trade. Find it on the dock and don't expect anything more complicated than prawns and soda.

The **Tiende y Restaurante Don Blas** ($) serves up snacks, drinks and simple fish-and-rice meals for less than 10,000COP to eat in or take-away. Look out for this family-run eatery in the centre of town – it has dayglo green walls.

Nearby, the red-painted **Venta de Jugos Naturales** ($) whips up endless fresh tropical juices, such as papaya, mango, pineapple and orange.

For big plates of meat head to the **Restaurante Doña Fatima** ($) – a popular *carne a la plancha* joint located opposite the juice bar, where seasoned beef with plantain and a beer will set you back less than 9,000COP.

The **Restaurante Mi Barcito** ($) has a menu of grilled meat and chicken, fried fish and *sancocho* soup. You'll find it near the artisan vendors at the dock end of town.

Doña Ofelia ($) serves traditional *trópico chocóano* food using regional recipes and is renowned for delicious *arepa con carne* (meat *arepa*), *frijole* beans and *maza morra* (maize soup) – a real treat and very cheap.

There are chips, chips and more chips at the aptly named **El Palacio del Frito** ($) ('Palace of Fries') located opposite the Restaurante Café where a basic fare is served at tables on a corner shingle plot. If it's fried chicken and fries you want, head to **Chocó Pollo** on the park, a greasy spoon popular with Capurgana's drinking crowd on a Sunday afternoon.

ENTERTAINMENT AND NIGHTLIFE Capurgana's main park is little more than a square patch of grass that doubles as a town plaza-cum-soccer-field. It is also a popular grazing spot for horses and chickens. A small string of noisy local bars and a solitary disco pump out music until dawn each day, each playing competing tracks at deafening volume until the sound systems explode. The worst offenders are **El Empate**, **Guayabo Loco**, **El Wasa** and **Sohido Nitido**. Each has a set of mile-high distorted speakers and is located opposite the goalposts. At the nearby Estadero del Almendro old men stagger around a makeshift dance floor swigging from bottles of *aguardiente*. However, most gringos choose to give the local drinking dens a miss in favour of the beach bars and restaurants by the dock.

SHOPPING In the centre of town, along the Calle del Comercial, a string of handicraft shops and vendors sell jewellery, bags, trinkets, baskets and souvenirs.

There's also a stall selling local crafts outside the Hotel Almar – the **Arte el Machi** sets up early in the morning and closes at dusk and proudly displays a sign guaranteeing '50% discount' year-round. By the park, Almacén Accesorios Mannix stocks a nice range of jewellery, jeans, beachwear and belts. There are also a couple of souvenir shops at the airport. María Canamo and Helados both stock Kuna *molas*, jewellery and other handicrafts.

OTHER PRACTICALITIES Capurgana's city chiefs have dissuaded traders from hawking their wares on the beach and it is very rare to be hassled on Playa Caleta – or anywhere in the town. Pack a torch as Capurgana has many unlit paths due to an electric supply that only runs until 02.00. Capurgana's **CLARO office** in the centre of town offers a fax and airmail service with national and international calls and also sells mobile-phone chargers. Next door, the town's small **ADA airline office** has a stock of timetables and a ticket desk (✆ *682 8817*).

WHAT TO SEE AND DO
Beaches The picturesque palm-edged sandy stretch of **Playa Caleta** fronts some of Capurgana's largest hotels but is gorgeous nonetheless. It's easily accessible and a popular place for a morning stroll or jog. Pristine sands are swept daily and there are plenty of shady spots under palms in which to escape the rays. The sweeping **Playa Soledad** (aka Playa Alta) is a popular stop-off with day trippers while **Playa Media** is an idyllic 100m strip of golden soft sand fanned by palms. This Robinson Crusoe Beach is accessible by boat or a 6-hour hike on foot and is a gorgeous picture-postcard stretch. **Playa la Mora** (Blackberry Beach) is named after the fruit-laden bushes that edge the sand. Other small beaches within reach of Capurgana include **Playa Los Locos**, **Playa Bélen** and **Playa Sucia**.

Bahía Aguacarte (Avocado Bay) Most people visit Bahía Aguacarte as part of an organised boat trip, arriving to snorkel in the middle of the morning before a lunch of fried fish overlooking the bay. With this in mind, those arriving under their own steam may be wise to give it a wide berth between 11.30 and 14.00 as the place is much less likely to be crowded once the lunchtime rush has died down. Bahía Aguacarte is a beautiful spot with an avocado-shaped bay edged by thick jungle slopes and crimson San Joaquín blooms. Diners can enjoy views from the open-sided **Restaurante Doña Diana** (known locally as simply 'La Aguacarte') of bobbing fishing boats and open seas. The food is great and served at rustic wooden tables with plastic chairs set out under a thatched awning. Choose from the catch of the day with *patacones* and salad, grilled beef or seafood soup – all for less than 8,000COP. Four-hour tours on horseback depart from Capurgana with boat trips daily from the dock at around 09.30.

🏠 *Where to stay and eat*
🏠 **Bahía Lodge** (sleeps 35) m 314 812 2727; e info@bahia-lodge.com; www.bahia-lodge. com. German-owned & with a truly idyllic setting, this lodge offers 5 individual thatched-roof cabins (sleeping 2–4) plus a building for groups (with 4 rooms that can sleep up to 15). Meals are optional, but a really nice experience is the moonlit dinner that the staff can organise amidst flickering candles on the beach. Expect tours, transfers & lots of extras. All accommodation has private bathrooms & palm-trimmed terraces with sea views. **$$**

Isla de los Pájaros (aka Isla Sucre) Although renowned for its many species of nesting seabirds, this island has a dual persona as Sugar Island – a name born out

A couple of local dive operators offer trips out around the bays and islands to five prime spots. Most hotels will book this for you – and some include snorkelling within the price. A diving lesson generally costs around 110,000–160,000COP per person, including all equipment. Dolphins, nurse sharks and turtles are all common sights in these waters. The area's nicest diving spots are as follows:

* Aguacate (a small bay 10 minutes from Capurgana's Playa Caleta)
* La Miel (Panama's border town, 20 minutes away)
* Piedra del Centro (a calm diving spot, 10 minutes away)
* La Brieta (nice clear waters, 10 minutes from the centre of town)
* Piscina de los Dioses (Pool of the Gods, 10 minutes from Playa Caleta)
* Carreto (in Panamanian waters, 2 hours from Playa Caleta)

The main office of the **Almar Capurgana Centro de Buceo** (Dive Centre) (🕿 421 4969; e almar@epm.net.co) is in Medellín where it specialises in diving trips to Capurgana. However, local bookings can be made at the Hotel Almar (page 460).

of its sugar-like 'frosting' of crystallised salt. As a protected breeding site, the island is not accessible to humans. However, large numbers of birds can be easily sighted from the surrounding waters (especially at around 16.30). A trio of bottle-nosed dolphins can also often be spotted here.

El Hoyo Soplador (The Blowhole) Madcap Dario Gonzales (the Alcazar Hotel's medallion-wearing sexagenarian) claims to have first discovered Capurgana's blowhole decades ago. Today, this spouting cavity forms part of the daily tour schedule – a natural phenomenon that lies at the inland end of a rocky outcrop washed by waves. Water is funnelled up towards a gap in the rocks to create some spectacular soaring jets of water, although the height of the gushes very much depends on the state of the weather. In the right conditions, air is either blown out or sucked into the hole at considerable pressure with resulting spouts that reach speeds of 20mph.

El Cielo (The Sky) A simple walking tour along this rocky rainforest trail costs around 10,000COP with horseback a popular alternative option at 12,000COP – the trek is a 10km round trip along a gradual slope upwards. By horse, it is 45 minutes each way. Expect to spot titi monkeys high above waterfalls, sandy creeks and rocky rivers. A nice little rustic eatery – the **Esmeralda Restaurante** – serves fish-and-rice meals, sodas and beers at El Cielo. Thick jungle and creekside views make this a memorable pit stop ahead of the trek back down. Another option is **La María Restaurante** towards the end of the journey or the **Ultimo Recurso** at the point the trail begins.

Piscina de Los Dioses (Pool of the Gods) Plunging into the sparkling waters of this deep, natural pool from the surrounding rocky ledges is a popular daredevil pursuit. However, those less fearless will still enjoy swimming in the pristine depths of this beautiful spot – Mother Nature's own jacuzzi.

Kuna Yala (San Blas) Kuna Yala is an autonomous region of 400 islands and a 230km needle-thin strip of mainland coastline in Panama inhabited solely by indigenous Kuna people. Meaning 'Kuna-land' in Dulegaya, the unique language of its people, Kuna Yala has been self-ruled since 1930, when the Panamanian government granted the tribe the right to govern its own land. Many of these beautiful palm-fringed islands surpass every travel brochure 'paradise island' cliché. Most have white-sand beaches, some have thatch-and-mud villages, but all are blessed with uncluttered ocean views. Only 40 are inhabited, with communities that range in size from five to 5,000. The people of Kuna Yala are believed to be descendants of people from the land known today as Colombia, whose tribes migrated to Darién to escape disease in the Colombian jungle in the 1600s. Since settling on the archipelago the Kuna have struggled as outsiders in Panama, isolated by culture and location. The last 130 years have been a period of immense change for people who have fought to retain their traditions against a background of economic, discriminatory and political challenge.

Declining fish stocks in recent years have caused the Kuna Yala to look elsewhere for revenue, and its modern-day economy is becoming increasingly reliant on the exploitation of its culture. Tourism is a contentious issue that is endorsed by some but not all Kuna. Traditionally a barter economy, the sale of *mola* to tourists is bringing greater cash orientation to the islands, a cause of some social tension. Yet in many respects there are few discernable differences between the people of Kuna Yala and those olden settlements in northern Colombia. Men fish and hunt wild tapir, agouti, monkey, deer, bird, peccary and iguana using blowguns, spears, bow and arrow and a variety of traps and pits. Women cook on open fires in one-room bamboo-and-thatch huts while children play in the rivers and on the shoreline with coconut husks and palm fronds. All are practised oarsmen whose only method of transport is dugout canoe (*ulu*).

To the Kuna the world is a dual civilisation containing the 'world of spirit' and the 'world of subsistence'. The world of spirit surrounds and resides inside every material thing, underpinning the world of subsistence and giving it power. Spirits respect those who reinforce tradition and so the Kuna respect 'spirit sanctuaries' where these spirits dwell. These sanctuaries are usually on what would be quality agricultural land but because of the Kuna belief, it remains forested and intact. Violation of these sanctuaries would cause the spirits to rise up in rage and harm the community, a principle based on the earth as the body of the Great Mother who in union with the Great Father gave birth to all plant, animal and human life.

The distinctive dress of the Kuna women comprises a *mola* (blouse), gold nose rings, a long skirt, a red-and-yellow headdress, gold breastplates and colourful long strands of beaded leg wraps (*uini*). A long black line is painted on the face from the tip of the nose to the forehead and women adopt this dress after puberty rites when they are properly named. Until this point they are known only by a nickname but after menarche a woman's position is reinforced in matrilineal Kuna society by a formal name. This strong female status is further strengthened by the income generated by *mola* sales, a practice that began in 1945 after a missionary purchased one as a souvenir. Today making *molas* for tourist revenue represents an important part of the region's economy, and one that is wholly reliant on its women.

Many Kuna are keen to connect with foreigners and are curious, candid and engaging. However, they often do not understand the blatant disrespect they receive from visiting tourists. Many feel their cultural sensibilities are ignored by 'guests' who should know better. That tourists can disregard Kuna values has horrified entire communities in the archipelago, resulting in a further tightening of the grip on tourism. Skimpy clothes may be *de rigueur* in Acapulco but it is alien attire in

Kuna Yala. Nudity is strictly prohibited and men are asked not to go shirtless. The offence it causes and the image it creates present the Kuna with an unfavourable picture of the 'outsiders' and often breeds cynicism in those once keen to show their homeland to the world.

Each of the 400 islands is privately owned by the communities of Kuna Yala. At the time of writing, none of the nine communities on the mainland is geared up for visits by '*wagas*' (the Kuna word for foreigner) and the archipelago is the focus of visitor activities. Every visitor that steps on to any island in Kuna Yala needs to pay a fee to its people. The rate varies from island to island but is about US$35. This is generally included in the cost of a tour and is paid to the village elders. Visitors should be sure to carry plenty of US$1 bills, as a dollar fee is payable to the subject of each photograph that you take. The photogenic Kuna and their colourful clothes make striking subjects, but visitors should never take a photo without first gaining permission. The issue of photography is a sensitive one in Kuna Yala and can lead to some misunderstanding. However the rule is simple ('no fee, no photo') and is rarely wavered. Kuna elders enforced this law after learning that photographs of Kuna Yala were being used for commercial gain without any financial benefit to its people. Today the value of its culture in terms of 'bankability' has been a valuable lesson learned, especially by the many Kuna with a photogenic smile. The 2-hour trip to Kuna Yala is offered by almost every hotel tour desk and operator. Prices include a guide and lunch at around 110,000COP for adults (80,000COP for children), with 24-hour permission to visit granted by the Kuna elders. Trips generally depart at 08.00 and return to Capurgana at 17.00.

AROUND CAPURGANA

SAPZURRO   It is difficult not to take this tiny seaside community to your heart, such is its charm, beauty and laid-back seafront feel. Just 150 inhabitants live in this 120-year-old settlement, located right on the Panamanian border – Colombia's so-called 'Last Town of The North-West'. A yellow-and-black-striped wooden jetty leads to Sapzurro's main drag – a colourful 100m waterfront stretch. A couple of bars and restaurants overlook bobbing boats and rainforest-clad slopes along the bay. Sandy paths wriggle with burrowing crabs in flower-filled neighbourhoods of candy-coloured wooden houses. Fruit trees bearing mango, avocado, lemon, lime, kumquat and tamarind edge a thick emerald-green jungle mass tumbling down to bright-blue waters.

Safety   Colombia's military forces have successfully pushed the FARC guerrillas that once controlled the region back deep into the jungle and FARC operatives are now based in Panamanian territory in the Darién. Here, FARC's Frente 57 continues to engage mainly in logistical planning. Today, local residents boast that the town is the 'safest place in Colombia' as it has a four-to-one ratio of lawmen (local police, army, coastguard and federal police) for every citizen. The entire border region is heavily guarded by both the Colombian and Panamanian armies – and with posts every half-mile it feels exceedingly safe now that the guerrillas have been pushed deep into the surrounding jungle tracts.

Getting there   Timetabled **tour boats** leave from Capurgana throughout the day, but for a more direct route find a boatman prepared to do the short trip. However, don't be rushed to board a vessel clearly not fit for the purpose, especially in rain or high seas. Over the past couple of years at least one elderly boat has broken in half during the trip from Capurgana. The motor immediately sank and although everyone aboard was eventually rescued (or was able to swim the miles to shore) an absence of insurance, life vests and radio in choppy seas wasn't a recipe for a carefree journey.

Getting around Sightseeing on foot is your only option in pedestrianised Sapzurro, but that's just fine as the pretty paths are a pleasure to walk and the jungle treks totally stunning.

Tour guides **Martha Rubio** (m *314 622 3149*) is an excellent independent tour guide who offers a wide range of trips from jungle treks and visits to Kuna tribes to birding, fishing and 'meet the people' tours. Martha speaks a little English and is also involved in conservation projects in Sapzurro. She can arrange tailor-made camping and snorkelling trips and trips to local farms. Martha is a member of the Colombian Ornithological Society and a practised birding guide.

Andrés Buendia (m *313 624 1329*) knows his way around the islands, bays and jungle tracks (from short stomps to full-day hikes and three-day camping trips). He can also organise a boat and guides across the border into Panama.

Where to stay and eat For a teeny-weeny town, Sapzurro sure has a lot of places to stay. A collection of cabins, homestays and campsites offer well over 150 beds a night – an incredible achievement that should make many of Colombia's larger resorts take note.

Hotel Uvalí (4 rooms) 75m back from the beach. This simple family-run hotel has fan-cooled rooms at rates including b/fast & a seafood lunch (or dinner). A guide to La Miel is included in the room rate. **$$**

Restaurant & Hotel Doña Triny (10 rooms) m 312 751 8626; e gerenciadonatriny@gmail. com; www.hoteltriny.com. In front of the main dock. Patron Triny is proud of her hotel & restaurant – & it shows. This spotlessly clean yellow-&-lime waterfront building is immaculately maintained with pretty rooms at rates including b/fast & lunch (or dinner). Seafood & chicken dishes in the restaurant are priced at around 9,000COP for red snapper with delicious soups & snacks from 3,000COP. **$$**

Cabaña Cabo Tiburon (2 rooms) m 314 632 4890. Owner Yadiva Barrios offers double fan-cooled rooms with an ample b/fast. **$**

Cabaña Narza (2 rooms) Twin rooms are available at this pleasant B&B where the owner can also arrange walking tours & fishing trips. **$**

Cabañas Barracuda (6 cabins) ☎824 3042. Budget travellers rave about this beachfront set of cabins on a backdrop of jungle & palms. Facilities are rustic with few frills & fuss – rates vary so be prepared to haggle. **$**

Cabañas Teonila (1 room) A large fan-cooled family-sized room can accommodate 4 people in this simple B&B. **$**

Casa del Monte (2 rooms) m 313 593 8265. Patron Guillermina Borrio has guest rooms in her family-run B&B. **$**

Donde De Mauro (7 rooms) Rooms of various sizes & configurations with discounts available for longer stays. **$**

Hotel Chileno (commonly referred to as the 'Hotel Chileno' on account of its Chilean owner) (sleeps 8) Playa Diana, at the end of the beach; m 313 685 9862. This nice little hotel has 2 rooms sleeping up to 8 people plus camping & hammocks. The patron 'El Chileno' also arranges boat launches to Panama & local tours. **$**

La Punta (4 rooms) m 314 666 5210. Without a doubt, this is one of Sapzurro's nicest places to stay, on account of its stunning location. Owner Mirium Serrano has a great eye for detail & each of her guest rooms is beautifully decorated. Find La Punta 5mins out of the town centre (reachable on foot or by boat). **$**

Ⓧ Donde Guille There are few sophisticated amenities on this family-run campsite, apart from washing facilities & a bathroom. However, it can accommodate 20 people & costs just 7,000COP in high season (5,000COP off-peak). **$**

Ⓧ Nawaly There's sufficient room for 50 people on this decent-sized campsite. On-site amenities include a shower block with prices from 5,000COP. **$**

Entertainment and nightlife It's fair to say that apart from a trio of bars and a couple of restaurants Sapzurro doesn't have much to offer once the sun sets. However, **Martha Rubio** (page 466) organises 'meet the people' evenings to offer interaction with Sapzurro's elderly storytellers over local food and drink.

Shopping For a great selection of funky bags, jewellery, handicrafts, local produce, souvenirs, T-shirts, swimwear, flip-flops, sunhats, scarves, shorts, Kuna *molas* and carvings, pop into **Tatuajes en Jagua** on the waterfront.

Other practicalities Sapzurro has an excellent CLARO mobile signal, unlike many of Colombia's other remote jungle villages. An international telephone service is offered at the Servicio shop next door to Tatuajes en Jagua on the waterfront. Generator-powered electricity runs 09.00–02.00 so you may need a torch to be on the safe side. Snack shops (such as Los Almendros and Doña Marta on the waterfront) offer food supplies for jungle treks and camping trips. Muddy trails, high humidity and biting insects make boots, water, sun block and bug repellent essential items.

What to see and do
Coqueria de Agua Viva For a henna tattoo (using *jagun* ink) and a range of handicrafts ask a guide to direct you to this pretty private home. The owners are a couple of Argentine expatriates and welcome visitors – their home is near to the waterfall Cascada Agua Viva.

Kuna settlement In order to visit the Kuna settlement in Carreto (a 45-minute trip to the north and a more 'authentic' non-touristy experience than some Kuna villages), contact **Martha Rubio** (page 466) – she makes the bookings with the *zaila* (chief) and is also the guide (she speaks some English) at 60,000COP per person.

Turtle protection Martha Rubio is also involved in a local turtle protection programme – *Protección, Monitoreo E Investigación Tortuga Caña* – led by local conservationist Emigdo Pertuz (e *emigdiopertuz@hotmail.com*). Aside from protecting nesting sites and breeding turtles, education initiatives include teaching local communities about conservation and dissuading against eating turtle meat and turtle eggs. Martha can organise volunteer placements and visits to the project, which remains in dire need of funding and resources.

LA MIEL La Miel means 'honey' on account of this small town's soft, sweet tranquillity, but a cluster of burnt-out buildings is testament to the fact that peace

---

CROSSING INTO PANAMA

A 45-minute gluey trail leads from the back of Sapzurro up 180 impossibly steep muddy steps to the Panamanian government checkpoint (a kind of pre-border border), called Cabo Tiburón. An obelisk bearing Panama's heraldic coat of arms marks a change in territory and from here the trip down into Panamanian soil is slippery, slidy and ungainly. Traversing this mud-fest eventually leads to the frontier settlement of La Miel – Panama's last (or first) town. Expect to arrive in an undignified sludge-like state, especially if it happens to be raining.

11

hasn't always reigned. Residents fled their homes in 1999 when 200 rebels from the Colombian Revolutionary Armed Forces (FARC) invaded their home town, launching an assult from the densely forested hills in nearby Panama – the perfect hiding place for drug labs and guerrilla camps and, in recent years, even coca plantations. More than 120 La Miel inhabitants fled to safer provinces, concerned that AUC paramilitaries would move into the area and kill villagers thought to be supporting FARC guerrillas.

But take a stroll through tiny La Miel now to spot giggling toddlers and snoozing elders in porch-fronted homes of painted wood. At the end, coralline rocks form a craggy mass in the water by buildings destroyed to rubble in the troubles of the past. Thankfully, today, La Miel is peaceful and laid-back – even if a large proportion of the village's 142 population are children. Most villagers earn a living from coconut trading and fishing. Playa Blanca is a 25m curved stretch of white sand that is truly idyllic. If you have time, order a bowl of the dish of the day (see below) and find a spot on the beach and do nothing but soak up the views – pure bliss. Snorkel gear can also be rented at Playa Blanca where a boat to Puerto Obaldia (Panama's official border) costs US$65 and takes 20 minutes. This is also where you can pick up a boat back into Colombian waters, along a route that passes vast volcanic cliffs that signify the end of Panamanian territory in truly dramatic style.

Where to stay This is a pre-border frontier town, and tourists aren't permitted to stay overnight in La Miel. There are no hotels and camping is illegal, so head on to Puerto Obaldia.

Where to eat and drink Many of La Miel's womenfolk offer meals for sale when they spot a tourist in town. Dishes tend to consist of shrimp, snail and fried fish with coconut and rice and are usually served on Playa Blanca. Expect to pay 6,000–7,000COP (around US$3.50) for a bowl of caracol stew (*la cigua*) – with a generous portion usually part of the deal. Look out for the Atlas signs in the centre of town for a chance to sup one of Panama's finest beers.

PUERTO OBALDIA Panama's military checkpoint town of Puerto Obaldia is full of travellers keen to leave, so expect to encounter penniless backpackers frustrated by Panama's reams of red tape. Puerto Obaldia is a tatty transit town with few endearing qualities for travellers passing through. Hotels are shabby with the nicest accommodation available at the very basic **Pensión Conde** – expect to pay around 20,000COP for little more than an airless, soulless box with its fair share of wildlife. A handful of mediocre restaurants offer a limited menu with a couple of bars that tend to get rowdy after dark. Pack plenty of patience ahead of a trip to Puerto Obaldia as immigration officials are slow, cheerless and woefully inefficient – and that's if they just happen to be awake.

Getting there Get an exit stamp at the DAS office in Capurgana by the harbour where a **launch** to Puerto Obaldia costs about 60,000COP. This is a price for the whole boat, regardless of the number of passengers – so it makes sense to ask around to see if any fellow travellers are planning the journey. From La Miel, the price tends to be higher – in fact it can often double to around US$65. Head to Playa Blanca and ask around for a boatman prepared to do the trip. Officially, the immigration office stipulates that all travellers exiting Colombia to Panama require proof of yellow fever jabs and sufficient funds – but in practice this rarely happens. However, to be on the safe side, keep a credit-card statement to hand –

although it's likely that border staff will cast an eye over it for a couple of seconds and decide it's good enough.

Getting around Walking is the only way to navigate this small settlement unless you prefer to hitch a ride with a jeep on its way to the dock.

Getting away The four-times-a-week flight from Puerto Obaldia to Panama City on Wednesday, Thursday, Saturday and Sunday tends to be fully booked, so build in a contingency for making a reservation at the Air Panama office in town or pre-arrange it via the internet or central booking system (☏ *+507 299 9042; www. airpanama.com*). Tickets cost around US$65 for the hour-long flight.

Other practicalities It's important to sort out US dollars before travelling into Panama. Although there are money changers in Puerto Obaldia the peso–US dollar exchange is truly pitiful. Credit cards aren't welcome anywhere in La Miel or Puerto Obaldia and nobody will touch Colombian currency. At the time of writing, there isn't an ATM in either town. In La Miel there is no mains electricity or water supplies – so power and utilities can be iffy and bottled water recommended. Travellers can keep up to date via a local radio station to check what's going on – simply tune into 96.1 FM, 'Ecos del Darién'.

Appendix 1

Taken from Amazon: the Bradt Travel *Guide and edited by Mike Unwin*

AMAZON PLANTS Warmth, constant sunlight and heavy rainfall speed up photosynthesis in rainforests, allowing prolific plant growth, and at least 50,000 woody plants are recorded from the Amazon – around a fifth of all plant species known.

Trees Rainforest trees collectively take up and release so much water that they affect global weather patterns. Their trunks, stems, branches, leaves, fruits and roots also provide microhabitats for countless animals and smaller plants.

Rainforest layering The forest's vertical structure comprises four to six overlapping layers, differing in the amount of light and moisture they receive, and hence their species composition. The **emergent layer** comprises such giants as fig, teak, mahogany and kapok, which tower above the canopy, reaching 40m or more. The **middle (or closed-canopy) layer** consists of uniform-looking trees, 12–30m tall, with tall, narrow crowns; one tree never overlaps another of the same species. The **understorey (or shrub layer)** comprises typically a sparse growth of treelets and shrubs, from 1m to 6m, as well as small palms, tree-ferns and cycads. At **ground level** in mature forest, the closed canopy cuts off up to 98% of the light, allowing only shade-tolerant herbs, ferns, tree seedlings and fungi to grow. Many herbs have long, narrow, often variegated leaves; some are popular as houseplants.

Animal niches correspond to this layered structure. Birds and insects dominate emergent tree crowns, while the canopy has the greatest biodiversity, with birds, mammals and reptiles. Below the canopy, lianas and other parts of trees and shrubs are colonised by miniature ferns, mosses, lichens and other simple plants, creating a mini forest for micro-animals, which break down dead plant matter and provide food for micro-predators such as centipedes and hunting spiders. On the forest floor, jaguar and other predators hunt a range of prey, while anteaters feast on ants and termites. Meanwhile in the soil and leaf litter invertebrates help fungi and microbes decompose organic matter to recycle the forest's nutrients.

Forest edges and gaps Numerous plants thrive where light is abundant. Acacias and mimosas are common beside water. Acacias often have elaborate red-orange flowers and large seedpods, like giant beans. Mimosas produce globular yellow or creamy-white flowers and have feathery leaves. Cecropia, with its large five-lobed leaves, is a common tree of river edges and is protected from insects and epiphytes by aggressive stinging ants. Heliconia has waxy red-and-yellow flowers that resemble crab claws, and is pollinated by hummingbirds.

Epiphytes The treetops are ideal habitat for epiphytes. These 'plants on plants' perch on tree limbs, rooted in soil accumulated on branches or crevices and using their host tree to raise themselves to canopy height. The biggest are bromeliads and arum lilies. Others include orchids, philodendrons, peperomias, forest cacti and ferns. Velvet-green moss carpets every surface, and lichens and algae encrust branches and tree trunks.

Lianas and vines Lianas and vines are rooted on the ground, getting their nutrients from the thin forest soil. They hitch a ride upwards on new trees growing in forest gaps, or work their way into the canopy up the trunks of existing trees, connecting trees with one another and creating arboreal walkways for animals. There are over 15,000 liana species in the Amazon. *Ayahuasca*, also known as 'spirit vine' or 'vine of the soul', is widely used in religious ceremonies because of its powerful hallucinogenic properties. Vines tend to have spindly, often thorny stems and most are shorter-lived. They grow around forest edges and riverbanks, draping trees and shrubs with a mass of green. The delicate trumpet-shaped flowers of morning glories open early in the day to attract bees for a frenzy of nectar-feeding, but wither by the afternoon. Commercially important vines include *uña de gato*, or cat's claw, which has medicinal properties, while the passion vine has edible fruits used to make a soft drink.

Water plants Water plants form so-called 'floating meadows' that provide food for fish, arthropods and the manatee. Underwater roots and above-water vegetation shelter a community of small animals, including fish, amphibians and numerous invertebrates, which in turn provide sustenance for many predators. Water plants quickly colonise oxbow lakes and slow-flowing rivers, especially if manatee are absent. Most impressive is the Amazon or Victoria water lily, which grows pads up to 2m across that bristle underneath with large spines to deter manatees and herbivorous fish.

ANIMALS OF THE FOREST Rainforest harbours at least 50% of the planet's known animal species, a figure that would probably exceed 90% in the unlikely event that all the fauna were ever described.

Rainforest mammals Most rainforest mammals are very inconspicuous, being small, camouflaged, shy and nocturnal, and even larger creatures are mostly hidden by the dense vegetation. Many canopy mammals play a vital ecological role: nectar-feeding bats and rodents pollinate trees, while luscious fruit tempts monkeys who inadvertently disperse the seeds.

Primates Your expectation of seeing monkeys swinging from every branch quickly vanishes on entering the rainforest. Monkeys' activities rarely bring them within sight or sound of humans – especially in areas where they have been heavily hunted.

Pygmy marmoset

Some 30–35 lowland forest monkeys are known, with new ones still being discovered. South American monkeys, known as cebid monkeys, differ from Old-World monkeys in having a prehensile tail, which acts as a fifth limb. The most commonly seen species is the **squirrel monkey** (*Saimiri sciureus*), although this one lacks a prehensile tail. Squirrel-sized and slender, it has a handsome gold-green coat with yellow-orange forelimbs. During the day, troops roam in search of fruiting trees. Often kept as pets, squirrel monkeys run free at the zoo in Leticia where their antics provide amusing entertainment.

Squirrel monkey

Marmosets and tamarins are not true monkeys. They are smaller, with non-prehensile tails and have claws instead of fingernails. The **pygmy marmoset** (*Callithrix pygmaea*) has a maximum body length of 15cm, weighing no more than 141g. Its tawny colouring and mane around its face give rise to the local name *leoncito*, meaning 'little lion'. It is common and found throughout western Amazonia, where it prefers lowland flooded-forest areas. The saddle-back tamarin (*Saguinus fuscicollis*) is the primate most likely to be seen in the wild after the squirrel monkey, and gets its name from the large 'saddle' of dark red-brown fur on its shoulders.

Carnivores
A variety of carnivores (order Carnivora) hunt both in the trees and on the ground, including members of the cat, dog, racoon and weasel families.

Cats
All South American cat species (family Felidae) are officially endangered and extremely unlikely to be seen in the wild on an average-length visit. They are rare, wary of humans and usually nocturnal, but you might spot evidence of activity, such as tracks by muddy rivers or claw marks on a tree. Largest, and top of the rainforest food chain, is the **jaguar** (*Panthera onca*), which is thinly distributed across the Neotropics. Its name comes from the Amerindian word *yaguar* meaning 'he who kills with one leap', and this powerful, spotted predator can take prey up to the size of a tapir. Next down is the **puma** (*Felis concolor*), which varies greatly in colour, but is generally a plain golden-brown. Smaller spotted cats include the **ocelot** and the similar but smaller margay, both strictly nocturnal and seldom seen, though the plain-brown **jaguarundi** is sometimes encountered by day. These small cats prey on rodents, small reptiles, birds and reptiles.

Jaguar

Ocelot

Jaguarundi

Other carnivores
The most common member of the raccoon family (Procyonidae) is the sociable **coati**, which has a ringed tail and long, flexible snout. Its omnivorous diet includes insects, small vertebrates, fruits, nuts and flowers. The rather less racoon-like **kinkajou** wins the cutest rainforest animal contest, with its thick golden fur, wide brown eyes and docile manner. Uniquely among its family, it also has a prehensile tail. Among various rainforest members of the weasel family (Mustelidae) is the skunk-like grison, which eats small animals and sometimes fruit. The only two wild dogs (family Canidae) are the bush dog and the short-eared dog; both are small and exceedingly rare, with little known of their natural history.

Kinkajou

Coati

Sloths   Sloths (family Bradypodidae) are the commonest large canopy mammals. They are also the world's slowest and, arguably, laziest land animals, moving along branches at 4.5m a minute and spending up to 80% of their lives asleep or dozing. A slow metabolism enables them to survive on a low-energy diet of leaves, but they must eat lots to meet their nutritional needs. Sloths' excellent camouflage helps them evade predators. Their grooved fur encourages algae growth, creating a greenish hue, and grows in an opposite direction to that of other mammals so that rain runs off their inverted body. Sloths' main predators are eagles, though they may also fall prey to cats as they move across the forest floor to new feeding trees or make their weekly descent to ground level to defecate.

Hoffman's two-toed sloth

Anteaters and armadillos   Anteaters belong to the same order (Pilosa) as sloths. The 2m-long giant anteater is among the largest rainforest animals. It searches the forest floor for ants and termites, using powerful claws to rip open their nests and a long sticky tongue to lap up the food. Armadillos (family Dasipodidae) are protected by their distinctive body armour. The **nine-banded armadillo** is the most widespread species, while the largest is the giant armadillo, which may weigh up to 60kg. Armadillos are shy, nocturnal and solitary. They feed on insects, small vertebrates, carrion, fungi and fruit.

Nine-banded armadillo

Bats   These winged mammals are especially numerous and diverse in tropical rainforest. About 150–200 species are recorded from Amazonia, constituting 40% of the region's mammal species. The majority feed on flying insects. But there are also frog-eating bats, bird-eating bats and even bat-eating bats, while many are fruit- and nectar-feeders – the former dispersing seeds and the latter pollinating trees. Best-known of all are vampire bats. These will feed from cattle or wild mammals, but rarely humans. They do not suck blood, but cut a small flap of skin with their sharp incisors, from which they lap blood – anti-coagulant saliva preventing clotting. Another specialist is the greater bulldog or fishing bat, which plucks fish from the water like an osprey.

Ungulates   Hoofed mammals of the rainforest are shy, retiring and seldom seen. They include the **Brazilian tapir**, which – at up to 250kg – is the biggest South American land mammal. Tapirs are related to horses, but have an elongated, highly mobile snout, useful for searching out fruits, berries, tubers, fungi and herbs. The smaller peccaries are related to pigs. The collared peccary, or *sajino*, is omnivorous and roams in groups of ten or more, often revealed by their pungent cheesy smell. It defends itself aggressively with its 8cm-long tusks. Both tapirs and peccaries are threatened due to intensive hunting. More common and widespread is the

Red-brocket deer

Brazilian tapir

nocturnal **red brocket deer**, which often ventures into forest clearings or even to the edge of gardens and plantations.

Other mammals

A great variety of rodents (order Rodentia) inhabits the rainforest, most of which are small, nocturnal and hard to see, let alone identify. Those found in the canopy include porcupines (family Erithizontidae) and squirrels (family Sciuridae), while ground-dwellers include the agouti and paca, which resemble giant-long-legged guinea pigs. The **capybara** is the world's largest rodent, reaching 113kg, and leads a semi-aquatic life beside river and swamps, where it browses water plants. Superficially rodent-like are the 40 species of opossum (Didelphidae) found in Amazonia, which range in size from a mouse to a racoon. These marsupials sleep by day and forage at night.

Capybara

Rainforest birds

Lowland Amazonia is home to at least 1,800–2,000 types of bird – about four times more than Europe, an area half as big again. The number fluctuates seasonally with migrants from Patagonia or North America. Many forest species, including the well-known toucans and macaws, remain largely hidden until they fly out across a river or clearing. But some perch more conspicuously in the open, including hawks, kingfishers, orioles and flycatchers. Many small birds are very hard to identify, with differences in song or behaviour often being the only clues.

Parrots and macaws

Parrots (family Psittacidae) are the quintessential tropical birds, and often kept as pets in lodges, or jungle villages – though the pet trade has hastened the decline of many species. They use their powerful curved bill to break open hard nuts and seeds. Macaws are the largest. Nearly always seen in pairs, they have long tail-feathers and are easily identified by their colouring. Other parrots are smaller, with shorter tails, and generally fly in flocks. Most are difficult to distinguish in the field – especially since colour is hard to see as they fly overhead in silhouette.

Toucans

Toucans (Ramphastidae) are rainforest icons and have the biggest bill, relative to body size, of any bird. As well as fruit, they also eat small animals and even the eggs and nestlings of other birds. One of the largest species is the white-throated toucan, which is black with a white chest, yellow rump and blue skin around the eye. Smaller toucans include araçaris and toucanets.

Hummingbirds

Harpy eagle

Colombia is a hots pot for hummingbirds (family Trochilidae), with up to 132 species claimed by some authorities – more than any other country. These small nectar-feeding birds, hailed as messengers to the gods by pre-Columbian cultures, are rarely seen for long. They zip around between plants, and you will probably first hear the humming of their wings, which – at more than 80 beats per second in some species – are the fastest of any bird. The dazzling colours of hummingbirds have given rise to such evocative species names as glittering-throated emerald, golden-tailed sapphire and black-eared fairy. Hummingbirds are also ecologically essential as pollinators to many plants – notably of those with red, orange and yellow flowers.

Raptors

The massive **harpy eagle** is the world's most powerful bird of prey, standing up to 1m in height, with huge yellow talons. This rare raptor is a major predator of monkeys and sloths, and may sometimes be glimpsed soaring above the canopy. Among a range of other raptors are the yellow-headed caracara, the black-collared hawk and the roadside hawk. The black vulture is abundant around settlements, especially around rubbish tips, while away from towns the turkey vulture and the greater yellow-headed vulture are more common.

Hoatzin The hoatzin (*Opisthocomus hoazin*) is a pheasant-like bird with a 'mohican' crest, large blue eye-rings and bare facial skin. It is a poor flyer, with pectoral muscles reduced in size to allow space for its oversized crop, which stores its diet of 60% leaves. Gut bacteria ferment the material for up to four times longer than in most birds, which may explain the hoatzin's unpleasant smell, hence its nickname of 'stink bird'. Chicks, when threatened by a predator, fling themselves from the nest into the water below, before clambering back when the coast is clear, using their bill, feet and unique wing-claws. Hoatzins may be abundant in good habitat, forming surprisingly tame flocks of 25–30.

Hoatzin

Night birds Several owls (families Strigidae, Tytonidae) are endemic to the Amazon. The tropical screech owl has a cooing whistle often heard just after nightfall or before dawn. Nighthawks and nightjars (family Caprimulidae) are seen flitting around at dusk, catching insects on the wing, and are often mistaken for bats. When perched, their eye-shine may be reflected in torchlight. Potoos hide during the day by mimicking a dead branch.

Other forest birds Numerous other birds inhabit the forest, from finches and flycatchers to antbirds and cotingas. It is impossible here to do justice to them all, but the following selection comprises some that the visitor might encounter. **Foliage-gleaners**, **horneros** and **spinetails** (Furnariidae) construct big, distinctive nests, ranging from the dome-shaped mud structures of horneros to the tangled stick nests of spinetails. **Honeycreepers** (Thraupidae), such as the bananaquit, feed on nectar, often piercing flower petals near the base. **Jacamars** (Galbulidae) are kingfisher-like birds with lance-like bills and glossy green plumage. **Manakins** (Pipridae) feed in the canopy on fruits and insects. Breeding males perform in groups called 'leks', clearing an area of forest floor for their courtship dance. **Motmots** (Momotidae) have a distinctive tail ending in two racquet-shaped tufts. **Oropendolas** (Psarocolius spp) are common riverside birds, with a loud burbling call and woven nests that hang from branches like large pendulous fruits. **Pigeons** (Columbidae) are fruit-eating specialists. About a dozen species occur in lowland rainforest. **Puffbirds** (Bucconidae) have a tuft of bristles around the bill that may help them catch aerial insects. **Swallows and martins** (Hirundinidae) are recognised in flight by their forked tails and swept-back wings. **Swifts** (Apodidae) are supreme aerial insectivores, spending almost their entire life on the wing. **Tinamous** (Tinamidae) are poor flyers with loud calls that are heard more often than seen. **Tanagers** (Thraupidae) are colourful finch-like birds that feed mostly on fruit. **Trogons and quetzals** (Trogonidae) are elusive canopy birds with colourful plumage that feed on both fruit and insects. **Trumpeters** (Psophiidae) are ground birds with loud calls that enable them to communicate through thick undergrowth. **Woodcreepers** (Furnariidae) forage along branches, prising out insects from crevices. **Woodpeckers** (Picidae) are usually betrayed by their loud drumming, but are hard to glimpse among the branches, let alone identify. **Wrens** (Trogolodytidae) have beautiful, complex songs, and are more often heard than seen.

Aquatic birds The rivers, streams, lakes and swamps of the Amazon provide a haven for numerous aquatic and shore birds. Herons vary from the easily identified great and snowy egrets and little blue heron, to the white-necked heron, striated heron and rufescent tiger heron, with the small zigzag heron being a special rarity for birders. Nocturnal herons include the black-crowned night heron and the boat-billed heron, the latter's capacious bill being ideal for capturing shrimps, fish and insects. The only common stork species is the stately jabiru. Rarer waterbirds include the sunbittern and the sungrebe, each unusual enough to be classified in its own family.

Amazon kingfisher

Along muddy banks, various species of sandpiper, ibis and rail are also present, while birds hunting lakes for fish include the osprey, anhinga and olivaceous cormorant. Kingfishers include the common ringed kingfisher and **Amazon kingfisher**, which inhabit the edges of wide rivers and open lakes. The wattled jacana inhabits quiet wetlands and backwaters, where its long toes help it walk across floating vegetation. The horned screamer is a goose-sized bird with a prominent quill or 'horn' projecting from its forehead and a loud call that sounds a bit like 'Yoo-hoo!'

Rainforest reptiles
Land reptiles, including snakes, lizards and tortoises, are all represented in the Amazon. Aquatic reptiles are covered later in the appendix (page 479).

Snakes
The anaconda (see box, pages 268–9) is the world's heaviest snake and may exceptionally exceed 7m in length. This huge semi-aquatic constrictor asphyxiates prey within its powerful coils. Other constrictors include the rainbow boa, which has an iridescent skin that reflects all colours of the spectrum, the emerald tree boa which is nocturnal and hunts near water, and the boa constrictor, which is diurnal and hunts mostly large rodents.

Few Amazonian snakes pose any threat to humans, with only five or six species considered potentially dangerous. Of these, the fer-de-lance, common along trails, cultivated areas and around dwellings, is the most feared – but not as deadly as its reputation suggests. More imposing is the much rarer bushmaster, which – at 3m – is Amazonia's biggest poisonous snake. Coral snakes have powerful venom, and a vivid banded pattern that varies between species. They may be active day or night and are usually found under logs and rocks. Arboreal snakes include the slender vine snakes and green tree-snakes, while spindle snakes are adapted to burrowing in the forest floor.

Lizards
The prehistoric-looking green iguana often basks on a branch overhanging water and dives in at any hint of danger. Individuals may grow over 1.8m long, of which more than half is tail. This species, also known as 'chicken of the forest', is a popular local food, and there are even hopes that it can replace beef and so eliminate one cause of deforestation. Geckos (Gekkonidae) are generally nocturnal and often seen prowling around lights on walls and ceilings of hotels and lodges. They use adhesive toes to cling to the wall, and munch their way through any insect they can capture.

Rainforest amphibians
Frog and toad voices are an integral part of the rainforest chorus. Come dusk, croaks, whistles, trills, burps and grunts prove their abundance as they prepare for amorous encounters of the night. Expandable throat pouches greatly amplify the calls of the males, allowing females to choose the most impressive. Different calls ensure species remain separate and enable a skilled listener to identify them. Some species prey on others and will even mimic their calls, so when a curious female arrives she is promptly eaten! Other amphibians include salamanders, which sometimes turn up in damp leaf litter or tree holes, and the legless, wormlike Caecilians.

Poison frogs So-called poison-dart frogs, properly called poison frogs, are dayglo-coloured to warn predators of their highly poisonous skin. However, only 55 of 135 known species are actually toxic. Toxicity is diet-dependent: captive animals lose their poison after being fed different food. Some species rank among the smallest terrestrial vertebrates.

Other frogs and toads Tree frogs blend in with vegetation or mimic natural objects to escape predators, and use sucker pads on their feet to climb acrobatically. Glass frogs have colourless, virtually transparent skin and muscles, which reveal their heart, digestive system and bones underneath. The cane toad grows to around 30cm. Though native to Latin America, it is now established in the US and Australia and has become a serious pest in places.

Rainforest insects and other invertebrates The rainforest hosts a staggering
wealth of invertebrates (creatures without a backbone). Of these, the insects show the greatest number and diversity, with 34 different orders compared with 16 orders of mammal, and – according to recent studies of rainforest canopies – an estimated 30 million species. Without them, the rainforest would not function or even exist. They recycle nutrients, maintain soil structure and fertility, pollinate plants, disperse seeds, control populations of other organisms and are a major food source for birds, mammals, reptiles, amphibians, other invertebrates and even carnivorous plants.

Beetles Of the world's 1.75 million animal species so far described, a third are beetles. Notable rainforest beetles include the exquisite golden tortoise beetle, which resembles an Egyptian scarab carved in gold, as well as giants such as the titan-longhorn, one of the world's largest insects, and the 12cm-long rhinoceros beetle, which sports impressive horns. Fireflies, really beetles, are responsible for spectacular luminous displays along river edges and lowland areas at certain times of year, with each species using its own identification code of short and long flashes to attract a mate. The metallic-green wing-cases of wood-boring beetles, also called jewel beetles because of their dazzling iridescence, are used locally in necklaces and other adornments. Weevils look like miniature tanks, armed with a nozzle-like proboscis and a rounded carapace. Locals harvest the thumb-sized grubs of the palm beetle for a handy, nutritious snack, called *suri*.

Wasps Wasps vary greatly in size, from the tiny to the worryingly large. Among the biggest is the tarantula hawk, which uses its sting to paralyse tarantulas, laying its eggs in the victim. Most wasps are communal, living in hives from five–ten individuals to many tens of thousands. Many are impressive architects: common wasps use chewed wood pulp to build finger-shaped nests 2m long; potter wasps use clay to build compact globular nests. One Colombian species moulds a spherical clay nest about 10cm across, which has a covering of clay and sand cement that is virtually impenetrable, except via a small entrance hole.

Ants and termites Ants are the most abundant rainforest insects, comprising up to one-tenth of the total animal biomass. Some consume the waste products of herbivorous insects, while others eat the insects themselves. Strictly speaking, even leaf-cutter ants are not herbivorous: the pieces of leaf that workers harvest and cut into neat shapes become compost for a fungus, which feeds every ant in the colony and is incessantly tended by workers.

Other ants include Azteca ants, which aggressively defend their host plant, the cecropia tree (page 470), and honey ants, which 'farm' plant-sucking aphids. Army ants plunder other ant nests for eggs and larvae, and the flurry of activity caused by insects trying to escape draws insectivorous creatures, such as antbirds, to the scene. The glossy black bullet ant is the world's largest ant and has an excruciating sting. These ants are solitary by day, but at night they gather in small bands of a dozen or so and head out to collect their prey.

Termites, like ants, are master builders, but are more primitive insects that are closely related to cockroaches. The grey, pencil-wide tunnels that you see on the sides of trees are highways from the termites' food sources to their nests high above flood levels.

Butterflies and moths We do not know the precise number of butterfly and moth (Lepidoptera) species found in the lowland Amazon, though some 4,000 butterflies have been described from Peru alone. The trays of mounted butterflies and other insects sold by hawkers at tourist sites often include specimens imported from Asia, so are not representative of the local fauna. Do not encourage this destructive trade by buying them.

Morpho butterflies are distinguished by their large size and iridescent blue wings, which sport eye-spots on the underside that deter or confuse a predator. The caligo, like the morpho, has superb eye-spots – perfect replicas of owl eyes – while, to complete the deception, the rest of its wings and body mimic the bird's 'ears' and beak.

Many heliconiid butterflies are highly poisonous. They are thought to derive their toxins from the host plant, ingested by the caterpillar or butterfly and sequestered for later use. Different species of heliconiid have evolved to mimic one another, sharing similar wing patterns. This is known as Müllerian mimicry: a taste or two of a poisonous species leads a predator to associate its pattern with poison, thus all butterflies that share this pattern will benefit from being off the menu.

Hawkmoths resemble hummingbirds in form and size, and feed in a similar way by extracting nectar from flowers during their nocturnal forays. The rapid wingbeats of the larger species create a 'hum' while hovering.

Spiders: a world of web sights Spiders and other arachnids are distinguished from insects by their eight legs, and a body divided into two, not three, segments. Many rainforest species make distinctive webs. On jungle walks or canoe rides, look for the large, funnel-shaped webs woven by communal spiders, which are designed to catch prey that drops from the canopy. The elegant golden orb-weaver, which has long legs and an elongated black-and-silver body, spins a giant web of strong gold silk across forest gaps and trails, which is most disconcerting (though harmless) to walk into.

Tarantulas fit our preconception of a rainforest spider. These impressive creatures do not trap prey in webs but actively hunt it in swamp vegetation or other damp habitats. Most are harmless, with a bite no more painful than a bee sting. It is quite safe to let one walk across your arm, but you should not handle their hairy bodies, which may irritate the skin.

Some spiders are dangerous, with cytolytic venom that causes cells to break down, hindering the healing process. Among tens of thousands of species, however, only two or three are potentially life-threatening. One of these is considered the world's most venomous spider: the Brazilian wandering spider, which lives in the thatch or walls of jungle huts. The terrifying-looking tailless whip scorpion, by contrast, is all bluff, being harmless and lacking a sting.

Millipedes and centipedes These arthropods look like armoured caterpillars. Most millipedes (class Diplopoda) are cylindrical in cross-section, but one common rainforest species, greyish and up to 13cm long, has a flattened body with horizontal projections from each of its body segments. Centipedes (class Chilopoda), unlike the herbivorous millipedes, are hunters that prey on small insects and other invertebrates. They are flattened in cross-section and have only one pair of legs per segment. All centipedes have a venomous bite. Most are harmless to humans, but they should be avoided.

WATERWORLD The Amazon has the most diverse freshwater fauna on the planet. There are, for example, at least 2,000 fish species and perhaps 1,000 more to be described, by contrast with a paltry 150 or so in Europe.

Aquatic mammals A number of specialised mammals have adapted to life in the waterways of the Amazon.

Freshwater dolphins Amazon dolphins are smaller than their marine relatives. They are most common at river mouths, where fish are abundant. Locals generally have taboos against eating dolphin. However, fishermen occasionally kill them by accident – or deliberately when they become entangled in nets. Some are also killed for medicinal or shamanistic purposes.

Size, colour and behaviour distinguish the two Amazon species. The pink river dolphin (boto) is about 2.4m long, with a low dorsal ridge in place of a fin. It swims slowly, feeding on fish, crabs and small river turtles. Pink river dolphins are active day and night, and you will often see a bachelor male, or sometimes a small family pod, swim by. Their body does not clear the water when they leap. The grey dolphin is smaller and shaped more like a marine dolphin, with a curved dorsal fin, and its body clears the water when jumping. It feeds mainly on fast-swimming fish close to the surface.

Manatee The Amazon manatee is a strictly freshwater species. Weighing up to 500kg, it is the largest Amazon mammal – though it wins no beauty contests. Nostrils positioned on top of its squarish muzzle enable it to breathe with its body and head submerged, while a paddle-like tail propels it ponderously through the water. Manatees are purely vegetarian, consuming over 45kg a day of waterweeds – which would otherwise quickly clog waterways. Unfortunately, unlike dolphins, no taboos protect the manatee, and hunting is virtually uncontrolled. Docile, slow-moving and conspicuous, it is easy prey, and high prices provide a strong incentive to a poor *ribereño*.

Otters Otters, which belong to the weasel family (Mustelidae), are supreme underwater fish catchers. The southern river otter is dark brown above and creamy below, while the Brazilian or giant otter is the world's largest freshwater otter. Unfortunately, otters' loud, playful antics do little to disguise their whereabouts from hunters. Formerly common and widespread, both species are now endangered.

Aquatic reptiles The Amazon's two main groups of aquatic reptiles are crocodilians and turtles. These are evolved from ancestors that were isolated when South America became an island continent.

Caiman Caiman are South American crocodilians. They eat mostly fish, but turtles, frogs and other reptiles also fall prey. The largest species is the black caiman, which can reach an impressive 5m. On night boat rides, you might see the red eye-shine of the common or spectacled caiman, which does not exceed 2.5m. Caiman make nests of vegetation in which they lay 30–60 eggs at a time, though just one or two individuals in a clutch survive. Their populations are under severe hunting pressure throughout the Amazon.

River turtles The 13 Amazon river turtle species are all side-necked turtles, so-called because they retract their head sideways into the shell. The giant river turtle is the largest, weighing up to 75kg. The matamata has a long neck, a tube-like snout that acts as a snorkel, and a carapace that resembles floating leaves to fool approaching prey. It feeds by opening its wide mouth suddenly to draw in small fish like a vacuum cleaner.

Fabulous fish Around 80% of the Amazon's fish species are characins. This is the largest family of Neotropical freshwater fish and includes such well-known groups as catfish, lungfish and piranhas.

A1

Piranhas B-movies would have us believe that there is only one type of Amazon fish: the reputedly deadly piranha. In fact records show not a single human fatality, although fishermen have been known to lose toes and fingers. The best-known species is the red-bellied piranha, which has a silvery back, an orange-red underside and extremely sharp teeth that are serrated and triangular, like a tiny shark's. Piranhas' feeding habits depend on the season, with low water levels being likely to reduce food availability and thus increase competition – leading, on occasion, to the famous feeding frenzies. At this time they are easy to catch on a hook baited with raw meat, though their hundreds of tiny bones and rather greasy flesh make them rather an acquired taste. (See box, page 266.)

Electric eel A number of documented cases report fatalities caused by the infamous electric eel. It discharges a shock of up to 1,000 volts to knock out prey and defend itself against predators. The current is usually non-lethal for humans, but powerful enough to cause temporary paralysis – which can, on occasion, lead to drowning.

Other characins Jewel tetras, found in murky waters, are tiny living gems and among the most sought-after aquarium fish, their brilliant primary colours glowing under lights. Flying hatchet fish use their pectoral fins like wings to propel them through the air as a defence against predatory fish, and may even land in a speeding canoe. The more sedate headstanders spend the most of their lives with their tail up in the air, whereas pencil fish live mostly head-up.

Candirú The candirú family comprises a number of small, scaleless fish, one of which normally dwells within another fish's waste tract and is reputed to wriggle up the orifices of human swimmers. Apparently attracted by the warmth of urine, it zooms inside the opening, whereupon its sharp spines project into the tender flesh and it is removable only by surgery. Stay safe: wear a bathing suit and don't pee in the water while swimming. (See box, page 262.)

Catfishes Most of the hundred or more species of catfish are bottom-feeders, and use their long whiskers (barbels) to search the river mud for worms, crustaceans and snails. One of Amazonia's biggest fish, with a scientific name to match, is *Brachyplatystoma filamentosum*, up to 3m long. The more common dorado is a staple food for people along the river, and in fish markets you may also see the smaller suckermouth catfish, which has ornate horns on its heavy scales.

Arapaima and arowana One of the world's largest freshwater fish, the predatory arapaima is shaped like a huge pike. Specimens over 4m long and weighing 250kg have been known, but this fish's huge size and tasty flesh make local mouths drool during arapaima seasons! Its large greenish-bronze scales turn white when removed, and are used for decoration or jewellery. The closely related arowana, or water monkey, can leap out of the water to snatch unsuspecting meals from a branch, including birds, reptiles and even baby sloths.

Cichlids Many cichlids are commercially important, either as food or sport fish, or for the aquarium trade. The peacock bass grows to 30kg and is golden-yellow with black dorsal bars, and an eye-spot on the tail to distract predators. Discus fish have a round, compressed body and their attractive markings make them popular in the aquarium trade.

Other Amazon fishes The leaf fish mimics a dead leaf floating on water. Drifting around, pointing downward, it preys on unsuspecting fish that swim by. A transparent tail and pectoral fins allow it to move without being detected. Tiny killifish spend most of their lives as tough, drought-resistant eggs in shallow, ephemeral ponds. Some complete their entire life cycle in places where water lasts no more than three weeks. Sting rays, notably those of the strictly freshwater genus *Potamotrygon*, are the only freshwater cartilaginous fishes (although some sharks roam upriver from the ocean), and rest half-covered in sand on the beds of shallow rivers. The 'sting' is a venomous barbed fin at the base of the tail.

Appendix 2

LANGUAGE

Of the more than 400 million people who speak Spanish (or Castilian) as their mother tongue, more than 300 million are in Latin America. Castillan Spanish is the official language of Colombia and there are close ties between the Spanish and Colombian language academies. Accents vary throughout the country and the dialect is full of local jargon and numerous Colombianisms, although in many ways it is similar to the style of Spanish observed in the southern parts of Spain.

The Caro y Cuervo Institute in Bogotá promotes the good use of the Spanish language in Colombia. Generally Spanish pronunciation and grammar are straightforward, with few irregularities. However, the singular second-person pronoun *tú* is widely used in informal talk, while *usted* is used in formal talk. Most people in Bogotá use *tú* when addressing strangers. As a paradox, when talking with very close relatives such as parents, siblings or spouses the more formal *usted* is mostly used. Mixing formal pronouns and informal verbal forms is common, eg: '*Usted que piensas?*' (What do you [formal] think [informal]?). Another characteristic of Colombian Spanish is the use of diminutive forms -ico, -ica, used in words ending in 't', eg: *gato* (cat). . . *gatico* (small cat), something that it shares with Costa Rican and Cuban Spanish. Words ending in a vowel, 'n' or 's' take the stress on the penultimate syllable; all words that end in other consonants take the stress on the last syllable. Irregular stresses are marked with an accent.

The strongest dialects in Colombia are found in Antioquia, Quindío, Risaralda and Caldas where people speak Spanish with a distinct Castilian-sounding 's'. In Bogotá, the city's clipped dialect is referred to as *cachaco* (meaning 'educated' or 'refined'), while on the Caribbean the coastal (*costeño*) dialect is characterised by a suppressive drawl almost as if speaking with a boiled egg in their mouth.

The Afro-Colombian communities in the department of Chocó have their own idioms and local terminology, as do the population of the San Andrés Archipelago where on Isla Providencia English patois is spoken. In addition to Spanish there are more than 180 indigenous languages and dialects belonging to such major linguistic groups as Arawakan, Chibchan, Cariban, Tupi-Guaraní, and Yuruman. Many tribes also use a form of communicative sign language wholly unique to their own communities.

PRONUNCIATION
Consonants

c	as in 'cat', before 'a', 'o', or 'u'; like 's' before 'e' or 'i'
d	as 'd' in 'dog', except between vowels, then like 'th' in 'that'
g	before 'e' or 'i', like the 'ch' in Scottish 'loch'; elsewhere like 'g' in 'get'
h	always silent
j	like the English 'h' in 'hotel', but stronger
ll	like the 'y' in 'yellow'
ñ	like the 'ni' in 'onion'

r   always pronounced as strong 'r'

rr   trilled 'rr'

v   similar to the 'b' in 'boy' (not as English 'v')

y   similar to English, but with a slight 'j' sound. When y stands alone it is pronounced like the 'e' in 'me'.

z   like 's' in 'same'

b, f, k, l, m, n, p, q, s, t, w, x as in English

Vowels

a   as in 'father' but shorter

e   as in 'hen'

i   as in 'machine'

o   as in 'phone'

u   usually as in 'rule'; when it follows a 'q' the 'u' is silent; when it follows an 'h' or 'g' it's pronounced like 'w', except when it comes between 'g' and 'e' or 'i', when it's also silent

USEFUL WORDS AND PHRASES *with Larissa Banting*
Essentials

Hello	*Hola*	I'm sorry	*Lo siento*
Good morning	*Buenos días*	Goodbye	*Adiós*
Good afternoon	*Buenas tardes*	See you later	*Hasta luego*
Good evening	*Buenas noches*	more	*más*
How are you?	*¿Cómo está?*	less	*menos*
Fine	*Muy bien*	better	*major*
And you?	*¿y Usted?* (formal)	much	*mucho*
	or *¿y vos?* (informal)	a little	*un poco*
Thank you	*Gracias*	large	*grande*
Thank you very	*Muchas gracias*	small	*pequeño*
much		quick	*rápido*
You are very kind	*Usted es muy amable*	slowly	*despacio*
You are welcome	*Con gusto*	good	*bueno*
Yes	*Sí*	bad	*malo*
No	*No*	difficult	*difícil*
I don't know	*Yo no sé*	easy	*fácil*
It's fine	*Está bien*	I don't speak	*No hablo español*
Please	*Por favor*	Spanish	
Pleased to meet you	*Mucho gusto*	I don't understand	*No entiendo*
Excuse me	*Discúlpeme*	Do you speak	*¿habla inglés?*
	Perdóneme	English	
	(figuratively)		

Numbers

0	*cero*	7	*siete*
1	*uno* (masculine)	8	*ocho*
1	*una* (feminine)	9	*nueve*
2	*dos*	10	*diez*
3	*tres*	11	*once*
4	*cuatro*	12	*doce*
5	*cinco*	13	*trece*
6	*seis*	14	*catorce*

15	quince	200	doscientos
16	dieciséis	300	trescientos
17	diecisiete	400	cuatrocientos
18	dieciocho	500	quinientos
19	diecinueve	600	seiscientos
20	veinte	700	setecientos
30	treinta	800	ochocientos
40	cuarenta	900	novecientos
50	cincuenta	1,000	mil
60	sesenta	2,000	dos mil
70	setenta	3,000	tres mil
80	ochenta	4,000	cuatro mil
90	noventa	5,000	cinco mil
100	cien	10,000	diez mil
101	ciento uno	15,000	quince mil

Days of the week

Sunday	domingo	Thursday	jueves
Monday	lunes	Friday	viernes
Tuesday	martes	Saturday	sábado
Wednesday	miércoles		

Time

What time is it?	¿Qué hora es?	tomorrow	mañana
one o'clock	la una	morning	la mañana
two o'clock	las dos	yesterday	ayer
at two o'clock	a las dos	week	semana
ten past three	las tres y diez	month	mes
06.00	las seis de la mañana	year	año
18.00	las seis de la tarde	last night	anoche
today	hoy	next day	al día siguiente

Terms of address

I	yo	Miss, young lady	señorita
you (formal)	usted	wife	esposa
you (informal)	vos, tu	husband	esposo or marido
he/him	él	friend	amigo (male)
she/her	ella		amiga (female)
we/us	nosotros	girlfriend	novia
you (plural)	ustedes	boyfriend	novio
they/them (males or mixed gender)	ellos	father	padre
		mother	madre
they/them (females)	ellas	son	hijo
		daughter	hija
Mr, Sir	señor	brother	hermano
Mrs, Ms, Madam	señora	sister	hermana

Getting around

Where is…?	¿Dónde está…?	highway	la carretera
How far is…?	¿Qué tan lejos está…?	road	el camino
From… to	De… a	street	la calle

block	la cuadra	east	este
kilometre	kilómetro	straight ahead	adelante
north	norte	to the right	a la derecha
south	sur	to the left	a la izquierda
west	oeste		

Accommodation

Can I see a room?	¿Puedo ver una habitación?	hot water	agua caliente
		cold water	agua fría
What is the rate?	¿Cuál es el precio?	towel	toalla
a single room	una habitación sencilla	soap	jabón
a double room	una habitación doble	toilet paper	papel higiénico
key	llave	air conditioning	aire acondicionado
bathroom	baño	blanket	cobija or manta

Public transport

bus stop	parada de bus	Here, please	Aquí, por favor
airport	aeropuerto	Where is this bus going?	¿Dónde va este bus?
ferry terminal	terminal de ferry		
I want a ticket to…	Quiero un pasaje/tiquete a…	round trip	ida y vuelta
		What do I owe?	¿Cuánto le debo?
I want to get off at…	Quiero bajar en…		

Food and drink

menu	menu	eggs	huevos
glass	vaso	bread	pan
mug	taza	watermelon	sandía
fork	tenedor	banana	banano
knife	cuchillo	apple	manzana
spoon	cuchara	orange	naranja
napkin	servilleta	meat (without)	(sin) carne
soft drink	gaseosa	chicken	pollo
coffee	café	fish	pescado
cream	crema	shellfish	camarones, mariscos
tea	té	fried	frito
sugar	azúcar	roasted	asado
drinking water	agua potable	barbecue	a la parilla
beer	cerveza	breakfast	desayuno
wine	vino	lunch	almuerzo
milk	leche	dinner	cena
juice	jugo	the bill	la cuenta

Making purchases

I need…	necesito…	I'm just looking	Estoy buscando
I want…	quiero…	Can I see…?	¿Puedo ver…?
I would like…	quisiera…	this one	ésto/ésta
How much does it cost?	¿Cuánto cuesta?	expensive	caro
		cheap	barato
What is the exchange rate?	¿Cuál es el tipo de cambio?	cheaper	más barato
		too much	demasiado

Health

Help me, please	*Ayúdeme, por favor*	chemist	*farmacia*
I am ill	*Estoy enfermo*	medicine	*medicina*
pain	*dolor*	pill, tablet	*pastilla*
fever	*fiebre*	birth control pills	*pastillas*
stomach ache	*dolor de estómago*		*anticonceptivas*
vomiting	*vomitar*	condoms	*preservativos*
diarrhoea	*diarrea*		

SLANG Colombia's street language is more colourful than its carnivals. Slang is widespread and has strong regional distinctions. It is particularly used in the Paisa region where it is known as 'Parlache'. Many of Colombia's slang expressions have been adopted by people living outside of their place of origin and are commonly understood countrywide.

Some of the most common slang terms with literal translation are listed below. Master a few and you'll significantly up your cred as a gringo on Colombian soil.

Slang	Meaning	Literal translation
abrirse	to leave	to open
Ala	Hey man	wing
almacén	shop	warehouse
andén	pavement, sidewalk	platform
armar videos	to lie	to do videos
atorarse	to choke	to get stuck
avión	a clever person	airplane
bacano	cool	good
barra	peso (currency unit)	bar
baúl	boot, trunk (of a car)	chest (furniture)
birra	beer	Italian for beer
bomba	baloon; also fuel pump	bomb
buzo	turtleneck sweater	diver
café	brown (colour)	coffee
camello	job, (heavy) work	camel
cana	gaol, jail	white hair
caneca	trash basket/waste bin	earthenware bottle
cantaleta	repetitive scolding	repetitive song
caña	bluff, bragging; also rhum	fishing rod
capar	to play truant	to castrate
carpeta	doily	folder
caspa	senseless speech	dandruff
catorce	favour	fourteen
chimba	excellent	fake
chino	kid, boy	Chinese
chupa	police officer	sucker
colorete	rouge	lipstick
cotejo	soccer/football match	comparison
culebra	debt	snake
duro	Skilful	hard
embarrarla	to make a grave mistake	to cover with mud
esfero	pen	sphere (masculine form)
Eye! Pilas!	be careful!	batteries!
filo	hunger	edge

gonorrea	vile person	gonorrheoa
guayabo	hangover	guava tree
güevón	dude, bro	mispronunciation of '*huevón*'
hacerse el gringo	to feign ignorance	to act as an American
hueco	pot hole; also gaol, jail	hole
huevón	dude, bro	sluggish or idiot
jurgo	plethora, lot	massive amount
levantar	to seduce/to beat, thrash	to raise
ligar	to give money, bribe	to tie
listo	all right	ready
llave	friend	key
lobo	bad taste	wolf
luca	a thousand	Colombian pesos
mamar	to bore	to suck
man	guy	man (English loanword)
marica	dude, bro	queer
marimba	marijuana	marimba
mono	blond(e), fair-haired	monkey
mosca (estar mosca)	be clever for a while; also annoyed	fly (as an adjective, 'be fly')
No joda!	Nuh-uh!/Get outta here!	Don't fuck
No me joda!	Don't bother me!	Don't fuck me!
Ojo!	Be careful!	Watch out!
olla	place where drugs are sold	saucepan
paila	bad luck	frying pan
paja	lie, falsehood; also masturbation	hay
parar bolas	to pay attention	to stand balls
parche	band	patch
pata	marijuana roach	leg
pedo	big problem	fart
perder el año	to die	to get an F (grade)
piedra	anger	stone
pilo	good student	battery (masculine form)
poner bolas	to pay attention	to put balls
poner los cachos	to cheat (relationships)	set the horns
puto	enraged	male prostitute
Qué boleta!	How embarrassing!	What a ticket!
Qué hubo? (Quiubo)	What's up?	What was there?
Qué mamera!	That's boring!	What a sucker!
Qué más?	What's up?	What else?
rascado	drunk	scratched
rata	robber	rat
sapo	meddler, snitch	frog
sobar	to disturb	to handle, touch
tinto	black coffee	red wine
tomba	the police/police officer	fuzz
vaina	thing	scabbard
Vientos o maletas?	How are you?	winds or suitcases

Appendix 3

FURTHER INFORMATION

BOOKS
Art
Basualdo, Carlos, Princenthal, Nancy and Huyssen, Andreas *Doris Salcedo* Phaidon Press, 2000. A collection of the Colombian sculptor's work, made from objects found in the abandoned homes of missing Colombians.

Botero, Werner Fernando *Spies* Prestel Verlag, 1997. An excellent overview of the broad range of works of this world-acclaimed Colombian figurative artist.

Cardale Schrimpff, M (ed) *Calima and Malagana: Art and Archaeology in Southwestern Colombia* Pro Calima Foundation, 2005. Based on 25 years of research by a multi-national team, this detailed chronicle centres on the cultural and artistic development from 8000BC to the early colonial period along with recent excavations of gold and pottery in the context of Colombia's social and political changes and indigenous belief systems.

Perez, Roberto, Botero, Clara and Londono, Santiago *The Art of Gold* Skira Editore, 2007. Traces the legacy of gold in pre-Hispanic Colombia with 250 gold objects taken from the Gold Museum of Bogotá.

Autobiographies/biographies
Betancourt, Ingrid *Even Silence Has An End: My Six Years of Captivity in the Colombian Jungle* Virago Press, 2010. This is Betancourt's own story of her capture, kidnap and eventual release. A deeply moving book that redresses the often critical accounts of her behaviour at the hands of FARC published by her fellow captives (see Gozalves below).

Betancourt, Ingrid *Until Death Do Us Part: My Struggle to Reclaim Colombia* Phoenix Press, 2003. A personal political memoir of a Colombian presidential candidate who was kidnapped by FARC after the publication of this international bestseller. She was released in 2009 and some editions include an update.

Gozalves, Mark and Howes, Tom *Out of Captivity: Surviving 1967 Days in the Colombian Jungle* Harper Paperbacks, reprint edition, 2010. An interesting account of three Americans captured by FARC including their time spent with Ingrid Betancourt (see above).

Lynch, John *Simón Bolívar: A Life* Yale University Press, 2006. Bolívar was the very first president of Colombia, and known throughout South America as 'The Liberator'. This is his story.

Paternostro, Silvana *My Colombian War: A Journey through the Country I left Behind* Henry Holt, 2007. An intimate portrait from the perspective of a journalist and part of the Colombian diaspora in the United States forced into leaving due to violence and wishing to come back to visit. An interesting take on the Colombian class system.

Business
Buchelo, Marcelo *Bananas and Business: The United Fruit Company in Colombia 1899–2000* New York University Press, 2005. A critical analysis of the United Fruit Company's century-long presence in Colombia with a look at its widespread influence in the political, consumer, labour and historical arenas.

Colombian Government and Business Contacts Handbook International Business Publications USA, 2004. Colombia's indispensable commercial bible.

Erlick, June Carolyn *A Gringa in Bogotá: Living Colombia's Invisible War* University of Texas Press, first edition, 2010

Cuisine

Fleetwood, Jenni *South American Food and Cooking: Ingredients, Techniques and Signature Recipes from the Undiscovered Traditional Cuisines of Brazil, Argentina, Uruguay, Ecuador, Mexico, Colombia and Venezuela* Southwater, 2006

McCausland-Gallo, Patricia *Secrets of Colombian Cooking* Hippocrene Books, US, 2004. Over 175 tasty and authentic Colombian recipes. Contains dishes using fish from the Caribbean Sea, the Pacific Ocean and the Amazon, Magdalena and Cauca rivers and features the hearty stews of the Andes.

Drugs

Kirk, Robin *More Terrible than Death: Drugs, Violence and America's War in Colombia* Publicaffairs Ltd, 2004. A personal, contemporary history of Colombia and the drug war, told by an employee of Human Rights Watch who was posted in Colombia for 12 years.

Leech, Garry *Beyond Bogotá – Diary of a Drug War Journalist in Colombia* Beacon Press, first edition, 2010

Molano, Alfredo *Loyal Soldiers in the Cocaine Kingdom: Tales of Drugs, Mules, and Gunmen* Colombia University Press, 2004. Testimonials of ordinary Colombian people who have become involved in smuggling in search of a better life, and the consequences that they have faced for their decisions. The translation has made this book confusing in parts, but it's worth a read.

Otis, John *Law of the Jungle: The Hunt for Colombian Guerrillas, American Hostages and Buried Treasure* William Morrow, 2010. A very digestible and journalistic account of contemporary Colombia, the guerrillas and the drugs trade by a foreign correspondent based in Colombia.

Porter, Bruce *Blow: How A Small-Town Boy Made $100 Million With the Medellín Cocaine Cartel and Lost it All* Saint Martín's Press, 2001. The true story of how George Jung introduced cocaine to the US mass market. This was the basis of a successful film starring Johnny Depp in 2001.

Fiction

Isaacs, Jorge *María* Losada, 2005. This famous novel represents the Colombian literary period known as Spanish-American Romanticism. Wildside Press edition in English, 2007.

Márquez, Gabriel García *One Hundred Years of Solitude* Penguin, new edition, 1998. Tells the story of a poor Colombian family living through a century of extraordinary events in the Caribbean lowlands. Márquez was the winner of the 1982 Nobel Prize in literature, and is credited for developing the 'magical realism' style of writing.

Rainier, Peter W *The Bogotá Connection* Authorhouse, 2005. Espionage thriller based at an emerald mine in 1930s Colombia.

Silva, José Asunción *Obra Poetica* Ediciones Sa, 1996. A collection of the poet's *modernismo* work (Spanish).

Geography and natural history

Colombia Map International Travel Maps and Books, second edition, 2012. By far the best map on the market.

Corwin, Jeff *Into Wild Amazon* Blackbirch Press, 2004. A chronicle of the flora and fauna found in the Amazon region.

Defler, Thomas Richard *Primates of Colombia* Conservation International, 2005. Illustrated field guide.

Hart Dyke, Tom and Winder, Paul *The Cloud Garden: A True Story of Adventure, Survival, and Extreme Horticulture* Lyons Press, 2004

Pollard, Michael *Great Rivers: The Amazon* Evans Brothers, 2003. Detailed look at the plants, terrain, birds and wildlife found in the Amazon watershed. Von Humboldt, Alexander *Personal Narrative of Travels to the Equinoctial Regions of America During the Years 1799–1804* Indypublish.com, 2006. Three-volume studies and explorations of a German botanist.

Guidebooks

Harris, Roger *Amazon Highlights* Bradt Travel Guides, first edition, 2011. Selected highlights of the Amazon in Colombia, Brazil, Peru and Ecuador.

Harris, Roger and Hutchinson, Peter *The Amazon* Bradt Travel Guides, third edition, 2007. The most comprehensive Amazon travel guide with detailed information on the biodiversity of the region, expedition planning and jungle routes.

Woods, Sarah *Panama* Bradt Travel Guides, second edition, 2011

Health

Duke, James A *The CRC Handbook of Alternative Cash Crops for the Tropics and the Amazonian Ethnobotanical Dictionary: The Green Pharmacy* US Aid for International Development, 2003

Schultes, Richard Evans *Vine of the Soul: Medicine Men, Their Plants and Rituals in the Colombian Amazonia* Synergetic Press Inc, 2004

These two excellent books provide a fascinating insight into traditional healing. Both explore roles of shaman in ancient medicine and the origins and potency of plants, while also examining the powers associated with the sacred ground of the Amazon region.

Wilson-Howarth, Jane *Bugs, Bites & Bowels* Cadogan, 2006

Winsor, Shane (ed) *Expedition Medicine* Profile Books, 2004. This essential guide to treating accidents and illnesses when travelling to remote areas includes how to handle remote medical emergencies and common infections. Lots of detail and advice comes with illustrations with tips for first-aid kit items to pack and information on specific emergency procedures, including treatment of acute mountain sickness.

Young, Isabelle *Healthy Travel: Central and South America* Lonely Planet, 2000

History

Dudley, Steven *Walking Ghosts: Murder and Guerrilla Politics in Colombia* Routledge, 2004. This powerful account details the political genocide that eliminated the Patriotic Unión Party in the late 1980s and early 90s.

Hemming, John *The Search for El Dorado* Weidenfeld & Nicolson, 2001. Provides some useful background information on the colonisation of Colombia with plenty of pre-Columbian insight.

Kellaway, Victoria and Lievano, Sergio J *Colombia a Comedy of Errors* Kauf Book, 2014. At first appearing to be a lightweight book regarding Colombian identity, culture, economics and justice, this amusingly illustrated book pulls no punches and is a must for first-time visitors to Colombia wishing to learn more.

Rolddan, M *Blood and Fire: La Violencia in Antioquia, Colombia, 1946–53* Duke University Press, 2002. Examines the period of terror that led to the death of over 200,000 Colombians.

Simons, Geoff *Colombia: A Brutal History* Saqi Books, 2004. A revealing insight into the violent drug cartels, foreign interference, corporate exploitation, paramilitary death squads and civil war of Colombia's past.

Taussig, Michael T *Law in a Lawless Land: Diary of a Limpieza in Colombia* University of

Chicago Press, 2003. Anthropologist Michael Taussig's dramatic exposé of Colombia's paramilitary death squads is based on witness statements from friends and relatives of the victims of 'social cleansing', and his own experiences in a small Colombian village.

Language

Campbell, Lyle *American Indian Languages: The Historical Linguistics of Native America* Oxford University Press, USA, 2000. A useful examination of Native American languages, and the relationships between them.

Latin American Spanish Lonely Planet, fifth edition, 2008

Latin American Spanish Phrasebook Rough Guides, second edition, 2011. A decent phrasebook for everyday situations.

McVey Gill, Mary and Wegmann, Brenda *Streetwise Spanish: The User-Friendly Guide to Spanish Slang and Idioms* McGraw-Hill, 1998. An indispensable guide to the irregularities of Spanish language – including proper street slang for gossip, swearing and undying love – and everything else you can imagine.

Strom, Clay *Studies in the Languages of Colombia* Summer Institute of Linguistics, 1993. A thorough look at the 60-plus languages and umpteen dialects of the Colombian peoples.

Literature

Borda, Juan Gustavo *Historia de la Poesia Colombiana* Siglo XX Editores Villegas, Colombia, 2006. A compilation of significant Colombian works, selected by a prolific Colombian poet (Spanish).

Doherty de Novoa, Caroline, Kellaway, Victoria and McColl, Richard *Was Gabo an Irishman? Tales from Gabriel García Márquez's Colombia* Papen Press, 2015. A well-edited collection of essays written by journalists and García Márquez enthusiasts on their Macondo-style experiences in Colombia.

Gonzalez, Anibal *A Companion to Spanish American Modernismo* Tamesis Books, 2007. Paperback edition, 2010.

Jrade, Cathy *Modernismo, Modernity and the Development of Spanish American Literature* University of Texas Press, 1998. Details the evolution of Spanish-language contemporary literature.

McKnight, Kathryn Joy *The Mystic of Tunja: Writings of Madre Castillo, 1671–1742* University of Massachusetts Press, 1997. Pioneering nun Madre Castillo's struggle to balance her literary aspirations with the demands of religious service.

Suárez-Araúz, Nicomedes *Literary Amazonia: Modern Writing by Amazonian Authors* University Press of Florida, 2004. This remarkable selection of 20th-century Amazonian literature contains work from the Amazon's indigenous and *mestizo* people. Some 24 poets and 12 prose writers capture the spirit of the region and many of the community's forgotten voices, collected and translated into English for the first time.

Music

Bennion, Neil *Dancing Feat: One Man's Mission to Dance Like a Colombian* Amazon, 2014. Join inveterate dance coward Neil Bennion as he romps through this land of swashbuckling peaks and luscious coastlines, learning new dances as he goes. When he's not doing everything in his power to avoid them, that is.

Ellingham, Mark, McConnachie, James and Broughton, Simon (eds) *World Music, vol 2 (including Latin & North America, Caribbean, India, Asia and Pacific)*, Rough Guides, 2000. In particular, see pages 372–85.

Wade, Peter *Music, Race and Nation: Música Tropical in Colombia* University of Chicago Press, 2000. The rise of '*musica tropical*', incorporating *porro*, *cumbia* and *vallenato* styles of music.

Waxer, Lise A *The City of Musical Memory: Salsa, Record Grooves and Popular Culture in Cali,*

Colombia Wesleyan University Press, 2002. A thorough history of salsa and its importance to Cali's traditions and culture.

Xemina, Diego *Shakira: Woman Full of Grace* Simon & Schuster, 2001. Biography of Colombia's chart-topping singer/songwriter that chronicles her early days as a rising star and recent award-winning pop-music success.

Older travellers

Gardener, Alison *Travel Unlimited: Uncommon Adventures for the Mature Traveler* Avalon Travel Publishing, 2000. Despite being in need of an update, this remains a valuable real first-of-its-kind, covering alternative worldwide travel options for adventurous older travellers. Detailed reviews explore ecological, cultural and volunteer opportunities for people aged 50-plus who are still keen to indulge their irrepressible travel spirit.

Toland, James *Travel Tips and Trips for Seniors* Bridgeway Press, 2002. Humorous quips, anecdotes and insight make this an entertaining read for any 50-plus traveller looking for advice on great destinations that are ideal for an active older person keen to hit the ground running.

Photography

Hurtado García, Andrés *Secret Vistas of Colombia* Villegas Editores, 2005. A photographic collection focuses on panorama shots of Colombia's regional landscape and fine colonial cities.

Villegas, María *Bogotá from the Air* Villegas Asociados SA, 2002. A stunning photographic tour of Bogotá.

Von Rothkirch, Cristóbal *Bogotá Viva* Villegas Asociados SA, 2006. An anthology of urban photography, offering an honest reflection of both positive and negative aspects of city life.

Politics

Kline, Harvey F *Chronicle of a Failure Foretold: The Peace Process of Colombian President Andrés Pastrana* University of Alabama Press, 2007

Lozano, Carlos *Guerra O Paz En Colombia?* Ocean Press, 2007. A historical perspective on the Colombian conflict, analysing the role of the US and the war on drugs, the right-wing paramilitaries and the left-wing guerrilla movements – and the real possibilities for achieving peace (Spanish).

Murillo, Mario A and Avirama, Jesús Rey *Colombia and the United States: War, Terrorism and Destabilization* Seven Stories Press, 2003. Discusses the origins of the Colombian conflict, the myths behind Colombian democracy and how the involvement of the US has contributed to the problems.

San Andrés y Providencia: Tradiciones culturales y coyuntura política Uniandes, 1989. A look at the political, social and cultural history of the San Andrés Archipelago.

Stokes, Doug *America's Other War: Terrorizing Colombia* Zed Books, 2004. A highly critical political analysis of US political involvement in Colombian policy.

Religion

Eliade, Mircea *Shamanism: Archaic Techniques of Ecstasy* Arkana Publishing, 2004. A look at the hallucinogenic properties of traditional plants and their curative powers in indigenous groups.

Greco, David *Dios Sana Mi Nacion Colombia* Vida Publishing, 2002. A look at Colombian society from a healing perspective that examines God's provision for modern Christians and the nation's history of using the power of religion in a curative form (Spanish).

Levine, Daniel H *Popular Voices in Latin American Catholicism* Princeton University Press, 1992. Combining interviews and community studies with analysis of broad ideological and institutional transformations, this is a fascinating look at religious and cultural change in Venezuela and Colombia.

Londono-Vega, Patricia *Religion, Society and Culture in Colombia: Medellín and Antioquia, 1850–1930* Clarendon Press, 2002. An exemplary debate about the role of the Catholic Church in the Antioquia department and its capital, Medellín.

Schultes, Richard Evans and Raffauf, Robert F *Vine of the Soul: Medicine Men, Their Plants and Rituals in the Colombian Amazonia* Synergetic Press, 2004. Over 12 years Evans Schultes and Raffauf collected 30,000 specimens, discovered 300 species and chronicled 2,000 novel medicinal plants to become two of the most important Amazonian plant explorers of the 20th century. This first-hand photographic account of life in the Colombian Amazon takes an incredible journey through the use of plants in some of the most fascinating indigenous cultures on the planet.

Taussig, Michael T *Shamanism, Colonialism and the Wild Man: A Study in Terror and Healing* University of Chicago Press, 1991. Examines the role of the shaman and healing practices used in the Colombian jungles.

Society

Cathey, Kate *Culture Smart!: The Essential Guide to Customs and Culture* Kuperard, 2011

Helen Kellogg Institute for International Studies *Peace, Democracy, and Human Rights in Colombia* University of Notre Dame Press, 2007. A scholarly collection of analyses and debate on the war in Colombia, the human rights of its people, the corruption and the political fragmentation.

Livingstone, Grace and Pearce, Jenny *Inside Colombia: Drugs, Democracy and War* Rutgers University Press, 2006. Intricate examination of the make-up of Colombia's conflict and the role of drugs and power in its turmoil.

Safford, Frank *Colombia: Fragmented Land, Divided Society* Oxford University Press, 2001. Background on the divisive issue of societal structure and classes in Colombia.

Wade, Peter *Black Culture and Social Inequality in Colombia* Institute for Cultural Research, 2006

Sport

Hilton, Christopher *Juan Pablo Montoya* J H Haynes & Co Ltd, 2003. Story of former Formula One racing driver and current NASCAR professional, now a UN Goodwill Ambassador.

Josephs, Allen *Ritual and Sacrifice in the Corrida: The Saga of César Rincón* University Press of Florida, 2002. Demonstrates the importance of the bullfight in Colombian culture.

Rendel, Matt *Kings of the Mountains: How Colombia's Cycling Heroes Changed Their Nation's History* Aurum Press, 2003. Part cycling history, part travelogue and part social analysis, this captures the raw emotion perfectly. Rendel not only pays homage to Colombia's sporting heroes but links a passion for sport with nationalism in an almost religious understanding of cycling's pride, pain and glory.

Travel narratives

Feiling, Tom *Short Walks from Bogota: Journeys in the New Colombia* Allen Lane, London, 2012. Fascinating insight into contemporary Colombia through the eyes of a true Colombiaphile. Political in parts but very well informed.

Heggstad, Glen *Two Wheels Through Terror: Diary of a South American Motorcycle Odyssey* Whitehorse Press, 2004. The shocking travelogue of adventure motorcyclist Heggstad's journey through the southern tip of South America, where he was captured by Colombia's rebel ELN army.

Jacobs, Michael *The Robber of Memories: A River Journey Through Colombia* Granta, 2012. In 2011, Michael Jacobs travelled the whole length of the Magdalena River, from its source high up in the Andean moorlands controlled by guerrillas. In spellbinding prose, *The Robber of Memories* charts the dangers he negotiated – including a terrifying three-day encounter with the FARC – while uncovering the river's history of pioneering explorations, environmental decline and political violence.

Kelly, B and London, M *Amazon* Harcourt, 1983. A travelogue along the river by boat and plane during the pre-tourist era in the 1970s.

Mann, Mark *The Gringo Trail* Summersdale Publishers, 2001. A terrifically raw, unglamorised account of backpacking around South America, including a harrowing experience in Colombia. A tumultuous read.

Nicholl, Charles *The Fruit Palace* Vintage, 1998. An amusing and eye-popping cutting-edge travelogue based on the author's amblings through Colombia in the 1980s.

Smith, Steven *Cocaine Train* Abacus, 2000. Captivating tale of Smith's journey from the UK to Colombia to trace the second family and history of his enigmatic grandfather, a railway pioneer.

Young readers

Cherry, Lynn *The Great Kapoc Tree: A Tale of the Amazon Rainforest* Harcourt Brace International, 2000. A good introduction to the issues of deforestation in the Amazon rainforest.

Harding, Colin *Colombia in Focus: A Guide to the People, Politics and Culture* Latin America Bureau, 1996. Suitable for older children.

Jennings, Terry *Our World: Living in the Rainforest* 4Learning, 2002. Depicts the wildlife, birds and plants in the planet's rainforest regions, including the Amazon.

Streissguth, Thomas *Colombia in Pictures* Lerner Publications, 2004. A children's book of photographs aimed at readers aged nine–12.

WEBSITES

www.bananaskinflipflops.com Nicely written blog about the life of a single Englishwoman in Bogotá.

www.britishcouncil.org/colombia.htm (English/Spanish).

www.colombia.com Describes itself as the website of everything (Spanish).

www.colombiacallingradio.com Listings to a weekly podcast about life in Colombia.

www.colombiaemb.org Colombian e-embassy.

www.colombia-politics.com The only English-language website dedicated to Colombian politics.

www.colombia.travel The official government Colombia website.

www.ethnologue.com An encyclopaedic reference cataloguing the world's 6,912 known languages.

www.juanvaldez.com Well-designed site containing news about the country's coffee industry, set up by Colombia's National Federation of Coffee Growers in order to honour the industry's rich coffee tradition and history and celebrate its iconic figurehead, Juan Valdez.

www.off2colombia.com Vital resource for travel to Colombia.

www.procolombia.co Colombian government trade body.

www.richardmccoll.com Articles and blogs from an Anglo-Canadian foreign correspondent and travel writer in Colombia.

www.seecolombia.travel Interesting and witty blogs perfect to whet your appetite for a trip to Colombia.

www.thebogotapost.com One of Colombia's Anglo-newspapers available to read online.

www.thecitypaperbogota.com Bogotá's longest-running Anglo-newspaper online.

www.theotherlookofcolombia.com A cracking site dedicated to promoting the positive aspects of Colombia, from its sporting world champions to its pioneering physicists and peace campaigners.

www.travelhealth.co.uk Some useful health advice to bear in mind before you travel.

ukincolombia.fco.gov.uk British embassy in Bogotá.

Business

www.**banrep.gov.co** Central Bank – Banco de la República.
www.**dnp.gov.co** National Planning Department.
www.**ft.com** *Financial Times* (UK issue).
www.**investincolombia.com.co** Invest In Colombia.
www.**larepublica.com.co** *La República* (finance/business news).
www.**mincomercio.gov.co** Ministry of Commerce, Industry and Tourism.
www.**portafolio.com.co** *Portafolio* (finance/business news).

Index

INDEX OF ADVERTISERS